KT-173-911

Organizational behaviour and work

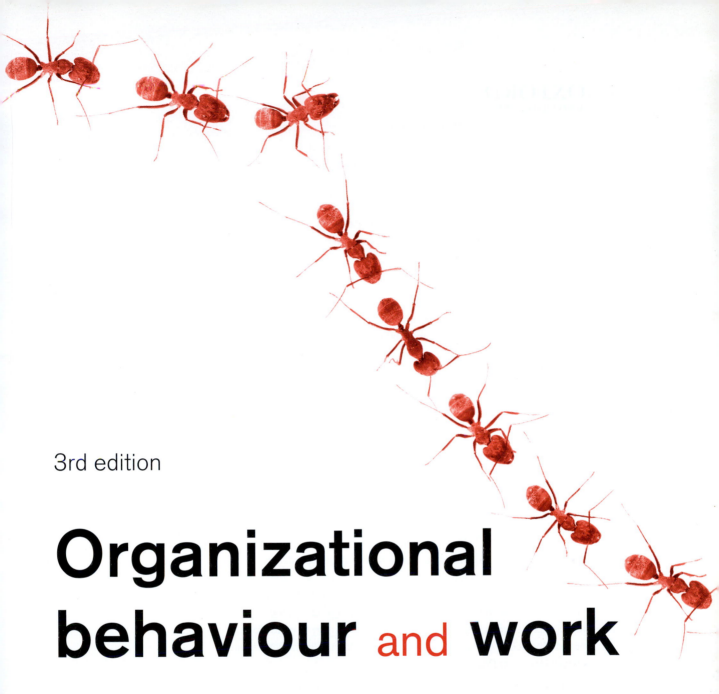

3rd edition

Organizational behaviour and work

a critical introduction

Fiona M. Wilson

OXFORD
UNIVERSITY PRESS

OXFORD
UNIVERSITY PRESS

Great Clarendon Street, Oxford ox2 6DP

Oxford University Press is a department of the University of Oxford.
It furthers the University's objective of excellence in research, scholarship,
and education by publishing worldwide in

Oxford New York

Auckland Cape Town Dar es Salaam Hong Kong Karachi
Kuala Lumpur Madrid Melbourne Mexico City Nairobi
New Delhi Shanghai Taipei Toronto

With offices in

Argentina Austria Brazil Chile Czech Republic France Greece
Guatemala Hungary Italy Japan Poland Portugal Singapore
South Korea Switzerland Thailand Turkey Ukraine Vietnam

Oxford is a registered trade mark of Oxford University Press
in the UK and in certain other countries

Published in the United States
by Oxford University Press Inc., New York

© Fiona Wilson 2010

The moral rights of the authors have been asserted
Database right Oxford University Press (maker)

First edition published 1999
Second edition published 2004
Third edition published 2010

All rights reserved. No part of this publication may be reproduced,
stored in a retrieval system, or transmitted, in any form or by any means,
without the prior permission in writing of Oxford University Press,
or as expressly permitted by law, or under terms agreed with the appropriate
reprographics rights organization. Enquiries concerning reproduction
outside the scope of the above should be sent to the Rights Department,
Oxford University Press, at the address above

You must not circulate this book in any other binding or cover
and you must impose the same condition on any acquirer

British Library Cataloguing in Publication Data

Data available

Library of Congress Cataloging in Publication Data

Data available

MPS Limited, A Macmillan Company
Printed in Italy
on acid-free paper by L.E.G.O. S.p.A

ISBN 978-0-19-953488-3

7 9 10 8 6

Acknowledgements

The author would like to acknowledge the enormous assistance in the development of this third edition given by the various reviewers; they provided the best and most useful constructive feedback. Emily Medina Davis, development editor with Oxford University Press, has worked closely with the author, researching the market to develop this book from a second to a third edition, merging chapters and producing new ones. The author would like to thank her for her support, encouragement, and detailed comment.

Walk-through preface

Each chapter contains a range of learning features that enrich the main text, and help you to reflect upon your reading, reinforcing your study of organizational behaviour and encouraging you to question and critique what you have learnt. This guided tour shows you how to get the most out of your textbook.

Example boxes

Example boxes throughout the text provide additional illustrations of the topic under discussion. Examples are drawn both from research and from organizational life.

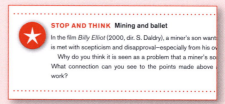

EXAMPLE More expensive placebos bring more relie...

In marketing, it has been found that perception really counts. A ...sion of higher value, just as the placebo pill can reduce pai... effects and found that a $2.50 (£1.25) placebo works better than one th... explain the popularity of some high-cost drugs over cheaper alternatives a... generic drugs are less effective than brand-name ones, although their activ...

(*Source:* Carey, 2008; Waber et al., 2008)

Stop and Think boxes

Stop and Think boxes encourage you to pause your reading and reflect on a question about, or implication of, the point under discussion. These are key to the critical approach, encouraging you to draw from your own experience.

STOP AND THINK Mining and ballet

In the film *Billy Elliot* (2000, dir. S. Daldry), a miner's son want... is met with scepticism and disapproval—especially from his ov...

Why do you think it is seen as a problem that a miner's so... What connection can you see to the points made above ... work?

Key Points

Each main chapter section ends with a set of Key Points that draw out the most important arguments developed within that chapter topic, to help consolidate your learning.

KEY POINTS

- Alienation is a good starting point from which to discuss ... work can be dehumanizing rather than fulfilling.

- Those who are alienated are more likely to be in jobs ... and call centre jobs. These jobs have been well descr... researchers.

Case study

End-of-chapter case studies with questions provide further illustration and opportunity to engage actively with your reading.

CASE STUDY

Cases of organizational structure: Two church...

Churches, like other organizations, make choices about hov... Church of Scotland has a relatively flat organizational struc... organizations in Scotland, with around 600,000 members and... professional and administrative support staff. The support staf... level for the Church—that is, the day-to-day policymaking and p...

Further Reading

An annotated further reading list is provided at the end of every chapter, to help you to take your learning further and to locate the key academic literature relevant to the chapter topic. It is also designed to guide you towards reading which will help you prepare for exams and essays.

FURTHER READING

Collinson, D. (2000) 'Strategies of resistance: Power, knowle
K. Grint (ed.), *Work and Society: A Reader*, Cambridge: F
options, knowledge, and agencies through which opposi

Gabriel, Y., Fineman, S., and Sims, D. (2000) *Organizing and*
3, 'Rules are rules', discusses the rationality and rules in o
chapter about bureaucracy and rationality.

Links to film and novels

An annotated list of films and novels which relate in some way to the chapter topic, help you to see OB operating in a variety of contexts.

LINKS TO FILMS AND NOVELS

Blue Collar (1978) dir. P. Schrader   Film about a trio of Det
are living at the mercy of a heartless corporation and a c

Titanic (1997) dir. J. Cameron   This film uses class as a cer

Lee, H. (1960) *To Kill a Mocking Bird; To Kill a Mocking B*
its screen adaptation focus on class and race.

vii

Research Questions

A set of carefully devised questions is provided at the end of every chapter to help you to take your learning further, and may also be used as the basis of seminar discussion and coursework.

RESEARCH QUESTIONS

1. Given what you now know about personality testing, wha
   recruiting a new manager?

2. What personality traits are being tested for by organizati
   narcissism, or petty tyranny?

3. Review the evidence for and against emotional intellige

Glossary Terms

Key terms appear in bold in the text and are defined in a glossary at the end of the book to aid you in exam revision.

in employment in which they are unable to control their immediate
they do. As a result, they cannot develop a sense of purpose, or s
in the production process, or feel that work is a mode of personal
might be argued that the person is 'alienated'.

The concept of alienation forms, for many, a useful starting poi
about work. It helps us to understand why work might be dehuman
Economic and Political Manuscript, Karl Marx, a founding father of so
aspects to the experience. When people feel alienated, work, accord

Guided tour of the Online Resource Centre

http://www.oxfordtextbooks.co.uk/orc/wilson_ob3e/

The Online Resource Centre that accompanies this book provides students and instructors with ready-to-use teaching and learning resources.

For Students

Glossary

A series of key terms and concepts has been provided to test your understanding of terminology from the book. Terms are taken from the textbook and from OUP's *A Dictionary of Business and Management*.

Web links

Web links relating to each chapter topic have been provided for further reading and research.

Further Reading

Additional readings are provided to help you to deepen your knowledge and understanding of organizational behaviour.

For Lecturers

Questions for research and discussion

Discussion and research questions relating to each chapter topic have been provided for use in seminars and lectures.

Chapter 11: Culture

Questions for research and discussion

1. Goffman (1961) gives us a detailed account of life in asylums. What insight can we gain from this work to help us understand the working and culture of organizations like universities?

2. Hopfl (1995) draws the analogy between acting and customer service. Read her paper and critically assess the similarities.

3. What evidence is there to suggest that the culture within police forces is discriminatory

PowerPoint® slides

A suite of customizable PowerPoint® slides has been included for use in lectures. Arranged by chapter, the slides may also be used as handouts in class.

Typology of work orientation

- *Instrumental* - work as a means to an end: car workers, oil rig, electrical supply.
- *Bureaucratic* - service to an organization in return for career progress (found among white collar workers: e.g. administrator, manager).

Additional Case Studies

Additional case studies and related questions are provided for use in seminars, lectures or to set as coursework.

Case Study: A Tale of Two Friends and of Jobs Worth Having

(Adapted from a piece by Wythe Holt and found on Alabama Public Radio's web site (see www.wual.ua.edu). Wythe Holt is a lawyer, historian, and writer who lives in Alabama, USA. He is University Research Professor of Law at the University of Alabama.)

I have a friend who took a job at the Mercedes plant in Tuscaloosa County. A high school graduate, my friend had worked steadily for several years as a pipefitter in a much smaller local plant. He was glad when Mercedes called him, thinking it was a dream job. The pay is better than $17 an hour and he began to accrue sick leave and vacation leave from the moment he signed the contract.

Group Exercises

Group exercises relating to each chapter topic are provided for use in seminars and lectures.

Chapter 10: Learning

Group exercise

As a student, one summer, I worked in a hotel in a small community on the west coast of Scotland. The hotel was owned and run by an ex-army colonel. He enforced strict rules that he told you about verbally. For example, you may not entertain guests in your room, may not have visitors, receive phone calls, or use the public phone in the hotel. The only ways to keep in touch with friends and family were by public phone (using a phone box in the village in the afternoon break or after 9 p.m.), by letter, or by arranging to meet them away from the hotel. This way he ensured that you defined yourself as a lowly servant and less than a guest, and noted the superiority of the guest. The culture and rules he created operated as a 'boundary device' (see Grint 1995:167), marking the privileged from the unprivileged. But there were also some rules that you only learned about when you broke them. For example I discovered that you might not sing in the empty dining room while setting the tables. What rules have you learned, in a work setting, only by having broken them?

Brief contents

Detailed contents

xiv

xv

About the author

Fiona Wilson is a Professor of Organizational Behaviour in the Department of Management at the University of Glasgow. Before moving to Glasgow, she worked at the University of St Andrews: first as a lecturer; then as a senior lecturer. Previously, Fiona had been employed as a researcher at Manchester Business School and University of Bradford Management Centre. Fiona completed a PhD at Manchester Business School.

Introduction

Work occupies a substantial proportion of most of our lives. It can be a symbol of personal value, and it can provide status, economic reward, and a potential. Work can also be a provider of friends, gossip, networks, fun, creativity, identity, and even love. It can also be regarded as a punishment or even as an addiction. Work, people, and employment structure our lives and shape the inequalities that we face. Employers—and, in particular, managers—have the hierarchical power to influence, if not to determine, the shape and degree of those inequalities in their organizations.

If you are, want to be, or were a practising manager, what would you want to know about people, work, and organizational behaviour (OB)? You might want to know how to motivate or lead employees. You might want to know how to manage a team. This book discusses some functionalist management ideas—that is, ideas of management as a function, serving a purpose, and managing a consensus. A good deal of what is known about management, people, and work comes from studies that aim to contribute to the effectiveness of managerial practice, or to build a better model or gain a better understanding of management. Research has tried to answer questions that practising managers might pose. For example, those studying management might want to know what a manager does, how managers have attempted to control absence from work, or what are the causes and consequences of stress. There are answers, from research, to those questions in this book.

The book does not, however, take a functionalist approach. A functionalist approach to people management would treat employees as reactive players pursuing objectives that are congruent with those of the organization. From this perspective, the employee is seen as a functionary who is selected, trained, and developed in accordance with organizational objectives that are clearly defined and unproblematic. Organizations are assumed to be unitary wholes, characterized by order and consensus. The functionalist view is evident in classical management theory. For example, the work of scientific management believes that there is one best way in which to organize work, and prescribes the careful selection and training of employees. We also find the functionalist view in leadership theory and among those advocating the management of culture (for example, Deal and Kennedy, 1982).

The book does not take a managerialist approach. A managerialist approach would look at OB from the exclusive perspective of the manager, within which managers are the functional agents who ensure the survival, growth, and prosperity of an organization by deploying scientific management techniques. This book does not accept the assumption that the performance of all organizations can be optimized by the application of generic management skills and theory; nor does it accept that there is one best way in which to manage in all situations. Management textbooks might lead you to believe that this is possible—that all you need to do is learn about how to manage, and then go off and do it. But if this were the case, there would be no organizations that are poorly managed and all organizations would demonstrate continual improvement. And there would be no competing theories of leadership and motivation.

One of the purposes of this book is to help you to question just how realistic the managerialist or functionalist approach might prove to be, by generating doubt and helping you to frame a number of questions. For example, what does 'greater organizational efficiency and effectiveness' really mean? Whose interests might it serve? Can greater efficiency and effectiveness always be achieved?

The following example illustrates the kind of managerial problem that an organization might face and why management skills that fit every situation cannot be taught.

EXAMPLE A problem faced by managers in one organization

Lillian Ladele, a registrar (who presides over wedding ceremonies) refused to perform civil partnership ceremonies. As a result, her employer—a council—took disciplinary action against her, concluding that she was in breach of its 'Dignity for All' policy. Lillian took her case to an employment tribunal alleging religious discrimination; she won.

In this case, the management faced a situation in which there was a conflict of the interests, rights, and freedoms of the gay community, who want civil partnership ceremonies, and the interests and rights of Lillian Ladele and her religious beliefs (Koster, 2008; Williams, 2008). The organization found it impossible then to tell the individual what to do and preserve her rights as an employee.

2

The book is sympathetic to an interpretive perspective, which regards the employee as a creative individual whose commitment must be earned and who is capable of—and able to exercise—choice and taking action that influences the organization. While there is no single way of demarcating a critical approach (Fournier and Grey, 2000; Parker, 2002), this book might be considered critical in its approach—that is, critical in that it views organizations as places of struggle and domination, and questions how effectively managers can manage. It asks you to stand back from management, work, and organizations, and to look with a critical eye and reflect on what you see. It needs you to be aware of how the social, political, and historical circumstances of the times in which we live condition our ideas and assumptions. It highlights where there is ambiguity and debate about behaviour and organizations. It considers issues such as power and inequality.

This book is designed to encourage you to appreciate why there are no simple answers to the questions that practising managers might pose and why there is no single 'best' way in which to manage. It is designed to encourage critical thinking and reflection on your part. You will be asked, for example, to look at assumptions about the priority assigned to certain interests over others: why is there a recurring bias in organizations in favour of privileging objectives such as 'rationality', 'profitability', 'effectiveness', and 'efficiency' over values such as 'equity', 'justice', and 'security' (Reed, 1992: 95)? What kind of organizations do you usually consider in management courses: manufacturing companies, and those from the service industry such as banks and call centres? Why do you not also consider credit unions, farms, cooperatives, voluntary groups, charities, and work councils? Are all organizations necessarily structured in a hierarchy? You will be encouraged to question whether managers are 'saviours' within organizations who protect us from chaos and inefficiency—or actually creators of cruelty and inequality (Parker, 2002). Should managers be designing or creating jobs that are 'too small for the human spirit' (Cohen, 2004)? And is it possible for managers to pursue objectives that are in everyone's interests—and can they be trusted to do so?

As Adam Smith, moral philosopher and political economist, pointed out in 1776, if company directors manage other people's money rather than their own, 'it cannot well be expected that they will watch over it with the same anxious vigilance' (Smith, 1776: 233). In the early eighteenth century, deliberate fraud and incompetence played a significant part in the failure of companies (Pollard, 1968: 25–6). In the early nineteenth century, managers were, more often than not, attracted to management positions because they gave the managers power to hire their spouses and children to work in the factory (Wren, 1994: 45).

How much evidence is there to suggest that managers should be trusted more today? (See, for example, Knights et al., 2001.)

This book also asks you to look outside what are normally thought of as organizations and how we usually think of work. (In management textbooks, work is often conceived of in very narrow terms.) In fact, work can be divided into four types.

1. *Recognized and rewarded work*, which is paid, takes the individual into a labour market to sell his or her skills, time, and energy to an employer, such as a university, a private or public company, or his or her family, if the individual works in the family business.

2. *Reproductive labour* concerns the efforts involved in raising one or more children to adulthood.

3. *Maintenance labour* refers to the chores that are necessary to maintain yourself and other members of your family by cooking, paying the bills, food shopping, gardening, laundry, house-work, and so on.

4. *Unpaid work* includes voluntary work for charities, churches and other religious groups, hospitals, and political parties.

'Deviant' work—including work in the sex industry, such as prostitution—tends to be excluded from mainstream management textbooks. Everett Hughes, a sociologist, encouraged his students to look at 'dirty' or deviant types of occupation. These occupations are interesting in their own right and can help to highlight factors of general relevance to work experience that we might not notice in conventional work, where we too easily take them for granted (Watson, 2003). There is little mention of sex, violence, pain, and power in organizational life in the mainstream literature. Gibson Burrell (1997: 52) suggests that this is because organization studies tend to ignore or hide that which is thought to be unacceptable in polite company and that management writers have acted like funeral directors or morticians, using cosmetics and 'rouge of excellence' to cover the 'necrotic collapse' of organizational structures.

We can also gain insight into OB by looking at less organized work, such as work 'on the fiddle', which has been examined by both psychologists and social anthropologists, and what work means to the unemployed. This book asks you to question what OB is and how it is influenced. What are the common characteristics to be found in organizations and what behaviour draws our attention? For you, is it all about work—or do rest and play have a part too?

The book is therefore designed to challenge what constitutes the very term 'organizational behaviour'. The meaning of the term is far from clear. Is it behaviour that occurs in some specified place and not in others, or behaviour that is controlled by an organization (Weick, 1969: 25)? Should we discuss behaviour in organizations from the point of view of the manager and what he or she can do to improve it, or should we also discuss how behaviour might look from the point of view of those further down the organization, including some of the realities of organizational life and presenting a more complete picture? Should we be interested only in behaviour that happens within organizations? What happens within organizations affects what happens outside and vice versa, so should we not consider that too? OB is seen here as chiefly being about the particular ways in which individual dispositions are expressed in an organizational setting and about the effects of this expression. While at work, there is rest and play; what happens in rest and play, both inside and outside the organization, impacts on organizational life.

There is plenty of research that reveals the difficulties, problems, and realities of organizational life, and plenty from outside organizations that might help to inform our understanding about what happens in organizations—but, so far, little of this research has appeared in mainstream management textbooks. Most of those reading this book will already be in work or be intending to enter into employment in the near future. Because work is a familiar topic, many treat it as if it is something about which they already know. But much of the knowledge from research that we have about people in workplaces and OB is not at all obvious or common sense. We need to question and research in order to gain insight, doubting what we otherwise might accept as obvious or common sense. For example, is it obvious that students in universities (a type of organization), when warned that excessive drinking is putting many of their peers at risk, might actually drink more (Perkins et al., 2005)? Or that the majority of people could be persuaded to electrocute someone to death merely by being asked to by a scientist in a white coat (Milgram, 1974)? We may think that it is obvious that making teenagers take part-time employment through secondary school is character building and generally a positive thing to do—but research has shown that work can harm academic work; it can also make teenagers cynical about corporate culture and the value of hard work. Further, it has been shown to promote some forms of delinquent behaviour (Steinberg et al., 1993). We therefore need to question, and be informed by, research in order to understand people's behaviour in organizations. Things that people consider obvious do not comprise a coherent theory of human behaviour or understanding (Stafford, 2007).

Research may also lead to interesting findings about people's behaviour in organizations that may need to be investigated and researched further. For example, it has been found that popcorn eaters at cinemas are three times more likely to cry than non-popcorn eaters (Ebenkamp, 2001). Why? Is it likely that there is a causal link? Remember that research can lead to some spurious conclusions being drawn. For example, there is a significant relationship to be found between the number of fire engines attending fires and the amount of damage caused (Burns, 1996). One might easily conclude that fire engines and firefighters cause the damage, which would be an absurd conclusion; it is much more likely that more fire engines are sent to the fires that cause the most damage. So while research helps us to gain insight and question our assumptions, we do need to think carefully about research findings and their conclusions about people at work.

The purpose of the book is to provide a fresh critical look at management and organizations, to uncover the issues and assumptions underlying the world of management, and subject them to scrutiny. The emphasis here is on exposing and discussing deep-seated features of organizational life, such as inequality, conflict, domination, subordination, and manipulation. It was written particularly for those people who acknowledge that there are few certainties about how to manage and many difficulties, uncertain tensions, irrationalities, and dilemmas to face in the mundane realities of work. This book aims to offer an introduction to a view of OB that has a long history, but which, as yet, has not been included in many of the introductory texts.

Textbooks on OB usually include chapters on perception, personality, motivation, job satisfaction, job design, leadership, learning, and socialization. We seem to have accepted the litany of topics that fall under the heading of 'organizational behaviour'—but this litany does not reflect the much wider range of issues and topics that are under discussion in management and OB journals. Nor are these topics usually dealt with from a critical perspective, examining, for example, the weaknesses in the research from the 'gurus' such as Herzberg and Belbin, or the ability of managers to manage. Organizational or occupational psychology has mainly informed the discipline that is cited in textbooks, yet is only one small part of what currently is recognized as constituting OB.

The psychology approach takes a 'scientific' view; its mission is to construct and validate theories that can explain and predict OB. Science provides a justification for believing that there is no problem with the status of knowledge: knowledge produced through scientific methods is seen as unproblematically true and scientists are potentially 'neutral', 'objective' agents in the process (Hollway, 1991).

The individual is usually the unit of analysis. Theory construction in organizational psychology is based on a highly analytic and experiment-based form of science, rooted in the natural sciences. There has, in the past, been an unwillingness to reflect on and critique the discipline (Steffy and Grimes, 1992), although there are now a few books that do so (for example, Fox and Prilleltensky, 1997; Trew and Kremer, 1998). Another problem with organizational psychology is that the bulk of the research does not focus on dynamic issues such as organizational power, conflict, class, politics, and ideology; as a result, there is a very tidy and sanitized view of what goes on in organizations—even though we all know that work issues and behaviour in organizations are much more than this. There is uncertainty, chaos, and confusion in organizing. There is control and resistance, with work also being degraded and deskilled. Workplaces are not peopled by high-performing, highly committed individuals bound together in a common cause by a corporate mission enshrined within a strong organizational culture (Noon and Blyton, 2002); rather, workplaces are sites of inequalities, divided by class, levels of education, race, and gender (Acker, 2006). Workplaces are places in which romances occur—places in which people find others with whom they develop relationships outside work. They are also places in which harassment, bullying, lying, and other negative behaviours take place. And this book discusses these messy issues—issues that other texts have ignored.

We need, then, a critical approach, taking a critical or radical view of contemporary behaviour in organizations, considering fun, exploitation, repression, unfairness, and unequal power relations. Sociology must inform the 'textbook' definition of OB. Since the 1990s, management, work, and organizations have been increasingly subject to critical analysis. If the dream of management and practising managers was the establishment of a recognized managerial science (a stable, confident, and established set of techniques), it is clear that the dream has proven both unrealized and unrealizable (Fournier and Grey, 2000).

Mainstream management texts have also largely neglected to take account of gender. Much of what we read in textbooks about work is about men and their work, how they are motivated, how they gain job satisfaction, how they are stressed, and so on. As Crompton (1989: 129) has noted, much of the empirical research and theorizing on work—particularly in sociology—is derived from outdated studies of predominantly white male production workers, working in factories. It can be argued that the theory of organizations and work is mainly a chronology of men's writings, research, and theory. And female management theorists—such as Mary Parker Follett (Graham, 1995; Stewart, 1996), Joan Woodward (Tancred-Sheriff and Campbell, 1992), and Simone Weil (Grey, 1996)—have been written out of, or marginalized from, the history and development of management ideas, and are rarely discussed in management texts. Classical theory in management comes from the early twentieth century, from the intellectual 'fathers' such as Max Weber and Frederick Winslow Taylor. The fathers' ideas formed the foundation for the theory and research methods of organizational behaviour—meaning that women's experiences are conspicuously absent from theory, methods, and data.

Practically all OB analysis and theory focuses on the male world. The topics that preoccupy it are topics that preoccupy men—power, leadership, technology, stress, the world of the (mainly male) manager and the work that he does, and so on—with women seen only as adjuncts to men. If women are dealt with, it is usually in a chapter thrown in as an extra, almost as 'beside the point' rather than as an intrinsic component of behaviour in organizations. Half of the population of organizations is left at the edge of, or just tagged onto, OB texts (Wilson, 1996). Very little in OB texts deals with the nature, structure, and functioning of female-dominated jobs, such as in service industries (for example, hairdressing, catering, and nursing).

Despite the fact that authors such as Richard Brown (1976) and Janet Wolff (1977) argued nearly three decades ago that gender should figure more largely in organizational analysis, little progress has been made (Wilson, 2003). A great deal of research focuses on men with no reference at all to women, but when research is focused on women, it is almost always with reference to men. If comparisons are not made with men, the research is viewed as incomplete (Bernard, 1998); research on women in their own right is often viewed as not worthy of male attention. Yet gender is universal: gender is not only about women, but also about men; both men and women play out gendered roles, and exhibit gendered behaviours (for example, in the way they talk, dress, or stand). Gender is more than an individual trait or set of roles. The differences between women and men are not essential to either sex. This book is written—like others such as Grint (1998), and Noon and Blyton (2002)—with the intention of discussing women's work in balance with that of men and thinking about the implications of unpaid domestic work. (If, when reading this book, you feel that there is too much on women and work, you might want to ask yourself why you feel this way when half of the population of organizations is female.)

Gender is systematically and inextricably tied to other inequality issues, such as race, sexual orientation, and class. Race, like gender, offers itself as a kind of performance—that is, a set of practices and language. The issues of the racial and ethical foundations of organizational power and control have emerged recently in the literature—for example, in relation to the police and the low numbers of ethnic minorities found in management. If we were to include a more comprehensive consideration of race—that is, to 'colour' organizational studies—we would need to think more about what 'colour' means and take apart the grammars of race (black/white, African/American/Asian American, native/indigenous) to track racial identity and search ideological commitments (Ferguson, 1994: 93). It is, for example, debatable whether British Asian people are excluded by the term 'black' or whether they support its use as a political tool.

Finally, another area from which OB draws profitably—and which is also often excluded from mainstream management textbooks—is emotion and feeling. As Fineman (1996) notes, a scan of the indexes of textbooks on OB and theory reveals few, if any, entries under 'emotions' or 'feelings'. Yet gripes, joy, drudgery, anger, anxiety, frustrations, glee, surprise, embarrassment, and tedium are part of the social creation and personal expression of work and organizational life. Activities such as recruiting, firing, negotiating, and persuading are felt and shaped by feelings. Emotion, therefore, emerges as an issue in many of the chapters here and you are asked to consider the place of emotion in organizations.

 STOP AND THINK Revenge in the workplace

Cary Cooper is head of occupational psychology at Lancaster University's Management School, and is concerned about the effect of greater frustration and anger in the workplace.

'I expect to see more revenge,' he says. 'The number of potential sources are enormous. The problem is that people store revenge up. They don't confront what is responsible for the problem.'

Why do you think these emotions are rarely acknowledged in textbooks on OB and management?

(*Source:* Richardson, 2004)

This book is structured so that the scene is first set, introducing the context in which work is done, the views of workers and managers on work, and rationality and its place in how work is organized. Next, we look at the classic management topics: structure (including bureaucracy), motivation, leadership, perception, personality, learning, teams, culture, and change. These topics are discussed in such a way that the main ideas are articulated, but they are also critiqued. Finally, we consider the more critical approaches, issues of power, control resistance, alternative forms of organization, the place of emotion, and stress in work and organization.

The theory on which much of the book is based is drawn from psychology, industrial sociology, and organization theory. While the prevailing theory in management is a unitary theory (to be found in much of the literature on human resource management, empowerment, and team building that assumes that management and workers are striving together to achieve common goals) or pluralist (assuming that diverse interests in organizations are pursued through continuous compromise), the theory proposed here is more radical, and would argue that there is no balance of power between those who own and manage capital (property, machines, money), and labour (those who work); rather, there is an asymmetry of power—owners and managers having much more power than workers. It also draws on critical theory, critiquing the contemporary world of organizations, management, and work, re-examining what we know, analysing the strengths and weaknesses of existing research and ideas, and looking towards new possibilities, rather than reproducing the status quo.

FURTHER READING

All of the following texts will help you to develop a more critical approach to the realities of work organization.

Barry, J., Chandler, J., Clark, H., Johnston, R., and Needle, D. (2000) *Organization and Management: A Critical Text*, London: Thomson Learning.

Knights, D. and Willmott, H. (2007) *Introducing Organizational Behaviour and Management*, London: Thomson Learning.

Thomas, B. (2003) *Controversies in Management: Issues, Debates, Answers*, London: Routledge.

Thompson, L., Linstead, S., Fulop, L., and Lilley, S. (2004) *Management and Organization: A Critical Text*, Houndmills: Palgrave Macmillan.

Thompson, P. and McHugh, D. (2002) *Work Organizations*, Houndmills: Palgrave.

Watson, T. (2002) *Organizing and Managing Work*, Harlow: Pearson Education.

REVIEW QUESTIONS

7

1. Should the work that you do as a student be classed as work? If not, why not? Where does 'student work' fit in? What category would you need to add to the four types described above, given that it is not paid work, reproductive, maintenance, or simply unpaid work? Look at the contents pages of other management and organizational behaviour texts, and see what kind of work is typically discussed.

2. If you were a practising manager, what would you want to know about people, work, and organization?

REFERENCES

Acker, J. (2006) 'Inequality regimes: Gender, class and race in organizations', *Gender and Society*, 20(4): 441–64.

Bernard, J. (1998) 'My four revolutions: An autobiographical history of the ASA', in K.A. Myers, C.D. Anderson, and B.J. Risman (eds), *Feminist Foundations: Towards Transforming Sociology*, London: Sage, ch. 1.

Brown, R. (1976) 'Women as Employees: Some comments on research in industrial sociology', in D.L. Barker and S. Allen (eds), *Dependence and Exploitation in Work and Marriage*, Harlow: Longman, ch. 2.

Burns, W.C. (1996) 'Spurious Correlations', available online at http://www.burns.com/wcbspurcorl.htm

Burrell, G. (1997) *Pandemonium: Towards a Retro-Organizational Theory*, London: Sage.

Cohen, A. (2004) 'What Studs Turkel's working says about worker malaise today', *New York Times*, 31 May, available online at http://www.nytimes.com/2004/05/31/opinion/31MON3.html

Crompton, R. (1989) 'Review of Y. Gabriel (1988) *Working Lives in Catering*', *Work, Employment and Society*, 3(1):129–30.

Deal, T.E. and Kennedy, A.A. (1982) *Corporate Cultures: The Rites and Rituals of Corporate Life*, Reading, MA: Addison Wesley.

Ebenkamp, B. (2001) 'A kernel of truth: Survey relates popcorn consumption with movie satisfaction', BPI Communications, available online at http://findarticles.com/p/articles/mi_m0BDW/is_24_42/ai_75617339/

Ferguson, K. (1994) 'On bringing more theory, more voices, more politics to the study of organization', *Organization*, 1(1): 81–100.

Fineman, S. (1996) 'Emotion and organizing', in S.R. Clegg, C. Hardy, and W.R. Nord (eds), *Handbook of Organization Studies*. London: Sage, ch. 3.3.

Fournier, V. and Grey, C. (2000) 'At the critical moment: Conditions and prospects for critical management studies', *Human Relations*, 53(1): 7–32.

Fox, D. and Prilleltensky, I. (1997) *Critical Psychology: An Introduction*, London: Sage.

Graham, P. (ed.) (1995) *Mary Parker Follett: Prophet of Management*, Boston, MA: Harvard Business School Press.

Grey, C. (1996) 'Towards a critique of managerialism: The contribution of Simone Weil', *Journal of Management Studies*, 33(5): 591–611.

Grint, K. (1998) *The Sociology of Work: An Introduction*, 2nd edn, Cambridge: Polity.

Hollway, W. (1991) *Work Psychology and Organizational Behaviour: Managing the Individual at Work*, London: Sage.

Knights, D., Noble, F., and Vurdubakis, T. (2001) 'Chasing shadows: Control, virtuality and the production of trust', *Organization Studies*, 22(2): 311–36.

Koster, O. (2008) 'Victory for Christian registrar bullied for refusing to perform "sinful" gay weddings', *Mail Online*, 10 July, available online at http://www.dailymail.co.uk/news/article-1033955/Victory-Christian-registrar-bullied-refusing-perform-sinful-gay-weddings.html

Kynaston, C. (1996) 'The everyday exploitation of women: housework and the patriarchal mode of production', Women's Studies International Forum, 19(3): 228, 232–3.

Milgram, S. (1963) 'Behavioral study of obedience', *Journal of Abnormal and Social Psychology, 67(4):* 371–8

_____ (1974) *Obedience to Authority: An Experimental View*, New York: Harper Collins.

Noon, M. and Blyton, P. (2002) *The Realities of Work*, 2nd edn, Basingstoke: Palgrave Macmillan.

Parker, M. (2002) *Against Management: Organizations in the Age of Managerialism*, Blackwell, Oxford.

Perkins, H.W., Haines, M.P., and Rice, R. (2005) 'Misperceiving the college drinking norm and related problems', *Journal of Studies in Alcohol*, 66: 470–8.

Pollard, S. (1968) *The Genesis of Modern Management*, London: Penguin.

Reed, M. (1992) *The Sociology of Organizations: Themes, Perspectives and Prospects*, London: Harvester Wheatsheaf.

_____ (1996) 'Organizational theorizing: A historically contested terrain', in S.R. Clegg, C. Hardy, and W.R. Nord (eds), *Handbook of Organization Studies*, London: Sage. ch. 1.1.

Richardson, B. (2004) 'When office work turns ugly', BBC News, 12 August, available online at http://news.bbc.co.uk/1/hi/business/3811937.stm

Smith, A. (1776; 1904) *The Wealth of Nations*, London: Methuen.

Stafford, T. (2007) 'Isn't it all just obvious?', *The Psychologist*, 20(2): 94–5.

Steffy, B.D. and Grimes, A.J. (1992) 'Personnel/organizational psychology: A critique of the discipline', in M. Alvesson and H. Wilmott (eds), *Critical Management Studies*, London: Sage, ch. 9.

Steinberg, L., Fegley, S., and Dornbusch, S.M. (1993) 'Negative impact of part time work on adolescent adjustment: Evidence from a longitudinal study', *Developmental Psychology*, 29(3): 171–80.

Stewart, R. (1996) 'Why the neglect?', *Organization*, 3: 175–9.

Tancred-Sheriff, P. and Campbell, E.J. (1992) 'Room for women: A case study in the sociology of organizations', in A.J. Mills and P. Tancred (eds), *Gendering Organizational Analysis*, London: Sage, ch. 2.

Trew, K. and Kremer, J. (eds) (1998) *Gender and Psychology*, London: Arnold Publishers.

Watson, T.J. (2003) *Sociology, Work and Industry*, 4th edn, London: Routledge.

Weick, K.E. (1969) The Social Psychology of Organizing, Reading, MA: Addison-Wesley.

Williams, A. (2008) 'Faith at work: A journey without maps', *Guardian Online*, 8 July, available online at http://www.guardian.co.uk/society/2008/jul/18/equality.discriminationatwork

Wilson, F.M. (1996) 'Research note: Organizational theory—Blind and deaf to gender?', *Organization Studies*, 17(5): 825–42.

_____ (2003) *Organizational Behaviour and Gender*, 2nd edn, Aldershot: Ashgate.

Wolff, J. (1977) 'Women in organizations', in S. Clegg and D. Dunkerley (eds), *Critical issues in Organizations*, London: Routledge & Kegan Paul, pp. 7–20.

Wren, D. (1994) *The Evolution of Management Thought*, New York: John Wiley.

Approaching Management Critically

Setting the Scene

Introduction

This chapter aims to provide a context for understanding work and behaviour in organizations. While other textbooks might describe the environment in which organizations operate in terms of finance, stakeholders, and other influences or constraints on organizational behaviour, this chapter describes some key facts about trends, topical issues, people, and work in order to set the scene for the rest of the book.

You are asked to consider what information you might find useful if you were a manager observing people and how they behave. You are encouraged to think about how these scene-setting issues might impact on organizations and how managers have choices to make about these issues: for example, who is employed, how employees are contracted to work, what they are paid, how fair that payment is, and how they are appraised and promoted. Management is enmeshed in moral relations, decisions, and activity to do with growth, globalization, and the terms under which people are employed; some management is involved in trafficking and exploitation, while some brings about more positive outcomes. Organizations such as

schools and universities play their part in the improvement—or otherwise—of social mobility.

By the end of the chapter, you will have learnt more about some of the key issues relating to people and work. In particular, you will learn about the context in which managers make decisions that affect people and their work. You will also be able to see how managers could make decisions that might change how work is experienced.

The chapter explores:

- some scene-setting issues;
- globalization;
- human trafficking and modern-day slavery;
- the growth of the enterprise economy;
- trends in the working population;
- income and social mobility;
- men and women working;
- men, women, and management;
- mothers' and fathers' attitudes to work and family;
- working hours;
- part-time working;
- homeworking;
- other scene-setting issues.

Some scene-setting issues

Chapters on the business environment in management textbooks tend to concentrate on how to analyse the general business environment and identify environmental influences—that is, the political, legal, economic, sociocultural, and technological influences. The examples given usually relate to manufacturing organizations based in the developed world; rarely do examples include the developing world, the farming industry, service organizations, not-for-profit organizations, or charities.

The scene-setting information that you need, as a manager, depends on the kind of organization in which you are employed. For example, if you work as a manager for an organization that is a charity, it might be useful to know that 57 per cent of the UK adult population donates to charity at least once a month and that women are more likely to give than men (although men give more per donor than women) (NCVO, 2007), or that those who are less wealthy have been found to give proportionately more than the rich (Egan, 2001). If you are a manager in social services, then you may need to know that more households have become poor over the last fifteen years, but that fewer are very poor (Dorling et al., 2007). These are the kinds of behaviour and facts with which you will be most concerned—facts and behaviours that require constant monitoring and research. You will then make choices if you are a charity manager, for example, about to whom you appeal in your campaigns.

The farming industry receives a lot of media attention, but virtually no attention in mainstream management texts. Farming is increasingly being dominated by large corporations who have an interest, for example, in promoting genetically modified (GM) crops. Interesting questions for managers in this arena include:

- could better management reduce the reality of hunger for over 800 million people in the world?
- will GM crops stop hundreds of millions going without enough to eat?
- famine might be a management problem—but is it a situation that can be managed?
- has the promise of globalization, which was to lift underdeveloped economies onto a level playing field with the developed ones, failed?

This last issue—globalization—is an area in which management has had a large part to play. Many work in globalized companies, or for companies that source their goods or services globally, and organizations are affected by the global context: a company going global, for example, can challenge its organizational design and structure.

Globalization

The term 'globalization' was originally used to describe the gradual connection between different societies. It is a shorthand term to describe the global circulation of goods, services and capital, information, ideas, and people. The term often refers to the global presence and expansion of organizations such as *Christian Dior*, *McDonald's*, or *Exxon*, and products such as *Coca Cola*, as well as global production methods such as 'just in time', 'total quality management (TQM)', and 'lean production'. Coupled with the increasing role of worldwide telecommunications and e-commerce, there has been an unprecedented global flow of capital, goods, services, and labour (Jones et al., 2007). And globalization has played an important catalytic role in global prosperity, lifting more people out of poverty than in all human history (World Bank, 2000).

Some scholars make the mistake of equating large organizations with globalization. For example, while *Walmart* (which operates *Asda* in the UK) is the biggest company in the world, as measured by sales, it is not a global company; rather, it is primarily a North American business, with only 9.6 per cent of its stores being outside its home region. Similarly, *Carrefour* of France has 9,200 stores, but only 19 per cent of its revenues originate from outside Europe, so while it may source globally, it cannot be called a 'global company' (Rugman and Girod, 2003).

Globalization is a strongly contested concept—one reason being that there is no consensus as to its meaning and significance, and another the debate over the desirability of its effects. There is also debate on the extent to which globalization is occurring. For example, Hirst and Thompson (1999) claim that the extent of globalization is greatly exaggerated and that the globalization of the British economy, in particular, is nothing new. Further, because the UK has surrendered a very large part of its internationally competitive manufacturing sector and much of service sector to international investors, it has become vulnerable to externally initiated shocks or crises in foreign financial markets, and decisions by foreign business managers and their interests (Hirst and Thompson, 2000).

Another debate concerns the generation of greater inequalities. Globalization is thought—for example, by Steeten (2001) and Isaak (2005)—to lead not to bland sameness across countries, but to sharpened inequalities. Sociologists are concerned that national and regional cultures may be submerged within a common global capitalist culture and that globalization will increase existing inequalities, as well as the pace of growth of individualism (Herriot and Scott-Jackson, 2002). Protestors around the world have drawn attention to these inequalities and while globalization has played an important part in reducing poverty in developing countries through its impact on growth, there are significant variations in the levels of that growth (World Bank, 2000).

There is a need, then, for behaviours that help to reduce levels of poverty. Fair trade has emerged as a market-based mechanism to improve the lives of producers in developing countries, by prescribing the behaviour within fair trade companies. For example, within fair trade companies, farmers and workers are organized democratically. On fair trade estates and plantations, farm workers form democratically controlled groups that manage the disbursement of the fair trade social premia. Child and slave labour abuse is prohibited, and workers must be allowed to be unionize (Nickolls and Opal, 2005).

EXAMPLE **Fair organizational behaviour: Paying fair wages in a fair trade organization**

Fair trade is not about paying developed world wages in a developing world; rather, fair wages are determined by a number of factors, including the amount of time, skill, and effort involved in production, minimum and living wages in the local context, the purchasing power in a community or area, and other costs of living in the local context. Wages are determined independently from wage structures in developed countries and are designed to provide fair compensation based on the true cost of production.

Human trafficking and modern-day slavery

One of the dark sides of globalization has been human trafficking—that is, the supply human beings for prostitution, sweat shop labour, street begging, domestic work, marriage, adoption, agricultural work, construction, armed conflicts, and other forms of exploitative labour or services. Trafficking is behaviour that is organized and managed, and it has been estimated that about 27 million people are victims (Jones et al., 2007).

EXAMPLE **A case of exploitative labour**

A group of illegal immigrants smuggled out of China by gangsters became cockle pickers in Morecambe Bay in 2004. Police believe that twenty-three of them died, drowned in rising waters on 5 February 2004 (two bodies were never found). Up to seventy illegal Chinese workers were employed for the cockle harvest and were crammed into four properties rented in Liverpool. Survivors told police that they were forced to give gangmasters most of their wages for accommodation, food, and transportation, leaving them only £1 per day for over nine hours of work. They were forced to work in all weather conditions.

(*Source: Times Online*, 2006, 'Gangmaster guilty of 21 cockle picker deaths', 24 March; *Anti-Slavery International*, 2006, 'Gangmaster convicted for cocklepicker deaths', 24 March)

Modern-day slavery is being monitored by organizations such as the International *Labour Organization* (ILO), the *UK Human Trafficking Centre*, and the campaign group *Anti-Slavery International*. Workers from abroad can be subject to deception, systematic underpayment, intimidation, the removal of documents, excessive charges for accommodation and transport, and the exploitation of their irregular immigration status or the fact that they are in debt in order to force them to work in conditions to which they do not agree. Recently, an organization called the *Gangmasters Licensing Authority* has been set up in the UK to curb the exploitation of workers in the agricultural, horticultural, shellfish gathering, and associated processing and packing industries (see http://www.gla.gov.uk).

EXAMPLE **Modern-day slavery**

Nasir was a qualified chef from Pakistan who was offered work in Ireland. He worked from 8 A.M. to 2 A.M.—that is, eighteen hours a day—seven days a week. As well as cooking, he was required to clear and wash up, and deliver menus and takeaway meals. Instead of the €300–400 a week he was promised, he was given €150, from which his employer deducted €50 a week to pay for a work permit. He was verbally abused, continually threatened with deportation, unsure of his rights, demoralized, and exhausted.

(*Source:* B. O'Brien, 2007, 'Opinion and analysis', *Irish Times*, 30 June; see also http://www.europeanslavery.com)

The growth of the enterprise economy

With globalization has come the growth in interest in the enterprise economy. Entrepreneurship has been at the centre of economic and industrial policy across many of the *Organisation for Economic Cooperation and Development* (OECD) countries since the 1980s. The Global Entrepreneurship Monitor seeks to ascertain the amount of entrepreneurial activity in the world and investigate its relationship with economic growth (Reynolds et al., 2002). In the European Union, 99 per cent of businesses are small and medium-sized enterprises (SMEs)—that is, those employing fewer than 250 people (European Community, 2006); of all business in Europe, 91 per cent are micro-businesses—that is, businesses employing fewer than ten people. Within the UK, SMEs account for more than half of the employment (58.7 per cent) and turnover (51.1 per cent) (DTI, 2006). While the importance of new firms to economic growth and competitiveness has been widely recognized, and the encouragement of enterprise has been central to the economic strategies of successive governments, the success of the 'enterprise economy' depends on a flow of individuals who are willing and able to start up in business. In the UK, in 2005, the number of enterprises was at its highest, having grown in eight successive years (ibid.); the UK also has higher rates of entrepreneurship than every other major economy outside the USA (Work Foundation, 2006).

More men than women are defined as 'entrepreneurs'. While 8.9 per cent of men are classed as entrepreneurs in Britain, the figure stands at only 3.8 per cent for women (see http://www.startups.co.uk). And while small businesses may, or may not, be entrepreneurial, a recent UK study of SMEs found that 75 per cent are majority-owned by men, compared with only 25 per cent by women (Fraser, 2004).

Trends in the working population

Age

Because the general population in the UK is gradually rising, so the number of those of working age is increasing. The population is expected to rise from 59.2 million in 1998 to over 63.5 million by 2021 and to peak around 2036, then gradually fall. The aging population is expected to produce more demand for informal caring. By 2026, more than 10 per cent of the population is likely to be over 75 years old (Government Actuaries Department, 2005), and by 2008, it is expected that the population of pensionable age will exceed the number of children (Shaw, 2000).

One reason for this is increased life expectancy, which is expected to rise from 74.9 to 78.5 years for men, and from 79.7 to 82.7 years for women, by 2020. Will the increase in pensioners bring increased pressure on health and social services, or will tomorrow's older population be wealthier and healthier? If the working population is ageing, will today's youth have to support an increasingly large elderly population? Is age discrimination stopping older workers from supporting themselves? These are all questions that are regularly raised in the media. There have been some alarmist projections of demographic 'time bombs' in the UK—including a 'pensions crisis'—arising from the combination of an ageing population and declining fertility. As a result—and to reflect parity between the genders—the state retirement age for women is to be raised from 60 to 65 years old by 2020, increasing the size of the female working age population. But there are other demographic differences within the older population in terms of socio-economic status, employment patterns and stability, education, ethnicity, and gender.

As people live longer and medical advances help older people to lead active lives, they may want to work longer or may welcome early retirement as a way in which to establish their own businesses and take control of their working lives. The alarmist projections were fuelled by just such a trend among older people—particularly older men (those over the age of 50)—during the 1990s (Loretto and White, 2006). The phenomenon of early exit from employment—on grounds including early retirement, voluntary or compulsory redundancy, dismissal, and retirement on grounds of ill health—has been described as 'one of the most dramatic economic transformations of labour markets in modern industrial economies' (Rein and Jacobs, 1993: 53) and, in most cases, that exit proves permanent (Duncan, 2003). The trend is widespread across both the public and private sectors, and in growth industries as well as those experiencing employment decline. And, at one stage, it was thought that this trend would create jobs for the young and reduce official rates of unemployment, it was found that older workers should actually be persuaded to stay at work in order to offset the decline in the numbers of young workers.

Early exit is now seen as a phenomenon that derives from ageism—a term that came into existence around the same time as 'sexism', in the late 1960s in the USA, but which only entered public discourse in the UK in the 1980s. It refers to the systematic stereotyping of, and discrimination against, people because they are old (Loretto et al., 2000). Although the UK government outlawed age discrimination in March 2006—setting a default retirement age of 65, and prohibiting age discrimination in recruitment, training, and promotion—much 'voluntary' early retirement masks individual willingness, intention, or need to continue working. Jobs taken after early exit or retirement can lead to downshifting in terms of levels of pay and responsibility. Many American and British male workers, in particular, have been forced or 'encouraged' out of their main career to take up lower-paid and less skilled work in another sector (Vickerstaff et al., 2003); by contrast, in Sweden, men are more likely to downshift within their main career organization (Jacobs and Rein, 1994).

While research has clearly shown that older workers experience ageism, the issue of age prejudice and age discrimination remains under-researched—largely because the definition of who is an 'older worker' is ambiguous and contingent. It may be those over the age of 45 (Warr, 2001), 50 per cent of the population (Loretto et al., 2005), or those over the age of 55 (OECD, 2004). The definition of 'older worker' also varies with industry, occupation, and gender: for example, women report experiencing age discrimination or being considered too old for employment at earlier ages than men (Encel and Studencki, 1997; Onyx, 1998; Duncan and Loretto, 2004). Research for the *Department for Education and Employment* did, however, find widespread evidence of discrimination against older workers (DfEE, 2001b). Around one in four older workers reported experiencing age discrimination in relation to job applications; one in twenty reported experiencing age discrimination in relation to promotions, training, and development, as well as compulsory retirement. Further, studies of performance appraisal showed older workers receiving lower performance ratings than their younger counterparts (Saks and Waldman, 1998).

Employers, it has been found, think that older workers are less productive and have less relevant skills. They think that they are resistant to change, resist training, and can be inflexible (Chiu et al., 2001; Redman and Snape, 2002). Older workers are less likely to undergo training and less likely to be offered training by employers (Taylor and Urwin, 2001). Yet age has been found to be a poor proxy for performance (Grimley Evans et al., 1992). Some perceive the older worker to have positive attributes, including reliability, loyalty, enthusiasm, superior interpersonal skills, and scarce skills (Taylor and Walker, 1994; McGregor, 2001; IRS, 2003; Loretto and White, 2006; Riach, 2007), and discrimination against older workers can lead to suboptimal use of human resources and a narrow pool of talent from which to draw. Early exit due to discrimination has resulted in skill shortages, a loss of 'collective memory', and the good relations—coupled with an understanding of the ageing market—that can be generated by ageing employees working with ageing customers.

Finally, while more negative attitudes are held toward older than younger adults (Kite et al., 2005), it should be noted that is not only those in the older age groups who are discriminated against in employment: a quarter of those aged between 16 and 24 claimed to have experienced age discrimination in employment (Age Concern, 1998).

Disability

Research indicates that, as life expectancy increases, there will be a rise in the proportion of people experiencing light to moderate disabilities, but a fall in those with severe disabilities (Evandrou and Falkingham, 2000). The prevalence of disability increases with age. Disabled women and men each have lower employment rates and higher unemployment rates than women and men who are not disabled (ONS, 2005a).

There have been changes in understanding about disability. Prior to 1995, the medical model was the most common frame of reference for employers and others—a model that constructed the disabled as 'problems', often to be regarded by employers as unproductive in comparison with the able-bodied. Disabled activists and academics such as Thomas (2007) have worked towards changing this view, so that disability is not perceived as a medical condition, but as a socially constructed concept formed on the basis of a narrow viewpoint about what is 'normal' and about how tasks should be performed. The problem is not the disabled themselves, but rather the 'disabling world'; society must change for the better to facilitate the participation of disabled people more fairly.

The law now requires organizations to make 'reasonable adjustments' for the disabled. This might include altering a person's working hours, acquiring special equipment, allowing absences for medial or therapeutic appointments, or providing additional supervision. Nonetheless, those with disabilities remain more likely to be unemployed or underemployed.

Unemployment

When the male partner in a couple becomes unemployed, it might be expected that the female partner will find a job to supplement the household income—but research has indicated the opposite (McGinnity, 2002). In the UK, the employment rate of the wives of unemployed men is considerably lower than the employment rate of the wives of employed men. There has been a rise in both 'work rich' households and those that are 'work poor' (Gregg and Wadsworth, 1999). This may be because both partners lack education, or because the leisure times of husbands and wives may complement each other, and so the couple may prefer to spend time together rather than the wife to work when the husband is unemployed. Alternatively, it may be that they negatively view the benefit system or the prospect of the woman becoming the breadwinner.

Race and ethnicity

'Race' refers to socially defined differences based on physical characteristics, culture, and historical domination and oppression, justified by entrenched beliefs. 'Ethnicity' may accompany race or stand alone as a basis for inequality.

Data on the ethnic origin of the UK population show that 92 per cent are classified as 'white'. Only 3.5 per cent are Asian or Asian British, while 2 per cent are black or black British. Those who are classified as Chinese make up just 0.3 per cent (ONS, 2001). The ethnic population makes up 9 per cent of the population of England, but only 2 per cent of Scotland and Wales. In terms of religion, Muslims form the largest group belonging to a non-Christian religion and have the lowest employment rates of all religious groups (ONS, 2005b).

While we might like to believe that racial discrimination is a thing of the past, racial inequalities undeniably persist (Brown et al., 2003). The relative position for ethnic minorities does not appear to have improved since the 1970s. Native ethnic minorities appear to be faring little better than their parents (Blackaby et al., 2002). The subtleties and discrepancies of the workplace mean that the white person is frequently favoured over someone who is black (Royster, 2003). Despite legislation to combat racial discrimination, Britain's non-white ethnic minority does not appear to face a level playing field in the labour market. Within this group, the unemployment rate among Pakistani, Bangladeshi, Black African, and Black-Caribbean men is twice that for white men (6 per cent). And Pakistani and Bangladeshi women are at least three times as likely to be unemployed as white women (4 per cent) (EOC, 2004).

Even with higher-level qualifications, Pakistani and Bangladeshi women experience considerable barriers to employment, and have high levels of unemployment. There are major differences in the employment of Indian women, and those from Pakistan and Bangladesh. Women of Pakistani and Bangladeshi origin have low levels of economic activity—particularly married women and women with dependent children. By contrast, Indian women have much higher levels of economic activity, which are similar to those of white women. Differences in employment patterns are related to migration, level of education, language ability, local labour markets, and employment opportunities (Dale et al., 2002a).

Black women (those of African-Caribbean descent) are continually concentrated in specific occupations and sectors of the labour market. In the early post-migration years, black women were concentrated in nursing or semi-skilled manual work, such as catering. Today, most black women are employed in public administration (central and local government), retail, and distribution (Bhavnani, 1994). Within these occupations, black women are over-represented in the lower-paid and lower-status jobs; their presence as senior managers is virtually negligible (Modood, 1997). Black women continue to work in settings in which sexism and racism are everyday aspects of paid work (Reynolds, 2001). Ethnic minority men are also concentrated in particular sectors: high percentages of Chinese men (40 per cent) and Bangladeshi men (45 per cent) work in hotels and restaurants—an especially low-paid sector—compared to 3 per cent of white men (EOC, 2004).

EXAMPLE How to counter racism?

Black police officers in the *Metropolitan Police* in London (the 'Met') are four times more likely to leave during their first two years of employment than their white counterparts. The Met needs to increase the number of minority officers because it is failing to hit Home Office recruitment targets. In order to help to counter public perception of the organization as racist, the Met trialled a 'refer a friend' scheme, which would have paid black officers a £350 'bounty' for every minority recruit that they attracted. The staff felt, however, that it evoked images of slavery and the idea that you could 'buy' a black person. The *Black Police Association* also felt it to be demeaning and warned that officers keen to make money could abuse it.

(*Source:* Muir, 2003)

STOP AND THINK Cloning and the reproduction of sameness

Essed and Goldberg (2002) provocatively ask who, in the future, will be biologically cloned? It seems likely that, in the biological cloning of humans the preference will be for male, white, able-bodied, heterosexual, and highly intelligent beings.

While biological cloning is still to be realized, cultural cloning brings exclusion into focus. The preference for reproducing white (European) masculine privileges in terms of race, ethnicity, gender, or profession is not contested with the same force of indignation as might be the case with biological cloning. The exclusiveness of the whiteness of the highest European echelons remains silenced and thirty years of equal opportunities has done little to change the reproduction of sameness (see also Foroohar, 2002; Sanglin-Grant, 2002). Preferences for sameness are even embedded in our allegiance to copy culture, mass-produce, consumerism, and the promise of eternal growth (Schwartz, 1996; Klein, 1999).

Income and social mobility

The national income in the UK doubled between 1970 and 2000. As a nation, we are twice as well off as we were thirty or so years ago—but there are many indications that inequality and social mobility are worse now than they were in the past. The gap between the rich and poor has widened (Atkinson, 2001; ONS, 2005b; Dorling et al., 2007): the wealthiest 1 per cent owned 21 per cent of the UK's marketable wealth in 2003 (ONS, 2007), and the earnings gap between the highest and lowest paid workers has widened out by a considerable amount (Machin, 1999). Some of the best-paid workers are currently health professionals (with a median pay for full-time employees of £1,038 a week) followed by corporate managers (£668 a week). The lowest paid of all full-time employees in the UK are found in sales occupations (£259 a week). The estimated number of jobs paying below the national minimum wage in the UK amounts to 1.3 per cent of all jobs (ONS, 2007).

STOP AND THINK Are premiership footballers 'grossly overpaid'?

Premiership footballers earn an average of £676,000 a year, while the prime minister currently earns £187,000. According to a recent poll (Fabian Society, 2007), people think that top footballers should only be paid £62,000, whereas £135,000 is reasonable for a prime minister; respondents thought that it would be reasonable if the prime minister were to be at the top of the earning league, above J.K. Rowling, managing directors of the FTSE100 companies, and premiership footballers. The poll also found that wages for fast-food restaurant and supermarket checkout staff are considered too low.

Do you think that the distribution of rewards, as it is, is fair?

(Source: Fabian Society, 2007)

There are, of course, those working in countries such as Pakistan and Bangladesh—for example, in companies manufacturing clothes for British high streets—who are paid far less than those working in the UK. For example, while the living wage is £30 a month in Bangladesh, the minimum wage is only £7 per month (Labour Behind the Label, 2008). But definitions of 'poverty' differ. The UK government defines a household in poverty as having income that is below 60 per cent of the median income. According to this definition, 21 per cent of children and pensioners, and 14 per cent of adults in the UK live below the poverty line (BBC News, 22 April 2005). If the definition is slightly changed to focus on those whose income is below the average, there has been massive rise in the proportion of children growing up in poverty: in 1979, 13 per cent of children lived in such households; by 1996, this had risen to 33 per cent (Gregg et al., 1999).

Relative social mobility—that is, the relative chances of people from different social backgrounds moving into a given social class—has remained fairly stable for most of the century (Goldthorpe and Payne, 1986; Aldridge, 2001; Sutton Trust, 2008). Contrary to many expectations, the UK and the USA have the lowest levels of gross generational mobility, lying well below those of Canada and the Nordic countries. Higher education is one way of achieving social mobility: almost one in two school leavers go to university now; in the 1970s, only one in eight did so. But the expansion of higher education in the UK since the late 1980s has, so far, disproportionately benefited those from the more affluent families (Blanden et al., 2005)—particularly those in the higher social classes. Data from the *Office of National Statistics* (ONS) show that, in 1991–92, 35 per cent of those in the top three social classes went to university, compared with 11 per cent from the bottom three (a gap of 24 percentage points). Ten years later, although the proportions of both higher and lower social class students had increased because of the expansion of university places, the 'gap' between the social classes had increased to 31 percentage points (Sutton Trust, 2008).

One of the reasons for lack of social mobility may be the cost of education: prospective students from lower socio-economic backgrounds are more likely than those from better-off ones to report that they are deterred by the cost of higher education and fear building up large debts (Forsyth and Furlong, 2000; 2003; Christie and Munro, 2003). Students from poorer backgrounds are also generally ignorant of the system of grants and bursaries on offer (Sutton Trust, 2008), meaning that students from low-income families are paying more for higher education and receive less help with repayments once they graduate (Furlong and Cartmel, 2005). Financial pressures mean that they are then more likely to take jobs that do not require a degree when they leave university, often feeling compelled to take the first job that comes along—particularly if they lack significant financial support from their families. This, in turn, makes it harder to gain a job that leads to a graduate career and move to jobs in which they are better able to repay debts.

In the USA, there has been talk of the 'fortunate fifth'—that is, the top 20 per cent of society in terms of wealth and wages, most of whom will have benefited from higher education. Their earnings and wealth have increased faster than among the other 80 per cent of society, and they are accused of separating themselves from others by wealth, where they live, and where they choose to educate their children. They are accused of having abdicated their social responsibility (*University Week*, 2000): to improve the economic position of the bottom four-fifths requires that the fortunate fifth share its wealth (Reich, 1991).

STOP AND THINK **Social mobility and the middle class**

Barbara Ehrenreich (1989) castigates the middle classes as elitist, self-absorbed, and selfish. According to Ehrenreich, the middle classes have status anxiety and so live with a constant 'fear of falling' from their privileged place in society.

Do you think that Ehrenreich is right?

Men and women working

In the UK, since 1975, men's employment has declined from around nine out of ten to eight out of ten (79 per cent) for men of working age (that is, aged 16–64). At the same time, women's employment has increased from around six out of ten to seven out of ten (70 per cent) for women of working age (ONS, 2005b). Despite this, women in the labour force continue to face inequality. Women still lag behind men in terms of income: in 2005, average hourly earnings for women working full-time were £11.67, while for men they were £14.08, representing a full-time gender pay gap of 17.1 per cent (ONS, 2005b). And surveys regularly uncover pay gaps among managers.

STOP AND THINK Why are women workers still going cheap?

A study by the *Equal Opportunities Commission* (EOC) found that an awareness of the gap between men's and women's pay was low among students. It launched a campaign entitled '15% off: why are women workers still going cheap?', which aimed to encourage students to ask prospective employers if they could demonstrate that their pay systems were fair to women.

Would you be comfortable asking prospective employers this question?

Jobs tend to be seen as either 'male' or 'female' jobs. Men dominate some industries, such as construction (90 per cent male) and manufacturing (75 per cent male), while women dominate in health and social work (79 per cent female) and education (73 per cent female). Less than 1 per cent of plumbers are women and only 2 per cent of childcare workers are men (ONS, 2005b).

Students are also finding it necessary to take on paid work. A bank survey found that 52 per cent of students work in the UK; on average, they work for 17.8 hours a week. Male students earn about £122 per week, compared with female students, who earn £107—but who work slightly longer hours. Far fewer males are, however, in paid employment than their female counterparts (Hunter, 2007).

Academic qualifications have a crucial impact on employment prospects and earnings potential. While the qualification levels of women and men under the age of 25 are now very similar, currently, a higher percentage of males have qualifications (EOC, 2003). Qualifications and the presence of dependent children influence the very different patterns of employment of men and women. Following the birth of their children, some women are able to return to full-time work, but many work part-time and others withdraw from the labour market altogether. During the past twenty-five years, there has been an increase in poverty among mothers—particularly lone mothers (who head 90 per cent of one-parent families) (ibid.).

The number of children that parents have is also changing: rather than the average family having 2.5 children, it is now expected that they will have 1.8 children (Evandrou and Falkingham, 2000). Women still take the major share of responsibility for housework and childcare, even when both partners work (Bianchi et al., 1999). Women, on average, do about 70 per cent of domestic work (Baxter, 2000)—even when husbands are retired or unemployed. Husbands' household labour is 'remarkably unresponsive' to decreases in their overall working hours, to increases in their wives' working hours, and to the fact that their wife is a high earner (Kynaston, 1996). But the context in which work is defined as men's or women's work must be considered: men's lives 'continue to be consistently enhanced by their appropriation of female labour' (ibid.: 233)—little mention of which made in books on work or organizational behaviour.

Finally, the proportion of women remaining childless has almost doubled in recent decades, from one in ten born in 1940, to nearly one in five born in 1959 (Simpson, 2006). And while it might be assumed that never-married women without children would not experience work–life conflict, research has shown that they do—often at similar levels to those experienced by other groups of working women (Hamilton et al., 2006). This may be because never-married women without children are often viewed as prime candidates for extra projects, staying late, or working weekends (Wilson, 2004). They also often allow work to completely consume them (Anderson et al., 1994).

Men, women, and management

Although global data show that women continue to increase their share of managerial positions, the rate of progress is slow and uneven. For example, in a study of forty-eight countries, women's share of managerial jobs increased by only between 1 and 5 per cent in twenty-six countries between 1996 and 1999, and 2000 and 2002. While a few countries such as Costa Rica showed steep increases in women in managerial positions (23.5 per cent), others experienced declines, including Canada (-3.7 per cent) and Ireland (-5.6 per cent) (ILO, 2004). Women hold few of the top managerial jobs: the higher the organizational level, the more glaring the gender gap (Schein, 2007). For example, in the USA, among the Fortune 500 companies, women hold 14.7 per cent of all board places (Catalyst, 2006). In the UK, women held 10.5 per cent of all directorships among the FTSE100 companies (Singh and Vinnicombe, 2005). And while 50 per cent of graduate recruits are female, the proportion reaching senior levels falls to 30 per cent and to just 15 per cent in executive roles (Treanor, 2006).

STOP AND THINK **Why is the number of women in top positions falling?**

How would you explain why there is evidence that the number of women in top positions in UK companies has been found to be falling? *The Guardian*'s pay survey, published in October 2006, found that there were only twelve female executive directors at FTSE100 companies during 2005—down from twenty. The twelve women were spread among just ten companies.

The major barrier to women's progress in management continues to be the gender stereotyping of the managerial position, which is viewed as intrinsically 'male'. In the last thirty years, while the managerial gender stereotype has changed among women, male managers and male management students have been found to hold attitudes similar to those held in the 1970s (Schein, 2007). Women in management are not considered natural allies (Hite, 2005; Mavin, 2006). The nature of senior management—in particular, the behaviours and actions required to gain entry and remain within this environment—does little to sustain notions of 'sisterhood' or solidarity behaviour. Women in senior management have consequently been seen to fight amongst themselves (Mavin, 2006).

23

Mothers' and fathers' attitudes to work and family

While the volume of research on fathers has increased, discussion about work and family life still tends to be focused on 'working mothers': rarely do we hear of 'working fathers'. Mothers undertake the majority of childcare in all European countries (Smith, 2007); the majority of mothers make significant changes to their working lives to accommodate children. They are likely to take prime responsibility for childcare because of the pay gap, the fact that they tend to earn less than their partner, and high childcare costs (Hatten et al., 2002). Mothers are also more likely than fathers to take time off work when children are sick (O'Brien and Shemilt, 2003).

Men generally want to work, and few men want to reduce their hours or stop work altogether, yet fathers continue to work long hours. Some fathers work longer hours when children are born, feeling a greater pressure to provide financially; others compress their work into fewer hours, so that they can get home earlier. Only a small minority of fathers make major changes that enable them to be more involved in family life. About one in five of European fathers of children under the age of 6 spend 'substantial paternal time' (more than 28 hours a week) looking after their children; there are, however, considerable differences between countries in the percentage of fathers who do so—for example, 43 per cent in Denmark and 8 per cent in Portugal (Smith, 2007).

Fathers' use of flexible working practices is low in the UK. Flexitime, part-time or reduced hours, and job sharing are used by 20 per cent, 6 per cent, and 2 per cent of fathers, respectively (O'Brien and Shemilt, 2003). New parental rights at work came into force in 2003: statutory maternity leave rose from eighteen to twenty-six weeks and, for the first time, men were given the right to two weeks' paid paternity leave and flexible working hours. It remains to be seen, however, whether many men will take up the latter rights, because a man who works long hours is a cultural paradigm.

Men now have the right to two weeks of paid paternity leave, can request flexible hours, and are eligible for up to thirteen weeks of parental leave for children under 6 or disabled children under the age of 18. Men are more actively involved in childcare than they were twenty years ago (Sweet, 2003)—but men want to use paid work as an excuse not to do work (at home), which they perceive as low status and unpaid (Cary Cooper, quoted ibid.).

Is this true in your experience?

Male professional workers appear to be caught in their own cultural stereotypes, so are unlikely to lower barriers to flexible working. There seems to be an 'executive hourglass' created by a club of workaholics addicted to working long hours, which sets the performance standard for themselves and those seeking promotion. A survey of male professional workers (Knell and Savage, 1999) found that while 84 per cent believed that organizations should offer flexible working and over half indicated that they would like greater flexibility at work, the majority displayed a clear preference for full-time working. They did not want to work part-time and were not prepared to work shorter hours for less money. The male workers felt that flexible working practices would be abused and that being flexible would lead to 'career death' in terms of lack of promotional opportunities; 90 per cent thought that senior roles require more commitment than a 9–5 working day. The authors concluded that if these entrenched attitudes are left unchecked and unchallenged, it will continue to prove difficult for individuals to balance a serious working career with their life responsibilities. It will also be hard for those who do work flexibly to reach senior management positions unless they work at the same pace as their colleagues.

Working hours

Not so long ago, the conventional wisdom was that technological advances would lead to a 'problem of leisure'; on the contrary, working hours rose in the 1990s. While the average blue-collar worker in Europe now puts in around 41 hours a week, the figure rises to 43 hours for professionals and 50 hours for managers. About 30–40 per cent of managers are working in excess of their contractual hours (Bunting, 2004)—doing so because of economic factors, such as job insecurity. As a result, Bunting calls those who do so 'willing slaves': life is work and work is life for the willing slaves who hand over large chunks of themselves to their employers in return for the pay.

STOP AND THINK Cases of enslavement?

Bunting (2004), in *Willing Slaves*, argues that instead of hard work bringing wealth and satisfaction, it brings worry, illness, poverty, and debt. She argues that we are enslaved by work when we are overworked and stressed. Further, we are coerced by 'brand'. Companies such as *Microsoft*, *Asda*, and *Orange* use concepts such as brand loyalty and teamwork to give the illusion that the company is bringing some sort of meaning into people's lives.

Asda, for example, encourages its employees to believe that they are lucky to be part of a caring family. Managers look for cheerful souls who are team players. One *Asda* manager describes an occasion on which employees were asked to wear a pink item of clothing for Breast Cancer Awareness Day. Two dissenters forgot and were told to go home by the manager, who added: 'You're not in the team.' They went off, bought pink shirts, and came back.

Is this an example of 'willing slaves' or are there alternative explanations for this behaviour?

(*Source:* Hodgkinson, 2004)

The USA has the longest working hours in the developed world; the UK comes in just behind. Recent surveys estimate that only 44 per cent of workers use up their full entitlement of annual leave, while 65 per cent of UK workers do not use their full lunch allowance (Gillan, 2005). Evidence shows that if you work consistently long hours, over 45 hours a week every week, it will damage your health. In 1987, the Japanese Ministry of Labour acknowledged that it had a problem with death from overwork and began to publish statistics. In 2001, the numbers in Japan reached a record level, with forty-three workers dying (ibid.).

Part-time working

Another change that has come about over recent years relates to the number of part-time jobs. Part-time working is mainly found in restaurants, hotels, and retail establishments, and other sectors of the 'leisure' industry. Currently, every fourth job is part-time, and it is predicted that, between 2002 and 2012, most of the jobs that will be created will be part-time and taken by women (Tomlinson, 2007). In the recent past, as employment levels have recovered following recessions, most job growth has been in part-time work and the bulk of the new jobs have been taken by women, although some part-time work has gone to men. Part-time hours are adopted by 42 per cent of women employees and 9 per cent of men (ONS, 2005a)—but while the vast majority of part-timers (94 per cent) have been said to have 'voluntarily' chosen to work fewer hours (ONS, 2003a), a significant minority do not.

Many believe that part-time work offers flexibility and choice—particularly in terms of time that can be spent with the family. Part-time jobs tend, however, to represent lower skill levels, wage rates, and promotion prospects than those that are full-time. While part-time work is not associated with job insecurity and unemployment, it constitutes a trap that lowers women's lifetime employment prospects and earnings; there is a 'part-time penalty' (Manning and Petrongolo, 2004). Many women working part-time are working below their potential (Grant et al., 2005); it has also been found that women are increasingly dissatisfied with poor-quality part-time work (Taylor, 2002; Tomlinson, 2007). Part-time work can be difficult to obtain in some jobs, such as management, in which only 6 per cent of managers and senior officials are employed part-time; there are, then, still far too few opportunities for flexible working at senior levels in organizations (EOC, 2002). But in addition to reducing a job to part-time hours, employers might consider splitting a full-time job between two people (job sharing) as a way of sharing heavy management responsibilities. Alternatively, the manager might be allowed to work from home.

Homeworking

Working from home is a global phenomenon (Felstead and Jewson, 2000). Official statistics on homeworking can be found for the USA, Canada, Australia, New Zealand, the European Union, Japan, India, and Hong Kong, as well as some developing nations; it appears to be a growing phenomenon—particularly in the USA, Australia, Canada, and Europe. The extent of homeworking in the UK has increased dramatically in the past two decades (see http://www.homeworking.gn.apc.org). Home-workers perform a huge range of jobs, such as sewing, knitting, engraving, inspecting industrial seals, assembling greeting cards, and packing gift tags or tights, while others work in telesales or data inputting.

While it is difficult to gain access to, and measure the exact numbers of, homeworkers (Phizacklea and Wolkowitz, 1995), it has been estimated that they grew in number over the period 1981–98 from 1.5 per cent of the workforce to 2.5 per cent (Felstead and Jewson, 2000). Ethnic minorities are, however, over-represented among those working at home in manual occupations. It is thought that nearly half of all homeworkers are from ethnic minorities and that over a third are of Pakistani, Indian, or Bangladeshi origin (Low Pay Commission, 1998). Asian women continue to experience greater difficulties in finding employment outside the home than equivalent white women (Dale et al., 2002b), and while those working from home rank among the lowest paid in the labour market, white homeworkers fare better than non-white (Felstead and Jewson, 2000).

Other scene-setting issues

Chapters in texts on organizational behaviour—particularly those on organizational culture—usually fail to acknowledge that those seeking to be recruited have often considered the values and culture of the organization to which they have applied. For example, if you are against testing on animals, you are unlikely to apply for a job at *Huntingdon Life Sciences* near Cambridge, England. Similarly, *Nestlé*, *Nike*, *McDonald's*, and *Coca Cola* are well-known companies providing employment for graduates, but they are also the most boycotted brands on the planet (Tran, 2005). In addition, organizational cultures and behaviours can be racist, elitist, sexist, and ageist; they can also be heterosexist (Smith and Ingram, 2004). There are strains inherent in being a member of a minority whose needs, values, culture, and experience are at odds with those of the majority.

It might be useful to know about organizational behaviours such as corruption, which is a global phenomenon. It has been estimated, for example, that about £200 billion flows out of Africa into UK and other banks through corrupt practices, money laundering, and other criminal means. As much as $30 billion in aid for Africa has ended up in foreign bank accounts (Christian Aid, 2008), and some $1 trillion dollars of 'dirty money'—that is, money derived from criminal or corrupt activities or tax avoidance—is stashed in offshore tax havens (Baker, 2005).

It might be interesting to look at not-for-profit organizations, and see whether organizational behaviour and work is radically different from that in profit-making organizations. A not-for-profit organization aims to support an issue or matter of private interest or public concern and, as the name suggests, without concern for profit. The *Bill and Melinda Gates Foundation* is thought to be among the largest of these organizations. Some will be charities, others will be in arts or sports, and some will focus on social entrepreneurship, including companies that make biodiesel fuel from weeds in India, or lend money to micro-businesses in Bangladesh (see Day, 2006).

EXAMPLE **A not-for-profit organization in the sporting world**

The *British Cheerleading Association* is the governing body for the athletic discipline of cheerleading in the UK and is a non-profit, community-based organization that represents numerous cheerleading clubs. Russell Crowe recently hit the sports news headlines when he banned cheerleaders at the rugby team that he co-owns following complaints about the sexism inherent in scantily clad women shaking their pompoms for male rugby fans.

(*Source:* Jeffries, 2007)

What further scene-setting issues would you need to consider? Having looked at the context in which work is organized and set the scene in this chapter, the next chapters will begin looking at the realities of work and non-work, the work that managers do, the rationale behind how jobs are designed, and how people are fitted into jobs.

KEY POINTS

- Scene-setting issues—that is, context issues—may include a consideration of issues such as who is employed (including gender, parental responsibilities, age, race, etc.), on what terms, and how organizations contribute or act to increase equality or to prevent or counter inequality for individuals or groups in society.

- Prejudice and discrimination are common behaviours in organizations.

- Managing might mean exploiting labour; more positively, it might mean helping to grow the economy through the development of new enterprise.

- The scene-setting information, or knowledge, that is required will depend on the kind of organizations in which you are involved, employed or interested. You need to decide what kinds of facts and behaviours you want to consider as relevant.

- You may be interested in scene-setting issues and facts on management in certain sectors of the economy, or in questions such as how far can it be said that managers are responsible for maintaining famine, poverty, or inequality, and whether globalization and organizations' involvement in it is contributing towards greater inequality. You may, however, have no interest in any of these wider issues. The chapter challenges you to think about what scene-setting issues you see as relevant to people and work, and to develop your knowledge and understanding of them, and of how they may impact on organizational behaviour.

CASE STUDY
Organizing against injustice

This case study focuses on an unusual organization that has been set up for a specific purpose: to organize against injustices such as the following.

Those who stay in expensive hotel rooms and leave a disgusting mess behind can spend £500 a night; those who clean it up can work six days a week and yet take home less than £200. There is a yawning gap between rich and poor in Britain.

An organization has been set up to revolt and organize against injustices such as these. It is a registered charity called the *Citizen Organizing Foundation* and has been operating for about ten years. It brings together religious and community groups, schools, students unions, and trade unions into local alliances. It aims to create networks of competent, informed, and organized citizens to influence, for the common good, decisions that impact on their community. It starts with community matters, such as clean and safe streets, and then goes on to build other campaigns. Priorities are determined democratically. One of the Foundation's biggest triumphs has related to pay amongst cleaners in London. In the Midlands, where many members are Muslims, it has carried out cultural awareness training with the police.

(*Sources: The Guardian*, Tuesday 21 November 2006; 'Get back to our roots', Neal Lawson and www.cof.org.uk)

Questions

1. Do organizations such as this appeal to you? If yes, why? If no, why not?

FURTHER READING

Bradley, H., Erikson, M., Stephenson, C., and Williams, S. (2000) *Myths at Work*, Cambridge: Polity Press
Includes chapters on the debates about business and organization: for example, on globalization.

Curran, J. and Blackburn, R.A. (2001) *Researching the Small Enterprise*, London: Sage Small and medium-sized businesses are clearly important to the economy, and this book is a good introduction to the subject area.

Erikson, M., Stephenson, C., Bradley, H., and Williams, S. (2009) *Business in Society*, Cambridge: Polity Press Includes chapters on the debates about business and organization: for example, on globalization.

Grint, K. (2005) *The Sociology of Work*, 3rd edn, Cambridge: Polity Press, ch. 1 Offers contrasting views on work.

Various newspapers Offer online search facilities that allow you to use a key word for the topical organizational issues of the day.

Various Office for National Statistics (ONS) publications Offer a context for behaviour that can be observed in organizations.

Various publications from charities such as the Joseph Rowntree Foundation Offer insight into a broad range of current topics, as well as organizations and how they might function.

LINKS TO FILMS AND NOVELS

Blue Collar (1978) dir. P. Schrader Film about a trio of Detroit car workers (including Richard Pryor), who are living at the mercy of a heartless corporation and a corrupt union.

Titanic (1997) dir. J. Cameron This film uses class as a central theme.

Lee, H. (1960) *To Kill a Mocking Bird; To Kill a Mocking Bird* (1962) dir. R. Mulligan Both the book and its screen adaptation focus on class and race.

Lewycka, M. (2007) *Two Caravans* A novel depicting the exploitation of migrant labour, along with issues such as prostitution and factory farming. It tells the story of strawberry pickers who find themselves working for some unethical employers. Despite its bleak subject matter, the novel is also humorous and charming in places.

RESEARCH QUESTIONS

1. How accessible and affordable is childcare for working parents? The Daycare Trust, a charity, found that the cost of full-time childcare in 2007 was, on average, £152 a week in England—as compared to the average gross weekly earnings of £447. A quarter of all mothers of preschool children are not able to access the type of childcare that they would prefer (Gaber, 2003).

2. Should chief executives and managers of charities be paid wages that match those found in other organizations? Would those who give to charity be 'put off' doing so if they were to know how much goes towards manager's salaries?

REFERENCES

Age Concern (1998) *Age Discrimination: Make It a Thing of the Past*, London: Age Concern.

Ainsworth, S. (2002) 'The "feminine advantage": A discursive analysis of the invisibility of older women workers', *Gender, Work and Organization*, 9(5): 579–601.

Aldridge, S. (2001) *Social Mobility: A Discussion Paper*, London: Cabinet Office Performance and Innovation Unit.

Anderson, C.M., Stewart, S., and Dimidjian, S. (1994) *Flying Solo: Single Women in Midlife*, New York: W.W. Norton & Co.

Atkinson, M. (2001) 'New technology creates a larger rift between rich and poor', *The Guardian*, 24 January, available online at http://www.guardian.co.uk/technology/2001/jan/24/internetnews.business1

Baker, R. (2005) *Capitalism's Achilles Heel: Dirty Money and How to Renew the Free Market System*, New Jersey: John Wiley & Sons.

Baxter, J. (2000) 'The joys and justice of housework', *Sociology,* 34(4): 609–31.

Bhavnani, R. (1994) *Black Women in the Labour Market: A Research Review*, London: Equal Opportunities Commission.

Bianchi, S., Robinson, J.P., Sayer, L., and Milkie, M. (1999) 'Is anyone cleaning the bathroom? Trends in gender differentials in housework', Paper presented at the American Sociological Association Meetings, Chicago, IL, August.

Blackaby, D.H., Leslie, D.G., Murphy, P.D., and O'Leary, N.C. (2002) 'White/ethnic minority earnings and employment differentials in Britain: Evidence from the LFS', *Oxford Economic Papers*, 54/270–97.

Blanden, J., Goodman, A., Gregg, P., and Machin, S. (2002) *Changes in Intergenerational Mobility in Britain*, LSE Centre for Economic Performance, Paper No. 517, January.

_____, Gregg, P., and Machin, S. (2005) *Intergenerational Mobility in Europe and North America: A Report by the Sutton Trust*, LSE Centre for Economic Performance, April.

Bradley, H., Erikson, M., Stephenson, C., and Williams, S. (2000) *Myths at Work*, Cambridge: Polity Press.

Brady, B. (2003) 'Army battle to hold on to their bear necessities', *Scotland on Sunday,* 11 May, p. 8.

British Social Attitudes (2000) *Women's Attitudes to Combining Paid Work and Family Life*, London: Women's Unit of the Cabinet Office.

Brown, M.K., Carnoy, M., Currie, E., Duster, T., and Oppenheimer, D.B. (2003) *Whitewashing Race: The Myth Of A Color-Blind Society*, Berkeley, CA: University of California Press.

Bunting, M. (2004) *Willing Slaves: How The Overwork Culture is Ruling Our Lives*, London: Harper Collins.

Catalyst (2006) *Catalyst Census of Women Board Directors of the Fortune 500*, New York: Catalyst.

Chiu, W.C., Chan, A.W., Snape, E., and Redman, R. (2001) 'Age stereotypes and discriminatory attitudes towards older workers: An East–West comparison', *Human Relations*, 54(5): 629–61.

Christian Aid (2008) 'From local to global: Stopping corruption from stunting development', December, available online at http://www.christianaid.org.uk/images/from-local-to-global.pdf

Christie, H. and Munro, M. (2003) 'The logic of loans', *British Journal of Sociology of Education*, 24(50): 621–36.

_____, _____, and Rettig, H. (2001) 'Making ends meet', *Studies in Higher Education*, 26(3): 363–83.

Clegg, S., Kornberger, M., and Pitsis, T. (2008) *Managing and Organizations: An Introduction to Theory and Practice*, 2nd edn, London: Sage.

Dale, A., Kalra, V., and Fieldhouse, E. (2002a) 'Routes into education and employment for young Pakistani and Bangladeshi women in the UK', *Ethnic and Racial Studies*, 25(6): 942–68.

_____, Shaheen, N., Fieldhouse, E., and Kalra, V. (2002b) 'The labour market prospects for Pakistani and Bangladeshi women', *Work, Employment and Society*, 16(1): 5–25.

Day, P. (2006) 'Young, gifted and not for profit', *BBC News*, 25 April, available online at http://news.bbc.co.uk

Department for Education and Employment (DfEE) (2001a) *Age Diversity: Summary of Research Findings*, London: HMSO.

_____ (2001b) *Action on Age: Report on the Consultation on Age Discrimination in Employment*, March, London: HMSO.

Department of Trade and Industry (DTI) (2006) Statistical Press Release URN 06/92, 31 August, London.

Dorling, D., Rigby, J., Wheeler, B., Ballas, D., Thomas, B., Fahmy, E, Gordon, D., and Lupton, R. (2007) *Poverty, Wealth and Place in Britain 1968 to 2005*, London: Joseph Rowntree Foundation/Policy Press.

Duncan, C. (2003) 'Assessing anti-ageism routes to older worker re-engagement', *Work, Employment and Society*, 17(1):101–20.

29

_____ and Loretto, W. (2004) 'Never the right age? Gender and age-based discrimination in employment', *Gender, Work and Organization*, 11(1): 95–115.

Egan, B. (2001) *The Widow's Might: How Charities Depend on the Poor*, London: Social Market Foundation.

Ehrenreich, B. (1989) *Fear of Falling: The Inner Life of the Middle Class*, New York: Pantheon Books.

Encel, S. and Studencki, H. (1997), *Gendered Ageism: Job Search Experiences of Older Women*, NSW Committee on Ageism and the Department for Women, Sydney (cited in Ainsworth, 2002).

Equal Opportunities Commission (2001) *EOC Analysis of Labour Force Survey*, Spring, London: ONS.

_____ (2002) *Women and Men in Britain: Management*, Manchester: EOC.

_____ (2003) *The Lifecycle of Inequality*, Manchester: EOC.

_____ (2004) *Ethnic Minority Women and Men*, Briefing, December.

Erikson, M., Stephenson, C., Bradley, H., and Williams, S. (2009) *Business in Society*, Cambridge: Polity Press.

Essed, P. and Goldberg, D.T. (2002) 'Cloning cultures: The social injustices of sameness', *Ethnic and Racial Studies*, 25(6):1066–82.

European Community (2006) *Enterprise and Industry Facts and Figures*, available online at http://ec.europa.eu/enterprise/entrepreneurship/facts_figures.htm

Evandrou, M. and Falkingham, J. (2000) 'Looking back to look forward: Lessons from four birth cohorts for ageing in the 21st century', *Population Trends*, 99: 27–36.

Fabian Society (2007) *Report on Equality in Britain*, London: Fabian Society.

Felstead, A. and Jewson, N. (2000) *In Work, at Home: Towards an Understanding of Homeworking*, London: Routledge.

Foroohar, R. (2002) 'Race in the boardroom', *Newsweek*, 18 February, available online at http://www.newsweek.com/id/63793

Forsyth, A. and Furlong, A. (2000) *Socioeconomic Disadvantage and Access to Higher Education*, Bristol: Policy Press.

_____ _____ (2003) 'Access to higher education and disadvantaged young people', *British Educational Research Journal*, 29(2): 205–25.

Fraser, S. (2004) *Finance for Small and Medium-Sized Enterprises*, Warwick: Warwick Business School Centre for Small and Medium Sized Enterprises.

Furlong, A. and Cartmel, F. (2005) *Graduates from Disadvantaged Families: Early Labour Market Experiences*, Bristol: Joseph Rowntree Foundation/Policy Press.

Gaber, I. (2003) 'Childcare still failing', *The Guardian*, 16 April, available online at http://www.guardian.co.uk/society/2003/apr/16/guardiansocietysupplement5

Gillan, A. (2005) 'Work until you drop: How the long-hours culture is killing us', *The Guardian*, Saturday 20 August.

Goldthorpe, J.H. and Payne, C. (1986) 'Trends in intergenerational class mobility in England and Wales', *Sociology*, 20: 1024.

Government Actuaries Department (2005) '2004-based population projections by age at last birthday', available online at http://www.gad.gov.uk/Documents/Demography/Projections/2004-based_national_population_projections.pdf

Grant, L. Yeandle, S., and Buckner, L. (2005) *Working Below Potential: Women and Part-Time Work*, Manchester: EOC.

Gregg, P. and Machin, S. (1999) 'Childhood disadvantage and success or failure in the labour market', in D. Blanchflower and R. Freeman (eds.), *Youth Employment and Joblessness in Advanced Countries*, Cambridge, MA: National Bureau of Economic Research, ch. 6.

_____ and Wadsworth, J. (eds) (1999) *The State of Working Britain*, Manchester: Manchester University Press.

_____, Hansen, K., and Wadsworth, J. (1999) 'The rise of the workless household', in Gregg and Wadsworth (eds) *The State of Working Britain*, Manchester: Manchester University Press, ch. 5.

Grimley Evans, J., Goldacre, M.J., Hodkinson, M., Lamb, S., and Savory, M. (1992) *Health: Abilities and Well Being in the Third Age*, The Carnegie Inquiry into the Third Age Research Paper No. 9, Dunfermline: The Carnegie Trust.

Hamilton, E.A., Gordon, J.R., and Whelan-Berry, K.S. (2006) 'Understanding the work–life conflict of never-married women without children', *Women in Management Review*, 21(5): 393–415.

Hatten, W., Vinter, L., and Williams, R. (2002) *Dads on Dads: Needs and Expectations at Home and at Work*, Mori Social Research Institute Research Discussion Series, Manchester: EOC.

Herriot, P. and Scott-Jackson, W. (2002) 'Globalization, social identities and employment', *British Journal of Management*, 13: 249–57.

Hilpern, K. (2003) 'Ageism in reverse', *The Guardian,* 14 April, available online at http://www.guardian.co.uk/money/2003/apr/14/careers.jobsadvice4

Hirst, P.Q. and Thompson, G.F. (1999) *Globalization in Question: The International Economy and the Possibilities of Governance*, 2nd edn, Cambridge: Polity Press.

_____ _____ (2000) 'Globalization in one country? The peculiarities of the British', *Economy and Society*, 29(3), 335–56.

Hite, S. (2005) 'The psychology with which women regard other women', available online at http://www.hite-research.com/artpsychology.html

Hodgkinson, T. (2004) 'Branded for life', *The Guardian*, 3 July, available online at http://www.guardian.co.uk/books/2004/jul/03/highereducation.news2

Hunter, T. (2007) 'Working students lose out on pay', *Scotland on Sunday*, 12 August, p. 9.

Internal Revenue Service (IRS) (2003) 'Legislation comes of age', *IRS Employment Review*, 782: 8–15.

International Labour Organization (ILO) (2004) *Global Employment Trends*, January, available online at http://www.ilo.org/public/english/employment/strat/download/trends.pdf

Isaak, R.A. (2005) *The Globalization Gap: How the Rich Get Richer and the Poor Get Left Further Behind*, Upper Saddle River, NJ: Pearson Education.

Jacobs, K. and Rein, M. (1994) 'Early retirement: stability, reversal or redefinition', in F. Naschold and B. de Vroom (eds) *Regulating Employment Welfare*, Berlin: De Gruyter, pp. 1–17.

Jeffries, S. (2007) 'Give me an "ow"! Give me an "argh"!', *The Guardian*, 9 April, available online at http://www.guardian.co.uk/world/2007/apr/09/usa.americansports

Jones L., Engstrom, D., Hilliard, T., and Diaz, M. (2007) 'Globalization and human trafficking', *Journal of Sociology and Social Welfare*, XXXIV(2): 107–22.

Kite, M.E., Stockdale, G.D., Whitley, B.E., and Johnson, B.T. (2005) 'Attitudes toward younger and older adults: An updated meta-analytic review', *Journal of Social Issues*, 61(2): 241–66.

Klein, N. (1999) *No Logo*, New York: Picador.

Knell, J. and Savage, C. (1999) 'Flexible working and male professionals: Can't change, won't change', in *Industrial Society*, London: The Resource Connection.

Kynaston, C. (1996) 'The everyday exploitation of women: Housework and the patriarchal mode of production', *Women's Studies International Forum*, 19: 221–37.

Labour Behind the Label (2008) 'Let's clean up fashion: The state of pay behind the UK high street', available online at http://www.cleanupfashion.co.uk

Loretto, W. and White, P. (2006) 'Employers' attitudes, practices and policies towards older workers', *Human Resource Management Journal*, 16(3): 313–30.

_____, Duncan, C., and White, P. (2000) 'Ageism and employment: Controversies and ambiguities and younger people's perceptions', *Ageing and Society*, 20: 279–302.

_____, Vickerstaff, S., and White, P. (2005) *Older Workers and Options for Flexible Work*, Manchester: EOC.

31

Low Pay Commission (1998) *The National Minimum Wage: First Report of the Low Pay Commission*, London: HMSO.

Machin, S. (1999) 'Wage inequality in the 1970s, 1980s and 1990s', in Gregg and Wadsworth (eds) *The State of Working Britain*, Manchester: Manchester University Press, ch. 12.

Manning, A. and Petrongolo, B. (2004) *The Part-Time Pay Penalty*, Centre for Economic Performance Discussion Paper No. 679, March, available online at http:/cep.lse.ac.uk/pubs/download/dp0679.pdf

Mavin, S. (2006) 'Venus envy 2: Sisterhood, queen bees and female misogyny in management', *Women in Management Review*, 21(5): 349–64.

McGinnity, F. (2002) 'The labour-force participation of the wives of unemployed men: Comparing Britain and West Germany using longitudinal data', *European Sociological Review*, 18(4): 473–88.

McGregor, J. (2001) *Employment of the Older Worker*, Palmerston North, NZ: Massey University.

Modood, T. (1997) *Ethnic Minorities in Britain*, London: PSI.

Muir, H. (2003) 'Met's "black bounty" recruitment plan shelved', *The Guardian*, 20 May, available online at http://www.guardian.co.uk/society/2003/may/20/raceequality.uknews

National Council for Voluntary Organizations (NCVO) (2007) *UK Giving 2005/6*, available online at http://www.ncvo-vol.org.uk

Nickolls, A. and Opal, C. (2005) *Fair Trade: Market-Driven Ethical Consumption*, London: Sage.

O'Brien, M. and Shemilt, I. (2003) *Working Fathers: Earning and Caring*, Manchester: EOC.

Office for National Statistics (1999) *Social Focus on Older People*, London: HMSO.

_____ (2000) *Population Trends*, London: HMSO.

_____ (2001) *Labour Force Survey*, London: HMSO, available online at http://www.dcsf.gov.uk/rsgateway/DB/VOL/v000303/index.shtml

_____ (2003a) 'Labour market spotlight: Reasons given for working part-time for employees and self-employed', *Labour Market Trends*, March, London: HMSO.

_____ (2003b) *New Earnings Survey Data 2003: Analysis by Occupation*, London: ONS.

_____ (2005a) *Labour Market Statistics: Time Series Data and Labour Force Survey*, Spring, London: HMSO.

_____ (2005b) *Social Trends No. 35*, London: HMSO.

_____ (2007) 'Society share of the wealth, and labour market earnings and low-paid jobs', available onilne at http://www.statistics.gov.uk/cci/nugget.asp?id=2

Onyx, J. (1998) Older women workers: A double jeopardy', in M. Patrickson and L. Harmann (eds), *Managing an Ageing Workforce*, Warriewood, NSW: Woodlane.

Organisation for Economic Cooperation and Development (OECD) (2004) *Ageing and Employment Policies: United Kingdom*, Paris: OECD.

Oviatt, B. and McDougall, P. (1995) 'Global start-ups: Entrepreneurs on a worldwide stage', *Academy of Management Executive*, 9(2): 30–44.

Phizacklea, A. and Walters, S. (2000) *A Statistical Portrait of Working at Home in the UK: Evidence from the Labour Force Survey*, Economic and Social Research Council Future of Work Programme Paper Series, Swindon: ESRC.

_____ and Wolkowitz, C. (1995) *Homeworking Women: Gender, Racism and Class at Work*, London: Sage.

Redman, T. and Snape, E. (2002) 'Ageism in teaching: Stereotypical beliefs and discriminatory attitudes towards the over-50s', *Work, Employment and Society*, 16(2): 353–69.

Reich, R.B. (1991) 'What is a nation?', *Political Science Quarterly*, 106(2): 193–209.

Rein, M. and Jacobs, K. (1993) 'Ageing and employment trends: A comparative analysis for OECD countries', in P. Johnson and K. Zimmerman (eds), *Labour Markets in an Ageing Europe*, Cambridge: Cambridge University Press, pp. 53–76.

Reynolds, P.B., Bygrave, B., Autio, E., and Hay, M. (2002) *Global Entrepreneurship Monitor (GEM) Summary Report*, Babson Park, MA/London: Babson College/London Business School.

Reynolds, T. (2001) 'Black mothering, paid work and identity', *Ethnic and Racial Studies*, 24(6): 1046–64.

Riach, K. (2007) '"Othering" older worker identity in recruitment', *Human Relations*, 60: 1701–26.

Royster, D.A. (2003) *Race and the Invisible Hand*, Berkeley, CA: University of California Press.

Rubery, J. and Fagan, C. (1994) 'Occupational segregation: Plus ça change', in R. Lindley (ed.), *Labour Market Structures and Prospects for Women*, Warwick: University of Warwick Institute for Employment Research.

Rugman, A. and Girod, S. (2003) 'Retail multinationals and globalization: The evidence is regional', *European Management Journal*, 21(1): 24–37.

Saks, A. and Waldman, D. (1998) 'The relationship between age and job performance evaluations for entry-level professionals', *Journal of Organizational Behavior*, 19(4): 409–19.

Sanglin-Grant, S. (2002) *Widening the Talent Pool: Racial Equality in FTSE-100 Companies*, Runnymede Trust Briefing Paper, April, available online at http://www.runnymedetrust.org/uploads/publications/pdfs/wideningTheTalentPool.pdf

Schein, V.E. (2007) 'Women in management: Reflections and projections', *Women in Management*, 22(1): 6–18.

Schwartz, H. (1996) *The Culture of Copy: Striking Likeness, Unreasonable Facsimiles*, New York: Zone Books.

Shaw, C. (2000) '1998-based national population projections for the United Kingdom and constituent countries', *ONS Population Trends* (Spring), London: HMSO.

Simpson, R. (2006) *Childbearing on Hold: Delayed Childbearing and Childlessness in Britain*, Centre for Research on Families and Relationships Research Briefing No. 29, Edinburgh: University of Edinburgh.

Singh, V. and Vinnicombe, S. (2005) *The Female FTSE Index 2005*, Cranfield: Cranfield School of Management, available online at http://www.som.cranfield.ac.uk

Smith, A. (2007) *Working Fathers in Europe: Earning and Caring?*, Centre for Research on Families and Relationships Research Briefing No. 30, Edinburgh: University of Edinburgh.

Smith, N.G. and Ingram, K.M. (2004) 'Workplace heterosexism and adjustment among lesbian, gay and bisexual individuals: The role of unsupportive social interactions', *Journal of Counseling Psychology*, 51(1), 57–67.

Steeten, P. (2001) *Globalisation: Threat or Opportunity?*, Copenhagen: Copenhagen Business School Press.

Sullivan, O. and Gershuny, J. (2001) 'Cross-national changes in time-use: some sociological (hi)stories re-examined', *British Journal of Sociology*, 52(2): 331–47.

Sutton Trust (2008) 'Low social mobility in the UK has not improved in 30 years', available online at http://www.suttontrust.com/news.asp

Sweet, C. (2003) 'Will it change your life?', *The Guardian,* 12 May, available online at http://www.guardian.co.uk/women/story/0,3604,931092,00.html

Taylor, P. and Urwin, P. (2001) 'Age and participation in vocational education', *Work, Employment and Society*, 15(4): 763–79.

_____ and Walker, A. (1994) 'The ageing workforce: Employers' attitudes towards older people', *Work, Employment and Society*, 8(4): 569–91.

Taylor, R. (2002) 'Diversity in Britain's labour market', Economic and Social Research Council Future of Work Programme Seminar Series, available online at http://www.esrc.ac.uk/ESRCInfoCentre/Images/fow_publication_4_tcm6-6058.pdf

Thomas, C. (2007) *Female Forms: Experiencing and Understanding Disability*, Maidenhead: Open University Press.

Thomas, M. (2008) *Belching Out the Devil*, London: Ebury Press.

Tomlinson, J. (2007) 'Female part-time worker's experiences of occupational mobility in the UK service sector', *Women in Management Review*, 22(4): 305–18.

Tran, M. (2005) 'Branded', *The Guardian*, 1 September, available online at http://blogs.guardian.co.uk/businessinsight/archives/2005/09/01/branded.html

33

Treanor, J. (2006) 'Campaign for more women at the top', *The Guardian*, 30 October, available online at http://money.guardian.co.uk/businessnews/story/0,,-1934772,00.html

University Week (2000) 'Carnegie scholar issues educational wake up call', 3 February, available online at http://depts.washington.edu/uweek/archives/2000.02.FEB_03/_article3.html

Vickerstaff, S., Cox, J., and Keen, L. (2003) 'Employers and the management of retirement', *Social Policy and Administration*, 37(3): 271–87.

Warr, P.B. (2001) 'Age and work behaviour: Physical attributes, cognitive abilities, knowledge, personality traits and motives', in C.L. Cooper and I.T. Robertson (eds), *International Review of Industrial and Organizational Psychology*, London: Wiley, ch. 1.

Wilson, R. (2004) 'Singular mistreatment', *The Chronicle of Higher Education*, 50(33), available online at http://chronicle.com/weekly/v50/i33/33a01001.htm

Work Foundation (2006) 'UK increasingly a nation of entrepreneurs', News release, 9 January.

World Bank (2000) *Poverty in an Age of Globalization*, Briefing paper available online at http://www.sph.umich.edu/symposium/2004/pdf/povertyglobalization.pdf

The View from Below

2

Introduction

This chapter examines the research that tells us what employees—principally those at the bottom of the hierarchy—feel about work. How do they view their jobs? What does work mean to people? How passionate or alienated can they be said to be—that is, for whom is work a central life interest and who sees work as a means to an end? Managing people requires an understanding of how they think about their jobs and how those from different social groups experience work. For this knowledge, we draw heavily on the sociology of work, developed to provide a critical understanding of the world of work.

By the end of this chapter, you will understand more about how work for those with the less satisfying jobs has been described and researched, and what has been learned about what these jobs mean to those who do them. You will understand how attempts have been made to improve the meaning of work by redesigning jobs. You will have insight into work that might be described as 'dirty'—particularly how people who do these jobs maintain their dignity—and understand how class and work are interlinked. While the view of the employee tends to be ignored by many key

textbooks in organizational behaviour, this 'view from below' offers managers a good foundation for going on to look at the thorny issue of motivation in Chapter 6. It might help, for example, to explain why some people might be more difficult—if not impossible—to motivate.

This chapter explores:

- alienation;
- the experience of the assembly line;
- making work manageable;
- the experience of the call centre;
- class and orientation to work;
- what work means;
- measuring meaning;
- job redesign to improve the intrinsic meaning of work;
- class, gender, and the meaning of work;
- more 'not so good' and 'unskilled' low-paid jobs;
- doing 'dirty work';
- the experience of catering work;
- working-class kids, working-class jobs, and the case of care assistants;
- the experience of homeworking.

Alienation

'Many people are consumed by work because it is the element of their lives which is most affirming' (Trinca and Fox, 2004: 69). This statement may hold true for those who run their own businesses or for 'knowledge workers' (Reich, 1991)—such as research scientists, lawyers, architects, musicians, film and television producers—and those who have challenging and satisfying jobs with freedom to make their own decisions about when and how they work, but it is not the case for all of those who work. Some are in employment in which they are unable to control their immediate work processes—that is, the job that they do. As a result, they cannot develop a sense of purpose, or see how their job connects to others in the production process, or feel that work is a mode of personal expression. And if this is the case, it might be argued that the person is 'alienated'.

The concept of alienation forms, for many, a useful starting point for understanding how people feel about work. It helps us to understand why work might be dehumanizing rather than fulfilling. In his 1844 *Economic and Political Manuscript*, Karl Marx, a founding father of sociology, argued that there are various aspects to the experience. When people feel alienated, work, according to Marx, is external to the worker:

[Work] is not part of his nature, ... consequently he does not fulfil himself in his work but denies himself, has a feeling of misery, not of well being, does not develop freely a physical and mental energy, but is physically exhausted and mentally debased. A worker therefore only feels at home in his leisure, whereas at work he feels homeless. His work is not voluntary but imposed, forced labour.

(Bottomore and Rubel, 1963: 177–8).

Max Weber (1864–1920), a second 'founding father', was a German sociologist who also argued that alienation is a state or a feeling in which the job is external to the individual (Weber, 1926; 1947). It results primarily from lack of autonomy at work. This has implications for the individual's learning, because, over time, work alienation is established in the minds of employees in a continuing sequence of conditioning (Argyris, 1985; 1990). For example, employees are conditioned not to ask questions, answer back, or question management authority; this results in increased organizational rigidity and inefficiency as organizational members experience job dissatisfaction and low levels of organizational commitment (Efraty et al., 1991). There are also implications for leadership, because research (Sarros et al., 2002) has shown that transformational leadership (that is, considerate leadership based on more personal relationships between managers and followers) is associated with lower work alienation. Leadership style can therefore have a significant impact on feelings of work alienation, influencing how employees feel about their jobs and either hindering or improving employees' learning.

Marx (1963) and Braverman (1974) identify structural conditions and technologies as generating alienation in the workplace. For example, centralization and work technology may impact on an individual's sense of job autonomy, levels of participation, and sense of well-being (Zeffane and MacDonald, 1993). Further, structural conditions and technology can impact on an individual's perceptions, feelings, and consciousness of alienation within specified work conditions and relationships (Kanungo 1982; Kakabadse, 1986; Ashforth, 1989). Work alienation occurs when employees perceive that the work environment is personally detrimental to their needs, values, and sense of well-being (Kanungo, 1982).

The meaning and measurement of work alienation is, however, problematic and fraught with ambiguity (Geyer and Schweitzer, 1981). A number of different interpretations of the concept have consequently emerged, but it is usually thought of as consisting of three main components, as follows.

1. *Powerlessness*—that is, a lack of control over the work activities, a lack of autonomy, and a lack of participation.

2. *Meaninglessness*—that is, the inability to comprehend the relationship of one's own work contribution to a larger purpose. Workers feel that they contribute little to the overall production process and do not see the significance of their role in it; employees therefore experience meaninglessness at work, particularly when their job tasks are dull, boring, unchallenging, and separate from other work activities.

3. *Self-estrangement*—that is, when the work process is perceived as alien to the individual and independent of their contributions (for example, where external rewards serve to limit the creative contributions of employees). It occurs where jobs are narrow in scope and depth, and are unable to provide employees with intrinsic job satisfaction and fulfilment. Researchers have attempted to

tap into the extent of self-estrangement by asking individuals about how central work is to their life (Dubin, 1956) and whether the employees prized self-image is fulfilled at work (Wilensky, 1964). The more work is a central life interest and fulfilling, the less the employee feels estranged.

Some writers, following Marx, would argue that workers, such as assembly line workers and those who have jobs that can be described as a 'drudge', are being exploited and alienated. There is a fundamental tension between the needs of capital and the needs of labour within capitalist economies, so workers are exploited. The worker is robbed of part of the value of the labour: 'In reality [workers] are paid only the equivalent in monetary terms of the value they produce in part of the working day, say five out of eight hours' (Burawoy, 1979: 23). As well as being exploited economically, they are alienated from the products of their labour. Since they do not own or control the products of their labour, their needs and capacities are subordinated to the requirements of capital accumulation. The psychological consequence is that the worker feels a stranger to his or her work (Thomson and McHugh, 1990).

We are now going to turn to look at the experience of alienation and degrading work as it is documented in research. While a good deal of research on this topic has been based on assembly line work, this is not the only environment in which an employee can feel alienated.

The experience of the assembly line

The experience of alienation and degrading work has been well documented by researchers and journalists who have spent time working on assembly lines. An early account of the concrete experiences of factory work can be found in the work of Simone Weil (see Grey, 1996), who worked in an electrical plant and a metalworking factory in Paris in 1934–35. The highly mechanized work was degrading, humiliating, and shaming for the individual. For example, she describes how she worked on a stamping press under which the pieces were difficult to position, producing 600 pieces in less than three hours before having a half-hour to reset the machine. She had to adapt to the 'slavery'; she clearly felt powerless. She felt disgust at being forced to strain and exhaust herself, 'with the certainty of being bawled out either for being slow or for botching' (Weil, 1987: 159). According to Weil, workers are oppressed: they are treated as means rather than as ends in themselves. The clearest manifestation of oppression is to be found not in class, but in the organization of production, she says.

Michael Moore, the North American filmmaker, describes another, more modern, experience of the assembly line. 'This insane system known as the assembly line is designed to deny individuality and eliminate self-worth', says Moore in the Foreword to Ben Hamper's (1992) *Rivethead*. Written by a journalist, this book recounts how he found work at General Motors' truck and bus plant in Michigan. Initially, Hamper worked on an assembly line, installing clips and screws inside rear wheel wells. He then learned how to spot-weld, so that he could also do his neighbour's job on the line and they could 'double up'—that is, do two jobs for an hour or two and then have one or two hours' break. Hamper complains about the monotony of the job (being faced with the same job every few minutes) in spite of being able to take these long breaks during which he could read two newspapers, a magazine, and a good chunk of a novel each evening. In this world, Ben Hamper says, 'workers suffer and cope through drink or madness'.

Joseph and Suzy Fucini (1990), a husband-and-wife journalist team, tell the story of working at the Mazda Flat Rock plant in Michigan from the point of view of the employees. They discuss the incredible time pressure under which the assembly workers there laboured. The torrid pace of the assembly line kept the worker in motion for 57 seconds of every minute—12 seconds longer than at a typical US car plant. The average working week was 60 hours; when workers entered the plant in the morning, they did not know when they would be leaving in the evening. The workers were chronically stressed and exhausted—particularly during record-breaking summer temperatures. Disputes flared up over issues such as whether the American workers had to wear 'voluntary' baseball caps or attend 'voluntary' morning exercise classes.

Some further realities of working on assembly lines in the UK and France are captured in accounts from researchers Ruth Cavendish (1989) and Robert Linhart (1989), who vividly describe the endless pressure and the continual fear of slipping behind with work. They want to do a good job; the control system hooks the worker into a manic concern for throughput (Littler, 1989). Few aspects of work provide intrinsic satisfaction, but individuals become resigned to the daily drudge. These workers would not be in a strong position in a labour market: the job did not offer scope for personal development. But in order to counter the lack of satisfaction, employees were found to use their initiative.

Making work manageable

To counter the negative effects of the drudge, workers are known to find ways of making work manageable. Ditton (1979: 160) describes how the workers in a bakery broke the day up into 'digestible fragments to make it psychologically manageable'.

EXAMPLE **Making work manageable: Banana, peach, and 'other' time**

Between 1944 and 1945, Donald Roy worked as a drill operator in a factory. He was a secret participant observer, particularly interested in restriction of output—that is, why workers did not work harder. Roy (1960) outlines how workers who are subject to monotonous tasks make their experiences bearable by adding meaning to their day. Work at the factory was tedious (simple machine operation) and comprised a 12-hour day, six days a week. The group in which Roy worked had established a series of events for structuring the day. There was a 'peach time', instigated by Sammy, during which two peaches would be shared. There was 'banana time' (during which Sammy provided a banana, but Ike ate it, because he had stolen it from Sammy's lunch box; Sammy made futile protests). 'Window time', 'pick-up time' (during which a man came to cart away boxes), 'fish time', and 'coke time' followed in quick succession. Various pranks and food consumption were linked with these 'times'.

Roy also describes horseplay—that is, boisterous play—in this work setting. One worker, Ike, would regularly switch off the power to Sammy's machine whenever Sammy went to the toilet or water fountain. Sammy invariably fell victim to the plot by attempting to operate his machine on his return. This blind stumbling into the trap was always followed by indignation and reproach from Sammy, smirking satisfaction from Ike, and a mild scolding from a third worker. When would Ike weary of the prank or when would Sammy learn to check his power switch?

There was, Roy observed, a pattern to the interaction. A system of roles had formed: a sort of pecking order or hierarchy. It was a controlling frame of status—a matter of who can do what to whom and get away with it. Roy concludes that one source of job satisfaction lay in the interaction between members of the group. Horseplay, conversation, and the sharing of food and drink reduced the monotony of simple, repetitive operations to the point that the long workdays became manageable.

(*Source*: Excerpts from *Banana Time*, quoted in Salaman and Thompson, 1973)

Burawoy (1979) worked as a machine operator at the engine division of Allied Corporation, producing, among other things, agricultural equipment. This was the same plant at which Donald Roy had worked (see the Example above) and researched thirty years before. The central question for Burawoy was: 'Why do workers work as hard as they do?' He describes a series of games that the operators played in order to achieve levels of production that earned incentive pay. The rules of the game were experienced as a set of externally imposed relationships, like informal alliances. The art of 'making out' (that is, maximizing bonus pay in a piece-rate system) was to manipulate those relationships with, for example, the foreman, superintendent, scheduling man, other operators, or truck drivers to a worker's best advantage. For example, truck drivers were responsible for bringing the stock from the aisles, where it was kept, to the machine. They could delay an operater considerably if he or she had not befriended them—particularly at the beginning of the shift, when they were in great demand. The foreman acted as a referee and expediter in the game of making out. The foreman could point out more efficient set-ups, help make special tools, persuade inspectors to pass work, and so on, so that the job could be done faster and an operator could earn more.

The shop-floor culture revolved around making out. Each worker was sucked into a distinctive set of activities and language. The pressure to make out could also lead to conflict between workers. The games that workers play are not usually created in opposition to management, but emerge out of struggle and bargaining. Management participates in the game by organizing it and enforcing the rules. The game is entered into for its 'relative satisfactions'; the satisfaction of that need reproduces consent from both managers and workers, as well as material wealth. But Burawoy has described the games that workers play as a way of creating space outside managerial surveillance (see also Pahl, 1988).

EXAMPLE **An example of the game**

Stewart Clegg (1987) produces an interesting example of 'making out' in the 'inclemency rule'.

Clegg worked on a building site. On construction sites in the UK, joiners have an agreement that they do not have to work in 'inclement' weather. There is, however, no operational definition of how bad the weather has to be before it is called 'inclement'. One day, the worker unit leader decided that it was such, so the workmen downed tools, went to their hut, and brewed tea. After about ten minutes, the site foreman came and asked them to go back to work. It was drizzling lightly with rain. The first time that this happened, Clegg thought: 'OK. I know the joiners don't like getting wet and we don't work when it is raining.' But when it happened again a few days later and the men downed tools, it was hardly raining at all. This went on several times over a period of two or three weeks. Clegg's explanation was that the joiners were using the inclemency rule to put pressure on incompetent managers to organize the job more effectively so that the materials and supplies that the joiners needed to do the job were there on time and the joiners could increase their bonus. Because supplies were not arriving, the joiners were taking up slack time for 'inclemency'. They were putting pressure on management to increase control and thus more effectively exploit them.

Burawoy (1979)—as Jermier et al. (1994: 7) note—did not, however, draw out the implications for understanding shop-floor resistance from this analysis. Burawoy's account has been critiqued in some detail (Knights, 1990; Thompson, 1990; Willmott, 1990; Collinson, 1992). He is criticized for not investigating workplace subjectivity enough: for example, neglecting gender and sexual identity.

The experience of the call centre

It is not only in factories that we find dehumanized work or alienated workers. Call centres have attracted an enormous amount of academic and media attention in recent years, as the latest 'dark satanic mills', the 'new sweatshops', or 'battery phone farms' (Beirne et al., 2004).

Call centres are dedicated operations in which employees using computers receive inbound, or make outbound, telephone calls, with those calls being processed and controlled by either an automatic call distribution or predictive dialing system (Taylor and Bain, 1999). Agents or advisers sit in front of a visual display unit and keyboard, and make or take calls though a headset comprising an earpiece and a small microphone.

Call centre workers have joined with flight attendants, shop assistants, fast-food waiting staff, and others to swell the ranks of service workers whose performance at work is shaped by the objective of customer satisfaction. All are required, in various ways, to conform to predetermined scripts and modes of behaviour and delivery. They are subject to monitoring and pressure to conform. A call centre operator, in particular, has to listen intently to the voice on the phone, think through the response, and promptly give an appropriate reply, while simultaneously scanning a screen and manipulating a keyboard. Sore throats and voice loss are common, as are physical strain to fingers, wrists, and arms. A predictive dialer for an outbound operator in an insurance company, for example, can bring the call centre worker eighty calls in a single 4-hour shift (Taylor and Bain, 1999); this leads to very intense work that can be highly constrained, oppressive, monotonous, repetitive, stressful, and exhausting (Taylor et al., 2002). Staff turnover can be high (Krishnamurthy, 2004), in which boredom is a major factor (Mann, 2007). Some employers have, however, tried to compensate for the rigidity or tightness of their online controls with teamwork activities, fun events, 'friendly' human resource policies, and other methods (Kinnie et al., 2000); the workers may have their own ways of making the job more manageable.

EXAMPLE Making work more manageable in a call centre

Dealing with angry or threatening customers is a feature of work that many call centre operators have to face. While management may not support these actions, the operator can put the customer on hold, wait for him or her to say something about the call centre operator, then embarrass the customer by saying 'I'm still here!' They can also make obscene hand gestures to colleagues about particular callers. Further, the system can be 'tripped' to allow time for the operator to 'chill out' after dealing with a difficult customer.

(*Sources:* Callaghan and Thompson, 2001; Beirne et al., 2004)

Class and orientation to work

How people think, react, and behave in the workplace is influenced by their background and community. A person's attitude and feelings to work, and what work means to them, can be described as their 'orientation to work'. Goldthorpe et al. (1968) differentiate between three categories of worker, in terms of their orientation to work.

1. The first group has an *instrumental* orientation, within which the primary meaning of work is as a means to an end—that is, work is experienced as mere labour. Workers' involvement in the organization that employs them is primarily calculative and will be maintained only as long as the economic return for the effort is seen as the best available. Their jobs do not form a part of their central life interests; work is not a source of emotionally significant experiences, nor of social relationships or self-realization.

2. The second group has a *bureaucratic* orientation to work—that is, the primary meaning of work for the individual is as service to an organization, in return for steadily increasing income, social status, long-term security, and a career. Economic rewards are regarded not as payment for work done, but as rewards for grade, function, and length of service. Faithful service is given in return for a relatively secure and privileged existence. Position and prospects are a source of social identity, and work represents a central life interest.

3. The third group has a *solidaristic* orientation. In this case, while work has an economic meaning, it is also experienced as group activity. Economic returns would be sacrificed where 'maximizing' behaviour—that is, behaviour that leads to making the maximum amount of

income—would offend group norms and threaten group solidarity. The social relationships and shared activity of work are found to be emotionally rewarding. Work provides a central life interest, in addition to its instrumental significance; work implies a whole way of life, of which mining is one example.

STOP AND THINK Mining and ballet

In the film *Billy Elliot* (2000, dir. S. Daldry), a miner's son wants to be a ballet dancer, but his dream is met with scepticism and disapproval—especially from his own family.

Why do you think it is seen as a problem that a miner's son wants to become a ballet dancer? What connection can you see to the points made above about the solidaristic orientation to work?

STOP AND THINK How useful is the idea of work orientation?

Goldthorpe et al.'s typology of work orientation, described above, was compiled to facilitate a discussion of the differences among the workers in their study.

How useful is it in a broader context? Do you think that work orientation is 'fixed' in a person?

One of the influences on a person's orientation to work will be their class and background—but can work influence a person's class? Do manual workers who achieve relatively high incomes and living standards—that is, those who become affluent, more bourgeois—assume a way of life that is more middle class and become progressively assimilated into the middle class? Is there a process of working class embourgeoisement happening?

These were the research questions posed by Goldthorpe et al. (1968; 1969), who questioned the assumption that the political and social habits of the working class become more middle class with rising affluence. They set their research in three leading manufacturing firms in Luton, England. A sample of male manual workers was selected, all of whom were aged between 21 and 46, married, and living with their wives. The sample were already prime candidates for embourgeoisement, because they were all looking to improve their lot. Seventy-one of these men had moved to Luton after marriage: 61 per cent due to availability of housing or better housing than they already had; 46 per cent in search of better paid work. Fifty-seven per cent owned, or were buying, their houses. The men earned well above the average wages for men in the manufacturing industry, but their jobs were described as 'physically unpleasant and stressful if not actually hazardous' (Goldthorpe et al., 1969: 34). Only a minority appeared to find the work that they performed inherently reward-ing. Work-related stress of one kind or another was quite frequently reported and, in some groups, was quite acute. Among the assemblers and machinists, the jobs were particularly fragmented, divided into small jobs, and rationalized. The number of those who stated that their work was monotonous, that their job did not absorb their full attention, and that the pace of work was too fast, was notably high.

Why, then, did these men do these jobs? The affluent workers were attracted to these jobs primarily by the extrinsic economic returns—that is, the pay. Their orientation to work was instrumental. The level of pay was given as the reason for staying for half of the process workers, two-thirds of the more skilled men, and three-quarters of the assemblers and machinists. In no occupational group did as many as a third of the affluent workers make any mention of staying in their jobs because they liked the work that they did. Affluence was therefore achieved at a price: that of accepting work that affords little in the way of intrinsic rewards, such as job satisfaction.

STOP AND THINK Is work within an organization always instrumental?

It might be argued that all work activity in an organizational context tends to have a basically instrumental component.

To what extent is this true?

Although the workers' orientation to work was found to be instrumental' and they became more affluent, a major finding of the study was that there was no process of embourgeoisement in terms of political behaviour. Despite being middle class in terms of incomes and possessions, and living in communities markedly different from those of the more traditional working class, there was no evidence of any shift away from their political loyalties—that is, loyalty to the Labour Party. Further, middle-class social norms were not widely followed and middle-class lifestyles were not consciously emulated; these affluent workers were still fairly distinctively working class.

The orientation to work view proposed by Goldthorpe et al. was not without its critics (for example, Daniel, 1969; Wheelan, 1976; Russell, 1980). Goldthorpe et al. contended that orientations have a 'fixed' quality: they are not necessarily responsive to contextual organizational factors and orientation to work can explain much—for example, why workers may not be interested in maximizing their earnings. Daniel (1969) argued that explanations of choice of job, behaviour in a job, and leaving a job are likely to be different, that it should not be assumed that orientations to work are fairly stable over time and in different contexts. For example, the instrumental worker of one context may become much more interested in what a job offers intrinsically—for example, in terms of job satisfaction—in another context. Perceived levels of interest will change, depending on the social situation. An overemphasis on orientations can therefore seriously reduce the analytical potential of an investigation. There is no single generalized set of priorities against which all occupational experience is measured.

Bechhofer (1973: 134), one of the Goldthorpe et al. research team, later admitted that the dynamic nature—the *changing* nature—of orientation was 'perhaps insufficiently emphasized' in the original study. This consequently poses a problem for managers: it appears that orientation to work can neither be assumed from context, nor from previously expressed attitudes and behaviours.

What work means

We have seen how one of the prime reasons that individuals give for working is to earn money—but there are other reasons, too: to use our skills; for a feeling of worth; for a sense of dignity. These are aspects of a job over which a manager may have control.

Most people will say that earning money is the prime reason that they go to work. In a British survey (Rose, 1994), 68 per cent of respondents said that they worked for the money to provide money for basic essentials, or to buy extras and enjoy some economic independence from the primary earner in a household. Economic need may be contingent on family composition: for example, if you have many dependants, you may need to earn more than someone who has none. It may also be that the earnings of minority ethnic women are more important to their households than are those of women in many white households if there is a large family to support (Westwood, 1988; Phizacklea and Wolkowitz, 1993).

In the same survey (Rose, 1994), however, 26 per cent said that they did not work for money, but for 'expressive' reasons—that is, intrinsic rewards, such as a sense of enjoyment, satisfaction, and a sense of achievement. So although work can usually be described as an economic activity, economic reasons are not, in themselves, a sufficient explanation for the decision to work.

STOP AND THINK The lottery question

Ask yourself the 'lottery question' (Corbett, 1994). Imagine that you have won a lottery or inherited a large sum of money and could live comfortably for the rest of your life without working: what would you do about work? Would you continue working or could you imagine stopping work altogether?

Further, economic reasons may not account for the decision *not* to work. For example, racism and prejudice may explain 'economic inactivity': Pakistani and Bangladeshi women record the lowest levels of economic activity despite living in the most disadvantaged households; they are also around four times as likely to be unemployed as white British women (EOC, 2007). It may therefore be that, for cultural and family reasons, these women may not work (Kamenou, 2008), or it may be that they face—or fear that they will face—discrimination in the labour market or at work itself (see Buchner et al., 2007). Widespread ignorance about different cultures means that women from ethnic minorities women may face a daily barrage of questions and stereotyped comments, especially in working environments in which they are in a minority. Research has shown that women with Islamic names are not called for interview even when they have good qualifications and experience (EOC, 2007); this is a clear example of discrimination. Two-thirds of Bangladeshi and Pakistani girls feel that they cannot apply for certain jobs because of their race, gender, or faith (Bhavnani, 2006). So some people will have reasons why they do or do not work that will not only be about earning money.

Maintaining dignity at work is something that workers from all walks of life struggle to achieve (Hodson, 2001; Bolton, 2007). Dignity can be achieved through taking pride in productive accomplishments, even if those accomplishments may be modest by someone else's standards. Dignity is also realized through resistance against abusive bosses or bad management. In defending dignity, workers establish themselves as active agents with some control over their work lives. Without dignity, work can become unbearable: employees can find themselves confronting abusive conditions and a chaotic, mismanaged workplace (Juravich, 1985), chronic overwork and exhaustion (Cavendish, 1982), defending their competence and autonomy (Bosk, 1979), or avoiding downsizing and lay-offs (Smith, 1990). Each of these conditions presents challenges to working with dignity, and shows how dignity is attained and defended (Hodson, 2001). Dignity is, then, about self-command and autonomy, and is crucial for people's well-being (Sayer, 2007).

Work has, then, more meaning than as a means towards the end of earning a living. If work were purely a means to an economic end, there would be no way of explaining the dislocation and deprivation that individuals feel when they retire. Intrinsic reward is clearly important too—perhaps more so than money. Both qualitative research (for example, through individual interviews) and quantitative survey research have shown similar findings. For example, interviewees in a study by Sharpe (1984: 78) expressed that they are less concerned about earning than they are about somebody wanting them 'for what I can do' (see also Sayers, 1988).

So what about people who do not have to work? Some people who win the pools or the lottery continue to work even if they hold jobs that could be described as dull, routine, and repetitive (Brown, 1954). If individuals are asked whether they would continue working if they were to have enough money to live comfortably for the rest of their life, the majority say that they would continue to work (Morse and Weiss, 1955; Gallie and White, 1993). Men in middle-class occupations will point to the loss of interest and accomplishment that they find in their current jobs; those in working-class jobs typically mention the lack of activity that they would experience (Morse and Weiss, 1955). But where the status of work is low, money is more likely to be stressed as the principal reward (Friedmann and Havighurst, 1954). At higher occupational levels, intrinsic job components, such as opportunity for self-expression, interest, and value of work, tend to be more valued; at lower occupational levels, extrinsic job components, such as pay and security, are more valued (Centers and Bugental, 1966). One explanation might be that those in higher-level jobs, with intrinsic job components, design jobs for those in lower levels and have no interest in designing them with the same intrinsic components.

43

Work can be also be a vocation or a calling. An ethic of vocational care or an ethic of social care might be found in those who are, for example, ministers, social workers, or nurses. Nursing was promoted as a vocation in the 1940s and 1950s, in particular (Hallam, 2002). The strict disciplinary regime gave the impression of nursing as being like a religious community: the uniform made reference to a religious past; the veiled hat worn by novice nurses evoked notions of purity and a 'calling' to a higher ideal, similar to those of the religious sisterhoods. Aware of the melodramatic sentimentality of how nurses were portrayed in popular films of the time—for example, *The Lady with the Lamp* (1951, dir. H. Wilcox) and *The Lamp Still Burns* (1943, dir. M. Elvey)—Monica Dickens (1957: 9) described, with more than a hint of irony, how she was encouraged to undertake nursing training: 'I was going to be a nurse in a pure white halo cap, and glide swiftly about with oxygen cylinders and, if necessary, give my life for a patient.'

Measuring meaning

So work can have meaning for people, as well as offer them economic reward—but measuring what constitutes meaningful work is a complex task (Hodson, 2002). Job satisfaction is one measure, but there are other indicators. The experience of creativity can contribute significantly to meaning and dignity at work. The ability to take pride in work is a core foundation for meaningful work: for example, if a worker is able to boast that he or she has delivered a year's production work without any rejects. Conversely, conflict—either with managers or with co-workers—can undermine satisfaction. Further, work groups that are diverse, less integrated, and cohesive report greater dissatisfaction (Maznevski, 1994). Research shows that groups that are diverse have lower levels of member satisfaction and higher rates of labour turnover than more homogeneous groups (Milliken and Martins, 1996). Respect for workers' rights as organizational stakeholders is another contributor to satisfaction: for example, managers refraining from abusive practices (Adler and Borys, 1996), providing job security, and avoiding lay-offs. Management leadership manifested through the maintenance of a viable and well-functioning organization, and a respect for workers, are of crucial importance for satisfaction and meaning of work (Hodson, 2002).

We saw earlier how some groups of workers—for example, miners—may have a solidaristic orientation to work and how work may be a whole way of life. Classic studies of male workers by Dennis et al. (1969) showed how the dangerous difficult conditions in mining created a male culture of mutual dependence that continued outside in leisure and other activities. The men defined themselves almost exclusively in terms of their work. But research from the USA shows that jobs in the new economy—that is, those in today's more service-oriented economy—are very mixed in what they offer in terms of meaning. Reich (1991) calculated that only 20 per cent of the jobs in the new economy were intrinsically satisfying and economically rewarding. These jobs belong to the journalists, designers, architects, and lecturers whose work has creativity at its core, because they communicate complex ideas. These are the 'fortunate fifth' (see Chapter 1), and they can be contrasted with the 25 per cent who regularly perform routine tasks and the 30 per cent who deliver a variety of mundane services.

When Vecchio (1980) revisited Morse and Weiss's (1955) findings about whether or not people would continue to work if they had enough money not to do so, he found that the majority of workers would want to continue working—but he also discovered a 39 per cent increase in the number of male workers who would stop working if given the opportunity. One explanation for this is that there has been a real decline in the perceived value and meaning of work. Alternatively, it may be that a leisure ethic is replacing the traditional work ethic.

'Meaning' may not be found in work at all, but in other life interests. Research by Dubin (1956) looked at how central work was to people's lives. Dubin concerned himself with looking at the 'central life interests' of workers. Work was seen as a central life interest of adults in most societies, and the capitalist system was seen to rest upon the moral and religious justification that the Reformation gave to work, as Weber (1930) pointed out. The Protestant work ethic, discussed by Weber, is the idea that work is valuable in itself—that is, that one should work hard and aim to succeed. Dubin, however, found that for almost three out of four industrial workers, work and the workplace were not central life interests. People's life histories had their centres outside work; this was where they looked for human relationships, feelings of enjoyment, happiness, and worth. Yet, as Dubin notes, much management activity is directed at restoring work to the status of central life interest through human relations: for example, through concern for jobs and how they are designed. Management's efforts therefore seem to be at odds with reality.

Job redesign to improve the intrinsic meaning of work

In spite of Dubin's findings that work was not a central life interest for so many industrial workers, managements and researchers have sought to discover more about what work means to people and what can be done to increase productivity. Researchers moved on to dedicate themselves to trying to understand what motivated employees or what satisfied them (for example, Herzberg, 1966; 1968). Some researchers saw both employee productivity and alienation as a problem (Hackman and Oldham, 1975) to which job enrichment and job redesign were seen as solutions.

Job redesign meant any attempt to alter jobs with the intention of increasing the quality of work experience and productivity. This would include rotating people around jobs, or enriching them to make them more challenging or interesting, or using socio-technical systems design—that is, giving the technical and social aspects of the work equal weight, and taking each into account at the point of job (re)design. Typically, changes involved providing employees with additional responsibilities for planning, setting up, checking their own work, making decisions about methods and procedures, establishing their own work pace (within limits), and sometimes relating directly with the client who sees the results of their work (Hackman, 1977). For example, a basic job involved the assembly of a small pump used in a washing machine. The assembly line worker assembled a particular part of the job along with five others on an assembly line. The job was redesigned so that each worker assembled a whole pump, inspected it, and placed his own identifying mark on it; workers were given more freedom to control their pace of work. As a result, total assembly time decreased, quality improved, and cost savings were realized (ibid.: 99).

In order to measure and understand what happened to jobs when they were changed, Turner and Lawrence (1965) measured employee perceptions of task attributes in the USA. Based on that work, Hackman and Oldham (1975) developed the job diagnostic survey (JDS). The theory underlying the tool was that experienced meaningfulness of work is enhanced by skill variety (that is, using different skills and talents), task identity (that is, doing a job from beginning to end with a visible outcome), and task significance (that is, the degree to which the job has a substantial impact on the work or lives of other people). Hackman et al. (1975: 61) claimed that the JDS gauged the 'objective characteristics of the jobs themselves'. Similarly, Sims et al. (1976) developed the job characteristics inventory (JCI), while in the UK, Banks et al. (1983a) developed a job components inventory. The JDS and JCI would diagnose existing jobs as an input to planned job redesign.

There were, however, some serious problems with the measures of job characteristics (Salancik and Pfeffer, 1977; Aldag et al., 1981; Stone and Gueutal, 1985). The job characteristics that were measured had been derived from a search of the literature, reflective thinking, and by trial and error. The dimensions may or may not have consequently coincided with the dimensions along which individuals generally perceive jobs to vary; they may only represent the idiosyncratic way in which Turner and Lawrence (1965) viewed jobs.

Some social scientists had much to say about how jobs should be redesigned—an international 'quality of working life' movement began, in 1972, with a conference (Davis and Cherns, 1975)—but other social scientists—particularly sociologists and political scientists—were more critical of the job redesign movement (Blacker and Brown, 1978) and what it sought to achieve. One of these criticisms was that attempts to improve quality of working life amounted to little more than 'human relations' management (that is, showing concern for employee's social needs and personal problems, and making them feel important) and a cosmetic activity to help managers to increase productivity (Blacker and Brown, 1980). Job redesign was thought only to serve to control behaviour: for example, to limit the scope, responsibility, and autonomy of the job.

For many modern teachers of organizational behaviour, job redesign is consequently seen as a dated 1970s fad. Examples are to be found in the literature of new work designs that failed because, for example, of cost (Klein, 1982, cited in Clegg, 1984), because the role of supervisors was threatened (Lawler et al., 1973; Cummings, 1978), or because changes were resented and opposed by other groups (Clegg, 1982). And complex job design can be exceptionally difficult to implement for a mixture of historical, economic, and psychological reasons (Clegg, 1984), so it is little wonder that few major initiatives of this kind have been attempted and survived.

The questions for us now are whether job redesign could have been 'sold' to employers if it did not bring with it the promise of increased efficiency and productivity. Were employers really interested in what jobs meant to individuals, with a view to increasing what they might mean and offer in terms of intrinsic rewards? Did employers have altruistic motives and were they interested in their employee's quality of work life?

Alan Fox (1973: 219) argued that job redesign did not address the principle of hierarchical rewards (that is, how those with better intrinsically satisfying jobs earned more) or the possibility of increases in intrinsic reward at the cost of efficiency. Job design could therefore be described as a management control device: instead of bringing fundamental change, job redesign only addressed marginal issues, while the legitimacy of prevailing power structures and current business frameworks remained constant. Impartial science was claimed, but poor research designs were used. The criteria used in evaluation studies were usually managerially, rather than psychologically—with emphasis on organizational efficiency rather than an individual's psychological growth (Blacker and Brown, 1978). And while management had a definite interest in seeing workers as thinking social beings with the potential to work together more productively, they also had an interest in limiting these potentials.

Fineman (1996) says that the managers implementing job redesign presented their employees as 'emotionally anorexic': while employees may feel dissatisfaction and satisfaction, be alienated or stressed, and have preferences, attitudes, and interests, these were noted only as variables for managerial control. Managers had no wish to forfeit control and there were limits to what they could 'sensibly', in their view, do (Nichols, 1976: 22; see also Thompson and McHugh, 2002). So while job redesign was implemented ostensibly to increase intrinsic reward or to bring meaning to work, commentators have suggested that these aims were sought only as long as high levels of efficiency were achieved, and managerial control and its prerogative remained the same. The changes that were wrought were condemned as only peripheral (Blacker and Brown, 1980)—and a significant effect of job redesign was seen to be 'to divert attention away from a recognition of more fundamental sources of inequality' (Child, 1973: 243).

Class, gender, and the meaning of work

If class and work orientation may influence what people might expect from work, what influence does gender have? Focusing on issues of class and gender at work, Anna Pollert (1981) has described the differing situations and identities of men and women in a cigarette factory in Bristol. She talks about how, in this situation, the women were subject to a double burden of male oppression and capitalist exploitation. According to Pollert, women were pushed down, discriminated against, and unfree—much like black and minority ethnic workers, immigrants, and other oppressed groups. She describes, in some detail, the lived experience of factory life and work in the home, which domestic background was a distinctive part of the women workers' consciousness. She concludes that these women workers were workers in a man's world, yet also created their own: women remain separate, importing their own world and maintaining a dual existence.

STOP AND THINK Being a woman at work

Anna Pollert (1981) asks: 'Does it make any difference being a woman worker? Is work seen or felt differently from a man?'

How would you answer these questions?

Similarly, Westwood (1984) describes how home and work are part of the one world for women working in a company she calls *Stitchco*. Westwood is an anthropologist and was a participant observer for over a year, working with the women on a wide variety of machines producing socks, tights, sweaters, and cardigans. She uses a Marxist framework to explain her findings, beginning with the point that these women—previously free labourers in the home—sell their labour power to employers for wages, and so enter the world of social production and relations of exploitation in the workplace, which gives them a class position. But these women were also workers in the home and, according to Westwood, they were exploited through the gift of unpaid labour to men who were husbands and fathers. Both Westwood and Cynthia Cockburn (1983) would argue that the sex-gender system and class structure are two interlocking systems from which women's subordination is generated and reproduced.

Westwood's book examines both the way in which women enter waged employment and the way in which they become classed subjects. Women in the labour market are affected by their domestic lives: being a woman counts. The factory in Westwood's research employed over 2,000 workers; women made up nearly two-thirds of these workers. The gendered division of labour was clear: while the men were knitters, mechanics, dyers, and top managers, the women worked in the finishing process, in personnel, and in other white-collar jobs. The finishing jobs that women did were low-paid, repetitive, and based upon dexterity, which is conceived of as a natural attribute of women, rather than a skill: they joined fabric together, bar-tacked hems, and operated button-sewing machines. A woman might sew side seams all day, every day, for weeks at a time. Unlike the assembly line that controlled the flow of work, the machinist was dependent on the supervisor to bring work to her. This could be an endless source of frustration and aggravation. The individual worker had no control over what she would do, but tried to boost her speed on each operation in order to secure the highest rate for the job. The women disliked being moved between jobs, but management looked for flexibility in the use of their labour power.

The work was physically tiring, noisy, and monotonous. Illness was a common response to the job. The women were expected to meet targets of production each day and had to work under tremendous pressure to earn a bonus. Monotony was eased through conversation, jokes, fierce quarrels, and passing sweets around. Like the women in Anna Pollert's study, the women domesticated their work: they used the phrases 'my machine' and 'my chair', and adorned their machines with family photos or a picture of the current heart-throb; they would even wear slippers at work. They made aprons from company fabrics to protect their clothing—aprons that were embroidered and edged—and engagements and weddings were major events to be celebrated by all. Although it is likely that men also bring objects from home to work and reinforce gender identity in the workplace (see Roper, 1991), these collusive practices reinforced a definition of 'woman' that was securely tied to domestic work in the home.

STOP AND THINK Personalizing objects

Might the way in which people personalize objects at work—'my machine', 'my chair'—be to do with ownership and power—'my secretary', 'my office'—or the need for personal space?

What examples of these kinds of practices have you seen at work? How might these behaviours be expressions of men's and women's relation to power at work?

47

More 'not so good' and 'unskilled' low-paid jobs

When looking at class, gender, and the meaning of work, the jobs at which we have looked have been low in skill. Those in the lowest classes are more likely to be in unskilled and low-paid work. In *Hard Work*, journalist Polly Toynbee (2003) writes about her experiences of a series of low-paid jobs in London, working for hourly wages as a hospital porter (£4.35), a school dinner lady (£4.12), a temporary nursery assistant (£6), a call centre operator (£4.08 plus bonus), an office cleaner (£4.10), a bakery assistant (£4.00), and a care worker (£4.85). Toynbee describes the jobs, highlights the struggle of those who live on low wages, and finds that the poor effectively earn less than they did thirty years ago. The minimum wage in 2003 was £4.10 an hour—but it was calculated by the Family Budget Unit that a living wage (that is, a wage that offers an adequate standard of living) would have been £6.30 an hour, while a 'decency threshold' (a figure used by the Low Pay Unit) would have been £7.32 (a sum representing two-thirds of the male median earnings).

In the USA, a 'good' job is defined as one that offers at least $16 an hour, and which provides employer-paid health insurance and a pension (Center for Economic and Policy Research, 2005). Yet despite huge improvements in the average educational level of the workforce, technological advances and the fact that inflation-adjusted gross domestic product (GDP) per person increased 60 per cent since 1979, only 25.2 per cent of US workers have such a job. Barbara Ehrenreich (2001), a journalist working in the USA, also investigated the jobs that we usually describe as 'unskilled' or 'low-skilled': jobs such as waitress, hotel maid, house cleaner, nursing home aide, and *WalMart* salesperson. She argues that the work requires feats of stamina, focus, memory, quick thinking, and fast learning. She worked in jobs, as millions of others do, for poverty-level wages—that is, around $6–7 an hour, which is only half of the living wage (about $14 an hour). Even with all of the advantages of education, health, a car, and money for the first month's rent, she had to work in two jobs, seven days a week, and still found it hard to find the necessary transportation to work costs and rent. In the end, she failed to achieve a sustainable lifestyle on the low wages. She combats the 'too lazy to work' and 'a job will defeat poverty' ideals held by many middle-class and upper-class citizens, arguing that hard work in these low-skilled jobs fails to live up to its reputation as the ticket out of poverty. Work for these people trapped in these types of employment does not mean 'betterment' or social mobility.

STOP AND THINK Imagine you are a manager

As a manager, you will potentially have choices to make about what people earn. Will this research influence what you pay people?

Doing 'dirty work'

'Dirty work' was a term originally coined by Everett Hughes, a North American sociologist, in 1951, to describe jobs that are physically disgusting, which symbolize degradation, which wound the individual's dignity, or which 'run counter to the more heroic of our moral conceptions' (Hughes, 1958: 50)—that is, jobs that might be considered 'deviant' or somehow morally dubious by the public. He wanted to know how people coped with doing these jobs and how they maintained their identity.

The study of these jobs is interesting in its own way, but also helps highlight factors of general relevance to work experience and meaning that we might otherwise take for granted. A very varied topic in the research literature, the study of dirty work focuses on jobs from gynaecology nurse (Bolton, 2005)—doing difficult work associated with infertility, miscarriage, and foetal abnormalities, and distasteful work associated with urinary incontinence, termination of pregnancy, or sexually transmitted disease—through bike messengers working in a physically dirty and dangerous occupation, with low pay and no benefits (Dennerlein and Meeker, 2003; Kidder, 2006), slaughterhouse work (Thompson, 1983), the 'deviance' of topless or exotic dancing (Thompson and Harred, 1992; Trautner, 2005), and building workers being the 'scum' of the earth (Thiel, 2007), to the demeaning nature of scavenging and collecting rubbish (Perry, 1978). Even police work is 'dirty' when it involves duties that inflict harm on people (Bittner, 1990; Waddington, 1999; Dick, 2005), as is psychiatric nursing when it involves coercion to bring patients under control (May and Kelly, 1982; Godin, 2000). Being a funeral director is dirty work, because it involves dealing with dead bodies, and is seen as both polluting and polluted (Cahill, 1996).

One of the interesting questions raised by the concept of intrinsic reward in work is how those who do dirty work find meaning in their work and maintain a positive sense of self. This question was considered by Kidder (2006) in a study focusing on bike messengers. Kidder finds that, despite the dirt and danger, the creativity and spontaneity of courier labour allows messengers to become emotionally attached to their jobs: being a bike messenger brings thrill-seeking leisure behaviour into work. Kidder argues that the work is meaningful for these workers; games such as avoiding danger and doing the job as fast as possible, building stamina and physical ability, also help to make the occupation a central life interest.

When Perry (1978) worked alongside rubbish collectors in San Francisco, he found that workers coped with the demeaning aspects of their work and managed to maintain their self-esteem in various ways. These workers overcame stigma partially by forming a cooperative type of ownership, in which they purchased shares.

The slaughterhouse job is similarly dirty work in the literal sense—that is, of being drenched in perspiration and beef blood (Thompson, 1983)—but also in a figurative sense of performing low-status, routine, and demeaning work. Butchering cattle is generally viewed as an undesirable and repugnant job. The slaughterhouse job considered by Thompson was an assembly job; the rate was 187 head of cattle each hour. The job was physically exhausting and, like the courier's job, dangerous. During the second week of Thompson's nine weeks of being a participant observer in the slaughterhouse, a death occurred when a crane operator's skull was crushed. Working with large very sharp knives also made the job hazardous. Thompson examined how workers attempted to maintain their sense of self-worth despite these demeaning and dehumanizing aspects of their jobs.

Social relations between labourers was marked by anonymity, due to the way in which work was organized and the noise (so loud that they wore ear plugs), so it was not uncommon for two workers who had worked alongside each other for ten years to know only each other's first names—and only then because they were written on pieces of plastic tape on the front of their hard hats. Yet the workers shared a sense of unity: work on the line was described as 'uncooperative teamwork'—meaning that the assembly line demanded coordinated teamwork to some extent, but that each worker had a separate specialized task, so that it was 'every man for himself'. If a worker were to fall behind, however, fellow workers would help him or her out, because not to do so would have slowed their own work. A more subtle sense of unity also existed in the sense that they were 'all in this together'. They shared a common bond—a common language even, referring to themselves as 'beefers'—and had developed an occupational culture.

Despite a profit-sharing scheme, the workers viewed themselves as distant from management; management were referred to as 'they' and workers referred to themselves as 'we'. Employee social relations often take precedence over production, efficiency, and promise of material rewards (Roethslinger, 1941). It was this social force that bound the workers together that provided a sense of meaning and worth. Although their job might not be highly respected by outsiders, they derived mutual self-respect from their sense of belonging. To deal with the monotony of the work, the 'beefers' would sing to themselves, tap their feet to imaginary music, daydream, or have conversations with themselves. To deal with the dehumanizing aspect of the job, they would indulge in horseplay (which was strictly forbidden), daydream, take unscheduled breaks, indulge in social interaction with other employees, or occasionally engage in sabotage (see Chapter 15). Further, the high wages and fringe benefits seemed to override the negative aspect of the daily work. In fact, Thompson describes how the high wages led to the men being financially trapped: the 'contagious' spending patterns that they adopted made leaving the plant almost impossible.

The research on dirty work is usually ignored in textbooks with a more managerialist framework, but this research contains some important messages about the view from below—that is, the views of workers themselves, about their identity, and how they cope. The research shows how individuals draw on different meanings to make sense of themselves and their activities—and these findings may be relevant to other jobs, not only 'dirty' ones.

The experience of catering work

Researchers argue that little has been written on class relations at the point of production, that the experience and meaning of class has not been explored from the workers' point of view. Helping to redress the balance—like the other researchers in this chapter—Gabriel (1988) documents working lives in catering. He says that catering workers frequently complain that they are taken for granted and academic researchers who talk about the 'service sector' rarely trouble themselves to find out what catering work is like. Even the public with whom the catering workers come into daily contact seldom seem to register their existence.

Work in hotels and catering differs little in kind and quality from similar work in manufacturing, argues Wood (1992: 16). Jobs in catering are low paid, have poor job security and union representation, and are mainly done by part-time employees and women workers. Catering jobs have a sense of subservience that is not associated with other jobs. Gabriel (1988) interviewed both ancillary workers and cooks in a hospital kitchen, and reported that the job had become like a prison for the ancillary workers: they felt trapped in their jobs because they lacked training, because their command of English was limited, or because of age, nationality, and background. In contrast, the cooks in the hospital kitchen did not feel trapped, and expressed pride and achievement in their jobs. But the cooks in a cook-freeze kitchen were far less happy, because here the kitchen was a faithful adoption of rationalized, Taylorist principles (see Chapter 4) in mass catering: splitting cooking from planning, making tasks simple and tightly controlled, and reducing the skill, initiative, and thinking required of cooks to a bare minimum. There were pockets of resistance: for example, one of the supervisors started cooking curried and vegetarian meals, and used her initiative, ability, and skill. Like the workers in Anna Pollert's study (1981), domestic responsibilities dominated the women's thinking about work: the main asset of the job was that the hours of work and holidays fitted with the schools.

The literature does not only document a single researcher's findings: Wood (1992) draws on a range of studies in the hotel and catering industry to construct a sociological account of employment in that sector. He argues that the hospitality industry has attracted little research attention compared with manufacturing, and aims to relate what is known about hotel and catering work to wider issues in industrial sociology-led trends towards deskilling and flexible working and trends in industrial conflict. He shows how hotel and catering work is largely exploitative, degrading, poorly paid, unpleasant, insecure, and taken as a last resort or because it can be tolerated in the light of family commitments and other constraints. Some will value and enjoy their work in the industry, but they are in the minority. How, then, do people cope?

An in-depth study by Paules (1991) of women who waited tables in a family-style restaurant in New Jersey used participant observation to demonstrate how the dictates of management can be resisted. She describes how these women protected and enhanced their position at work while absorbing the abuse of a hurried and often abusive public. Paules notes how the waitress's subordination to her customers is proclaimed: she is directed to wear a uniform that recalls a housemaid's dress, and is prohibited from eating, drinking, and resting in public view. She is to address each customer as 'sir' or 'ma'am', while the customers call her by her first name. The greater part of her income comes from tips—conferred as gifts by strangers—because her wages are below the national minimum wage. Despite this, she is not passive and powerless: she can boost tip income by increasing the number of customers whom she serves—that is, by securing the largest and busiest sets of tables, 'turning' the tables quickly (taking the order, delivering the food, clearing, and resetting the table as fast as possible), and by controlling the flow of customers through the restaurant. In order to compete effectively with other waitresses, she does not take formal breaks. Waitresses had even been known to refuse to serve customers who had not tipped them on an earlier occasion. She can resist the demands of management and customer either silently or with open confrontation. Despite the demeaning features of jobs, this study illustrates how workers can inject into them meaning and control.

Working-class kids, working-class jobs, and the case of care assistants

We have looked at the links between class and the jobs that people are now doing, but here we will look at how people's choices of jobs are shaped by class. Why do working-class individuals continue to enter working-class, gender-stereotyped jobs? Why do working-class boys look for heavy manual work (Willis, 1977), in trades such as plumbing, electrical engineering, and forestry? Why do working-class girls still swarm towards traditional female occupations, such as, nursing and rarely, for example, seek training as electricians, joiners, technicians, and computer operators? We might expect that new production patterns, and new systems of education and training, coupled with the promise of lifting barriers to opportunity, might have dislocated the processes of class and gender reproduction of careers—but little has happened to counteract the influence of class, race, and gender on career choice (Cockburn, 1987; Jones and Wallace, 1990; Mirza, 1992).

Bates (1993) explored the experiences of a group of young women who chose jobs in the field of institutional care. Care workers, like many other female workers, find that they are using a wide range of domestic skills. The work can be physically and emotionally demanding, involving a range of tasks from bed making, food serving, bathing, lifting the elderly, sitting with the dying, and laying out the dead. It is low paid, and involves long and often socially inconvenient hours of work. Some of the tasks that care workers have to do are stressful and traumatic, including dealing with violence, incontinence, and death. In order to cope, they have been found to 'switch off' from their job (ibid.). Swearing and being sworn at, getting a 'belt'—and occasionally delivering one—were seen as given parts of a day's round. There was a perpetual tension between taking time to care for people and appearing to be simply processing them, making sure that they are fed and cleaned. The limits to the caring came not from the women themselves, but from the occupational culture and levels of resourcing—that is, the amount of time and money that could be spent on those who were being cared for. The girls expressed a pride in what they did, in how they coped with death, and in their growing 'toughness' in becoming unflinching in the face of harsh facts of life.

The paradox was that, despite the gruelling nature of the work, the girls came to accept it and even became enthusiastic. These jobs were not their initial choices at school (they would have preferred jobs such as nursery nurse, beauty therapist, or typist), but they failed to gain entry into the relevant courses or jobs, so found themselves on a Youth Training Scheme (YTS) 'Caring' course. Bates found that the girls changed their definitions of themselves and their approach to the job in order to accommodate it in the light of labour market realities—that is, high unemployment and job scarcity. They were able to challenge feelings of disgust, inferiority, and shame, and convert them into feelings of pride and a job that was 'right' for them. And the fact that their family lives had often exposed them to experiences such as care of the young or elderly, crowded conditions, demanding physical work, verbal and physical aggression, so that they appeared to be the ideal candidates for care jobs, is a possible explanation as to why these young women took jobs in institutional care.

EXAMPLE **The case of an institutional care cat**

The following is the case of a cat that is able to influence organizational behaviour—a very literal 'view from below'.

Oscar, a cat, has been found to predict accurately which patient is going to die next in an advanced dementia unit in the USA. His predictions in this organization are so accurate that, as soon as he curls up with one of the patients, staff immediately start summoning family and clergy to the anticipated deathbed. 'No one dies on the third floor unless Oscar pays a visit and stays awhile,' writes Dr David Dosa in the *New England Journal of Medicine.*

So far, Oscar has presided over the deaths of more than twenty-five residents—but the patients have not yet spotted Oscar's uncanny powers.

(Source: *Agence France-Presse,* 26 July 2007)

The experience of homeworking

Homeworking is usually considered to be unskilled, or low-skilled, and low-paid work and so constitutes another 'view from below'—but what is the reality of homeworking for individuals? Allen and Wolkowitz (1987) showed how it involved long hours, punctuated by strict deadlines from employers and demanding family members, and was relied upon for a regular household income. A key factor in homeworking was women's responsibility for unpaid work—that is, looking after young children and elderly relatives. Racism in the labour market and discrimination against the disabled were other factors leading to the choice of homeworking.

'Teleworking' is a type of homeworking in which telecommunication links home offices with corporations and the employee works from home. This form of working has received a good deal of attention in the media, directed largely at professional jobs; the more mundane data-entry clerk or women preparing your bills do not usually feature in these stories. Teleworking, Huws et al. (1990) showed, is only adopted by managers who see it as solving an immediate, concrete problem, such as the retention of valued staff or cutting costs. The teleworkers do the work for equally practical reasons, such as having no alternative or for childcare reasons. The need to combine work and childcare was a primary motive for predominately European female group studied by Huws et al. Similarly, Christensen (1989), in a sample of 7,000 US women, found that values related to family, work, and money drove the initial decision to work at home. In contrast, Olson's (1989) largely male US sample gave work-related reasons. Over 50 per cent said that the reason they first decided to work at home was to increase productivity; only 8 per cent said that it was to take care of their family.

Christensen (1989) directly challenges media images of homeworking as computer-based work that offers freedom and independence. Firstly, she found that computers are not the central factor in the proliferation of homework: only one in four clerical workers and one in three professional workers were using them. Secondly, a large number of clerical homeworkers had the legal status of independent contractor, but worked for only one employer, and therefore had little control over the amount and timing of their work. Further, in some cases, the women had worked in offices for the same company and the shift to home-based work meant the loss of employee status, rights, and benefits. Christensen also showed that homework did not reconcile the tension between the need to earn money and the need, or desire, to care for children. The majority of women in the survey did not manage to work when their children were around or awake. Homeworking was stressful and isolating.

Phizacklea and Wolkowitz (1995) provide evidence of the realities of homeworking for a sample of thirty white English-speaking and nineteen Asian homeworkers in Coventry. The nine clerical workers (all white) were paid between £2.90 and £3.25 an hour, but none of these workers received holiday leave, and only one paid National Insurance and was therefore eligible for Statutory Sick Pay. Despite the absence of employment rights, levels of job satisfaction among clerical homeworkers were comparatively high: they had relatively high earnings for homework, relatively low hours, and little variation in the flow of work.

The forty manual homeworkers in the survey were sewing or knitting machinists, dressmakers, undertaking other forms of assembly and packing work, or childminders. Manual homework was found to be sharply divided along ethnic lines: all of the clothing assembly was done by Asian women; fifteen of the nineteen Asian women either assembled whole garments or stitched pieces, such as collars and cuffs—and hourly earnings varied between £0.75 and £3.50. In contrast, the white manual homeworkers were spread over a larger range of occupations, worked shorter hours than the Asian women, and had slightly higher average hourly earnings. And despite the cultural stereotype being Asian women homeworkers choosing to work from home because their husbands want them to, only 10 per cent of the Asian women said that they preferred to do so.

Further research (Felstead and Jewson, 2000; Felstead, 2007) has shown the way in which female homeworkers were segregated into female occupational ghettos, from which few women would be able to use homework to escape. These workers had little access to the assistance offered to the self-employed and perceptions of the disadvantages of homeworking were widely shared: there were more responses to the question about the disadvantages of homeworking than to that which asked about its advantages. The realities of homeworking are, then, low or unpredictable earnings, work-related health problems, and the inconvenience of working at home.

Conclusion

So what can we conclude about the 'view from below'? Firstly, it is clear that it is worth researching and understanding in order to gain insight into how employees feel and think about work. People can feel alienated from their jobs: this is most likely in jobs that lack autonomy or jobs that are narrow in scope, and it is particularly likely for those working on assembly lines and perhaps for those working in call centres if their jobs are tightly prescribed. How people feel and react will be shaped by their class, gender, and background, as well as the context and content of work. They may counteract some of the negative experiences of work with more positive ones—that is, fun experiences—but the nature of their resistance will vary, depending on the workplace and the people. Most employees are not, however, class-conscious revolutionaries about to overthrow managerial ownership or control; nor are they passive docile automatons, as this chapter has shown. Employees can be very innovative in how they counteract the more negative features of work. Attempts have nonetheless been made to redesign work to make it more challenging and interesting, rather than to leave it up to the individual to do so.

In later chapters, we will look at sexuality and the sex-typing of jobs, and resistance and misbehaviour, and how they may be construed, because these contribute towards our knowledge of the view from below. We will also examine the experience of unemployment, because that gives us a greater understanding of what work means. But before doing so, we will turn to look at what managerial work is like, what it means, and how it has been researched.

KEY POINTS

- Alienation is a good starting point from which to discuss 'the view from below', because it highlights how work can be dehumanizing rather than fulfilling.

- Those who are alienated are more likely to be in jobs that are a drudge—particularly assembly line and call centre jobs. These jobs have been well described in the literature by both journalists and researchers.

- To counter the negative effects of drudge, people use innovative ways to make work more manageable.

- How people think, behave, and react at work will be influenced by their class, gender, background, and orientation to work.

- Work is about more than simply making money.

- Meaning may be found not only at work, but also in other life interests.

- Job design has been used to counter some of the negative features of work and to increase productivity.

- People maintain their dignity in jobs that might be described as 'dirty' in a number of innovative ways.

- We have also seen what work might mean for those in less skilled jobs, those working at home, and those working in care homes.

CASE STUDY
Meaningful work

One innovation company—*What If!*—claims to celebrate the ideal of 'meaningful work', and was voted the best workplace in Britain in 2004 and 2005 by the *Financial Times*. It says that it works with clients who want to innovate and grow, and that it helps clients to 'release the creative potential of their people, products and brands'. *What If!* employs over 300 'of the world's brightest and nicest' people in offices across the UK, the USA, China, and Australia. The business claims to be built on five key values that are embedded in how it works: freshness, passion, action, love, and bravery. These can be felt, says the company, in all of its offices worldwide. Sal Pajwani, company director, argues that great people are motivated by being surrounded by other great people and that, if you can break down the distinction between 'work' and 'home', and think more of work as part of your life, the better off you will be. The long hours put in by staff are a consequence, he believes, of hiring and empowering talented and motivated staff.

(*Source*: http://www.whatifinnovation.com/default; http://www.greatplacetowork.com/best/list-eu-2005.htm)

Questions

1. Are these employees, in your view, best defined as 'willing slaves' (see Chapter 1 for a definition)?

2. There are other companies that are ranked as 'best workplaces'. *Beaverbrooks the Jewellers* won the title in 2007. What can you find out about that organization that makes it one of the best workplaces in the UK?

3. Do you have doubts about the claims that these companies make? If yes, why? Can they avoid all staff being alienated regardless of the job that they do? Do you suspect that some staff—maybe those with less autonomy and scope in their jobs, for example, the cleaners or other support staff—might not say that these are great places in which to work?

FURTHER READING

Ackroyd, S. and Thompson, P. (1999) 'Only joking?', in *Organizational Misbehaviour*, London: Sage, ch. 5 This chapter discusses the use of humour and makes links to counter-culture.

Beynon, H. (1984) *Working for Ford*, Harmondsworth: Penguin Considered a classic of its time, this book describes the attitudes of the men towards the assembly line, the company, and the unions.

Burawoy, M. (1979) *Manufacturing Consent: Changes in the Labour Process under Monopoly Capitalism*, Chicago, IL: University of Chicago Press Also considered a classic, this is an example of how participant observation is done. Burawoy questions why workers work as hard as they do.

Gabriel, Y., Fineman, S., and Sims, D. (2000) 'Serious joking', in *Organizing and Organizations*, 2nd edn, London: Sage, ch. 14 This chapter includes some interesting examples of how humour is used in organizations.

Noon, M. and Blyton, P. (2007) *The Realities of Work*, 3rd edn, Houndmills: Palgrave Macmillan Covers survival strategies at work and critiques Burawoy. One chapter provides an answer to the question of 'why work?', including a look at the influence of culture and religion on answers to this question. The issue of the 'work ethic' is also discussed.

Pahl, R.E. (1988) *On Work: Thirty Years of Making Out*, Oxford: Basil Blackwell, ch. 8 This chapter provides more on Burawoy's work.

Roy, D. (1960) 'Banana time: Job satisfaction and informal interaction,' *Human Organization*, 18: 156–68 This lively description of behaviour and its interpretation makes for great reading.

Thompson, P. and McHugh, D. (2002) *Work Organizations*, 3rd edn, Houndmills: Palgrave Macmillan, ch. 19 This chapter discusses Roy's work in the context of motivation and the drive for satisfaction.

55

LINKS TO FILMS AND NOVELS

Dirty Harry (1971) dir. D. Siegal A film in which a police officer does 'dirty work': a good 'cop' is seen to act immorally in order to bring a criminal to justice.

Roger and Me (1989) dir. M. Moore A documentary in which Michael Moore challenges General Motors' decision to close a car manufacturing plant in Flint, Michigan. In his quest to discover why GM would want to do such a thing, Moore tries to meet the chairman, Roger Smith, and invites him out for a few beers up in Flint to 'talk things over'.

Orwell, G. (1933) *Down and Out in Paris and London* This book depicts the daily grind for those who have nothing to do and who are trying to survive.

RESEARCH QUESTIONS

1. Hakim (1991) argues that women—particularly homeworkers—who willingly marry and accept the authority of husbands who have traditional views of women should take the blame for their poor situation in the labour market. According to Hakim, some women gratefully accept slave status. Phizacklea and Wolkowitz (1995) argue against this view. How do both sides present the argument and with whom would you agree?

2. How would you explain how working-class kids continue to get working-class jobs (see Bates, 1991; Mirza, 1992; Willis, 1977)? Why is it so inevitable? Can you find any research that demonstrates that this process is not inevitable?

3. Reeves (2001) argues that work gets a bad press because it is constantly portrayed as an endurance task rather than one of enjoyment—but work has changed. Read Reeves (2001) and Toynbee (2003): is Reeves right?

REFERENCES

Adler, P.S. and Borys, B. (1996) 'Two types of bureaucracy: Enabling and coercive', *Administrative Science Quarterly*, 41(1): 61–89.

Aldag, R.J., Barr, S.H., and Brief, A.P. (1981) 'Measurement of perceived task characteristics', *Psychological Bulletin*, 90(3): 415–31.

Allen, S. and Wolkowitz, C. (1987) *Homeworking: Myths and Realities*, London: Macmillan.

Argyris, C. (1985) *Strategy, Change and Defensive Routines*, Boston, MA: Pitman.

_____ (1990) *Overcoming Organizational Defenses: Facilitating Organizational Learning*, Boston, MA: Allyn & Bacon.

Ashforth, B.E. (1989) 'The experience of powerlessness in organizations,' *Organizational Behavior and Human Decision Processes*, 43(2): 207–42.

Banks, M.H., Jackson, P.R., Stafford, E.M., and Warr, P.B. (1983) 'The job components inventory and the analysis of jobs requiring limited skill', *Personnel Psychology*, 36(1): 57–66.

Bates, I. (1991) 'Closely observed training: An exploration of links between social structures, training and identity', *International Studies of Sociology of Education*, 1: 225–43.

_____ (1993) 'A job which is "right for me"? Social class, gender and individualization', in I. Bates and G. Riseborough (eds), *Youth and Inequality*, Buckingham: Open University Press, ch. 1.

Bechhoffer, F. (1973) 'The relationship between technology and shop-floor behaviour: A less heated look at the controversy', in D.O. Edge and J.N. Wolfe (eds), *Meaning and Control: Essays in Social Aspects of Science and Technology*, London: Tavistock.

Beirne, M., Riach, K., and Wilson, F. (2004) 'Controlling business? Agency and constraint in call centre working', *New Technology, Work and Employment*, 19(2): 96–109.

Beynon, H. (1984) *Working for Ford*, Harmondsworth: Penguin.

Bhavnani, R. (2006) *Ahead of the Game: The Changing Aspirations of Young Ethnic Minority Women*, Manchester: EOC.

Bittner, E. (1990) *Aspects of Police Work*, Boston, MA: Northwestern University Press.

Blackburn, R., Dale, A., and Jarman, J. (1997) 'Ethnic differences in attainment in education, occupation and lifestyle', in V. Karn (ed.), *Employment, Education and Housing Among Ethnic Minorities in Britain*, London: HMSO.

Blacker, F.H. and Brown, C.A. (1978) *Job Redesign and Management Control*, London: Saxon House.

_____ _____ (1980) 'Job redesign and social change: Case studies at Volvo', in K.D. Duncan, M.M. Gruneberg, and D. Wallis (eds), *Changes in Working Life*, Chichester: Wiley, ch. 8.

Bolton, S. (2005) 'Women's work, dirty work: The gynaecology nurse as "other"', *Gender, Work and Organization*, 12(2): 169–86.

_____ (ed.) (2007) *Dimensions of Dignity at Work*, London: Butterworth Heinman.

Bosk, C.L. (1979) *Forgive and Remember*, Chicago, IL: University of Chicago Press.

Bottomore, T. and Rubel, M. (1963) *Karl Marx: Selected Writings in Sociology and Social Philosophy*, Harmondsworth: Penguin.

Bradley, H. (1997) 'Gender and change in employment', in R. Brown (ed.), *The Changing Shape of Work*, Basingstoke: Macmillan, ch. 5.

Braverman, H. (1974) *Labor and Monopoly Capital*, New York: Monthly Review Press.

Brown, J.C. (1954) *The Social Psychology of Industry*, Baltimore, MD: Penguin.

Buchner, L., Yeandle, S., and Botcherby, S. (2007) *Ethnic Minority Women and Local Labour Markets*, Manchester: EOC.

Burawoy, M. (1979) *Manufacturing Consent: Changes in the Labour Process under Monopoly Capitalism*, Chicago, IL: University of Chicago Press.

Cahill, S.E. (1906) 'The boundaries of professionalization: The case of North American funeral direction', *Symbolic Interaction*, 22(2): 105–19.

Callaghan, G. and Thompson, P. (2001) 'Edwards revisited: Technical control and call centres', *Economic and Industrial Democracy*, 22(1): 1–37.

Cavendish, R. (1982) *Women on the Line*, Boston, MA: Routledge & Kegan Paul.

_____ (1989) 'Women on the line', in C. Littler (ed.), *The Experience of Work*, Milton Keynes: Open University Press, ch. 8.

Center for Economic and Policy Research (2005) *How Good is the Economy at Creating Good Jobs?*, Report from the Center for Economic and Policy Research, Washington DC.

Centers, R. and Bugental, D.E. (1966) 'Intrinsic and extrinsic job motivations among different segments of the working population', *Journal of Applied Psychology*, 50(3): 193–7.

Child, J. (1973) 'Organization: A choice for man', in J. Child (ed.), *Man and the Organization*, London: Allen & Unwin.

Christensen, K. (1989) 'Home-based clerical work: No simple truth, no simple reality', in E. Boris and C. Daniels (eds), *Homework: Historical and Contemporary Perspectives on Paid Labour at Home*, Chicago, IL: University of Illinois Press, ch. 9.

Clegg, C.W. (1982) 'Modelling the practice of job design', in J.E. Kelly and C.W. Clegg (eds), *Autonomy and Control at the Workplace: Contexts for Job Redesign*, London: Croom Helm.

_____ (1984) 'The derivations of job designs', *Journal of Occupational Behaviour*, 5: 131–46.

Clegg, S. (1987) 'The language of power and the power of language', *Organization Studies*, 8(1): 61–70.

Cockburn, C. (1983) *Brothers: Male Dominance and Technological Change*, London: Pluto Press.

_____ (1987) *Two-Track Training: Sex Inequalities and the YTS*, London: Macmillan.

Collinson, D.L. (1992) *Managing the Shopfloor: Subjectivity, Masculinity and Workplace Culture*, Berlin: De Gruyter.

Corbett, M. (1994) *Critical Cases in Organizational Behaviour*, Houndmills: Macmillan.

Coward, R. (1992) *Our Treacherous Hearts*, London: Fontana.

Cummings, T.G. (1978) 'Self-regulating work groups: A socio-technical synthesis', *Academy of Management Review*, 3: 625–34.

Daniel, W.W. (1969) 'Industrial behaviour and orientation to work: A critique', *Journal of Management Studies*, 6(3): 366–75.

Davis, L.E. and Cherns, A.B. (1975) *The Quality of Working Life, Vols I and II*, New York: Free Press.

Dennerlein, J.T. and Meeker, J.D. (2003) 'Occupational injuries among Boston bicycle messengers', *American Journal of Industrial Medicine*, 42: 519–25.

Dennis, N., Henriques, F., and Slaughter, C. (1969) *Coal is our Life*, London: Tavistock.

Dick, P. (2005) 'Dirty work designations: How police officers account for their use of coercive force', *Human Relations*, 58(11): 1363–90.

Dickens, M. (1957) *One Pair of Feet*, Harmondsworth: Penguin.

Ditton, J. (1979) 'Baking time', *Sociological Review*, 27: 157–67.

Dubin, R. (1956) 'Industrial workers' worlds: A study of the "central life interests" of industrial workers', *Social Problems*, 5: 138–42.

Du Gay, P. (1996) *Consumption and Identity at Work*, London: Sage.

Efraty, D., Sirgy, J.M., and Claiborne, C.B. (1991) 'The effects of personal alienation of organizational identification: A quality-of-work-life model,' *Journal of Business and Psychology*, 6(1): 57–78.

Ehrenreich, B. (2001) *Nickel and Dimed: Undercover in Low-Wage USA*, London: Granta Books.

Equal Opportunities Commission (2007) *Moving on Up? The Way Forward*, Report on the EOC's investigation into Bangladeshi, Pakistani and Black Caribbean women and work, March, Manchester: EOC.

57

Felstead, A. (2007) 'Homeworking in Britain: The national picture in the mid 1990s', *Industrial Relations Journal*, 27(3): 225–328.

_____ and Jewson, N. (2000) *In Work, at Home: Towards an Understanding of Homeworking*, London: Routledge.

Fineman, S. (1996) 'Emotion and organizing', in S.R. Clegg, C. Hardy, and W.R. Nord (eds), *Handbook of Organization Studies*, London: Sage, ch. 3.3.

Fox, A. (1973) 'Industrial relations: A social critique of pluralist ideology', in J. Child (ed.), *Man and Organisation*, London: Allen & Unwin.

Friedmann, E.L. and Havighurst, R.J. (1954) *The Meaning of Work and Retirement*, Chicago, IL: University of Chicago Press.

Fucini, J.J. and Fucini, S. (1990) *Inside Mazda's American Auto Plant*, New York: Free Press.

Gabriel, Y. (1988) *Working Lives in Catering*, London: Routledge & Kegan Paul.

Gallie, D. and White, M. (1993) *Employee Commitment and the Skills Revolution*, London: Policy Studies Institute.

Geyer, R.F. and Schweitzer, D. (eds) (1981) *Alienation: Problems of Meaning, Theory and Method*, London: Routledge & Kegan Paul.

Godin, P. (2000) 'A dirty business: Caring for people who are a nuisance or a danger', *Journal of Advanced Nursing*, 32(6): 1396–1402.

Goldthorpe. J.H., Lockwood, D., Bechhofer, F., and Platt, J. (1968) *The Affluent Worker: Political Attitudes and Behaviour*, Cambridge: Cambridge University Press.

_____ _____ _____ _____ (1969) *The Affluent Worker in the Class Structure*, Cambridge: Cambridge University Press.

Grey, C. (1996) 'Towards a critique of managerialism: The contribution of Simone Weil', *Journal of Management Studies*, 33(5): 591–611.

Hackman, J.R. (1977) 'Work Design', in J.R. Hackman and J.L. Suttle (eds), *Improving Life at Work*, Santa Monica, CA: Goodyear, ch. 3.

_____ and Oldham, G.R. (1975) 'Development of the job diagnostic survey', *Journal of Applied Psychology*, 60(2): 159–70.

_____, Janson, R., and Purdy, K. (1975) 'A new strategy for job enrichment', *California Management Review*, 17: 57–71.

Hakim, C. (1991) 'Grateful slaves and self-made women: Fact and fantasy in women's work orientations', *European Sociological Review*, 7(2): 101–21.

Hallam, J. (2002) 'Vocation to profession: Changing images of nursing in Britain', *Journal of Organizational Change Management*, 15(1): 35–47.

Hamper, B. (1992) *Rivethead: Tales from the Assembly Line*, London: Fourth Estate.

Hassard, J. (1996) 'Images of time in work and organization', in S. Clegg, C. Hardy, and W.R. Nord (eds), *Handbook of Organization Studies*, London: Sage, ch. 3.5; also published in K. Grint (ed.) (2000), *Work and Society: A Reader*, Cambridge: Polity Press, pp. 14–40.

Herzberg, F. (1966) *Work and the Nature of Man*, New York: Staples Press.

_____ (1968) 'One more time: How do you motivate employees?', *Harvard Business Review*, 46(1): 53–62.

Hodson, R. (2001) *Dignity at Work*, Cambridge: Cambridge University Press.

_____ (2002) 'Demography or respect? Work group demography versus organizational dynamics as determinants of meaning and satisfaction at work', *British Journal of Sociology*, 53(2): 291–317.

Hughes, E. (1958) *Men and Their Work*, Glencoe, IL: The Free Press.

Huws, U., Korte, V., and Robinson, S. (1990) *Telework: Towards the Elusive Office*, Chichester: Wiley.

Jermier, J.M., Knights, D., and Nord, W.R. (1994) 'Resistance and power in organizations: Agency, subjectivity and the labour process', in J. Jermier, D. Knights, and W.R. Nord (eds), *Introduction to Resistance and Power in Organizations*, London: Routledge, pp. 1–24.

Jones, G. and Wallace, C. (1990) 'Beyond individualization: What sort of social change?', in L. Chisholm, P. Buchner, H. Kruger, and P. Brown (eds), *Childhood, Youth and Social Change*, Lewes: Falmer Press.

Juravich, T. (1985) *Chaos on the Shop Floor*, Philadelphia, PA: Temple University Press.

Kakabadse, A. (1986) 'Organizational alienation and job climate: A comparative study of structural conditions and psychological adjustment', *Small Group Behavior*, 17(4): 458–71.

Kamenou, N. (2008) 'Reconsidering work–life balance debates: Challenging limited understandings of the "life" component in the context of ethnic minority women's experiences', *British Journal of Management*, 19: S99–S109.

Kanungo, R.N. (1982) *Work Alienation: An Integrative Approach*, New York: Praeger.

Kidder, J. (2006) 'It's the job that I love: Bike messengers and edgework', *Sociological Forum*, 21(1): 31–54.

Kinnie, N., Hutchinson, S., and Purcell, J. (2000) 'Fun and surveillance: The paradox of high commitment management in call centres', *International Journal of Human Resource Management*, 11(5): 967–85.

Klein, L. (1982) *Design Strategies in Theory and Practice*, Paper presented at the 20th International Congress of Applied Psychology, University of Edinburgh.

Knights, D. (1990) 'Subjectivity, power and the labour process', in D. Knights and H. Wilmott (eds), *Labour Process Theory*, London: Macmillan, ch. 10.

Krishnamurthy, M. (2004) 'Resources and Rebels: A study of identity management in Indian call centres', *Anthropology of Work Review*, XXV(3–4): 9–18.

Lawler, E.E., Hackman, J.R., and Kaufman, S. (1973) 'Effects of job redesign: A field experiment', *Journal of Applied Social Psychology*, 3: 49–62.

Linhart, R. (1989) 'The assembly line', in C. Littler (ed.), *The Experience of Work*, Milton Keynes: Open University Press.

Littler, C. (1989) 'Introduction: The texture of work', in C. Littler (ed.), *The Experience of Work*, Milton Keynes: Open University Press.

Mann, S. (2007) 'The boredom boom', *The Psychologist*, 20(2): 90–3.

Marx, K. (1963) *Early Writings*, ed. and trans. T.B. Bottomore, London: C.A. Watts.

May, D. and Kelly, M.P. (1982) 'Chancers, pets and poor wee souls: Problems of legitimation in psychiatric nursing', *Sociology of Health and Illness*, 4(3): 279–99.

Maznevski, M.L. (1994) 'Understanding our differences: Performance in decision-making groups with diverse members', *Human Relations*, 47(5): 531–52.

Milliken, F.J. and Martins, L.L. (1996) 'Searching for common threads: Understanding the multiple effects of diversity in organizational groups', *Academy of Management Review*, 21(2): 402–33.

Mirza, H. (1992) *Young, Female and Black*, London: Routledge.

Morse, N.C. and Weiss, R.S. (1955) 'The function and meaning of work and the job', *American Sociological Review*, 20: 191–8.

Nichols, T. (1976) 'Management, ideology and practice', in *People at Work*, Block 5, Unit 15, Milton Keynes: The Open University Press.

Olson, M. (1989) 'Organizational barriers to professional telework', in E. Boris and C. Daniels (eds), *Homework: Historical and Contemporary Perspectives on Paid Labour at Home*, Chicago, IL: University of Illinois Press, ch. 11.

Orzak, L. (1959) 'Work as a central life interest of professionals', *Social Problems*, 7: 125–32.

Pahl, R. (1984) *Divisions of Labour*, Oxford: Blackwell.

_____ (1988) *On Work, Thirty Years of Making out*, Oxford: Basil Blackwell.

Paules, G.F. (1991), *Dishing It Out: Power and Resistance Among Waitresses in a New Jersey Restaurant*, Philadelphia, PA: Temple University Press.

Perry, S.E. (1978) *San Francisco Scavengers: Dirty Work and the Pride of Ownership*, Berkeley, CA: University of California Press.

Phizacklea, A. and Wolkowitz, C. (1993; 1995) *Homeworking Women: Gender, Racism and Class at Work*, London: Sage.

Pollert, A. (1981) *Girls, Wives and Factory Lives*, London: Macmillan.

Reeves, R. (2001) *Happy Mondays: Putting the Pleasure Back into Work*, Harlow: Pearson.

Reich, R. (1991) *The Work of Nations*, New York: Knopf.

Roethslinger, F.J. (1941) *Management and Morale*, Cambridge, MA: Harvard University Press.

Roper, M. (1991) 'Yesterday's model: Product fetishism and the British company man 1945–85', in M. Roper and J. Tosh (eds), *Manful Assertions: Masculinities in Britain since 1800*, London: Routledge, ch. 9.

Rose, M. (1994) 'Skill and Samuel Smiles: Changing the British work ethic', in R. Penn, M. Rose, and J. Rubery (eds), *Skill and Occupational Change*, Oxford: Oxford University Press, ch. 10.

Roy, D. (1960) 'Banana time: Job satisfaction and informal interaction', *Human Organization*, 18: 156–68; repr. in J. Hassard (ed.) (1990) *The Sociology of Time*, London: Macmillan, ch. 9.

Russell, K.J. (1980) 'The orientation to work controversy and the social construction of work value systems', *Journal of Management Studies*, 17(2), 164–84.

Salaman, G. and Thompson, K. (eds) (1973) *People and Organisations*, Harlow: Longman for the Open University Press.

Salancik, G.R. and Pfeffer, J. (1977) 'An examination of the need–satisfaction models of job attributes', *Administrative Science Quarterly*, 22: 427–57.

Sarros, J.C., Tanewski, G.A., Winter, R.P., Santora, J.C., and Densten, I.L. (2002) 'Work alienation and organizational leadership', *British Journal of Management*, 13: 285–304.

Sayer, A. (2007) 'Dignity at work: broadening the agenda', *Organization*, 14(4): 565–81.

Sayers, S. (1988) 'The need to work: A perspective from philosophy', in R.E. Pahl (ed.), *On Work: Historical, Comparative and Theoretical Approaches*, Oxford: Basil Blackwell, ch. 33.

Sharpe, S. (1984) *Double Identity: The Lives of Working Mothers*, Harmondsworth: Penguin.

Sims, H.P., Szilagyi, A.D., and Keller, R.T. (1976) 'The measurement of job characteristics', *Academy of Management Journal*, June: 195–212.

Smith, V. (1990) *Managing the Corporate Interest: Control and Resistance in an American Bank*, Berkeley, CA: University of California Press.

Spencer, L. and Taylor, S. (1994) *Participation and Progress in the Labour Market: Key Issues for Women*, Department of Employment Research Series No. 35., Sheffield: Department of Employment.

Stone, E.F. and Gueutal, H.G. (1985) 'An empirical derivation of the dimensions along which characteristics of jobs are perceived', *Academy of Management Journal*, 28(2): 376–96.

Taylor, P. and Bain, P. (1999) 'An assembly line in the head: Work and employee relations in the call centre', *Industrial Relations Journal*, 30(2): 101–17.

_____, Hyman, J., Mulvey, G., and Bain, P. (2002) 'Work organization, control and the experience of work in call centres', *Work, Employment and Society*, 16: 133–50.

Thiel, D. (2007) 'Class in construction: London building workers, dirty work and physical cultures', *The British Journal of Sociology*, 58(2): 227–51.

Thompson, P. (1990) 'Crawling from the wreckage: The labour process and the politics of production', in D. Knights and H. Wilmott (eds), *Labour Process Theory*, London: Macmillan.

_____ and McHugh, D. (1990) *Work Organizations*, Basingstoke: Macmillan.

_____ _____ (2002) *Work Organisations*, 3rd edn, Houndmills: Palgrave.

Thompson, W.E. (1983) 'Hanging tongues: A sociological encounter with the assembly line', *Qualitative Sociology*, 6: 215–37.

_____ and Harred, J.L. (1992) 'Topless dancers: Managing stigma in a deviant occupation', *Deviant Behavior*, 13: 291–311.

Toynbee, P. (2003) *Hard Work: Life in Low-Pay Britain*, London: Bloomsbury.

Trautner, M.N. (2005) 'Doing gender, doing class: The performance of sexuality in exotic dance clubs', *Gender and Society*, 19(6): 771–88.

Trinca, H. and Fox, C. (2004) *Better Than Sex: How a Whole Generation Got Hooked on Work*, Sydney: Random House.

Turner, A.N. and Lawrence, P.R. (1965) *Industrial Jobs and the Worker*, Cambridge, MA: Harvard University Press.

Vecchio, R.P. (1980) 'The function and meaning of work and the job: Morse and Weiss (1955) revisited', *Academy of Management Journal*, 23(2): 361–7.

Waddington, P.A. (1999) 'Police (canteen) sub-culture: An appreciation', *British Journal of Criminology*, 39(2): 287–309.

Walter, N. (1996) 'Bringing out the women in New Labour', *The Guardian*, 29 February.

Weber, M. (1926; 1947) *The Theory of Social and Economic Organization*, ed. Talcott Parsons, New York: Free Press.

_____ (1930) *The Protestant Ethic and the Spirit of Capitalism*, London: Allen & Unwin.

Weil, S. (1987) *Formative Writings 1929–1941*, London: Routledge.

Westwood, S. (1984) *All Day Every Day: Factory and Family in the Making of Women's Lives*, London: Pluto Press.

_____ (1988) 'Workers and wives: Continuities and discontinuities in the lives of Gujarati women', in S. Westwood and P. Bhachu (eds), *Enterprising Women: Ethnicity, Economy and Gender Relations*, London: Routledge, pp. 103–31.

Wheelan, C.T. (1976) 'Orientations to work: Some theoretical and methodological problems', *British Journal of Industrial Relations*, 14(2): 145.

Wilensky, H.L. (1964) 'Varieties of work experiences', in H. Borrow (ed.), *Man in a World of Work*, Boston, MA: Houghton Mifflin.

Willis, P. (1977) *Learning to Labour*, Farnborough: Saxon House.

Willmott, H. (1990) 'Subjectivity and the dialectics of praxis: Opening the core of labour process analysis', in D. Knights and H. Wilmott (eds), *Labour Process Theory*, London: Macmillan.

Wood, R.C. (1992) *Working in Hotels and Catering*, London: Routledge.

Zeffane, R. and Macdonald, D. (1993) 'Uncertainty, participation and alienation: Lessons from workplace restructuring', *International Journal of Sociology and Social Policy*, 13(5–6): 22–52.

The View from Above

Introduction

In Chapter 2, we looked at the realities of work, mainly from a worker's perspective—but what about managers? What do they do and what are their jobs like?

'Managing' usually means being in charge, and being responsible for the smooth running and rational conduct of an organization or unit. In some ways, however, we all 'manage'. In all societies, people are involved in the complex and demanding work of organizing their lives, accomplishing ordinary tasks, and maintaining routines. We manage our resources, our time, and sometimes those of others, but we are not called 'managers'. Those who are called managers will be those who are trained and employed to shape, organize, and regulate within a particular organization. They will be managing large, medium-sized, and small production or service organizations—stores, hospitals, theatres, hotels, factories, voluntary organizations, cooperatives—so the job of manager will differ from organization to organization. Additionally, many people are managers without having the title of manager: for example, nursing administrators, farmers, head teachers, prison governors, and bishops are all managers of people and resources. All are vested with formal authority—that is, a legitimate right to manage—within their organizations. They may also

be gangmasters or be involved in managing other illegal activity; in these cases, they are even less likely to be called 'managers', but will nevertheless believe that they have a legitimate right to manage. Management is about having power and control over people, while achieving a measure of voluntary compliance from them.

This chapter looks at the research on managerial work. By the end of the chapter, you will be able to explain how management is defined and researched; you will also understand some of the realities of managerial life.

This chapter covers:

- the definition of 'management';
- research on the role of the manager;
- management as a profession;
- middle management;
- success in management;
- management and men;
- the reality for the woman manager;
- double jeopardy—the reality for the black and ethnic minority woman manager;
- hotel management;
- surprises in managerial work;
- standing back from managerial work.

The definition of 'management'

Management can be defined as 'mental (thinking, intuiting, feeling) work performed by people in an organizational context' (Kast and Rosenzweig, 1985). Stewart (1994: 2) defines management as a level: a position above foreman and above first-level supervision. It is power and social context that differentiate managers from non-managers. As Grint (1995) notes, what managers do is little different from what anyone might do, but the context within which the act of management occurs differentiates the manager from the non-manager.

WHAT DO MANAGERS DO? A JOKE

A big corporation hired several cannibals. 'You are all part of our team now,' said the human resources officer during the welcoming briefing. 'You get all of the usual benefits and you can go to the cafeteria for something to eat, but please don't eat any of the other employees.' The cannibals promised not to do so.

Four weeks later, their boss remarked: 'You're all working very hard, and I'm satisfied with you. But one of our secretaries has disappeared. Do any of you know what happened to her?' The cannibals all shook their heads.

After the boss had left, the leader of the cannibals asked the others: 'Which one of you idiots ate the secretary?'

A hand was raised hesitantly. The leader of the cannibals continued: 'You fool! For four weeks, we've been eating managers and no one noticed anything, but you had to go and eat the secretary!'

Research on the role of the manager

Henri Fayol (1949), a French businessman, was one of the first managers—along with others including Gulick and Urwick (1937)—to use his experience to theorize about the manager's job and to generalize about all managerial work. He described the functions that all managers perform as planning, organizing, motivating, controlling, and coordinating. (He then went on to list the fourteen general principles of management that guide the manager in his or her activities.) This very clear-cut traditional account of what managers do can still be found in current management textbooks—but while it offers us a theory, what is the everyday reality of what managers do?

STOP AND THINK **Are managers always motivating?**

Fayol believed that all managers plan, organize, motivate, control, and coordinate. Does this fit with your experience and view of reality? For example, are managers always motivating?

Mintzberg (1970; 1973), Kotter (1982a; 1982b), and Stewart (1974; 1982a) all criticized Fayol's simplistic functional view of management. Mintzberg (1975) described the classical functions as 'folklore'. But Fayol's contribution to management has recently been re-evaluated in a more favourable light by Parker and Ritson (2005), who argue that his management theories embraced a wider spectrum of approaches and concepts than are traditionally identified with him.

Research to discover what managers actually did began in earnest with a study by Carlson in 1951 (Stewart, 1994; Hales, 1999). Carlson looked at the work of seven Swedish and two French executives over a four-week period. He described managers as reactive socializers, rather than machine-like decision makers, who, in the words of Grint (1995: 48) 'fought fires with words and networks of colleagues and subordinates'. In *Men Who Manage*, Dalton (1959) became an observer of managerial work in order to study it. He exposed much of the underlife of organizations in which informal arrangements replace, impede, and are mixed with formal official procedures. He showed how managers manage with feelings and political skill. There is an 'orderly disorder' of managerial cliques endlessly struggling for power and respect.

Rosemary Stewart (1967; 1988) researched the question of what managers do by asking 160 middle and senior managers—mainly in production, marketing, sales, and accounting, across a large number of different companies—to keep a specially designed diary for four weeks. All of the managers were men. Stewart was particularly interested in studying the similarities and differences between managers' jobs for a functional end: to show ways in which the selection and training of managers could be improved. Information on such differences could influence both the content of the courses and the decisions on who should attend them. She also wanted to classify managers' jobs on the basis of differences and to discover the ways in which managers may use their time inefficiently.

Stewart found that the managers worked an average of 43–44 hours a week. They spent, on average, 75 per cent of their time in their own organization. Time spent outside the organization varied considerably from manager to manager, as did the time that they spent on writing, dictating, reading, figure work, and inspection. Discussions were the dominant activity of nearly all of the managers, occupying half of their time. On average, they spent about a third of their time alone, although this varied widely from job to job. The traditional Fayol description of a manager who plans, organizes, coordinates, and controls was not the reality she witnessed‘ rather, managerial work was characterized by the brevity of most activities. Managers switch their attention frequently from one person and activity to another, spending so little time uninterrupted that many complained that they had no time to think. In this study, managers spent, on average, only nine periods of half an hour or longer alone during the four weeks. The interruptions were found to be generated by the managers themselves, not only by other people, because managers will frequently think of something else and switch activity rather than continue with the task at hand.

Stewart categorized the managers into five groups, or job profiles, in order to describe the variability between jobs better.

1. The *emissaries* spent much of their time away from the company, talking to people on the outside. They worked the longest hours compared with managers in other groups. The most numerous were sales managers, then general managers. Of the 160, 45 fell into this group.

2. The *writers* spent more time by themselves, reading, writing, dictating, and performing figure work. They spent half of their time with other people. They spent the least time in group contacts because they rarely had to attend committees and worked shorter hours. Most of this group comprised middle managers, but it included some top managers.

3. The *discussers* spent most time with other people and with their colleagues. This group contained a wide variety of managers.

4. The *troubleshooters* had the most fragmented work pattern and a large number of fleeting contacts. As their name suggests, they frequently had to cope with crises. Even though they may have planned carefully to avoid trouble, much of their time was spent dealing with problems that needed a speedy solution. They spent longer with their subordinates than any other group.

5. The *committee men*, as might be guessed, spent a large amount of time in committees and group discussion. They had the widest range of internal contacts, but few contacts outside the company.

It is clear from Stewart's work that management cannot be discussed as though it were a single activity that requires uniform abilities and a common body of knowledge. It can be misleading, then, to talk about the manager's job or how the average manager spends his or her time. The way in which managers spent their time may have been determined by the kind of organization for which they worked, by the kind of job that they had, or by their own individual ways of doing their jobs.

Henry Mintzberg (1973) took a different approach and based his theories on having observed five chief executives work for only a week. In *Mintzberg on Management* (1989), he describes how he used a stopwatch (much as Frederick Taylor had done before him) to observe, in the course of one intensive week, the activities of five chief executives of a major consulting firm, a well-known teaching hospital, a school system, a high-technology firm, and a manufacturer of consumer goods. He says that if you ask managers what they do, they will most likely tell you that they plan, organize, coordinate, and control—giving you a traditional account in Fayol's terms. But if you watch them, you will be unlikely to relate what you see to those four words. Where, for example, would the activity of presenting a gold watch to a retiring employee fit into those four Fayol categories?

There are four myths, Mintzberg says, about managers' jobs that do not bear up under scrutiny.

1. The manager is a reflective, systematic planner.

2. The effective manager has no regular duties to perform.

3. The senior manager needs aggregated information that a formal management information system best provides.

4. Management is becoming a science and a profession.

Evidence suggests that managers work at an unrelenting pace. Again, Mintzberg noted that the work was characterized by brevity: for example, half of the activities in which the five chief executives engaged lasted less than nine minutes and only 10 per cent exceeded one hour. The work of management is also characterized by variety and discontinuity. Chief executives are strongly oriented to action and dislike reflective activities. There are a number of regular duties to perform, including negotiating, ceremonies (such as presiding at special dinners), and processing information that connects the organization with its environment. Managers favour telephone calls and meetings, rather than formal information systems. In two British studies (Mintzberg, 1989), for example, managers spent an average of 66 and 80 per cent of their time in oral communication—helping to explain, at least in part, why managers are reluctant to delegate tasks: most of the important information that they carry is in their heads and has not been recorded. Managers certainly do not, in Mintzberg's view, practise a science. They seek information by word of mouth, and rely on what they call 'judgement' and 'intuition'—that is, what Mintzberg would call 'ignorance'. As a result, the job of a manager is enormously difficult and complicated. They are overburdened, yet cannot delegate, meaning that they are forced to do tasks only superficially. But scientific attempts to improve managerial work have proven impossible.

IS THIS WHAT MANAGERS DO: ARRANGE MEETINGS?

Are you lonely?
Hate having to make decisions?
Rather talk about it than do it?

Then why not HOLD A MEETING?

At a meeting, you can:
See other people
Sleep in peace
Offload decisions
Learn to write volumes of meaningless notes
Feel important
Impress (or bore) your colleagues
All in work time!

MEETINGS: The practical alternative to work

Mintzberg (1989) defines the manager as a person in charge of an organization or one of its subunits, which can include bishops, prime ministers, and vice-presidents. What all of these people have in common is that they have all been vested with formal authority over the unit. From formal authority comes status, which leads to various interpersonal relations, from which comes access to information—information that is used to make decisions and to build strategy. As a result of looking at managerial work and describing it, Mintzberg distinguishes between three main roles that the manager plays:

- his or her role in interpersonal aspects;
- his or her role in receiving and disseminating information (that is, as a nerve centre for information);
- his or her role as decision maker.

Mintzberg then divided these three roles yet further, as Table 3.1 illustrates.

For the 'figurehead', there are duties of a ceremonial nature, such as meeting local dignitaries. As the people in charge, managers are responsible for the work of the people in their unit; they are therefore 'leaders'. As a 'liaison', managers are making contact outside their vertical chain of command, spending as much time with peers and others outside their units (including clients, suppliers, and government officials) as with their own subordinates.

Due to interpersonal contact with those below in the hierarchy and a network of contacts, managers are at the nerve centre of their unit. They will not know everything, but will typically know more than their subordinates. This information needs to be processed. As a 'monitor', they scan their environment for information (including gossip and speculation), which information they then share and distribute as 'disseminator'. In their role as 'spokesperson', managers send some of their information to people outside their units: for example, to consumer groups.

Managers also play a major role in decision making. As 'entrepreneur', they seek to improve the unit and adapt it to changes in the environment; they seek and initiate new ideas. Some of the chief executives that Mintzberg studied had as many as fifty development projects running at any one time. In the role of 'disturbance handler', the managers respond to pressures: for example, a threatened strike or the bankruptcy of a major customer. As 'resource allocator', they decide what resources go where, and the role of 'negotiator' is, for the manager, a way of life.

These roles are not easily separated and form an integrated whole from which no single role can be withdrawn. Mintzberg believes that this description of managerial work should be more important to managers than any prescription that can be offered: for Mintzberg, a manager's effectiveness is significantly influenced by insight into his or her own work. His or her performance is dependent on how well he or she understands and responds to the pressures and dilemmas of the job. Managers are challenged systematically to share their privileged information with subordinates, to step back to see the broader picture on offer, and to make use of analytical inputs—and they need to control their time carefully.

A few studies have attempted to test Mintzberg's roles in actual operating situations (Lau et al., 1980; McCall and Segrist, 1980; Snyder and Wheelan, 1981; Kurke and Aldrich, 1983). Minzberg's role theory is accused of failing to deliver something that it promises—that is, explanation of managerial behaviour.

TABLE 3.1 Mintzberg's managerial roles

Interpersonal roles	Informational roles	Decisional roles
Figurehead	Monitor	Entrepreneur
Leader	Disseminator	Disturbance handler
Liaison	Spokesperson	Resource allocator
		Negotiator

It does not answer the question of why managerial behaviour is as it is; rather, it simply categorizes that behaviour (Hales, 1999). It is criticized for lacking specificity, and for not pointing out the relationship between the role types and organizational effectiveness. It is developed on the basis of the questionable practice of not going beyond the observable work activities themselves. Managers might be thinking about job-related problems long after they leave work; we know, for example, that some managers may work many hours even before coming into the office (Carroll and Gillen, 1987). Consequently, because much managerial work is mental, it is not directly observable: the physical activities of managers do not indicate exactly what they do. It is consequently impossible to measure managerial work without questioning managers about the purpose of their telephone calls, conversations, and so on. And although managers may make only brief contacts, this does not mean that they are not planning, controlling, or investigating—all of which require information (ibid.). Mintzberg is also criticized for ignoring the historical and political processes that underpin, channel, and provide rationales for the work that managers do (Willmott, 2005).

Kotter (1982a) conducted a detailed analysis of how fifteen successful general managers spent their time. He compared his data with those of Mintzberg (1973), in the USA, and Stewart (1967; 1988), in the UK. All three agreed that managers' work is largely reactive rather than proactive, and is varied, fragmented, and frequently interrupted—giving a different picture of the hectic day that contrasts with the theorist's view of a manager who plans, organizes, and controls. The research also shows how important interpersonal skills are to managers: successful managers spend time establishing informal networks, and creating or being involved in cooperative relationships with people. The emphasis is on frenetic, disjointed activity, using informal methods of disseminating and collecting information, and a realization of the paramount importance of people skills. As Alimo-Metcalfe (1992) notes, these skills are difficult to measure and simulate. Equally difficult to measure are the necessary political skills. Kotter (1982a) shows how power is exercised and replenished through the successful management of interpersonal networks that are central to management activity (Willmott, 2005). Studies of British and US managers have shown how they spend nearly all of their time with other people, trying to find out what is happening, trying to persuade others to cooperate, and (less often) trying to decide what ought to be done. They need to know how to trade, bargain, and compromise. And the more senior they are, the more political will be the world in which they live (Stewart, 1997).

Studies have repeatedly shown that managerial activity is high on oral communication (see Kanter, 1977). Gowler and Legge (1996) go beyond this assertion to say that such verbal activity involves the use of rhetoric—that is, the use of a form of word delivery that is lavish in symbolism and involves several layers or textures of meaning. Managers use a political rhetoric of bureaucratic control that is highly expressive, constructing and legitimizing managerial prerogative in terms of a rational, goal-directed image of organizational effectiveness. And not only do managers spend most of their time talking, but they also generate a culture, in an anthropological sense, which is maintained and transmitted from one generation to another. Meaning may be generated through rituals, myths, magic, totemism, and taboo, in the same way as is documented by social anthropologists studying distant cultures. This talk—especially the rhetoric—may be the way in which social control is maintained.

The issue of social control arises again when we look at the hours for which managers are required to work. Pahl (1995) notes the consistent patterns of long work hours and few holidays that characterize managerial work. Watson (1994) undertook participant observation to study managers, which demonstrated how long work hours—especially in the evening—were seen as a measure of commitment to the organization. Male managers, in particular, deliberately stayed at work late in the evening, wasted time, artificially extended meetings, and criticized managers who left at 7.15 p.m. Similarly, Coyle (1995) notes the long hours for which managers worked in the five UK organizations within which she conducted research (see Collinson and Collinson, 1997). National surveys have also shown how managers are working increasingly long hours: responding to Austin Knight UK (1995), 45 per cent of senior male managers said that they were working more than 50 hours a week; the Institute of Management (1995) found that 60 per cent of respondents felt that their workload had 'greatly increased' over the past two years. The Institute of Management's subsequent annual survey (1996) saw that response rise to 80 per cent. As a result, most managers were experiencing signs of stress. Many now experience job insecurity and uncertainty—and fear of redundancy can make it imperative to appear visibly committed to the job, to maximize limited promotion opportunities. Such 'presenteeism' has, however, been found to be highly gendered: it is more likely to be recognized by women, but practised by men (Simpson, 1998).

While many similarities can be found in managerial jobs, there can also be differences. Kotter (1982a) found that the jobs of the general managers that he studied differed. He also found that managers did their jobs differently, as similarly noted by Stewart (1982b). Stewart showed how every manager does the job in his or her own way, choosing, for example, to be outward-focused—that is, spending much time with people outside the organization building business—or inward-looking—that is, spending most of his or her time developing relations with and managing his or her own staff. Johnson and Gill (1993) believe that there is little consensus about what managers' everyday activities are. This is made worse by the fact that management is not an undifferentiated, homogeneous occupational group. But there must be some consensus to be found: Grint (1995) concludes that—in the UK, at least—management seems to be mainly concerned with talk and manic attempts to stamp out numerous 'fires'. They dash from one emergency to the next, resolving short-term problems and crises, while keeping production going. The typical manager's day involves 'keeping the show on the road, and managing to keep one's head above water when all around are losing theirs to stress' (ibid.: 66).

Drucker (1989) does not describe what the manager does, but describes instead what a manager *should* do. His is a very practical approach to management: a guide for those working in management. Drucker says, for example, that managers should put economic performance first, because they can only justify their existence and authority by economic results. The ultimate test of management is business performance. Their second function is to make a productive enterprise out of human and material resources, the transmutation of which requires management. The third and final function of management, for Drucker, is the managing of workers and work. In practice, managers discharge these three functions in every action.

In a similarly prescriptive vein, Kanter (1987) examined the conditions that support innovation and change, coupled with the experiences and activities of the innovators that bring this about. She looked at how people acquire and use power in empowering organizations, and how this contributes to innovation and the mastery of change. She used ten core research companies and found that, to manage effectively, corporate entrepreneurs need to work through participative teams to produce small changes that will add up later to big ones. They need 'power skills' to persuade others to invest information, support, and resources in new initiatives driven by an entrepreneur. They need the ability to manage the problems associated with the greater use of teams and participation, as well as an understanding of how change is designed and constructed in an organization.

Some, like Burnham (1945), have argued that a managerial revolution has come about. Specialist knowledge and skills of managerial experts have become crucial to the successful running of increasingly large and complex businesses and bureaucracies. The dominance of owners of wealth is undermined and a new class of professional salaried managers exercises control. The counter-argument is that the criteria of performance under which managers operate are oriented to ownership interest: the more successful managers tend to be those who internalize profit-oriented values and priorities. Corporate profits are prerequisites for high managerial income and status (Zeitlin, 1989). The ownership of wealth and control of work are closely related: both managers and owners play their parts in the same 'constellations of interest' (Scott, 1979; see also Watson, 1997).

A power approach to manager and management—that is, an approach that looks at who appears to possess power—would tend to say that the distinguishing feature of the professions is their ability to gain societal recognition as professions. This approach emerges from the (second) Chicago School, who used symbolic interactionism—that is, a perspective that emphasizes the individual's views and interpretations of social reality—to argue that professions are essentially the same as other occupations. There is no precise and unique definition of professions; rather, it is a title claimed by certain occupations at certain points in time. Professional rewards are sufficient for people to want and to strive for professional status.

The taxonomic, or classification, approach would argue that a profession possesses specialized skills, the necessity of intellectual and practical training, and the perceived collective responsibility for maintaining the integrity of the profession as a whole via a professional body (see Dietrich and Roberts, 1997: 23)—all of which is achieved through, for example, barriers to entry and occupational closure.

Management as a profession

During the 1980s, British management education and training became a matter for public concern, debate, and action. A number of reports (Mangham and Silver, 1986; Constable and McCormick, 1987; Handy, 1987) showed that the range and quality of provision of education and training fell well below that of the USA, Europe, and Japan (Reed and Anthony, 1992). British management was, in some areas, a 'spurious elite' (Handy et al., 1988: 168). British managers were embedded in centuries-old technique and a culture of rule that emphasized stability at the expense of innovation, and compromise at the expense of confrontation (Fox, 1983: 33). They seemed to lack the entrepreneurial zeal and basic technical competence of managerial elites in other countries. British managers relied on a model of status, rather than occupational professionalism. They lacked developmental, educational, and training opportunities. While other professionals—in law, medicine, accountancy, and architecture, for example—spent up to seven years in apprenticeship and further study, British managers did nothing to apply the procedures of professionalism to management. And because the practice of management is so diversified, and bereft of occupational organization and control, it is hard for the manager to generate effective professional authority and closure.

> **EXAMPLE An example of managerial work**
>
> Smith (1980) researched and analysed the jobs of three managers in a bakery in the north-west of England. The job titles were 'general manager', 'factory manager', and 'product development manager'. Each manager kept a log of his activities for a period of ten days.
>
> Results showed that the general manager's job required the ability to deal with people, and involved specialist knowledge and accuracy. The main component of the job involved organizing and administering. Both the factory manager and product development manager reported to the general manager. The factory manager's job involved making checks of staff, taking disciplinary action, and making checks on machinery. While the general manager's job was basically that of an 'emissary' (Stewart, 1979), the factory manager was typical of Stewart's 'troubleshooter', and was, as Mintzberg (1973) would have predicted, subject to much brevity, variety, and fragmentation of work. The product development manager had a job that lay somewhere in between. This job was a specialist job, requiring some time to work in isolation on ideas, and other time on administrative routine, planning activities, and running meetings.
>
> The results are consistent with everyday expectations of these kinds of job, and fit with the descriptions and categorizations of other researchers of managerial work. Taking a managerialist perspective (that is, assuming that research can serve the objectives of managers), this kind of research and analysis can be said to help to develop a necessary 'person specification'—that is, a document that sets out the education, qualifications, training, experience, and personal attributes or competences of the job candidates—for use in recruitment and selection. Taking a more critical perspective, however, it might be argued that this is not a cost-effective solution. In addition, the method involved—that is, asking the managers to describe their own jobs—means that the job description would be constrained by the perceptions of the particular job incumbent, which might lead to jobs being evaluated and rated unfairly.

69

Middle management

There are some gloomy views of middle management. There are a number of reasons why middle managers may be frustrated, disillusioned individuals, according to Dopson and Stewart (1990).

1. They are in the middle of a long hierarchy and may have been bypassed by top management's efforts to increase employee involvement.

2. They have to cope with conflicting expectations of those above and below them in the hierarchy. They are squeezed between the demands of the strategies that they cannot influence and the ambitions of independent-minded employees (Kanter, 1986). They can get caught in cross-fire between departments and customers or suppliers.

3. They have lost technical expertise to administrative tasks.

4. There is career disillusionment among middle managers: they express frustration, dissatisfaction, and powerlessness. The middle manager can no longer expect a lifetime career, and some commentators have talked about the 'end of the career' in management (Handy, 1989; Osterman, 1996).

As if this were not bad enough, middle managers have been under attack throughout the 1980s and 1990s as organizational downsizing and re-engineering have reduced their numbers (Scarborough and Burrell, 1996). While opinions vary as to the extent of the reduction (Dopson and Stewart, 1990), middle managers have been a target: they are seen to add costs, slow down decisions, and obstruct flow of information (Dopson and Neumann, 1998; Thomas and Dunkerley, 1999). The downsized, re-engineered, flatter organization has less need for people whose primary role is to transmit senior manager's orders down through the hierarchy—particularly when they fail to perform the role effectively. They have also been considered to have a negative impact on change, being obstructive and resistant to change.

This gloomy view is counterbalanced by a number of writers who show that information technology has led to a reshaping of the middle manager's role rather than to its demise. For example, Dopson and Stewart (1990) found that a smaller number of middle managers now had a greater responsibility for a wider range of duties, for which they were clearly accountable. They were described as more important than in the past, because they are in slimmer, flatter organizations, have more responsibility, and are seen by top management as having a major role in implementing change. Most managers were positive about the changes and how their jobs had changed: middle managers found themselves closer to top management and strategic decisions; they had their own clear areas of responsibility, with more control over resources, and could more legitimately take decisions within these areas. The traditional career model for managers must therefore be revised (McGovern et al., 1998).

Success in management

While there is little question that restructuring has spelt the end of de facto lifetime employment guarantees for managers, managers in general have done well: their earnings have grown faster than those of most employees and their employment opportunities continue to develop. They are also optimistic about their career futures (Wajcman and Martin, 2001; Martin, 2005).

Careers in organizations have undergone a transformation as organizations have reformed and reshaped, culling layers of the management hierarchy, rethinking employment contracts, and revising what they are prepared to offer in terms of career progression (Arnold, 1997). The meaning of 'career success' needs therefore to be revisited by organizations. Career success has frequently been presented as something that can be objectively quantified through external criteria, such as hierarchical position and salary level (O'Reilly and Chatman, 1994; Melamed, 1995). Managers' own conceptions of success have generally been excluded from research into careers (Herriot et al., 1994)—but when own concep-tions of success are researched, only a minority of individuals include reaching the most senior levels of management as criteria for success; the majority use a range of internal and intangible criteria, such as achievement, accomplishment, personal recognition, and influence, to define career success in their own terms (Sturges, 1999).

While salary and rank have nonetheless been shown to correlate with career satisfaction for men (Russo et al., 1991), Sturges (1999) found that women managers and older managers appear less inclined to define career success in terms of hierarchical and financial progression. Women managers have been found to view career success as a process of personal development that involves interest-ing and challenging work, coupled with balance with the rest of their life (Marshall, 1984; Powell and Mainiero, 1992). Women managers' different ideas about career success are likely to be influenced by their socialization as women. Also the constraints that they perceive are likely to affect their careers in organizations, in which they remain in a minority and in which hierarchical success is seen to be very difficult to achieve (Davidson and Cooper, 1992; Poole et al., 1993; Davidson and Burke, 2004).

Management and men

It is interesting to note—as Collinson and Hearn (1996) have done—how Mintzberg uses 'manager' and 'he' interchangeably; Mintzberg remains silent about the inherently gendered assumptions that he makes about management. Drucker does the same, intending his book *The Practice of Manage-ment* (1989: Preface) to be 'a guide for men in major management positions … For younger men in management—and for men who plan to make management their career'.

Most managers are men and men are associated with organizational power—yet male domination of management is a subject that has received little scrutiny (Collinson and Hearn, 1996). Management has been portrayed as a masculine concept, about controlling, taking charge, and directing. Journalistic profiles of male executives and 'captains of industry' imagine macho heroes, emphasizing struggle, battle, a willingness to be ruthless, brutality, a rebellious nature, and an aggressive, rugged individualism (Neale, 1995). Managers have frequently depicted as masculine, abrasive, and highly autocratic 'hard men' who insist on the 'divine right of managers to manage' (Purcell, 1982).

Kanter (1977) has, however, studied men and women in management. She notes how the 'masculine ethic' can be identified as part of the early image of managers in the writings of Taylor, Weber, and Ches-ter Barnard. This masculine ethic elevates the traits that are supposed intrinsically male to necessities for effective management: a tough-minded approach to problems; the analytic ability to abstract and plan; a capacity to set aside personal, emotional considerations in the interests of task accomplishment; and a cognitive superiority in problem solving and decision making. And when women tried to enter management jobs, the masculine ethic was invoked as an exclusionary principle.

The reality for the woman manager

Since the 1980s, there has been talk of a 'glass ceiling' preventing women managers from progressing—and this invisible barrier appears still to be in place (Weyer, 2007). While the number of women occupy-ing jobs defined as 'management positions' is greater than it ever has been, there are still only half as many women in management in the UK as there are men: of the 4.3 million managers in the UK, some 2.8 million are men and around 1.4 million are women (ONS, 2006). And while the number of women at director level has tripled since 1998, they still only account for 14.4 per cent of directors (Chartered Management Institute, 2005). Female managers earned an average of £43,571 in 2006, which was £6,076 less than the male equivalent of £49,647; at director level, the gap is £49,233, or 23 per cent.

Women have been found recently, however, to be promoted at a quicker rate than men and to be more likely to receive a bonus (Chartered Management Institute, 2007).

'Double jeopardy': The reality for the black and ethnic minority woman manager

The US literature on women managers has been accused of making African American women managers invisible (Nkomo, 1988). The 'double jeopardy' faced by African American women managers helps to secure their position at the very bottom of the managerial hierarchy: they represent only 1.1 per cent of corporate officers in Fortune 500 companies. Barriers facing African American women in business include negative, race-based stereotypes, more frequent questioning of their credibility and authority, and a lack of institutional support (Catalyst, 2004).

Those who are young, female, and black in the UK also have only a slim chance of finding a job that reflects their academic ability or potential (Mirza, 1992). Ethnic minority women are under-represented in the professional field in comparison with white women (Bhavnani, 1994). Black and Asian women are entirely 'missing' from a third of workplaces in some areas of the UK, and only 9 per cent of African Caribbean and Pakistani women are senior managers, compared with 11 per cent of white women (Gabriel, 2007). Yet little research has been devoted to the plight of the black and ethnic manager woman in the UK (Davidson, 1997).

In her study of thirty black and ethnic minority managers, Davidson shows how these women face the doubly negative effects of sexism and racism. These women had fewer, if any, role models and were more likely to feel isolated. They had to contend with stereotypical images based on gender and ethnic origin, and were more likely to experience performance pressure. As one noted: 'I feel under enormous pressure to perform well. White people always seem to be looking to me to fail. If I fail, though, I let down all black women' (ibid.: 46). They have greater home/social/work conflicts—particularly in relation to the family and the black community—and, as a result, 80 per cent reported negative psychosocial and health outcomes that were related to sexism and racism at work. Bhavnani (1994) notes that there is some evidence from local government suggesting that the segregated patterns of black women's professional areas actually block access into senior management positions. For example, black women in education were given opportunities to use their background as relevant experience, but when they attempted to move out of these areas, their work experience became a barrier to parity of status. There is also evidence that black staff employed at managerial level in local government are primarily recruited for directing services towards black users. There may, then, be new forms of resegregation emerging.

Similarly, there is little research evidence on the likelihood of racism being experienced by black male managers. Both the army and the Prison Service have recently been attacked for discriminating on grounds of race: for example, only 6 per cent of those employed in prisons are from black and minority ethnic groups, compared with 25 per cent of the inmates (Prison Reform Trust, 2006).

Hotel management

Research into hotel management took place mainly in the 1980s. In comparison with management in other industries, hotel management has been found to be notoriously insular (Wood, 1992: 80): those training in hotel and catering management are generally separated off from those studying management or business more generally. Hotel and catering trainees are usually required to do periods of industrial placement as a form of pre-entry socialization, and two-thirds of hotel managers have been found to have had no work experience outside the hotel industry (Guerrier, 1987; Baum, 1989). Formal qualifications do not seem to affect the position on entry, promotion prospects, or career patterns of hotel managers: for example, most managers find themselves in very junior positions at first, in spite of their qualifications. Most managers will have to move jobs in order to gain experience of specific functions and different types of hotel.

Hotel managers engaged in a larger number of activities than their counterparts in other industries, saw less of their peers, and were rarely involved in group situations. They spent less time alone because of time spent directly supervising staff and because of customer contact. Generally, they appeared to dislike sitting behind a desk, and saw the important job as being out and about in the hotel; like other managers, however, they worked long hours. In Mintzberg's terms, hotel managers were found to place emphasis on leadership and entrepreneurial roles (Wood, 1992).

Surprises in managerial work

While events cannot always be predicted or controlled, managers will always seek to control their consequences. To be surprised is to encounter suddenly or unexpectedly a phenomenon that has not previously been considered—that is, to be taken unawares with neither preparation nor anticipation (Cunha et al., 2006).

Managers might prize predictability, control and routine, but these are not always the conditions under which they must work—and it is their tendency to overestimate control and predictability that may have led to ignorance and apparent incompetence (Weick, 2003). Gonzales (2003: 120) argues that disasters such as Bhopal in India, the space shuttle Challenger explosion, the Chernobyl nuclear meltdown, and countless airline crashes 'all happened in part while people were denying the clear warnings before them'. Honda was surprised when launching the 50cc motorbikes in the USA: it had assumed that motorcycle dealers would sell them, but found that it was sporting goods stores that wanted to sell them (Pascale, 1983). And the case of Post-it™ notes is also often cited as a surprise: a 3M scientist developed a repositional adhesive in 1968, but this was not developed into what was to become a successful innovation until 1974, when another 3M scientist—singing in his church choir and tired of losing his place in the hymnal—dreamt of a bookmark that was lightly adhesive. Post-it notepads were first marketed in the USA ten years after the adhesive was discovered (see http://www.3m.com).

Standing back from managerial work

For managers, then, there is no best way in which to manage; rather, there are 'only partial routes to failure' (Hyman, 1987: 30). Managers face complexities in their social and organizational worlds. With management, we have a highly structured order permeated by relational networks that, according to Reed (1989: 93), 'simultaneously sustain and undermine the viability of the former'. Whether managers are able or willing to overcome the obstacles that stand in the way of constructing a more meaningful and satisfactory work environment remains to be seen.

We saw, in the Introduction, that if we were to take a unitary perspective—that is, to stand back and take a look at managerial work—we would be assuming that management and workers are striving

73

together to achieve common goals. From a unitary standpoint, managers' jobs appear to be about developing the most efficient and effective means of bringing about the common good, pursuing common interests and objectives. Strong traces of this perspective can be found in the studies of managerial work—particularly the work of Mintzberg.

From a pluralist perspective, the unitary perspective looks unconvincing (Willmott, 2005). The research discussed in this chapter demonstrates that managers have political interests and play political games in order, for example, to build coalitions. Managers' rhetoric is political; how they demonstrate commitment through long hours spent at work is a tactic that is designed to impress. Conflict between management and workers is endemic in organizations, as we will see in other chapters: managerial work is a continuous effort to gain consent, constrain conflict, prevent disaster, and maintain some form of control. The unitary perspective is, then, an unobtainable ideal: however desirable it might be, it should not be confused with reality.

A radical standpoint challenges the assumptions of both the pluralist and unitary views. The basic charge is that the division of labour and differentiation of tasks that individuals and groups do cannot be adequately explained by reference to functional imperatives. Who does what reflects and sustains the structure of power relations within society. For example, managers—who have jobs that usually contain lots of challenge, responsibility, and other good features—design jobs for those lower in the hierarchy—that is, jobs with lower discretion and control. They spend time maintaining their social advantage in a number of ways: for example, through strengthening their networks and coalitions. Managers are not, however, omniscient and they face difficulties (such as resistance), as well as dilemmas. This is a theme to which we will return in the next case study and in following chapters.

Conclusion

Management gives managers formal authority, power, and prerogative to manage. Managerial work may have been presented as a rational and politically neutral activity, yet it clearly is not so. Managerial work may be categorized by research, yet it is difficult to generalize about managerial work, because there is no common body of knowledge required by all managers or a set of uniform abilities. The reality is that the job is varied, difficult, demanding, complicated, and may require long hours of work. It often requires good interpersonal and political skills. Further, female managers—particularly those from ethnic minorities—can face barriers to their progression in management and we will look at this issue further in Chapter 7.

KEY POINTS

- Managing means being responsible for the running and conduct of an organization or unit. Managers' jobs are varied.

- Despite the variety of jobs that managers do, theorists such as Fayol have attempted to identify and categorize what managers have in common in terms of their functions, and to generalize about managerial work.

- Since the early 1950s, the reality of managerial work has been researched. This has resulted in the categorization of different kinds of manager and the roles that they play. Instead of being portrayed in functional terms as planning, organizing, and controlling, a picture is painted of the manager who has a hectic, varied, and largely reactive day; he or she also works long hours. Interpersonal skills are important, and the manager uses political rhetoric to generate a culture and to maintain social control.

- There are good reasons to look at managerial work from a critical perspective—that is, to understand better how managers have been vested with, and maintain, power and how they use that power, which may have detrimental impacts on those below them in the hierarchy. The manager is, however, not omniscient and faces difficulties in carrying out his or her work.

CASE STUDY

The difficulties that hotel managers face

This case study looks at some of the difficulties that managers face. Managers are always faced with dilemmas, such as those posed here by the need to standardize and customize, control and empower. For example, managers in luxury international hotels are required to deliver a highly standardized service, controlled and maintained with the help of volumes of operating manuals. Coupled with this, they need to provide an 'authentic' (that is, non-routinized and individualized) service in a variety of cultural contexts to gain competitive advantage (Jones et al., 1997). How do they ensure that rules are followed, standards are maintained, and staff act consistently, yet provide a non-routinized and individualized service? Managers are often reluctant to empower employees for fear, for example, that they will give too much to the customer. An example of how empowerment might be out of control, but a customer given the highest service delivery, can be found in Bowen and Lawler (1992: 35), who tell us the story of Willie, a doorman at the *Four Seasons Hotel*, who left work and took a flight to return a briefcase left behind by a guest.

How, then, do managers train empowered workers? Various methods are used, which include customer feedback, and the careful selection and training of employees who have internalized 'appropriate' corporately determined values. Well-trained, socialized, and informed employees can be empowered to make good decisions. Jones et al. (1997) give us the case of *Americo*, a multinational hospitality company. Here, empowered employees are asked to 'do whatever it takes' to ensure that every guest leaves satisfied. The company advertises this aim by showing a waiter on night duty driving round town to find a favourite night-time drink and a porter retracing a guest's journey on a tram to retrieve a lost wallet. But creating these empowered employees is not a simple task for managers if employees have already been socialized to accept a more directive management style or if employees feel that they are being asked to take on duties for which managers are paid. Empowerment also means that there is little need for many layers of management—meaning that some will lose their jobs.

(Sources in text)

Questions

1. How, then, should empowerment be managed? What are the boundaries for empowerment for the manager and for the worker? (See also Chapter 15 on empowerment.)

75

FURTHER READING

Gowler, D. and Legge, K. (1996) 'The meaning of management and the management of meaning', in S. Linstead, R. Grafton Small, and P. Jeffcutt (eds), *Understanding Management*, London: Sage, ch. 2 This chapter discusses the rhetoric of management and the moral necessity of hierarchy, accountability, and achievement.

Grint, K. (1995) *Management: A Sociological Introduction*, Cambridge: Polity This book presents a discussion of how rational managers' work is.

Noon, M. and Blyton, P. (2002; 2007) *The Realities of Work*, Houndmills: Palgrave This might help to answer the question of whether management is a profession.

Thomas, A.B. (2003) 'What is management? A term in search of a meaning', in *Controversies in Management*, 2nd edn, London: Routledge, ch. 2 This chapter provides a useful discussion of the meaning of 'management'.

Thompson, P. and McHugh, D. (2002) *Work Organizations*, Houndmills: Palgrave, ch. 7 This chapter discusses whether management can be a profession.

Watson, T. (2002) *Organising and Managing Work*, Harlow: Pearson, pp. 84–92 These pages attempt to make sense of what managers do.

LINKS TO FILMS AND NOVELS

The Damned United (2009) dir. T. Hooper In the football world, Brian Clough was considered a managerial genius. This film fictionalizes the 44 days Brian Clough managed Leeds United—during which he annoyed so many people that he was fired.

RESEARCH QUESTIONS

1. How rational is management (see Grint, 1995)? Are managers 'firefighters', because they are 'mimetic pyrophobes'—that is, because they are addicted to fear of fire—or because they are responsible for the 'chronically inflammable' (Hales, 1999)?

2. What are the differences between the findings of Stewart, Kotter, and Mintzberg on what managers do? How far do they help us to understand why managers do what they do? (See Hales, 1999.)

3. 'Representing management as a predominantly technical activity creates an illusion of neutrality' (Alvesson and Wilmott, 1996: 12). Discuss.

REFERENCES

Alimo-Metcalfe, B. (1992) 'Different gender—different rules', in P. Barrar and C.L. Cooper (eds), *Managing Organizations*, London: Routledge, ch. 11.

Alvesson, M. and Wilmott, H. (1996) *Making Sense of Management: A Critical Introduction*, London: Sage.

Arnold, J. (1997) *Managing Careers in the 21st Century*, London: Paul Chapman.

Austin Knight UK (1995) *The Family Friendly Workplace*, London: Austin Knight.

Balogun, J. (2003) 'From blaming the middle manager to harnessing its potential: Creating change intermediaries', *British Journal of Management*, 14(1): 69–84.

Baum, T. (1989) 'Managing hotels in Ireland: Research and development for change', *International Journal of Hospitality Management*, 8(2): 131–44.

Bhavnani, R. (1994) *Black Women in the Labour Market: A Research Review*, Manchester: EOC.

Bowen, D.E. and Lawler, E.E. (1992) 'The empowerment of service workers: What, why, how and when', *Sloan Management Review*, Spring: 31–9.

Burnham, J. (1945) *The Managerial Revolution*, Harmondsworth: Penguin.

Carlson, S. (1951) *Executive Behaviour: A Study of the Workload and Working Methods of Managing Directors*, Stockholm: Strombergs.

The Rationality of Management

4

Introduction

We have now looked at what managers do and how their work is described. Their work appears to have a rationality, because they make choices to achieve specific end results. 'Rationality' can be defined as intentional, reasoned, and goal-directed behaviour (Putnam and Mumby, 1993). For example, managers seek to recruit the best employees and then extract the best performance from them; they also seek to devise methods that ensure that individuals act in the organization's interest. This is the rationale, or rationality, of management.

So how have managers tried to do this? As we shall see in this chapter, historically, the emphasis was on finding the best way in which to manage the human resource through scientific and mechanical means. Frederick Taylor ('Taylorism') and Henry Ford ('Fordism') were looking to make labour more efficient by fitting workers to jobs. The job redesign and human relations movements counteracted some of the worst features of Taylorism, stressing the importance of an understanding of employees' social, rather than simply economic, needs.

While it is easy to trace a development of thinking from Taylorism and Fordism through to human relations and job redesign, ideas from Taylorism and Fordism remain present in much of today's management thinking and practice. It therefore remains pertinent to ask questions such as: what were Ford and Taylor trying to achieve? What is the rationale in *today's* job design? Is rationality within organizations all about better fitting workers to existing jobs within the organization? Or—using knowledge from psychology, intelligence, and psychometric testing—should rationality within organizations be about better aligning the goals of the job with workers?

This chapter covers:

- early management thinkers and rationality;
- the rationale of scientific management and Taylorism;
- Henry Ford;
- routinization, the detailed division of labour, and modern-day Taylorism;
- the rationale of the human relations movement;
- job redesign;
- the rationale of fitting workers to jobs;
- eugenics;
- intelligence testing;
- vocational guidance—testing, then fitting people to jobs.

Early management thinkers and rationality

Organizations depend on people for their competitive advantage: people possess skills, experience, and knowledge that have economic value to organizations. Demand is placed on employees to add value by helping to lower costs or provide greater output—but how has this been managed? Early management thinkers or theorists (Babbage, 1832; Ure, 1835; Taylor, 1911) sought to apply 'rational' scientific practices to organization with the view of improving its performance. They mainly thought of organizations as machines, while people were seen as both variable and unreliable. According to Ure (1835), for example, 'science now promises to rescue … business from handicraft caprice, and to place it … under the safeguard of automatic mechanism'. For Ure, there were 'right mechanisms' for managing; one 'mechanism' would be for the manager to remove jobs that require dexterity from the workman, who cannot be relied upon, placing these jobs in the safe hands of mechanization so simple that a child could supervise. Similar views can be found the writings of both Babbage and Taylor. This, then, is a 'functionalist' approach to management—that is, the employee is seen as a functionary who is selected, trained, and developed in accordance with organizational objectives.

The rationale of scientific management and Taylorism

Frederick Winslow Taylor (1856–1915) believed that the best management was true science 'resting upon clearly defined laws, rules and principles' (Taylor, 1911: 7). The problems of production lay in the hands of management, because they lacked knowledge of how to maximize production. The workers had a rationale for restricting output—that is, the fear of underpayment or redundancy—and payment systems lacked sufficient incentive. For Taylor, applying the principles of scientific management could solve all of these problems: it was the manager's job to gather together all of the traditional knowledge, held in the past by the workmen, and then classify, tabulate, and reduce this knowledge to rules, laws, and formulae that became a science.

The Spanish–American War of 1898 gave Taylor the opportunity to try his first experiment in scientific management at the *Bethlehem Steel Company*. With the war came an increase in the price of pig iron (that is, iron from the smelting furnace). The pig iron was stored in a field adjoining the works and needed to be moved inside to the furnaces. A railway was laid out to the field, with an inclined plank placed against the side of the railroad 'car'. Each man was required to pick up a 'pig of iron' weighing about 92 lbs, walk up the inclined plank, and drop it into the car. An average man could load about 12.5 tons a day, but it was found that the best men could handle between 47 and 48 tons. Four of the best pig-iron handlers were picked from among seventy-five workers. One was then selected to start the experiment: a man Taylor called 'Schmidt' and described as 'of the mentally sluggish type'. (Schmidt was, in fact, called Henry Knolle—Johnson and Gill, 1993—a Pennsylvanian Dutch man—Jacques, 1996—who had recently built his own house.)

This man was offered $1.85 per hour instead of $1.25 if he would follow another man's instructions on when to pick up the iron, when to walk, and when to rest. He had then to follow the 'science of pig iron handling' developed and taught to him by someone else (Taylor, 1911: 124–5). He managed to load 47.5 tons of iron a day, never failing to work at this pace and to do the task set him during the three years during which Taylor was at *Bethlehem*. The development of this 'science' amounted 'to so much that the man who is suited to pig iron cannot possibly understand it, nor even work in accordance with the laws of this science, without the help of those who are over him' (ibid.: 48). A fit pig-iron handler should be 'so stupid and so phlegmatic that he more nearly resembles in his mental make-up the ox than any other type ... He is so stupid that the word "percentage" has no meaning to him' (ibid.: 59). In this way, the man was selected, trained, and supervised. As a consequence, seven out of eight pig-iron handlers were thrown out of their jobs—but we are assured that they were given other jobs with the *Bethlehem Steel Company*.

Similar treatment is to be found in the second experiment to develop a 'science of shovelling'. A first-class shoveller was found to do his biggest day's work with a shovel load of about 21 lbs. Eight or ten different kinds of shovel were provided at the *Bethlehem Steel Company*, one for each type of material, depending on the weight of that material: for example, a small one for ore (a heavy material) and a large one for ashes (a light material). Providing the different shovels prevented the shoveller, who previously owned his own shovel, from alternating between shovelling ore with a load of about 30 lbs per shovel to handling rice coal with a load, on the same shovel, of less than 4 lbs. Every day, the shoveller would be given—and would implement—instructions for doing each new job; he would also be given feedback on his performance during the previous day. Clerks planned the work that the shovellers did and, this time, the work of 400 and 600 yard labourers was reduced to the work of 140.

Four duties emerge for the managers in developing the science.

1. They develop a science for each element of work, which replaces the old rule of thumb. (The rule of thumb was based on experience or practice, not on measurement and calculation.)

2. They scientifically select, then train, the worker.

3. They cooperate to ensure that all of the work is being done in accordance with the principles laid down.

4. They have an almost equal division of work and responsibility between manager and worker.

The management takes over all of the work for which it is better fitted than the worker. It plans out the work at least one day in advance; each worker should receive a set of written instructions describing in detail the task that he or she has to accomplish and the time that it should take, as well as the means by which it should be done. When the workers have done the work correctly, within the specified time limit, they should receive an addition to their ordinary wages (a bonus) of between 30 and 100 per cent. Workers should never be asked, if the job has been scientifically studied, to work at a pace that could injure their health. With the scheme in place, it was found that the workers and manager could profit considerably. The system was not designed to provide satisfying work, but to maximize rewards and increase the division of labour.

Similarly, Frank Gilbreth studied bricklaying, analysing the movement, speed, and tiring rate of the bricklayer (see Taylor, 1911). He developed the exact positions that the feet of the bricklayer should occupy in relation to the wall, the mortar box, and pile of bricks. He studied the best height for the mortar box and brick pile, then designed an adjustable scaffold to hold the materials. He asked that the bricks be sorted and packed in an orderly pile before being brought to the bricklayers, so that they were placed with their best edge up on a simple wooden frame; each brick could then be lifted in the quickest time in the most advantageous position. Gilbreth was thus able to reduce the motions of bricklayers from eighteen per brick to five. He also taught the bricklayers to pick up bricks with the left hand while at the same time taking a trowel full of mortar with the right hand. In this way, one person could lay 350 bricks in an hour, compared with the previous 120-brick average. To achieve this result, the standards and cooperation have to be enforced—and the duty of enforcement lies with management. If the workers agree to this enforcement, they should, however, receive higher pay.

While Taylor's 'men' were being scientifically selected and trained, in another plant, 'girls' were working for ten-and-a-half hours a day inspecting ball bearings for bicycles. Gradually, their hours were shortened to ten, nine-and-a-half, nine, then eight-and-a-half hours a day for the same pay. With each shortening of the day came an increase in output. The best workers were selected; some of the most intelligent, hardest working, and trustworthy girls were laid off, because they did not perceive the fault and discard defective ball bearings quickly, or accurately, enough. The honesty and accuracy of those remaining inspectors was checked. Senior inspectors checked one batch; the chief inspector, in turn, checked the work of the senior inspectors. The inspectors were also kept in check by another method. Every two or three days, a batch of balls was prepared by a foreman, so that it contained a definite number of perfect and defective balls; this was given to an inspector for checking and the inspector's accuracy was recorded. An accurate and daily record was kept of the quantity and quality of all of the work. The temptation to slight (neglect) the work or make false returns was, Taylor claimed, removed. The inspectors' ambition was 'stirred' by increasing the wages of those who turned out a large quantity of good quality, while those who did indifferent work found their wages lowered. Those who were slow or careless were discharged. The inspectors were seated so far apart that they could not conveniently talk while at work, but were given ten-minute breaks each hour-and-a-half, so that they could leave their seats, walk around, and talk. This was found to be the best way in which to gain steady work without overexertion. Taylor believed that feedback on performance was needed at regular intervals, such as every hour. Profit sharing would only be mildly effective (Taylor, 1911: 94). As a result of these changes, thirty-five 'girls' did the work formerly done by 120. The accuracy of the work at higher speed was two-thirds greater than at the former slow speed. In return, the women's average wage was 80 to 100 per cent higher with a day of eight-and-a-half hours and a half-day holiday on a Saturday than it had originally been.

A psychologist might explain the roots of Taylor's thinking in terms of his upbringing. His youth was preoccupied with order, control, and parsimony, clearly rooted in the puritanical strictures of his family. Fastidious analysis was made of his sporting activities, country walks, sleeping position, and even his dancing (Fineman, 2000). (In dancing, he would make an advanced list of the unattractive and attractive girls expected to attend, and then compute the time that he would spend with each on a precisely equal basis.) It also has to be noted, however, that Taylor emerged in a particular climate and time of thinking about how to apply rational scientific practices to organizations to increase performance.

From a job design perspective, Taylor's scheme rests upon the principle of the division of mental and manual labour. It also involved:

- a general principle of the maximum decomposition—that is, breaking-up—of tasks;
- the divorce of direct and indirect (setting-up, preparation, maintenance) labour;
- the minimization of skill requirements, leading to minimum job-learning time (Littler, 1985).

These were the principles of job design that were accepted in the USA and, more slowly, in the UK. But not all economies accepted Taylor's ideas. A different pattern is to be found in Japan, where factories depended on a tradition of work teams incorporating managerial and maintenance functions, and few staff specialists, which allowed for considerable job flexibility. Even there, however, Dore (1973) tells us that Taylor's time and motion studies were introduced for a period around the First World War.

Taylor's work was carried out in union-free or weakly unionized plants, while the *American Federation of Labour* (AFL) initiated an anti-scientific management campaign (Grint, 1991). Within weeks of its first major implementation, a strike broke out in Watertown Arsenal. A full investigation by the House of Representatives (a government assembly) found widespread malpractices, and so Taylorist methods were banned from all arsenals, navy yards, and (for 1916–49) from all government-funded operations (Noble, 1974). The *Society of Mechanical Engineers*—despite that fact that Taylor was its president—refused to publish his *Principles of Scientific Management* on the grounds that it was not scientific. Taylor was himself appalled at the strong hostility that he witnessed amongst rank and-file workers in response to his design of industrial organization (Stearns, 1989)—particularly because workers' feelings of anger, disaffection, and humiliation can breach organizational controls (Fineman, 1996).

Henry Ford

Despite the problems inherent in Taylor's work design, Henry Ford adopted the principles of Taylorism for his car plants, having seen a system of mass disassembly (taking animal carcasses to pieces) in the Chicago meat packing plants before the First World War (Ackroyd and Crowdy, 1990; Burrell, 1997: 138). Ford had the wit to appreciate that the process of disassembling animal carcasses could, in principle, be applied in reverse to the construction of complex products, such as cars. The following is an illustration of how the principles of mass assembly production were begun.

Ford began with the little pieces and found that one man took 20 minutes to produce an electrical alternator. When the process was spread over twenty-nine operations, assembly time was decreased to 13 minutes. Raising the height of the assembly line by 8 inches reduced this to seven minutes, while further rationalization cut it to five minutes (Sims et al., 1993; Gabriel et al., 2000). The closely monitored, machine-paced, short-cycle, and unremitting tasks were combined with an authoritarian work regime.

Ford was aware that some of the jobs were monotonous: they were 'so monotonous that it seems scarcely possible that any man would care to continue long at the same job' (Ford, 1923: 106). Ford's research showed, however, that no man's mind had been twisted or deadened by the work—and besides, if a person did not like the repetitive work, he did not have to stay in it (ibid.). But while the jobs were repetitive, the workers also had to devote themselves to a system of harsh discipline both at work and outside the factory gates. Ford had a missionary impulse to change the behaviour of men, as well as to make automobiles. He was passionately opposed to gambling, alcohol, smoking, and sex outside marriage, so insisted that any employee who was found to be indulging in any of these activities be expelled from the prosperity-sharing, five-dollar-a-day pay scheme. Fifty investigators were employed to monitor the behaviour of employees and midnight raids on employees' homes were not uncommon (Corbett, 1994: Case 27).

STOP AND THINK Henry Ford

A report in the *New York Times* (8 January 1928) described Henry Ford as the 'Mussolini of Detroit'. From what you have read, is this a fair description of the man in your opinion? (For further information, see Corbett, 1994: Case 27.)

In the early 1920s, Ford's share of the car market was two-thirds. Fifteen years later, it had fallen to 20 per cent. According to Drucker (1989), Henry Ford tried to run his billion-dollar business without managers. He ran a one-man tyranny within which he employed a 'secret police' that spied on Ford executives and informed him of any attempt on the part of executives to make decisions. When they seemed to acquire managerial authority or responsibility, they were generally fired. Henry Ford demoted first-line supervisors regularly every few years, so that they would not become 'uppity' and forget that they owed their job to him. Drucker believes that it was this absence of management that caused the fall of the *Ford Motor Company*.

After the Second World War, Henry Ford's grandson (Henry Ford II) took over the company. He rebuilt management, although he had no business experience at all, taking most of his concepts of management and organization, along with his top managers, from *General Motors*, *Ford's* biggest competitor.

Routinization, the detailed division of labour, and modern-day Taylorism

Why would you pay a highly skilled worker to do a job from start to finish when you could split the job into component parts, assign each task to minimally qualified workers, and so reduce costs and increase output? Designing jobs so that each worker repeatedly performs a limited number of tasks in accordance with instructions provided by management increases efficiency, results in uniform products, and gives management increased control. Management have no need to rely on the cooperation of workers to tell them how long a task takes, how many people are required to do a job, and how much work can be completed in one shift. Management has power over workers undertaking less skilled jobs to dictate wages, hours, and working conditions, and is more easily able to interchange workers or replace workers with technology. The logic of routinization of work is, then, simple, elegant, and compelling (Leidner, 1993)—but routinization and the detailed division of labour increases the potential of a few people to disrupt a whole production process.

This routinization—or deskilling—of work began in the manufacturing industry. As clerical work grew, the principles were applied there, so that the thinking work was removed, leaving jobs lacking in variety and opportunities for decision making (Braverman, 1974). For Braverman, there were three principles of Taylorism:

- the dissociation of the labour process from the skills of the workers;
- the separation of conception—that is, the 'thinking' about how work is done—from the execution—that is, the 'doing'—of the work;
- the managerial use of the monopoly of this knowledge to control each step of the labour process and its mode of execution.

Following Marx, Braverman argues that work under capitalism is geared to the creation of profit rather than the satisfaction of human needs, and that there is thus a conflict of interests between labour and capital. In these antagonistic conditions, it is necessary for managers to secure maximum possible control over the labour process. (The labour process, as defined by Marx, has three elements: purposeful human activity directed to work; the materials on which work is performed; and the instruments of work.) Braverman argues that the consequence of the extension of scientific management is degradation of the labour process, with jobs becoming increasingly specialized and routine. (For a critique of Braverman, see Edwards, 1978; Grint, 1991: 190–5.)

EXAMPLE **The deskilling and degradation of work**

Watanabe (1990) describes how labour was deskilled and degraded in the Japanese banking sector. Labour control was intensified and labour conditions deteriorated. The computer systems had book-keeping skills, for example, so the work of a large mass of employees became routine and monotonous, involving only the punching of computer keys, and so on. The work of middle management was also simplified, because functions requiring judgement and discretion became almost unnecessary. Branch managers were placed under the unified and centralized control of head office by means of computer networks, so their authority was reduced and accountability increased.

As a result, a polarization of labour occurred—that is, a separation of mental and physical labour. Mental labour was concentrated in fewer employees, such as top managers and systems analysts.

The effect on workers is well documented. Routinized jobs lack variety, job satisfaction, and meaning, and the process of deskilling is complemented by the application of technology to the labour process. But management has not always had its own way, as studies by Noble (1979), Zeitlin (1983), Buchanan (1985), and Wilson (1987) illustrated in relation to the engineering industry. Taylorism could never be a universal set of specific practices and is inappropriate in some industries, such as machine tools manufacture (Broadbent et al., 1997: 4). And while the developing trade union movement defended the interests of workers, employers worried about labour unrest were sceptical.

Taylorism does, however, inform a management philosophy that managers have a right to manage, and offers a 'scientific' rationale for the professional status and autonomy of managers. Despite its drawbacks, then, Taylorism remains very much in evidence in jobs around us—not least in the 'wise and knowing expert' selecting the right person for the right job (Jacques, 1996).

EXAMPLE Taylorism and the routinization of work in the service industry

Dealers in casinos are trained in exactly how to deal; the job is scripted and standardized—an example of modern-day Taylorism. Austrin and West (2005: 315) describe the work thus: '… dealing a card involves pulling out of a shoe with this finger with having the rest of your arm straight like this, don't have your elbow too high, don't turn your hand on the side, keep your fingers together … keep this thumb showing, take it down, flip it up, you put your thumb just like that and you have to practice where to put the card …'

Each movement is taught as a separate action and then has to be put into practice as a set of flowing motions, which require very considerable mind and body coordination.

EXAMPLE Taylorism and the routinization of work in the airline industry

The job of check-in staff at airports illustrates the nature of a routinized job—so much so that technology is now being used to do the job in an effort to reduce congestion at airports. By October 2007, more than half of all airlines offered online check-in facilities, while 89 per cent expected to offer the service within the next two years. Further, 76 per cent are planning mobile phone check-in. Among the top twenty-five low cost airlines (in terms of passenger numbers), the rate of availability of online check-in was 100 per cent.

(*Source*: Ferguson, 2007)

STOP AND THINK Taylorism today

When marking essays, lecturers often notice that students talk about 'Taylor' and 'Taylorism' as if it is history—that is, a management idea that existed in the past, but which is now outdated and old-fashioned. It is easy to see why: Taylor was writing and practising management at the start of the twentieth century. But his ideas are alive and well today.

What other examples can you think of that demonstrate that Taylorism is still of relevance and in use today?

Scientific management can best be identified by its most prominent features—time and motion studies, and incentive payments (Taska, 1995). It can, however, also be seen as bolstering middle-class professionals' social and political struggle for legitimacy, giving them a role in influencing the training given to workers (ibid.). And despite the limitations of Tayloristic job design and its negative effects, there are many benefits to be gained by the employer. Taylorism can bring about efficient working; efficiency was Taylor's guiding obsession.

EXAMPLE Taylorism in practice

United Parcel Service employs industrial engineering managers, who, for example, stipulate how fast their drivers walk: they are expected to walk at a pace of 3 ft per second. Until recently, drivers were even instructed in how to move, in an effort to maximize efficiency: packages were to be carried under the left arm and the driver was to step into the van with his or her right foot, while holding the van's keys on the middle finger of the right hand.

Neat and clean jobs may be found in the parcel delivery service, but Taylor's principles are also found applied in 'dirty' jobs, such as those in a chicken factory. Here, too, work can be segmented into simple repetitive operations. Packing the chicken, for example, involves four people doing one of four tasks: inserting the giblets and tucking the legs in; bagging the chicken; weighing it; and securing the top of the bag. An employee in a chicken factory was found to be checking over 2,000 chickens an hour—that is, 14,000 chickens a day. This involved checking that no chickens had been left with livers, hearts, or similar organs. In the words of the employee, this meant, 'putting your hand in the backside of a chicken, feeling around then bringing anything out, dropping it in the bin, and then going on to the next' (Noon and Blyton, 2007: 148). As might be expected, the employees found the work hard.

Numerous scholars have documented the unintentional and unfortunate consequences of the trend towards work simplification (for example, Walker and Guest, 1952; Herzberg et al., 1959; Argyris, 1964; Blauner, 1964). Routine, non-challenging jobs often led to high employee dissatisfaction, increased absenteeism and turnover, and substantial difficulties in effectively managing employees who worked on simplified jobs (Hackman and Lawler, 1971). And while scientific management has long been associated with behavioural problems at work, it has more recently become associated with inefficiencies arising from inflexibility. For those who design work organization in relation to a continuous, standardized product with homogeneous (that is, the same) throughput for a mass market, Taylorism may appear to be an extremely efficient way of organizing. But where there is no such mass market and a heterogeneous (that is, diverse), rapidly changing, and unpredictable throughput (due to customer demand or product innovation), then what may be required is a more flexible, committed, itinerant, and skilled workforce capable of exercising discretion to cope with uncertainties and fluctuations in demand and technology. The mechanistic conception of people therefore needs to be replaced with an alternative approach to human beings—that is, a more 'human–centred' approach.

The rationale of the human relations movement

The roots of human relations are to be found in the nineteenth century in, for example, Émile Durkheim's (1858–1917) analysis of anomie—that is, a pathology, a form of social breakdown (Durkheim, 1984)—and his concern with social solidarity and integration. The human relations movement began to emerge during the First World War, and was concerned with the selection, testing, and classification of army recruits, which required psychological testing. These developments sought to increase employees' productivity and personal satisfaction by easing difficulties, rather than by using sanctions (Lupton, 1971).

The starting point was a series of experiments at the *Western Electric Company*'s Hawthorne plant in Chicago in 1924. Firstly, the relationship between lighting, temperature, humidity, frequency of rest breaks, and employees' productivity was investigated (Roethlisberger and Dickson, 1939). Two groups of employees were selected and isolated in another part of the plant. One group experienced changes in their working conditions, while the other did not. The productivity of each group was monitored and it was found that output of the experimental group increased regardless of how illumination was manipulated. Even when lighting was reduced to the equivalent of a candle, output continued to increase. Output of the control group also steadily increased.

The second set of experiments took place in the relay assembly test room in 1927 and looked in more detail at the effect of working conditions (also reported by Homans, 1959). Here, six women were watched as they assembled telephone relays. They put together parts and fixed them with screws; they were expected to complete five relays in six minutes. For the experiment, they were assured that the object was to determine the effect of certain changes in working conditions, such as rest periods, lunches, and shorter working hours. They were told to work at a comfortable pace. Again, no matter what the researchers did—even lengthening the working day and reducing rest periods—productivity increased. The researchers explained this by saying that the employees had been made to feel special: they had been the centre of attention. They had been given a 'test room observer', they had frequent interviews with the superintendent ('a high officer in the company'), and their views about the experiment were sought. The operators knew that they were taking part in what was considered an important and interesting experiment. Their work was expected to produce results 'which would lead to the improvement of the working conditions of their fellow employees' (ibid.: 586). This had increased their morale, which led to the increase in productivity. Further, when they went for physical examinations to monitor their health, they were given ice cream and cake. Relationships within the group also improved during the period of the experiment, so that when one of them had a birthday, each of the others would bring her a present and she would respond by offering the group a box of chocolates. If one of them was tired, the others would 'carry' her—that is, they would agree to work especially fast to make up for the low output expected from her. They became friends and socialized together out of work. The group developed a self-appointed leader, who was ambitious, and who saw the experiment as a chance for personal distinction and advancement; this led to the development of an organized social group, which in turn led to improved output.

This behaviour is contrasted with that within the original department, which was discussed in conversations with each other and the observers. They had not enjoyed the constraints of supervision in their old department and were disparaging about their former supervisors, indicating that they felt 'relief from some form of constraint, particularly the constraint of supervision' in the test room (ibid.: 587). It is curious—as Homans notes (1959: 595)—that the women felt that they were free from the pressure of supervision in the test room, even though they were far more thoroughly supervised than they ever had been formerly.

Further interviews revealed that workers were banding together informally to protect themselves against practices that 'they interpreted as a menace to their welfare' (ibid.: 588). In response to the 'menace', they adopted a standard of what they felt to be a proper day's work and none of them exceeded it by very much. They resented the wage incentive system—usually some form of group piecework (under which system the group would be paid for the number of pieces that it produced)—and implied that it was not working satisfactorily; they used informal practices to punish and bring into line those who exceeded the accepted standard, and developed informal leadership to keep the group working together and enforcing its rules. They felt that seeking promotion was futile.

Interviews with another group in 1931 (ibid.) revealed that, while management thought that the adjustments that the group made to small parts in the telephone equipment were complex, they were actually quite simple. The operators had 'put a fence around the job' and took pride in relating how they had adjusted the apparatus—which no one else could make work properly. Even telephone engineers would seek their expertise. The operators would 'fool around', taking two hours to make all sorts of wrong adjustments; in this way, they prevented people 'on the outside' from finding out what they really did. They delighted in telling the interviewer how they were pulling the wool over everybody's eyes. An informal organization had developed a leader who dealt with, and answered any questions from, any outsiders—whether engineers, inspectors, or supervisors. Another leader emerged to keep new operators from exceeding group norms of output. But while supervisors were largely aware of this situation of informal leadership, they felt powerless to do anything about it.

Later research in the early 1930s involved the detailed observation over a seven-month period of a group of fourteen men, who worked in the bank-wiring observation room. This time, the men stayed in their normal work setting and a financial incentive scheme was introduced to reward group output. The men appeared to control their output, limiting it to what they thought was a 'fair day's work' for the pay that they received. The group determined the maximum and minimum output norm; any deviations were punished. If one of the employees did something that was not considered quite 'proper', one of his fellow workers had the right to 'bing' him—that is, to deliver a stiff blow to his upper arm. The person who was struck usually took the blow without protest and did not strike back. If he turned out too much work, he was called names such as 'Speed King' or 'The Slave' (ibid.: 592).

These studies are now famous for identifying the importance of social needs in the workplace and the way in which work groups can satisfy these needs by restricting output and engaging in all kinds of unplanned activities. In identifying the 'informal organization' based on friendship and groups, and unplanned interactions, existing alongside the formal organization designed by management, the research dealt an important blow to classical management theory. The informal organization included the emotional, non-rational, and sentimental aspects of human behaviour in organizations: the ties and loyalties that affected workers; the social relations that could not be encompassed by the organization chart, but which shaped behaviour regardless. Other theorists who influenced the development of this perspective included Mary Parker Follett (Kanter, 1977). Follett believed that communication was key: for example, that not only should workers understand management, but that managers should also 'get the workers' point of view' (Follett, 1982: 135). She promotes a theory of 'reciprocal leadership', at which we will look in the chapter of leadership.

The answer to problems of output restriction and resistance—according to Mayo (1949), writing on the Hawthorne research—was to develop managerial social skills so that the workers felt more disposed to work better with management. Morale and motivation could be improved if managers were better able to elicit cooperation through being more sensitive to workers' social needs. Management was encouraged to intervene in the informal organization and build a new moral order that would 'create and sustain consent' (Thompson and McHugh, 2002: 49). It is interesting, however, that researchers have noted that Mayo was deeply distrustful of collective sentiment. He wanted to reduce the likelihood of workplace unrest. Mayo believed in industrial harmony (Rose, 1988:115); he ignored power and politics, believing that 'political issues are illusions created by evil men' (Baritz, 2005). In some respects, his views were not too dissimilar from those of Frederick Taylor. He is also found to have allowed management to remove troublemakers from an experiment (Brewis and Linstead, 2004).

The Hawthorne experiments have come under close scrutiny by researchers and have been found to be inadequate. Carey (1967) made it clear that these studies are replete with erroneous interpretations and do not offer support many of their conclusions. For example, the finding that relaxed and friendly supervision causes higher productivity is refuted by Carey, who argues that because of higher productivity, the managers became more relaxed. Further, the increase in productivity was caused by a simple change of people in the work group: two recalcitrant male workers were dismissed halfway through the study and were replaced with two women who needed jobs to help with their financial problems. It was their efforts and prodding that led to the increase in group output, and it was only after this output increase that management relaxed its coercive style of supervision (Weick, 1969).

Similarly, Brown (1976) and, more recently, Acker and Van Houton (1992) have noted how the Hawthorne studies produced questionable or incomplete interpretations of their results, failing to consider adequately the gender dimensions of organizational processes. The men were observed under normal working conditions, while the female group was in an experimental situation. Despite the fact that the women increased and the men restricted output, the overall findings were presented as an explanation of the behaviour of employees per se.

It is also interesting to note—as Kanter (1977) has done—that, while the first thrust in management theory (that is, planning and decision making) put the 'rational man' into management, the second thrust concerning motivation and morale (that is, acknowledging the human order behind the machine) did not significantly change this aspect of the management image: the traits of the masculine ethic seen as integral to effective management (see Chapter 3) did not change. Human relations theories may have made inroads, adding a 'feminized' element to the old masculine ethic, and influencing new forms of organization using teams and project management systems, but the masculine ethic of rationality has dominated the spirit of managerialism and has given the manager role its defining image. It told men how to be successful as men in the new organizational world—and it provided a rationale for where women belong in management. If they belonged, it was only in people-handling staff functions such as personnel—that is, at the 'emotional' end of management, excluded from the centres of power (ibid.). (See Chapter 6 for more on the logic and critique of human relations—particularly that of Douglas McGregor.)

Job redesign

Researchers experimented with job enlargement and redesign to make jobs more meaningful and challenging. Support for job redesign was, however, hard to substantiate empirically. A major evaluative study of job redesign studies suggested missionary zeal, the publication of only positive results, and the employment of poor research designs (Blacker and Brown, 1978).

An understanding of job design requires recognition of the strategic choices open to managers (Child, 1972; Monanari, 1979). Management, for example, has choices about the techno-structural arrangements—that is, the sort of technology in which to invest and the type of structures used to manage the organization. Despite the wide variety of choices available, job designers use a common set of criteria (Davis et al., 1955; Taylor, 1979). They typically opt for a technology that minimizes the time required to perform the job, the skill level needed, the necessary training time, and the individual's contribution to the whole process. The choices usually made, then, seek to minimize immediate costs through specialization and routine. Management also has choices in relation to the pattern of local control. When information-processing requirements are low, then jobholders are usually subjected to a relatively direct form of control (Friedman, 1977; Clegg, 1984).

Economic and psychological values underpin these choices: those that are economic are Taylorist, and include ease of training and replacing staff, and the reduction of direct labour costs resulting from deskilling; those that are psychological rest in the belief that individuals need close external control—that is, the worker is seen as naturally lazy and unreliable (McGregor, 1960). These economic and psychological views may be widely held by both key decision makers and jobholders, and represent a strong pressure for, and expectation of, the design of relatively simple, closely supervised jobs. Employing easily replaced people in technologically simple jobs that are highly constrained and directly supervised goes a considerable way towards meeting the needs of managers to make their operations predictable and to maintain direct control over events.

The rationale of fitting workers to jobs

Frederick Taylor argued that jobs and individuals should be matched. Because employees are not universally similar, in the interests of efficiency, jobs and workers should be matched in terms of the necessary skills and intelligence required. It has always been in employers' interests to fit workers to jobs, but the First World War brought the issue into sharp relief. The provision of munitions and people for the war forced the government of the time to intervene in the management of factories to accelerate efficiency. When the USA entered the First World War in 1917, the scale of activities changed and the army's Committee for Psychology was established to place recruits—from the subnormal to officer material—using psychological tests; it claims to have tested almost 2 million men.

The *Industrial Fatigue Board* in Britain was set up in 1918 to investigate and promote mechanisms of efficiency. It looked at rest, working hours, ventilation, and lighting systems. Psychological tests were also developed at this time, meaning that individuals could be tested and placed. C.S. Myers, founder and director of the *National Institute of Industrial Psychology*, began his work in Britain in 1921; industrial psychology has been dominated by the need to use psychometric testing to fit workers to jobs since this time. Wartime produced the technology for mass psychometric selection. While, in the USA, this generally tested ability, in Britain, the tests were based on specific job needs to help to select, for example, pilots (see Rose, 1988; Hollway, 1991). Rose (1988: 92) notes: 'Applied psychology thus achieved much favourable publicity, massive development funds and full respectability.'

After the First World War, selection tests were used more widely, and spread to the spheres of education and business—but the tests were used for far more sophisticated purposes than those for which they were intended and, as a consequence, failed to meet expectation, resulting in a backlash. It was, inevitably, the Second World War that revived interest in ability testing, in which progress had been made and a number of tests developed to measure separate dimensions. It had now become possible to assess those aspects of individual's competence that were of specific relevance to the individual's situation and the organization's purpose.

Social Darwinism—that is, the application of Darwinist biology to society—provided the framework for a new psychology of individual differences. The relation of psychology of individual differences to psychometrics was 'symbiotic' (Hollway, 1991: 57)—that is, one fed off the other. Where psychometrics provided the method, the theory was individual differences. Darwinism had enabled theory, in terms of populations, rather than individuals; social Darwinism, at the turn of the century, was concerned with improving the fitness of the race, genetic inheritance, and national efficiency.

Eugenics

Eugenics gives political salience to the question of individual differences. Eugenics is the 'science' of improving stock, taking into account all influences that tend to give the preferred races, or strains of blood, a better chance of prevailing speedily over the others than they would otherwise have had (Hollway, 1991). It sees individual differences as determined largely by genetic inheritance: if an individual's performance is genetically determined, no attempt will be made to change it; it is only necessary to group, place, and regulate individuals. Bureaucracy—with its ideology of efficiency and rationality—can help to justify and enforce eugenics. For example, it was a US 'Eugenics Record Office' that, in the early twentieth century, restricted interracial marriage.

In the early twentieth century, a British scientist called Sir Francis Galton proposed that the British population be divided into 'desirables', 'undesirables', and 'passables'. The first group would be encouraged to have children, the second discouraged, and the third left alone. Bertrand Russell, who suggested the state issue colour-coded procreation tickets, also expressed the need for eugenics in Britain; those who reproduced without the ticket would be fined. And the author H.G. Wells hailed eugenics as the first step towards the removal of detrimental types and the fostering of more desirable ones. But eugenics appears to be a topic raised for discussion on a regular basis. It relatively recently returned to public attention when Scandinavian governments were found to have executed a plan to purify the Nordic race through enforced sterilization: more than 60,000 Swedish women branded 'low class' or 'mentally slow' were sterilized between 1935 and 1996. It has also been acknowledged that 60,000 Americans underwent forced sterilization in the name of science and improvement of the human breeding stock (Engel, 2002)—a practice that was ended only in 1979.

> **STOP AND THINK** **Organizations and technology help to make a custom-made baby**
>
> People should be able to choose the sex of their baby, argues Professor Lord Robert Winston (Ross, 2006). The story of the Masterton family was brought to the fore by the media as a result of their wish to ensure that their next child was female, having lost their only female child in a bonfire accident. A sperm-sorting machine called 'Microsort' has led to the birth of some 300 babies whose parents selected their gender. Some organizations sell the use of this technology, while others—such as the *Human Fertilization* and *Embryology Authority* (HFEA)—try to regulate its use.
>
> Can engineered gender selection be natural, or is this eugenics? Is it ethically acceptable? What do you think of the value judgement that is being made on the basis of gender?

Intelligence testing

Both eugenics and the psychology of individual differences are derived from a statistical theory of population distribution based on the normal curve. In the UK, Cyril Burt was the most prominent representative of the psychology of individual differences—in particular, the genetic determination of intelligence testing.

Burt (1924) compared the intelligence quotient (IQ) scores of identical twins with less closely related siblings. He gathered a large set of data on identical twins that were raised separately. After Burt's death, his work was closely scrutinized by Leon Kamin (1974; 1981). Carelessness and fraud was suggested, first by the *Sunday Times* (Gillie, 1976) and later by Burt's official biographer (Hearnshaw, 1979): Burt had failed to indicate which tests of intelligence he was using and had published his papers with co-authors who could not be located; the co-authors were unknown to the institutions listed as their place of employment and were unknown to members of the scientific community at that time (Cernovsky, 1997). His findings showed identical correlation coefficients for twin samples (see also Butler and Petrulis, 1999); since IQ tests are not a precise tool, it is unlikely that an identical IQ would be obtained even when testing the same person over time. These and other facts led to the uncomfortable conclusion that Burt had manufactured the data to support his belief that intelligence is largely inherited. Yet before being discredited, Burt influenced British social policies: for example, in schooling and the workplace.

Despite the assumption that IQ is static, Flynn (1987) is able to show data from fourteen countries indicating IQ gains ranging from five to twenty-five points in one generation. This increase suggests powerful environmental influences that affect performance in IQ tests. Howe (1998) shows how intervention can produce lasting change. Yet many write as if this is not the case (for example, Murray, 1996). Other environmental factors likely to influence IQ differences include such things as infant malnutrition and the consumption (or otherwise) of breakfast (Spring et al., 1992).

The public assumes, however, that intelligence testing is infallible and this has very negative consequences for those groups seen as 'genetically inferior', as 'proven' by 'science'. Intelligence tests have a very narrow focus on skills and tasks acquired in schooling; they do not test creativity or social intelligence (such as self-awareness or the perception of the emotional states or social behaviour of others). Many treat intelligence as if it were inherited through genes and as unchangeable during life (see Cernovsky, 1997). Despite classical textbooks warning that it is unlikely that any test can be fair to more than one cultural group, numerous psychologists still misinterpret IQ scores from other cultures as indicating the genetic inferiority of these groups. In the late 1960s, a scientific debate erupted over whether black peoples were genetically less intelligent than whites; the issue became less popular in the 1970s when some researchers demonstrated—using the same logic and tests—that, on average, Asians in the USA scored more highly than whites.

Intelligence testing is so unreliable that even those who have been described as 'geniuses' have been awarded low IQ scores. Cultural differences, for example, count for the ten-point gap in the IQ scores between white and black Americans. Yet in spite of this, there are still those—such as Christopher Brand, a psychologist at the University of Edinburgh—who continue to claim than it is a 'scientific fact' that white Americans and Asians are more intelligent than blacks. In the USA, Hernstein and Murray (1994) documented the alleged intellectual inferiority of African Americans. Not only did the result harm the research participants, who had been given Standford-Binet or other tests, but it weakened the available social support for those from black and minority groups by stigmatizing them as genetically inferior, thus strengthening the larger culture's racist attitudes (Brown, 1997). And it is difficult, if not impossible, to finds tests that are culture-free (Hofstede, 1997).

There is no inherent quality of intelligence that can indicate high potential (Howe, 1997); education and family background are better predictors of future success. Had George Stephenson, the nineteenth-century railway engineer, been given an intelligence test, he would probably have received a low score because he did not go to school, could not write his name, and could do no more than simple arithmetic by the age of 18. What intelligence tests have done is to set a threshold for entry into occupations that makes access to high-status jobs difficult for people with low scores. Large-scale research on army recruits from the Second World War found that the median IQ scores increased and the range of scores decreased with occupational status. The median score for accountants was 128, with a range of 94–154, while the median scores for labourers was 88, with range of 46–145 (Harrell and Harrell, 1945)—demonstrating that, if IQ scores are accepted as an accurate reflection of ability, some labourers have the capacity to be accountants and vice versa.

It is generally accepted that a high IQ is about being clever, being good at thinking, and being good at solving abstract problems. According to Beloff (1992), we also assume that such power lies in the domain of men. Three separate studies show how—compared with male self-perceptions—females invariably underestimate their IQs. Further, females project higher IQs onto their fathers than onto their mothers (Hogan, 1973; Higgins, 1987; Beloff, 1992). Young female students tend to see themselves as intellectually inferior to young men; women tend to see themselves as inferior to their fathers and men as superior to their mothers. Issues of power, self-perception, gender, and IQ are therefore clearly linked—an issue at which we will look again when considering individual differences and personality.

Primarily an educational psychologist, Burt testified to British government committees that children's intelligence levels were largely fixed by the age of 11 or so and were accurately measurable by standard tests given at that age. Burt claimed that the mental level of each child should be measured, then the education most appropriate to that level should be given, so that the child is guided into a career 'for which his measure of intelligence has marked him out' (Burt, 1924: 71). He helped to produce the '11 plus' examination, which streamed the top-scoring minority into grammar schools or top streams at comprehensive schools, and the rest into less challenging classes. It was virtually impossible for a child in a non-grammar secondary school to move—and grammar school education was required for acceptance into university (Fancher, 1985). In this way, Burt worked with industrial psychologists to develop an idea known as 'vocational guidance', in which the measurement of general intelligence in children and the interests of employers come together to fit the person to the job.

Vocational guidance: Testing, then fitting people to jobs

Cyril Burt claimed that the results of the measurement of intelligence corresponded with existing forms of classification of the school population and could also justify the sorts of jobs that less intelligent adults should choose. The Idea was that ensuring the right 'fit' between individuals and jobs would create a world of industrial harmony and productivity. 'Misfits' were those who, by virtue of being in the wrong job, did not match up to the new methods and speeds introduced into production (Hollway, 1991: 64). This notion of 'vocational guidance' assumes that, of all occupations, individuals are better suited to some than to others. Vocational selection uses such examination to choose the best fitted for the vacancies and assumes some are better fitted than others for any particular job.

Vocational guidance for school leavers was of interest to industrial psychologists, because if natural abilities and aptitudes could be measured, there would be no waste generated by those who found themselves in jobs with which they did not 'fit'. Because the vocational tests were applied almost entirely to mechanized jobs, all that was tested were aptitudes such as finger dexterity and hand—eye coordination. These ideas were adopted by producers such as J.S. Rowntree, the chocolate manufacturer, who believed that vocational selection would enable his company to reduce the number of cases in which work was experienced as monotonous. Automatic machinery would suit the lowest grade of worker; rational scientific management practices could enable the employer to select the right worker for the job.

Psychometric testing—that is, the measurement of mental ability—emerged from this basic assumption. The 'science' produces a battery of methodologies and techniques for selecting the 'right person for the job'. It is estimated that 100,000 psychometric tests are taken each day in Western countries (Cole, 1997). The tests are used to assist the recruitment process, for mid-career appraisal, and outplacement—but we will look at this topic further in Chapter 9.

STOP AND THINK Key performance indicators (KPIs)

Another method that managers use to increase efficiency and productivity is performance indicators, which must appear rational. If managers want to improve performance, it must be monitored, and key performance indicators (KPIs) must be agreed upon and measured. But those subjected to this rationale can sometimes see its weaknesses. The police, for example, working with between twenty and thirty KPIs at any one time, find that the theft of a milk bottle by a juvenile carries the same weight as a multimillion-pound fraud, so feel that they are being motivated to look after the easy detections rather than the harder ones (BBC News, 2008).

Have you come across examples of where the use of performance indicators does not appear to be so rational?

Conclusion

In this chapter, we have looked at the rationale behind the selection of the right people for jobs, and how management thinking has developed in terms of increasing efficiency and productivity, and gaining greater control. We have looked, in particular, at the logic of Taylorism and Fordism, which is applied to manual and white-collar work; good job design according to this rationale is making jobs more routine. In contrast, the human relations movement emphasized the emotional, non-rational, and sentimental aspects of human behaviour. Managers were encouraged to be more sensitive to workers' social needs; job redesign could accomplish this. But while job redesign might make jobs more meaningful and challenging, managers appear to use it only rarely to improve jobs or to redesign jobs to better fit social needs. The rational appears instead to be to fit people better to jobs.

In the next chapter, we will look at some of the other factors that might not be seen to contribute to this rationality.

KEY POINTS

- The rationality of management lies in intentional, reasoned, and goal-directed behaviour.

- Rationality has been achieved by applying scientific practices to better manage and control how work is done—but workers can have a rationale that runs counter to that of management, and may respond negatively to management's reasoning and goals by restricting output, for example.

- The human relations movement provided insight into workers' rationale for restricting output and engaging in unplanned activities. It drew attention to the emotional, non-rational, and sentimental aspects of human behaviour in organizations, and to the importance of social ties. It is, however, accused of ignoring the place of power and politics in organizations.

- While some management thinkers, such as Taylor and Ford, have employed a rationale of deskilling and simplifying jobs, others, such as those from the job redesign movement, have employed a different rationale in an attempt to make jobs more motivating, meaningful, and challenging.

- Intelligence testing and vocational guidance provide a further rationality: that of fitting the right person to the job.

CASE STUDY
Work and rationality

This case study looks at rationality and the response from the point of view of a university student working in a fast-food restaurant near the university campus and concerned about how the workers, including himself, were treated.

The student observed that the workers would steal food, make obscene statements about the boss behind his back, and complain about the low pay. The student argued that the work should be made more challenging and the indifferent management more democratic. He was asked why he thought that management was unresponsive to such suggestions. He considered the possibility that management was cruel and interested only in making a profit. He was then asked why employees would permit management to treat them in such a fashion—could they not simply quit their jobs? The student replied that the workers needed the money and that jobs were hard to obtain. It was precisely because there was an almost limitless pool of students looking for part-time employment that the operation was able to disregard the feelings of the workers. Because there were many who wanted work, the power of the individual was severely limited.

There is, then, a rationale to explain management's position: it was to be found in the organization's context, in the environment, in this case.

(*Source:* Adapted from Pfeffer and Salancik, 1978)

Questions

1. Is a plentiful supply of cheap labour a reasonable rationale explaining why managers should be indifferent to workers' views of the workplace?

2. What power do workers have to challenge these work conditions? What power do managers have?

FURTHER READING

Bramel, D. and Friend, R. (1981) 'Hawthorne, the myth of the docile worker, and class bias in psychology', *American Psychologist*, 36(8): 867–78; reprinted in M.J. Handel (2003) *The Sociology of Organizations*, London: Sage, ch. 8.

Cernovsky, Z.Z. (1997) 'A critical look at intelligence research', in D. Fox and I. Prilleltensky (eds), *Critical Psychology*: An Introduction, London: Sage, ch. 8 This chapter demands that you take a really critical view of intelligence research.

Hollway, W. (1991) *Work Psychology and Organizational Behaviour*, London: Sage Chapter 4 discusses fitting workers to jobs. Other chapters will help you to understand the history of work psychology.

Homans, G.C. (1941) 'The Hawthorne experiments', in M.J. Handel (2003) *The Sociology of Organizations*, London: Sage, ch. 7.

Noon, M. and Blyton, P. (2007) *The Realities of Work*, 3rd edn, Houndmills: Palgrave Macmillan See, particularly, the section entitled 'Work Routines and Skill Change', which is strong on Taylorism, Fordism, and the deskilling debate (that is, whether it is right to assume that there is a trend in which managers use technology to deskill jobs).

Rose, M. (1988) *Industrial Behaviour*, 2nd edn, Harmondsworth: Penguin This book is particularly good at describing, in greater depth, the thinking and rationale behind Taylorism and the human relations movement.

Thompson, P. and McHugh, D. (2002) *Work* Organizations, 3rd edn, Houndmills: Palgrave Chapter 3, in particular, asks you to think about the ideology underlying Taylorism, while Chapter 15 is useful on personality testing.

LINKS TO FILMS AND NOVELS

Modern Times (1936) dir. C. Chaplin As Gabriel et al. (2000) note, this Charlie Chaplin film memorably captures and criticizes the spirit of Taylorist ideas and Fordist applications.

RESEARCH QUESTIONS

1. What are the advantages of scientific management according to Taylor? What disadvantages in employing scientific principles have been shown to exist?

2. You have seen here the 'logic' of job design. Clegg (1984) shows how the processes of work simplification can be reversed. If you were a manager, would you try to humanize work? Why or why not?

3. What key performance indicators are used to measure the work of teachers, police, and other groups? What evidence can you find to describe the rationale of the approach and the inherent irrationality?

REFERENCES

Acker, J. and Van Houton, D.R. (1992) 'Differential recruitment and control: The sex structuring of organisations', in A.J. Mills and P. Tancred (eds), *Gendering Organizational Analysis*, London: Sage, ch. 1.

Ackroyd, S. and Crowdy, P.A. (1990) 'Can culture be managed?' *Personnel Review*, 19(5): 3–13.

Argyris, C. (1964) *Integrating the Individual and the Organization*, New York: Wiley.

Austrin, T. and West, J. (2005) 'Skills and surveillance in casino gaming: Work, consumption and regulation', *Work, Employment and Society*, 19: 305–26.

Babbage, C. (1832; 1989) *The Economy of Machinery and Manufactures*, 4th edn, London: William Pickering.

Baritz, L. (2005) 'The servants of power', in C. Grey and H. Willmott (eds), *Critical Management Studies: A Reader*, Oxford: Oxford University Press, ch. 3.

BBC News (2008) 'Chasing targets—not criminals', 14 August, available online at http://news.bbc.co.uk

Beloff, H. (1992) 'Mother, father and me: Our IQ', *Psychologist*, July: 309–11.

Blacker, F.H. and Brown, C.A. (1978) *Job Redesign and Management Control*, London: Saxon House.

Blauner, R. (1964) *Alienation and Freedom*, Chicago, IL: University of Chicago Press.

Braverman, H. (1974) *Labor and Monopoly Capital: The Degradation of Work in the Twentieth Century*, New York: Monthly Review Press.

Brewis, J. and Linstead, S. (2004) 'Gender and management', in S. Linstead, L. Fulop, and S. Lilley (eds), *Management and Organization: A Critical Text*, Houndmills: Palgrave Macmillan, ch. 2.

Broadbent, J., Dietrich, M., and Roberts, J. (1997) 'The end of the professions?', in J. Broadbent, M. Dietrich, and J. Roberts (eds), *The End of the Professions? The Restructuring of Professional Work*, London: Routledge, ch. 1.

Brown, L. (1997) 'Ethics in psychology: *Cui bono*?', in D. Fox and I. Prilleltensky (eds), *Critical Psychology: An Introduction*, London: Sage, ch. 4.

Brown, R. (1976) 'Women as employees: Some comments on research in industrial sociology', in D.L. Barker and S. Allen (eds), *Dependence and Exploitation in Work and Marriage*, Harlow: Longman, ch. 2.

Buchanan, D.A. (1985) *Canned Cycles and Dancing Tools: Who's Really in Control of Computer-Aided Machinery?*, Paper presented to the Third Annual Labour Process Conference, Manchester, 9–11 April.

Burrell, G. (1997) *Pandemonium: Towards a Retro-Organizational Theory*, London: Sage.

Burt, C. (1924) 'The mental differences between individuals', *Journal of the National Institute of Industrial Psychology*, 11(2): 67–74.

Butler, B.E. and Petrulis, J. (1999) 'Some further observations concerning Sir Cyril Burt', *British Journal of Psychology*, 90: 155–60.

Carey, A. (1967) 'The Hawthorne studies: A radical criticism', *American Sociological Review*, 32: 403–16.

Cernovsky, Z.Z. (1997) 'A critical look at intelligence research', in D. Fox and I. Prilleltensky (eds), *Critical Psychology: An Introduction*, London: Sage, ch. 8.

Child, J. (1972) 'Organizational structure, environment and performance: The role of strategic choice', *Sociology*, 6: 1–22.

Clegg, C.W. (1984) 'The derivations of job designs', *Journal of Occupational Behaviour*, 5: 131–46.

Cole, N. (1997) 'Personality put to the test', *The Scotsman,* 24 October, p. 1.

Corbett, M. (1994) *Critical Cases in Organizational Behaviour*, Houndmills: Macmillan.

Davis, L.E., Canter, R.R., and Hoffman, J. (1955) 'Current job design criteria', *Journal of Industrial Engineering*, 6: 5–11.

Dore, R.P. (1973) *British Factory—Japanese Factory*, London: Allen & Unwin.

Drucker, P.F. (1989) *The Practice of Management*, Oxford: Heinemann Professional Publishing.

Durkheim, E. (1984) *The Division of Labour in Society*, trans. W.D. Halls, London: Macmillan.

Edwards, R.C. (1978) 'The social relations at the point of production', *Insurgent Sociologist*, 8(2–3): 109–25.

Engel, M. (2002) 'State says sorry for forced sterilizations', *The Guardian*, 23 May, available online at http://www.guardian.co.uk

Fancher, R.E. (1985) *The Intelligence Men: Makers of the IQ Controversy*, London: Norton.

Ferguson, T. (2007) 'Airlines see passenger service take off', *Silicon.com*, 19 October, available online at http://networks.silicon.com/broadband/0,39024864,39168884,00.htm

Fineman, S. (1996) 'Emotion and organizing', in S.R. Clegg, C. Hardy, and W.R. Nord (eds), *Handbook of Organization Studies*, London: Sage, ch. 3.3.

_____ (ed.) (2000) *Emotion in Organizations*, London: Sage.

Flynn, J.R. (1987) 'Massive IQ gains in 14 nations: What IQ tests really measure', *Psychological Bulletin*, 101: 171–91.

Follett, M.P. (1982) 'The influence of employee representation in remoulding the accepted type of business manager', in E. Fox and L. Urwick (eds), *Dynamic Administration*, New York: Hippocrene Books, pp.132–47.

Ford, H. (1923) *My Life and Work*, London: William Heinemann.

Fox, D. and Prilleltensky, I. (eds) (1997) *Critical Psychology: An Introduction*, London: Sage.

Friedman, A. (1977) 'Responsible autonomy versus direct control over the labour process', *Capital and Class*, 1(Spring): 43–57.

Gabriel, Y., Fineman, S., and Sims, D. (2000) *Organizing and Organizations*, 2nd edn, London: Sage.

Gillie, O. (1976) 'Crucial data faked by eminent psychologist', *Sunday Times*, 24 October, cited online at http://www.indiana.edu/~intell/burtaffair.shtml

Grint, K. (1991) *The Sociology of Work: An Introduction*, Cambridge: Polity.

Hackman, J.R. and Lawler, E.E. (1971) 'Employee reactions to job characteristics', *Journal of Applied Psychology Monograph*, 55(3): 259–86.

Harrell, T.W. and Harrell, M.S. (1945) 'Army classification test scores of civilian occupations', *Educational and Psychological Measurement*, 5: 229–39.

Hearnshaw, L.S. (1979) *Cyril Burt: Psychologist*, London: Hodder & Stoughton.

Hernstein, R.C. and Murray, C. (1994) *The Bell Curve: Intelligence and Class Structure in American Life*, New York: Free Press.

Herzberg, F., Mausner, B., and Snyderman, B. (1959) *The Motivation to Work*, New York: Wiley.

Higgins, L. (1987) 'The knowing of intelligence', *The Guardian*, 10 February.

Hofstede, G. (1997) *Cultures and Organizations: Software of the Mind*, New York: McGraw Hill.

Hogan, H.W. (1973) 'IQ: Self estimates of males and females', *Journal of Social Psychology*, 106: 137–8.

Hollway, W. (1991) *Work Psychology and Organizational Behaviour: Managing the Individual at Work*, London: Sage.

Homans, G.C. (1959) 'Group factors in worker productivity', in E. Maccoby, T.M. Newcomb, and E.L. Hartley (eds), *Readings in Social Psychology*, 3rd edn, London: Methuen, pp. 583–95.

Howe, M. (1997) *IQ in Question,* London: Sage.

_____ (1998) 'Can IQ change?', *Psychologist*, February: 69–72.

Jacques, R. (1996) *Manufacturing the Employee: Management Knowledge From the 19th to 21st Centuries*, London: Sage.

Johnson, P. and Gill, J. (1993) *Management Control and Organizational Behaviour*, London: Paul Chapman.

Kamin, L. (1974) *The Science and Politics of I.Q.*, Potomac, MD: Erlbaum.

_____ (1981), in H. J. Eysenck and L. Kamin (eds), *Intelligence: The Battle for the Mind—H.J. Eysenck versus Leon Kamin*, London: Macmillan, chs 12–20 and 22.

Kanter, R. (1977) *Men and Women of the Corporation*, New York: Basic Books.

Leidner, R. (1993) *Fast Food, Fast Talk: Service Work and the Routinization of Everyday Life*, Berkeley, CA: University of California Press.

Littler, C.R. (1985) 'Taylorism, Fordism and job design', in D. Knights, H. Wilmott, and D. Collinson (eds), *Job Redesign: Critical Perspectives on the Labour Process*, Aldershot: Gower, ch. 2.

Lupton, T. (1971) *Management and the Social Sciences*, Harmondsworth: Penguin.

Mayo, G.E. (1949) *The Social Problems of Industrial Civilization*, London: Routledge & Kegan Paul.

McGregor, D. (1960) *The Human Side of Enterprise*, New York: McGraw Hill.

Monanari, J.R. (1979) 'Strategic choice: A theoretical analysis', *Journal of Management Studies*, 16: 202–21.

Murray, C. (1996) 'Murray's précis', *Current Anthropology*, 37(February supplement): S143–51.

Noble, D.F. (1974) *America by Design*, New York: Oxford University Press.

_____ (1979) 'Social choice in machine design: The case of automatically controlled machine tools', in A. Zimbalist (ed.), *Case Studies in the Labor Process*, New York: Monthly Review Press, pp. 1–50.

Noon, M. and Blyton, P. (2007) *The Realities of Work*, 3rd edn, Houndmills: Palgrave.

Pfeffer, J. and Salancik, G.R. (1978) *The External Control of Organizations: A Resource Dependence Perspective*, Upper Saddle River, NJ: Pearson Education.

Putnam, L. and Mumby, D. (1993) 'Organizations, emotions and the myth of rationality', in S. Fineman (ed.), *Emotion in Organizations*, London: Sage, pp. 36–57.

Radio Times (1997) 'Why am I on TV so much? Probably because I'm cheap', 4–10 October, pp. 15–16.

Roethlisberger, F.J., and Dickson, W.J. (1939) *Management and the Worker*, Cambridge, MA: Harvard University Press.

Rose, M. (1988) *Industrial Behaviour*, 2nd edn, Harmondsworth: Penguin.

Rose, N. (1990) *Governing the Soul: The Shaping of the Private Self*, London: Routledge.

_____ (1996) 'Identity, genealogy and history', in S. Hall and P. du Gay (eds), *Questions of Cultural Identity*, London: Sage, ch. 8.

Ross, P. (2006) 'Winston backs "social" embryo sex selection', *Sunday Herald*, 5 November, p. 22.

Sims, D., Fineman, S., and Gabriel, Y. (1993) *Organizing and Organizations*, London: Sage.

Smith, M. and George, D. (1994) 'Selection methods', in C.L. Cooper and I.T. Robertson (eds), *Key Reviews in Managerial Psychology: Concepts and Research in Practice*, Chichester: Wiley, ch. 2.

Spring, B., Pingitore, R., Bourgeois, M., Kessler, K.H., and Bruckner, E. (1992) *The Effects and Non-Effects of Skipping Breakfast: Results of Three Studies*, Paper presented at the 100th Annual Meeting of the American Psychological Association, Washington DC, August.

Stearns, P.N. (1989) 'Suppressing unpleasant emotions: The development of a twentieth-century American', in A.E. Barnes and P.N. Stearns (eds), *Social History and Issues of Human Consciousness*, New York: New York University Press.

Taska, L. (1995) 'The cultural diffusion of scientific management', *Journal of Industrial Relations*, 37(3): 427–61.

Taylor, F.W. (1911) *Principles of Scientific Management*, New York: Norton & Co.

Taylor, J.C. (1979) 'Job design criteria twenty years later', in L.E. Davis and J.C. Taylor (eds), *Design of Jobs*, 2nd edn, Santa Monica, CA: Goodyear.

Thompson, P. and McHugh, D. (2002) *Work Organizations: A Critical Introduction*, 3rd edn, Houndmills: Palgrave.

Ure, A. (1835) *The Philosophy of Manufactures*, London: Charles Knight.

Walker, C.R. and Guest, R.H. (1952) *The Man on the Assembly Line*, Cambridge, MA: Harvard University Press.

Watanabe, T. (1990) 'New office technology and the labour process in contemporary Japanese banking', *New Technology, Work and Employment*, 5(1): 56–67.

Weick, K. (1969) *The Social Psychology of Organizing*, Reading, MA: Addison-Wesley Publishing.

Wilson, F.M. (1987) 'Computer numerical control and constraint', in D. Knights and H. Wilmott (eds), *New Technology and the Labour Process*, London: Macmillan, ch. 4.

Zeitlin, J. (1983) 'The labour strategies of British engineering employers 1890–1922', in H. Gospel and C. Littler (eds), Managerial Strategies and Industrial Relations, London: Heinemann, ch. 2.

Sexuality, Sex Typing, and Gender

5

Introduction

In Chapter 2, we looked at the 'view from below'—that is, at the perspective of some employees. In Chapter 3, we looked at the 'view from above'—that is, the manager's reality. In the last chapter, we looked at the degree to which management might appear to be rational. But what about those aspects of organization that might not appear to contribute to this rationality: for example, what insights might be gained by looking at issues such as sexuality?

While it might not be seen to be an appropriate subject for those interested in the more 'rational'— and thus 'asexual'—world of organizations, workplace sexuality has been the focus of some lively discussion among researchers in organization studies for over twenty years. Despite this fact, it rarely finds a place in textbooks on organizational behaviour: scholars appear to have implicitly assumed that sexuality has no place at work.

In this chapter, we look into organizations, concentrating on issues that are normally treated in management and organizational behaviour as though they were external to organizations: sexuality, emotions, and feelings. These issues play an important role in the everyday experience of behaviour in organizations.

By the end of this chapter, you will understand more about how sex and sexuality are relevant to an understanding of behaviour in organizations—that is, how jobs are often seen as being 'for women' or 'for men', how labour can be sexualized, how gender affects the expectations and requirements of employees in terms of how they should look, act and talk, and how employees' behaviour has to be controlled. We will also consider whether romance and sexual harassment needs to be 'managed' within a work context. Finally, we will recognize the connections that can be made between the control that prostitutes have been found to exert, and other jobs in which acting and control are required.

This chapter covers:

- sexuality in organizations;
- the sex typing of male and female jobs;
- the sex stereotype and emotional labour;
- masculinity and managing feelings;
- feeling in control;
- accounting for emotion;
- organizational romance;
- sexual harassment.

Sexuality in organizations

Far from being marginal to the workplace, sexuality is pervasive. It is alluded to in dress (that is, in how we present ourselves), jokes, gossip, looks and flirtations, secret affairs, and sexual harassment (Pringle, 1990; Lerum, 2004). 'Sexuality' refers to sex roles, sexual preferences, sexual attractiveness, and notions of masculinity and femininity in organizations. It is sexuality that marks men and women out as different, and also that marks out differences between groups: for example, gay men and lesbian women. Individuals 'do gender' and simultaneously 'do sexuality' with an awareness of society norms and in anticipation of the judgment of others (West and Zimmerman, 1987; Miller et al., 2003): one of the first things that we notice about a person is their gender.

We are as preoccupied with sexuality as we are with gender, as a means of 'knowing' others and 'knowing' ourselves (Brewis, 2005). There are explicit and implicit displays of sexuality to be witnessed in the workplace—usually involving heterosexuality. It is interesting to note that most writing on sexuality in organizations assumes heterosexuality as given. Heterosexuality is the unassailable norm, while other sexualities are seen as 'abnormal' (Foucault, 1979). 'Heterosexual' (like 'white', 'male', and 'able-bodied') is almost always a silent term (Kitzinger et al., 1992) and it is only recently that studies have looked at lesbians and gay men in work—in the public sector (Skelton, 1999; Humphrey, 2000), in the police (Burke, 1993; Miller et al., 2003), and in the military (Hall, 1995)—or at those who are transgender (Schilt, 2006).

STOP AND THINK Can we be 'genderless'?

It is not possible to be 'genderless' or 'unmarked' by your gender and sexuality at work. This fact is brought into stark relief by experiences such as those of Moreno (1995), who was raped by one of her research assistants (Brewis, 2005). We are also perceived in terms of our ethnicity, age, and class.

What experiences have you had that confirm or deny that it is not possible to be genderless or unmarked by your sexuality?

So what about management and sexuality: do they mix? We will see, in Chapter 13, how women in bureaucracies are strangers in a male-defined world. There is evidence of women managers being perceived as threats to male self-image (Cockburn, 1991; Sargent, 1983). Women may play down their sexuality in order to 'blend in' (Sheppard, 1989). In this chapter, we will look further into the issue of sexuality and how it is pertinent to understanding organizational behaviour.

Issues of emotionality, sexuality, and intimacy are currently missing from descriptions of organizational life (Brewis and Grey, 1994): they are seen as belonging to a private sphere; women and sex are not welcome in the public sphere. Women—characterized as inherently passionate, sexual beings—are thought not to function as well as men in the rational public sphere, because they are overly prey to their basic emotions. Popular myth says that women are too neurotic to be able to cope with public positions of responsibility and are more suited to 'instinctive' roles, such as caring for the young or infirm, or in supportive, helping, administrative roles.

The sex typing of male and female jobs

Employers tend to assign people to jobs that are seen as suitable for their gender (Reskin, 1993)—a practice in which gender stereotypes play a large part. Men are seen to be more aggressive, ambitious, assertive, athletic, decisive, forceful, good at leadership, and willing to take risks; women are seen to be more cheerful, compassionate, sensitive to the needs of others, sympathetic, and understanding (Holt and Ellis, 1998). As a result, women tend to be perceived as unsuitable for, and excluded from, jobs high in authority, such as ownership or high-level management, jobs that require physical strength or blue-collar technical skills, those involving exposure to physical risk or physically uncomfortable working conditions, or those involving authoritative social control, as in much police work. Women are seen as suitable for, and are more likely to be found in, jobs requiring social skills.

Some jobs and professions have been sex-typed as male: the legal profession is a good example. Male lawyers (with a few exceptions) and the professional bodies in England fiercely resisted the entry of women into the profession for three reasons (Podmore and Spencer, 1982).

1. It is a very conservative profession that is opposed to change.

2. Most importantly for our purposes here, the men felt that professional standards would be dangerously compromised by the entry of women into the profession. Maleness was one of the attributes of professionalism; maleness was part of the profession's character, so the admission of women was seen as threatening the very identity of the institutions. Men lawyers referred to stereotypes that portrayed women as emotional, illogical, and irrational. Women were seen as successful only if they suppressed the feminine side of their characters. This would mean 'unsexing' women, which would be deplored by the male legal establishment. The only acceptable solution, then, was that women should be excluded.

3. The men wished to exclude the competition that women would present. Women in the profession feel that their careers have been shaped and fashioned by their gender: for example, they find themselves channelled into particular types of work seen as fit for females—that is, desk-bound work, such as conveyancing and divorce work. Women tend to be excluded from higher status and more remunerative work (particularly company and commercial law), because they are thought, by men, to be less effective in these areas (Podmore and Spencer, 1982).

The profession still contains inequality in terms of pay; the pay gap reaches its highest level at a point 21–25 years after qualifying (see http://www.lawscot.org.uk). There are also still proportionately fewer women who are partners than men (one in five women, compared with one in two men in 2005).

Social norms are often personified in sexual stereotypes. For example, a commonly held belief is that female bar staff should be attractive, warm-hearted, easy-going women, providing a shoulder for men to cry on, and capable of taking and giving a joke. Such consensual objectivity has a reality that is independent of fact. The barmaid who is not attractive, is embarrassed by risqué humour, or unsympathetic to cries for sympathy fails to comply with criteria for membership of the group 'barmaid' and is unlikely to be ignorant of that failure (Breakwell, 1979).

Rosemary Pringle, in her book *Secretaries Talk* (1989), shows how femininity and secretarial work are closely tied. Although most secretaries were men until the late nineteenth century and they retained a presence in secretarial work until the Second World War, secretarial work is now seen as quintessentially feminine. Moreover, all women are assumed to be capable of secretarial work: '... typing is seen as something every woman can do—like washing up!' (a secretary quoted in Pringle, 1989: 3.) Men may perceive any woman in an office (or a university department) as the secretary and expect her to perform secretarial service in the absence of such. Secretaries are also represented almost exclusively in familial or sexual terms as wives (for example, office wife), mothers, spinster aunts, mistresses, and femmes fatales. The image is often of the 'sexy secretary' and the 'mindless dolly bird'. It is virtually impossible to talk about secretaries without making a set of sexual associations. In fact, secretary–boss relations are seen by Pringle as the most sexualized of all employment relationships 'outside the sex industry itself' (ibid.: 158). Media images of secretaries sitting around filing their nails or doing their knitting reinforce the idea that they do little work.

But men's labour is also sexualized. Research undertaken by McDowell (1997) in the City of London shows how men 'do' masculinity. Organizations are structured by the social relations of sexuality (ibid.: 27). Men construct everyday work through heterosexual masculine discourse in different types of merchant banking. The stock exchange is a commercial marketplace—a space in which 'rampant male libido' (ibid.:169) is celebrated. Work itself was described in terms of explicit sexual metaphors, such as 'lift your skirt' (that is, reveal your position), 'hard on' (that is, rising market), 'rape the cards' (that is, exaggerate expenses), and the 'consummation' of deals (ibid.: 148). Women and gay men are 'others' in this heterosexual culture. The men used terms such as 'skirts', 'slags', 'brasses', and 'tarts' to describe women and to emphasize the ways in which they were illegitimate outsiders. Similarly, Knorr-Cetina and

Bruegger (2000) are struck by the sexual vocabulary of the training rooms: 'I got shafted ...'; 'I got bent over ...'; 'I got blown up ...'; 'I got raped ...'; 'I got stuffed ...'.

....

⭐ **STOP AND THINK** The cost of sex discrimination

Loutish behaviour in the finance industry can cost companies a lot of money. *American Express* (the travel and finance company) agreed to pay $31 million in a lawsuit for sex and age discrimination filed on behalf of more than 4,000 women. Two investment banks settled two sex discrimination cases in New York and London. In the London case, an employment tribunal awarded the claimant almost £1.5 million—a record amount for a sex discrimination case in the UK (*The Economist*, 2002).

....

While it might be argued that merchant banking jobs are not inherently masculine, some jobs are seen as very much the masculine domain. One example is butchery. Women make up less than 1 per cent of butchers (Pringle and Collings, 1993). Butchers continue to stress the inappropriateness of butchery for women. The 'woman butcher' is almost unthinkable as a cultural category. Women's place within the popularly mythologized butcher's shop is as the butcher's wife, as the cashier, or as the shop assistant; there has been a reluctance to allow them to cut the carcasses up. A physical strength discourse helps to keep women out of butchery: strength is needed to break up carcasses. It is also assumed that women will be afraid of knives and squeamish at the sight of blood (ibid.)—yet if this were the case, why would women doctors and nurses be working in operating theatres?

Just as there are jobs, such as merchant banking and butchery, that are sex-typed as male, so there are jobs that are sex-typed as female and in which fewer men are to be found. Examples include nursing, aircraft cabin crew, primary school teachers, and librarians. Men working in female-dominated occupations fear feminization (that is, being associated with female traits) and stigmatization (Lupton, 2000). But while 'token' women can be severely disadvantaged by their minority status, positive career outcomes appear to accrue for token men. Men working in non-traditional occupations have been found to benefit from their token status through the assumption of enhanced leadership and other skills, and being associated with a more careerist attitude to work. Male nurses often ascent the hierarchy more quickly than their female counterparts (Bradley, 1993). Minority status therefore appears to have mainly positive outcomes for men in female-dominated jobs (Simpson, 2004).

The sex stereotype and emotional labour

Sexuality and emotions are clearly brought into work. Women are often required to display the sex stereotype in order to be effective in their work. Arlie Russell Hochschild (1983) was among the first scholars to show how extensively individuals—particularly employed women—are expected to manage their emotions; she uses the metaphor of a 'managed heart' to underscore the emotional control that the women were required to exhibit. This research offers a new angle on the experience of work and the 'view from below': many workers must go beyond the suppression of negative emotion and express positive emotion (for example, cheerfulness) that they are not truly feeling—a process that Hochschild termed emotional labour.

Hochschild's study of US airline flight attendants demonstrates how the attendants were trained to display an emotional commitment to the welfare and comfort of airline passengers; they were required to show a caring, courteous, friendly, and efficient front even when passengers were rude or arrogant. There were rules for grooming and personal attitudes. Customers had to be met with warmth and smiles; the smiles were to be 'inside-out' ones—that is, felt and meant. Cabin crew at *Delta Airlines* were socialized during their training to believe not only that they had to make customers feel cosseted and valued, but also that they had genuinely to experience positive regard for them, and suppress both negative behaviour and negative emotions. This is emotional labour for the flight attendants—particularly when it involves the semi-institutionalized expectation of flirting expected between (mainly) female air stewardesses and male airline passengers, and is reflected in advertising taglines such as 'We really move our tails for you to make your every wish come true' (*Continental Airlines*) or 'Fly me, you'll like it' (*National Airlines*) (see ibid.: 93). The company, then, manufactured the response to the client. 'Professionalism' requires this behaviour.

There are two main ways in which emotional labour is engaged: surface acting; and deep acting. The former involves pretending to feel 'what we do not': we may be deceiving others about how we feel, but we do not deceive ourselves. Deep acting, however, means deceiving one's self as well as others. There is a cost attached to this labour: the labour 'affects the degree to which we listen to feeling and sometimes our very capacity to feel' (ibid.: 21–2). Employees become alienated from their real feelings—and this can cause psychological damage in the long term (Furnham, 2008). Hochschild goes on to imply that many—perhaps most—women have had the kinds of training that she observed among *Delta* flight attendants, who were taught 'that an obnoxious person could be reconceived in an honest and useful way'. Such lessons were part of their 'anger desensitization' (Hochschild, 1983: 25).

EXAMPLE Surface acting

Bolton and Boyd (2003) found that many airline staff admitted showing obviously false emotions—that is, that they were 'surface acting'. For example, they might offer polite words, but with a 'wooden smile' that did not reflect their true feelings.

This emotional labour cannot be regarded as 'gender neutral'. Jobs requiring significant amounts of emotional labour are dominated by women (Taylor and Tyler, 2000). The 'natural' skills and personality required to deliver quality service among telephone sales agents at *Flightpath* appeared to be female ones: 'We are looking for people who can chat to people, interact, build rapport. What we find is that women can do this more, they're definitely more natural when they do it anyway … women are naturally good at that sort of thing' (ibid.: 84). The women were expected to put up with sexualized encounters with men on the phone. Similarly, female flight attendants were thought to be best suited to the role because they were seen as more patient and caring of other's needs than men. The quality service delivered by flight attendants—that is, the 'personal servicing' of passengers—increases relative to the cost of the service itself. Flight attendants working with first-class travellers were trained to introduce themselves, use passenger names, memorize their drink and meal requirements, and to provide a more 'personal' service. They were instructed to walk softly though the cabin, make eye contact with each passenger, and always smile at him or her—all of which prescribed behaviours recall those required of Hugh Hefner's *Playboy* bunny girls.

EXAMPLE The prescribed behaviour of bunny girls

Bunny girls had a uniform: a very tight corset, cuffs, and bunny ears. They were required to work eight-hour shifts in 4-inch heels and were trained how to serve drinks: carrying the tray aloft and bending over the table backwards—that is, the 'bunny dip'. A 'bunny mother' would inspect every bunny before each shift to make sure that their nails were manicured and their seams straight. When sitting, they were required to keep their backs very straight and their legs crossed.

(*Source:* Wuamett, 2001)

Similar prescribed behaviour exists within a more common work context: a restaurant chain called *Hooters*.

EXAMPLE The prescribed behaviour of *Hooters'* waitresses

A new restaurant chain has come to the UK: *Hooters*—that is, 'a US-born franchise that specializes in men being served their chicken wings by a smiling nubile with enormous breasts, wearing a comically tight T-shirt emblazoned with the word *Hooters* and Kylie-sized scarlet hot pants (tagline: A fun place to work!)' (Patterson, 2008). The restaurant chain requires the women to sign a contract in which they agree to wear the *Hooter* Girl uniform, and interact with and entertain customers.

STOP AND THINK Your experience of prescribed behaviour

Can you think of other jobs in which behaviour and appearance is tightly prescribed and enforced? Does this only happen in jobs that women do?

Tyler and Abbott (1998) have documented how women flight attendants were also asked to manage themselves as 'ornamental objects' (West and Zimmerman, 1987: 141). Flight attendants were required to deploy skills and abilities that they are deemed to possess simply by virtue of their sexual difference from men: the flight attendant is 'part mother, part servant and part tart' (Tyler and Abbott, 1998: 440)—that is, essentialized, gendered, and sexualized. The skills are not remunerated or trained, but they are managed. These women are required to manage and monitor their bodies, be 'body conscious', and watch their weight. An efficient and effective airline is signified by a 'slender' flight attendant. Applicants can be rejected if their weight is not considered to be in proportion to their height. One airline company (*Indian Airlines*) recently hit the headlines when it temporarily suspended flight attendants without pay for being 'too fat to fly' (Gentleman, 2006).

The women flight attendants in Tyler and Abbot's study also needed to look after their bodies in other ways; rejection was associated with looking too old, having blemished skin, or having hair that was too short, too messy, or too severe. They could also be rejected if their nails were too short or bitten, their posture was poor, or their legs were too chubby. Others were rejected for having prominent teeth or having a weakness for chocolate. Poise and grooming are important for the image. All attendants are required to conform to company-specific formal uniform and grooming regulations, which stipulate clothing, shoes, hair, and make-up, and height–weight restrictions. Only female flight attendants were weighed periodically during grooming checks. While men have to look clean and socially attractive, the women have to look 'polished' and sexually attractive—and they are expected to do so at their own expense: no allowance is given for make-up, hairdressers, or fitness centres. (For more on flight attendants and emotional labour, see also Bolton and Boyd, 2003, and Williams, 2003.)

EXAMPLE Another example of emotional labour: The beauty salon

Beauty therapists are required to wax, manicure, and massage, but are also involved in the work of confidence and morale boosting, pampering, and stress management (Black, 2004). Emotional labour may well be vital for the long-term viability of the salon: a beauty therapist must work on the relationship with the client (Sharma and Black, 2001: 919). He or she needs to be responsive to the client in a non-rote fashion, offering reassurance, aligning him or herself with the client's concerns, and treating the client as an individual (Toerien and Kitzinger, 2007).

EXAMPLE **Further examples of emotional labour**

Other examples of emotional labour are to be found in studies focusing on: hospice nursing (James, 1989); nursing homes (Lopez, 2006); sex work (Sanders, 2004); call taking (Korczynski, 2003); food retailing (Peccei and Rosenthal, 2000); pubs (Seymour and Sandiford, 2005); and small business management (Mirchandani, 2003).

Masculinity and managing feelings

Emotions are, then, an integral and inseparable part of everyday organizational life. From moments of frustration or joy, and grief or fear, to an enduring sense of dissatisfaction or commitment, the experience of work is saturated with feeling and emotion. And research has shown that it is not only women who are required to manage their feelings and emotions at work; men also have to manage them, as the following report of a meeting in a law firm during which a senior partner criticized the way in which an attorney had handled a case illustrates:

> **During the twenty five minutes that the focus remained on his case, Jake said nothing. He reported that at first he was sure he had turned 'beet red' from embarrassment. Pretty quickly, though, the embarrassment turned to another emotion as he found himself with clenched fists at his sides. He then (literally) bit his lip in order to hold back a sharp retort or a sarcastic comment. In telling the story, he remarked that he would have 'decked the guy' if he had been a senior partner.**

(Plas and Hoover-Dempsey, 1988: 26–7, cited in Ashforth and Humphrey, 1995)

Management offers advice on how to handle emotion; it prescribes combinations of positive and negative feelings to help police officers and debt collectors adjust social interaction to organizational aims (Rafaeli and Sutton, 1991). Debt collectors are explicitly trained to adapt their display rules to the emotional reactions of debtors: they are taught to express warmth with anxious debtors, neutrality or calmness with angry respondents, and urgency and disapproval with reluctant customers. Rises, promotions, cash prizes, criticism, warnings, demotions, and firings are used to sanction those who deviate from the appropriate emotional displays.

Research has also shown how men are often reluctant to admit to vulnerability or fear at work. Prison officers, for example, view requests for help from colleagues as evidence of professional weakness. If a colleague were to ask for help, it would be tantamount to admitting that he is not 'man enough' for the job. Asking for help and showing fear or emotion are not occupationally acceptable (Carter, 1996).

Another example can be found in 'security' work at nightclubs and pubs—that is, being a 'bouncer' or 'door supervisor' (Monaghan, 2002). In this setting, fear can be hidden and managed through group solidarity. Research with over sixty door supervisors (only five of whom were female) showed the importance of demonstrating solidarity with the 'comrades'; solidarity was evidenced between door staff in a masculinist way. Greeting and departure rituals, such as the obligatory firm handshake, represented a mundane manifestation of in-group ties, while violence towards 'problematic' customers who physically assault door staff provides a more shocking indication of this commitment. Danger is an extremely important unifying factor and is implicated in dominating styles of body use. While the door staff face personal bodily injury, police arrest, and instant dismissal by the manager, this renders in-group cohesion salient at practical, cognitive, and emotional levels. And they do not only support staff at their own place of work: workers at different venues can be in radio contact with others in adjoining pubs and clubs.

If a violent incident were to erupt at one site, door teams could 'double up', with the intention of resolving the conflict quickly and reducing the risk of occupational injury. In this way, door staff were seen to 'keep warm together' in an insecure world.

As other research has shown, the strong male-coded emotions, such as anger, hatred, and aggression, sometimes actually prompted 'bloody revenge' (Mellor and Shilling, 1997: 201): '… you hit a doorman and, if the team is worth its salt, you'll pay in blood. That's the unwritten law' (Thompson, 2000: 151; Monaghan, 2002: 512). But 'masculinity' is very precarious, and may be usurped in a public and humiliating manner: for example, one doorman (Terry) 'took the piss' out of another (Paul) by refusing him access to a nightclub; Paul's reaction was tearful. Paul 'lost face', because he was, in this case, unable to tolerate the public exchange of insult and humour, and the overt conflict.

There is, however, research in this area that challenges stereotypes of 'masculinity' and 'femininity' both at work and at play.

EXAMPLE **When bingeing women spur the rise of the female bouncer**

Door security staff or 'bouncers' in pubs and clubs are mainly men, but women are being hired in larger numbers in order to tackle female violence; the proportion of women bouncers has risen from 2 per cent to 11 per cent (Times Online, 2006). Attacks by drunken women are now almost as common as men fighting and the number of females defined as 'binge drinkers' has doubled during the last decade. Contrary to the popular view, women do not simply act as a 'calming, diffusing' influence, but actually work in ways that echo the actions of male colleagues. The women bouncers in one study had been in just as many fights as the men with whom they worked (Open University, 2006).

Feeling in control

In a similar way to the way in which door security staff act to maintain control, strippers describe themselves as powerful:

'It's your show, you're higher than everyone else on that stage and you feel in control,' says Ninon. Melissa (a student at Oxford who works in the same show) says, 'It's the only sexual relationship I've had where I feel completely in control.'
(*Scotland on Sunday*, 3 August 1997, p. 4)

'When I am on stage I am a sex goddess, I'm revered by every man in the room. I'm all powerful, they all want me but they can't have me.'
(Melissa Butler, quoted in *The Guardian*, 28 August 1997)

A male stripper (Clarke, 2003) was advised by a female stripper about the behaviour that he should exhibit. Women expect to 'get interactive': 'They want to laugh, scream and howl. The male stripper has to get among them, dance, flirt and expect to get a bit mauled.' He had not anticipated that a woman would bite him on his buttock; he was bitten so badly that he needed four stitches. This time, he had lost control.

It is not only relationships with clients that sex workers manage. Relationships between prostitutes and police, for example, also have to be managed. For example, to reduce the chances of being arrested by the police, they use 'the courtesy of the road', which means that, if the police come along, the prostitutes will move, walk off, or even just look in the opposite direction (McKeganey and Barnard, 1996). Sharpe (1998) found that an unwritten rule with the police was that the women would not start working on the patch until 6 p.m. If they were to come out before this time, they would be immediately arrested and charged.

STOP AND THINK **Unwritten rules**

All jobs have unwritten rules attached to them. For example, when working as a temporary hospital cleaner, the author found that temporary cleaners were given all of the worst jobs to do, including cleaning up sewage from a broken ceiling pipe. Temporary cleaners could only use the cleaning equipment (floor polishers, etc.) when they were not needed by those with permanent cleaning jobs; the full-time cleaners had control.

What unwritten rules have applied in your experience of working?

Images of stereotypical femininity in contemporary culture are associated with the good wife and mother—that is, the 'good girl': reliable, passive, nurturing, often fragile, gentle, and emotional. Some prostitutes claim to challenge these stereotypes for all women by resisting the pressure to conform to the stereotype, and by bringing into the public sphere and to many men the services that women would usually perform in private for one man. They insist that prostitution is work and a service that anyone can offer or seek, and that they should have the same rights and liberties as other workers (O'Neill, 1997).

EXAMPLE **Student sex work**

A study by Kingston University found that one in ten of the 130 students whom they surveyed knew students who had stripped, lap danced, or worked in massage parlours and escort agencies, and that more than 6 per cent of surveyed students knew of students who worked as prostitutes. There has been a 50 per cent growth in student prostitution since 2000. This growth in student prostitution is thought to be linked to the increasing financial problems experienced by students (Milne, 2006).

109

O'Connell Davidson (1995) describes some of the many similarities between sex workers and other self-employed individuals. One of the most difficult aspects of the prostitute's business is the flow of custom and therefore cash. About 90 per cent of the men break their appointments, so it is difficult to control or reliably predict demand. One way in which the prostitute can do this is to build up a regular clientele who, more generally, do keep the appointments that they make. Some control can also be achieved over the nature and volume of demand through pricing systems, skills, and specialisms. The prostitute called 'Desiree' in O'Connell Davidson's study catered for men who were better off; they came to her premises, and had diverse and demanding requirements in terms of skill, equipment, and props. The clients were prepared to pay higher prices for these services than they would pay to a street prostitute. In this way, Desiree was seen to plan and control all aspects of her business: where and when to advertise; who to employ and tasks to assign; the pricing system; the services on offer; and the hours and days of business. She also was seen to exercise a great deal of control over the details of transactions with clients, and had a clearly defined split between her private and public self.

Issues concerning 'being in charge' or in control in both the public and private worlds seem to be important in managing sexuality in organizations. An interesting example of who is in charge can be found in research undertaken by Martin (1990). Taking as her example a television interview with a chief executive of a very large multinational organization, she shows how organizational practices can break down the separation between the individual's public and private lives. In this interview, the chief executive talks of how a young woman is important to the launch of a new product the next day. In order for her to be prepared for the launch, she had arranged to have a Caesarian section for the birth of her child. The company had 'insisted' that she stay at home, and her involvement with the product launch was going to be maintained and televised on closed-circuit television.

Accounting for emotion

We have seen how traditional organizational theory has stressed the functional and how managers try to shape worker behaviour to organizational objectives using an armoury of rules, regulation, and inducements. The view is of a 'passionless organization' (Fineman, 1994)—but organizational theory needs to account for the process and interaction of emotions, both felt and displayed, that are as diverse as pride, jealousy, love, hate, happiness, despair, anger, grief, joy, fear, and excitement; it has only begun to do so during the last two decades.

Feelings connect us with our realities and provide internal feedback on how we are doing, what we want, and what we might do next. We work over our feelings, have feelings about feelings, and are guided by previous experience and social scripts: for example, asking ourselves how we should really feel about what is happening; whether we should I be feeling upset; and why we are feeling angry. Some people are going to feel intrinsic pleasure from aesthetic work, such as dancing, designing, or painting; surgeons, computer programmers, and mathematicians are reputed to report similar feelings of deep involvement in work (Fineman, 1996). Being in organizations involves us in worry, envy, hurt, sadness, boredom, excitement, and other emotions. Boredom, for example, has been found to be the second most commonly suppressed emotion at work (Mann, 2007)—but even if you feel dull indifference to work, this is still feeling.

Of course, workers may also develop feelings for certain colleagues.

Organizational romance

While managements may historically have attempted to expunge erotic and romantic relations at work (Burrell, 1992) and sexual misconduct is often cited in dismissal cases (Kakabadse and Kakabadse, 2004), organizational romances are commonplace and it has been argued that the work environment has become 'increasingly conducive to the formation of workplace romance' (Powell, 2001). Organizations are natural breeding grounds for romantic involvements: there is abundant evidence that individuals tend to prefer others with similar attitudes (Smith et al., 1993) and similar attitudes are often found among people working together. A recent survey by *Personnel Today* (2006) found that about 50 per cent of respondents had already had a relationship with a colleague and that 40 per cent of UK workers were looking for love in the office. Lack of time is the main reason why people look to colleagues for romantic relationships, because 44 per cent of those interviewed are working more than 40 hours a week.

STOP AND THINK **Consensual relationships between staff and students at university**

University teachers are advised not to develop intimate relationships with students. If they do develop a consensual relationship, the university teacher is asked to declare that a relationship has developed and to ask that another member of staff assess the student's work.

Is this what you witness as good practice?

(*Source:* Fearn, 2008)

Romantic relationships can, however, produce a serious practical problem for managers, because they can distort the smooth functioning of organizations (Quinn, 1977). There have been some high-level cases of romantic entanglements that have had devastating effects on careers: for example, *Boeing*'s married chief executive was fired after his affair with a colleague was exposed (Guest, 2005).

Initially, couples usually try to keep their relationship a secret because some organizations have explicit rules against romantic relationships, and fear of gossip and disapproval fosters secrecy. Where one or both of the participants is married, the predominant fear is that family members will find out. There can be negative impacts if favouritism or special treatment is shown to the new partner in the relationship; this causes jealousy and resentment (Lobel et al., 1994). Sometimes, hostility can be generated by the romance in a work group, and output and productivity lowered (Mainiero, 1986). Couples can experience role conflict—that is, conflict between their personal and professional roles: for example, a couple might attend a presentation ceremony dinner along with the company's top executives; during dinner, someone at the table may suggest to the male executive that it is inappropriate to bring his lover along, because her corporate status is not the same as that of the other executive guests (Collins, 1983). A more disruptive impact can come about when the affair ends (Warfield, 1987). In office romances that cross the lines of authority in an organization, there is the potential for exploitation: for example, sexual favours to the boss might be offered in return for promotion; conversely, a boss may manipulate a subordinate by threatening to withdraw from the relationship unless a work deadline is met (Mainiero, 1993). In the most extreme cases, the affair can lead to a harassment claim, of which there have been a number of high-level cases: for example, Bill Clinton and Paula Jones (*American Lawyer*, 1997; Taylor, 1997; *Macleans*, 1998), and Anita Hill and Clarence Thomas (Trix and Sankar, 1998). But it is nonetheless questionable whether or not organizations can stop romances happening (Riach and Wilson, 2007).

It would be wrong, however, to leave the impression that the impact of romantic relationships is only ever negative. Mainiero (1989) describes several cases in which couples report that their personal and professional lives were enhanced by an office romantic involvement. For example, one couple found that, when a deadline had to be met, they worked together at home to meet that deadline. In another case, the couple reported that they had benefited from each other's critical comment on management style and work behaviour. The research literature on sexual harassment does tend to show, however, that for every happy outcome, there are many more unhappy ones.

Sexual harassment

A major catalyst that raised the profile of workplace sexuality in organization studies was the naming of sexual harassment in the mid-1970s (Hearn and Parkin, 2001). Sexual harassment, like bullying, is termed 'organizational violation' (Hunt et al., 2007) and is misbehaviour (Wilson, 2000; 2003; Wilson and Thompson, 2001).

Sexual harassment can take many forms, from leering, whistling, and suggestive gestures, through to sexual blackmail. It is defined by the European Parliament as unwanted conduct related to the sex of a person, with the purpose or effect of violating the dignity of a person and of creating an intimidating, hostile, degrading, humiliating or offensive environment. Much of the teasing, flirting, and joking that goes on at work between the sexes is not sexual harassment, because it is mutual; most sexual behaviour at work is seen as benign or positive (Witz et al., 1994). Sexual behaviour becomes harassment when it is unwanted and intrusive—that is, when it offends and threatens. It is for the individual to decide what behaviour is acceptable to him or her and what he or she regards as offensive. So although there is general agreement on what can constitute sexual harassment, the experience of sexual harassment is subjective in nature, partly due to problems of identification (Bimrose, 2004; Hunt et al., 2007).

In the workplace, harassers are usually male supervisors or managers. Although it is overwhelmingly women who experience sexual harassment, it is not exclusively so. For example, a recent survey found that two-fifths of employees in the UK who said that they had been sexually harassed were men (Grainger and Fitzner, 2006). Women are, however, more likely to define more experiences as harassing than men. Sexual harassment is a pervasive problem. Women are most likely to be harassed where they are in jobs dominated by men. For example, a study of the armed forces (Rutherford et al., 2006) found that sexualized behaviours (defined as jokes, stories, language, and other materials) had been experienced by almost all of the service women during the previous twelve months and 52 per cent had been in a situation in which they found it offensive. Two-thirds of respondents had encountered sexual behaviours directed at them personally during the same period. These behaviours varied from making unwelcome comments, sending sexually explicit material, and unwanted touching, through to sexual assaults; one in eight had experienced a sexual assault. Sexual harassment is more prevalent in some jobs than it is in others and some groups—for example, those from ethnic minorities (Kohlman, 2004), or lesbians, gays and bisexuals (Di Martino et al., 2003; TUC, 2007)—may be at greater risk of sexual harassment.

Sexual harassment has become widespread even over the telephone—particularly in call centres (Sczensky and Stahlberg, 2000). Most of those harassed do nothing about it; they simply hope that the offender will stop. The victims often fear not being taken seriously if they complain; they may also not want to challenge the position of the harasser, or may fear reprisals. Sexual harassment remains, then, common organizational behaviour.

EXAMPLE Organizational harassment

A 42-year-old balding lecturer with a beer gut and glasses has complained of being harassed by a young female student who emails him 'constantly' and rings him at home. When he mentioned this situation to his head of department, she found it funny and implied that he might have flirted with the student.

(*Source: Times Higher Education*, 5 January 2007)

Conclusion

Sexuality, emotions, and feelings play an important role in the everyday experience of organizations. Sexuality is a commodity that is often used in organizations, and emotion and feelings are key to an understanding of behaviour in organizations. The control and manipulation of employees' feelings is central to competitive advantage: emotional labour is a saleable commodity and emotions have to be managed. Some organizations will be found trying to mould employees to conform to rigid scripted emotion rules, while others may rely on existing emotional skills that the employee is seen to already possess. Adherence to emotion rules is expected. The management of emotions is particularly important in the case of romantic relationships at work—but sexual harassment must be managed.

Having looked at how management and organizational behaviour can be approached more critically, we now go on to look at more classical approaches—but including a critique. We begin by looking at motivation.

KEY POINTS

- Workplace sexuality has been a focus of discussion among organizational behaviour researchers for over twenty years—yet the topic remains absent from the textbooks.

- Sexuality, emotions, and feelings play an important role in the everyday experience of behaviour in organizations: we are all 'doing gender' and expressing our sexuality in our behaviour.

- 'Sexuality' refers to sex roles, sexual preference, sexual attractiveness, and notions of masculinity and feminity in organizations.

- 'Sex stereotyping' means that jobs become sex-typed as masculine or feminine—although this view of which jobs are suitable for men or women can change over time.

- 'Emotional labour' refers to the emotional control and commitment that workers are expected to exhibit—particularly when dealing with customers.

- While traditional organizational behaviour has stressed how managers should control behaviour at work through rules, regulations, and inducements—portraying a passionless organization—emotions and feelings are clearly evident in the research.

CASE STUDY

The case of prostitutes: managing emotions and the image of professionalism

We have seen how managing emotions is important for employees: it can indicate professional behaviour—that is, professionalism. Professionalism is also important for sex workers—that is, prostitutes. Prostitution has been described as the 'mutually voluntary exchange of sexual services for money or other consideration' (COYOTE, 1988: 290). Others might argue that prostitution is always by force, is always a violation against women, and is always an outrage to their dignity (for example, Barry, 1991, quoted in Van der Gaag, 1994). Some argue that a firm distinction must be made between 'free choice' prostitution, and all forms of forced and child prostitution (for example, Delacoste and Alexander, 1988). Organizations such as *Barnardos* and *The Children's Society* have campaigned to bring about change in how those under the age of 16 who work as prostitutes are seen, arguing that they should be treated as victims of abuse. But free-choice prostitution can be regarded as sex work and a form of work like any other. Many definitions rely on analogies with work or industry, calling prostitutes 'saleswomen', women 'sex workers', or women who perform 'erotic labour' (Boynton, 2002), although women and girls involved in prostitution may not always perceive what they do as work or prostitution.

Sex workers generate future business by adopting an equivalent professionalism to that found in other jobs. For example, both flight attendants and sex workers have been found to separate the realms of experience into private and public domains (McKeganey and Barnard, 1996). Publicly, they are required to act in order to present a certain 'face'; privately, they can let this go. Publicly, flight attendants' faces and feelings help to make money (although not directly for themselves); similarly, prostitutes' faces and bodies are a resource with which they make money.

Maintaining the public image requires individuals to distance themselves from the clients in some way. The most visible strategy that prostitutes use to distance themselves from clients is explicitness. From the outset, they make clear that they are sexually available—but at a price. Negotiation and contract are central concerns for prostitution. Prostitution is governed by unwritten 'rules', but because the 'rules of the game' are not fixed for clients, there are three considerations:

- what the prostitute is prepared to do;
- the nature of the client's request;
- the amount of money on offer.

All of these have to be negotiated and agreed. Throughout the process of initial negotiation, the women adopt an assertive, business-like stance in the hope of securing client compliance, so that they can dictate the terms and conditions of the sale. A large part of the rationale for this resides in an acute awareness of the potential dangers of providing sex to men who, for most part, are total strangers. Once the deal has been negotiated, additional income is dependent on the skill of the prostitute and level of naivety of the client; extra charges are incurred by the client for 'extras', such as touching (ibid.).

113

While the prostitutes describe themselves as being in charge of the encounter with the client, the client will similarly feel that he is in charge. Because the client has the money, he has the power. The business relationship is 'managed' so that both parties feel that they have control (ibid.). Sharpe (1998) describes the 'rules of the game'—that is, the unwritten code of conduct adopted by one group of prostitutes. These women claimed never to accept business without insisting that their clients use condoms. Information about whether the vice squad were patrolling, information about punters (particularly 'funny punters'), attacks, violent incidents, or strangers 'on the patch' (new prostitutes, new police in the vice squad, media people, and researchers) was exchanged, but the women never mixed socially beyond the boundaries of the patch. Most of the prostitutes developed a territorial affiliation and the 'poaching' of someone else's patch or customers was neither appreciated nor tolerated. The newcomer had to stand her ground and the war of attrition was played out until she was accepted or tolerated. The patch had a well-established internal market that controlled and regulated prices. If an individual moved her prices to attract more business, she laid herself open to retribution from the others: at least, verbal abuse, and at worst, a severe beating.

Sharpe also noted that negotiations with the clients followed 'rules'. Once it was ascertained what service the client required, he was informed of the prices and where the business would take place. It was at this point that the prostitute made the decision whether to accept or decline the business. Prices were invariably non-negotiable and the women always took the money before acting. The women always provided condoms; if a hotel room was used, the client would meet the cost. Again, being in control was a major issue for the women: being in control of the situation, the client, the location, and what their children understood were all-important for these women.

(Sources in text)

Questions

1. In what ways is sex workers' work similar and dissimilar to other paid work? (See Scambler and Scambler, 1997.)

2. What insight does the study of prostitution as work give us when we consider other types of work?

FURTHER READING

Barry, J., Chandler, J., Clark, H., Johnston, R., and Needle, D. (2000) *Organization and Management: A Critical Text*, London: Thomson Learning Chapter 1 discusses emotion, while chapter 5 discusses sex at work.

Fleming, P. (2006) 'Sexuality, power and resistance in the workplace', *Organization Studies*, 28(2): 239–56 This article investigates whether the expression of sexuality in organizations represents an opportunity for employee resistance or for increased managerial control.

Gabriel, Y., Fineman, S., and Sims, D. (2000) *Organizing and Organizations*, 2nd edn, London: Sage Chapter 12 discusses feelings and emotional control.

Linstead, S., Fulop, L., and Lilley, S. (2004) *Management and Organization: A Critical Text*, Houndmills: Palgrave Macmillan Chapter 2 focuses on gender and management.

Noon, M. and Blyton, P. (2002; 2007) *The Realities of Work*, Basingstoke: Macmillan The chapter on emotion work is excellent. It covers deep and surface acting, and how emotion and feelings are managed in service interaction.

Thompson, P. and McHugh, D. (2002) *Work Organizations: A Critical Approach*, 3rd edn, Basingstoke: Macmillan Chapter 10 covers gender, sexuality, and organizations.

LINKS TO FILMS AND NOVELS

Nine to Five (**1980**) dir. C. Higgins Starring Dolly Parton, Jane Fonda, and others, this film clearly illustrates the place that sexuality can have in the office.

RESEARCH QUESTIONS

1. In what ways can performing emotional labour be a stressful experience. (See Handy, 1995; Hochschild, 1983; Taylor and Tyler, 2000.)

2. What are the personal consequences of work? (See Sennett, 1998.)

3. 'The qualities of emotionality and rationality are dependent upon each other' (Ashforth and Humphrey, 1995). Discuss.

REFERENCES

American Lawyer (1997) 'Principles, politics and Paula Jones', *American Lawyer*, 19(1): 49.

Ashforth, B.E. and Humphrey, R.H. (1995) 'Emotion in the workplace', *Human Relations*, 48(2): 97–125.

Barry, K. (1991) *The Penn State Report on Sexual Exploitation, Violence and Prostitution*, Paris: Coalition Against Trafficking in Women/UNESCO.

Bimronse, J. (2004) 'Sexual harassment in the workplace: An ethical dilemma for career guidance practice?', *British Journal of Guidance and Counselling*, 32(1): 109–21.

Black, P. (2004) *The Beauty Industry: Gender, Culture, Pleasure*, London: Routledge.

Bolton, S. and Boyd, C. (2003) 'Trolley dolley or skilled emotion manager? Moving on from Hochschild's "emotional labour"', *Work, Employment and Society*, 17(2): 289–308.

Boynton, P. (2002) *'At the End of the Day, It's a Job': Discursive Practices around Sex Work*, London: Department of Psychiatry and Behavioural Sciences, Royal Free and University College Medical School.

Bradley, H. (1993) 'Across the great divide', in C. Williams (ed.), *Doing Women's Work: Men in Non Traditional Occupations*, London: Sage, pp. 10–28.

Breakwell, G. (1979) 'Women: group and identity?', *Women's Studies International*, 2: 9–17.

Brewis, J. (2005) 'Signing my life away? Researching sex and organization', *Organization*, 12: 493–510.

_____ and Grey, C. (1994) 'Re-eroticizing the organization: An exegesis and critique', *Gender, Work and Organization*, 1(2): 67–82.

Burke, M.E. (1993) *Coming Out of the Blue: British Police Officers Talk about their Lives in the Job as Lesbians, Gays and Bisexuals*, New York: Cassell.

Burrell, G. (1992) 'The organization of pleasure', in M. Alvesson and H. Wilmott (eds), *Critical Management Studies*, London: Sage, ch. 4.

Carter, K. (1996) 'Masculinity in prison', in J. Pilcher and A. Coffey (eds), *Gender and Qualitative Research*, Aldershot: Avebury, ch. 1.

Clarke, S. (2003) 'Would you lose more than your shirt to gain your PhD?', *Times Higher Education Supplement*, 17 January, pp. 18–19.

Cockburn, C. (1991) *In the Way of Women: Men's Resistance to Sex Equality in Organizations*, London: Macmillan.

Collins, E.G. (1983) 'Managers and lovers', *Harvard Business Review*, 16(5): 142–53.

COYOTE (1988) 'COYOTE/National Task Force on Prostitution', in F. Delacoste and P. Alexander (eds), *Sex Work: Writings by Women in the Sex Industry*, London: Virago.

Delacoste, F. and Alexander, P. (eds) (1988) *Sex Work: Writings by Women in the Sex Industry*, London: Virago.

Di Martino, V., Hoel, H., and Cooper, C.L. (2003) *Preventing Violence and Harassment in the Workplace*, Luxembourg: European Foundation for the Improvement of Living and Working Conditions, Office for the Official Publications of the European Communities.

The Economist (2002) 'Women in suits', 362(8262): 60–2.

Fearn, H. (2008) 'Sex and the university', *Times Higher Education*, 22 May, available online at http://www.timeshighereducation.co.uk/story.asp?sectioncode=26&storycode=401935

Fineman, S. (1994) 'Organizing and emotion: Towards a social construction', in J. Hassard and M. Parker (eds), *Towards a New Theory of Organizations*, London: Routledge, ch. 4.

_____ (1996), 'Emotion and organizing', in S.R. Clegg, C. Hardy, and W.R. Nord (eds), *Handbook of Organization Studies*, London: Sage, ch. 3.3.

Foucault, M. (1979) *The History of Sexuality, Vol. 1: An Introduction*, London: Allen Lane.

Furnham, A. (2008) *Personality and Intelligence at Work*, London: Routledge.

Gentleman, A. (2006) 'India grounds hostesses who are "too fat to fly"', *The Observer*, 5 November, available online at http://www.guardian.co.uk/business/2006/nov/05/theairlineindustry.india

Grainger, H. and Fitzner, G. (2006) *Fair Treatment at Work Survey 2005*, Employment Relations Research Series No. 63, London: Department of Trade and Industry.

Guest, K. (2005) 'Office affairs', *Independent on Sunday*, 13 March, available online at http://www.independent.co.uk/news/uk/this-britain/focus-the-truth-about-office-affairs-528224.html

Hall, E. (1995) *We Can't Even March Straight*, London: Vintage.

Handy, J. (1995) 'Rethinking stress: Seeing the collective', in T. Newton (ed.), *Managing Stress*, London: Sage, ch. 4.

Hearn, J. and Parkin, W. (1995) *Sex at Work: The Power and Paradox of Organizational Sexuality*, Hemel Hempstead: Prentice Hall/Harvester Wheatsheaf.

_____ (2001) *Gender, Sexuality and Violence in Organizations: The Unspoken Force of Organizational Violations*, London: Sage.

Hochschild, A.R. (1983) *The Managed Heart: Commercialisation of Human Feeling*, Berkeley, CA: University of California.

Holt, C.L. and Ellis, J.B. (1998) 'Assessing the current validity of the BEM sex-role inventory', *Sex Roles*, 39: 929–41.

Humphrey, J. (2000) 'Organizing sexualities, organization inequalities: Lesbians and gay men in public service occupations', *Gender, Work and Organization*, 6(3): 134–51.

Hunt, C., Davidson, M., Fielden, S., and Hoel, H. (2007) *Sexual Harassment in the Workplace: A Literature Review*, Working Paper Series No. 61, Manchester: Manchester Business School/EOC.

James, N. (1989) 'Emotional labour: Skill and work in the social regulation of feelings', *Sociological Review*, 37: 15–47.

Kakabadse, A. and Kakabadse, N. (2004) *Intimacy: An International Survey of the Sex Lives of People at Work*, Basingstoke: Palgrave.

Kitzinger, C., Wilkinson, S., and Perkins, R. (1992) 'Theorizing heterosexuality', *Feminism and Psychology*, 2(3): 293–324.

Knorr-Cetina, K. and Bruegger, U. (2000) 'The market as an object of attachment: Exploring postsocial relations in financial markets', *Canadian Journal of Sociology*, 25(2): 141–68.

Kohlman, M.H. (2004) 'Person or position? The demographics of sexual harassment in the workplace', *Equal Opportunities International*, 23(3–5): 143–62.

Korczynski, M. (2003) 'Communities of coping: Collective emotional labour in service work', *Organization*, 10(1): 55–79.

Lerum, K. (2004) 'Sexuality, power and camaraderie in service work', *Gender and Society*, 18(6): 756–76.

Lobel, S.A., Quinn, R.E., St Clair, L., and Warfield, A. (1994) 'Love without sex: The impact of psychological intimacy between men and women at work', *Organizational Dynamics*, 23: 5–16.

Lopez, S.H. (2006) Emotional labor and organized emotional care: Conceptualizing nursing home care work, *Work and Occupations*, 33: 133–60.

Lupton, B. (2000) 'Maintaining masculinity: Men who do women's work', *British Journal of Management*, 11: S33–48.

Macleans (1998) 'Is Clinton home free?', 111(15): 13.

Mainiero, L.A. (1986) 'A review and analysis of power dynamics in organizational romances', *Academy of Management Review*, 11(4): 750–62.

_____ (1989) *Office Romance: Love, Power and Sex in the Workplace*, New York: Macmillan.

_____ (1993) 'Dangerous liaisons? A review of current issues concerning male and female romantic relationships in the workplace', in E.A. Fagenson (ed.), *Women in Management: Trends, Issues and Challenges in Managerial Diversity*, London: Sage, ch. 6.

Mann, S. (2007) 'The boredom boom', *The Psychologist*, 20(2): 90–3.

Martin, J. (1990) 'Deconstructing organizational taboos: The suppression of gender conflict in organizations', *Organization Science*, 1(4): 339–59.

McDowell, L. (1997) *Capital Culture: Gender at Work in the City*, Oxford: Blackwell.

McKeganey, N. and Barnard, M. (1996) *Sex Work on the Streets: Prostitutes and their Clients*, Buckingham: Open University Press.

Mellor, P. and Shilling, C. (1997) *Re-Forming the Body: Religion, Community and Modernity*, London: Sage.

Miller, S.L., Forest, K.B., and Jurik, N.C. (2003) 'Diversity in blue: lesbian and gay police officers in a masculine occupation', *Men and Masculinities*, 5(4): 355–85.

Milne, J. (2006) 'Female students turn to prostitution to pay fees', *Sunday Times*, 8 October, available online at http://www.timesonline.co.uk

Mirchandani, K. (2003) 'Challenging racial silences in studies of emotion work: Contributions from anti-racist feminist theory', *Organization Studies*, 24(5): 721–42.

Monaghan, L.F. (2002) 'Embodying gender, work and organization: Solidarity, cool loyalties and contested hierarchy in a masculinist occupation, *Gender, Work and Organization*, 9(5): 504–36.

Moreno, E. (1995) 'Rape in the field: Reflections from a survivor', in D. Kulick and M. Willson (eds), *Taboo, Sex, Identity and Erotic Subjectivity in Anthropological Fieldwork*, London/ New York: Routledge, pp. 219–50.

Mumby, D.K. and Putnam, L.L. (1992) 'The politics of emotion: A feminist reading of bounded rationality', *Academy of Management Review*, 17: 466–85.

O'Connell Davidson, J. (1995) 'The anatomy of "free choice" prostitution', *Gender, Work and Organization*, 2(1): 1–10.

O'Neill, M. (1997) 'Prostitute women now', in G. Scambler and A. Scambler (eds), *Rethinking Prostitution: Purchasing Sex in the 1990s*, London: Routledge, ch. 1.

Open University (2006) 'Why women want to join the club', News and Events, available online at http://www.open.ac.uk/alumni/news-events/publications/openeye-bulletins/2006_archive/october-2006

Patterson, S. (2008) 'If we don't give a hoot about Hooters, we're all in Pottersville now', Opinion and Debate, *Sunday Herald*, 20 April, p. 40.

Peccei, R. and Rosenthal, P. (2000) 'Front-line responses to customer orientation programmes: A theoretical and empirical analysis', *International Journal of Human Resource Management*, 11(3): 562–90.

Personnel Today (2006) 'Two in five UK workers are looking for love in the office', 10 February, available online at http://www.personneltoday.com

Plas, J.M. and Hoover-Dempsey, K.V. (1988) *Working Up a Storm: Anger, Anxiety, Joy and Tears on the Job*, New York: Norton.

Podmore, D. and Spencer, A. (1982) 'Women lawyers in England: The experience of inequality', *Work and Occupations*, 9(3): 337–61.

Powell, G.N. (2001) 'Workplace romances between senior level executives and lower-level employees: An issue of work disruption and gender', *Human Relations*, 54(11): 1519–44.

Pringle, R. (1989) *Secretaries Talk: Sexuality, Power and Work*, London: Verso.

_____ (1990) 'Bureaucracy, rationality and sexuality: The case of secretaries', in J. Hearn, D. Sheppard., P. Tancred-Sheriff, and G. Burrell (eds), *The Sexuality of Organization*, London: Sage

_____ and Collings, S. (1993) 'Women and butchery: Some cultural taboos', *Australian Feminist Studies*, 17: 29–40.

Quinn, R.E. (1977) 'Coping with Cupid: The formation, impact and management of romantic relationships in organizations', *Administrative Science Quarterly*, 22: 30–45.

Rafaeli, A. and Sutton, R.I. (1991) 'Emotional contrast strategies as means of social influence: Lessons from criminal interrogators and bill collectors', *Academy of Management Journal*, 34: 749–75.

Reskin, B. (1993) 'Sex segregation in the workplace', *Annual Review of Sociology*, 19: 241–70.

Riach, K. and Wilson, F. (2007) 'Don't screw the crew: Exploring the rules of engagement in organizational romance', *British Journal of Management*, 18: 79–92.

Rutherford, S., Schneider, R., and Walmsley, A. (2006) *Agreement on Preventing and Dealing Effectively with Sexual Harassment: Quantitative and Qualitative Research into Sexual Harassment in the Armed Forces*, Ministry of Defence/EOC, available online at http://www.mod.uk/defenceinternet/home

Sanders, T. (2004) 'Controllable laughter: Managing sex work through humour', *Sociology*, 38(2): 273–91.

Sargent, A.G. (1983) *The Androgynous Manager*, New York: AMOCOM.

Scambler, G. and Scambler, A. (eds) (1997) *Rethinking Prostitution: Purchasing Sex in the 1990s*, London: Routledge.

Schilt, K. (2006) 'Just one of the guys? How transmen make gender visible at work', *Gender and Society*, 20(4): 465–90.

Sczensky, S. and Stahlberg, D. (2000) 'Sexual harassment over the telephone: Occupational risk at call centres', *Work and Stress*, 14(2): 121–36.

Sennett, R. (1998) *The Corrosion of Character: The Personal Consequences of Work in the New Capitalism*, New York: W.W. Norton.

Seymour, D. and Sandiford, P. (2005) 'Learning emotion rules in service organizations: Socialization and training in the UK public-house sector', *Work, Employment and Society*, 19: 547–64

Sharma, U. and Black, P. (2001) 'Look good, feel better: Beauty therapy as emotional labour', *Sociology*, 35(4): 913–31.

Sharpe, K. (1998) *Red Light, Blue Light: Prostitutes, Punters and the Police*, Aldershot: Ashgate Publishing.

Sheppard, D. (1989) 'Organizations, power and sexuality: The image and self image of women managers', in J. Hearn, D.L. Sheppard, P. Tancred Sheriff, and G. Burrell (eds), *The Sexuality of Organization*, London: Sage, ch. 10.

Simpson, R. (2004) 'Masculinity at work: The experiences of men in female-dominated occupations', *Work, Employment and Society*, 18: 349–68.

Skelton, A. (1999) 'The inclusive university? A case of the experiences of gay and bisexual higher education in the UK', in P. Fogelberg, J. Hearn, L. Husu, and T. Mankkinen (eds), *Hard Work in the Academy*, Helsinki: Helsinki University Press, pp. 190–209.

Smith, E.R., Becker, M.A., Byrne, D., and Przybyla, D.P. (1993) 'Sexual attitudes of males and females as predictors of interpersonal attraction and marital compatibility', *Journal of Applied Social Psychology*, 23(13): 1011–34.

Taylor, S. (1997) 'Her case against Clinton', *American Lawyer*, 18(9): 56.

_____ and Tyler, M. (2000) 'Emotional labour and sexual difference in the airline industry', *Work, Employment and Society*, 14(1): 77–95.

Thompson, G. (2000) *Watch My Back*, Chichester: Summersdale.

Times Online (2006) 'Bingeing women spur rise of the female bouncer', 5 February, available online at http://www.timesonline.co.uk

Toerien, M. and Kitzinger, C. (2007) 'Emotional labour in the beauty salon: Turn design of task-directed talk', *Feminism Psychology*, 17: 162–72.

Trades Union Congress (TUC) (2007) 'Union report highlights high levels of harassment for lesbian, gay and bisexual workers', Press release, 23 May, available online at http://www.tuc.org.uk/equality/tuc-13342-f0.cfm

Trix, F. and Sankar, A. (1998) 'Women's voices and experiences of the Hill-Thomas hearings', *American Anthropologist*, 100(1): 32.

Tyler, M. and Abbott, P. (1998) 'Chocs away: Weight watching in the contemporary airline industry', *Sociology*, 32(3): 433–50.

Van der Gaag, N. (1994) 'Prostitution: Soliciting for change', *New Internationalist*, 252(February): 4–7.

Warfield, A. (1987) 'Co-worker romances: Impact on the work group and on career-oriented Women', *Personnel*, 64(5): 22–35.

West, C. and Zimmerman, D.H. (1987) 'Doing gender', *Gender and Society*, 1: 125–51.

Williams, C. (2003) 'Sky service: The demands of emotional labour in the airline industry', *Gender, Work and Employment*, 10(5): 513–50.

Wilson, F.M. (2000) 'The subjective experience of sexual harassment: Cases of students', *Human Relations*, 53(8): 1081–97.

_____ (2003) *Organizational Behaviour and Gender*, London: McGraw Hill.

_____ and Thompson, P. (2001) 'Sexual harassment as an exercise of power', *Gender, Work and Organization*, 8(1): 61–83.

Witz, A., Halford, S., and Savage, M. (1994) *Organized Bodies: Gender, Sexuality, Bodies and Organizational Culture*, Paper presented to the British Sociological Association Conference 'Sexualities in the Social Context', University of Central Lancashire, March.

Wuamett, Y. (2001) 'I was a Playboy Bunny', *BBC News*, 6 April, available online at http://news.bbc.co.uk

Classic Organizational Behaviour and the Critique

Motivation

6

Introduction

How should managers motivate employees? Is motivating employees all about using common sense as a manager—or is there more to it than that?

Having looked at the rationale behind job design, and described what work means and how it might be experienced, this chapter turns to different theories of motivation, considering why and how they arose, and what attempts have—and can—be made to influence motivation or improve the quality of working life for employees.

But why would a manager want to know about motivation theory? The theory underlying motivation is—although rarely stated—that improving the motivation of the employee improves output and other factors. Managers are interested in motivating and creating

sufficient job satisfaction that work will be done adequately or, even better, continually improved.

This chapter covers both content and process theories of motivation. Content theories attempt to describe the individual's needs, drives, and goals, while process theories focus on the individual's interactions with the environment, as well as his or her cognitive processing—that is, his or her judgements about rewards, costs, and preferences.

This chapter covers:

- motivation as a problem;
- content theories of motivation;
- process theories of motivation;
- some further thoughts on motivation'
- job satisfaction and positive outcomes for organizations.

Motivation as a problem

It would appear that the motivation of employees is one the predominant problems faced by managers. The ability to influence employees' motivation is seen as crucial to the effective management of organizations. A better understanding of employees' motivation is supposed to enable management to cause its subordinates to act in a particular way. When chief executives say that people are their 'biggest asset' or their 'only source of competitive advantage', it suggests that they value their human resource. Advocates of humane work practices have long needed some proof that treating people well was good for business, as well as good ethical behaviour. Managers want to know how to get their employees to do what they want them to—and the 'right' theory of motivation potentially has much to offer. The right theory might explain a range of behaviours found in organizations, and may even provide the key to increased productivity and job satisfaction. A highly motivated worker is likely to be a happy and productive one. He or she might be easier to manage, and could help to realize the objectives that a manager has been set and on which they will be appraised.

Conventional management theory is managerialist—that is, premised on isolating what compels employees to work, to work at particular levels, or to specific standards and to keep working at them (Brewis et al., 2006). It is also unitarist, because it is presented as though managers and workers will be working together towards 'good' corporate behaviour (Fulop and Linstead, 2004)—that is, worker efforts will be aligned with management priorities.

Motivation theory tends to be dominated by psychology, but sociology also has an interesting contribution to make to our understanding of how motivation may be viewed as a social construction, shaped by people, rather than a scientific objective thing that can be manipulated to change behaviour. Motivation, as an idea, is useful to us when meaning is lost from jobs. Sievers (1986), for example, has argued that motivation only became an issue for management or organizational theorists when meaning was either lost or disappeared from work: the more jobs became meaningless and fragmented, due that 'rational' management process at which we looked earlier, the more motivation theories developed (Sievers, 1993). Motivation theories have then become surrogates for the search for meaning (Thompson and McHugh, 2002: 306). Sievers (1993) also notes that the assumption that people can only motivate themselves and that others can facilitate self-motivation only in a very indirect and limited way, through the management of tasks and other resources, seems to be totally untenable.

No fewer than 140 definitions of motivation have been found in the literature (Kleininga and Kleininga, 1981). While Vroom (1964) defines it as 'a process governing choices made by persons or lower organisms among alternative forms of voluntary activity', Dewsbury (1978) says that the concept of motivation tends to be used as a 'garbage pail' for a variety of factors, the nature of which is not well understood. Motivational models are commonly divided between those that focus on an individual's internal attributes, needs, drives, and goals—that is, content theories—and those that focus on the individual's interactions with the environment, and cognitive judgements about rewards, costs, and preferences—that is, process theories. Discussions of motivation theory usually start with content theories: principally, Maslow's need hierarchy and Herzberg's two-factor theory.

Content theories of motivation

Maslow's theory

Maslow's 'hierarchy of needs' tends to be treated as classical within the field of organizational behaviour; it has been referred to as a 'classic among classics' (Matteson and Ivancevich, 1989: 369). It remains a conceptual starting point for motivation theory and appears to have a common-sense appeal for which students develop a particular affection. In Maslow's (1943) theory of motivation, there are thought to be five sets of needs that people possess; as they satisfy most of the needs at one level, they move up to seek satisfaction at the next. These needs are innate, and so are universal and unchanging. Physiological needs—that is, the lowest needs for food and drink—are followed by safety needs, love needs, esteem needs, and finally, the need for self-actualization—that is, the desire to realize one's ultimate potential. 'Self-actualization' is defined as the 'desire to become more and more what one is, to become everything that one is capable of becoming' (Maslow, 1954: 92), a need that can be expressed in a range of ways both inside and outside of work.

Implicit in the idea that a person is motivated to satisfy needs is the idea that needs serve as inevitable determinants of action. Maslow (1943) speaks of self-actualizing behaviour as a compulsive thing, in evidence among musicians who must make music and artists who must paint. This formulation provides an explanation of behaviour—'I *had* to do it'—and can help in maintaining behaviour in the face of negative reactions about its worth or acceptability. But what about people who find themselves in jobs that will not help them to satisfy higher-order needs? Individuals in lower-level occupations are more likely to be motivated by lower-order needs—that is, physiological and safety needs—because these are not sufficiently gratified to allow needs at a higher order—that is, self-esteem and self-actualization—to become prepotent (more powerful).

The strength of the theory lies in the fact that it supports management practices that encourage employee autonomy and personal growth, because these will enable employees to satisfy esteem and self-actualization needs. Proper management of the ways in which people work and earn their living can improve them, and improve the world—and, in this sense, can be a utopian revolutionary technique (Maslow, 1965: 1). There are, however, limits to what can be achieved: it is, for example, appropriate only when employees are already developed (ibid.: 15–33).

STOP AND THINK Is Maslow's theory kitsch?

Linstead (2002) argues that Maslow's theory is kitsch (defined as 'worthless pretentiousness'). Is he right?

The critique of Maslow

Maslow's theory lacks empirical support (Wahba and Bridwell, 1976) as Maslow himself admitted when, in 1962, he wrote: 'My motivation theory was published 20 years ago and in all that time nobody repeated it, or tested it, or really analysed it or criticized it. They just used it, swallowed it whole with only the minor modifications' (Lowry, 1982: 63).

In 1972, Alderfer suggested a revision of Maslow's need hierarchy. In Maslow's model, if the individual is frustrated at a particular need level, he or she stays at that level until the need is satisfied. Once it is satisfied, the individual progresses to the next level of the hierarchy. Unfortunately, empirical research has consistently failed to confirm this (for example, Hall and Nougaim, 1968; Lawler and Suttle, 1972; Rauschenberger et al., 1980). Hall and Nougaim (1968) found that, as managers advanced, safety needs became less important, while higher-order needs were more important, but found also that a process of career change and advancement could explain this. Alderfer (1972) proposed that, when an individual becomes frustrated at a particular need level, he or she might regress to a lower level. He also suggested that instead of the five-level model, a more appropriate hierarchy would be based on three need levels: those for existence, relatedness, and growth. This theory has not, however, received much more empirical support than Maslow's.

Cullen (1994) goes one step further than Alderfer and says that Maslow's methodology is suspect. It has also been accused of being occupationally biased—that is, of not considering issues such as how occupation and class influence whether or not an we might aspire to self-actualization (Friedlander, 1965), culturally biased (Nevis, 1983), male biased (Cullen, 1994; Cullen and Gotell, 2002), better understood as a mythical quest for the meaning of life, and elitist (Shaw and Colimore, 1988). Further, the needs hierarchy has been accused of legitimating and perpetuating exploitative relations (Knights and Wilmott, 1974–75: 219; Buss, 1979): it legitimizes how and why people remain motivated, producing more for those who own and control capital. At the same time, it allows for finding imagination, ingenuity, and creativity in the average person (McGregor, 1960) and supports the move away from the more negative assumptions of human nature that underpin the practices of scientific management. It might be said, then, to contain contradictory premises: there is a 'democratic' one, which emphasizes authenticity, self-fulfilment, and respect for the choices, preferences, and values of each individual; at the same time, there is an 'aristocratic' premise, which emphasizes vocational competence, self-criticism, and deference to the choices, preferences, and values of the self-actualizing elite (Aron, 1977; Cullen, 1997). For Maslow, the 'good' society is one in which the 'biological elite' are given the opportunity to develop their superiority, but are protected from the 'almost inevitable malice of the biologically non-gifted' (Hoffman, 1996: 71), who cannot accept the reality that their inferiority is a matter of biological chance. The theory has intuitive appeal and influence, because it is concerned with individual superiority and social dominance (Cullen, 1997).

But do people, in reality, tend only to seek out the company of others once they have had enough to eat (Watson, 1996)? Might the hierarchy be accused of explaining away fetishes about sex, food, security, and social esteem by conceiving of them as healthy needs, only one or two steps away from the need to breathe (Knights and Wilmott, 1974–75: 219)? Does it allow people to think about being propelled by their needs and therefore shield them from the responsibility of choice? It is not difficult to think about problems with Maslow's hierarchy of needs. It is possible that they have structurally different hierarchies or that they differ in their concept formation, so that no two of us use identical categories or categorization rules. It is also possible that these needs are not hard-wired biological and/or psychological mechanisms, but rather cognitive processes. And uncertainty in the workplace might lead to an emphasis on affiliation motives: the more uncertain the environment, the more likely individuals are to exert more effort to develop and maintain relationships (Veroff et al., 1984).

STOP AND THINK How useful is Maslow's theory?

Watson (2002) argues that students only 'surface learn', so that motivation is linked with Maslow. This approach is typified in the phrase: 'Motivation, that's Maslow, isn't it?'

Is he right? Look at Watson's (1996; 2002; 2004) argument and evaluate for yourself the usefulness of Maslow's theory.

Herzberg's theory

Herzberg (1968) says that there is a manager in every audience who thinks that the simplest, surest, and most direct way of motivating someone is to 'kick them in the ass'—that is, the 'KITA', as he abbreviated it. There are various forms of this theory: the literal one is inelegant, contradicting the precious image of benevolence that most organizations cherish, and often resulting in the employee simply 'kicking' the manager in return; positive KITA, meanwhile, rewards the desired behaviour (like the autonomous working of Thompson and McHugh, 2002), but is not motivation. Herzberg's theory of motivation starts with the premise that the factors involved in producing job satisfaction and motivation are separate and distinct from the factors that lead to job dissatisfaction. These two feelings are not opposites of each other; rather, the opposite of job satisfaction is no job satisfaction, while the opposite of job dissatisfaction is no job dissatisfaction.

Herzberg believes that the growth or motivator factors that are intrinsic to work are achievement, recognition for achievement, the work itself, responsibility, and growth or advancement. These factors are to do with the job content. Motivators are the primary cause of job satisfaction. Motivators cause positive job attitudes, because they satisfy the worker's need for self-actualization (Maslow, 1954)—that is, the individual's ultimate goal.

Hygiene factors stand in contrast to motivators. Hygiene factors are the primary cause of unhappiness in work. The hygiene factors that are to do with the context of the job are extrinsic to the job and include company policy, administration, supervision, interpersonal relationships, working conditions, salary, status, and security.

Twelve different investigations informed the theory: research that covered a diverse range of employees, including lower-level supervisors, professional women, agricultural administrators, men about to retire from management positions, hospital maintenance personnel, nurses, food handlers, military officers, engineers, teachers, housekeepers, accountants, foremen, and engineers. Interviewees were asked open-ended questions about their jobs, and about when they felt bad or good about their jobs (Herzberg et al., 1959). They were asked what job events had occurred in their work that had led to extreme satisfaction or extreme dissatisfaction.

In an attempt to enrich jobs, management, Herzberg argues, has 'horizontally loaded' jobs. For example, management might challenge the employee by increasing the amount of production expected of him or her: instead of tightening 10,000 bolts a day, he or she might be challenged to see if he or she can tighten 20,000 bolts. But this merely enlarges the meaninglessness of the job. Instead, Herzberg recommends enriching work by 'vertical loading'. This can be achieved by removing some controls, while retaining accountability—that is, by increasing the accountability of individuals for their own work, perhaps by giving them a complete natural unit of work (for example, giving an employee a whole job rather than a small part). The supervisor or manager could grant additional authority to an employee, make periodic reports directly available to the worker rather than the supervisor, introduce new and more difficult tasks, or assign individual specialized tasks enabling him or her to become an 'expert'. But not all jobs can be enriched; nor do all jobs *need* to be enriched. (Visit http://www.youtube.com and search for 'Jumping for the jelly beans' to see Herzberg discuss his ideas.)

Herzberg's theory suggested that a job should enhance employee motivation to the extent that it provides opportunities for achievement, recognition, responsibility, advancement, and growth in competence. These principles gave rise to a series of generally successful job enlargement experiments in the *American Telephone and Telegraph Company*, summarized by Ford (1969). A number of researchers were, however, unable to provide empirical support for some of the major tenets of the theory (for example, Dunnette et al., 1967; Hinton, 1968; King, 1970). A more recent example of Herzberg-based job redesign can be found in the so-called 'empowerment' initiatives—such as the *Marriot Hotels* 'Whatever it takes' programme, which sought to empower staff to satisfy customer needs (Lashley, 1997: 49–50)—at which we will look further in Chapter 15.

The critique of Herzberg

Many critics find it a little strange—and a little more than coincidence—that Herzberg's two sets of factors fit so neatly into two boxes: 'intrinsic' contributing to job satisfaction, and 'extrinsic', to dissatisfaction. Researchers have questioned whether these are separate and distinct factors giving different outcomes. It is conceivable, for example, that a new company policy (a hygiene factor) could have a significant effect on a worker's interest in the work itself or his or her success with it (Locke, 1976; Tietjen and Myers, 1998). In a study by Ewan (1963), it was found that hygiene factors—that is, dissatisfiers—sometimes actually acted as satisfiers, while satisfiers (motivators) sometimes acted in the predicted manner, and sometimes caused both satisfaction and dissatisfaction.

Researchers have also questioned whether the differences in result reflect defensive processes at work within the individual. On the one hand, individuals may be more likely to perceive the causes of satisfaction within the self and therefore describe experiences invoking their own achievement—that is, a recognition of advancement in their job. On the other hand, dissatisfaction is attributed not to personal inadequacies, but rather to factors in the work environment (Vroom and Maier, 1961). Put simply, employees interviewed were taking credit for the satisfying events, such as advancement or recognition, while blaming others, such as supervisors, subordinates, and peers, for dissatisfying situations (Locke, 1976).

Locke (1976) also criticizes Herzberg's analysis for placing an emphasis on the number of times that a particular factor was mentioned. Even though a dissatisfying factor is recorded numerously, this does not necessarily imply that this factor is a significant problem or even an irritation to the worker. Locke suggests that the measurement of intensity of satisfaction or dissatisfaction, rather than frequency, might have been used.

Centers and Bugental (1966) set out to look at the strength of intrinsic and extrinsic job factors in a sample of the entire working population. Respondents were asked: 'Which of these things is the most important factor keeping you in your present job?' (ibid.: 194). Answers included extrinsic factors, such as pay, good coworkers, and job security, while the intrinsic included interesting work, skilled work, and job satisfaction. The researchers found that intrinsic job components were more valued among white-collar groups than blue-collar groups; the extrinsic job components were more valued in blue-collar groups. No consistent sex differences appeared in the extent to which they valued intrinsic or extrinsic job satisfaction in general, although men placed a slightly higher value than women on self-expression in their work. They concluded that the job motivations of workers at higher level stem from the work itself, the skill required, and the interest value of the work. At lower levels, job motivations are centred in facts that are external to the work itself. These findings are not surprising if one considers what else there is to value other than extrinsic factors in low-level jobs. Further, individuals in low-level occupations may not be sufficiently gratified to allow higher-order needs to become prepotent.

More recently, the issue of trust in a supervisor—fundamental to good relationships with the supervisor—was found to be an important variable in predicting job satisfaction (and therefore in reported absence and the desire to quit). Trust was found to be just as important as intrinsic factors (Barton Cunningham and MacGregor, 2000). Fostering or maintaining trusting relationships between individuals who have to work together could therefore help to enhance the benefits inherent to improving the design of a job.

McClelland's need for achievement theory

Motives are believed to function to energize and direct behaviour. David McClelland and his colleagues are specifically interested in how people are motivated to achieve—that is, in their need for achievement. The achievement motive is defined in McClelland's theory as a process of planning and striving for excellence (McClelland et al., 1953). People with a high need for achievement have a strong desire to assume personal responsibility for performing a task; they tend to set difficult goals and have a strong desire for feedback about their performance (ibid.). McClelland believes that there is a connection between the need for achievement and economic growth: the more individuals have a need for achievement, the greater the economic growth. Innate and early-learned need for achievement is an essential characteristic of entrepreneurs.

David McClelland and his colleagues believe that there are two types of motive that can be identified using different research instruments: 'implicit' motives develop early in childhood, at a preverbal stage, and tend to be poorly represented and difficult to articulate; 'self-attributed' motives are thought to develop later in childhood and are more readily accessible to consciousness. Implicit motives are assessed indirectly with projective instruments—typically, the thematic apperception test (TAT). Participants might be given four minutes in which to create a story in response to one of four–six black-and-white pictures used to assess need for achievement (for example, a picture of female scientists, or of an executive or architect at a desk). The supporting theory argues that people will project their own feelings, motives, and needs into the picture. Participants are asked to write a story in response to a question, or questions, about (for example) what is going on in this situation, what has led up to it, and what has happened in the past. The stories are then analysed by a coder, who has to interpret what has been said in the story; he or she searches for projected expressions of achievement. McClelland and his colleagues have devised a scoring system for need for achievement (ibid.).

The second technique for assessing need for achievement is through questionnaires. Self-attributed motives are assessed with self-report questionnaires containing, for example, true-or-false questions such as 'I enjoy difficult work'. (For a recent application, see Thrash and Elliot, 2002.) The scale and questions that have been most commonly used to look at need for achievement are the achievement scale, from the personality research form which assesses conscious motivation (Jackson, 1974). But it has been noted that it does not include the need for 'mastery' [sic], the need for work, and the need competitiveness, which are seen to overlap with, or be components of, the need for achievement (Helmreich and Spence, 1978). Goal commitment and perceived goal difficulty might also be components of the need for achievement (Johnson and Perlow, 1992). These are scales that are now likely to be added in research on need for achievement to give a multi-component view.

The critique of McClelland

There have been some questions raised about this relationship between the need for achievement and entrepreneurs (Frey, 1984; Gilleard, 1989). Other writers have argued that the influencing attributes of entrepreneurs are paramount (Furnham, 1992); the successful entrepreneur is some- one who can 'get things done through other people' (Timmons et al., 1985: 115). Entrepreneurs need managerial skills (Hisrich, 1990). The argument that need for achievement is the dominant motive disposition for entrepreneurs may be in conflict, then, with other research (Langan-Fox and Roth, 1995).

The projective test has been criticized for being complicated and time-consuming, both in adminis- tration and scoring (Gjesm and Nygard, 1970). It is seen by some to be subjective. It is difficult to inter- pret the stories and the interpreter may need experience in clinical psychology to be competent (see Hansemark, 1997). It is also criticized for having low predictive validity and reliability (Entwhistle, 1972; Fineman, 1977).

Early research using projective measurement techniques found that women have a lower need for achievement than men (McClelland et al., 1953; Veroff et al., 1953). This was explained in part by a perception of the need to compete as a masculine attribute. But later research showed that women, in general, actually possess a comparable need for achievement (Stein and Bailey, 1975; Lips and Colwill, 1978)—or even a higher need for achievement (Veroff et al., 1975; Chusmir, 1985)—than men.

The most obvious weakness with the questionnaire is that subjects make choices about what can be seen as socially acceptable: they can create an ideal picture of themselves. Further, links between questionnaires and projective tests are questionable: Fineman (1977) found no correlation between the results of questionnaires and TAT tests.

McGregor's Theory X and Theory Y

In the late 1950s, Douglas McGregor took a different approach to motivation theory and questioned the assumptions that were held about employees. McGregor (1957; 1960) argues that behind every managerial decision or actions are assumptions about human nature and human behaviour. He characterizes traditional management thinking on motivation as 'Theory X'—that is, a traditional view of direction and control, characterized by the following implicit assumptions.

1. The average human being has an inherent dislike of work and will avoid it if he or she can.

2. Because of this human characteristic of dislike of work, most people must be coerced, directed, and threatened with punishment to get them to put forth adequate effort toward the achievement of organizational objectives.

3. The average human being prefers to be directed, wishes to avoid responsibility, has relatively little ambition, and wants security above all.

STOP AND THINK

Are these your assumptions about work?

The inadequacy of Theory X is demonstrated by McGregor's reference to a number of common problems faced by managers. Individual incentive plans do not induce added productivity, because they run counter to major non-economic motives, such as the desire for group approval; performance appraisal, meanwhile, tends to keep employees in a state of childlike dependence. McGregor acknowledges that many of these criticisms were not new, of course; some had been more graphically illustrated in Dalton's (1959) *Men Who Manage*.

McGregor asks managers also to consider a Theory Y, with a different set of assumptions, as follows.

1. The expenditure of physical and mental effort in work is as natural as play or rest. The average human being does not inherently dislike work; work may be source of satisfaction or punishment.

2. External control and the threat of punishment are not the only means for bringing about effort towards organizational objectives. Individuals can exercise self-direction and self-control in the services of objectives to which they are committed.

3. Commitment to objectives is a function of the rewards associated with their achievement. The most significant of rewards—the satisfaction of ego and self-actualization needs—can be direct products of effort directed toward organizational objectives.

4. The average human being learns, under proper conditions, not only to accept, but also to seek, responsibility. Avoidance of responsibility, lack of ambition, and emphasis on security are general consequences of experience, not inherent human characteristics.

5. The capacity to exercise a relatively high degree of imagination, ingenuity, and creativity in the solution of organizational problems is widely, not narrowly, distributed in the population.

6. Under the conditions of modern industrial life, the intellectual potentialities of the average human being are only partly utilized.

McGregor is asking managers to look at their assumptions and to make them explicit. He is encouraging the realization that theory is important. He goes on to prescribe to managers how Theory Y assumptions may be put into practice.

The critique of McGregor

McGregor (along with Herzberg and other human relations theorists) is, in turn, asked to question his own assumptions. The goal of organization remains the same for traditional theorists of management and early human relations theorists: to maximize productivity in order to maximize profit. The assumptions are that there should be a coincidence between the goals of the individual and those of the organization; both should be dedicated to maximum productivity. Attending to the needs of the individual—for human relations theorists, needs for achievement, recognition, and companionship—will lead to increased productivity and greater profits. The overriding goal of the prescriptions for organizational reform is harmony. If the individual could be led to feel a significant and capable part of the organization, he or she would see that his or her own interests could be fulfilled by the harmonious interaction between him or herself and the organization.

STOP AND THINK Does organizational harmony lead to exploitation?

Overvold (1987) argues that harmony disvalues autonomy for the individual, discourages any critical stance towards organizational goals, and invites the kind of exploitation that excessive obedience permits. Is he right?

Overvold (1987) argues that much of human relations theory is naive: work is not a central life interest for all workers (Dubin et al., 1965) and it is not possible to escape conflict in organizations (Litterer, 1966). It is naive to believe that harmony and fulfilment are—or, generally, even could be—attained in an organization. Further, it is dubious that harmony should even be pursued, assuming it could be achieved. Harmony raises the spectre of the 'organization man', with the consequent loss of individuality, and the incumbent threat of a lack of creativity and devaluation as an autonomous person. Creativity and change are a product of conflict, not harmony (Dahrendorf, 1964; Litterer, 1966). (For more critique of McGregor and human relations, see also Kaplan et al., 1975; Ellerman, 2001.)

Process theories of motivation

The assumptions on which many of the theories of motivation are based need, therefore, to be questioned. Motivation is not simply about identifying a package of needs, or assuming that there is a simple relationship that can be identified between the needs of the individual and productivity. Process theories of motivation attempt to counter some of this alleged human relations naivety by conceiving of the individual as a thinking, rational actor, who is weighing up whether or not, for example, his or her greater efforts will be rewarded, or whether or not the reward for work is fair and equitable.

Equity theory

This is a cognitive, or process, theory of motivation that was put forward by Stacey Adams of the *General Electric Company* in 1963. It deals with two questions: what do people think is fair and equitable, and how do they respond when they feel that they are getting far more or far less than they deserve (Walster et al., 1978)? The theory suggests that people are capable and willing to perceive fairness in their immediate environment; people act in the light of what they regard as fair. They compare their input or 'investments' (Homans, 1961), such as ability, skill, age, education, effort, and training, to outcomes such as monetary rewards, praise, status, and improved promotion opportunities. They also compare their reward to that of others with whom they make the comparison. For example, if a skilled worker is currently earning a certain wage, but finds that other similarly skilled workers in a different company are earning more, then that skilled worker can be expected to experience feelings of deprivation if there is no obvious reason for the underpayment. He or she will then have to make a 'cognitive adjustment' in order to deal with the inequity. He or she might, for example, lower inputs and work contribution, or attempt to raise his or her outcomes, including pay. The individual may decide to redefine his or her reference group—that is, the individuals with whom he or she made the comparison—so, in this case, he or she might find another group of skilled workers in a different company with whom to make the comparison. The individual might also change his or her perceptions of the skills involved in the job, saying, for example, that the skills used in this job are not as many as those used in Company X. Alternatively, he or she could convince him or herself that he or she is well compensated in other ways. Adams (1963) lists eight different courses of action that might be taken to reduce inequity.

EXAMPLE In support of equity theory

One example that can be used to support the theory that Adams (1963) discusses is the case of checkout staff at supermarkets, which include a cashier and a 'bundler'—that is, a person who takes the bought goods out of the trolley and puts them in bags ready for the customer to take away.

Under normal conditions, the cashier's job was of a higher status, better paid, permanent, and full-time, whereas bundling was of lower status and lower pay, and was usually undertaken by part-time employees who were often young. Psychologically, bundlers were usually perceived as working for cashiers. Because the employees in both groups varied in sex, age, and education, a bundler could be directed to work for a cashier whose status (as determined by sex, age, and education) was lower than his or her own. For example, a male university student of 21 years of age could be ordered to work for a female school student cashier aged 17. The response of the bundlers to this perceived inequity was to reduce their work speed. Consequently, there was a cost to the store; those stores with greatest inequity between lower-status cashiers and higher-status bundlers experienced greater cost of operating the services. It cost approximately 27 per cent more to operate the stores in which the inequity was higher.

Evidence from other researchers has been found to support the theory. Some of the findings stress the negative ways in which workers can redress inequality. Underpayment leads to lowered job performance (Prichard et al., 1972; Lord and Hohenfeld, 1979). Underpaid workers paid on a piece-rate basis have been found to produce more goods of lower quality (Prichard, 1969). Another form of reaction to underpayment is disruptive, deviant behaviour, such as vandalism and theft (Hollinger and Clark, 1983). In fact, acts of employee theft may be an effective means of increasing outcomes in order to reduce feelings of underpayment inequity. Pilferage can be seen as 'a morally justified addition to wages … an entitlement due from exploiting employers' (Mars, 1974: 224). Greenberg (1990) found that, in manufacturing plants into which a temporary 15 per cent pay cut was introduced, the workers felt highly underpaid and employee theft rates were as much as 250 per cent higher than under normal pay conditions. Higher rates of theft were found where limited information was given in an insensitive manner; lower rates were found where the basis for underpayment had been thoroughly and sensitively explained to workers (ibid.).

But equity theory also shows that the cognitive adjustment can be more positive. Underpaid workers are motivated to perceive the tasks that they perform as highly interesting, in order to justify cognitively their performing them in exchange for low wages (Deci, 1975; Lepper and Greene, 1978). Employees also enhance the value of non-monetary aspects of their job in order to make up for being underpaid (Lepper and Greene, 1978; Greenberg, 1989): opportunities to work in large, private offices or to have large desks have been recognized as valued organizational rewards (Konar et al., 1982).

Currently, however, equity theory does not help us to understand fully when the various reactions to inequality will occur and how they are interrelated (Cook and Parcel, 1977; Greenberg, 1993).

EXAMPLE A problem of inequity at the bank

Paris-born bank clerks worked side by side with other clerks who did identical work and earned identical wages, but who were born in the Provinces. The Parisians were dissatisfied with their wages, because they considered that Parisian breeding was an input into the wage bargain that deserved monetary compensation. The bank management, while recognizing that place of birth distinguished the two groups, did not consider birthplace relevant in the exchange of services for pay (Crozier, 1960).

> **EXAMPLE** **A problem of inequity for the Gurkas**
>
> Former Gurkha soldiers from Nepal, who served in the British army, lost their battle for equal pay and pensions in the courts. Differential treatment was seen as lawful given the difference of living in Britain and Nepal (Tait, 2003). Yet only the year before, Gurkha war veterans, subjected to brutal treatment in Japanese prisoner of war camps, won a case of unequal treatment and racial discrimination. They were awarded £10,000 each in compensation. They had been excluded for compensation payments awarded to British survivors of the camps in the 1950s (Norton-Taylor, 2002). More recently, Gurkha veterans have been demonstrating about their rights to live in the UK (BBC News, 18 and 19 March 2008).
>
> Is this inequity what you would have anticipated or expected?

Finally, it is interesting that only some of the research on equity theory has examined whether there are differences in senses of equity among women and among men (for example, Greenberg, 1989). There appears to be no reported difference, yet it was a factor under consideration in the early studies (see Adams, 1963). Researchers who have followed Adams appear to ignore gender, referring to all subjects as 'he' (for example, Prichard, 1969), while others—for example, Harder (1991)—assume that it is recognized that, because the subjects are baseball players, they will all be men.

Expectancy theory

Expectancy theory is another process of cognitive theory, and can also be applied to pay and motivation. Expectancy theory admits the possibility that individuals may have different goals or needs, and that individuals may perceive different connections between actions and their achievement of goals. In 1957, Georgopolous et al. sketched the mechanics of expectancy theory in their path goal theory. Seven years later, Vroom (1964) published his expectancy theory of work motivation. Vroom's formulation postulates that the motivational force for an individual is a function of the expectancy that certain outcomes will result from their behaviour and the valence or desirability of these outcomes. It is suggested that individuals consider alternatives, weigh costs and benefits, and then choose a course of action of maximum utility. The decision by an individual then to work on a particular task and expend a certain amount of effort is a function of his or her probability estimate that he or she can accomplish the task and the probability estimate that accomplishing the task will be followed by certain outcomes. This is dependent on the valence—that is, the desirability of the outcomes. Different rewards can be accrued by the individual as a result of effort or performance. Extrinsic outcomes are rewards distributed by some external agent, such as the boss or the organization; intrinsic rewards are mediated by the individual and are personal rewards, such as self-fulfilment and self-esteem.

Expectancy theory proposes that motivation and work-related behaviour can be predicted if we know about the workers' strength of desire for various outcomes and the probability of achieving them. (For an application of the theory in an industrial setting, with a discussion of its weaknesses, see Reinharth and Wahba, 1976.) The following are some examples of how it works.

1. It assumes, as we have seen, that an individual perceives that effort is positively correlated with level of performance, so experienced secretaries who believe that they can increase the number of words that they type per minute by exerting greater effort have a high effort–performance expectancy. Less experienced typists may realize that no matter how much effort they put in, their performance is fixed at a low level; they have low effort–performance expectancy. The theory predicts that the person with the high effort–performance expectancy will be more motivated to perform.

2. It assumes that a person's expectations of reward will be tied to his or her level of performance. A sales person who is paid on commission is likely to have high performance–outcome expectancy.

A person who works with no prospect of receiving a bonus has low performance–outcome expectancy. The former will be more motivated to perform than the latter.

3. Valence—that is, the degree to which an individual values a particular reward—means that the more people value the reward they receive for their effort, the more motivated they will be to receive the reward. Rewards for which people generally have high valence include salaries, bonuses, promotion, and recognition. But individuals will differ.

As an employer, you can increase the effort that employees expend by increasing the expectation that greater effort will lead to a higher level of performance, by strengthening the perceived link between results and rewards, and by ensuring that employees value the rewards given for high performance.

This, then, is the basic theory, but it has been made more complex by the number of factors that are now recognized as affecting the basic components. Lawler (1970) first modified the basic theory by introducing two variables that affect the effort–performance expectancy. The first is ability—that is, the individual's skill level. An employee must not only possess the skills, but also be able to apply them. The more confident people are in their ability to apply their skills to solve new tasks, the higher the effort–performance expectancy. In this way, past experience will affect a person's confidence in his or her problem-solving approach—and this is the second variable. Satisfaction is a measure of how well the extrinsic and intrinsic rewards for performing a job satisfy the individual's needs and desires.

Wahba and House (1974) report that expectancy theory offers much in terms of potential for understanding job behaviour and work motivation. Research generally supports the predictions of expectancy theory—but the magnitude of the support varies from study to study. Most studies deal only with limited parts of the theory, rather than the whole. Consequently, the predictions of the whole theory are virtually unknown. Further, there are unresolved methodological and logical issues: for example, inadequate clarification of concepts such as expectancy and valence.

Arvey and Mussio (1973) found little support for expectancy theory, and job performance and satisfaction, in their study of female clerical workers. A common criticism of expectancy theory is that it is unlikely that individuals actually carry out all of the complicated calculations implied by the model. Wanous et al. (1983) imply that expectancy mechanisms only come into play when there is a period for reflection on the possible outcomes; they may, however, help us to understand the important decisions that an individual is making (Guest, 1984).

STOP AND THINK Does motivation theory lead to work addiction?

'Motivation theory leads us into addiction because it constructs work as a compulsion, and this renders us vulnerable to work addiction' (Boje and Rosile, 2006: 79). Do you agree?

Some further thoughts on motivation

Herzberg relied on individuals' verbal accounts of their motivation—but should we, as social scientists, always take a person's word and not question it? If we cannot see motives, how do we know that they are real? Do we know that motives are not produced to create a 'case' or a 'position'? These are the kinds of questions about motivation that Laurie Taylor (1972)—the sociologist turned radio journalist—has asked. People may lie, he argues, to continue their deviant behaviour or to explain the initial reason for their action. There is only a limited range of acceptable justifications for behaviour and these may be adopted as we are acting. Once articulated, they become reasons for continuance. People typically cite motives that they consider will be regarded as satisfactory or acceptable. Put crudely, we tell people what we think they want to hear (Taylor and Walton, 1971). If we are no longer able to articulate such motives, then we may give up the behaviour. Motives are not inner biological mainsprings of action, but linguistic constructs that organize acts. Motives are not mysterious internal states, but typical vocabularies with clear functions in particular social situations (Wright Mills, 1940). And each audience may be offered a different account.

To illustrate how motives serve a particular purpose and can have a clear function, Taylor (1972) uses the case of sexual deviants. Taylor investigated sexual deviancy, looking at the range of justifications that are available, the role of others in determining which are acceptable, and the variables that restrict the acceptance or development of motives. He discovered that friends will be told a similar story to that which is provided for the magistrate or psychiatrist. The majority of the responses had in common a reference to factors beyond the individual's control. They refer to certain forces or circumstances outside the person that impinge upon him or her, often in a sudden or unexpected manner. For example, the individual may say that he or she had a breakdown in mental functioning at the time of the offence, or that he or she was overcome by a desire that compelled him or her to act against his or her will. When magistrates were asked how likely they thought a statement to be true, it was found that the explanations offered by offenders were accorded significantly more credibility if the explanation was that the offender did not assert any conscious control over his or her behaviour. Magistrates rejected statements made by offenders who claimed that their action was intentional or meaningful, such as 'I get sexual satisfaction out of it' (see also Taylor and Walton, 1971). Taylor (1972) finishes by asking us if we are prepared to go on accepting that a large section of our society is subject to sudden blackouts and irresistible urges over which they lack any control; we ought therefore to question articulated motives.

Job satisfaction and positive outcomes for organizations

The majority of laypeople believe that there is a relationship between job satisfaction and performance (Fisher, 2003). Many leaders in organizations are likely also to believe that satisfaction causes performance and would expect that organizational efforts aimed at improving employee satisfaction will result in increases in performance (Bowling, 2007). But the literature debates the extent to which increased job satisfaction leads to improved performance: Brayfield and Crockett (1955) conclude that there is no evidence of a relationship between job satisfaction and performance; Iaffaldano and Muchinsky (1985) conclude that there is a weak relationship; Petty et al. (1984) demonstrate that there is a strong relationship. Studies have revealed, however, that satisfied employees are more likely to have low absenteeism and turnover (Tett and Meyer, 1993; Barling et al., 1990; Pierce et al., 1991; Eby et al., 1999). (For more on job satisfaction, see the Work Foundation, 2006.)

Job satisfaction and motivation are difficult subjects to study, because there are so many views on offer and so many of them offer contradictory positions. It is, then, a subject in relation to which arguments need to be weighed and balanced; there are few easy solutions to be found in this research. But one way in which managers have tried to increase motivation and efficiency is through empowerment, or through their leadership—and it is on this that we will focus in the next chapter.

Conclusion

Motivation appears to present a problem for management to solve. As a result, there are a range of theories or explanations on offer. As we have seen here, there are good reasons to be suspicious of some of the claims of motivation theories and their applications. You might have noticed that motivation theories are derived from Western—usually US—thinking, culture, and assumptions. There is, however, no single reliable theory or set of ideas on motivation that can be used as a solution by managers to the problem of motivation.

KEY POINTS

- Motivation theory aims to help managers continually to improve output and work satisfaction through means of a happy, productive worker. The 'right' theory may provide this, as well as explain a wide range of behaviours.

- Theories are usually divided into content theories (Marlow, Herzberg, McGregor, and McClelland) and process theories (equity and expectancy).

- Content theories refer to the content within us—that is, needs, drives, and goals—while process theories concern themselves with the cognitive processes involved in motivation—that is, the process, for example, of expecting equity or rewards and costs.

- Motivation and job satisfaction are both difficult subjects to study, because there are clearly no easy answers for managers asking how to achieve greater motivation and satisfaction. Developing a critical approach helps us to understand why this is the case.

CASE STUDY

A case of training for motivation

The following case study focuses on a company that tried to improve motivation.

A loan company called *Purple Loans* (part of the *GE Capital* group of finance brokers) invested in Special Air Service (SAS) military-style training to improve the motivation of staff. The company hoped, in particular, to improve teamworking and communication, and that the training would result in people working more closely together, which would therefore increase the number of sales. At the end of the training, one of the staff members said that she felt as though if she were to set her mind to any task, she would be able to do it. The training had made her feel more confident and motivated to achieve.

(*Source:* BBC, 2002, 'The Motivators', *Money Programme*)

Questions

1. What could be the potential benefits of SAS training for sales staff?

2. How would you research the impact of this type of training on a sales team?

3. How would you know if the team was more highly motivated?

FURTHER READING

Brewis, J., Linstead, S., Boje, D., and O'Shea, T. (eds) (2006) *The Passion of Organizing,* Malmö: Liber and Copenhagen Business School Press This book contains a number of readings that deal critically with theories of motivation.

Brooks, I. (2003) *Organizational Behaviour: Individuals, Groups and Organization*, 2nd edn, Harlow: Pearson Chapter 3, entitled 'Motivation to work', includes a good critique of Maslow.

Brotherton, C. (1999) *Social Psychology and Management: Issues for a Changing Society*, Buckingham: Open University Press Chapter 3, entitled 'Individual performance at work: The problem of motivation', provides critical appraisal of motivation that is frequently lacking in most mainstream texts.

Cullen, D., and Gotell, L. (2002) 'From orgasms to organizations: Maslow, women's sexuality and the gendered foundations of the needs hierarchy', *Gender, Work and Organization*, 9(5): 537–55 Includes further good critique of Maslow.

Fulop, L. and Linstead, S. (2004) 'Motivation and meaning', in S. Linstead, L. Fulop, and S. Lilley (eds), *Management and Organization: A Critical Text*, Houndmills: Palgrave Macmillan, ch. 9 This chapter usefully discusses motivation critically, linking motivation with concepts such as commitment, emotion, and trust.

Thompson, P. and McHugh, D. (2002) *Work Organizations*, 3rd edn, Houndmills: Palgrave Chapter 19, entitled 'Motivation: The drive for satisfaction', provides a critical introduction to motivation. Some comments are deliberately provocative, such as 'Managers often appear to be better at demotivating workers than at enthusing them with the spirit of the enterprise' (p. 314).

Watson, T. (2002) *Organizing and Managing Work*, Harlow: Pearson Chapter 9 critically discusses motivation theories.

LINKS TO FILMS AND NOVELS

Dead Poets Society (1989) dir. P. Weir This film shows a teacher using some unusual methods to motivate his students to think for themselves, 'seize the day', demonstrate non-conformity, and build self-confidence.

Why We Fight series (1942–45) dir. F. Capra During the Second World War, Frank Capra, a Hollywood film director, was commissioned by the US government to make a series of seven propaganda films aimed at motivating US soldiers. These soldiers had grown up between the two World Wars; the USA was now involved in a war that had to be fought—and won.

RESEARCH QUESTIONS

1. It can be argued that people have greater needs than self-actualization and greater management problems, including providing for those without food or clean water. What would be on your hierarchy of needs?

2. Martina Horner (1972) concluded that there was a high, and perhaps increasing, incidence of the motive to avoid success found in women. The predominant message was that highly competent women, when faced with conflict between their feminine image and expressing their competencies, adjust their behaviour to the sex stereotype. Do you think that this finding would be replicated today?

3. 'The pathway to company profit is also the pathway to self-actualisation' (Rose, 1996). Discuss.

REFERENCES

Adams, S. (1963) 'Toward an understanding of inequity', *Journal of Abnormal and Social Psychology*, 67(5): 422–36.

Alderfer, C.P. (1972) *Existence, Relatedness and Growth: Human Needs in Organisational Settings*, New York: Free Press.

Aron, A. (1977) 'Maslow's other child', *Journal of Humanistic Psychology*, 17(2): 9–24.

Arvey, R.D. and Mussio, S.J. (1973) 'A test of expectancy theory in a field setting using female clerical employees', *Journal of Vocational Behaviour*, 3: 421–32.

Barling, J., Wade, B., and Fullagar, C. (1990) 'Predicting employee commitment to company and union: divergent models', *Journal of Occupational Psychology*, 63(1): 49–63.

Barton Cunningham, J. and MacGregor, J. (2000) 'Trust and the design of work: Complementary constructs in satisfaction and performance', *Human Relations*, 53(12): 1575–91.

Boje, D.M. and Rosile, G.A. (2006) 'Death, terror and addiction in motivation theory', in J. Brewis, S. Linstead, D. Boje, and T. O'Shea (eds) *The Passion of Organizing*, Malmö: Liber and Copenhagen Business School Press, ch. 2.

Bowling, N.A. (2007) 'Is the job satisfaction–job performance relationship spurious? A meta-analytic examination', *Journal of Vocational Behavior*, 71(2): 167–85.

Brayfield, A.H. and Crockett, W.H. (1955) 'Employee attitudes and employee performance', *Psychological Bulletin*, 52: 396–424.

Brewis, J., Linstead, S., Boje, D., and O'Shea, T. (eds) (2006) *The Passion of Organizing*, Malmö: Liber and Copenhagen Business School Press.

Buss, A.R. (1979) 'Humanistic psychology as liberal ideology: The socio-historical roots of Maslow's theory of self actualization', *Journal of Humanistic Psychology*, 19(3): 43–5.

Centers, R. and Bugental, D.E. (1966) 'Intrinsic and extrinsic job motivations among different segments of the working population', *Journal of Applied Psychology*, 50(3): 193–7.

Chusmir, L.H. (1985) 'Motivation of managers: Is gender a factor?' *Psychology of Women Quarterly*, 9: 153–9.

Cook, K.S. and Parcel, T.L. (1977) 'Equity theory: Directions for future research', *Sociological Inquiry*, 47(2): 75–88.

Crozier, M. (1960) Personal communication, reported in S. Adams, 'Toward an understanding of inequity', *Journal of Abnormal and Social Psychology*, 67(5): 422–36.

Cullen, D. (1994) 'Feminism, management and self-actualization', *Gender, Work and Organization*, 1(3): 127–37.

_____ (1997) 'Maslow, monkeys and motivation theory', *Organization*, 4(3): 355–73.

_____ and Gotell, L. (2002) 'From orgasms to organizations: Maslow, women's sexuality and the gendered foundations of the needs hierarchy', *Gender, Work and Organization*, 9(5): 537–55.

Dahrendorf, R. (1964) 'Toward a theory of social conflict', in A. Etzoni and E. Etzoni (eds), *Social Change*, New York: Basic Books.

Dalton, M. (1959) *Men Who Manage*, New York: Wiley.

Deci, E.L. (1975) *Intrinsic Motivation*, New York: Plenum.

Dewsbury, D.A. (1978) *Comparative Animal Behavior*, New York: McGraw Hill.

Dubin, R., Homans, G.C., Mann, F.C., and Miller, D.C. (1965) *Leadership and Productivity: Facts of Industrial Life*, San Francisco, CA: Chandler Publishing Co.

Dunnette, M.D., Campbell, J.P., and Hakel, M.D. (1967) 'Factors contributing to job satisfaction and job dissatisfaction in six occupational groups', *Organizational Behaviour and Human Performance*, 2: 143–74.

Eby, L., Feeman, D.M., Rush, M.C., and Lance, C.E. (1999) 'Motivational bases of affective organizational commitment: A partial test of an integrative theoretical model', *Journal of Occupational and Organisational Psychology*, 72(4): 463–83.

Ellerman, D. (2001) 'McGregor's Theory Y vs Bentham's panopticism: Toward a critique of the economic theory of agency', *Knowledge, Technology and Policy*, 14(1): 34–49.

Entwhistle, D.R. (1972) 'To dispel fantasies about fantasy-based measures of achievement motivation', *Psychological Bulletin*, 77(6): 377–91.

Ewan, R.B. (1963) *Determinants of Job Satisfaction*, Paper read at American Psychological Association, Philadelphia, September, cited in Wernimont (1966).

Fineman, S. (1977) 'The achievement motive construct and its measurement: Where are we now?', *British Journal of Psychology*, 68: 1–22.

Fisher, C.D. (2003) 'Why do lay people believe that satisfaction and performance are correlated? Possible sources of a commonsense theory', *Journal of Organizational Behavior*, 24: 753–77.

Ford, R.N. (1969) *Motivation Through the Work Itself*, New York: American Management Association.

Frey, R.S. (1984) 'Need for achievement, entrepreneurship, and economic growth: A critique of the McClelland thesis', *Social Science Journal*, 21(2): 125–34.

Friedlander, F. (1965) 'Comparative work value systems', *Personnel Psychology*, 18: 1–20.

Fulop, L. and Linstead, S. (2004) 'Motivation and meaning', in S. Linstead, L. Fulop, and S. Lilley (eds), *Management and Organization: A Critical Text*, Houndmills: Palgrave Macmillan, ch. 9.

Furnham, A. (1992) *Personality at Work*, London: Routledge.

Georgopolous, B.S., Mahoney, G.M., and Jones, N.W. (1957) 'A path-goal approach to productivity', *Journal of Applied Psychology*, 41: 345–53.

Gilleard, C.J. (1989) 'The achieving society revisited: A further analysis of the relation between national growth and need achievement', *Journal of Economic Psychology*, 10(1): 21–34.

Gjesm, T. and Nygard, R. (1970) *Achievement-Related Motives, Theoretical Considerations and Construction of the Measuring Instrument*, Fear of Failure Project Report No. 2, September, Oslo: University of Oslo.

Greenberg, J. (1989) 'Cognitive re-evaluation of outcomes in response to underpayment inequity', *Academy of Management Journal*, 32(1): 174–84.

_____ (1990) 'Employee theft as a reaction to underpayment inequality: The hidden costs of pay cuts', *Journal of Applied Psychology*, 75: 561–8.

_____ (1993) 'Stealing in the name of justice: Informational and interpersonal moderators of theft reactions to underpayment inequality', *Organizational Behaviour and Human Decision Processes*, 54: 81–103.

Guest, D. (1984) 'What's new in motivation', *Personnel Management*, May: 20–3.

Hall, D. and Nougaim, K.E. (1968) 'An examination of Maslow's need hierarchy in an organizational setting', *Organizational Behaviour and Human Performance*, 3: 12–35.

Hansemark, O.C. (1997) 'Objective versus projective measurement of need for achievement: The relation between TAT and CMPS', *Journal of Managerial Psychology*, 12(4): 280–9.

Harder, J.W. (1991) 'Equity theory versus expectancy theory: The case of Major League Baseball free agents', *Journal of Applied Psychology*, 76(3): 458–64.

Helmreich, R.L. and Spence, J.T. (1978) 'The work and family orientation questionnaire: An objective instrument to assess components of achievement motivation and attitudes towards the family and career', *JSAS Catalog of Selected Documents in Psychology*, 8(35) (MS No. 1677).

Herzberg, F. (1968) 'One more time: How do you motivate employees?', *Harvard Business Review*, January–February: 53–62.

_____, Maunser, B., and Snyderman, B. (1959) *The Motivation to Work*, New York: John Wiley & Sons.

Hinton, B.L. (1968) 'An empirical investigation of the Herzberg methodology and two factor theory', *Organizational Behaviour and Human Performance*, 3: 286–309.

Hisrich, R.D. (1990) 'Entrepreneurship/intrapreneurship', *American Psychologist*, 45: 209–22.

Hoffman, E. (ed.) (1996) *Future Visions: The Unpublished Papers of Abraham Maslow*, Thousand Oaks, CA: Sage.

Hollinger, R.D. and Clark, J.P. (1983) *Theft by Employees*, Lexington, MA: Lexington Books.

Homans, G.C. (1961) *Social Behaviour: Its Elementary Forms*, London: Routledge & Kegan Paul.

Horner, M. (1972) 'Toward an understanding of achievement-related conflicts in women', *Journal of Social Issues*, 28(2): 157–75.

Iaffaldano, M.T. and Muchinsky, P.M. (1985) 'Job satisfaction and job performance: A meta- analysis', *Psychological Bulletin*, 97(2): 251–73.

Jackson, D.N. (1974) *Personality Research Form Manual*, Port Huron, MI: Research Psychologist Press.

139

Jaques, E. (1961) *Equitable Payment*, New York: John Wiley & Sons.

Johnson, D.S. and Perlow, R. (1992) 'The impact of need for achievement components on goal commitment and performance', *Journal of Applied Social Psychology*, 22(21): 1711–20.

Kaplan, H., Tausky, C., and Bolaria, B. (1975) 'Human relations: Fact or fantasy', *Harvard Business Review*, November–December.

King, N. (1970) 'A clarification and evaluation of the two factor theory of job satisfaction', *Psychological Bulletin*, 74: 18–31.

Kleinginna, P.R., and Kleinginna, A.M. (1981) 'A categorised list of motivation definitions with a suggestion for a consensual definition', *Motivation and Emotion*, 5: 263–92.

Knights, D. and Wilmott, H.C. (1974–75) 'Humanistic social science and the theory of needs', *Interpersonal Development*, 5: 213–22.

Konar, E., Sundstrom, E., Brady, C., Mandel, D., and Rice, R.W. (1982) 'Status demarcation in the office', *Environment and Behavior*, 14: 561–80.

Langan-Fox, J. and Roth, S. (1995) 'Achievement motivation and female entrepreneurs', *Journal of Occupational Psychology*, 68(3): 209–18.

Lashley, C. (1997) *Empowering Service Excellence: Beyond the Quick Fix*, London: Cassell.

Lawler, E.E. (1970) 'Job attitudes and employee motivation: theory, research and practice', *Personnel Psychology*, 23: 223–37.

_____ and Suttle, J.L. (1972) 'A causal correlation test of the need hierarchy concept', *Organizational Behavior and Human Performance*, 23: 251–67.

Lepper, M.R. and Greene, D. (eds) (1978) *The Hidden Costs of Reward*, Hillsdale, NJ: Lawrence Erlbaum Associates.

Linstead, S. (2002) 'Organizational kitsch', *Organization*, 9(4): 657–82.

Lips, H.M. and Colwill, N.J. (1978) *The Psychology of Sex Differences*, Englewood Cliffs, NJ: Prentice Hall.

Litterer, J. (1966) 'Conflict in organization: A reexamination', *Academy of Management Journal*, IX(3): 178–86.

Locke, E.A. (1976) 'The nature and causes of job satisfaction', in M.D. Dunnette (ed.), *Handbook of Industrial and Organizational Psychology*, Chicago, IL: Rand McNally, pp. 1297–349.

Lord, R.G. and Hohenfeld, J.A. (1979) 'A longitudinal field assessment of equity effects on the performance of Major League Baseball players', *Journal of Applied Psychology*, 64: 19–26.

Lowry, R.J. (ed.) (1982) *The Journals of Abraham Maslow*, Lexington, MA: Lewis.

Mars, G. (1974) 'Dock pilferage: A case study in occupational theft', in P. Rock and M. McIntosh (eds), *Deviance and Control*, London, Tavistock Institute, pp. 209–28.

Maslow, A.H. (1943) 'A theory of human motivation', *Psychological Review*, 50: 370–96.

_____ (1954) *Motivation and Personality*, New York: Harper.

_____ (1965) *Eupsychian Management*, Homewood, IL: Irwin.

Matteson, M.T. and Ivancevich, J.M. (eds) (1989) *Management and Organizational Behavior Classics*, Homewood, IL: BPI/Irwin.

McClelland, D.C., Atkinson, J.W., Clark, R.A., and Lowell, E.L. (1953) *The Achievement Motive*, New York: Appleton-Century-Crofts.

McGregor, D. (1957) 'The human side of enterprise', *Management Review*, November; reprinted in M.J. Handel (ed.) (2003) *The Sociology of Organizations*, London: Sage, ch. 9.

_____ (1960) *The Human Side of Enterprise*, New York: McGraw Hill.

Nevis, E.C. (1983) 'Using an American perspective in understanding another culture: Toward a hierarchy of needs for the People's Republic of China', *Journal of Applied Behavioral Science*, 19: 249–64.

Norton-Taylor, R. (2002) 'Racist MoD ordered to compensate Gurkha PoWs', *The Guardian*, 28 November, available online at http://www.guardian.co.uk/uk/2002/nov/28/race.military

Overvold, G.E. (1987) 'The imperative of organizational harmony: A critique of contemporary human relations theory', *Journal of Business Ethics*, 6: 559–65.

Petty, M.M., McGee, G.W., and Cavender, J.W. (1984) 'A meta-analysis of the relationships between individual performance', *Academy of Management Review*, 9(4): 712–21.

Pierce, J.L., Rubenfeld, S.A., and Morgan, S. (1991) 'Employee ownership: A conceptual model of process and effect', *Academy of Management Review*, 16(1): 121–44.

Prichard, R.A. (1969) 'Equity theory: A review and critique', *Organizational Behaviour and Human Performance*, 4: 75–94.

_____, Dunnette, M.D., and Jorgenson, D.O. (1972) 'Effects of perceptions of equity and inequity on worker performance and satisfaction', *Journal of Applied Psychology Monograph*, 56: 75–94.

Rauschenberger, J., Schmitt, N., and Hunter, T.E. (1980) 'A test of the need hierarchy concept', *Administrative Science Quarterly*, 25(4): 654–70.

Reinharth, L. and Wahba, M.A. (1976) 'A test of alternative models of expectancy theory', *Human Relations*, 29(3): 257–72.

Rose, N. (1996) 'Identity, genealogy and history', in S. Hall and P. Du Gay (eds), *Questions of Cultural Identity*, London: Sage, ch. 8.

Shaw, R. and Colimore, K. (1988) 'Humanistic psychology as ideology: An analysis of Maslow's contradictions', *Journal of Humanistic Psychology*, 28(3): 51–74.

Sievers, B. (1986) 'Beyond the surrogate of motivation', *Organization Studies*, 7(4): 353–67.

_____ (1993) *Work, Death and Life Itself: Essays on Management and Organization*, New York: De Gruyter.

Stein, A.H. and Bailey, M.M. (1975) 'The socialization of achievement motivation in females', in M.T. Mednick, S.S. Tangri, and L.W. Hoffman (eds), *Women and Achievement*, Washington DC: Hemisphere, pp. 151–7.

Tait, N. (2003) 'Gurkhas lose case on discrimination', *Financial Times*, 22 February, p. 2.

Taylor, L. (1972) 'The significance of interpretation of replies to motivational questions: The case of sex offenders', *Sociology*, 6(1): 23–40.

_____ and Walton, P. (1971) 'Industrial sabotage: Motives and meanings', in S. Cohen (ed.), *Images of Deviance*, Harmondsworth: Penguin, pp. 219–45.

Tett, R.P. and Meyer, J.P. (1993) 'Job satisfaction, organizational commitment, turnover intention and turnover: Path analyses based on meta-analytic findings', *Personnel Psychology*, 46(2): 259–93.

Thompson, P. and McHugh, D. (2002) *Work Organizations*, 3rd edn, Houndmills: Palgrave.

Thrash, T.M. and Elliot, A.J. (2002) 'Implicit and self-attributed achievement motives: Concordance and predictive validity', *Journal of Personality*, 70(5): 729–55.

Tietjen, M.A. and Myers, R.M. (1998) 'Motivation and job satisfaction', *Management Decision*, 36(4): 226–31.

Timmons, J., Smollen, L., and Dingee, A. (1985) *New Venture Creation*, 2nd edn, Homewood, IL: Irwin.

Veroff, J., McClelland, L., and Ruhland, D. (1975) 'Varieties of achievement motivation', in M.T. Mednick, S.S. Tangri, and L.W. Hoffman (eds), *Women and Achievement*, Washington, DC: Hemisphere, pp. 172–205.

_____, Reuman, D., and Feld, S. (1984) 'Motives in American men and women across the adult life span', *Developmental Psychology*, 20: 1142–58.

_____, Wilcox, S., and Atkinson, J.W. (1953) 'The achievement motive in high school and college age women', *Journal of Abnormal and Social Psychology*, 48: 108–9.

Vroom, V.H. (1964) *Work and Motivation*, New York: Wiley.

_____ and Maier, N.R. (1961) 'Industrial school psychology', *Annual Review of Psychology*, 12: 413–46.

Wahba, M.A. and Bridwell, L.G. (1976) 'Maslow reconsidered: A review of research on the need hierarchy theory', *Organizational Behavior and Human Performance*, 15: 212–40.

_____, and House, R.J. (1974) 'Expectancy theory in work and motivation: Some logical and methodological issues', *Human Relations*, 27(2): 121–47.

Walster, E., Walster, G.W., and Berscheid, E. (1978) *Equity: Theory and Research*, Boston, MA: Allyn & Bacon.

141

Wanous, J.P., Keon, T.L., and Latack, J.C. (1983) 'Expectancy theory and occupational and organizational choices: A review and test', *Organizational Behavior and Human Performance*, 32: 66–85.

Watson, T.J. (1996) 'Motivation: That's Maslow, isn't it?', *Management Learning*, 27(4): 447–64.

_____ (2002) *Organizing and Managing Work: Organizational, Managerial and Strategic Behaviour in Theory and Practice*, Harlow: Pearson Education Ltd.

_____ (2004) 'Motivation: That's Maslow, isn't it?', in C. Grey and E. Antonacopoulou (eds), *Essential Readings in Management Learning*, London: Sage, ch. 12.

Wernimont, P.F. (1966) 'Intrinsic and extrinsic factors in job satisfaction', *Journal of Applied Psychology*, 50(1): 41–50.

Work Foundation (2006) *The Good Worker: A Survey of Attitudes Towards Work in the UK*, London: The Work Foundation.

Wright Mills, C. (1940) 'Situated actions and vocabularies of motive', *American Sociological Review*, 15(Dec): 904–13.

Leadership

7

Introduction

Leadership ranks among the most researched and debated topics in organizational behaviour—but what is the difference between management and leadership? Are leaders really necessary in all kinds of organization? Does leadership make a difference? What are the traits—that is, the qualities—required of leaders? Which style of leadership is the most appropriate to adopt? Are there recipes for successful leadership? These are the kinds of questions that this chapter aims to tackle.

By the end of this chapter, you will be able to identify and discuss a number of different theories of leadership. You will understand the links between emotion, spirituality, gender, class, and leadership, and be able to discuss the topic critically.

This chapter covers:

- thinking about leadership;
- a trait theory of leadership;
- style theories and democratic leadership;
- task- versus relations-oriented leadership;
- consideration versus initiating structure;
- transactional versus transformational leadership;
- situational leadership;
- emotion and leadership;
- gender and leadership;
- spirituality and leadership;
- race and leadership;
- class and leadership.

Thinking about leadership

Leadership can be about being ahead of others, taking others forward with you, influencing and motivating them. Most of us start thinking about the topic of leadership with the assumption that leaders are necessary for the effective functioning of an organization. This thought is encapsulated in a quote from the beginning of Locke's (1991) book on leadership: 'There probably has never been a society, country, or organization that did not have a leader; if there has, it probably did not survive for long.' Belief in hierarchy and the necessity of leaders is often an unrecognized ideology—but perhaps we should question whether leaders are really necessary? The Quaker religion, for example, seems to manage without formal leaders in a hierarchy; Quakers believe that all can be led by the divine and they resist personal authority—particularly when exercised by people with formal positions of power. Perhaps leaders are only necessary because, when we are faced with uncertainty and ambiguity in organizations, we project them onto 'leadership' or the 'leader' role. We do this in order to avoid directly confronting our own emotions, including anxiety, discomfort, or fear of failure.

Some writers (for example, Gemmill and Oakley, 1992) believe, therefore, that the concepts of 'leader' and 'leadership' have become psychological prisons. Leadership is a process whereby 'followers' give up their mindfulness to a 'leader' (Smircich and Morgan, 1982). The necessity of leadership is seen as a social myth that induces helplessness—an inability to imagine or perceive viable options—with accompanying feelings of despair and resistance to any form of action. It is this social myth that maintains the status quo (Bennis, 1989; Sievers, 1993).

Another factor that maintains the status quo is the individual's own philosophy of leadership, convictions about the right and wrong way to lead, or implicit theories of leadership. When describing leaders, people apply 'information simplification heuristics' (Bryman, 1987) or implicit leadership theories (Schyns and Meindl, 2005), which influence their perceptions of leaders' behaviour and inform their descriptions of real leaders. This is particularly damaging to the questionnaire-based approaches to leadership, because implicit leadership theories underpin individuals' descriptions of leaders when answering batteries of questions. Questionnaire-based representations of leader behaviour will only partially capture actual behaviour. The validity and meaning of questionnaires is consequently a matter of concern. It has also been shown that people's views about the behaviour of leaders are influenced by knowledge of their performance (Bryman, 1987).

STOP AND THINK   Should we focus on followers or leaders?

Meindl (1990) would argue that leadership is more a creation in the minds of followers than a characteristic of those who occupy leadership roles and that perhaps we should concentrate on studying followers rather than leaders (Meindl, 1995; Shamir, 2007). Do you think that Meindl is right?

Some, such as Grint (2000), would argue that research on leadership has been too scientific for this highly interpretative subject matter. Allegedly objective conditions and situations surrounding leaders are contestable, and open to interpretation. Traditional scientific approaches to the study of leadership may therefore be inappropriate. Leadership might better be considered as an art rather than a science; we ought therefore to discard the 'recipe' approach to leadership, because there a no 'seven ways to guaranteed success' (Grint, 2005b).

Another weakness of the research on leadership is that experimental subjects have tended to be North American. There is, then, the possibility that the findings have less applicability outside the USA. We would have good reason to doubt the generalizability of findings outside the USA: there is evidence to suggest that there are differences between the UK and the USA in connection with issues relating to leadership. For example, Bass and Franke (1972) suggested that British university students are more likely than their US counterparts to believe that a manipulative approach to management is conducive to organizational success. Bass et al. (1979) found that British managers were more likely than US managers to prefer the use of authority to the use of persuasion.

STOP AND THINK   Do we need 'responsible followers'?

Keith Grint (2005b) argues that we need to learn how to lead without authority. He also says that seeing leaders as 'gifted', 'charismatic', or 'inspirational' promotes the assumption that the role of followers is to comply with the demands of the leader—that is, not to be responsible: 'This is fine providing the leader is an accomplished miracle-worker; in which case all we need to do is dig a lake for the boss to walk across on a daily basis.' If the leader fails, what is needed is 'responsible followers' to voice their dissent if they think that the leader was wrong.

Do you think that there is something in this argument?

(*Source:* Grint, 2005b; see also Grint, 2005a)

The controversy created by the subject of leadership is reflected in the very process of trying to define it. While everyone might have an opinion on the phenomenon, few seem to agree to what it really is. Is it really any different from management? Some—for example, Maccoby (2000b)—would argue that it is. Management is a function; it is about administration—that is, planning, facilitating, writing business plans, setting budgets, and monitoring progress. Leadership, in contrast, is a relationship; it is about motivating, coaching, and building trust. Leaders get organizations to change.

Kelly (2008) asks, however, whether there is a uniform reality of leadership. There are almost as many different definitions of leadership as there are people who have attempted to define it (Stogdill, 1974; Bass, 1990). The controversy is also reflected in the research literature. Bass's (1990) *Handbook of Leadership* lists several thousand references to research on leadership, most of which has been directed at the question of the determinants of effective leadership behaviour (Bryman, 1986). Leadership theory offers both instrumental knowledge for overcoming resistance among followers and the criteria for who will be recognized as having legitimate power to lead (Jacques, 1996). Leaders themselves clearly believe in effective leadership skills to ensure business success. In a relatively recent survey (Smith, 1997) of 250 British chief executives, when asked to identify the most important management skills for ensuring business success, leadership emerged as the top item. But can it even be defined and researched?

It might be useful, as a starting point, to know what characteristics leaders should have.

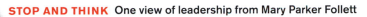

STOP AND THINK One view of leadership from Mary Parker Follett

Mary Parker Follett has been hailed as the 'prophet of management' and has recently received much attention (Graham, 1996). She is considered to be ahead of her time in her thinking about the nature of organizing (Wheelock and Callahan, 2006). She was writing at the turn of the twentieth century—at around the same time as Urwick and Taylor.

Follett discusses 'a reciprocal leadership' (Follett, 1982: 303), in which 'the leader guides the group and is at the same time himself guided by the group' (1918; 1998: 229); in addition, the leader has the key understanding to do the job. Her leader, in terms of traits or characteristics, is inspirational and visionary, leading change and exhibiting conduct that merits trust. He or she does not use persuasion. Follett advocates the coactive power of management and unions, arguing that society must merge labour and capital to form an integration of interests and motives, and of standards, becoming an integrative unity.

This, then, is a unitarist view of organization. How realistic is it, do you think?

A trait theory of leadership

The earliest research looked at the traits of leaders—that is, at the characteristics of effective leaders. Great leaders in history tend to be great orators, such as Martin Luther King and Nelson Mandela. If leaders are endowed with superior qualities that differentiate them from followers, it should be possible to identify these qualities. A 'great man' theory of leadership depicts great leaders, such as Ghandi or Churchill, centre stage and looks for the heroic characteristics that marks them out as having the ability to transform societies or organizations. But the 'great man' theory is controversial for a number of reasons—not least that women such as Joan of Arc, Elizabeth I, Catherine the Great, Mother Teresa, or business leaders such as Anita Roddick or Oprah Winfrey (who owns her own production and media company), are rarely used as the basis of the analysis. It has also been argued—for example, by Tolstoy (1957)—that although leaders are commonly believed to command events and appear to be the causes of them, they are, in fact, merely 'labels' used to explain outcomes that otherwise seem inexplicable—and, sometimes, the labels or traits seem to contradict each other.

146

STOP AND THINK Describing the leadership traits of Gordon Ramsay, the celebrity chef

Is Gordon Ramsey talented and charismatic, or a hotheaded perfectionist with a penchant for swearing?

(*Source: People Management,* 2005)

A classic survey by Stogdill (1948) looked at all of the studies of traits and personal factors associated with leadership in which factors had been studied by three or more investigators. He offers the following conclusions that are supported by positive evidence from fifteen or more of the studies surveyed: 'The average person who occupies a position of leadership exceeds the average member of his [sic] group in the following respects' (ibid.: 63)—that is, intelligence, scholarship, and dependability in exercising responsibilities, activity, and social participation and socio-economic status. As you might expect, the qualities, characteristics, and skills required in a leader are determined, to a large extent, by the demands of the situation in which the person functions as a leader. A person does not become a leader by virtue of the possession of some combination of traits, but rather the pattern of personal characteristics of the leader must bear some relevance to the characteristics, activities, and goals of the followers. These will be in constant flux. It will therefore not be very difficult to find leaders, but it will be difficult to place these people in different situations in which they will be able to function as leaders. The study of leadership should therefore involve not only a study of leaders, but also a study of situations.

STOP AND THINK Alan Sugar's view on leadership

The following are some quotes about leadership qualities from Alan Sugar, the ex-CEO of Amstrad and star of BBC's *The Apprentice*.

'A good leader is not necessarily the most popular person in their business, but the best ones are liked because they are respected for their clarity and vision.'

'Above all, in order to gain respect, you need to be true to yourself. There is no point in trying to be brutal if it's not in your nature; there is no point in trying to be suave and sophisticated if it doesn't come naturally.'

Do these quotes add anything to your current theory of leadership?

Before looking at leaders in different situations, however, we will look at leadership style and inclusiveness.

Style theories and democratic leadership

One of the major dilemmas facing leaders is how to balance the advantages of a democratic approach, which contributes better to the commitment, loyalty, involvement, and satisfaction of followers, with a more authoritative approach, which contributes to order, consistency, and the resolution of conflict. Should managers give directions and tell subordinates how to do the work, or should they share with subordinates the need for solving problems or handling situations, and involve them in working out what needs to be done and how? Most managers do both, depending on the circumstances, but in different amounts (Bass, 1990).

Kurt Lewin and his associates were very keen to demonstrate the advantages of democratic decision making (see the 'Case study' at the end of this chapter). Lewin and his associates—Ronald Lippitt and Ralph White (Lewin et al., 1939; Lippitt and White, 1959) explored the extent to which various aspects of leadership behaviour affect group behaviour. Using four clubs of 11-year-old children over a six-month period, they tried three styles of leadership: democratic, authoritarian, and laissez-faire. Four adults were selected as leaders and all of them took two or three different leadership roles with different groups during the course of the experiment. The groups of boys and types of activity remained constant, while the form of leadership changed.

- The authoritarian leader was told to determine practically all club activities and procedures. The techniques and activity steps were to be communicated one at a time and assigned.: 'The dominator should keeps his standards of praise and criticism to himself in evaluating individual group activities. He should also remain fairly aloof from active group participation except in demonstrating' (Lippitt and White, 1959: 498).

- The democratic leader was instructed to discuss and decide policies with the group. Wherever technical advice was needed, the leader was to try to suggest two or more alternatives from which group members could make a choice. Everyone was to be free to work with whomever they chose and divisions of responsibility were to be left to the group. The bases of praise and criticism of individual and group activities were to be communicated in an objective, fact-focused way. The leader was to try to be a 'regular' group member, but not do much of the work.

- The laissez-faire leader was asked to play a passive role and leave complete freedom to the group for decisions. He or she was to make it clear that various materials were available, and supply information and help when asked. The leader was to take a minimum of initiatives in making suggestions. No attempt was to be made to evaluate the behaviour of individuals or the group, and he or she was to be friendly, rather than 'stand-offish'.

About 60 per cent of the behaviour of the average authoritarian leader might be described in the following way. The authoritarian leader usually initiated individual or group activity with an order. He or she often disrupted ongoing activity with an order that started activity off in another direction. He or she fairly frequently criticized work in a manner that carried the meaning 'It is a bad job because I say it is a bad job' rather than 'It is a poor job because those nails are bent over instead of driven in'.

The democratic leader took the initiative where he or she felt that it was needed in making guiding suggestions. He or she did not take initiative for action away from the group. He or she stimulated child independence eight times as often as the authoritarian leader; he or she also had about eight times more social interaction than the authoritarian leader, during which he or she discussed personal matters about home or school, or joked with the children. The laissez-faire leader concentrated on giving out information when it was asked for, stimulating child independence half as much as the democratic leader.

Two types of reaction were found to the authoritarian leadership style. Three of the four clubs responded with dependent leaning on the adult leader, relatively low levels of frustration tension, and practically no capacity for initiating group action. For example, if the leader arrived late, no group initiative to start new work or to continue work already underway was found. The fourth club demonstrated considerable frustration and some aggression toward the leader. This was interpreted as a 'frustrated hopelessness in the face of overwhelming power' (Lippitt and White, 1959: 510). The group average of inter-member aggressiveness under the autocracy is either very high or low; in democracy, it is at a more medium level (Lippitt, 1940; Lippitt and White, 1943). It was thought that the 'we feeling', which tends to decrease inter-member aggression, is diminished in autocracy (Lewin, 1947: 20).

Demands for attention from the adult were greater than in the democratic and laissez-faire groups. In the democratic and laissez-faire groups, there was less discontent in relations with the adult leader and conversation was less restricted. Members of the democratic and laissez-faire clubs initiated more personal and friendly approaches to their leaders, and there was more spontaneous exchange of confidences about life outside the club.

In relation to the differences between the democratic and laissez-faire groups, members in the democratic group felt much freer and more inclined to make suggestions on matters of group policy than in other groups. The absence or presence of a leader had practically no effect: groups were already active in production if a leader arrived late. The lower level of suggestions in the laissez-faire situation was thought not to be caused by any feeling of restricted freedom, but rather by a lack of cooperative working relationships between the adult and the group members. The need for the laissez-faire club to gather its own information meant that about 37 per cent of its behaviour consisted of asking for information, compared with about 15 per cent in the other three clubs. The groups under laissez-faire leaders were active, but not productive.

The relationships between the club members also developed along different lines in the different groups. Expressions of irritability and aggressiveness toward fellow members occurred more frequently in both the authoritarian and laissez-faire groups than in the democratic. Further, the child members depended more on each other for social recognition, and were more ready to give recognition to each other, in the democratic and laissez-faire situations. It is interesting to discover that all but one boy preferred the democratic leader to the other two types, but there was disagreement about whether they preferred the laissez-faire or authoritarian type as a second choice.

No attempt is made by Lippitt and White, however, to discuss the implications of this research for behaviour among adults or the lessons for the management of people.

Despite the weaknesses of these conclusions, other researchers went on to advocate the democratic approach. These included Likert (1961; 1967; 1977) and the whole human relations movement (for example, Argyris, 1957; McGregor, 1960). Borrowing heavily from the original experimental concepts and results of Lewin and Lipitt (1938), Likert (1961) conceived of four systems of interpersonal relationship in large organizations: exploitative autocratic; benevolent autocratic; consultative; and democratic. In more than 500 studies completed, positive associations were generally found between measures of the organization's performance and whether they were closer to the democratic systems than the autocratic (Likert, 1977). This demonstrated the efficacy of democratic, as opposed to autocratic, systems of management. (For more detail on these studies, see Bass, 1990: 430–2.)

The more positive results are to be found in the large-scale field studies, rather than in small group laboratory experiments. Generally, the patterns of leadership behaviour included in democratic leadership are more satisfying than those associated with autocratic leadership (Bass, 1990). But autocratic leadership may enhance productivity in the short term—particularly if democratic leadership ignores the task and concern for production goals.

Task- versus relations-oriented leadership

Looking at more distinctive components of democratic leadership, such as consideration for subordinates and relations orientation, produces a sharper picture of leadership. Leaders differ in the extent to which they pursue a human relations approach and try to maintain friendly supportive relations with their followers. Those with a strong concern are identified as 'relations-oriented', or 'people-centred'. These types of leader will demonstrate a sense of trust in subordinates, less perceived need for control, and more general, rather than close, supervision. Those with a strong concern for group goals and the means to achieve them will be considered 'task-oriented' or 'production-oriented'. The leader's assumptions about his or her roles, purposes, and behaviour reflect his or her interest in completing assignments and getting the work done. The most effective managers are, however, those who can combine both concerns (Bass, 1990).

The best-known model prescribing the integration of both task and relations orientations is that supplied by Blake and Mouton (1964). Managers and leaders were attributed a score (of between 1 and 9) in relation to their concern for people and another in relation to their concern for production. The measurement of these concerns is based on a manager's endorsement of statements about assumptions and beliefs. Team leadership (9,9) is prescribed, and is achieved by participation, openness, trust and respect, involvement and commitment, open confrontation to resolve conflicts, consensus, mutually determined management by objectives, mutual support, and change through feedback. (For more on the development of the theory and thinking, and an interview with Blake and Mouton, see Oates, 1973.)

Blake and Mouton did not, however, leave much room for exceptions (Bass, 1990). Investigations of the success of the impact of the idea have been mixed or negative—particularly because situations may impact on the satisfaction and productivity of the followers.

Consideration versus initiating structure

Another attempt to describe individuals' behaviour while they act as leaders of groups or organizations was made by *Ohio State University*, which developed a 'leader behaviour description questionnaire' using 150 statements that described different aspects of the behaviour of leaders. Two factors were produced: consideration and the initiation of structure. Table 7.1 illustrates some of the kinds of statement with which people might be asked to agree or disagree (on a five-point scale), when looking at consideration versus initiating structure in a male leader.

Consideration—as you might guess from the above and as the label implies—describes the extent to which a leader exhibits concern for the welfare of the other members of the group. Considerate leaders express appreciation for good work, stress the importance of job satisfaction, maintain self-esteem, or subordinate and put their suggestions into action. Initiation of structure shows the extent to which a leader initiates activity in the group, organizes it, and defines the way in which work is to be done. The initiation of structure includes leaders insisting on maintaining standards and meeting deadlines, deciding in detail what will be done, and how it should be done (Bass, 1990).

We noted earlier how people's views about the behaviour of leaders are influenced by knowledge of their performance; performance cues have a clear effect on ratings of both consideration and initiating structure, irrespective of the behaviour of leaders, as implied by behavioural manipulations in experiments (Bryman, 1987). Findings such as these prompt a questioning of the meaning of research that shows that leaders who score high on both consideration and initiating structure are more effective or successful.

TABLE 7.1 Consideration vs initiating structure (Bryman, 1987)

Consideration	Initiating structure
Friendly and approachable	Asks that group members follow standard rules and regulations
Treats all members as his equals	Decides what shall be done and how it shall be done
Looks out for the personal welfare of group members	Assigns group members to tasks
Puts suggestions made by the group into operation	Lets group members know what is expected of them

EXAMPLE Research on leadership styles in higher education

A survey on leadership styles in higher education found that they were perceived to be predominantly reactive, secretive, inconsistent, demotivating, controlling, and indecisive. Only a third of university staff surveyed said that their leaders were caring, while fewer than a quarter felt that their organization was loyal to them and treated them fairly.

(*Source: Times Higher Education,* 27 March 2008, p. 4)

150

Transactional versus transformational leadership

Transactional and transformational leadership were first conceptualized by Burns (1978), and later developed by Bass (1985). Transactional leadership happens in circumstances under which goods, services, and other rewards are exchanged so that various parties achieve their goals. It is a bargain struck to help the individual interests of persons or groups going their separate ways (Burns, 1978), under which the emphasis is on exchange relationships between followers and leaders. The culture that results is likely to be one characterized by dissent, which may be more or less tolerated.

In transformational leadership, the leader changes the goals of followers or subordinates. New goals are assumed to be of a higher level and represent the collective good, or pooled interests, of leaders and followers (Burns, 1978). A 'vision' combines the members into a collective whole, with a shared set of aspirations that is capable of guiding their behaviour. The transformational leader inspires, intellectually stimulates, and is individually considerate to followers (Bass, 1999). Charisma is needed to communicate the vision—but while a transformational leader may have charisma, he or she may also display other less desirable leadership traits.

EXAMPLE Transformational leadership?

We will see, in Chapter 9, that Jack Welch, chief executive officer (CEO) of the *General Electric Company* between 1981 and 2000, while revered widely as charismatic and an exemplary CEO, was also described as arguably narcissistic. He was labelled 'Neutron Jack' for his ability to eliminate people and their jobs while leaving buildings intact. His rhetoric, found in annual report letters to stockholders, has been analysed by researchers (Amernic et al., 2007), and has been found to show how Welch offers little recognition of the positive contribution that debate and dissent can make to organizations. The language seems directed to shaping a uniform definition of reality that accords with his vision of the truth. He repeatedly asserts the assumed positive value of his approach to such fraught issues as sacking employees; he appears to assume that, if he defines actions—such as dismissing people—in positive terms, then the actions must be so.

We know that most managers do not exude charisma; indeed, quite a few have a reputation for being boring (Tourish and Pinnington, 2002). Maccoby (2000a) suggests that many charismatic leaders are likely to be narcissists—that is, people with a well-developed self-image in which they take great pride and on which they reflect frequently (see chapter on personality). They are also likely to have a strong need for power, high self-confidence, and strong convictions (De Vries et al., 1999). As Yukl (1999) has argued, expressing strong convictions, acting confidently, and taking decisive action may create an impression of exceptional expertise, but it can also discourage feedback from followers. Charismatic leadership is consequently an indispensable ingredient of cults and was observed in the Jonestown cult of the 1970s (Layton, 1999), the suicidal Heaven's Gate cult in California (Booth and Claiborne, 1997), and in the Aum cult in Japan (Lifton, 1999).

The assumption of 'greater' goals requires a leap of faith on behalf of the followers. By definition, the transformational leader needs more power than constraints in order to restrain the power of potential dissidents. The transformational leader may have to take unpopular decisions, reject conventional wisdom, and take reasonable risk (Bass, 1990)—and the dangers inherent to doing so are considerable. For example, research has shown that new group members—or those with low status—acquire influence within a group only by over-conforming to the norms (Brown, 2000). If they do not do so, they risk being penalized—usually through the withdrawal of valued social rewards.

Rosener (1990) argues that men are more likely than women to describe themselves in ways that are characteristic of transactional leadership: they exchange rewards for services rendered, or punishment for inadequate performance. The men are also more likely to use power that comes from their organization and formal authority. She posits that women describe themselves in ways that are characteristic of transformational leadership—that is, getting subordinates to transform their own self-interest into the interest of the group through concern for a broader goal. They ascribe their power to personal characteristics, such as charisma, interpersonal skills, hard work, or personal contacts, rather than to organizational stature. Women actively work to make their interactions with subordinates positive for everyone involved. They encourage participation, share power, and get others excited about their work. This reflects the belief that allowing employees to contribute makes them feel powerful and important.

It may be that, on average, women leaders are more democratic and participative than their male counterparts—or, at least, are perceived to be so (Bass et al., 1996). It may be that this is only how women describe their style and that they have stereotyped their behaviour according to cultural views of gender-appropriate behaviour: few women want to indicate that they are 'masculine' (Epstein, 1991). But the magnitude of the differences between male and female leaders has generally been small (Eagly, 1987), and organizational factors may make a difference. For example, a female nurse in the operating room, seen in a job 'appropriate' for her gender, may be very task-oriented, while men may be more task-oriented in roles that are consistent with their gender, such as coaching men's football teams (Bass, 1967). Situations may, then, make all the difference.

STOP AND THINK **The difference between managers and leaders**

Kelly (2008) found the following pinned to the wall within one organization that she studied: 'Managers do efficiency; leaders create change.'

Do you find this an inspirational thought or an irritating one?

Situational leadership

The situation may have some effect on the preferred leadership style. Contingency theories of leadership consequently allow for the situational effect on leadership. Situational leadership theory states that effective leadership depends on the ability of the leader to diagnose situational conditions accurately and to respond with the appropriate combination of behaviours. Hersey and Blanchard (1988) believe that leadership is contingent on the amount of guidance and direction that a leader gives, the amount of socio-emotional support a leader provides, and the readiness level that followers exhibit. The critical situational factor that determines preferred leadership style is the task-related readiness of followers, labelled 'employee maturity' in early descriptions. Readiness is the extent to which a follower has the ability and willingness to accomplish a specific task (ibid.: 174); this will depend on the ability and technical skills needed to do a task, and the employee's self-confidence in his or her ability.

Using four leadership styles and four readiness levels, Hersey and Blanchard make several recommendations for leaders. They summarize appropriate leader styles in terms of a leader primarily 'telling', 'selling', 'participating', or 'delegating' in relations with subordinates. If, for example, subordinates are at the lowest level of readiness (for example, in the case of a newly appointed employee), telling is the best leadership style; delegating is the least effective. For subordinates at the highest level of readiness, delegating is the best style.

Hersey and Blanchard are, however, criticized for providing little evidence in support of their theory (Yukl, 1981). They are also criticized for their lack of conceptual clarity and lack of theoretical justification (Bass, 1990). Vecchio (1987) tested the theory. His results strongly supported the theory's prescriptions at low levels of follower readiness, but the recommended matches were not confirmed for high-readiness subordinates. Goodson et al. (1989) also failed to support the theory's use as a prescriptive tool. The most valuable contribution to evolve from the theory is its emphasis on leader flexibility or adaptability (Yukl, 1981; Goodson et al., 1989): training leaders to develop adaptive skills is a more promising approach than training leaders to adopt one particular style. Blake and Mouton (1978)—who add that the leader must assess the nature of the task and the task environment, as well as subordinate characteristics—also advocate this conclusion.

It might be asked, however, whether leaders are free agents who can choose their style to suit the situation. Enmeshed in the organization, the individual leader is constrained; he or she is expected to conform to the expectations of peers, subordinates, and superiors (Pfeffer, 1978; Fulop et al., 2004).

152

Emotion and leadership

'Emotion' and 'leadership' are two terms that are rarely seen together. Emotionality has been cast in opposition to, and lesser than, rationality (Blackmore, 1996). In daily life, rationality is seen to be a virtue and revered, while emotionality is seen to be an encumbrance and reviled. Yet those in leadership positions are constantly being assailed by emotional demands placed on them by their peers and others (Sachs and Blackmore, 1998). Emotional investment and emotion management is particularly going to be found in organizations in which there is the uncertainty and ambiguity inherent in a changing environment. Disappointment arising from a lack of promotion, conflict over work tasks, and matters of policy and practice, for example, are going to be features of almost all organizations at times. As a result, individuals typically talk about controlling emotions and handling emotional situations, as well as emotional feelings, and dealing with people, situations, and emotions. The effective and efficient functioning of organizations therefore necessitates emotional control; carefully regulated and tempered emotions, such as warmth, patience, strength, calm, caring, concern, and expressing vulnerability, are likely to be privileged over anger, rage, and passion (Hargreaves, 1995).

Managers and leaders consequently have to have the ability to assess feelings. Every time they handle an office quarrel, an interdepartmental rivalry, or a family emergency, they function as a sort of judge, assessing who is under too much stress, or who feels angry or jealous (Hochschild, 1993). They decide which feelings seem 'healthy' and which are 'sick' (Parkin, 1993)—and company culture sets the social boundaries between the right and wrong thing to do.

Charisma appears to be important for some when considering leadership (Lindholm, 1990; Conger and Kanungo, 1998)—and charisma and emotion, it can be argued, are linked. In making judgements about how 'charismatic' a leader is, we are articulating our emotional response to that leader.

EXAMPLE Research on mood and leadership

Mood and the feelings of the leader may play an important role in leadership. George and Bettenhausen (1990) found that the extent to which leaders of work groups experienced positive moods was positively related to levels of pro-social behaviour performed by group members and negatively related to group labour turnover rates. George (1995) found that work groups led by sales managers who tended to experience positive moods at work provided higher-quality customer service than groups led by managers who did not tend to experience positive moods at work.

Mood and emotion capabilities are addressed by emotion intelligence theory and research (George, 2000; see also Chapter 2).

Views of emotion tend to be highly gendered. The expression of anger has been seen as culturally acceptable for men, but not for women. Negative terms such as 'dragon', 'bitch', and 'nag' are applied to women, but not to men. Women's anger is associated with characteristics of being sharp-tongued, cruel, nasty, whining, and unpleasant, while expressing her anger with tears will lead to her being described as emotional or manipulative (Court, 1995). Feminine managerial or leadership traits and emotions—for example, expressing empathy and being sensitive—are viewed in negative terms, as 'not masculine' (Fondas, 1997; Lewis and Simpson, 2007).

Gender and leadership

Until recently, women were extremely rare in major positions of public leadership. In world history, only forty-two women have ever served as presidents or prime ministers and twenty-five of those have come to office in the 1990s (Adler, 1999). The *Wall Street Journal* (1986) is credited with being the first to use the term 'glass ceiling' to acknowledge the invisible, but powerful, barrier that allows women to advance only to a certain level. The glass ceiling is a metaphor for prejudice and discrimination, which takes a number of forms; evidence supports the metaphor. In 2007, in US Fortune 500 companies, women held only 14.8 per cent of all board seats (Catalyst, 2007).

STOP AND THINK

Why do you think that men continue to have far more access to elite leadership positions than do women?

The traits that are characteristic of leaders and followers are similar to those that have historically been attributed to men and women, respectively. Leaders are expected to be assertive and influential, while followers are expected to be accommodating and responsive (Stogdill, 1950; Bass, 1973). The research on male–female leadership styles concludes that women are generally viewed as more nurturing, understanding, helpful, collaborative, empathetic, socially sensitive, cooperative, and expressive than their male counterparts (Eagly, 1987; Eagly and Johnson, 1990); in contrast, men are expected to be more independent, masterful, assertive, and competent. Females demonstrate more transformational leadership behaviour (individual consideration) than males (Bass et al., 1996).

These differences are thought to arise from socialization patterns, rather than genetics. It has been argued that men and women seek work roles that are most appropriate and consistent with their gender, resulting in gender differences in leadership styles that may be, to some extent, self-fulfilling (Eagly, 1987). Managerial positions may therefore still be described as requiring characteristics such as assertiveness, competitiveness, and tough mindedness, which are associated primarily with men (Powell and Butterfield, 1989); female personality traits and behaviour patterns may make females appear less suited for leadership roles involving dominance and assertiveness (Morrison and Von Glinow, 1990).

STOP AND THINK Offering advice to women in leadership

Women are advised in books about women and leadership to maintain their sense of humour. This can be demonstrated in one-liners such as 'Better to be big in the backside than have bullshit for brains', which is the retort attributed to a female Australian government minister after a male opponent made some unflattering comments about her appearance (Stewart, 2002). More examples are to be found in Kirner and Rayner (1999).

What advice might you offer?

Evidence on leadership style offers a number of different conclusions. This subject is confusing, because contradictory research findings exist (Wilson, 2003). There is a large volume of research that has shown that men and women do not actually differ in leadership style (Eagly and Johnson, 1990; Eagly and Karu, 1991; Bass et al., 1996). The paradox is that men and women have been perceived as possessing different strengths—but whether those differences result in either perceived or actual differences in leadership styles remains a noot point in the literature.

These perceived differences between men and women come to the forefront again in research on discipline and leadership. If, as individuals, we have beliefs about the behaviour that women and men should exhibit, and they violate those beliefs, we may regard them negatively as a consequence. For example, if women are expected to be warm, sensitive, passive, and supportive, then it might be expected to be more difficult for them to discipline. It is, in fact, more difficult for women to discipline if they are getting cues from subordinates that discipline from them is unwelcome; this could serve to reduce their confidence at discipline delivery, which, in turn, impacts on their behaviour and the way in which their disciplining is perceived. Women delivering discipline are perceived to be less effective and less fair than men (Atwater et al., 2001). Further, males may perceive women in positions of power as a threat (Hale, 1996).

STOP AND THINK Do women leaders have to be tougher than men?

Alice Eagly (2008) argues that some women who have risen to high places (Margaret Thatcher was a good example) may have had to emulate men and in fact 'overachieve'—that is, be more extreme—to gain legitimacy as a leader. She notes that leaders such as Golda Meir and Indira Gandhi adopted quite commanding, masculine leadership styles too.

She also notes, however, that in settings in which women leaders are more common, they tend to develop a more differentiated, nuanced style. Women can even take on a more maternal role, as in the case of Ellen Johnson-Sirleaf, who is president of Liberia. Eagly comments that Johnson-Sirleaf presented herself as a maternal leader capable of healing the nation's problems.

Do you think that women leaders have to be tougher than men?

Spirituality and leadership

Spiritual leadership theory has recently been posited as a new development. It claims to be based on vision, altruistic love, hope, and faith, grounded in an intrinsic motivation theory (Fry et al., 2007). Spiritual leadership taps into the fundamental needs of both leader and follower for spiritual survival through 'calling'—that is, a sense that one's life has meaning and makes a difference— and 'membership'—that is, a sense that one is understood, appreciated, and accepted unconditionally (Fleishman, 1994; Maddock and Fulton, 1998). The purpose of spiritual leadership is to create a vision coupled with value congruence across the individual, empowered team and organizational levels, and ultimately foster higher levels of both organizational commitment and productivity.

In a similar vein, a small stream of literature has emerged that emphasizes the leader as servant first, commonly described as the 'servant leader' (Greenleaf, 1977). Servant leadership is similar to transformational leadership (Farling et al., 1999). Patterson (2003) describes servant leadership, placing the highest priority on the needs and purposes of the individual followers above the goals and objectives of the organization. This, then, is clearly a unitary theory of leadership.

THE UNIVERSAL VALUES OF SPIRITUAL LEADERSHIP

1. Trust/loyalty in chosen relationships: being faithful; having faith in the character, ability, strength and truth of others.

2. Forgiveness/acceptance/gratitude: choosing the power of forgiveness through acceptance and gratitude.

3. Integrity: saying what you will do and doing what you say.

4. Honesty: seeking the truth and rejoicing in it; basing actions on it.

5. Courage: firmness of mind and will, as well as mental and moral strength to maintain morale and prevail in the face of extreme difficulty, opposition, threat, danger, hardship, and fear.

6. Humility: modesty; courteousy; not jealous, rude or arrogant.

7. Kindness: warm-hearted; considerate; humane; sympathetic to the feelings and needs of others.

8. Empathy/compassion: the ability to read and understand the feelings of others.

9. Patience/meekness/endurance: the ability to bear trials and pain, calmly and without complaint; constancy to any purpose, idea, or task in the face of obstacles or discouragement.

10. Excellence: recognizing, rejoicing in, and celebrating the efforts of others.

11. Fun: seeing daily activities and work as reasons for smiling, and having a terrific day in serving others.

Does this bear any resemblance to the values of any leaders whom you currently know or have known?

(*Source:* Fry et al., 2007)

Race and leadership

Like emotion and leadership, 'race' and 'leadership' are terms that are rarely seen together in the research literature or in textbooks about people and work. We saw in earlier chapters that racism is still prevalent in the jobs market—a fact that is described as 'shocking' by the BBC (BBC News, 12 July 2004). Lenny Henry, the comedian, believes that the lack of black and ethnic minority faces in top jobs is 'scandalous' (Pettengell, 2008). Twenty per cent of black managers believe that racial discrimination stands in the way of their career progression; this contrasts with only 1 per cent of white managers (*Management Today*, 2008). The statistics show that the numbers of ethnic minorities in managerial and professional jobs varies by ethnic group. While Chinese men and women improved their representation in managerial jobs in retail between 1992 and 2000, and are found in greater proportions than white workers, the proportions of black Caribbean and Pakistani managers remains low (Wright and Pollert, 2005).

There are very few studies of racism in the workplace. The little that there is—for example, Deitch et al. (2003)—shows that black people experience everyday discrimination in the form of minor pervasive mistreatment and unfairness at work. While the formal practice of racism has become less acceptable over the last sixty years, and legal protection is now afforded to those subject to racism and discrimination, this has not fully guaranteed equality. And if people deny that racism now exists for certain ethnic groups, or do not pay attention to the lack of some ethnic minorities in leadership positions, the situation is likely to remain the same.

Class and leadership

It may be worth touching on the topic of class and leadership. We saw in Chapter 1 how research evidence consistently demonstrates that there is a virtual stability in class mobility rates. There is a strong link between the class into which we are born into and the class in which we end up. While we might like to believe that society is meritocratic—that is, that individual merit, such as educational qualifications, should be the principal determinant of subsequent class position—empirical work addressing the role of education in class mobility has been far from conclusive in proving that this is actually the case. Even after controlling for educational qualifications, significant relationships between origins and class destinations remain (Breen, 1998). While merit certainly counts, 'children of disadvantaged class origins have to display far more merit than do children of more advantaged origins in order to attain similar class positions' (Breen and Goldthorpe, 1999: 21). People from lower classes 'learn' their place (Willis, 1977).

Leaders, then, are not likely to be evenly drawn from each class. The highest demand for qualifications is in the managerial and professional class (Jackson, 2001), but non-meritocratic characteristics, such as criteria with which to judge the suitability of an individual for a particular job, remains a significant part of the recruitment process. Those from certain class backgrounds are therefore likely to fit the employer's ideal type of employee better than those from other class backgrounds (Brown and Scase, 1994).

The class composition of senior management in the developed world has changed very little in the post-war period (Child, 1969). Most of the 'new' managerial groups that emerged in the 1970s came from old professional, administrative, and military backgrounds—that is, from a very limited social setting (Sampson, 1996; Burrell, 2002). Studies documenting the clear links between class and leadership include that of Lupton and Wilson (1974) on the aristocracy and their close associates, who acted as 'top decision makers' in the City of London in 1957, and the analysis of Barings Bank undertaken by Gapper and Denton (1996).

Conclusion

The literature on leadership is vast, yet still poses more questions than it offers answers about leadership and how it should, or can, be done. In this chapter, we have seen how one way in which to research leadership is through observing individual leaders, and analysing their personality traits and styles for the commonalities that make them good leaders. But this can potentially create a 'one size fits all' theory of leadership and ignores context. Situational or contingency leadership theory leaves us with a different set of problems.

In the absence of compelling evidence on the significance of leadership, we are forced back, to a considerable extent, on our convictions and beliefs. A belief in the potency of leaders is perhaps one of the most deeply rooted and 'magical' of human assumptions (Thomas, 2003). Some would argue that, as it is being researched, it appears to dissolve and disappear (Alvesson and Sveningsson, 2003), while Sinclair (2007) argues: 'Leadership should be aimed at helping to free people from oppressive structures, practices and habits encountered in societies and institutions as well as within the shady recesses of ourselves. Good leaders liberate.'

KEY POINTS

- Leadership, as a topic, appears to raise many questions, but provide few answers. The necessity of leadership may be a social myth that maintains the status quo.

- There are many definitions of leadership. The earliest theories looked at the traits of leaders.

- Style theorists have looked at how democratic leaders are or how they could transform their own self-interest into the interest of the group.

- The situation may influence leadership style.

- An understanding of leadership and emotion may help us to understand more of the challenges and realities of leadership.

- Spiritual leadership has constituted a new development in thinking about leadership.

- The chapter has also paid attention to the role of gender, race, and class as factors that can be considered when looking at inequality and leadership.

CASE STUDY
Democratic decision making

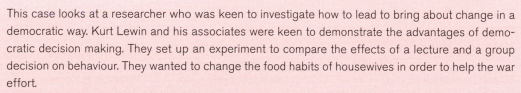

This case looks at a researcher who was keen to investigate how to lead to bring about change in a democratic way. Kurt Lewin and his associates were keen to demonstrate the advantages of democratic decision making. They set up an experiment to compare the effects of a lecture and a group decision on behaviour. They wanted to change the food habits of housewives in order to help the war effort.

Six groups of *Red Cross* volunteers, ranging in size from thirteen members to seventeen, were used. The objective was to increase the use in cooking of cow's hearts, sweetbreads (pancreas or thymus gland), and kidneys. In three groups, 'attractive' lectures (Lewin, 1959: 202) were given, which likened the problem of nutrition with the war effort, emphasized the vitamin and mineral value of the three meats, and gave detailed explanations with the aid of charts. Both the health and economic aspects were stressed. The preparation of these meats was discussed in detail, including techniques for avoiding aversion to odour, texture, and appearance. Recipes were distributed; the lecturer gave hints on her own methods for preparing these 'delicious dishes' and mentioned her success with her own family (ibid.).

In the other three groups, the problem of nutrition was linked to the war effort and general health in a discussion. Could the housewives be induced to participate in a programme of change without attempting any 'high-pressure salesmanship' (ibid.)? The group discussion about 'housewives like themselves' led to an elaboration of the obstacles that this change would encounter, such as distaste, or smell during cooking. The nutrition expert offered the same remedies and recipes for preparation that had been presented in the lectures to the other groups—but in these groups, preparation techniques were offered after the groups had become sufficiently involved to be interested in whether certain obstacles could be removed.

Near the start of the meeting, a show of hands demonstrated how many women had served any of these foods in the past. At the end of the meeting, the women were asked whether they were willing to try one of these meats in the next week. Only 3 per cent of those who heard the lectures served one of the meats never served before; of those attending the group decision, 32 per cent served one of the meats.

Lewin (1959) explained why the group discussion produced these results. Firstly, lecturing is a procedure in which the audience is chiefly passive; discussion is likely to lead to a much higher degree of involvement. Further, it is easier to change the ideologies and social practices of a small group handled together than those of single individuals. An individual in a small group is more likely to change if the group changes. (This is the practice adopted by those involved with alcoholics.)

It is interesting that Lewin himself notes that the difference between the results of the lectures and the group decision may be due to the fact that only after the group decision did the discussion leader mention that an inquiry would be made later as to whether a new food was introduced into the family diet. The 'threat' of follow-up in itself may therefore have influenced the results. It is also interesting that no mention is made of the gender of the nutrition 'expert'—but the discussion group appears to have been run by a male called Mr Bavelas, who was an experienced group worker 'and doubtless of unusual ability in this field' (Lewin, 1959: 204), while the lecture was given by a female, a 'housewife'. This, too, may have influenced the results—but Lewin does not consider the effect of this variable.

(*Source:* Lewin, 1959)

Questions

1. What are the main lessons of Lewin's experiment for leaders and managers trying to influence groups in organizations?

2. What are the flaws with Lewin's food experiment?

FURTHER READING

Fulop, L., Linstead, S., and Dunford, R. (2004) 'Leading and managing', in S. Linstead, L. Fulop, and S. Lilley (eds), *Management and Organization: A Critical Text*, Houndmills: Palgrave Macmillan, ch. 10 This chapter asks some uncomfortable questions such as whether leaders can change their styles or behaviours and whether we need leaders; it also provides some answers.

Jackson, B. and Parry, B. (2008) *A Very Short, Fairly Interesting and Reasonably Cheap Book About Studying Leadership*, London: Sage This book is, as Keith Grint notes on the cover, extremely interesting rather than fairly so. It manages to say a huge amount about leadership in about 150 pages and will answer questions such as whether leaders are born or made.

Sinclair, A. (1999) *Doing Leadership Differently: Gender, Power and Sexuality in a Changing Business Culture*, Melbourne: Melbourne University Press This book critically assesses the concept of leadership. It particularly questions the traditional tough heterosexual male form of leadership and why our faith in it is so misplaced. If you like this, you may also like Sinclair (2009), in which the author argues that leadership development is a process of seduction.

Thomas, A.B. (2003) *Controversies in Management: Issues, Debates, Answers*, 2nd edn, London: Routledge Chapter 8, entitled 'Organizational leadership: Does it make a difference?', offers a counterpoint to much of the research on leadership, which can appear prescriptive (for example, 'participative and democratic managers are best'). It throws into sharp relief a more confused picture, with contradictory findings, and invites us to ask interesting questions such as whether leadership even makes a difference and whether effective leadership exists.

Thompson, P. and McHugh, D. (2002) *Work Organizations*, 3rd edn, Houndmills: Palgrave Chapter 12, entitled 'Open to persuasion: Communication and leadership', critically discusses how managers buy into ideologies of control and how that is more or less taken for granted.

Western, S. (2008) *Leadership: A Critical Text*, London: Sage This book takes a very original approach to leadership: for example, it deals with challenging issues, such as religious fundamentalism and leadership.

LINKS TO FILMS AND NOVELS

Ghandi (1982) dir. R. Attenborough   This film focuses on Mahatma Ghandi's leadership during the Indian revolt against the British.

Hotel Rwanda (2004) dir. T. George   This film tells the story of Paul Rusesabagina, a hotel manager whose leadership offered succour to over a thousand Tutsi refugees during their struggle against the Hutu militia in Rwanda.

RESEARCH QUESTIONS

1. Tourish and Pinnington (2002) draw on the similarities between the components of transformational leadership and the characteristics of leadership found in cults. How do they do this? To what effect?

2. 'A frightening irony is that those who actively seek leadership are perceived as narcissistic and grandiose, wanting it too badly, and those who are emotionally healthy and could be exceptional leaders shrink from publically exerting their leadership abilities' (Herman, 2007). Discuss.

3. Is it time to stop talking about gender differences between men and women in leadership? (See Epstein, 1991; Eagly and Carli, 2007.)

REFERENCES

Adler, N.J. (1999) 'Global leaders: women of influence', in G. Powell (ed.), *Handbook of Gender and Work*, Thousand Oaks, CA: Sage, pp. 239–61.

Alvesson, M. and Sveningsson, S. (2003) 'The great disappearance act: Difficulties in doing leadership', *Leadership Quarterly*, 14: 359–81.

Amernic, J., Craig, R., and Tourish, D. (2007) 'The transformational leader as pedagogue, physician, architect, commander and saint: Five root metaphors in Jack Welch's letters to stockholders of General Electric', *Human Relations*, 60: 1839–72

Argyris, C. (1957) *Personality and Organization*, New York: Harper.

Atwater, L.E., Carey, J.A., and Waldman, D.A. (2001) 'Gender and discipline in the workplace: Wait until your father gets home', *Journal of Management*, 27: 537–61.

Bass, B.M. (1967) 'Social behaviour and the orientation inventory: A review', *Psychological Bulletin*, 68: 260–92.

_____ (1973) *Leadership, Psychology and Organizational Behaviour*, Westport, CT: Greenwood Press.

_____ (1985) *Leadership and Performance: Beyond Expectations*, New York: Free Press.

_____ (1990) *Bass and Stogdill's Handbook of Leadership: Theory, Research and Managerial Applications*, New York: Free Press.

_____ (1999) 'Two decades of research and development in transformational leadership', *European Journal of Work and Organizational Psychology*, 8: 9–26.

_____ and Franke, R.H. (1972) 'Societal influences on student perceptions of how to succeed in organizations', *Journal of Applied Psychology*, 56: 312–18.

_____, Alvio, B.J., and Atwater, L. (1996) 'Transformational and transactional leadership of men and women', *Applied Psychology: An International Review*, 45(1): 5–34.

_____, Burger, P.C., Doktor, R., and Barrett, G.V. (1979) *Assessment of Managers: An International Comparison*, New York: Free Press.

Bennis, W. (1989) *Why Leaders Can't Lead: The Unconscious Conspiracy Continues*, San Francisco, CA: Jossey Bass.

Bies, R. and Tripp, T. (1998) 'Two faces of the powerless: Coping with tyranny in organizations', in R. Kramer and M. Neale (eds), *Power and Influence in Organizations*, London: Sage, ch. 9.

Blackmore, J. (1996) 'Doing emotional "labour" in the education market place: Stories from the field of women in management', *Discourse*, 17: 337–50.

Blake, R.R. and Mouton, J.S. (1964) *The Managerial Grid*, Houston, TX: Gulf.

_____ _____ (1978) *The New Managerial Grid*, Houston, TX: Gulf.

Booth, W. and Claiborne, W. (1997) 'Cult group's leader among suicides', *Washington Post*, 29 March, p. A01.

Breen, R. (1998) 'The persistence of class origin inequalities among school leavers in the Republic of Ireland, 1984–1993', *British Journal of Sociology*, 49(2): 275–98.

_____ and Goldthorpe, J. (1999) 'Class inequality and meritocracy: A critique of Saunders and an alternative analysis', *British Journal of Sociology*, 50(1): 1–27.

Brown, P. and Scase, R. (1994) *Higher Education and Corporate Realities: Class, Culture and the Decline of Graduate Careers*, London: UCL Press.

Brown, R. (2000) *Group Processes*, 2nd edn, Oxford: Blackwell.

Bryman, A. (1986) *Leadership and Organizations*, London: Routledge & Kegan Paul.

_____ (1987) 'The generalizability of implicit leadership theory', *Journal of Social Psychology*, 127(2): 129–41.

Burns, J.M. (1978) *Leadership*, New York: Academic Press/Harper & Row.

Burrell, G. (2002) 'Twentieth-century quadrilles: Aristocracy, owners, managers and professionals', *International Studies of Management and Organization*, 2: 25–50.

Catalyst (2000) *Census of Women Corporate Officers and Top Earners*, New York: Catalyst.

_____ (2007) *2007 Catalyst Census of Women Board Directors of the FP500: Voices From the Boardroom*, New York: Catalyst.

Child, J. (1969) *The Business Enterprise in Modern Industrial Society*, London: Collier Macmillan.

Conger, J.A. and Kanugo, R.N. (1998) *Charismatic Leadership in Organizations*, Thousand Oaks, CA: Sage.

Court, M. (1995) 'Good girls and naughty girls: Rewriting the scripts for women's anger', in B. Limerick and R. Lingard (eds), *Gender and Changing Educational Management*, Sydney: Hodder & Stoughton.

Deitch, E.A., Barsky, A., Butz, R.M., Chan, S., Brief, A.P., and Bradley, J.C. (2003) 'Subtle yet significant: The existence and impact of everyday racial discrimination in the workplace', *Human Relations*, 56: 1299–1324.

De Vries, R., Roe, R., and Thaillieu, T. (1999) 'On charisma and need for leadership', *European Journal of Work and Organizational Psychology*, 8: 109–26.

Eagly, A.H. (1987) *Sex Differences in Social Behavior: A Social Role Interpretation*, Hillsdale, NJ: Lawrence Erlbaum Associates.

_____ (2008) 'Men, women and leadership', The Interview, *Psychologist*, 21(3): 216–17.

_____ and Carli, L.L. (2007) *Through the Labyrinth: The Truth About How Women Become Leaders*, Boston, MA: Harvard Business School Press.

_____ and Johnson, B.T. (1990) 'Gender and leadership style: A meta-analysis', *Psychological Bulletin*, 108: 233–56.

_____ and Karu, S.S. (1991) 'Gender and the emergence of leaders: A meta-analysis', *Journal of Personality and Social Psychology*, 60: 685–710.

Epstein, C.F. (1991) 'Ways men and women lead', *Harvard Business Review*, January–February: 150–1.

Farling, M.L., Stone, A.G., and Winston, B.E. (1999) 'Servant leadership: Setting the stage for empirical research', *Journal of Leadership and Organizational Studies*, 6(1–2): 49–72.

Fleischman, P.R. (1994) *The Healing Spirit: Explorations in Religion and Psychotherapy*, Cleveland, OH: Bonne Chance Press.

Follett, M.P. (1982) 'The teacher–student relation', in E. Fox and L Urwick (eds), *Dynamic Administration*, New York, Hippocrene Books, pp. 303–25.

_____ (1918; 1998) *The New State–Group Organization: The Solution for Popular Government*, University Park, PA: The Pennsylvania State University Press.

Fondas, N. (1997) 'Feminization unveiled: Management qualities in contemporary writings', *Academy of Management Review*, 22(1): 257–82.

Fry, L.W., Matherly, L.L., Whittington, J.L., and Winston, B.E. (2007) 'Spiritual leadership as an integrating paradigm for servant leadership', in S. Sengupta (ed.), *Integrating Spirituality and Organizational Leadership*, Bangalore: Macmillan India, pp. 70–82.

Fulop, L., Linstead, S., and Dunford, R. (2004) 'Leading and managing', in S. Linstead, L. Fulop, and S. Lilley (eds), *Management and Organization: A Critical Text*, Houndmills: Palgrave Macmillan, ch. 10.

Gapper, J. and Denton, N. (1996) *All That Glitters: The Fall of Barings*, Harmondsworth: Penguin.

Gemmill, G. and Oakley, J. (1992) 'Leadership: An alienating social myth?', *Human Relations*, 45(2): 113–29.

George, J.M. (1995) 'Leader positive mood and group performance: The case of customer service', *Journal of Applied Social Psychology*, 25: 778–94.

_____ (2000) 'Emotions and leadership: The role of emotional intelligence', *Human Relations*, 8: 1027–55.

_____ and Bettenhausen, K. (1990) 'Understanding prosocial behaviour, sales performance and turnover: A group level analysis in a service context', *Journal of Applied Psychology*, 75: 698–709.

Goodson, J.R., McGee, G.W., and Cashman, J.F. (1989) 'Situational leadership theory: A test of leadership prescriptions', *Group and Organization Studies*, 14(4): 446–61.

Graham, P. (ed.) (1996) *Mary Parker Follett: Prophet of Management*, Boston, MA: Harvard Business School Press.

Greenleaf, R.K. (1977) *Servant Leadership: A Journey Into the Nature of Legitimate Power and Greatness*, New York: Paulist Press.

Grint, K. (2000) *The Arts of Leadership*, Oxford: Oxford University Press.

_____ (2005a) *Leadership: Limits and Possibilities*, New York: Palgrave Macmillan.

_____ (2005b) 'Public opinion: Keith Grint', *The Times*, 8 March, available online at http://www.lums.lancs.ac.uk/news/5150/timesgrintopinion

Hale, M. (1996) 'Gender equality in organizations', *Review of Public Personnel Administration*, Winter: 7–18.

Hargreaves, A. (1995) 'Development and desire: A postmodern perspective', in T. Guskey and H. Huberman (eds), *Professional Development in Education*, New York: Teachers College Press, ch. 1.

Herman, S. (2007) 'Leadership training in a "not-leadership" society', *Journal of Management Education*, 31: 151–5.

Hersey, P. and Blanchard, K.H. (1988) *Management of Organizational Behavior: Utilising Human Resources*, 4th edn, Englewood Cliffs, NJ: Prentice Hall.

Hochschild, A. (1993) *Preface to Emotion in Organizations*, ed. S. Fineman, London: Sage.

Jackson, M. (2001) 'Non-meritocratic job requirements and the reproduction of class inequality: An investigation', *Work, Employment and Society*, 15: 619–30.

Jacques, R. (1996) *Manufacturing the Employee: Management Knowledge From the 19th to 21st Centuries*, London: Sage.

Kelly, S. (2008) 'Leadership: A categorical mistake?', *Human Relations*, 61: 763–82.

Kirner, J. and Rayner, M. (1999) *The Women's Power Handbook*, Melbourne: Viking.

Layton, D. (1999) *Seductive Poison: A Jonestown Survivor's Story of Life and Death in the People's Temple*, London: Aurum Press.

161

Lewin, K. (1947) 'Frontiers in group dynamics: Concept, method and reality in social science—Social equilibria and social change', *Human Relations*, 1(1): 5–41.

_____ (1959) 'Group decision and social change', in E. Maccoby, T.M. Newcomb, and E.L. Hartley (eds), *Readings in Social Psychology*, 3rd edn, London: Methuen, pp. 197–211.

_____ and Lippitt, R. (1938) 'An experimental approach to the study of autocracy and democracy: A preliminary note', *Sociometry*, 1: 292–300.

_____, Lippitt, R., and White, R.K. (1939) 'Patterns of aggressive behavior in experimentally created "social climates"', *Journal of Social Psychology*, 10: 271–99.

Lewis, P. and Simpson, R. (2007) *Gendering Emotions in Organizations*, Basingstoke: Palgrave Macmillan.

Lifton, R. (1999) *Destroying the World to Save it: Aum Shinrikyo, Apocalyptic Violence and the New Global Terrorism*, New York: Holt.

Likert, R. (1961) *New Patterns of Management*, New York: McGraw Hill.

_____ (1967) *The Human Organization*, New York: McGraw Hill.

_____ (1977) *Past and Future Perspectives on System 4*, Orlando, FL: Academy of Management.

Lindholm, C. (1990) *Charisma*, Cambridge, MA: Basil Blackwell.

Lippitt, R. (1940) *An Experimental Study of Authoritarian and Democratic Group Atmospheres*, Studies in Topological and Vector Psychology I, Iowa City, IO: University of Iowa Press.

_____ and White, R. (1943) 'The "social climate" of children's groups', in R. Barker, J. Kounin, and B. Wright (eds), *Child Behaviour and Development*, New York: McGraw Hill.

_____ (1959) 'An experimental study of leadership and group life', in E. Maccoby, T.M. Newcomb, and E.L. Hartley (eds), *Readings in Social Psychology*, 3rd edn, London: Methuen.

Locke, E.A. (1991) *The Essence of Leadership: The Four Keys to Leading Successfully*, New York: Lexington Books.

Lupton, T. and Wilson, S. (1974) 'The social background and connections of top decision makers', in J. Urry and J. Wakeford (eds), *Power in Britain*, London: Heinemann, pp. 185–204.

Maccoby, M. (2000a) 'Narcissistic leaders: The incredible pros and the inevitable cons', *Harvard Business Review*, 78: 69–77.

_____ (2000b) 'Understanding the difference between management and leadership', *Research Technology Management*, 43(1): 57–9.

Maddock, R.C. and Fulton, R.L. (1998) *Motivation, Emotions and Leadership: The Silent Side of Management*, Westport, CT: Quorum Books.

Management Today (2008) 'Racial discrimination still rife', 19 June, available online at http://www.managementtoday.co.uk/search/article/821744/racial-discrimination-rife/

McGregor, D. (1960) *The Human Side of Enterprise*, New York: McGraw Hill.

Meindl, J.R. (1990) 'On leadership: An alternative to the conventional wisdom' in B.M. Staw and L.L. Cummings (eds), *Research in Organizational Behavior, Vol XII*, Greenwich, CT: JAI Press, pp. 159–203.

_____ (1995) 'The romance of leadership as a follower-centric theory: A social constructionist approach', *The Leadership Quarterly*, 6(3): 329–41.

Morrison, A. and Von Glinow, M. (1990) 'Women and minorities in management', *American Psychologist*, 45: 200–8.

Oates, D. (1973) 'Ways to change managerial behaviour', *International Management*, 28(4): 54–8.

Parkin, W. (1993) 'The public and the private: Gender, sexuality and emotion', in S. Fineman (ed.), *Emotion in Organizations*, London: Sage, ch. 8.

Patterson, K.A. (2003) 'Servant leadership: A theoretical model', *Dissertation Abstracts International*, 64(2): 570.

People Management (2005) 'One hell of a guy', 24 March, pp. 26–8.

Pettengell, T. (2008) 'Off message: No laughing matter', *Personnel Today*, 25 February, available online at http://www.personneltoday.com/articles/2008/02/25/44548/off-message-no-laughing-matter.html

Pfeffer, J. (1978) 'The ambiguity of leadership', in M.W. McCall and M.M. Lombardo (eds), *Leadership: Where Else Can We Go?*, Durham: Duke University Press, pp. 13–34.

Powell, G.N. and Butterfield, D.A. (1989) 'The "good manager": Did androgyny fare better in the 1980s?', *Group and Organization Studies*, 14: 216–33.

Rosener, J.B. (1990) 'Ways women lead', *Harvard Business Review*, November–December: 119–25.

Sachs, J. and Blackmore, J. (1998) 'You never show you can't cope: Women in school leadership roles managing their emotions', *Gender and Education*, 10(3): 265–79.

Sampson, A. (1996) *Company Man*, London: Harper Collins.

Schyns, B. and Meindl, J.R. (2005) *Implicit Leadership Theories*, Greenwich, CT: Information Age Publishing.

Shamir, B (2007) *Follower-Centered Perspectives on Leadership*, Greenwich, CT: Information Age Publishing.

Sievers, B. (1993) *Work, Death and Life Itself: Essays on Management and Organization*, New York: De Gruyter.

Sinclair, A. (2007) *Leadership for the Disillusioned*, Crows Nest, NSW: Allen and Unwin.

_____ (2009) 'Seducing leadership: Stories of leadership development', *Gender, Work and Organization*, 16(2): 266–84.

Smircich, L. and Morgan, G. (1982) 'Leadership: The management of meaning', *Journal of Applied Behavioral Science*, 18(3): 257–73.

Smith, D. (1997) 'Managers lack proper skills', *Sunday Times*, 14 September.

Stewart, C. (2002) 'It's Amanda's world', *Weekend Australian*, 1–2 July.

Stogdill, R.M. (1948) 'Personal factors associated with leadership: A survey of the literature', *Journal of Psychology*, 25: 35–71.

_____ (1950) 'Leadership, membership and organization', *Psychological Bulletin*, 47: 1–14.

_____ (1974) *Handbook of Leadership: A Survey of Theory and Research*, New York: The Free Press.

Thomas, A.B. (2003) *Controversies in Management: Issues, Debates, Answers*, 2nd edn, London: Routledge.

Tolstoy, L.N. (1869; 1957) *War and Peace*, 2 vols, trans. R. Edmonds, Harmondsworth: Penguin.

Tourish, D. and Pinnington, A. (2002) 'Transformational leadership, corporate cultism and the spirituality paradigm: An unholy trinity in the workplace?', *Human Relations*, 55(2): 147–72.

Vecchio, R.P. (1987) 'Situational leadership theory: An examination of a prescriptive theory', *Journal of Applied Psychology*, 72(3): 444–51.

Wall Street Journal (1986) 'The corporate woman: A special report', 24 March, supplement.

Wheelock, L.D. and Callahan, J.L. (2006) 'Mary Parker Follett: A rediscovered voice informing the field of human resource development', *Human Resource Development Review*, 5: 258–73.

Willis, P. (1977) *Learning to Labour*, Brighton: Saxon House.

Wilson, F.M. (2003) *Organizational Behaviour and Gender*, Aldershot: Ashgate.

Wright, T. and Pollert, A. (2005) *The Experience of Ethnic Minority Workers in Hotel and Catering Industry: Routes to Support and Advice on Workplace Problems: A Review of the Issues*, Working Lives Research Institute Working Paper No. 1, London: London Metropolitan University.

Yukl, G.A. (1981) *Leadership in Organizations*, Englewood Cliffs, NJ: Prentice Hall.

_____ (1999) 'An evaluative essay on current conceptions of effective leadership', *European Journal of Work and Organizational Psychology*, 8: 33–48.

8

Perception

Introduction

This chapter is about how we perceive people in organizations. This appears to be a topic that the critical texts in organizational behaviour tend to miss—perhaps because it has not been subject to much critical scrutiny in the research literature. It could be argued that all management starts from perception, because we manage what we perceive to be happening (Clegg et al., 2008). The research from psychology on perception helps each of us to understand how we make sense of the information that we receive through our eyes, ears, and other senses—that is, the process of perceptions. Psychology has examined how the process of perception can significantly affect how we are evaluated and how we evaluate others in organizations. It challenges us to question the accuracy of our own perceptions, and to think about the positive and negative consequences of our perceptions, as well as some of the fundamental errors that are made in the perceptual process—that is, about bias, prejudice, and stereotyping. These errors have important implications for our roles in organizations and in life in general. We need to reflect critically on the process of perception in order to understand how we may see things differently. We also need to be aware of possible pitfalls in order to overcome them.

The aim of the chapter is make you think about how you perceive people and how you may have reason to doubt the accuracy of your own perceptual process. You may also think about how others perceive you. It is important that we have an understanding of our own and other's perceptions in order to gain insight into the behaviour that we witness in organizations and to have the ability to assess this process critically. It is also important to see how class and other factors may influence, or even determine, what we think we perceive. Fortunately, there are theories that can help to give us insight into thinking about this issue.

This chapter covers:

- the study of perception;
- Gestalt psychology and perception;
- attribution theory;
- conformity;
- implicit personality theory;
- the logical error;
- stereotypes and prejudice;
- the distortion of perception;
- the halo effect;
- frames and their effect on perception;
- classifications and their consequences;
- perceptions of employers by employees and the psychological contract;
- self-perception;
- further ways in which perception can be shaped.

The study of perception

The study of perception is a study that includes how we make sense of the information that we receive through the sense organs of the body. Most of the research on perception has focused on what we see— that is, on visual perception— rather than on what we hear or feel. Information received directly from the sense organs is known as 'sensation'—but perception is not the same as sensation, because we do not receive sensory information passively. We know this because if we were to pick up all information—that is, what we currently smell, what we feel through our nerve endings, and what we hear—we would be over-whelmed with information. Instead, we pay attention to the information that is important and we are able to ignore the rest. For example, we are able to ignore the constant hum of the central heating or air con-ditioning. We analyse, organize, and interpret stimuli picked up by the sense organs to make use of it.

Perception is not necessarily truthful; it may not coincide with realities. An individual's perceptions may be influenced by many factors, including his or her needs, wishes, and expectations. The implication of this is that 'we tend to perceive what we wish or expect to perceive' (Merton, 1957).

PERCEPTION DEPENDS ON HOW WE SEE OURSELVES ...

Dolly Parton is quoted as saying: 'I don't believe blondes are dumb. On the other hand, I've never believed I am a blonde.'

(*Source:* http://www.imdb.com/name/nm0000573/bio)

PERCEPTION DEPENDS ON HOW OTHERS SEE US: WHEN PERCEIVED BEAUTY BRINGS BIAS

Giam Cipriani and Angelo Zago looked at the exam results of 885 economics students in Verona, Italy, over three years. They discovered that those who were more beautiful than others performed much better in their exams than those who were not so good-looking. It may be, then, that those who are perceived as more beauti-ful are given more attention by teachers and therefore a greater chance to excel.

(*Source:* David Astle, *The Sun Herald,* 22 April 2007)

PERCEPTION MAY DEPEND ON CLASS: PERCEIVING STUDENT DEBT

Student's perceptions of, and attitudes to, debt appear to be influenced by class. Those from low social classes are more debt-averse than those from other social classes and are far more likely to be deterred from going to university because of their fear of debt.

(*Source:* Callender and Jackson, 2005)

PERCEPTION MAY DEPEND ON EXTERNAL INFLUENCES UPON THE OBSERVER

Even the simple act of holding a cold or hot drink can exert a powerful effect on your personal perception. University students were asked to hold a cup of either hot or iced coffee while they answered a few questions. Next, they had a brief chat with another researcher. He left and the participants were asked whether they would recommend him for a job. The participants who, several minutes earlier, had held the cold drink said that they would not hire him, whereas those who had held the warm drink said that they would. The potential practical applications are startling.

(*Source:* Williams and Bargh, 2007)

Gestalt psychology and perception

Gestalt means a unified or meaningful whole. Gestalt psychology is a school of psychology that emphasizes a human tendency towards wholeness of perception or experience; we interpret information to organize it to make patterns or to give it meaning. Gestalt is a theory that focuses on the ways in which the brain organizes information. Regarding perception, Gestalt psychology suggests that what we perceive is influenced by how we organize sensory information. For example, dots, lines, and shapes can have meaning for us. We do not only see in the image below a number of dots; what we see is a pattern of dots—that is, four groups of two dots.

■ ■ ■ ■

During the 1930s, the Gestalt psychologists—such as Max Wertheimer and Kurt Koffka—showed how some of the ways in which we classify visual information appear to be 'built into' our perceptual system. For the Gestalt psychologists, the whole is more than the sum of its parts. Perception appears to be loaded with meaning, so we attribute meaning of some sort to even the simplest collections of visual stimuli, as we saw above. We do this by automatically grouping stimuli together rather than viewing each stimulus as separate from everything around it. In the Gestalt 'principle of similarity', if all things are equal, we automatically perceive similar items as belonging together. For example, in a textbook, we will instantly and automatically see pictures and diagrams as similar and different from the body of the text. Even if things are not equal, this can be overridden by the Gestalt 'principle of proximity', under which stimuli that are close to each other are seen as forming a group, as we saw in the example above.

One of the strongest of the Gestalt principles of perception is the 'principle of closure'. According to this principle, we have a strong tendency to prefer closed figures to fragmented or unconnected lines. For example, if you were to see a circle made up of lines with gaps in between, you would still perceive it as a circle rather than as disconnected lines. In a similar way, the 'principle of good' also affects our perception, according to which we prefer figures that appear to be well rounded or symmetrical to those that seem fragmented or messy. We also tend to see things in terms of figures against backgrounds.

It would appear, then, that by organizing what we see, we interpret what we see, thus influencing our perception. Cognition is a primary determinant of perception and is affected by our needs, values, education, and personal history. Knowing about the perceptual process could be important for advertisers, designers, or those involved with health and safety in organizations. In the case of those involved in health and safety, knowledge of the perceptual process might help them understand how their messages could be perceived, or how they might communicate the message more effectively. It also helps us all to understand why we might perceive the same event, or person, differently.

Attribution theory

A variation of the theory of perception derives from attribution theory, which helps us to explain more about people perception in organizations, because it develops explanations of how we judge people differently depending on the meaning that we attribute to given behaviour (Kelley, 1971).

Attribution theory suggests that we observe a person's behaviour and then try to establish whether internal or external forces caused it. If it is judged to be internal, it is seen as being under the person's control; if it is judged to be external, it is seen as a result of the situation. Attribution is said to be subjected to a number of considerations, because we judge actions in a context. For example, we judge how distinctive behaviour is and whether behaviour is unusual for a particular person. If, for example, the person is absent from work and the circumstances are that his or her attendance record is exemplary, then the behaviour could be considered unusual and an external cause (that is, that the behaviour is outside the control of the individual) will be attributed. If the absenteeism fits in with the general pattern of behaviour, then an internal attribution will be attached (that is, it will be seen as being under the person's control).

We also judge how consistent the behaviour is: if it is consistent, then we are more likely to attribute the behaviour to internal causes. Further, we judge whether there is 'consensus'—that is, whether everyone faced with a similar situation would react in the same way—and we draw inferences. And we attribute causes to success or failure: ability, effort, luck, or task difficulty (Weiner et al., 1971). Even rape, for example, has been attributed to the individual: research has found that females who are raped are often perceived as having 'caused' it, or as being responsible in some way due to the way in which they have dressed or their behaviour.

> **EXAMPLE Attribution and date rape**
>
> Research has found that many people believe that the occurrence of date rape is aggravated by how the woman dresses. Male and female students, shown a photograph of a female rape victim in provocative clothing, were most likely to indicate that the victim was responsible for her assailant's behaviour and that his behaviour was justified, and were least likely to judge the act of unwanted sexual intercourse as rape. No differences between men and women were found. Even a minimal cue, such as a three-inch difference in skirt length, resulted in differences in responsibility attributed to a victim of a date rape. Convicted rapists endorse the view that victims cause rape through their appearance or behaviour.
>
> (*Source:* Workman and Freeburg, 1999)

Conformity

Perception may also be influenced by a need to conform. A group—or simply the people around us—can affect our perception. Solomon Asch, a Jewish Polish professor of psychology working in the USA, dramatically illustrated this in an experiment in 1951. He showed how people would deny the evidence of their own senses if others were to disagree with their judgements. Asch showed a group of eight people three black lines on a card and asked them to indicate which of the three lines was equal in length to a fourth vertical line, shown on a separate card.

The task was very easy and hardly anyone made a mistake when working alone; while in the group, unknown to the subject of the experiment, seven 'stooges' had been instructed to give the wrong answer. The stooges gave their answers first. When the naive subject was asked to respond, he or she yielded to the will of the bogus majority about one third of the time (listen to the programme available online at http://www.bbc.co.uk/radio4/science/mindchangers1.shtml and see Levine, 1999). Conformity to group pressure caused the participants to agree with the others even when these others were apparently wrong. The participants were not, in any sense, forced to conform, because they did not receive persuasion or threats from other group members. This experiment consequently helps us to understand more about how and why people conform in organizations, even when not under any threat.

Stanley Milgram was, for a time, Asch's research assistant and became familiar with Asch's conformity experiments. Milgram was interested in the study of conformity and obedience—partly as a result of his identification with the suffering of fellow Jews at the hands of the Nazis and in an attempt to fathom how the Holocaust could have happened. Firstly, Milgram modified Asch's procedure, using sound (Milgram, 1963). In each trial, subjects had to indicate which of a pair of tones was longer. Before giving an answer, the naive subject heard the tape-recorded answers of five other subjects. In a cross-cultural comparison of conformity with Norwegian and French participants, Milgram found the Norwegian participants to be more conforming than the French. He wondered whether it would be possible to demonstrate the power of social influence with something more than simple line judgements: how would changing aspects of the experimental situation alter the person's willingness to obey?

Subsequently, in one of the most significant and controversial psychological studies of the twentieth century, Milgram designed an experiment in which people were asked to inflict what they believed were increasingly painful shocks on innocent people when the experimenter told them to do so. Milgram found that an average person would readily inflict very painful, and even harmful, electric shocks on innocent victims in order to remain obedient. In the experiment, subjects believed that they were part of an experiment dealing with the relationship between punishment and learning. An experimenter instructed participants to shock a learner—a man described by most observers as 'mild-mannered and likeable' (Milgram, 1974:16)—which meant that they pressed a lever on a machine each time the learner made a mistake on a word-matching task. Each incorrect answer warranted, for the learner, a shock one level higher than its predecessor; the intensity of the shock increased in 15-volt increments, from 15 to 450 volts. Switches were labelled from 'Slight shock', through 'Very strong shock' and 'Danger: severe shock', to the final two switches at 435 and 450 volts, ominously labelled 'XXX'. The participants themselves were given a sample 45-volt shock, but the shock box that they 'gave' was a well-crafted prop and the learner, an actor, did not actually receive shocks. As the 'shocks' increased in intensity, the ostensible pain being experienced by the learner became increasingly apparent by way of shouts and protests emanating from the learner from behind a partition. Typically, the participants expressed concern over the learner's well-being, but the experimenter insisted that they continue—even when the learner was in apparent agony. When the learner was heard banging on the walls at 300–315 volt levels, the participants began to experience a new source of perceptual strain—and yet the results showed that a majority of subjects continued to obey, believing that they were delivering 450-volt shocks simply because the experimenter commanded them to do so.

In justifying why they were prepared to render severe shocks, these participants tended to devalue the learner by perceiving him as in some way deserving of the punishment, saying, for example: 'He is so dumb he deserves to get shocked.' As a result of the experiment, Milgram warned that when an individual 'merges … into an organizational structure, a new creature replaces the autonomous man, unhindered by the limitations of individual morality, freed of human inhibition, mindful only of the sanctions of authority' (Blass, 2002).

The Milgram experiments speak strongly to us of how the morally and socially 'undoable' becomes 'doable' (Russell and Gregory, 2006). A person's perception of what is morally or socially acceptable can be manipulated; it is not difficult, then, to think of situations in which individuals are requested to be obedient in organizations—to follow an order even if those orders entail harming another person.

Implicit personality theory

People perception is probably the most relevant for our purposes in understanding organizational behaviour. We each have an 'implicit personality theory'—that is, a set of concepts and assumptions that we use to describe, compare, and understand people. We have ideas about the personality characteristics that go together. For example, we have an idea of what the workplace bully or harasser might be like—but this 'profile' of the workplace bully might be implicit rather than explicit, and so we might experience difficulties if required to articulate its characteristics.

STOP AND THINK **Expectations and perceptions**

Lord Kitchener is best known for the famous First World War recruitment posters bearing his heavily moustachioed face and pointing hand over the legend 'Your country needs YOU'. Kitchener organized armies on an unprecedented scale and became a symbol of the national will to win.

Would your perception of the symbolism associated with Lord Kitchener lead you to anticipate that he was also a flower arranger?

(*Source:* BBC Radio 4, *Lord Kitchener's Image,* 10 November 2007)

STOP AND THINK **Further expectations and perceptions**

Brian May is lead guitarist and vocalist with the rock group Queen. He has a PhD in Astrophysics, and does not drink or smoke.

Teri Hatcher, who plays Susan Mayer in *Desperate Housewives* and played 'Bond Girl' Paris Carver in *Tomorrow Never Dies,* was an undergraduate on a mathematics and engineering course.

How well do the images or perceptions of rock legend and stunning actress fit with the other information that you now have about these people? What, then, does this tell us about implicit personality theory and the perceptions that we might hold about people in organizations?

The logical error

Our implicit personality theory might lead us to form hypotheses, or assumptions, about what traits fit together in a person. When faced with incomplete information, we form a more extensive and consistent view that is often referred to as the 'logical error'.

The logical error assumes that certain traits will always be found together. We use cues to lead to our view, as illustrated dramatically in experiments by Asch (1946) and Kelley (1950). Asch (1946) found that certain crucial cues, or labels, could transform the entire impression of the person, leading to further attributions. He read a list of adjectives that described a particular person, then asked the subjects to characterize that person. He found that the inclusion in the list of what he called 'central qualities'—such as 'warm' as opposed to 'cold'—produced a widespread change in the entire impression. The 'warm' person was subsequently also described by participants in the experiment as 'sociable', 'popular', 'good-natured', 'generous', and 'humorous'. Peripheral qualities such as 'polite' rather than 'blunt' did not, however, produce such strong effects. Kelley (1950) found that those given the favourable impression (the 'warm' cue) tended to interact more with the person. More recently, it has been found that when observers think positively about someone, believing him or her to be attractive, likeable, or interesting (that is, making positive dispositional attributions), they will also tend to believe that he or she is telling the truth (O'Sullivan, 2003).

169

Haire and Grunes (1950) designed an experiment in which they constructed a list of hypothetical personality characteristics of two factory workers, which were identical, except that one man was said to go to union meetings, while this point was not raised in the other. Respondents (students in a Psychology class) were then asked to describe the individual. Early pre-testing showed that the word 'intelligent', which was contained in the list, caused the respondents some difficulty: it did not fit well into their picture of a factory worker and consequently took up what was 'an inordinately large amount of their time' (ibid.: 405), leading to a number of different responses. Five of the forty-three respondents denied the existence of the word 'intelligent' in the list, while others were able to manage it by saying such things as 'He is intelligent but not too much so, since he works in a factory' (ibid.: 407). Others explained away the apparent conflict by joining intelligence with another item: for example, eight people postulated a lack of drive to account for the fact that this factory worker was intelligent; five people resolved the conflict by denying that he was a factory worker and promoting him to foreman; while three people recognised a disparity and responded by saying, for example, 'the traits seem to be conflicting … most factory workers I have heard about aren't too intelligent' (ibid.: 409).

In contrast, the descriptions of the factory worker who was not specified as either intelligent or a union member were very uniform. Respondents described a likeable and well-liked, mildly sociable, healthy, happy, uncomplicated, and well-adjusted sort of person, who, while not very intelligent, tried to keep abreast of current trends and sports. The descriptions were thought by Haire and Grunes to be 'a little patronising and snobbish' (ibid.: 406). For example, one of the respondents described the worker as 'probably not too cultured' and 'easily influenced by newspapers and movies and can be led to do something by following the crowd'. It can be concluded, therefore, that the students had a clear, well-organized picture of a 'working man' and that the attribute 'intelligent' did not fit their picture—that is, their stereotype—well.

A SMART BLONDE JOKE

A blonde walks into a bank and asks for the loan officer. She says that she is going to the USA on business for two weeks and needs to borrow £3,000. The bank loan officer says that the bank will need some kind of security for the loan, so the blonde hands over the keys to her new Rolls Royce. The car is parked in the bank's underground car park. The bank agrees to accept the car as collateral for the loan. The bank staff all enjoy a good laugh at the blonde for using a very expensive Rolls as collateral against a £3,000 loan.

Two weeks later, the blonde returns, and repays the loan and the interest, which comes to about £10. The loan officer says, 'Miss, we are very happy to have had your business and this transaction has worked out very nicely, but we are a little puzzled. While you were away, we checked you out and found that you are a multimillionaire. What puzzles us is why would you bother to borrow £3,000?'

The blonde replies: 'Where else in this city can I safely park my car for two weeks for only £10 and expect it to be there when I return?'

Stereotypes and prejudice

Stereotypes

'Stereotypes' are particular types of knowledge or thinking that link group membership to certain traits: for example, that all blondes are stupid. Allport (1954) suggested that the purpose of a stereotype was to enable people to manage information in an efficient manner. The human brain can only process a fine amount of detail; beyond that, information must be categorized. People oversimplify their experience by selectively attending to certain features of information, and then forming categories, concepts, and generalizations with which to deal with the vast quantities of information available. A stereotype can be defined as the general inclination to place a person in categories according to some easily and quickly identifiable characteristic, such as age, sex, ethnic membership, nationality, or occupation, and then to attribute to that person those qualities believed to be typical of members of that category (Tajfel, 1969). Examples would include stereotyping elderly people as hard of hearing, or foreigners as having trouble understanding English. In the past, black people have been stereotyped as more violent than white. As evidence of this stereotype, Duncan (1976) produced some disquieting results from an experiment examining perceptions of violence and race. White subjects who viewed a videotape of inter-group violence labelled an ambiguous shove as more violent when it was performed by a black man than when the same act was perpetrated by a white. A replication of this study with children found similar effects (Sagar and Schofield, 1980). Children have also been found to distort or change their memories of a story to fit their stereotypes (Bigler and Liben, 1993).

Given this research, it is perhaps not surprising that stereotypes can also serve as self-fulfilling prophecies. In another classic experiment, Rosenthal and Jackobson (1968) demonstrated how this could occur. After testing children in a variety of classes at the start of the school year, teachers were informed that a handful of students in their classes were 'late bloomers'. The academic performance of these students was expected to improve dramatically during the year. When the late bloomers were tested at the end of the school year, their performance had improved more dramatically than that of other students. The late bloomers had not been identified on the basis of test scores, but had been chosen randomly. By identifying these students as having potential, the researchers induced positive expectations in the teachers and the students met these expectations. The research concluded that they reflected the self-fulfilling prophecy.

Stereotypes can have the power, then, to boost performance. For example, if you belong to a group that is always exposed to the message 'We are the best', this can promote personal achievement. But as well as producing positive results and success, stereotypes can also cause poor performance when a person or group believes that he, she, or it should do badly. For example, according to Haslam et al. (2008), one reason that the England football team performs badly in penalty shootouts (winning only one of seven in major tournaments) is that performance is impeded by a history of failure. Similarly, performance may be affected by negative stereotypes, such as women underperform in maths tests, in negotiation, or career advancement (Bergeron et al., 2006).

An essential feature of stereotypes is that they are negative and so offensive. But it is easy to also easy to think of positive stereotypes, such as black people are good athletes. Black people may, however, object to the positive generalization that they are superior athletes on the grounds that this generalization fits only a minority of the black population and suggests that they are less gifted at academic pursuits (Macrae et al., 1996).

STOP AND THINK Challenging stereotypes

What is your stereotype of a person who falls victim to drink spiking in pubs? Is it an 18-year-old 'Essex girl', wearing high heels and a short skirt, and out with her friends? The statistics challenge such a stereotype and show that women aged 30–50 are most at risk—yet no awareness campaign has ever been created to target this age group. Surprisingly, many people have their drinks spiked at work-related events. Of the 675 reported cases of drug rape and sexual abuse in 2006, sixty-two were reported by men.

(*Source:* Roofie Foundation, 2008)

Prejudice

'Prejudice' is an attitude—usually negative—that is directed toward a group as a whole, or an individual member of that group (Allport, 1954). Unlike stereotypes, prejudice tends to be driven by emotion. While stereotypes might distort people's memory or perception of others, prejudice can lead to the dehumanization of others, and to inter-group hostility and violence. Prejudicial attitudes reinforce a superiority–inferiority belief system in which the object of prejudice is generally placed in a disadvantaged position (Loden and Rosener, 1991). People with high levels of prejudice are more likely to use cultural stereotypes; high levels of prejudice correspond with more negative stereotypes (Kawakami et al., 1998).

EXAMPLE Prejudice or bias from research

Purkis et al. (2006) found that, in employment interviews, judgements, and decisions, ethnic names, coupled with speaking with an accent, will lead to unfavourable judgements about the applicant. Frazer and Wiersma (2001) found that, although interviewers hired black and white applicants in equal proportion, one week later, they recalled the answers to the interview questions given by the black applicants as having been significantly less intelligent than those of whites.

STOP AND THINK The importance of perception in racist incidents

A racist incident is 'any … which is perceived to be racist by the victim or any other person'—a definition found in the Macpherson inquiry into the Stephen Lawrence murder investigation. Note how important perception is in the definition. Figures show that there were 18,253 racist incidents in London during 2000–01. This is double the number recorded in 1999 (Hopkins, 2002).

Do you think that the increase in number of reported incidents might be due the rise in awareness of racism, or awareness that it will be acknowledged?

Just as perception plays a part in racism, it also has a part to play in how we view disability. There are two dominant ways in which disability is seen: the medical model considers the person with a disability as sick or unhealthy; the social model looks at society's response to a person with a disability. People with a disability may choose to embrace, reject, conceal, or reveal their disability. They may choose not to adopt a self-perception as being 'disabled' (Watson, 2002). There is no objective perception of what constitutes a disability; rather, perceptions are shaped by factors associated with both the medical and social models (LoBianco and Sheppard-Jones, 2007).

In a similar way, different perceptions can be found of anger among men and women in organizations: men have been found to earn social status by displaying anger, whereas women who get angry are likely to be judged as incompetent and unsuitable for employment (Brescoll and Uhlmann, 2008; *The Psychologist*, 2008).

We may have to accept that different people will have different perceptions, but what can be done to change perceptions—especially prejudice? One of the most effective ways of reducing your reliance on stereotype and decreasing prejudice is trying to 'put yourself in another person's shoes' (Galisnky and Moskowitz, 2000). Studies focusing on this technique have asked individuals to imagine a day in the life of another person, as if they *were* that person. The results of such temporary changes in perspective have been the decreased use of stereotypes in making judgements of others, as well as a decrease in the degree to which people discriminate against stereotyped individuals. We need, then, to be aware of our judgements in order to decrease discrimination—and a decrease in discrimination might lead to more fairness, justice, and equality in organizations.

The distortion of perception

There is, then, no objective perception of a single reality; there are always differences in perception in organizations—a theme that plays out in a number of different ways. For example, you may think that you have good dress sense, but a potential employer may consider your dress sense bad, or poor—and poor appearance or 'bad dress sense' can prevent you being offered a job. Research has shown that appearance is an important consideration when retailers choose staff (Warhurst, 2008). The 'right' personality and appearance were rated 'very important', or 'essential', by between 68–80 per cent of employers. More than four-fifths of retailers surveyed had an 'appearance policy' covering personal hygiene, tidiness, and clothing style, and more than half of the respondents said that staff would be disciplined for failing to conform to clothing or appearance policies.

Further difficulties arise when perception is distorted—something that members of an organization may wish to avoid, but of which there is strong research evidence. One of the dramatic ways in which perception might be found to be defective or distorted is in experiments on eyewitness accounts. In a classic experiment, watched by an audience, Allport and Postman (1947) gave a group of six or seven people a task. All of the six or seven subjects were asked to leave the room. They were told that, when they returned, they had to listen carefully to what they heard and repeat it 'as exactly as possible'. A slide depicting a situation was thrown onto the screen as the audience watched. A member of the audience was asked to describe it to the first subject, who was called back into the room. That first subject did not see the picture on the screen. A second subject was then called back into the room and the first subject repeated, as accurately as he or she could, what he or she had heard about the scene. (Again, the subject did not see the picture.) A third subject then took up a position next to the second and listened to the report given by the second. This procedure continued, until all had heard from the previous subject what had been seen. The experiment demonstrated that the description of the scene often changed dramatically as it was passed from person to person. By the time that the last subject was given the description of the slide, the audience was usually laughing at how the description of the situation had become distorted. One particularly interesting finding was that when a scene showed a white man holding a straight razor, apparently confronting a black man on a tube train, in over half of the experiments using the picture, at some stage in the series of reports, the black man (rather than the white man) was said to hold the razor in his hand (ibid.: 111).

Ironically, Allport and Postman's study has since itself been distorted in historical accounts (Treadway and McCloskey, 1987; 1989). As Treadway and McCloskey note, the findings are not evidence of biases in eyewitnesses, because only the first person had viewed the picture; rather, they show how perceptions can become distorted by racial stereotypes as they are passed from person to person. But Treadway and McCloskey (1989) found no support for these claims about the effects of racial stereotypes on eyewitness accounts.

EXAMPLE Knife crime and perception

At the time of writing, the perception propagated by the media is that knife crime in the UK is on the increase. Twenty people died in knife attacks in London between the first day of the year and 10 July 2008. But according to the statistics, knife crimes actually fell by 15.5 per cent—from 11,986 to 10,131—between 2006–07 and 2007–08. Perceptions of knife crime, then, are distorted—demonstrating the need for accurate facts.

(*Source:* Summers, 2008)

The halo effect

A tendency similar to the logical error is the 'halo effect', or 'halo error', which involves a tendency to let our assessment of an individual be influenced by only one trait or characteristic. We see a person as better than he or she really is, because we associate that person with one positive attribute.

A study by Thorndike (1920) demonstrated that individuals are frequently seen as 'all good' or 'all bad' on the basis of having a single good or bad characteristic. He took the case of army officers being rated by their superiors and found that the superiors tended to think of the person, in general, as 'rather good' or 'rather inferior', and this then coloured the superiors' judgements of the officers' separate qualities. Individuals fail to discriminate properly between distinct and potentially independent aspects of ratees' behaviour (Saal, 1980)—yet, according to Feldman (1986: 173), 'halo error, like death and taxes, seems inevitable'.

EXAMPLE **Perception from research: The Lucifer effect**

In 1971, Phillip Zimbardo set up the Stanford Prison Experiment in which eighteen young, middle-class white men were randomly allocated to the role of guards and prisoners for the next six days. The experiment was prepared as if it were a play or a film, but the dramatization quickly became believable: the perceived roles were played out as if for real. When the prisoners rebelled, the guards' perception of the prisoners changed, so that it was no longer only an experiment. The guards saw the prisoners as troublemakers and 'out to get them'. The guards imposed severe penalties on the prisoners. One prisoner broke down after 36 hours and another after 48 hours, despite being ratified as psychologically healthy beforehand; this meant that the experiment had to be cut short.

The experiment demonstrated how people were liable to both vicious aggression and self-confirming victim-hood. Most prisoners believed that the subjects selected to be guards were chosen because they were bigger than those who were made prisoners, but, actually, there was no difference in the average height of the two groups.

What do you think caused this misperception?

More recently, prison guards in Abu Ghraib have been accused of setting dogs on naked prisoners, pretending to electrocute them, and forcing them to simulate sex. How then did these prison officers perceive their role?

(*Source:* Zimbardo, 2008; http://www.lucifereffect.com; http://www.prisonexp.org)

While not all organizations will have features similar to those of prisons, many will; some may see their organization as 'prison-like'. Perception is important, then, in helping us to understand behaviour in organizations—that is, how and why people behave as they do. We need to see how people see their roles, and how and why different perceptions and misperception can occur.

Frames and their effect on perception

So much for person perception—but what about the situation, an image, or an idea? Psychologists and sociologists talk about 'frames' in this context. A 'frame' is a personal perspective of a situation—that is, a well-learned set of associations that focus people's attention in, and label some aspects of, a situation to the exclusion of others (Goffman, 1974)—much as implicit personality theory relates to our personal perceptions of people. Lakoff (2004) suggests that the term 'tax relief' is a successful framing device, because the frame relates to the cultural metaphor of something positive: the individual is relieved of the strain of tax. It may be that he or she perceives taxes as an affliction, and the proponents of taxes as villains. The taxpayer is then the afflicted (the victim) and the proponents of tax relief are the heroes who deserve the taxpayer's gratitude. Using these positive terms casts any arguer in a negative light. (It is possible, of course, also to argue that taxation is not an affliction.)

There has been a good deal of interest in the behaviour found in casinos and amusement arcades, as interest and research in gambling have grown (see Davies, 2007). In this arena, perception also plays a part, because hardened gamblers do not perceive that they are constantly losing, but instead as 'nearly missing winning'; the gamblers, then, are framing the losing experiences as 'near wins' (Griffiths, 1991; 1994). Near misses encourage the gambler and raise hopes for future success.

Research has also shown how secondary school teachers seriously underestimate the proportion of state school students at Oxford and Cambridge universities (Sutton Trust, 2008). More than a third of those who made a valid response believed that 20 per cent or fewer of undergraduates at the two universities came from the state sector, and the majority (three-fifths) thought that the numbers of undergraduates were 30 per cent or fewer, even though 93 per cent of school-aged children attend state schools. Only 8 per cent of teachers picked the correct answer of 'between 51−60 per cent' (the actual figure being 54 per cent). The majority of teachers also thought that it was more expensive for students to study at Oxbridge, whereas the two universities charge the same tuition fees as the vast majority of other English universities and, in fact, offer some of the most generous bursary provision.

Secondary school teachers must therefore be 'framing' Oxford and Cambridge as being dominated by students from private schools; they are also seeing these universities as more expensive places to study. As a result, this may have an impact on the number of state school students applying to Oxford and Cambridge. Forty-five per cent of the teachers said that they would never—or only rarely—recommend that their brightest students apply to Oxbridge. This misperception means, therefore, that fewer secondary school students from state schools are going to Oxbridge and the Oxbridge universities are unlikely, if this misperception is not changed, to widen their access to more state school students.

Frames are fundamentally interpretative: they process the raw material of perception and deduce certain actions that the person should take in a given situation. Frames also create 'blind spots'—that is, defects in the perceptual field that can cloud judgement. It is also thought that, when people perceive one another, they separate judgements into two frames: one concerning the person's competence; the other, his or her moral character (Wojciszke, 1994). The competence frame includes traits such as 'capable', 'smart', 'efficient', 'creative', and 'strong', while the moral frame includes 'honest', 'generous', 'altruistic', and 'kind'. Wojciszke et al. (1998) argue that not only are these categories or frames separate, but also that, together, they almost exhaust the overall assessment of a person. Further, individuals assess each other more on the basis of moral than competence traits, because we are interested in defending ourselves against being victimized by moral misbehaviour. And negative assessments are more salient that positive ones (Baumeister et al., 2001), which may help explain why whistleblowers are seen more as betrayers than as virtuous people.

Everyone believes him or herself to be moral—even known liars and convicted criminals (Baumeister, 1998). In the case of person perception, it appears that the competence frame dominates rather than the morality frame. Personal ethics blind spots exist, so that, in developing a competent self, we can overlook the substance and expression of the moral self. In other words, we are blinded by the competence in ourselves and others rather than by their morality.

But this may not be the case when it comes to our perceptions of superiors, in which case it appears that the moral frame is highly salient (Kouzes et al., 2002). The moral dominance effect holds when the target of perception is a more powerful figure (Emler and Cook, 2000), so we scrutinize our superiors for their moral competence. Superiors do not necessarily, however, focus on morality traits among their subordinates; they are more likely to focus on competence traits. This may help to explain why Nick Leeson, the former investment officer in the Singapore branch of Barings Bank, was able to build up $1.3 billion in losses without detection (Moberg, 2006). Some framing will also include categorization: for example, 'competent' or 'incompetent' employees.

Classifications and their consequences

Individuals and organizations sort perceived characteristics into categories. 'Classification' is the systematic categorization of entities into meaningful content. Selecting how the world, the organization, its employees, or its customers are categorized is dependent upon perception, as well as judgement, and allows us to segregate. The use of classification also influences human behaviour. For example, categorizing a population based on genealogy can influence an individual's social, economic, and political status. During apartheid in South Africa, racial classification by government bureaucracy played a key role in unjustly segregating the population based on physical characteristics (Bowker and Leigh, 1999). More positively and with less serious consequences, airlines might classify a customer as a frequent flyer or non-frequent flyer; frequent flyers will be given incentives and rewards not offered to non-frequent flyers. The airline may then go on to classify frequent flyers further into 'blue', 'gold', or 'platinum' frequent flyers.

EXAMPLE Uncovering the classification and making it explicit

Howard Becker, a sociologist and criminologist, tells the story about his classification by an airline. He had heard, from a relative who worked for this airline, the way in which desk clerks were trained to deal with complaints. They were told that they should first try to solve the problem. If the customer was still dissatisfied. they were to call their supervisor, saying 'I have an irate on the line'. The dissatisfied customer was then classified as an 'irate'.

One day, Becker, who had a complaint, phoned the airline. He said in a calm voice: 'Hello, I'm Howard Becker and I'm an irate. Can you help me?' The clerk began to splutter: 'How did you know that word?'

(*Source:* Bowker and Leigh, 1999)

Perceptions of employers by employees and the psychological contract

Another example of groups and perception at work is found in the perception of employers by employees. The perception of employee and employer in terms of their mutual obligations towards each other is usually referred to as the 'psychological contract'. The obligations will often be informal and imprecise; they may be inferred from actions, or from what has happened before. Some obligations may be seen as promises, while others will be seen as expectations. The obligations—and how they are perceived—are important for the employee, in terms of his or her relationship with the employer. The psychological contract is based on an employee's sense of fairness and trust, and his or her belief that the employer is honouring the deal between them. It is assumed that, when the psychological contract is positive, this will increase employee commitment and that, in turn, this will have an effect on business performance. When employees believe that management has broken promises or has failed to deliver on commitments, this has a negative effect on job satisfaction and commitment, as well as on the psychological contract.

While press reports suggest that UK employees are dissatisfied, insecure, and lacking in commitment, surveys—for example, those carried out by the *Chartered Institute of Personnel and Development* (CIPD)

between 1996 and 2004 (available online at http://www.cipd.co.uk)—show that the majority of employees report that they are satisfied with their jobs. Levels of commitment have remained unchanged. Trust in the organization has, however, declined somewhat in both private and public sectors—and this is an area of research that you may wish to pursue at a later date.

Self-perception

Throughout time, philosophers, theologians, and others have stressed the importance of accurate self-knowledge—encapsulated in the phrase 'know thyself'. Yet many studies show that there is a tenuous association between perception and reality of self (see Dunning et al., 2004, for a review). For example, a medical doctor's impressions of his or her communication skills may show little correlation with impressions held by patients or supervisors, although the impressions of patients and supervisors correlate rather highly (Millis et al., 2002). Research has also shown that people overestimate how quickly they can get things done. For example, people filing income tax returns commonly mail their forms a week later than they thought they had (Buehler et al., 2002). In addition, companies trying to acquire other firms typically offer to pay 41 per cent more for the target firm's stock than its current price. Essentially, this is a statement that they believe that they can run the target firm much more profitably than its current management (Dunning, 2006). Among elderly drivers referred for driving evaluation, those who rate themselves 'above average' are four times more likely to be classified as 'unsafe' following a 30-minute driving simulation than those who describe their driving ability more modestly (Freund et al., 2005). And students who flunk, or nearly flunk, exams think that they have outscored most other students in the class (Dunning, 2006). Self-perception, then, appears to be shown by research to be relatively inaccurate.

177

 EXAMPLE **How the perception of exercise affects how our bodies actually look**

Research by Ellen Langer, a Harvard psychologist, found that hotel maids did not see themselves as physically active: 67 per cent reported that they did not exercise, yet cleaning is a very physically active job. Despite the fact that all of the women in the study far exceeded the US Surgeon General's recommendation for daily exercise, the women's bodies did not seem to benefit from their activity.

Langer set about changing perceptions, dividing the maids into two groups. In one group, researchers carefully went through each of the tasks that the maids did each day and explained how many calories they burned. They were informed that the activity met the Surgeon General's definition of an 'active lifestyle'. The other group were given no information at all. A month later, it was found that the group that had been educated had started losing weight.

(*Source:* Spiegel, 2008)

When it comes to self-perception, we even stereotype ourselves. According to self-categorization theory (an extension of social identity theory), the process of stereotyping arises from the same process that we use to categorize and understand the kind of person that we are in relations to others. Part of that self-concept will come from the social groups to which we belong and with whom we identify: our age, group, gender, social class, and our interests—for example, sports—and the type of music we like or other interests that we have. As we stereotype, we simplify—that is, take shortcuts in our process of perception. The effect is to minimize the differences between individuals within groups and maximize the distinction between groups. We make these simplified social comparisons to reduce uncertainty and work out how to behave; these distinctions also help us to maintain social esteem. Further, we tend to perceive favourably the group to which we belong (these are our ingroups), whereas we perceive less favourably those who belong to other groups (these are known as outgroups). This research on stereotyping and self-categorization consequently helps us again to call into question our own abilities to perceive ourselves completely, as well as accurately. We need to reflect on how we judge ourselves and others, base that judgement or perception on sound, more complete, information, and use critical reflection.

Further ways in which perception can be shaped

'Social constructionism' is a perspective from psychology that helps us to question our perception one stage further. Social constructionism denies that our knowledge is a direct perception of reality; rather, we are seen to construct our own versions of reality between us. There is no such thing as an 'objective fact'. All knowledge is derived from looking at the world from some perspective or other, and is in the service of some interests rather than others. Each person perceives the world differently and actively creates his or her own meanings from events. Some psychologists—for example, Kelly (1955)—would argue that we have the capacity to change our constructions of the world to create new possibilities for our own actions. And in narrative psychology (Gergen and Gergen, 1988), we tell each other—as well as ourselves—stories that powerfully shape our possibilities (Burr, 2003).

Finally, the marketing activity of organizations is particularly aimed at shaping our perceptions, beliefs, and assumptions. It is, however, not a topic that is central to a book on people, work, and organization—but there are clear links between perception, marketing to people, and organization.

EXAMPLE **More expensive placebos bring more relief from pain**

In marketing, it has been found that perception really counts. A higher price can create the impression of higher value, just as the placebo pill can reduce pain. Research has combined the two effects and found that a $2.50 (£1.25) placebo works better than one that costs 10 cents. This finding may explain the popularity of some high-cost drugs over cheaper alternatives and account for patients' reports that generic drugs are less effective than brand-name ones, although their active ingredients are identical.

(*Source:* Carey, 2008; Waber et al., 2008)

Conclusion

The research literature on perception helps us to question the process and accuracy of our perceptions, as well as those of others. It is important for us to understand the process of perception because it is through this process that we decide what 'reality' is. That 'reality' will be different for each of us because perceptions differ. In organizations, we manage what we perceive to be happening (Clegg et al., 2008). We may fail to see how our 'reality' is different from that of others, or to think why that might be the case.

The research highlights how our perceptions are influenced both positively and negatively, and the errors that we make in judgements, interpretations, assumptions, and beliefs about people and organizations. Often, the errors happen because we do not question, or reflect on, our beliefs, assumptions, or inferences. There is a need, then, to reflect critically on our perceptions and what we perceive to be happening in organizations: one person's views about what the organization promises and expects may not be fully—or even partly—shared by other employees or managers.

KEY POINTS

- Perception is an active process in which we pay attention to what is important to us. We also tend to perceive what we wish or expect to perceive.

- What we perceive may be influenced by many factors, such as our class, how we view others, or how they view us.

- Gestalt psychology has shown how we organize and interpret what we see, make patterns, or give it meaning. Perception is loaded with meaning and, again, it is acknowledged that we may perceive the same thing differently.

- Attribution theory alerts us to how we attribute meaning or cause to people's actions or behaviour.

- The need to conform can influence our perception.

- We also have implicit personality theories that influence what we expect of people and what their personality 'profile' might look like. When faced with incomplete information, we form a more extensive and consistent view often referred to as the 'logical error'.

- Perception can be easily distorted by, for example, the use of stereotypes—that is, a particular type of knowledge or thinking that links group membership with certain traits. Stereotypes can be either positive or negative (although they are usually negative) and serve self-fulfilling prophecies.

- Similarly, prejudice is usually negative and can be directed towards a group as a whole or an individual.

- In the halo effect, our perception or assessment of a person is influenced by one trait or characteristic.

- Frames also influence our perceptions; these are well-learned sets of associations that focus attention on some aspect of a situation.

- We also sort perceived characteristics into categories and classifications.

179

CASE STUDY
Organizations attempting to change perceptions

It is in the interest of organizations to try to manage the perceptions that people have of them as employers. *Goldman Sachs* and *Pfizer* are companies that appear to be trying to change perceptions of as firms in which women are welcomed. *Goldman Sachs* is a global banking firm with 20,000 employees world-wide, in forty-seven offices across twenty-five countries; in Europe, it employs 5,000 staff. It believes that recruiting a diverse workforce will aid all levels of its business—but finds that women are not drawn to its business because of preconceived ideas of roles in investment banking (including 'pounding the City floor', 'a 24-hour job'). As a result, *Goldman Sachs* started its 'A Level Girls' programme in 2000. This initiative is supported by senior managing directors and has to report into the European Union Diversity Committee on a regular basis.

Annabel Smith, executive director for global leadership and diversity at *Goldman Sachs*, informs us that the company has developed a relationship with sixty state and public schools, within which it targets female A level students. The girls are invited to attend a two-day event at which they look at the variety of roles in a global banking business and undertake activities relating to these roles. For example, to illustrate sales and trading, the firm gave the students Destiny's Child tickets and asked to see for what they could sell or trade them. The firm proactively retains these relationships with the girls throughout university, with the aim of asking them to attend a summer school once they have graduated. It has also developed a half-day conference for teachers, which includes lesson plans on how to write a CV and other job-related skills

Goldman Sachs maintains its relationships with young women and the schools through diversity networks of its existing staff. Staff participation in this network is recognized in staff annual reviews.

Pfizer is a pharmaceutical company. It wanted to focus on taking the stress out of the return to work—particularly for women returning after maternity leave. At the time of writing, less than half (44 per cent) of its staff are female and the company aims to retain its female talent.

Pfizer already has in place the following initiatives:

- 148 on-site childcare places;
- childcare services;
- holiday clubs;
- mentoring;
- a Daphne Jackson Fellowship for returnees;
- flexible working (for which the company feels there is a strong business case);
- a phased return programme;
- various networks (including women's, carers' support, rainbow, further education, and French).

The company has recently developed a new initiative called 'Freetime', which is to address the practical problems that people face on their return to work (for example, new IT systems, or new policies or practices). This initiative was developed by a senior manager and is therefore said to have full senior management support.

Freetime consists of packs developed for the individual, the manager, and colleagues, and addresses three situations: a maternity break; a career break; and long-term sick leave. The manager's pack looks at issues around communication, including demonstrating a considerate manner, and developing a reintroduction programme for returnees. In the case of maternity leave, the pack also considers the three key times for a woman: prior to going on leave; during leave; and on her return. The colleague pack has a checklist of new information to pass on to the returning colleague, and includes weekly and monthly updates and checklists.

Pfizer has found that the earlier the intervention, the more seamless the transition to returning to work, because it makes the employee feel valued by her manager and the company. Research has shown that women are more likely not to return to work after their second child, so the company believes that if it makes the first experience as supportive as possible, it is more likely to retain the woman's talent in the company.

(*Sources:* http://www.opportunitynow.org.uk/awards/awards_2009/2009_case_studies/global_award/goldman_sachs.html;
http://www.opportunitynow.org.uk/best_practice/exemplar_employers/women_returners/case_studies/pfizer_global.html)

Questions

1. What evidence is there that these companies have been successful in their mission to recruit more female employees?

2. What would you do in these circumstances?

3. What would you do to recruit those from ethnic backgrounds?

FURTHER READING

Blass, T. (2002) 'The man who shocked the world', *Psychology Today*, March–April: 68–74 This article discusses Milgram, the experiments that he designed on conformity, and their results.

Clegg, S., Kornberger, M., and Pitsis, T. (2008) *Managing and Organizations*, London: Sage This book contains a good chapter on perception.

Conway, N. and Briner, R. (2005) *Understanding Psychological Contracts at Work: A Critical Evaluation of Theory and Research*, Oxford: Oxford University Press.

Cullinane, N. and Dundon, T. (2006) 'The psychological contract: A critical review', *International Journal of Management Reviews*, 8(2): 113–29.

Thompson, P. and McHugh, D. (2002) *Work Organizations*, 3rd edn, Houndmills: Palgrave Chapter 15 includes a discussion of perception.

LINKS TO FILMS AND NOVELS

Bend it Like Beckam (2002) dir. G. Chadha This film follows a young woman's interest in football. It both challenges and reinforces stereotypes of Asians in Britain and among footballers.

Rogue Trader (1999) dir. J. Dearden This film tells the true story of Nick Leeson, an ambitious derivatives trader with *Barings Bank*. He breaks trading rules and gambles, leading to the bankruptcy of the bank. It is possible that Nick Leeson's perception of himself and his abilities in trading were inaccurate?

Schindler's List (1993) dir. S. Spielberg This film is the true story of Czech-born Oskar Schindler, a businessman who tried to make his fortune during the Second World War by exploiting cheap Jewish labour, but ended up penniless, having saved over a thousand Polish Jews from almost certain death during the Holocaust. It is a lesson in how perceptions of people can change.

181

RESEARCH QUESTIONS

1. Companies test for competencies (that is, attributes that they perceive are valuable in employees) in both the recruitment and appraisal processes. What are these competencies? Do organizations differ in the competencies that they perceive as valuable? What place does moral competency appear to have?

2. Does how you see yourself impact on how you subsequently perform? For example, if you see yourself as a capable knowledgeable student, does this impact on exam or essay performance? (Research on student self-efficacy and self-esteem will help you here.)

3. Sir Patrick Moore, presenter of the TV programme *The Sky at Night*, perceives that the *BBC* is worse than it used to be because it is 'run by women' (Sky News, Tuesday 18 May 2007). What evidence can you find to support or refute his perception?

REFERENCES

Allport, G.W. (1954) *The Nature of Prejudice*, Cambridge, MA: Addison-Wesley.

_____ and Postman, L. (1947) *The Psychology of Rumour*, New York: Henry Holt and Co.

Asch, S.E. (1946) 'Forming impressions of personality', *Journal of Abnormal Social Psychology*, 41: 258–90.

_____ (1951) 'Effects of group pressure on the modification and distortion of judgements', in H. Guetzhow (ed.), *Groups, Leadership, Men*, Pittsburgh, PA: Carnegie Press.

Baumeister, R.F. (1998) 'The self', in D.T. Gilbert, S.T. Fiske, and G. Lindsey (eds), *Handbook of Social Psychology*, New York: McGraw Hill, pp. 680–740.

_____, Bratslavsky, F.E., Finkenauer, C., and Vohs, K.D. (2001) 'Bad is stronger than good', *Review of General Psychology*, 5: 323–70.

Bergeron, D.M., Block, C.J., and Echtenkamp, A. (2006) 'Disabling the able: Stereotype threat and women's work performance', *Human Performance*, 19(2): 133–58.

Beuhler, R., Griffin, D., and Ross, M. (2002) 'Inside the planning fallacy: The causes and consequences of optimistic time predictions', in T. Gilovich, D. Griffin, and D Kahneman (eds), *Heuristics and Biases: The Psychology of Intuitive Judgement*, Cambridge: Cambridge University Press, pp. 251–70.

Bigler, R.S. and Liben, L.S. (1993) 'A cognitive-developmental approach to racial stereotyping and reconstructive memory in Euro-American children', *Child Development*, 64: 1507–18.

Blass, T. (2002) 'The man who shocked the world', *Psychology Today*, March–April: 68–74.

Bowker, G.C. and Leigh, S.S. (1999) *Sorting Things Out: Classification and Its Consequences*, Cambridge, MA: MIT Press.

Brescoll, V.L. and Uhlmann, E.L. (2008) 'Can an angry woman get ahead? Status conferral, gender, and expression of emotion in the workplace', *Psychological Science*, 19(3): 268–75.

Burr, V. (2003) *Social Constructionism*, 2nd edn, London: Routledge.

Callender, C. and Jackson, J. (2005) 'Does the fear of debt deter students from higher education?', *Journal of Social Policy*, 34(4): 509–40.

Carey, B. (2008) 'More expensive placebos bring more relief', *New York Times*, 5 March, available online at http://www.nytimes.com/2008/03/05/health/research/05placebo.html

Clegg, S., Kornberger, M., and Pitsis, T. (2008) *Managing and Organizations*, London: Sage.

Davies, J. (2007) 'Interview: The gambling man—Prof. Mark Griffiths', 16 July, available online at http://www.psychblog.co.uk/interview-the-gambling-man-prof-mark-griffiths-119.html

Duncan, B.L. (1976) 'Differential social perception and attribution of inter group violence: Testing the lower limits of stereotyping of blacks', *Journal of Personality and Social Psychology*, 34(4): 590–8.

Dunning, D. (2006) 'Strangers to ourselves?', *The Psychologist*, 19(10): 600–3.

_____, Heath, C., and Suls, J.M. (2004) 'Flawed self-assessment: Implications for health, education, and the workplace', *Psychology in the Public Interest*, 5: 69–106.

Emler, N. and Cook, T. (2000) 'Moral integrity in leadership: Why it matters and why it might be difficult to achieve', in B.W. Roberts and R. Hogan (eds), *Personality Psychology in the Workplace*, Washington DC: American Psychological Association, pp. 277–98.

Feldman, J.M. (1986) 'A note on the statistical correction of halo error', *Journal of Applied Psychology*, 71: 173–6.

Frazer, R.A. and Wiersma, I.U.J. (2001) 'Prejudice versus discrimination in the employment interview: We may hire equally but our memories harbour prejudice', *Human Relations*, 54(2): 173–91.

Freund, B., Colgrove, L.A., Burke, B.L., and McLeod, R. (2005) 'Self rated driving performance among elderly drivers referred for driving evaluation', *Accidents: Analysis and Prevention*, 37: 613–18.

Galinsky, A.D. and Moskowitz, G.B. (2000) 'Perspective taking: Decreasing stereotype expression, stereotype accessibility and in-group favouritism', *Journal of Personality and Social Psychology*, 78(4): 708–24.

Gergen, K.J. and Gergen, M.M. (1988) 'Narrative and the self as relationship', in L. Berkowitz (ed.), *Advances in Experimental Social Psychology*, New York: Academic Press, pp. 17–56.

Goffman, E. (1974) *Frame Analysis: An Essay on the Organization of Experience*, Cambridge, MA: Harvard University Press.

Griffiths, M.D. (1991) 'The psychobiology of the near miss in fruit machine gambling', *Journal of Psychology*, 125: 347–57.

_____ (1994) 'The role of cognitive bias and skill in fruit machine gambling', *British Journal of Psychology*, 85: 351–69.

Haire, M. and Grunes, W.F. (1950) 'Perceptual defences: processes protecting an organized perception of another personality', *Human Relations*, 3(4): 403–12.

Haslam, S.A., Salvatore, J., Kessler, T., and Reicher, S.D. (2008) 'The social psychology of success', *Scientific American Mind*, 19(2): 24–31.

Hopkins, N. (2002) 'Fifth of racist crime involves neighbours', *The Guardian*, 22 February, available online at http://www.guardian.co.uk/uk/2002/feb/22/race.ukcrime1

Kawakami, K., Dion, K.L., and Dovidio, J.F. (1998) 'Racial prejudice and stereotype activation', *Personality and Social Psychology Bulletin*, 24: 407–16.

Kelley, H.H. (1950) 'The warm–cold variable in the first impressions of person', *Journal of Personality*, 8(4): 431–9.

_____ (1971) *Attribution in Social Interaction*, Morristown, NL: General Leaning Press.

Kelly, G.A. (1955) *The Psychology of Personal Constructs*, 2 vols, New York: Norton.

Kouzes, J., Posner, B.Z., and Peters, T. (2002) *The Leadership Challenge*, San Francisco, CA: Jossey Bass.

Lackoff, G. (2004) *Don't Think of an Elephant: Know Your Values and Frame the Debate*, White River Junction, VT: Chelsea Green.

Levine, J.M. (1999) 'Solomon Asch's legacy for group research', *Personality and Social Psychology Review*, 3(4): 358–64.

LoBianco, A.F. and Sheppard-Jones, K. (2007) 'Perceptions of disability as related to medical and social factors', *Journal of Applied Social Psychology*, 37(1): 1–13.

Loden, M. and Rosener, B.J. (1991) *Workforce America!*, Homewood, IL: Business One Irwin.

Macrae, C.N, Strangor, C., and Hewston, M. (1996) *Stereotypes and Stereotyping*, New York: Guldford Press.

Martel, R. (2008) 'More than meets the eye', *Channel 4 News online*, 24 April, available online at http://www.channel4.com/news/articles/business_money/more+than+meets+the+eye/2075747

Merton, R.K. (1957) *Social Theory and Social Structure*, New York: Free Press.

Milgram, S. (1963) 'Behavioural study of obedience', *Journal of Abnormal Psychology*, 67: 371–8.

_____ (1974) *Obedience to Authority: An Experimental View*, New York: Harper and Row.

Millis, S.R., Jain, S.S., Eyles, M., Tulsky, D., Nadler, S.F., Foye, P.M., Elovic, E., and De Lisa J.A. (2002) 'Assessing physicians' interpersonal skills: Do patients and physicians see eye to eye?', *American Journal of Physical Medicine and Rehabilitation*, 81: 946–51.

Moberg, D.J. (2006) 'Ethics blind spots in organizations: How systematic errors in person perception undermine moral agency', *Organization Studies*, 27(3): 413–28.

O'Sullivan, M. (2003) 'The fundamental attribution error in detecting deception: The boy who cried wolf effect', *Personality and Social Psychology Bulletin*, 29(10): 1316–28.

The Psychologist (2008) 'Differing perceptions of anger', 21(4): 473.

Purkis, S.L., Perrewe, P.L., Gillespie, T.L., Mayes, B.T., and Ferris, G.R. (2006) 'Implicit sources of bias in employment interview judgements and decisions', *Organizational Behavior and Human Decision Processes*, 101(2): 152–67.

Roofie Foundation (2008) 'The Roofie Foundation statistics', available online at http://www.roofie.com

Rosenthal, R. and Jacobson, L.F. (1968) *Pygmalion in the Classroom: Teacher Expectations and Student Intellectual Development*, New York, NY: Holt Rinehart and Winston.

Russell, N. and Gregory, R. (2006) 'Making the undoable doable: Milgram, the Holocaust and modern government', *The American Review of Public Administration*, 35: 327–49.

Saal, F.E. (1980) 'Rating the ratings: Assessing the psychometric quality of rating data', *Psychological Bulletin*, 88: 413–28.

Sagar, H.A. and Schofield, J.W. (1980) 'Racial and behavioural cues in black and white children's perceptions of ambiguously aggressive acts', *Journal of Personality and Social Psychology*, 39(4): 590–8.

183

Speigal, A. (2008) 'Hotel maids challenge the placebo effect', *NPR*, 3 January, available online at http://www.npr.org/templates/story/story.php?storyId=17792517

Summers, C. (2008) 'Crime's growing perception gap', *BBC News*, 29 May, available online at http://news.bbc.co.uk/1/hi/uk/7425742.stm

Sutton Trust (2008) 'Teachers show alarming misconceptions about Oxbridge', available online at http://www.suttontrust.com/news.asp

Tajfel, H. (1969) 'Social and cultural factors in perception', in G Lindzey and E. Aronson (eds), *Handbook of Social Psychology*, Reading, MA: Addison-Wesley.

Thorndike, E.L. (1920) 'A constant error in psychological rating', *Journal of Applied Psychology*, 4: 25–9.

Treadway, M. and McCloskey, M. (1987) 'Cite unseen: Distortions of the Allport and Postman rumour study in the eyewitness testimony literature', *Law and Human Behaviour*, 11(1): 19–25.

_____ _____ (1989) 'Effects of racial stereotypes on eyewitness performance: Implications of the real and rumoured Allport and Postman studies', *Applied Cognitive Psychology*, 3: 53–63.

Waber, R.L., Carmon, Z., and Ariely, D. (2008) 'Commercial features of placebo and therapeutic efficacy', *Journal Of the American Medical Association*, 299: 1016–67.

Warhurst, C. (2008) 'Bad dress sense could keep unemployed out of work', available online at http://www.strath.ac.uk/press/newsreleases/2008/headline_141278_en.html

Watson, N. (2002) 'Well, I know this is going to sound very strange to you, but I don't see myself as a disabled person: identity and disability', *Disability and Society*, 17: 509–27.

Weiner, B., Frieze, I., Kukla, A., Reid, L., Rest, S., and Rosenbaum, R.M. (1971) *Perceiving the Causes of Success and Failure*, New York: General Learning Press.

Williams, L.E. and Bargh, J.A. (2007) 'Temperature to temperament: Warm objects alter personality impressions', Manuscript submitted for publication; Reported in *The Psychologist* (2008), 21(4): 295.

Wojciszke, B. (1994) 'Multiple meanings of behavior: Construing actions in terms of competence or morality', *Journal of Personality, and Social Psychology*, 67: 222–32.

_____, Bazinska, R., and Jaworski, M. (1998) 'On the dominance of moral categories in impression formation', *Personality and Social Psychology Bulletin*, 24: 1245–57.

Workman, J.E. and Freeburg, E.W. (1999) 'An examination of date rape, victim dress, perceiver variables within the context of attribution theory', *Sex Roles*, 41(3): 261–77.

Zimbardo, P. (2008) *The Lucifer Effect: How Good People Turn to Evil*, New York/London: Random House/Ebury.

Personality

9

Introduction

Thinking about personality involves considering people's behaviour, drawing heavily on psychology and using terms such as 'human nature', 'individuality', 'experience', 'character', and 'identity'. Personality can be influential for people when considering with whom they want to work, their team or leader preferences, or who they want to employ or not employ. Management is about managing people and personalities.

In this chapter, we will look at the theories, research, and practice that have been influential in organizations and management, and which help us to understand behaviour at work. Personality is important in understanding how people behave, think, and feel as they do, and may affect what they choose to do, as well as how they perform at work.

By the end of the chapter, you will be able to appreciate how personality is thought of and measured in organizations. Thinking critically about the topic will help you to examine the limitations of personality theories, the tests, and their measurement. You will be aware of some of the weaknesses inherent in the testing and measurement of personality.

This chapter covers:

- personality and personality theory;
- personality traits and tests;
- intelligence testing and personality;
- emotional intelligence and psychometric testing;
- some difficulties with measuring and testing personality;
- personality theory and problematic behaviour;
- personality, integrity, and dishonesty at work;
- judging competence at work;
- personality and leadership;
- is looking at personality traits enough?

Personality and personality theory

Personality consists of the mental, physical, moral, and social qualities of an individual. It comprises the relatively stable and enduring aspects of the individual that distinguish them from other people, and form the basis of our predictions concerning their future behaviour. A theory of personality is a set of concepts for understanding the actions and experiences of individuals. The immense challenge of producing a theory of personality has only been achieved by a few individuals, including B.F. Skinner, Abraham Maslow, Sigmund Freud, and Carl Jung. While they all vary widely in scope, intent, and style, all of the theories tend to address enduring questions such as whether personality remains roughly the same throughout life, or can be changed in significant ways: for example, through training. How much of personality is determined by nature and how much by nurture? What is the degree to which a person should be viewed as unique?

While psychology discusses theories of personality, sociology tends to talk about self-identity. Individuals have an internal sense of self and their identity; they are compelled to make significant choices throughout their lives about how they dress, their appearance, their leisure activities, their beliefs, and their occupations. There are connections between an individual's internal sense of self and identity, and more macro aspects of society, such as the state, multinationals, mass media, and globalization. Individuals have to work out for themselves what they do, how they act, and who to be. These questions of identity are both a consequence and a cause of change at institutional level (Giddens, 1991). There are clear links between the identity that we choose and the personality that we are seen to portray.

Theorizing about personality has tended to maintain the status quo. Sloan (1997) argues that theories of personality reflect a historical view of individuality, and yet make generalizations about all societies and historical periods. One may quickly jump to the conclusion that, because people will always be more or less the same (for example, greedy or aggressive)—as a personality theory might suggest—then we need not bother improving individuals collectively. The theories also lead to a definition of problems to be solved by personal growth or self-actualization, thus diverting attention away from seeking collective solutions to social problems. These individualistic theories also ignore that the luxury and leisure required to be concerned with personal growth is available mainly to the privileged classes. In short, individualistic perspectives tend to blame the individual and leave social inequality unchallenged.

STOP AND THINK **Does psychology justify a lack of societal equality?**

Do you agree with Sloan (1997) that theories of personality maintain the status quo and that it is mainly the privileged who can afford the luxury of concern with personal growth?

Cernovsky (1997) goes one stage further and argues that psychology supports an *unjust* status quo. One way in which it does this is to use psychological tests to explain—or, in effect, justify—a lack of societal equality. Administering and interpreting intelligence tests are primary examples of this. Because psychological tests are 'research tools', the public often assumes that their results or interpretations are infallible. This assumption is a mistake—and it is one that has serious negative consequences for members of groups seen as 'genetically inferior' as 'proven by science'. What do you think?

Despite this, in organizational behaviour, personality theory often serves as a source of concepts or categories that chart the ways in which individuals differ from one another in enduring ways. The practical aim of personality theory in organizational behaviour is to create assessments of an individual's personality, in order to make a fit between personality, predispositions, and jobs, or to predict the future behaviour of members of an organization, for example, in recruitment and selection. Such assessments allow subjective judgements to be replaced by supposedly objective personality descriptors. Debate still continues as to which traits are the most central to human personality and which make the best predictors of future behaviour (Sloan, 1997).

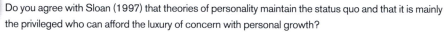

EXAMPLE **Personality traits and the prediction of behaviour: Narcissism**

What do Oprah Winfrey, Jack Welch, Martha Stewart, and Bill Gates all have in common? According to Michael Maccoby (2007), it is not only enormous success and celebrity, but also narcissism. Maccoby argues that today's most innovative leaders are not consensus-building bureaucrats; rather, they are 'productive narcissists'—that is, people who tend to think very highly of themselves. This is the personality best suited to lead during times of rapid social and economic change.

Is this a personality trait that you would like to see in your leader?

EXAMPLE Personality traits and the prediction of behaviour: Self-monitoring

High self-monitors tend to be highly attuned to cues, and adapt their behaviours and attitudes to suit the requirements of the situation—that is, they are 'chameleon-like'. Faced with a social situation, high self-monitors ask: 'Who does this situation want me to be and how can I be that person?' By contrast, low self-monitors faced with a social situation ask: 'Who am I and how can I be me in this situation?' High self-monitors tend to benefit from more numerous promotions (Kilduff and Day, 1994) and higher supervisory evaluations (Mehra et al., 2001). They have come to be seen as the preferred employee in work settings (Day and Shleicher, 2006). But they also pay the price of greater role conflict (Mehra and Schenkel, 2008), so may experience more stress (at which we look in Chapter 18).

Personality traits and tests

There are almost 20,000 words used to describe traits in the English language (Furnham, 2008). Managers are interested in personality traits, particularly if there is a link to be found between them and job fit, and/or performance. Most research concerning the effects of personality on job performance is based on five personality factors, or the 'Big Five': neuroticism; extraversion; openness to experience; agreeableness; and conscientiousness. These, and other, personality factors are said to be measurable through psychometric tests; psychometric tests can then be used to predict future behaviour. A psychometric test is a way of assessing a person's ability or personality in a measured and structured way. It is usually a test that has been thoroughly investigated to examine its reliability (that is, to ensure that it gives similar answers on various occasions) and validity (that is, that it measures what it says it measures).

There are three main types of test: ability; personality; and interest. Some tests are used by employers to help them in their recruitment process. It is common for graduate employers, for example, to use psychometric tests as part of their selection process. Organizations believe that tests help them to recruit the right people, with the right mix of abilities and personal qualities. They are also useful for 'sifting out' large numbers of applicants at an early stage, saving the employer both time and money. Tests can be administered by pencil and paper, or by computer, and often take the form of multiple-choice questions. Employers may set a particular score that the job applicant needs to achieve in order to proceed. (Examples of psychometric tests can be found at http://www.prospects.ac.uk, http://www.kent.ac.uk/careers/psychotests.htm, or http://www.shldirect.com/example_questions.html.)

The best-known psychometric tests are personality tests: for example, Cattell's 16PF personality questionnaire (now in its fifth edition); the Eysenck personality inventory/questionnaire; and the Myers-Briggs type indicator.

- The 16PF consists of sixteen factors, such as 'unassertive/dominant' and 'objective/sensitive', measured through 185 multiple-choice questions and completed in 45–60 minutes. The *Institute for Personality and Ability Testing* copyrights the questionnaires. Those administering the tests should be trained. But most researchers outside the Cattell establishment (that is, those using the Cattell questionnaire)—including Eysenck—have been unable to replicate the sixteen factors.

- Eysenck's personality test looks at a small number of different types, or basic dimensions, on which people differ: 'unstable/stable' and 'introvert/extrovert', for example. The dimensions are bipolar, meaning that if you score highly on extroversion, then you will be low on introversion. The types, or dimensions, are made up of traits; traits of the extrovert would be 'sociable', 'excitable', and 'impulsive', for example.

- The Myers-Briggs type indicator (MBTI) claims to be the most widely used psychometric test in the world (Case and Phillipson, 2004) and examines four bipolar personality dimensions: 'extraversion/introversion'; 'sensing/intuition'; 'thinking/feeling'; and 'judging/perceiving'. It is designed to make Jung's theory of psychological types understandable and useful in everyday life (Myers, 1993).

When these tests have been used during recruitment and promotion exercises, research has shown that they can predict job performance. Traits such as 'conscientiousness' have been consistently correlated with job performance, while 'neuroticism' has been found to be negatively correlated (Moutafi et al., 2007).

EXAMPLE **An organization putting personality theory into practice**

Furnham (1992) discusses the case of a South African bus company looking to recruit those bus drivers who were least likely to have accidents. He says that personality theory suggests that people who are extroverted—that is, those who are lively, somewhat impulsive, and sensation-seeking, etc.—and people who are emotionally unstable—that is, suffering from anxieties, over-reacting emotionally to dangerous situations, and tending to be tense—would be more likely to be involved in traffic accidents.

This proved to be the case. Accident categories were established on the basis of the driver's history, classifying them as a 'good', 'fair', 'poor', or 'bad' driver. Of the good drivers, 80 per cent had a 'good' personality test rating—that is, they were stable and introverted. Of the bad drivers, only 3 per cent had such a rating. Conversely, of the bad drivers, 80 per cent had a 'bad' personality test rating—that is, extroverted and unstable—compared with only 2 per cent of the 'good' drivers.

In light of this research, the accident rate of bus drivers was reduced considerably.

Psychometric testing grew substantially in popularity in the 1980s, largely for three reasons. Firstly, there were unprecedented large numbers of applicants for jobs. Secondly, Sir Michael Edwards, then the new head of *British Leyland*, was alleged to have claimed that, through the use of judicious tests (albeit applied in order to fire rather than to hire people), he was able to turn the whole company around. Thirdly, the test publishers were established and they marketed their goods aggressively. As a result, consultants have made a good deal of money testing people, writing reports, or training human resource managers to use the tests (Furnham, 2008). (We will look at the drawbacks more in a later section.)

Despite some of the concern over personality tests and psychometric testing, over 95 per cent of the FTSE100 companies use psychometric testing to select their staff, as do the police, the civil service, airlines, and even football clubs such as AC Milan, which has used profiling to understand what motivates its players.

STOP AND THINK **How should the social desirability factor be measured?**

Social desirability, or presenting yourself in the best possible light, is thought to be best measured by statements such as 'I am always happy to help someone, however inconvenient', or 'As a child, I always did as I was told to do', or 'I have no undesirable habits or vices'. If you were to agree with any of these statements, you may be identified as deliberately distorting the result, self-deceiving, or producing a highly positive—if not inaccurate—self-image. Would this be fair?

The personality test interpreter is expected to gather supportive evidence to assess whether or not genuine socially desirable behaviour is part of your disposition. How would he or she gather this evidence?

Intelligence testing and personality

Intelligence is relatively easy to measure reliably and accurately. We looked critically at intelligence testing in Chapter 4, where we looked at the rationality of management; here, we look at the link between intelligence and personality. Personality traits do significantly and systematically relate to intelligence test scores

(Furnham, 2008). For example, anxiety is fairly strongly linked to reduced academic performance: anxiety causes worry and tension, which affects working memory; low self-efficacy leads to worry and anxiety, and then poor test performance. Believing themselves to be poor at tests, these individuals then feel less interested in preparing for, or trying hard, during tests, leading to poor results, which circles back to further anxiety.

Gottfredson (2002) has examined the topic of intelligence in some depth and concludes that the better paid, more demanding, more socially desirable jobs recruit workers from the higher reaches of the IQ distribution. Across all jobs and all ratings of success, intelligence is very important. The more intellectually and technically demanding the job, the more important is intelligence for success. This is not to deny that there are other important factors: not all intelligent people do particularly well in the workplace. Gottfredson and Deary (2004) go on to show that intelligence is also a good predictor of health and longevity. Less intelligent people adhere less often to treatment regimes, learn and understand less about how to protect their health, seek less preventative care even when it is free, and less often practise healthy behaviours for slowing and preventing chronic disease.

Emotional intelligence and psychometric testing

There is no doubt that the social skills and emotional sensitivity of managers at work is very important. If you are kind, warm, and friendly, then this might lead to success (Paul, 1999). Recently, there has been a growth of interest in emotional intelligence; the topic has enjoyed remarkable popularity in professional and popular literature (Fineman, 2000; Hughes, 2005). A new lucrative market for test distributors and training consultancies has consequently opened up (Cartwright and Pappas, 2008). Daniel Goleman (1996; 1998) has established himself as a leading authority on the topic and has become a high-profile corporate consultant.

Emotional intelligence (EI) is defined as 'the ability to perceive emotions, to access and generate emotions so as to assist thought, to understand emotions and emotional knowledge, and to reflectively regulate emotions so as to promote emotional and intellectual growth' (Mayer and Salovey, 1997: 5). It is about effectively joining emotions and reasoning. (For a fuller description, see George, 2000, or Landon, 2002.) It has four elements:

- how aware you are of your own emotions;
- your ability to express your emotions accurately;
- your awareness of others' emotions;
- your ability to express others' emotions accurately and express empathy.

Emotional intelligence is thought to lead to enhanced functioning in a variety of aspects of life, such as achievement and close relationships (Goleman, 1995), but it may play a particularly important role in leadership effectiveness (George, 2000). For example, emotional intelligence is thought to contribute to constructive thinking—that is, the ability to solve problems—with a minimum of stress (Epstein, 1990). Further, because leaders who are high on emotional intelligence are better able to understand and manage their own emotions, they may be more likely to engage in constructive thinking to build and maintain high levels of cooperation and trust. Goleman (1995) claims that insurance sales agents who scored high on emotional competencies achieved sales figures that were more than twice those of the less emotionally competent colleagues, while Bachman et al. (2000) similarly suggest that highly emotionally competent debt collectors recovered double the amount of revenue of their more typical co-workers.

Several measures of emotional intelligence have been developed (Salovey et al., 1995; Mayer et al., 1997). These are 'diagnostic instruments' with self-report rating scales designed to profile emotional intelligence. But while a number of measures have been developed, in an exhaustive review,

189

Perez et al. (2005) found, described, and evaluated five ability emotional intelligence quotient (EQ) tests, establishing that many have been poorly constructed and validated (Furnham, 2008). Despite this, according to the *American Society for Training and Development* (Goleman, 1998), four out of five companies are actively trying to raise the emotional intelligence of their staff as a means of increasing sales, improving customer service (Cavelzani et al., 2003), and ensuring that their international managers perform successfully in global assignments (Gabel et al., 2005).

Emotional intelligence has been described as 'weak on hard evidence' (Zeidner et al., 2004). When promoting products such as the emotional intelligence profile, it is rarely acknowledged that the individual probably understands only a tiny fraction of his or her motives, intentions, or feelings (Scheff, 1997). Further, how would you, as a potential employer, be able to judge whether the self-report instrument had been completed with compliance, self-interest, and an instrumental orientation in mind? You may only be selecting the person on the basis of his or her ability to display certain emotions—that is, performing 'emotional eugenics' (Briner, 1999). Emotional intelligence is one way in which the individual can be aligned with a set of categories dictated by an organizational ideal. Making emotions calculable makes them amenable to management and control; emotions can be treated as a commodity and given a market value, just like other forms of capital (Landon, 2002).

Hughes (2005) has also provided a critique on the basis that emotional intelligence can be understood as constituting a reinvention and redefinition of character within the 'iron cage' of rationality. Emotional intelligence can be understood to signal 'new rules' for work, involving demands on workers to develop a moral character that is better attuned to the dynamics of the workplace—a character that would be more intelligent, adaptive, and reflective. Emotional intelligence may also signal diminished scope for worker resistance. It is unlikely, then, that promotional literature will note that engaging with employees' feelings is the most fragile of all managerial activities (Warhurst and Thompson, 1998).

190

Some difficulties with measuring and testing personality

There is little agreement among psychologists about how the term 'personality' is defined, or which aspects of personality can be measured. Personality is tested through a definition and measurement of traits—but there is little consistency between psychologists regarding the number of factors that should be considered: Eysenck (1992) claims that there are three factors, Cattell (1957), sixteen; and Brand (1994) specifies six factors. Furthermore, even the labelling of the factors within the 'Big Five' tradition is not consistent (Furnham, 2008). Consequently, no personality test will ever be totally accurate.

There are several potential problems with personality tests. Firstly, behaviour and personality will vary over time; a personality test has a 'shelf life' of only six months, which must make longitudinal research (that is, research with the same people over a period of time) particularly problematic. Secondly, behaviour will change depending on the situation: people cannot be expected to behave consistently regardless of context (Mischel, 1968). Further, the tests rely on self-report data, which means that respondents need to have some insight into their most characteristic behaviour—a level of insight that will vary from person to person. Some people do not have sufficient self-insight to give accurate answers about themselves. Interestingly, however, the '16PF' test attempts to control this factor by including a measure of the extent to which respondents attempt to present themselves in a favourable or unfavourable manner.

It is acknowledged, therefore, that personality tests can be distorted and that people may want to present themselves in the best possible light; they may even have practised the test before. 'Faking' in personality testing has been noted, for example, by personality trait theorist Cattell and his colleagues (1970). One of the major criticisms of personality questionnaires is that they are susceptible to deliberate 'faking-good' responding by candidates. Yet despite the fact that research has shown that personnel professionals know that personality tests can be faked easily and that some participants are likely to 'fake-good' in the future, these tests remain in wide use (Rees and Metcalfe, 2003).

⭐ **STOP AND THINK** **Do personality traits change over time?**

It has been argued that behaviour and personality will change over time. You might imagine that personality will change with personal growth if you believe in self-actualization (at which we looked in Chapter 6). Many people like to think that they change for the better over time (becoming wiser, more mature, and more insightful), but there is also research that shows an impressive level of stability in personality traits (particularly extraversion, neuroticism, and conscientiousness), and intelligence over time (Costa and McCrae, 1992; Deary, 2004).

Which view would you prefer to believe and why?

The tests can be unreliable for a host of reasons: for example, anxiety, boredom, or headaches may mean that people will give different answers on different occasions. Tests are unlikely to offer information on, for example, the person's propensity (or likelihood) to being absent. Further, the tests are unfair, so that middle-class, white people tend to do better or get a more attractive profile; they consequently 'fly in the face of anti-discriminatory legislation' (Furnham, 2008: 70) and create no meritocracy.

As a consequence, many hold personality research in poor regard. Murphy and Dzieweczynski (2005) conclude that 'the validity of measures of broad personality traits is still low, personality tests used in organizations are still poorly chosen and links between personality and jobs are poorly understood'. Case and Phillipson (2004) note that while the Myers-Briggs type indicator is often presented as a form of scientific psychology par excellence, its origins in Jungian personality typology mean that it is founded on astrology and alchemy. Contemporary practitioners of this brand of psychometrics inadvertently find themselves conducting a form of astrological character analysis. In addition, there is little agreement on a research agenda for personality research and test publishers seem quite unconcerned with measurement validity (Hogan, 2005). It should be noted that, in a review of managerial psychology, Smith and George (1994) say that non-work-related personality tests used as selection tools are poor predictors of job success and should be treated with caution.

Despite this poor validity, personality tests remain used by management consultants to dupe clients and to satisfy the demand for assessment of personality. Smith and George (1994) argue that there is worldwide abuse of personality testing. Thompson and McHugh (2002: 234) note further that personality testing and inventories effectively perform the same function for an organization as stereotypes do for an individual or group: they help to sort a bewildering variety of information about a person into categories that can be more easily comprehended and evaluated. They aim to point to characteristics that are useful or damaging to an organization.

The psychometric testing industry is particularly adept at making sweeping claims, providing evidence, for example, of women's inadequacies as employees. Glenn Wilson (1994: 62–3) says that the reason why 95 per cent of bank managers, company directors, judges, and university professors in the UK are men is because men are 'more competitive' and because 'dominance is a personality characteristic determined by male hormones'. According to this view, women who do achieve promotion to top management positions 'may have brains that are masculinized' (ibid.: 65). Psychology is thus deeply implicated in the patriarchal control of women (Wilkinson, 1997). Women's alleged limited achievements are seen as being due to biological differences and therefore unchangeable, or as a problem of social skills to which the solution can be found in assertiveness training. The effect of this is to locate women as the problem, saying nothing about the social context, organizational structures, policies, or procedures that discriminate against women. The underlying assumption behind personality testing is that managerial ability is related to personality factors—factors that will not include the ability to hold down a job, run a household, and bring up children simultaneously. It does fulfil the expectations of existing managers—mainly white, male, middle-class, and middle-aged—about what makes a good manager (Hollway, 1984) and it is probably for this reason that the use of personality questionnaires has become an established element in the selection of managers (IRS, 1997). People unable or unwilling to make the correct responses in psychometric tests automatically select themselves out, regardless of managerial potential.

The utility of psychometric testing is its cost-saving ability to predict who is capable or willing to be trained. The pragmatic psychology of Taylorism is at work here: if the person can do the job, as long as he or she has the 'right' personality, he or she will be a 'fit' employee.

Personality theory and problematic behaviour

So far in this chapter, we have looked at how psychology has used personality theory in organizations for the purposes of prediction, based on assessment of individual differences. But personality theory can also serve as a source of descriptive concepts or categories to help to explain a problematic aspect of an individual's behaviour, and then guide intervention to change it. For example, the personality features of the bully—or of the manager under stress—might be identified, and then training designed to intervene.

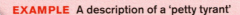

EXAMPLE **A description of a 'petty tyrant'**

'In the three months since [the new owner of the pharmacy] has been in charge [he] has made it clear that he is at liberty to fire employees at will ... change their positions, decrease their bonus percentages, and refuse time-off and vacation choices. Furthermore, he has established an authoritarian work structure characterized by distrust, cut-backs on many items deemed essential to work comfort, disrespect, rigidity and poor-to-no communication ... [He regards employees as] potential thieves and squanderers of work time. As a result, he consistently spies on employees ... These changes have been so pervasive that ... the employees no longer refer to the [pharmacy] as a "small family", but as the "third Reich", with [him] in the role of Hitler.' (Giarrusso, 1990: 5–6)

(*Source:* Ashforth, 1997)

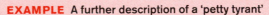

EXAMPLE **A further description of a 'petty tyrant'**

'[Harry Figgie] can be the nicest fellow in the world one day and totally abusive the next: "Men running $100 million divisions would come into my office and ask if it was safe to see Harry that day" ... "Figgie takes no prisoners when it comes to an insult. He'll call anyone a horse's ass anywhere" ... "Headquarters was like a tomb. People were scared. Harry chewed me out again and again and again. Every day he'd work me over. I lost 40 pounds putting in six days a week until ten o'clock every night, never sure I'd have a job in the morning."' (Nulty, 1989: 41)

(*Source:* Ashforth, 1997)

Other research has identified difficult types of personality. Similar to the 'petty tyrant' are the authoritarian personality (Adorno et al., 1950), the 'System 1 manager' who believes that it is the job of employees to abide by the manager's decision, who uses no teamwork, and who will use threat to make sure that work is completed (Likert, 1967), the 'bureaupathic individual' whose characteristics include petty insistence on the rights of office and ritualistic attachment to routines and procedures (Thompson, 1961) and the 'dictator' (Rubin, 1987). Recurring themes in these descriptions of difficult personalities are close and coercive supervision, an emphasis on authority and status differences, arbitrary actions, severe and punitive treatment of subordinates, and the deterrence of subordinates' initiative and dissent. There is, then, a tendency by these types of personality to overcontrol others, and to treat them in an arbitrary, uncaring, and punitive manner. (Ashforth, 1994; 1997).

Furnham (2007) has identified three categories, or types, of personality that have been commonly implicated in management derailment—that is, in individual management failure.

1. The psychopath is selfish, callous, superficially charming, and lacking in empathy and remorse. 'Psychopaths' are probably the most common and dangerous at work (Babiak and Hare, 2006).

2. The narcissist is attention-seeking, vain, self-focused, and exploitative.

3. The Machiavellian personality is deceptive, manipulative, and deeply self-interested.

Paradoxically, these are the disorders that prove to be an asset in acquiring and temporarily holding down senior management positions. The charm of the psychopath, the self-confidence of the narcissist, and the clever deceptiveness of the Machiavellian may be useful business traits. If these are coupled with physical attractiveness, good education, and intelligence, it is not difficult to see why people with these traits are selected for senior positions in management.

Personality, integrity, and dishonesty at work

People steal money, goods, and time at work. Counterproductive behaviours at work have attracted an ever-growing research literature (Griffin and O'Leary-Kelly, 2004; Fox and Spector, 2005) at which we will look further in Chapter 16. Concentrating on personality, one finding has been that the trait of 'conscientiousness' is correlated with 'integrity' (Murphy and Lee, 1994). Research has also indicated that it is possible to find a relationship between certain personality profiles (as revealed by Eysenck's personality test) and deviant behaviour at work. Eysenck (1964) has argued, for example, that criminals are more extroverted and neurotic than non-criminals, while Eysenck and Gudjonsson (1989) have argued that criminals are also relatively high on psychoticism, because high scorers on this trait tend to be uncaring about people and therefore unlikely to feel guilt, empathy, or sensitivity to the feelings of others. Certainly, the literature on delinquency supports the view that there is a relationship between certain personality profiles and deviant behaviours (Furnham and Thompson, 1991). Results from the 'Big Five' perspective are similar (Heaven, 1996). Young people low on conscientiousness and agreeableness (as well as on excitement-seeking) are those most prone to vandalism, theft, and violence. A functionalist manager might conclude from this that all that he or she need do is test future employees for these traits—but the issue is more complex, so more research, critical thinking, and analysis is needed. The situation—that is, external factors—also play their part, such as financial need or life stressors.

EXAMPLE Putting psychology into practice

It has been found that a photograph of a pair of eyes is enough to increase people's honesty. Researchers found that people put nearly three times as much money in a coffee-room honesty box when a nearby poster displayed a pair of staring eyes as compared with a bunch of flowers (Bateson et al., 2006). Inspired by the research, *West Midlands Police* subsequently launched 'Operation Momentum', featuring posters with eyes and the tagline 'We've got our eyes on criminals' (Jarrett, 2008).

Not surprisingly, 'integrity testing' has become popular with employers who want to select out potentially problem candidates. Around 5,000 companies use pre-employment integrity tests and there are some forty or fifty available tests on the market (Furnham, 2008). These tests can be useful and do provide some information—but they do not necessarily measure honesty: they do not tell us, with any degree of certainty, whether an individual will commit, or has committed, a dishonest act. They are certainly not the solution to the problems of employee theft and counterproductivity; they may even do more harm than good, in terms of the negative reactions that they might invoke (Murphy, 1994). They may be culturally dependent: for example, a gift in one culture might be a bribe in another. People may also be very honest in one situation and very dishonest in another. Further, paradoxically, it is the more honest people that admit to dishonesty in the past, so tests, it might be argued, are better are detecting 'goodies' than they are 'baddies' (Furnham, 2008).

EXAMPLE **A question in an integrity test**

You are a new clerk in a clothing store and you are being trained by Angie, a veteran employee. She quietly tells you that because employees are paid minimum wage most people take clothes for themselves. Employees who do not do so are considered dumb and arrogant. At closing time, Angie hands you a scarf to take home. Which of the following are you most likely to do?

1. Take home the scarf and keep your mouth shut. (If you select this answer you will score −1.)

2. Take home the scarf, but return it to the shelf later without letting other employees see you. (If you select this answer, you will score −1.)

3. Politely tell Angie that you do not need any more scarves. (If you select this answer, you will score 0.)

4. Tell Angie that you do not want to take home any clothes, now or ever. (If you select this answer, you will score 1.)

If you score 1 for any question, you will be deemed to have integrity.

(*Source:* Becker, 2005: 234)

Judging competence at work

Because many writers and researchers in psychology and management have been disappointed in the ability of personality and ability tests to predict job success, it was hoped that competencies might provide a solution. A 'competence' is an ability or skill, or know-how, that it is thought could be identified in order to recruit, select, train, and appraise employees. The concept was popularized by McClelland (1973), who developed tests to measure competencies by comparing above-average, average, and below-average managers to understand how they did their jobs and what competencies they used, in an attempt to identify generic competencies. The popularity of the concept was raised again by Richard Boyatzis (1982) in his book *The Competent Manager*. Boyatzis defined a 'competence' as an underlying characteristic of a person, which might be a motive, trait, skill, aspect of self-image or social role, or a body of knowledge that he or she uses.

The problem with Boyatzis' definition is that it appears to cover everything and does not define a common denominator; there are no specific competencies to test for in this list. It may consequently not be a very helpful concept (Furnham, 2000). McClelland has also been criticized—on the ground that his competencies concern past, rather than future, behaviour. The assumption is that demonstration of competencies used in the past is a predictor of future use of the same competencies. His methods were also criticized. Identifying competences also brought with it a lot of meaningless 'psychobabble' of individual differences, such as the ability to 'take the helicopter view' or 'think outside the box', which resist clear definition or use (ibid.).

Competencies may therefore initially appear to be a good way of measuring, then judging, aspects of an individual's personality—particularly in terms of work behaviour—but a little research and critical thinking on the topic soon uncovers their weaknesses.

Personality and leadership

There are links to be found in the research between personality and leadership, as we have seen in the research that highlights features such as narcissism. There remains a recognized need—especially among those who recruit leaders—to answer the question of what qualities should be sought and found in leaders. In order to answer this question, headhunters Neff and Citrin interviewed the USA's top fifty CEOs (Neff et al., 1999). Similarly, Harrison and Cough (2006) examined the personality characteristics of fifteen 'state of the art' leaders, finding that while eleven of the thirteen demonstrated personal humility, just over two-thirds showed signs of egotistical behaviour, and 85 per cent displayed aloof behaviours. Presumably, being egotistical and aloof are not characteristics that one would necessarily wish to recommend for leadership.

EXAMPLE The personality of the entrepreneur

We may intuitively think of entrepreneurs as rational, calculating people and predict that this may be the behaviour that they would exemplify—but stories about entrepreneurs tell of unruly, elusive creatures who do not obey the rules of logical economic behaviour. For example, they embark on schemes for which they cannot predict the outcome, and follow passions and hunches (Jones and Spicer, 2006). They indulge in excessive behaviour. For example, Richard Branson is described by one biographer as letting off fire extinguishers, initiating a food fight, and dressing up in fishnet stockings for the fancy dress party when his company (*Virgin*) had taken over a hotel for three or four days (Brown, 1998). He has also expended vast sums of money in order to become the first person to fly around the world in a hot-air balloon.

Is looking at personality traits enough?

As we have seen in this chapter, personality tends to be examined by looking at the individual's traits or competencies, adopting a 'nomothetic' approach—that is, an approach that has as its objective the isolation of one or more variables or traits of personality. Perhaps rather than looking simply at the traits of personality or competencies, a more 'ideographic' approach to personality should be adopted. This approach would view the individual as not only a collection of separate traits, but as an integrated individual; the present behaviour of the individual draws on both past experiences and future intentions in various situations. In this way, the ideographic approach is said to capture the wholeness and unique-ness of the personality, as it functions in the many and diverse situations in which it finds itself.

STOP AND THINK What makes a good boss?

Research involving a survey of 2,000 British people by the *Learning and Skills Council* in 2008 showed that the person whom most would like as their boss is Richard Branson: 51 per cent would like to work for him. Giving credit for great ideas, patience, and a commitment to training were the most popular personality features. Employers who organize social events, who let staff go early on Fridays, and who do not impose a dress code were, surprisingly, at the bottom of the list (*The Scotsman*, 28 July 2008). Yet those who discuss Google as an employer find that people love working for the company because it organizes social events and lets people dress unconventionally (see, for example, Holmquist, 2008).

How do you reconcile these two pieces of information?

Conclusion

It may seem self-evident that people have stable personalities, that personalities can be measured, and that we can predict how people will behave in organizations if we understand their personality traits. As this chapter has shown, this is clearly not the case. Organizational behaviour has drawn on psychology, and its study of individual traits and competencies, to try to predict individual behaviour and performance at work. It has done little to look at the wider aspect of the individual, such as his or her beliefs, values, and preferences, as contributors to organizations. A good personality theory may be expected to increase our ability to explain and predict behaviour in organizations—but a personality theory may only help understanding.

Understanding personality and personality theory is difficult and complex. It is by no means clear how personality should be best conceived of or measured. While consultants may profile individuals to assess their strengths and weaknesses, tests do not always have much validity and, as we have seen, there are other weaknesses inherent in the testing of individuals. Tests are also poor at predicting job performance. This may be because much may be hidden, immeasurable, unobvious, or unclear.

KEY POINTS

- Management is interested in individual personalities to understand how people behave, think, and feel, because this may affect what they do and how well they perform.

- Personality theories are designed to help us to understand, explain, or predict behaviour. Psychological tests, such as intelligence testing or tests for traits such as narcissism, are designed to help managers do this better.

- There is, however, little agreement among psychologists as to how personality is defined or which aspects can be measured.

- There are also potential problems with personality tests including: that personality will vary over time; that people may not have sufficient insight to give accurate answers about themselves; that people may want to present themselves in a favourable light; and that the tests may have poor validity—that is, they may not measure what they are supposed to measure.

- Despite the inherent problems, psychological testing has become a big industry, and tests for emotional intelligence and integrity testing have become particularly popular.

- Recently, competence testing has also become popular in order to help with recruitment, selection, training, and appraising employees.

CASE STUDY
Leader or narcissist?

In this following case, we see how a personality can be seen and described quite differently: as both a model leader and as a narcissist.

In the 1980s, Jan Carlzon, CEO of Scandinavian airline *SAS*, was described by Tom Peters as a model leader. By 2004, he was described by Maccoby (2004) as a narcissist. In Greek mythology, Narcissus was a man so vain and proud that he fell in love with his own image; narcissism is a personality trait encompassing grandiosity, arrogance, self-absorption, entitlement, fragile self-esteem, and hostility. Narcissists lack empathy, value competition over cooperation, and are interpersonally dismissive and abrasive (Sedikides et al., 2004);

they do not make good 'team players'. They have also been found to derogate those close to them who outperform them (Morf and Rhodewalt, 1993; 2001). But as well as having negative traits, narcissistic personalities also possess the charisma and grand vision that have been said to be 'vital to effective leadership' (Rosenthal and Pittinksy, 2006); it is an attribute of many powerful leaders and can be seen—as evident in the examples above cited by Maccoby (2004; 2007)—as a personality characteristic of successful leaders.

Recently, a business psychologist, Professor Binna Kandola, has commented that he feels that the banking bosses have been displaying signs of narcissism, characterized by a certain grandiosity and a strong sense of envy. They also seem to think that the rules do not apply to them. The very personality characteristics that made the banking bosses successful in the first place—that is, ambition, drive, and ruthlessness—have ultimately proven to be the very characteristics that brought them down.

(*Source: Management Today* (2009) 'Leadership: Were our big banks run by psychopaths?', 23 February, available online at http://www.managementtoday.co.uk)

Questions

1. Given that narcissism is socially undesirable, and that few people would wish to be described as vain, self-absorbed, egotistical, selfish, conceited and grandiose, lacking in empathy, or poor team players, would you expect organizations to screen these people out at hiring stage?

2. How do you think a narcissistic employee might respond to appraisal? (See Bushman and Baumeister, 1998.)

3. There appears to be no research that investigates how narcissists react to negative feedback (Judge et al., 2006). How difficult might it be to research this?

197

FURTHER READING

Ashforth, B. (1994) 'Petty tyranny in organizations', *Human Relations*, 47: 755–78 This article is good at provoking thoughts on further research questions, such as how common is petty tyranny and what becomes of the tyrannical manager.

Clegg, S., Kornberger, M., and Pitsis, T. (2008) *Managing and Organizations*, London: Sage This book contains a good section on personality.

Furnham, A. (2008) *Personality and Individual Differences at Work*, London: Routledge A good text for those who want to know more about this topic.

Landon, M. (2002) 'Emotion management: Dabbling in mystery—white witchcraft or black art?', *Human Resource Development International*, 5(4): 507–21 This article makes some interesting cases for being wary of psychometric testing—particularly those relating to emotional intelligence.

O'Doherty D. (2007) 'Individual differences, personality and self', in D. Knights and H. Wilmott (eds), *Introducing Organizational Behaviour and Management*, London: Thompson, ch. 3 This chapter discusses personality theory critically.

Thompson, P. and McHugh, D. (2002) *Work Organizations*, 3rd edn, Houndmills: Palgrave Chapter 15 includes a discussion on personality.

LINKS TO FILMS AND NOVELS

Blade Runner (1982) dir. R. Scott A science fiction film that poses the question: how do we know that we are human and, if we are human, what does it mean to be human? In this film, the main character is tasked with identifying and killing artificially created human beings—known as 'replicants'—who have free will and some of the same emotions as humans, including fear and love, but who lack empathy—that is, the ability to identify with the sufferings and joys of other sentient creatures. Empathy is portrayed as the key feature of personality that marks out humans. The film challenges us to think about what it means to be human and what features of humanity are needed in organizations. How essential is empathy as a personality trait?

The Corporation (2003) dir. M. Achbar and J. Abbott In the mid-1800s, the corporation emerged as a legal 'person' imbued with a 'personality' of pure self-interest. It appears in this film to be an anti-social personality: self-interested, inherently amoral, callous, and deceitful—meeting the criteria that would, in a human, lead to a diagnosis of psychopathy.

Last King of Scotland (2006) dir. K. Macdonald This is a powerful thriller that combines fact and fiction. It carves a portrait of one personality: Idi Amin, the 'charismatic but psychopathic ruler' of Uganda.

RESEARCH QUESTIONS

1. Given what you now know about personality testing, what best advice would you offer to someone recruiting a new manager?

2. What personality traits are being tested for by organizations? Are they screening for authoritarianism, narcissism, or petty tyranny?

3. Review the evidence for and against emotional intelligence, and draw your own conclusions. (See, in particular, Cartwright and Pappas, 2008.)

REFERENCES

Adorno, T.W., Frenkel-Brunswik, E., Levinson, D.J., and Sanford, R.N. (1950) *The Authoritarian Personality*, New York: Harper and Row.

Ashforth, B.E. (1994) 'Petty tyranny in organizations', *Human Relations*, 47: 755–78.

_____ (1997) 'Petty tyranny in organizations: A preliminary examination of antecedents and consequences', *Revue Canadienne des Sciences de l'Administration*, June: 1–11.

Babiak, P. and Hare, R. (2006) *Snakes in Suits*, New York: Regan Books.

Bachman, J., Stein, S., Campbell, K., and Sitarenios, A. (2000) 'Emotional intelligence in the collection of debt', *International Journal of Selection and Assessment*, 8(3): 14–20.

Bateson, M., Nettle, D., and Roberts, G. (2006) 'Cues of being watched enhance cooperation in a real world setting', *Biology Letters*, 2: 412–14.

Becker, T (2005) 'Development and validation of situational judgment test of employee integrity', *International Journal of Selection and Assessment*, 13: 225–323.

Boyatzis, R. (1982) *The Competent Manager: A Model for Effective Performance*, New York: Wiley.

Brand, C. (1994) 'Open to experience: Closed to intelligence', *European Journal of Personality*, 8: 299–310.

Briner, R. (1999) 'The neglect and importance of emotion at work', *European Journal of Work and Organizational Psychology*, 8(3): 323–46.

Brown, M. (1998) *Richard Branson*, London: Headline.

Bushman, B.J. and Baumeister, R.F. (1998) 'Threatened egotism, narcissism, self-esteem and direct aggression: Does self-love or self-hate lead to violence?', *Journal of Personality and Social Psychology*, 75: 219–29.

_____ Bonacci, A.M., van Dijk, M., and Baumeister, R.F. (2003) 'Narcissism, sexual refusal and aggression: Testing a narcissistic reactance model of sexual coercion', *Journal of Personality and Social Psychology*, 84: 1027–40.

Cartwright, S. and Pappas, C. (2008) 'Emotional intelligence, its measurement and implications for the workplace', *International Journal of Management Reviews*, 10(2): 149–71.

Case, P. and Phillipson, G. (2004) 'Astrology, alchemy and retro-organization theory: An astro-genealogical critique of the Myers-Briggs Type Indicator', *Organization*, 11(4): 473–95.

Cattell, R.B. (1957) *Personality, Motivation, Structure And Measurement*, Yonkers, NY: World Book Company.

_____, Eber, H.W., and Tatsuoka, M.M. (1970) *Handbook of the Cattell 16PF Questionnaire*, Champaign, IL: Institute of Personality and Ability Testing.

Cavelzani, A.S., Lee, I.A., Locatelli, V., Monti, G., and Villamira, M.A. (2003) 'Emotional intelligence and tourist services: The tour operator as a mediator between tourists and residents', *International Journal of Hospitality and Tourism Administration*, 4(4): 1–24.

Cernovsky, Z.Z. (1997), 'A critical look at intelligence research', in D. Fox and I. Prilleltensky (eds), *Critical Psychology: An Introduction*, London: Sage, ch. 8.

Costa, R. and McCrae, R. (1992) *Revised NEO Personality Inventory (NEO-P-I-R) and NEO Five-Factor Inventory (NEO-FFI): Professional Manual*, Odessa, FL: Psychological Assessment Resources.

Day, D.V. and Schleicher, D.J. (2006) 'Self-monitoring at work: A motive-based perspective', *Journal of Personality*, 74(3): 685–710.

Deary, I. (2004) *Looking Down on Intelligence*, Oxford: Oxford University Press.

Epstein, S. (1990) 'Cognitive-experimental self-theory', in L. Pervin (ed.), *Handbook of Personality Theory and Research*, New York: Guilford Press, pp. 165–91.

Eysenck, H.J. (1964) *Crime and Personality*, London: Routledge and Kegan Paul.

_____ (1992) 'Four ways five factors are *not* basic', *Personality and Individual Differences*, 13: 667–73.

_____ and Gudjonsson, G. (1989) *The Causes and Consequences of Crime*, New York: Plenum.

Fineman, S. (ed.) (2000) *Emotion in Organizations*, London: Sage.

Fox, A. and Spector, P. (2005) *Counterproductive Work Behaviour*, Washington DC: APA.

Furnham, A. (1992) *Personality at Work: The Role of Individual Differences*, London: Routledge.

_____ (2000) *Managerial Competency Frameworks*, London: Career Research Forum.

_____ (2007) 'Personality disorders and derailment at work', in J. Langan-Fox, C. Cooper, and R. Klimoski (eds), *Management Challenges and Symptoms of the Dysfunctional Workplace*, Cheltenham: Edward Elgar, ch. 2.

_____ (2008) *Personality and Intelligence at Work*, London: Routledge.

_____ and Thompson, J. (1991) 'Personality and self-reported delinquency', *Personality and Individual Differences*, 12: 585–93.

Gabel, R.S., Dolan, S.L., and Cerdin, J.L. (2005) 'Emotional intelligence as a predictor of cultural adjustment for success in global assignments', *Career Development International*, 10(5): 375–95.

George, J.M. (2000), 'Emotions and leadership: The role of emotional intelligence', *Human Relations*, 8: 1027–55.

Giarruso, N. (1990) 'An issue of job satisfaction', Unpublished term paper, Concordia University, Montreal, cited in B. Ashforth (1994) 'Petty tyranny in organizations', *Human Relations*, 47: 755–78.

Giddens, A. (1991) *Modernity and Identity*, London: Polity Press.

Gottfredson, L.S. (2002) 'Where and why matters: Not a mystery', *Human Performance*, 15: 25–46.

_____ and Deary, I. (2004) 'Intelligence predicts health and longevity, but why?', *Current Direction in Psychological Science*, 13: 1–4.

Goleman, D. (1995) *Emotional Intelligence*, New York: Bantam Books.

_____ (1996) *Emotional Intelligence: Why It Can Matter More Than IQ*, London: Bloomsbury.

_____ (1998) *Working with Emotional Intelligence*, London: Bloomsbury.

Griffin, R. and O'Leary-Kelly, A. (2004) *The Dark Side of Organizational Behaviour*, San Francisco, CA: Jossey Bass.

Harrison, J.K. and Clough, M.W. (2006) 'Characteristics of "state of the art" leaders: Productive narcissism versus emotional intelligence and Level 5 capabilities', *The Social Science Journal*, 43: 287–92.

Heaven, P. (1996) 'Personality and self-reported delinquency: Analysis of the "Big Five" personality dimensions', *Personality and Individual Differences*, 20: 47–54.

Hogan, B. (2005) 'In defence of personality measures', *Human Performance*, 18: 331–41.

Hollway, W. (1984) 'Fitting work: Psychological assessment in organizations', in J. Henriques, W. Hollway, C. Urwin, C. Venn, and V. Walkerdine (eds), *Changing the Subject: Psychology, Social Regulation and Subjectivity*, London: Methuen, ch. 1.

Holmquist, K. (2008) 'Google me the perfect job', *Irish Times*, 4 August, p. 15.

Hughes, J. (2005) 'Bringing emotion to work: Emotional intelligence, employee resistance and the reinvention of character', *Work, Employment and Society*, 19: 603–25.

IRS (1997) 'The state of selection: An IRS survey', *Employee Development Bulletin*, 85: 8–17.

Jarrett, C. (2008) 'Mind wide open', *The Psychologist*, 21(4): 294–7.

Jones, C. and Spicer, A. (2006) 'Entrepreneurial excess', in J. Brewis, S. Linstead, D. Boje, and T. O'Shea (eds), *The Passion of Organizing*, Malmö: Liber and Copenhagen Business School Press, ch. 7.

Judge, T.A., LePine, J.E., and Rich, B.L. (2006) 'Loving yourself abundantly: Relationship of the narcissistic personality to self and other perceptions of workplace deviance, leadership and task and contextual performance', *Journal of Applied Psychology*, 91(4): 762–76.

Kilduff, M. and Day, D.V. (1994) 'Do chameleons get ahead? The effects of self-monitoring on managerial careers', *Academy of Management Journal*, 37(4): 1047–60.

Landon, M. (2002) 'Emotion management: Dabbling in mystery—white witchcraft or black art?', *Human Resource Development International*, 5(4): 507–21.

Likert, R. (1967) *The Human Organization: Its Management and Value*, New York: McGraw Hill.

Maccoby, M. (2004) 'Narcissistic leaders: The incredible pros, the inevitable cons', *Harvard Business Review*, 82(1): 92–101.

_____ (2007) *Narcissistic Leaders: Who Succeeds and Who Fails*, Boston, MA: Harvard Business School Press.

Mayer, J.D. and Caruso, D. (1997), 'Multifactor emotional intelligence scale', New Caanan, CT: unpublished manuscript.

_____ and Salovey, P. (1997) 'What is emotional intelligence: Implications for educators', in P. Salovey and D. Sluyter (eds), *Emotional Development, Emotional Literacy and Emotional Intelligence*, New York: Basic Books, pp. 3–31.

McClelland, D. (1973) 'Testing for competency rather than intelligence', *American Psychologist*, 28: 1–14.

Mehra, A. and Shenkel, M.T. (2008) 'The price chameleons pay: Self-monitoring, boundary spanning and role conflict in the workplace', *British Journal of Management*, 19: 138–44.

_____, Kilduff, M. and Brass, D.J. (2001) 'The social networks of high and low self-monitors: Implications for workplace performance', *Administrative Science Quarterly*, 46(1): 121–46.

Mischel, W. (1968) *Personality and Assessment*, New York: Wiley.

Morf, C.C. and Rhodewalt, F. (1993) 'Narcissism and self-evaluation maintenance: Explorations in object relations', *Personality and Social Psychology Bulletin*, 19: 668–76.

_____ _____ (2001) 'Unravelling the paradoxes of narcissism: A dynamic self-regulating processing model', *Psychological Inquiry*, 1(2): 177–96.

Moutafi, J., Furnham, A., and Crump, J. (2007) 'Is managerial level related to personality?', *British Journal of Management*, 18: 272–80.

Murphy, K. (1994) *Honesty in the Workplace*, Pacific Grove, LA: Brooks.

_____ and Dzieweczynski, J. (2005) 'Why don't measures of broad dimensions of personality perform better as predictors of job performance', *Human Performance*, 18: 343–57.

200

_____ and Lee, S. (1994) 'Personality variables related to integrity test scores', *Journal of Business and Psychology*, 8: 413–24.

Myers, I.B. (1993) *Introduction to Type*, 5th edn, rev. L.K. Kirby and K. Myers, Palo Also, CA: Consulting Psychologists Press.

Neff, T.J. and Critrin, J.M. (1999) *Lessons from the Top: The Search for America's Best Business Leaders*, New York: Currency and Doubleday.

Nulty, P. (1989) 'America's toughest boss', *Fortune*, 27 February, available online at http://money.cnn.com/magazines/fortune/fortune_archive/1989/02/27/71697/index.htm

Paul, A.M. (1999) 'Promotional intelligence', *Salon.com*, available online at http://www.salon.com/books/it/1999/06/28/emotional

Perez, J., Petrides, K.V., and Furnham, A. (2005) 'Measuring trait emotional intelligence', in R. Schulze and R. Roberts (eds), *Emotional Intelligence: An International Handbook*, Gottingen: Hogrefe, pp. 181–201.

Rees, C.J. and Metcalfe, B. (2003) 'The faking of personality questionnaire results: Who's kidding whom?', *Journal of Managerial Psychology*, 18(2): 156–65.

Rosenthal, S. and Pittinsky, T.L. (2006) 'Narcissistic leadership', *Leadership Quarterly*, 17(6): 617–33.

Rubin, R. (1987) *Modern Dictators: Third World Coup Makers, Strongmen and Populist Tyrants*, New York: McGraw Hill.

Salovey, P., Mayer. J.D., Goldman, S.L., Turvey, C., and Palfai, T.P. (1995) 'Emotional attention, clarity, and repair: Exploring emotional intelligence using the trait meta-mood scale', in J.W. Pennebaker (ed.), *Emotion, Disclosure and Health*, Washington DC: American Psychological Association, pp. 125–54.

Scheff, T.J. (1997), *Emotions, the Social Bond and Human Reality*, Cambridge: Cambridge University Press.

Sedikides, C., Rudich, E.A., Gregg, A.P., Kumashiro, M., and Rusbult, C. (2004) 'Are normal narcissists psychologically healthy? Self-esteem matters', *Journal of Personality and Social Psychology*, 87: 400–16.

Sloan, T. (1997) 'Theories of personality: Ideology and beyond', in D. Fox and I Prilleltensky (eds), *Critical Psychology: An Introduction*, London: Sage, ch. 6.

Smith, M. and George, D. (1994) 'Selection methods', in C.L. Cooper and I.T. Robertson (eds), *Key Reviews in Managerial Psychology: Concepts and Research in Practice*, Chichester: Wiley.

Thompson, P. and McHugh, D. (2002) *Work Organizations: A Critical Introduction*, 3rd edn, Houndmills: Palgrave.

Thompson, V.A. (1961) *Modern Organization*, New York: Alfred A. Knopf.

Warhurst, C. and Thompson, P. (1998) 'Hands, hearts and minds: Changing work and workers at the end of the century', in P. Thompson and C. Warhurst (eds), *Workplaces of the Future*, Basingstoke: Macmillan.

Wilkinson, S. (1997) 'Feminist psychology', in D. Fox and I. Prilleltensky (eds), *Critical Psychology: An Introduction*, London: Sage, ch. 16.

Wilson, G. (1994) 'Biology, sex roles and work', in C. Quest (ed.), *Liberating Women … from Modern Feminism*, London: Institute of Economic Affairs, Health and Welfare Unit, pp. 59–71.

Zeidner, M., Matthews, G., and Roberts, R.D. (2004) 'Emotional intelligence in the workplace: A critical review', *Applied Psychology*, 53(3): 371–99.

10 Organizational Learning

Introduction

You might argue that organizations and individuals need the ability to learn in order to remain viable in a world characterized by uncertainty and change. So how do organizations learn? It might be said that organizational learning is undertaken by individuals, by groups, and by organizations as a whole. We will look at each of these areas in turn.

By the end of the chapter, you will be able to discuss what organizational learning might mean. You will be able to describe and contrast different theories of learning, and will understand some aspects of how the topic has been discussed in the research literature. While most textbooks discuss the topic as if it is always a good thing for individuals, groups, and organizations to learn—as if the process of learning is unproblematic—this book adopts a more questioning approach to the topic, including whether organizations are able to—and should—learn.

This chapter covers:

- the concept of organizational learning;
- individual learning;
- group learning;
- organizational learning;
- learning about language in organizations;
- developing a critical consciousness.

The concept of organizational learning

The concepts of 'organizational learning' (Schon, 1983) and the 'learning organization' (Senge, 1990) became prevalent and stylish in the 1990s. 'Organizational learning' means the learning undertaken or achieved by individuals within organizations (Argyris, 1992). It is, then, very similar to individual learning. Organizations learn when the knowledge that their members have is explicitly known and codified by the organization. Learning is 'a purposeful activity aimed at the acquisition and development of skills and knowledge and their application' (Dale, 1994: 24). Learning can be seen to have occurred when organizations perform in changed and better ways. The management and innovation literature sees organizational learning as a purposive quest to retain and improve competitiveness, productivity, and innovativeness in uncertain technological and market circumstances (Dodgson, 1993).

Early work on the learning organization focused on finding examples of good practice so that the learning organization might be replicated (Dale, 1994). For example, an organization could learn from the tacit knowledge and experience of, and improvements introduced by, its members. What happened, however, was that some of the organizations held up as role models were subsequently found to be flawed: there is no perfect organization and all organizations are peopled by fallible human beings. Mistakes and setbacks are features of development and learning. Also, as Grey (2001) notes, it is unproblematically assumed that learning—like vitamins and stopping smoking—is a good thing.

 STOP AND THINK **When learning may not be such a good thing**

Paul Willis (1977) documented, in his research on schoolboys in the UK's Midlands, how the official and unofficial learning at school fitted them for the limited kinds of work—mainly manual work—that they would perform when they left. But is it a good thing that these schoolboys were fitted to limited kinds of work?

The literature in this area is mainly prescriptive, and aims to help individuals, groups, and organizations learn more effectively. As Mumford (1994) notes, much of the literature on organizational learning has a flavour of the organizational development (OD) movement of the 1970s, within which organizational problems would be analysed and solutions offered by OD consultants. Yet there is little learning from the OD movement that remains in current managerial thinking. Most managers are unwilling to accept, for example, the values usually held by OD practitioners: openness, trust, and confrontation.

Individual learning

One way of learning in organizations is to watch what goes on, or how a job is done. This has historically been known as 'sitting by Nelly'. 'Nelly' would show the new employee how to do the job; he or she would watch and learn, then be able to do the job him or herself. Charles Handy, the management writer, was, in his first job as a manager, asked to sit and watch the general manager of his office—a man named Ian. Handy was asked to sit in the manager's room, in a corner, and be as inconspicuous as possible. He was told not to speak when anyone else was in the room and never to leave the room, no matter what was going on. The manager explained, 'You will learn more about this business from watching me for a month than by sitting by some other Nelly, and I will learn too from having to explain to you what is going on and why I did what I did' (Handy, 2000: 116). Handy says that he learned some important lessons in management, the biggest of which was the thrill of being trusted.

Classical and operant conditioning

Psychology has traditionally focused on the individual when considering learning. The 'golden age of learning' theory dominated experimental psychology from about 1940 to 1960. Texts on organizational behaviour usually acknowledge individual theories of learning—that is, the behaviourist approach, personified in the work of I.P. Pavlov, B.F. Skinner, and J.B. Watson. The behaviourists focused on the smallest unit of behaviour: the learned stimulus–response link. Essentially, behaviourism sees animals and people as 'black boxes'. Behaviourists observe what goes into the box—that is, input in the form of stimulus—and observe what comes out of the black box—that is, output in the form of behaviour. It is not the job of the behaviourist to speculate about what was going on 'inside the box'—that is, inside the learner's head: for example, thinking or reasoning. Direct observation of behaviour is seen by behaviourists as a rigorous and objective exercise. Anything else is seen as 'unknowable' and irrelevant.

Skinner and Pavlov saw behaviour as learned—that is, acquired through the learning mechanism of classical and operant conditioning. 'Classical conditioning' arises when a learned link—an association between a stimulus and a response—can be forged simply by repeating the two together often enough. Pavlov found that, in this way, a response could become 'conditioned'. He believed that all learning was no more than a result of conditioning—that is, a conditioned reflex. Classical conditioning is usually discussed in relation to animal behaviour—in particular, experiments in salivation with dogs, in which dogs learned to salivate when a bell was rung. Classical conditioning can also be found in experiments with humans. For example, if a person's hand is plunged into ice-cold water, vasoconstriction (the contracting and withdrawing of blood vessels from the skin's surface) occurs (Menzies, 1937); if this is done at the same time as the person hears a buzzer, after a few trials, it is found that the sound of the buzzer itself elicits the response of vasoconstriction. It is important to bear in mind that this is the autonomic nature of learning: we do not have to think about it. As such, it is not easy to break a conditioned response by thinking or reasoning, and classical conditioning tends to be associated with automatic responses, such as emotional reactions or reflexes.

EXAMPLE A conditioned response

Many jobs require a conditioned response. Driving, for example, requires reflexive behaviour, including knowing how hard to brake in various situations. If you normally drive a car with manual transmission and change to an automatic, you will find your left foot stomping on a non-existent clutch pedal: this is your conditioned response.

'Operant conditioning', in contrast, is mainly concerned with voluntary behaviour—that is, acts that can be deliberately controlled. It is used to create new forms of behaviours or to shape behaviour. Skinner believed that learning could become a conditioned response through positive or negative feedback—that is, that behaviour could be modified by its consequences. For example, reward or punishment can shape behaviour: if a manager wishes to see behaviour, such as an example of good customer care, learned and repeated, he or she may wish to praise the employee for demonstrating the required behaviour. This is known as 'positive reinforcement', an example of which is the case of the manager at IBM (see Chapter 11), who wrote out cheques for employees exhibiting behaviours or achieving goals that he wished to reinforce as he wandered around the organization. This would be 'intermittent reinforcement', because it is not continuous—that is, positive behaviour is not reinforced each time that it occurs. A higher and more constant response is elicited with intermittent reinforcement, because people have no idea when the reinforcement will occur and do not know when it will happen again. It is this very irregularity of the reward schedule that makes gambling so difficult to eradicate, because the gambler always feels that he or she may be lucky 'next time'.

Organizations use positive reinforcement regularly when they reward attendance, accident prevention, productivity, and other goals. Negative reinforcement is not generally recommended—which does not mean that managers do not use it.

EXAMPLE Negative reinforcement

A manager called Richard Grote was faced with a disgruntled worker who had written a vulgar message on a corn chip that was discovered by a customer. Grote gave the employee a day off with pay and called it 'positive discipline'. He found that this had a positive effect on morale and cut down on labour turnover. Others have adopted the idea when they tell an employee to take the day off and decide whether they want their job. After the day off, the employee has to agree, in writing, that he or she will not repeat the behaviour.

Other theories of individual learning

There are other theories of individual learning. E.L. Thorndike believed that learning might be achieved on the basis of trial and error. We looked briefly at the Gestalt theorists in Chapter 8; in relation to learning, the Gestalt psychologists—such as Max Wertheimer and Wolfgang Kohler—proposed that human consciousness cannot be understood adequately by unscrambling the components parts, but only by investigating its overall shape or pattern—that is, that we should look at the wholeness of learning. Kohler argued that there is 'insight learning'—that is, that you can learn by gaining an understanding of important elements within a problem and the relationship between them.

Texts usually go on to look at the cognitive approach. The assumption is that many of the laws of learning are common to a wide variety of species, including humans. The use of animals leads to a relatively 'mechanistic' view of conditioning in humans and 'a crude slot machine model of behavior' (Koestler, 1967: 3–18). Yet animal behaviour is not the same as that of humans (Davey, 1988). Even when principles that govern the behaviour are discovered, they may be specific to both the situation and the species under investigation (Schwartz and Lacey, 1988).

Researchers have examined the relevance of animal-based experiments for human operant conditioning. They have found, for example, that it is useful to tell human subjects what to do in order to receive reward or avoid punishment (Perone et al., 1988). (This, of course, cannot be done in conventional experiments with animals.) Ayllon and Azrin (1964) arranged for psychiatric patients to receive treats contingent upon appropriate behaviour at mealtime. After twenty meals with no improvement, the problem was solved by instructing the patients about the contingency—that is, about the fact that they would receive a treat if they demonstrated the right behaviour. For example, a specially designed token was given if the patient did what was asked; these tokens could them be exchanged for attention, privacy, or consumables. The desired behaviour was then being conditioned and reinforced.

STOP AND THINK Behaviour modification

The following story encourages us to think twice about what behaviour modification can achieve.

Don Bannister, a psychologist who worked at a psychiatric hospital near Leeds, told me how staff at the hospital had tried to use behaviour modification on psychiatric patients. The patients' behaviour was very bad (too much shouting, swearing, and disagreeing with staff's requests). The staff decided to reward good behaviour with tokens that could be 'spent' in the hospital shop on sweets, newspapers, cigarettes, and other goods. The result was that all of the patients bar one behaved worse than ever. When the staff asked what was happening, they found that the one well-behaved patient (an old man) was being rewarded with all of the tokens. He was rewarding the other patients for their bad behaviour with the same tokens.

The experiment was, then, unsuccessful and gives us insight into how people may manipulate the outcomes of simple behaviourist learning experiments.

Kolb and the learning cycle

A key theoretical model of individual learning that has developed in management has been Kolb's learning cycle. Kolb (1984: 26) maintains that 'learning is a process whereby knowledge is created through the transformation of experience', as Figure 10.1 represents.

Kolb's theory is that ideas are continually formed and reformed through experience, and that this process stimulates inquiry and skill in getting knowledge. Learning is a continuous process grounded in experience. At the heart of the approach is the idea that an individual can manage his or her own learning through reflecting on experience and will then be in control of his or her own self-development.

205

Concrete experience

Testing the
implications of
concepts in new
situations

Observation
and
reflection

Forming abstract
concepts and
generalizations

Figure 10.1 Kolb's learning cycle (Vince, 1998)

Experience is not, in Kolb's view, constructed, shaped, or contained by social power relations; yet in oppressive relationships, an individual's experience can be denied or called into question. (For more on Kolb and a critique of the approach, see Vince, 1998.)

Taylorism and scientific management

The principles of Taylorism and scientific management at which we looked in Chapter 4 are virtually identical to those of behaviour theory. Tacit and informal knowledge was rendered explicit; traditional practices were suppressed, and workplaces became describable and explicable in informative detail in terms of principles of reinforcement. Taylor and his present-day followers reward positive behaviour with wages.

Individual learning may be recognizing new ways of doing things or new possibilities. These may be based on prior experiences or images (Weick, 1995; Crossan et al., 1999). But we cannot be sure that individuals always want to learn.

 EXAMPLE **When an individual may not want to learn in an organizational setting**

A journalist has documented his experience of those who may not want to learn. He spent an afternoon in Haiti watching staff at a health clinic trying to educate young people about AIDS and problems associated with it. By the end of the 90-minute session, it was clear that two of the teenage girls—both of them mothers—would not be budged from their conviction that they knew two sure-fire ways to avoid AIDS. One was having sex in the sea; the other was getting their boyfriends to drink a potion made of the water they used to wash their private parts. Nothing, it seemed, was going to persuade them otherwise—and neither had much hope of persuading their boyfriends to use a condom.

(*Source:* Renton, 2007)

Group learning

When learning in a group, individuals share their own thinking and learning, engaging in individual and collective interpreting, or 'sensemaking' (Weick, 1995). During the interpretation process, existing views are revised and new ways of learning develop (Huff, 1990). It may be that this results in new rules, routines, information systems, or strategy for the organization (Crossan et al., 1999)—that is, groups can bring about organizational learning.

EXAMPLE **Craft skill and seeing organizational learning**

Yanow (2000) discusses the case of flute makers. Imagine that you are watching people sitting side by side working at a table making flutes. Each person adds a piece, then hands it to the next. At every point along the line, as a piece is passed, each maker assesses the work of the previous flute maker. If the flute 'does not feel right', the worker will say so, while handing the piece back to the previous flute maker for further work. One flute maker does not make an entire flute; making a flute requires the group to act as a whole.

Yanow (2000) goes on to infer that the flute makers held knowledge together, collectively; collectively, they had mastered the practice of flute making. The knowledge was not inborn and new organizational members could be trained to produce flutes in the company way, so it was inferred that learning took place. It is in the handing back and forth, in evaluating the flute's feel, and accepting or rejecting them, and in evaluating the rejection, that organizational learning takes place. Knowledge was shared by the makers and known tacitly within the collective; that tacit knowledge could be communicated. This was, then, collective organizational learning.

Organizational learning

Organizational learning has been seen as the aggregation of individual learning in an organizational context (for example, by Cangelosi and Dill, 1965; March and Olsen, 1976; Simon, 1991). This perspective views organizational learning as dependent on the cognitive processes of individuals in the organization and focuses on the detection of errors, so that individuals can learn to do things correctly (Bolman, 1976; Argyris and Schon, 1978).

Other scholars take the term 'organizational learning' literally, arguing that an organization is not simply a collection of individuals, but an entity that is capable of learning on a collective basis (for example, Hutchins, 1991; Cook and Yanow, 1993). Organizations are not only cognitive entities, but also cultural ones. Learning is seen as an integral part of successful organizational functioning: organizations need to learn in order to transform in response to rapidly changing environmental conditions. This model of the learning organization is popular with practitioners, as well as business school academics, and has a problem-solving orientation using specific diagnostic tools to identify, promote, and evaluate the quality of the learning processes within an organization (Easterby-Smith and Araujo, 1999). There is, however, very little empirical evidence to support the concepts and models of organizational learning that have been proposed (Evans and Easterby Smith, 2001; Dyck et al., 2005).

Theories of organizational learning

There are several key theories of organizational learning. Peter Senge (1990) provides a broad theory of organizational learning, which he separates into five types or disciplines:

- 'personal mastery', which includes education, training, and development, but also how that knowledge is brought to organizations to keep individuals and organizations responsive to the changing environment;
- the formation and examination of the mindsets that we use to analyse our organizations, the competition, and ourselves;
- the creation of a shared vision;
- team learning;
- 'systems thinking', which he suggests is the element that makes the other types work in harmony.

This view, then, is very different from the typical approach to learning, which would emphasize the individual learning alone, rather than as part of an organization or its units.

Socio-technical systems theory focuses a concept of a learning organization on the idea of collective participation by teams of individuals—especially workers—in developing new patterns of work, career paths, and arrangements for combining family and work. According to this theory, work must be redesigned by workers and supervisors, and managers must learn to create the context in which this can be done (Argyris, 1999). The socio-technical theorists—and others, such as Peter Senge and Edgar Schein—offer prescriptions to the kinds of structure, process, and condition that may function as enablers of productive organizational learning. These prescriptions include creating a flat, decentralized structure, information systems that provide fast public feedback on performance of the organization, measures of organizational performance, systems of incentives to promote learning, and ideologies, such as total quality, continuous learning, and excellence.

One of the best-known writers in this area is Argyris, who believes that organizational learning is a competence that all organizations should develop. He defines significant learning in organizations as the ability to detect and correct errors (Argyris, 1999). An error (technical, administrative, or human) is any mismatch between plan or intention and what actually happened when either is implemented. He and Donald Schon (1974; 1978) distinguish between 'single-loop learning' and 'double-loop learning'. Single-loop learning means optimizing skills, refining abilities, and acquiring knowledge to solve a problem. It produces behavioural changes that are adaptive, but which do not produce significant value changes—for example, changes in underlying thinking, norms, or strategy—such as choosing to deal with a person who is angry when a particular topic is raised by either avoiding the topic, or by manipulating the way in which it is discussed.

Conversely, double-loop learning means changing the frame of reference that normally guides behaviour. Double-loop learning produces a value change from which behaviour changes flow; for this to happen in the example just given, it would be necessary to explore the reasons for the angers and design suitable behaviours in response to those reasons. Argyris (1993) argues that double-loop learning is more powerful than single-loop learning and that double-loop learning can be taught to individuals—but accepts that this requires a strong motivation on the part of the individual to change.

Single-loop learning takes place when the organization identifies the error, but carries on without altering present policies or objectives. It is appropriate for routine, repetitive issues and helps to get the everyday job done. Double-loop learning is achieved 'if the error is detected and corrected in ways that involve the modification of an organization's underlying norms, policies and objectives' (Argyris and Schon, 1978: 3). Double-loop learning is more relevant for the complex, non-programmable issues: '… it assures that there will be another day in the future of the organization' (Argyris, 1992: 9). But Argyris suggests that most organizations have great difficulties in learning in this manner. The double-loop model assumes that individuals have the ability to learn new behaviour and are prepared to correct their old behaviours (Argyris, 1996).

Argyris also defined a third type of organizational learning: 'triple-loop learning'. Triple-loop learning is about increasing the breadth and depth of the learning about the diversity of issues and dilemmas faced (Flood and Romm, 1996). With triple-loop learning, organizational members discover how they and their predecessors have facilitated or inhibited learning in the past, and produce new structures and strategies for learning.

There can also be 'zero learning'. In organizational terms, the learning level is zero if members fail to take corrective action in response to problems encountered within the organization. The process of becoming a 'learning organization' has been described as an 'evolutionary journey' (Pedler et al., 1997). Organizations can be seen as committed to organizational learning by providing both formal and informal learning opportunities, within which people within the organization are encouraged to take responsibility for their own learning and development. Organizational learning can take place if the organization facilitates the learning of all its members (ibid.). It is assumed, in most cases, that there is some notion of consensus and unitarism (Fox, 1974). The 'learning organization' (Pedler et al., 1997) assumes a shared vision and shared values (Handy, 1995).

Researchers are, however, beginning to document situations in which identities are not shared, and in which conceptions and ideologies are diverse, and even in conflict. Power, politics, and diversity influence organizational learning (Easterby-Smith et al., 2000; Huzzard and Ostergren, 2002); an understanding and appreciation of the place of power and politics will be crucial to a critical perspective on this topic.

★ **STOP AND THINK** **Challenging questions on the concept of the learning organization**

The 'learning organization' is one that facilitates the learning of all of its members and continuously transforms itself (Pedlar et al., 1991). But how can we test whether a particular organization does so? Are organizations that transform themselves necessarily learning organizations and must an organization transform itself in order to qualify as a learning organization. Organizations can fail to learn (Noat et al., 2004)?

Some researchers have distinguished between 'hard' learning, which is formalized, prescriptive development and training, and 'softer', process-based learning, which is based on language development, relationships with others, memory, and identity. If learning is limited to training and self-development, only in order to fulfil organizational goals, then the soft learning, through which individuals make sense of their world, is not utilized (Jones and Hendry, 1994).

Self-development and continuous development has been acknowledged as important for organizational success (London and Smither, 1999). There are thought to be three essential elements that are required in order for self-development and continuous development to take place: the availability of choices; informational, non-threatening feedback; and empathy (ibid.). Organizations therefore have to shift away from a control model of management to facilitate self-development.

209

Questioning organizational learning

Some academics have questioned whether or not organizations learn at all, arguing that individuals within organizations learn, not organizations themselves. The counter-argument to this is that organizations do learn, in the sense that they 'encode inferences from history into routines that guide behaviour' (Leavitt and March, 1988). In other words, an organization has learned if any of its units have acquired information and are able to use this information on behalf of the organization (Huber, 1989). Further, Argyris (1999) would argue that thought and action carried out by individuals in interaction with one another, on behalf of the organization, can change that organization and become embedded in organizational artefacts, such as maps, memories, and programmes. It is possible for individuals to think and act on behalf of the organization, because organizations are political entities that make collective decisions. On behalf of organizations, individuals can therefore undertake learning that, in turn, yields outcomes reflected in changes in action and in organizational artefacts.

According to some researchers, it is possible to predict successful learning by paying attention to certain factors. (Findlay et al., 2000). For example, managerial and organizational justice was found to be one of the predominant predictors of a positive attitude towards organizational learning. Where management is seen to be fair and employees have trust in the leadership, they feel more positive about learning. Further, individuals tend to perceive greater procedural justice when they believe that they have had the chance to participate in decision making. But older employees have been found to have more negative perceptions of learning than their younger counterparts. This may be because older employees do not believe that training will bring them any benefit (Schuller and Bostyn, 1992; Findlay et al., 2000). Alternatively, it may be that companies decide that it is not worthwhile investing in older workers: if older workers are seen as not as flexible as younger employees, they may not be given the same opportunities for learning (Findlay et al., 1999).

It might be assumed that organizational learning should always be sought—but organizational learning is not always beneficial. The term should not, then, be treated as if it is neutral. For example, in the Nazi period, the bureaucracy became more efficient at extermination—that is, the organization 'learned' to be more efficient. Less dramatically, it might be said that those who have power and use the term 'organizational learning' as a vehicle of rhetoric—that is, as a vehicle of normative control (controlling the hearts and minds of employees) to gain compliance and commitment among subordinates—are doing so for their own good, but not for that of those subordinated. As Kunda (1992) notes, under normative control, members act in the best interests of the company, because they are driven by commitment, strong identification with company goals, managerial appeals, and exhortations, rather than because they are driven by force—but it is the employee's self that is claimed in the name of corporate interest. We cannot escape the need, then, to declare what kinds of organizational learning we will take to be desirable or undesirable, and why (Argyris, 1999).

Organizational learning also implies rationality, and being able to remember past events, analyse alternatives, and evaluate the results of action. Some authors would argue that organizations are political systems made up of subgroups, each with their own interests and powers, engaged in battle for control, or avoidance of control, and incapable of acting as agents of learning (Crozier, 1963). Perhaps organizations are inherently chaotic—at best, organized anarchies (March and Olsen, 1976). March has also cast doubt on the ability of organizations to learn in his concept of 'competence traps', in which organizations falsely project into the future the strategies of action that have worked for them in the past. He describes 'superstitious learning' (Leavitt and March, 1988: 325), which happens when the experience of learning appears compelling, but the connections between actions and outcomes are mis-specified. Further, learning does not always lead to intelligent behaviour: the behavioural theory of the firm (Cyert and March, 1963; Simon, 1976) notes that threats to effective action exist—for example, dysfunctional patterns of behaviour undermine learning. Organizations depend on control systems that set up conflicts between rule-setter and rule-followers, which lead to cheating, so that everyone appears to be rational and no one can be trusted.

Another problem in learning is 'unlearning', or forgetting past behaviour that is redundant or unsuccessful. Knowledge grows and simultaneously becomes obsolete as reality changes. New knowledge is learned and obsolete misleading knowledge must be discarded, or unlearned. Slow unlearning can be a further crucial weakness for many organizations (Hedberg, 1981). And forgetting past behaviour may also create problems: perhaps the organization cannot remember what it has learned because it did not efficiently reinforce what it knew in the first place (Walsh, 1995).

Of course, organizations, groups, and individuals can fail to learn in the first instance. The learning process is neither systematic, nor necessarily effective. In research carried out by Doyle et al. (2000), it was found that while a majority of managers considered their organization to be a learning organization, repeat mistakes were made, because there was no time to learn from what happened in the past. Managers do not necessarily have the luxury of time to pause and reflect on change. The principle of the learning organization therefore finds fragile support in the findings of this research.

In addition, what we learn is not always obvious and it does not always initially appear to be common sense. For example, firefighters dealing with forest fires have learned that it is not sensible for a fresh crew to replace a tired crew when a blaze is at its height, such as in the heat of the day when a strong wind is blowing. It might be supposed that fresh resources would produce redoubled effort and faster fire suppression; firefighters have learned that a change of command when a fire is at its most dynamic and volatile makes it harder for the incoming crew to catch up with its rapidly changing character. The incoming crew will always be behind, because the crew will not be able to learn what it faces; its idea of what is happening would tend to lag behind what is actually happening and, if it fails to get on top of the situation, the level of danger increases significantly (Weick, 2002).

Some organizations or groups may even refuse to learn, as we saw earlier in the chapter. Another interesting example comes from learning in the London Fire Service (Salaman and Butler, 1994). Seminars were designed to identify and, when necessary, modify attitudes towards the introduction of non-white and non-male firefighters—but resistance was evident. The station officers were markedly unsympathetic to the messages and refused to accept the validity of arguments presented to them. They were refusing to learn. One explanation may lie in the conservatism, racism, or sexism of the officers; a more plausible explanation, it is argued by Salaman and Butler, is that the refusal to learn developed because the implementation of equality of opportunity would mean having a formalized open system. This would bring about a significant reduction in the traditional authority of fire station personnel to intervene in the recruitment and selection of new officers, and to allocate advantage in these processes to applicants from among their own family and friends. (One wonders why their family and friends did not include women and those of ethnic origin.) The context was one of 'insiders' and 'outsiders', or 'them' and 'us'. Firefighters—that is, the station officers and crews ('us', 'the insiders')— worked shifts. They were separate and distinct from the next layer of management, who worked office hours and were based in regional offices, perceived to be far from the realities of firefighting. Close relationships developed between members of a watch: they had a shared world composed of danger and boredom, jokes, memories, and myths. And this loyalty and resistance got in the way of learning.

In some occupations, such as firefighting, security work, and the armed forces, we have learned that men are the norm—but our assumption that this is the case is sometimes challenged. For example, a war photograph was published in the international newspapers and outraged many people. The photo was of a US soldier searching an Afghan woman: 'To most Pakistanis and Afghans, this photo is hyper-offensive, showing a demure Islamic beauty disrespected by an American brute' (McGirk, 2002). If you look closely at the photo, however, you can see that the soldier is female and has her long hair bunched at the neck, under her helmet. The photo was, however, published in Pakistan without the original caption identifying the soldier as 'Sergeant Nicola Hall'. This example clearly shows how our learning—in this case, that men are always the norm in the armed forces—must be questioned.

Learning about language in organizations

The language that people have learned to use in an organization tells us a good deal about the views held by organizational members about what goes on both within the organization and outside. For example, if a logging company portrays environmentalists as 'deviant', 'lying', 'stinking', and 'zealots', while the environmentalists regard logging as the equivalent of 'forest rape' and forest companies as 'greedy corporate pigs' (Wilson, 1998), you know that there is little meeting of minds between the two groups.

Research has shown how actions, such as organizational change, can be legitimized through language. Language helps us to learn about the change. Organizational change can be made rationally accountable, and can help to define ingroups and outgroups. The language of warfare has been noted in the literature on takeovers and the introduction of new technology (Wilson, 1992). And the language of religion can help to define the 'saints' and the 'sinners'; it helps to highlight and make coherent aspects of change and 'good practice' that may lead to improved systems. One commentator goes as far as to say that the language of the apocalyptic vision, missions, and doom scenario is far more prevalent in business thinking than in most churches (Pattison, 1991).

The language used in organizations can also be sexist. The ridicule in the media of the concerns about sexism in language is one form of evidence that words are not neutral, but deeply ideological. Rules about language and standards of correct speech reveal information about patterns of power and privilege in the wider society (Cameron, 1995) and the organization. Language therefore transmits social information (which we have learned) about discrimination against women.

For example, organizations ask for titles. The titles 'Miss' or 'Mrs' supply information about a woman's sexual availability, and group single women together with the young and inexperienced (Miller and Swift, 1975). The title 'Ms' is often seen as an unattractive option and also, in fact, provides information about the woman, because Ms is associated with feminism, divorce, and widowhood (Wood, 1997). Pauwels (1998) has suggested that the only way to address the gender imbalance might be to introduce new titles for men that would provide information about marital status. The use of 'Mr', 'Miss', or 'Ms' can be understood as another demonstration of the dominant social order.

Another way in which gender is marked is by the use of suffixes or adjuncts. One suffix in common use to indicate a female is '–ess' ('stewardess', 'hostess', 'waitress'). This marks women as being different from, or less important than, men who do the same job. Adjuncts are found in terms such as 'woman doctor' or 'female surgeon'—and these demonstrate that the world is male unless proven otherwise (Weatherall, 2002).

Further, masculine forms of words tend to have more positive connotations than feminine ones. For example, 'bachelor' is more positive than 'spinster', and when being referred to in terms of the opposite gender, 'tomboy' has positive connotations, while 'sissy' is used as an insult. A woman might feel complimented if it were to be said that she thinks like a man, but it would be an insult if a man were to be likened to an old woman. Choice of language therefore demonstrates the social and moral order, in which men and masculinity are valued more than women and femininity. Awareness of the language that is used in an organization therefore tells us what has been learned by people in an organization—and developing a critical consciousness can assist in that initial awareness.

Developing a critical consciousness

Developing a critical consciousness is one way in which people can question what they have learned in organizational settings. 'Critical consciousness' is the ability to perceive social, political, and economic oppression, and to take action against it. It is a concept developed by Paulo Freire, in his book *Pedagogy of the Oppressed*, first published in Portuguese in 1968 (Freire, 2007). Instead, for example, of simply accepting knowledge passively or simply accepting instructions and adopting a passive role, organizational members would develop a critical consciousness, which would mean that they would question what they were being asked to learn, whose interests that served, and where power lies, and raise awareness of how they were oppressed (if they were being oppressed) and take action against that oppression.

We might question what is learned: for example, is management know-how universal or culture-bounded? Research on the cross-cultural transfer of management know-how has been growing since the 1960s. (We look at the transfer of Japanese management know-how in Chapter 14.) The research has found that management know-how is culture-bounded and that the US philosophy of management is not universally acceptable (Fan, 2004). Uncritical use of Western management theories and techniques in Eastern countries might therefore contribute towards feelings of resentment and other negative feelings, possibly associated with the perception of being subject to cultural imperialism.

Conclusion

In this chapter, we have looked at how the individual, the group, and the organization might learn. We have looked at conventional and newer theories of leaning in organizations. We know that behaviourism is alive and well in organizations when we see people being rewarded or punished for their behaviour. But conventional or traditional theories of learning appear to ignore issues, such as the individual's motivation to learn and a consideration of the place of power or gender.

KEY POINTS

- Learning is purposeful activity for acquiring and developing skills and knowledge.

- Learning within organizations can take place at individual, group, and/or organizational levels.

- Behaviourist learning theorists would say that all individual behaviours are learned through either classical or operant conditioning. Other theorists of learning—for example, the Gestalt psychologists—would argue that you need to look at the overall shape, pattern, and wholeness of learning.

- While organizations may want to make knowledge and learning explicit, and positively reward desirable behaviour, it would be wrong to assume that all individuals always wish to learn and see the benefit in learning, or that all learning is good for the individual and the organization. 'Un-learning', or forgetting past learning or knowledge, could also be a problem.

213

CASE STUDY
Organizing against injustice

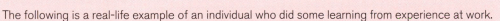

The following is a real-life example of an individual who did some learning from experience at work.

Annabel Brown, an academic, was passed over for promotion in favour of a far less qualified male employee, whom she had recently helped recruit. The post had not been advertised, nor had selection criteria been drawn up. She complained to the line manager, asked how the appointment could have been made in that way, and said that she felt that her qualifications, work experience, and current performance made her the best qualified for the role. Her manager suddenly proposed a U-turn solution: the original offer to the male colleague would be withdrawn, and she and the man would be left to decide who should have the job. Annabel turned this offer down, saying that she wanted an assurance from her department and the human resource department that, in future, all jobs would be properly advertised. The line manager referred Annabel to his manager, who made it clear that she believed that the case was clearly discrimination. She agreed that the appointment procedure had not been carried out properly. Annabel then asked the management to back down and advertise the post. By this time, the male colleague had a potential case for grievance, but agreed not to pursue it.

Because no acceptable solution could be reached, the post was withdrawn. Annabel was assured that all future posts would be advertised. The main lesson that Annabel learned was that, while her efforts were time-consuming and stressful, they did achieve a positive result. She would now recommend others to challenge similar unjust appointments. She also learned that you should keep matters completely confidential. In her case, she spoke only to the union, to those colleagues who were directly concerned with the situation, and to her partner. By acting in this way, she ensured that no damaging gossip was spread around her institution. During the experience, she was better able to appear calm, professional, and rational—even though she may not have felt it. She managed to maintain good relations with her managers and her male colleague.

(*Source:* Adapted from AUTLOOK (2003) 223: 30–1)

Questions

1. We have seen what Annabel learned—but do you think that the organization also learned some lessons from the experience, or can you say only that key individuals might have done so?

2. How would you decide whether or not organizational learning had taken place? What would need to happen?

FURTHER READING

Fulop, L. and Rifkin, W.D. (2004) 'Management knowledge and learning', in L. Fulop, S. Linstead, and S. Lilley (eds), *Management and Organization: A Critical Text*, Houndmills: Palgrave Macmillan, ch. 1 This chapter adopts a critical stance on learning and knowledge.

Gabriel, Y., Fineman, S., and Sims, D. (2000) *Organizing and Organizations*, London: Sage Chapter 8 on 'Learning the ropes' challenges us to think about the nature of knowledge and learning; Chapter 2 discusses the learning involved in entering and leaving an organization.

Grey, C. and Antonacopoulou, E. (eds) (2004) *Essential Reading in Management Learning*, London: Sage This book reprints a selection of the 'best and most innovative' writing on learning. The book also contains a case study, by Bente Elkjaer, on the undelivered promise of a learning organization.

Management Learning This journal will provide more in-depth knowledge on this topic.

Noon, M. and Blyton, P. (2002; 2007) *The Realities of Work*, Houndmills: Palgrave Macmillan One chapter discusses knowledge and work.

Thompson, P. and McHugh, D. (2002) *Work Organizations*, 3rd edn, Houndmills: Palgrave The first half of Chapter 16 on learning, change, and innovation is particularly strong.

RESEARCH QUESTIONS

1. Sambrook and Stewart (2000) have looked at twenty-eight European case studies and a further twenty organizations to understand the factors that affect the level of organizational learning and strategies to support it. What are their main findings? In the light of what you have learned here, how would you critique their work?

2. 'Learning organization initiatives are essentially technologies of regulation aimed at facilitating change processes' (Thompson and McHugh, 2002: 240). Discuss.

3. How do managers learn about management? (See Fulop and Rifkin, 2004.)

4. Our culture and socialization dictates that 'boys don't cry', but that it is acceptable for girls to weep. Research has found that, before the age of 12, boys and girls cry as frequently as each other, but that after they reach that age, boys cry four times less than girls. Boys are discouraged from crying as part of a larger programme of socialization into masculinity. This socialization involves teaching boys to 'tough it out' and refrain from expressing their feelings—except for anger; yet footballers cry when they miss a penalty and penitential presidents cry on TV (see Witchalls, 2003). What, then, are the 'rules' that we have been required to learn about crying in organizations?

REFERENCES

Argyris, C. (1992) *On Organizational Learning*, Cambridge, MA: Blackwell,

_____ (1993) *Knowledge for Action: A Guide to Overcoming Barriers to Organizational Change*, San Francisco, CA: Jossey Bass.

_____ (1996) 'Unrecognized defenses of scholars: Impact on theory and research', *Organization Science*, 7: 79–87.

_____ (1999) *On Organizational Learning*, 2nd edn, Oxford: Blackwell.

_____ and Schon, D.A. (1974) *Theory in Practice*, San Francisco, CA: Jossey Bass.

_____ _____ (1978) *Organizational Learning: A Theory of Action Perspective*, Reading, MA: Addison-Wesley.

Ayllon, T. and Azrin, N.H. (1964) 'Reinforcement and instructions with mental patients', *Journal of the Experimental Analysis of Behavior*, 7: 327–31.

Bennett, H.L. (1983–84) 'Remembering drink orders: The memory skills of cocktail waitresses', *Human Learning*, 2: 157–69; reprinted in P. Barnes, J. Oakes, J. Chapman, V. Lee, and P. Czerniewska (eds) (1984) *Personality, Development and Learning: A Reader*, Milton Keynes: Open University Press, ch. 2.4.

Bolman, L. (1976) 'Organizational learning', in C. Argyris (ed.), *Increasing Leadership Effectiveness*, New York: Wiley.

Cameron, D. (1995) *Verbal Hygiene*, London: Routledge.

Cangelosi, V.E. and Dill, W.R. (1965) 'Organizational learning: Observations toward a theory', *Administrative Science Quarterly*, 10: 175–203.

Cook, S.D. and Yanow, D. (1993) 'Culture and organizational learning', *Journal of Management Inquiry*, 2(4): 373–90.

Coopey, J. (1995) 'The learning organization, power, politics and ideology', *Management Learning*, 26(2): 193–213.

Crossan, M.M., Lane, H.W., and White, R.E. (1999) 'An organizational learning framework: From intuition to institutionalisation', *Academy of Management Review*, 24: 522–37.

Crozier, M. (1963) *The Bureaucratic Phenomenon*, Chicago, IL: Chicago University Press.

Cyert, R.M. and March, J.G. (1963) *A Behavioral Theory of the Firm*, Englewood Cliffs, NJ: Prentice Hall.

Dale, M. (1994) 'Learning organizations', in C. Mabey and P. Iles (eds), *Managing Learning*, Milton Keynes: Open University Press, ch. 2.

Davey, G.C. (1988) 'Trends in human operant theory', in G. Davey and C. Cullen (eds), *Human Operant Conditioning and Behavior Modification*, Chichester: John Wiley & Sons, ch. 1.

Dodgson, M. (1993) 'Organizational learning: A review of some literatures', *Organization Studies*, 14(3): 375–94.

Doyle, M., Claydon, T., and Buchanan, D. (2000) 'Mixed results, lousy process: The management experience of organizational change', *British Journal of Management*, 11(Special issue): S59–S80.

Dyck, B., Starke, F.A., Mischke, G.A., and Mauws, M. (2005) 'Learning to build a care: An empirical investigation of organizational learning', *Journal of Management Studies*, 42(2): 387–416.

Easterby-Smith, M. and Araujo, L. (1999) 'Organizational learning: Current debates and opportunities', in M. Easterby-Smith, J. Burgoyne, and L. Arujo (eds), *Organizational Learning and the Learning Organization*, London: Sage.

_____ M., Crossan, M., and Nicolini, D. (2000) 'Organizational learning: Debates, past, present and future', *Journal of Management Studies*, 37(6): 783–96.

Evans, N. and Easterby-Smith, M. (2001) 'Three types of organizational knowledge: Implications for the tacit-explicit and knowledge creations debates', in M. Crossan and F. Olivera (eds), *Organizational Learning and Knowledge Management*, London/Ontario: The University of Western Ontario, pp. 135–54.

215

Fan, Y. (2004) 'The transfer of western management to China', in C. Grey and E. Antonacopoulou (eds), *Essential Readings in Management Learning*, London: Sage. pp. 321–42.

Findlay, P., McKinlay, A., Marks, A., and Thompson, P. (1999) 'Flexible when it suits them: The use and abuse of teamwork skills', in S. Proctor and F. Mueller (eds), *Teamworking*, London: Macmillan, ch. 12.

_____ _____ _____ _____ (2000) 'Labouring to learn: Organizational learning and mutual gains', *Employee Relations*, 22(5): 485–502.

Flood, R.M. and Romm, N.R. (1996) *Diversity Management: Triple Loop Learning*, Chichester: Wiley.

Fox, A. (1974) *Beyond Contract: Power, Work and Trust Relations*, London: Faber and Faber.

Freire, P. (2007) *Pedagogy of the Oppressed*, New York: Continuum.

Fulop, L. and Rifkin, W.D. (2004) 'Management knowledge and learning', in L. Fulop, S. Linstead, and S. Lilley (eds), *Management and Organization: A Critical Text*, Houndmills: Palgrave Macmillan, ch. 1.

Grey, C. (2001) *Against Learning*, Research Papers in Management Studies, Cambridge: The Judge Institute of Management Studies, University of Cambridge.

Grint, K. (1995) *Management: A Sociological Introduction*, Cambridge: Polity.

Handy, C. (1995) 'Managing the dream', in S. Chawla and J. Renesch (eds), *Learning Organizations: Developing Cultures for Tomorrow's Workplace*, Portland: Productivity Press, ch. 2.

_____ (2000) *21 Ideas for Managers*, San Francisco, CA: Jossey Bass.

Hedberg, B. (1981) 'How organizations learn and unlearn', in P. Nystrom and W. Starbuck (eds), *Handbook of Organizational Design, Vol. 1*, Oxford: Oxford University Press, pp. 3–27.

Huber, G.P. (1989) *Organizational Learning: An Examination of the Contributing Processes and a Review of the Literature*, Paper prepared for the NSF-sponsored conference on Organizational Learning, Carnegie-Mellon University, 18–20 May, cited in Argyris (1999).

Huff, A.S. (1990) *Mapping Strategic Thought*, Chichester: John Wiley.

Hutchins, E. (1991) 'Organizing work by adaptation', *Organization Science*, 2(1): 14–39.

Huzzard, T. and Ostergren, K. (2002) 'When norms collide: Learning under organizational hypocrisy', *British Journal of Management*, 13(Special issue): S47–S59.

Jones, A.M. and Hendry, C. (1994) 'The learning organization: Adult learning and organizational transformation', *British Journal of Management*, 5: 153–62.

Koestler, A. (1967) *The Ghost in the Machine*, London: Hutchinson.

Kolb, D. (1984) *Experiential Learning*, Englewood Cliffs, NJ: Prentice Hall.

Kunda, G. (1992) *Engineering Culture*, Philadelphia, PA: Temple University Press.

Leavitt, B. and March, J. (1988) 'Organizational learning', *Annual Review of Sociology*, 14: 319–40.

London, M. and Smither, J.W. (1999) 'Empowered self-development and continuous learning', *Human Resource Management* (USA), 38(1): 3–16.

March, J.G. and Olsen, J.P. (1975) 'The uncertainty of the past: Organization learning under ambiguity', *European Journal of Political Research*, 3: 147–71.

_____ _____ (1976) *Ambiguity and Choice in Organizations*, Bergen: Universitetsforlaget.

McGirk, J. (2002) 'GI Janes flaunt their sports bras as body search arrives in cultural minefield of Afghan frontier', *The Independent*, 14 December, available online at http://www.independent.co.uk/news/world/asia/in-foreign-parts-gi-janes-flaunt-their-sports-bras-as-body-search-arrives-in-cultural-minefield-of-afghan-frontier-610892.html

Menzies, R. (1937) 'Conditioned vasomotor responses in human subjects', *Journal of Psychology*, 4: 75–120.

Miller, C. and Swift, K. (1975) *Words and Women*, New York: Anchor Books.

Mumford, A. (1994) 'Individual and organizational learning: The pursuit of change', in C. Mabey and P. Iles (eds), *Managing Learning*, Milton Keynes: Open University Press, ch. 7.

Naot, Y.B.-H., Lipshitz, R., and Popper, M. (2004) 'Discerning the quality of organizational learning', *Management Learning*, 35(4): 451–72.

216

Noon, M. and Blyton, P. (2002) *The Realities of Work*, Houndmills: Palgrave Macmillan.

Pattison, S. (1991) 'Strange theology of management', *The Guardian*, 27 May, p. 27.

Pauwels, A. (1998) *Women Changing Language*, London: Addison Wesley.

Pedler, M., Boydell, T., and Burgoyne, J. (1991) *The Learning Company*, cited in P. Hawkins, 'Organizational learning: Taking stock and facing the challenge', *Management Learning*, 25(1): 71–82.

_____ Burgoyne, J., and Boydell, T. (1997) *The Learning Company: A Strategy for Sustainable Development*, Maidenhead: McGraw Hill.

Perone, M., Galisio, M., and Baron, A. (1988) 'The relevance of animal-based principles in the laboratory study of human operant conditioning', in G. Davey and C. Cullen (eds), *Human Operant Conditioning and Behavior Modification*, Chichester: John Wiley and Sons, ch. 5.

Renton, A. (2007) 'The rape epidemic', *The Observer*, 2 December, available online at http://www.guardian.co.uk/lifeandstyle/2007/dec/02/women.features3

Salaman, G. and Butler, J. (1994) 'Why managers won't learn', in C. Mabey and P. Iles (eds), *Managing Learning*, Milton Keynes: Open University Press, ch. 3.

Sambrook, S. and Stewart, J. (2000) 'Factors influencing learning in European learning oriented organizations: Issues for management', *Journal of European Industrial Training* (UK), 24(2–4): 209–20.

Schon, D. (1983) 'Organizational learning', in G. Morgan (ed.), *Beyond Method*, Thousand Oaks, CA: Sage, pp. 114–29.

Schuller, T. and Bostyn, A.M. (1992) *Education, Training and Information in the Third Age*, The Carnegie Inquiry into the Third Age Research Paper No. 3, London: Centurion Press.

Schwartz, B. and Lacey, H. (1988) 'What applied studies of human operant conditioning tell us about humans and operant conditioning', in G. Davey and C. Cullen (eds), *Human Operant Conditioning and Behavior Modification*, Chichester: John Wiley & Sons, ch. 3.

Senge, P. (1990) *The Fifth Discipline: The Art and Practice of the Learning Organization*, New York: Doubleday.

Simon, H.A. (1976) *The Sciences of the Artificial*, Cambridge, MA: MIT Press.

_____ (1991) 'Bounded rationality and organizational learning', *Organization Science*, 2: 125–34.

Thompson, P. and McHugh, D. (2002) *Work Organizations*, 3rd edn, Basingstoke: Palgrave.

Vince, R. (1998) 'Behind and beyond Kolb's learning cycle', *Journal of Management Education*, 22(3): 304–19.

Walsh, J.P. (1995) 'Managerial and organizational cognition: Notes from a trip down Memory Lane', *Organization Science*, 6(3): 280–321.

Weatherall, A. (2002) *Gender, Language and Discourse*, London: Psychology Press.

Weick, K.E. (1995) *Sensemaking*, Thousand Oaks, CA: Sage.

_____ (2002) 'Puzzles in organizational learning: An exercise in disciplined imagination', *British Journal of Management*, 13(Special issue): S7–S16.

Willis, P. (1977) *Learning to Labour*, Brighton: Saxon House.

Wilson, F.M. (1992) 'Language, technology, gender and power', *Human Relations*, 45(9): 883–904.

Wilson, J. (1998) *Talk and Log: Wilderness Politics in British Columbia, 1965–1996*, Vancouver: UBC Press.

Witchalls, C. (2003) 'Boys don't cry', *The Guardian*, 5 February, available online at http://www.guardian.co.uk/lifeandstyle/2003/feb/05/familyandrelationships.features10

Wood, J. (1997) *Gendered Lives: Communication, Gender and Culture*, 2nd edn, Belmont, CA: Wadsworth.

Yanow, D. (2000) 'Seeing organizational learning: A "cultural" view', *Organization*, 7(2): 247–68.

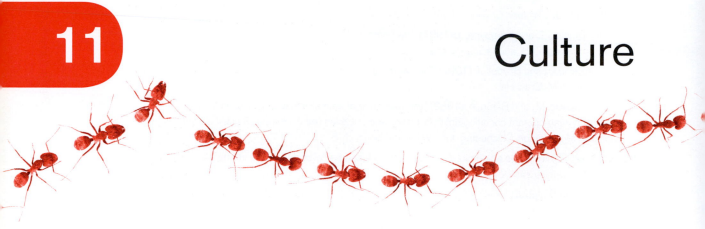

11 Culture

Introduction

Culture, as a concept, implies a stabilizing force that preserves the status quo—but organizations are seldom static. They are created, influenced, and transformed by many, not only by management, and are therefore not as susceptible to manipulation and control as many authors and management consultants might have us believe.

This chapter looks at what culture means in the context of behaviour in organizations. It wants you to question whether we can assume that we all mean the same thing when we are talking about culture. For example, in an age of globalization, does it make sense to talk about different cultures and how viable is it to consider changing culture?

By the end of the chapter, you should have an appreciation of how the concept of 'organizational culture' is defined and discussed in the literature. You will be able to assess the theory and evidence on offer critically, and have insight into a wide range of aspects of culture within organizations.

This chapter covers:

- the concept of culture;
- understanding culture;
- do the 'best' cultures lead to 'best' performance?
- critically assessing whether culture can be managed;
- national and organizational cultures;
- some problems with trying to manage culture;
- describing (rather than prescribing) culture;
- culture and change;
- culture and gender;
- culture and race;
- other aspects of culture.

The concept of culture

Culture is a popular explanatory concept frequently used to describe a company, a rationale for people's behaviour, a guideline for action, a cause for condemnation or praise, or a quality that makes a company 'what it is' (Kunda, 1992). The concept has been explicitly used only in the last few decades (Schein, 1990). It is a fascinating, but elusive, topic for researchers. Parker (2000) says that culture is one of the two or three most complicated words in the English language. Organizational culture is defined simply by Deal and Kennedy (1982: 4) as 'The way we do things round here', but more fully by Hofstede (1991: 262) as 'the collective programming of the mind which distinguishes the members of one organization from another'. Schein (1985: 6) claims that the term 'should be reserved for the deeper level of basic assumptions and beliefs that are shared by members of an organization, that operate unconsciously, and that define in a basic "taken-for-granted" fashion an organization's view of itself and its environment'.

It would be reasonable to expect that organizations that are set up for similar purposes would have similar cultures; it would be reasonable to expect this to be especially so in those sectors in which people move freely between organizations. But this has been found not to be the case. The *National Health Service* in the UK provides us with an example. Until recently, each health authority was run according to the same tight guidelines set down by central government. Doctors were trained using a rotation scheme that required them to move between hospitals and specialties. The doctors found that each authority had its own distinctive features that made the experience of each novel (Dale, 1994).

Culture is carefully defined by Schein (1990: 111) as (a) a pattern of basic assumptions, (b) invented, discovered, or developed by a given group (c) as it learns to cope with its problems of external adaptation and internal integration, (d) which has worked well enough to be considered valid, and therefore (e) is to be taught to new members as the (f) correct way to perceive, think, and feel in relation to those problems. The culture of a particular group or organization can be distinguished at three fundamental levels at which the culture manifests itself: observable artefacts; values; and basic underlying assumptions (ibid.).

Understanding culture

Culture is commonly theorized as a pervasive, eclectic, layered, and socially constructed phenomenon that is generated through values, artefacts, structures, and behaviours (Silvester et al., 1999; Detert et al., 2000). Geertz (1973) sees organizational cultures as webs of meaning; culture itself is an ongoing creation of those who live within its influence. Meanings around which consensus has already evolved are incorporated as norms, beliefs, symbols, and values of organizational culture, and become part and parcel of the way in which future interpretations are made. Values, beliefs, and shared meanings may be researched through interviews. Open-ended interviews can be very useful in getting at the level of how people feel and think about the culture. Questionnaires and survey instruments may prejudge the dimensions to be studied. There is no way of knowing whether the dimensions that are asked are relevant or salient in that culture until the deeper levels are examined. Assumptions are usually unconscious and may be observed through intensive observation, more focused questions, or self-analysis by members of a group.

Schein (1985) argues that we can gain some understanding at a superficial level of any culture by analysing artefacts produced and consumed by that culture. These are visible, and can be deciphered or decoded by observation and analysis. To get a better feel for the ideas and orientations that have shaped the character and form of these artefacts, we need to understand the deeper value system. A 'value system' is like a code of practice or behaviour; artefacts offer us clues to this deeper value system. Beneath the level of values, there is a deeper level of 'taken-for-granted', unconscious assumptions. Unlike values and beliefs that exist at a conscious level, and which may therefore be challenged, the cultural forms and our ideas are not open to challenge. The unconscious shapes our norms, such as standards of behaviour, dress, personal interaction, and our values and beliefs. Schein has been criticized by, for example, Collins (1998) for implying that cultural norms and values act as templates for thought and action, and appear not to be open to change; in fact, unconscious assumptions must be open to change and negotiation. They should be thought of as dynamic and social phenomena that will tend to evolve and change as people attempt to negotiate and bend the rules.

But if this gives us only a superficial understanding, is this all that we can expect to gain? Grint (1995: 162) appears to think so when he notes: 'Culture is rather like a black hole: the closer you get to it the less light is thrown upon the topic and the less chance you have of surviving the experience.' There is a lack of consensus about the nature of culture and its amenability to managerial manipulation (Wilmott, 2000). Yet despite the fact that there is a lack of consensus as to what culture might be and how it may be best defined, management consultants, in particular, have been keen to sell the idea that it can be managed and that strong cultures can be manufactured.

Do the 'best' cultures lead to 'best' performance?

Since the late 1970s, a vast body of literature has looked at the importance of organizational culture for organizational outcomes. Early writings on culture management were premised on the assumption that culture management could lead to significant performance improvements (Deal and Kennedy, 1982; Peters and Waterman, 1982)—that is, that a strong culture could be 'manufactured'. For example, Deal and Kennedy (1982: 15) claimed: 'The impact of a strong culture on productivity is amazing. In the extreme, we estimate that a company can gain as much as one or two hours of productive work per employee per day'. The emphasis was on improving efficiency, growth, and success. Ouchi (1981), for example, proposed that this could be achieved through the creation of a strong, unifying organizational culture. 'Strong' cultures emphasized the values of 'being the best', of flexibility, initiative, and innovation, of superior quality and service, and of being open participative companies in which employees were seen as the most important asset (Peters and Waterman, 1982: 285).

Peters and Waterman (1982) were employed as consultants by *McKinsay*, a large, well-known management consultancy firm. In looking at excellence in organizational culture, they say that there is a common culture to be found in excellent companies. This culture displays certain attributes, such as a bias for action (meaning that they make innovative decisions promptly), closeness to the customer (meaning that they focus upon meeting and exceeding customer expectations), and values innovation. They place considerable emphasis on the importance of positive reinforcement, rewarding desirable behaviour. We noted in the last chapter that, at *IBM*, one senior manager adopted the practice of writing out a cheque as a reward for achievements that he observed as he wandered about the organization. Well-known examples of companies who claim to have changed their culture are *British Airways*, which attempted to change the emphasis on flying routes to an emphasis on company service, and *Nissan*, which claimed that it achieved an entirely new sentiment and identification from its labour force (Ackroyd and Crowdy, 1990). Culture, under this functionalist view, is seen as a variable subject to management manipulation and control.

Many culture interventions consequently continue to focus on creating strongly unified values and are promoted as performance-enhancing (Fey et al., 1999)—but not all fully understand the concepts of organizational culture and change in the same way.

EXAMPLE **Organizational culture and misperception**

Some uncertainty over the concept of organizational culture is well illustrated in a story told by Deal and Kennedy (1984). They tell us that, in one company, they presented the concept of culture, its functions, and elements to the senior executives.

At the end of the presentation, the chairman of the board remarked that it was the finest presentation that he had heard in ten years. He then turned to his CEO and said forcefully: 'George, I want a culture installed here next Monday.'

'With all due respect,' interrupted Deal and Kennedy, 'we believe you have a culture here now; that's one of our key points.'

'Bullshit!' said the chairman. 'We don't have one, and as you pointed out, that's the problem. George, I want a culture here and I want it now— by next week. Your butt is on the line.'

In *Change Masters* (1985), Rosabeth Moss Kanter tries to encourage North American companies to rekindle the spirit of innovation and enterprise. *Change Masters* studies ten major companies in depth. Moss Kanter concludes that if corporations are to flourish, then the 'change masters' must be allowed to redesign, to tap the talents and skills of employees. Successful companies will create a climate that encourages change, will encourage anticipation of external pressures, and will listen to new ideas. In similar terms to Peters and Waterman, she argues for the bias for action—that is, companies that work through people, allow autonomy, and are value driven. In her later work, *When Giants Learn to Dance* (1989) Moss Kanter tells us that organizations must be fast, flexible, focused on their customers, and friendly, allowing staff to experiment and develop their skills.

Interest in culture was sparked too by Japanese business success, which was thought to arise from competitive advantage secured through national and corporate culture (Ouchi, 1981; Pascale and Athos, 1982). Throughout the 1970s, Japanese industry managed to establish a solid reputation for quality, reliability, value, and service—attributes that others wished to emulate. A large and profitable literature capitalized on the idea that culture can be diagnosed and changed to improve organizational effectiveness. It was thought that where US companies had adopted management practices that resembled those of the Japanese, as discussed by Peters and Waterman, and Ouchi, they achieved financial success (but see Chapter 14 for more on the Japanese model).

Functionalist management writers have prescribed how culture change may be achieved. Some have provided models for culture intervention, based on a typology or taxonomy of organizational culture: for example, Harrison (1972) and Schneider (1994). Targeted change models espouse the adoption of focused means of culture change. For example, Wilkinson et al. (1996) report a culture change effort dominated by training methods designed to change values. Gap or analytical frameworks champion culture change through analysing current culture, identifying the desired culture, and developing a programme of change to achieve the desired culture (for example, Hawkins, 1997).

Deal and Kennedy (1982: 15) claim that, with a strong culture, 'a company can gain as much as one or two hours of productive work per employee per day'. The prescriptive view shows how organizational culture can be designed and managed through the 'hearts and minds' of employees. The ideal employees are those who have internalized the organization's goals and values, and who no longer require rigid control. The trend has been towards a 'normative control' (Etzioni, 1961)—that is, an attempt to direct the efforts of employees by controlling the underlying experiences, thoughts, and feelings that guide their actions (Kunda, 1992: 11). It is thought that inherent conflict can be transformed into cooperation in the interests of both employee and employer; through education, personal development, growth, and maturity, employees become better, healthier people—and are saved from alienation and conflict.

Critically assessing whether culture can be managed

As Johnson and Gill (1993: 33) note, it is not clear whether the organizations that Deal and Kennedy, and Peters and Waterman, observed developed as they did through chance and spontaneity (that is, social control), or through conscious intent (that is, administrative control). Some have argued that organizational culture management is designed more to improve control than directly to increase profitability. Wilmott (1993: 522), for example, claims that cultural control is an intense and effective 'medium of domination'. The idea of equating the use of Japanese management practices with success in US companies was shaky, to say the least (Legge, 1994). Even Deal and Kennedy (1999) have themselves had to admit that the downsizing, outsourcing, and mergers that have characterized so much of management practice over the past twenty years have undermined relationships, trust, cohesion, and corporate culture. And the design and empirical basis of Peters and Waterman's research is highly suspect, as Guest (1992) and Collins (1998) demonstrate.

The more critical researchers have consequently raised concerns regarding the conceptual feasibility of culture management (Ackroyd and Crowdy, 1990; Legge, 1994). Some reject the view that culture can be managed, while others accept that culture may be malleable, but argue that change will be fraught with difficulties and ethical dilemmas. Some, like Ogbonna and Harris (1998a), would argue that culture is not easily controlled, but can be manipulated under certain—rare—organizational conditions. They believe that organizational culture is not unitary: culture cannot be viewed in a unidimensional manner; there are likely to be different subcultures or types of culture in existence within organizations. Attempts to change culture may evolve in unpredictable ways (Ogbonna and Harris, 1998b; Harris and Ogbonna, 2002).

Despite this scepticism, practitioners continue to attempt—often unsuccessfully—to bring about culture management initiatives—perhaps because only adaptable cultural traits are linked to performance (Gordon and DiTomaso, 1992), or because non-imitable, rare, and adaptable cultures may represent a source of competitive advantage (Barley, 1991). Whatever the truth, it has to be acknowledged that employees are not passive objects of control (Goffman, 1961). They may accept, deny, react, reshape, rethink, acquiesce, rebel, or conform, and create themselves within constraints imposed on them. Research, for example, on employee values and norms reflected in everyday practices (such as restriction of output), shows direct conflict with the aims and objectives of management (Roy, 1960; Lupton, 1963).

EXAMPLE Gender, culture, and control

An example of a company that attempted to change its culture and control the behaviour of its employees is *Emsite*, a mining company in Australia. The management believed that employing large numbers of females helped to improve the behaviour of male employees. Talking about the men, one of the managers said: 'I mean, they're just your average peacock and it's amazing how they dress better, stay cleaner, behave more appropriately, when there are females around than when there are not' (Eveline and Booth, 2002: 564). When women are part of the workforce, superintendents say that better care is taken of equipment, there is less antagonism among men, and the overall safety record improves. Management therefore sees the women as 'minders' of the men. The male employees consented to this designation of the women's 'housewifely' position. With women around, male operators said that the place was cleaner, that women took orders more readily, that there were fewer fights (between men), and that there was always someone different to talk to or to discuss family problems with (ibid.: 566).

But all was not positive. A number of men refused to be trained by women to use equipment on which women excelled—particularly the huge computerized trucks and the 824 dozer, which had been designated 'women's machines'. The men called the women offensive names, such as 'bush pigs' and 'dykes', and told sexually explicit stories and jokes. The 'belt shop' was designated 'male territory' and was lavishly adorned with lewd pin-ups. Men found that they could keep women away—or at least to a minimum—with pornography.

Hofstede (1998) believes that there are no shared values at the core of an organization's culture. While there is little doubt that practices are designed according to the values of the founder and significant top managers, this does not mean that all members of the organization share these values. Organizations can be composed of various subcultures that may be mutually antagonistic. These subcultures can compete overtly and covertly, as different groups of organizational members seek to establish or impose their distinctive meaning systems and definitions of reality. There may be various sites of culture embedded in the various groups that make up the organization, creating subcultures, or even counter-cultures (Smircich, 1983a; see Smircich, 1983b, for how networks of meaning can be researched). As Smircich (1983a) argues, organizations can change only those variables that they 'have', such as payment and information systems, mission statements, and corporate image; they cannot change what an organization 'is'—that is, the common values and beliefs that emerge from people's shared experiences. Individuals act out their work roles based on customary definitions and understandings. These meanings are themselves embedded in class, regional, and national cultures. There will therefore be distinctive patterns and connections that will be beyond the capacity of influence, never mind managerial control.

National and organizational cultures

Hofstede's work looks at the relationship between national and organizational cultures. He claims to have successfully uncovered the secrets of entire national cultures (Hofstede, 1980). Extracting primary data for employee attitude surveys within *IBM* subsidiaries in sixty-six countries between 1967 and 1973 (McSweeney, 2002), Hofstede (1991) studied differences in work-related values by analysing national cultures along five main dimensions: 'power distance'; 'individualism/collectivism'; 'masculinity/femininity'; 'uncertainty avoidance'; and 'Confucian dynamism'.

- Power distance refers to the extent to which the less powerful members of organizations, and institutions such as families, expect and accept that power will be distributed evenly. Those societies with high power distance scores tend to exhibit more authoritarian management styles.

- In cultures high in individualism, ties between individuals tend to be loose and there is an expectation that individuals are responsible for their own well-being. In collectivist societies, there is a high degree of social solidarity; it would be less acceptable in this culture to dismiss workers for economic reasons.

- In masculine forms of society, males are expected to be strong, tough, competitive, and assertive, while women are expected to be meek, gentle, modest, caring, and nurturing. In more feminine societies, both men and women are expected to demonstrate a degree of modesty, and a concern for the quality of life. More feminine organizations would operate using intuition and negotiation, while the masculine would use assertion and competition. Hofstede is, then, drawing on gender stereotypes here.

- Uncertainty avoidance refers to the extent to which members of a culture feel threatened by uncertainty and ambiguity. Those with high scores tend to have obvious routines and a need to be busy.

- Confucian dynamism is the extent to which societies adopt a short-term or long-term approach to life. Those with a short-term approach demand quick results, yet are respectful of traditions and social obligation. Those with a long-term approach also respect traditions, but would argue that they have to be adapted to meet modern contexts.

For Hofstede, culture is 'mental programming', 'software of the mind', subjective, and territorially unique. The inhabitants of a particular nation individually carry a unique national culture, which is itself a common component of a wider culture that contains both global and sub-national constituents.

223

The critique of Hofstede

A number of writers on culture have criticized Hofstede's work (see Hofstede, 2002; Smith, 2002; Williamson, 2002). There are richer conceptions of culture (for example, Geertz, 1973) and it is possible to dismiss his project as an attempt to measure the immeasurable (MacIntyre, 1971; Smelser, 1992). But it is mainly his presuppositions and methodology that come under fire. Schein (1990) notes how culture in Hofstede's research is viewed as the property of groups that can be measured by questionnaires leading to Likert-type profiles. The problem with this approach is that it assumes knowledge of the relevant dimensions to be studied. Even if these are statistically derived from large samples of items, it is not clear whether the initial item set is broad enough, or relevant enough, to capture what may be the critical cultural themes for any given organization. And it is not clear whether something as abstract as 'culture' can be measured with survey instruments at all. Further, the method is flawed, because it is assumed that national samples can be taken from a single company, and from mainly marketing and sales staff (McSweeney, 2002). It is therefore assumed that, in *IBM*, there is a single uniform monopolistic organizational culture—although Hofstede later acknowledged cultural heterogeneity.

Some problems with trying to manage culture

Organizational cultures are not mirror images of the cultures of the wider society. There are other factors that shape the cultures of organization. The founders, for example, can act to shape the nature and conduct of a business; the nature of the business, the markets that it serves, and the technology that it uses may all influence the culture to some degree. Stakeholders too, like customers, can influence the nature and characteristics of the products or services.

Harris and Ogbonna (1998) found that the initial objectives of management—that is, to inculcate clearly defined cultural values in staff—resulted in a range of undesired responses. Some employees apparently genuinely, or instrumentally, complied with the newly espoused organizational culture traits, but the majority of workers reacted to the culture change efforts in an ambivalent manner. They reinvented or reinterpreted the change in ways that were counter to the desires of management. Later research (Harris and Ogbonna, 2002) found that management efforts to impose time frames on culture change detrimentally ritualized the initiative, which led to negative interpretations of the change such as: 'Every three months or so we get a pack—yeah, yeah—"this is how we're supposed to act this month". Yeah, yeah—this is now your philosophy for life!' In some cases, the objectives were adulterated or hijacked by others for their own purposes. For example, in one company, the financial control department hijacked the aim of employee empowerment towards reducing the management by 4,000 managers. Further, cultural traits might become eroded by high staff turnover because there is not enough time to train all new staff.

Describing (rather than prescribing) culture

When and if we do find occupational cultures, shared values, and norms of behaviour, how can they best be described and researched? Stephen Barley (1991) argues that few organizational researchers have actually bothered to study the deep structure of a work setting; instead, they have focused on symbols, such as stories, myths, logos, heroes, and so on, while failing to reveal the core of the system that lends a culture its coherence. He looks at the occupation of funeral directors and analyses the meanings of funeral directors' activities, offering a seamlessly integrated interpretation of what may have otherwise appeared as disparate tasks. Closing the corpse's eyes, making the bed, opening the windows and curtains of the death room to allow fresh air to remove any odours, and embalming the body are all ways of making death seem lifelike. The strategic arrangement of the room is intended to reconstruct it to look as it would have done before it became a death room. The corpse's features are posed to make it look as though it is only engaged in restful sleep; peaceful sleep will appear familiar and natural to the mourners, so they are less likely to disrupt a smooth-flowing funeral. No emotionally disruptive hint of ambiguity or conflict is allowed to mar the funeral directors' choreographed presentation of a lifelike death. Barley (1991) provides us then with some insight and understanding of how the occupational culture created by the undertakers serves their purposes and makes their job easier.

For other researchers, the focus has been on describing, but not prescribing, the relationship between culture and ideological and discriminatory practices (for example, Collinson, 1987; 1992; Mills, 1988). One way of examining the culture of an organization is to look at its corporate image to see what and who is valued in the organization. A 'corporate image' is the mental picture that the clients, customers, employees, and others have of an organization. This impression is the combination of unconscious, unintended, conscious, and intended factors, found among annual reports, advertisements, or in-house magazines. Clues to the culture of an organization can be found in its norms, its values, and its rituals; the language of an organization, the metaphors, myths, and stories that are in common use, and the ceremonies, symbols, physical artefacts, taboos, and rites are also indicators.

EXAMPLE **Metaphors used to describe organizations**

The following are some examples of the metaphors that have been used to describe organizations and their cultures (Alvesson, 1993; Lloyd-Jones et al., 1999):

- the *machine*—that is, managed and designed like a machine made up of interlocking parts that each play a clearly defined role in the functioning of the whole;

- the *brain*—that is, drawing attention to the importance of information processing, learning, and intelligence;

- the *organism*—that is, a metaphor focusing attention on understanding and managing the organization's needs and environmental relations. Different organizations belong to different species, of which bureaucracy is only one. Different species are suited for coping with the demands of different environments.

For more examples, see Morgan (1986).

EXAMPLE **Culture as metaphor: The example of *Raleigh* bicycles**

Raleigh's culture was described as having a 'social glue' that held the company together. A reciprocal relationship was fostered between the firm and its employees, based upon the norms of loyalty and obligation. A high premium was placed on continuity and long service. It believed in 'growing its own timber' —that is, educating and training staff for internal promotion. Adopting a functionalist approach, the company evoked notes of culture as 'clan'. Articulating the notion of a unitary organization, all employers were members of the same team or 'same family'.

(*Source:* Lloyd-Jones et al., 1999)

Others who have looked at the language of organization include, for example, Gherardi (1994), who notes how the business environment echoes the great male saga of conquest (of new markets) and of campaigns (to launch new products), while the services echo the language of care and concern for needs, and relationality. The informal use of military, athletic, and sexual language in the workplace can produce a subtle separation between men and women, and alienates those who do not participate in its use (Bates, 1988; Wilson, 1992). Culture is a characteristic of the organization, not of individuals, but is manifested in—and can be measured from—the verbal and non-verbal behaviour of individuals. Traditionally, the study of organizational culture has centred on case studies, often involving participant observation (Hofstede, 1994). But while these studies provide interesting insights, the problem is that different researchers might arrive at different conclusions.

Downsizing and corporate anorexia: Does my bottom line look big in this?

In an interview with a manager in a declining industry, the manager talked of his fear that so many individuals would be made redundant that the organization would become 'anorexic'—that is, too thin to function when an upturn in business came about. Some academics and management practitioners (Tyler and Wilkinson, 2007) use slimming metaphors to talk about downsizing, delayering, and redundancy. Burrell (1992) talks of 'corporate liposuction', within which senior managers have to 'slim down' the 'bulky' middle layers of the organization.

What metaphors have you heard used recently to describe an organization and events?

In addition, occupational cultures consist of ideologies (that is, emotionally charged, taken-for-granted beliefs) and cultural forms (that is, mechanisms for affirming and expressing those beliefs); ideologies tell members what they ought to do (Trice, 1993). Culture is therefore a major carrier of social order. Cultures and subcultures bind people emotionally. Charismatic leaders are thought to be able to manage emotion: corporate leaders, for example, have crafted their words and arranged the physical setting to create emotional images intended to capture the imagination of their audience, and to 'move minds and hearts' (Fineman, 1993). Consequently, companies such as *IBM* offer an elaborate social calendar and extensive training to impress the company spirit on new recruits, so that employees report greater pride on seeing the *IBM* flag flying over corporate offices than when they see their national flag. Home sales organizations, such as *Tupperware*, create a cozy, warm, and cheery party feeling for their domestic sales teams. Regular sales meetings and reward ceremonies have a distinctly evangelical tone to keep spirits high (Fineman, 1993).

EXAMPLE **Creating a culture at *Consultancyco***

The founding owner-manager of this company created a 'distinctive culture' (Grugulis et al., 2000). When it was first founded, it consisted of a group of twelve friends who worked and socialized together. As the company grew, these social events continued and were seen as an important part of the way in which the organization was managed. 'Work hard and play hard' appeared to be the way in which to describe the company culture.

A 'culture manager' was appointed to manage the 'play'. The social events included weekends away, with families, nights out, competitions, and fund-raising. Employees were expected to want to participate actively. It was hoped that socializing together outside work would encourage employees to cooperate with one another in work and that subsidized social events would encourage loyalty. Families could join in on training days. The company's graduate open day was planned to coincide with Red Nose Day (a day of fun designed to raise money for charities).

But the whole image is not all positive. The selection process sought to replicate the characteristics of the small group of friends who founded the company. Almost all were white, male, and aged between 20 and 40. Those who chose not to participate voluntarily in the social activities, those who criticized the company, and those who did not immerse themselves in the company culture were sacked. In this way, the company recalls how home behaviour and regular church attendance were a condition of the $5 day for Henry Ford (Beynon, 1984).

Kunda (1992) provides us with a very detailed study of one organization and its culture, as an example of successful culture management. He concentrates on how the culture was 'engineered', exploring, describing, and evaluating the reality behind the rhetoric of corporate culture. The company at which he looked was called *Tech Engineering*, and represented an intense and complex environment. The rhetoric was taken seriously by management, and considerable time and energy was expended on embedding the rules, prescriptions, and admonitions of the culture into the fabric of everyday life. The company was portrayed as morally sound, organic, and undifferentiated. Kunda describes how social reality was formed around key words and strong images. Relentless repetition was the rule and the ideological formulations were to be found in the ready-made words of wisdom—that is, platitudes posing as insight and found in public places, in the mail, in workshops, and used in decoration, to the extent that they became constant background noise. Metaphors characterizing *Tech* as a social entity were based on imagery of the family or analogies with moral—religious or scientific—institutions. The ideal state was one of self-control and self-discipline. And while many members managed to maintain a sense of freedom, they also experienced a pull that was not easy to resist—that is, an escalating commitment to the corporation and its definitions of reality, coupled with a systematic and persistent attack on the boundaries of their privacy.

EXAMPLE **How to break the boundaries of personal time at work**

If an investment bank were to treat all of its employees, from clerk to partner, to a very good lunch, ordered from a menu and delivered to their desks, what will be the impact of this on the employees' behaviour?

The effect on the employees is likely to be that they feel that they must sit at their desk at lunchtime, eat lunch, and carry on working. It will be very hard for them to say 'Well, I think I'll take some time out now', having been given a gift of lunch.

While an organization may wish to engineer a culture, or a working atmosphere, it is not always totally successful in inducing harmonious relationships. Aktouf (1996) provides us with some excellent examples of how competence and promotability were displayed by charge-hands and workers in two breweries in Canada and Algeria in which he worked as a participant observer. He looks at the signs and indicators that made middle-level and lower-level employees look competent. They had to demonstrate that they had something extra or different from ordinary workers, for example, by being zealous and doing more work, by being ruthless, and by keeping their distance from other workers. There are some interesting omissions from the list of necessary attributes: for example, technical competence was not mentioned as an attribute necessary for being a foreman. Less surprisingly, the workers' idea of an 'ideal' foreman was found to be the exact opposite of that of management. Career-minded employees had to learn to use the language of the power holder and adhere to their values—for example, talking about costs, productivity, rates, and so on—when dealing with superiors—particularly if senior managers were around. The required non-verbal symbolic activity included adopting behaviour that conformed to management prescriptions (such as zeal in observing rules and quotas) and doing everything possible to help management, from 'seeing with the master's eye', to outright spying. Even more enlightening are the names given to promotion candidates, including 'blockheads', 'shit eaters', 'brown noses', and 'limp wrists' in Montreal, and 'traitors', 'lickers', 'porters', and 'yes-men' in Algiers. So however zealous management may be in trying to promote a culture, it may be undermined by the workforce. Further, there is a possibility—if not likelihood—that the culture will not be self-consistent.

EXAMPLE **Cultural ambiguity at *Hans Kardiner Design***

At *Hans Kardiner Design*, a small European luxury gift retailer, candour was seen as a central value in the company culture. It appeared in a written list of company values and could be seen in practice to guide much behaviour. Staff meetings were held with frank exchanges of views. But when harsh decisions were made, almost tortured contortions were adopted that obscured what had been decided. For example, the dismissal of staff was packaged in the guise of job opportunities, inviting staff to apply for posts that they could not get, or would not want, or would not like. This disguise appeared to go unnoticed.

(*Source*: Myers, 2002)

227

The way in which language in the organization culture differentiates managers' views of competence from the workers' can also be achieved through the use of symbols. An earlier study of symbolism by Thompson (1983) reports on his work in a slaughterhouse. He documents the workers' interaction as they cope with the danger, strain, and monotony of their jobs, as well as the consumer-spending norms that trap them in their jobs. Non-verbal gestures were the primary form of communication in this work culture. Knives were used to beat against the tubs to communicate time. Because managers had refused to install a clock in the work area, the gesture symbolized the workers' efforts to regain the control that management had taken from them—but these gestures could not free them from their oppressive jobs or an oppressive work culture.

Ackroyd and Crowdy (1990) also look at the case of slaughterhouse men and raise questions about how much control management had over the work culture. Much of the culture could not be explained by (and was highly resistant to) management action. Management did not decide the precise nature of the division of labour; the work cycle and therefore the pace of the line varied with the kind of animal being processed. The men worked fast and hard, habitually aiming to finish available batches of animals in the minimum time. Toughness and strength were the heroic qualities of the culture. Typically, they worked without a break until the work was done. Although management fixed meal breaks, the men would vary them, according to the batches that they had to process. High levels of sustained effort were needed to ensure large payouts from the piecework bonus system. This also removed the need for close managerial supervision. Each gang had a strong informal hierarchy dominated by the fastest and most accomplished workers. The gang decided how to distribute tasks and people, and fixed the pace of the line. The lead—that is, the most senior man—worked at the first work station, at which the animals were killed; he dictated the pace of work. The average pace of work led to a build-up at the work stations of the slower men; these men would be harassed (for example, by flying entrails) into working harder and faster. Liquid excreta would be sprayed or practical jokes played on the lower-status members of the gang. Very few seemed to resent the harassment and degradation to which they were subjected, believing that anyone was 'fair game'. Casual absenteeism was almost unknown and some of the men visited the plant while supposedly on vacation; they also brought their children to the plant and leisure activities were frequently communal. Would management therefore want to change the culture?

Culture and change

Studies of the impact of culture change have concentrated on the extent to which change objectives are achieved and the performance indicators of such change efforts (Denison, 1990; Gordon and DiTomaso, 1992). There is, however, a lack of attention paid to the unintended consequences that can impede or prevent the desired cultural change, as we noted earlier (Ackroyd and Crowdy, 1990; Legge, 1994; Harris and Ogbonna, 2002).

The culture of an organization is determined, in part, by its rules (see also the chapters on stress, emotional labour, and on routinization). If change is to be brought about, some of those rules will have to change. One change that six major supermarkets in the UK brought about was the development of 'surface-acting skills'—that is, staff were expected to tailor their responses carefully in order to please the customer (Ogbonna and Wilkinson, 1990). For example, cashiers were encouraged to smile all of the time and to note that the customer is 'always right'. The customer is 'king', not 'punter'. The cashiers adopt these values for instrumental reasons (because it disarms the customer) or under threat of sanction ('I smile because I am told to'). Random visits by mystery shoppers and head office management reinforce the threat of sanctions. But Ogbonna and Wilkinson argue that these are not changes in values at all; rather, they are changes in behaviour.

Other supermarkets have taken a different tack and decided to reward desired behaviour, such as the friendly smile. If an employee is 'caught' being friendly to a mystery shopper, he or she is rewarded with a gift ranging from $25 to a new car (Rafaeli and Sutton, 1987; 1989). In the UK, *McDonald's* restaurants rate surface-acting skills in their staff: whether there is a smile, the greeting is pleasant, audible, and sincere, the staff member looks the customer in the eye, and there is always a 'thank you' and some pleasant parting comment (Newton and Findlay, 1996). Interactive style is thus stripped of its improvisation; affective demeanour, precise words, and sometimes physical posture are scripted for production of the 'right' image.

Asda has tried to introduce a 'culture of service' (Du Gay, 1996: 121), finding that, in the *Disney Corporation*, people were recruited and interviewed in threes to see how they related to others. One girl had been fired because she was too introverted and did not have enough eye contact to go with the 'Have a nice day' routine. *Asda* thus wanted to move attention to the recruitment and training of employees, and to their effective 'enculturation' into its corporate norms and values.

Because consumers often resent the routinized interactions such as 'Have a nice day', seeing them as mechanical and phoney, organizations try to design routines that have some of the qualities of a more spontaneous interaction. For example, *Marriott* hotel porters were instructed to notice and comment on the home town of the guests whose bags they carried, to make the guests feel welcome. In this way, it becomes part of the service worker's job to hide the scripting through persuasive acting (Leidner, 1993).

Hopfl (1995) recounts the story of being on a *British Airways* domestic flight between Manchester and London. Having made the pre-landing announcements, a female member of the cabin staff announced: 'Ladies and gentlemen, I would just like to inform you that we have six cartons of milk left in the galley and if anyone is going home to an empty house or feels that they can make use of them, please make yourself known to the cabin staff in leaving the aircraft.' The response to hearing of this, by a member of *British Airways* cabin crew training, was shock. 'They're really not allowed to do that', she countered, with some consternation—despite emphasis in training on commitment to the customer. What was at issue was the extent to which improvisation around a specific role was possible or desirable, and the extent to which this behaviour indicates a deviation from a faithful reading of a prepared script. When organizations bring about cultural change through the scripting, rehearsing, and performing of roles, they cannot always guarantee the outcome that they might like to see. While the acquisition of a 'service ethic' has led to a conscious performance orientation and a belief in the importance of well-rehearsed actors, appropriate staging, and setting, and, in effect, a compelling illusion, they cannot define the degree of discretion over improvisation around the role.

Delayering and redundancy can also bring about change in culture and climate, producing an oppressive authoritarian climate that generates conformity (McKinley et al., 1995). Companies have targeted surviving managers with salary cuts, performance-related pay, stringent output targets, and early retirement. Collinson and Collinson (1997) have looked at the informal ways in which managers are assessed and monitored in an insurance company. The culture in this insurance company changed, so those managers worked longer hours. The CEO told managers that he did not expect them to be home 'in time to bath the baby' (ibid.: 388). Individuals started to compete to see how late they could be there in the evenings. There was an unquestioning enthusiasm for working long hours at the weekend, as well as during the week, and for minimizing holiday time and sick leave. The women took less time off on maternity leave, so the informal culture dictated that if women in management were going to insist on having children, then they must do so with the minimum impact on the smooth running of management. A more ruthless, macho, aggressive, and coercive management style was used. Managers were encouraged to look confident, in control, and optimistic. And clocks were banned to encourage everyone to work hard and stop 'clock watching'.

Junior managers tried to resist this change in the culture. They could make it appear that they worked even longer hours and that they were always there at work. For example, they left jackets on chairs during the day and overnight, or left their car keys on the desk (either taking public transport home or using a spare set of keys). They left the lights and computer on in their office and, if actually seen going home, would have a large pile of work to take with them for the evening (even though they may not do it). Of course, it is possible to reject a macho aggressive culture: Marshall (1995) documents how many women managers have decided to move on, having experienced these pressures, and build a more balanced life between work and home.

When it comes to parenthood, workplace cultures affect fathers, as well as mothers, and their ability to meet both their home and work commitments. Some fathers report a tension between the demands of work and home, and feel under pressure not to take time off work if a child is ill. If a father works in a culture in which family commitments are acknowledged and accepted, this can make the task of balancing work and family life much easier (Hatten et al., 2002). While some fathers accept the 'long hours' culture as an inevitable part of their job, a change in culture could be invaluable for many to enable them to balance work and home life. If cultures could be developed in which it is the norm to work only for contracted hours, rather than extra hours, this would take pressure off working fathers (ibid.).

Research by Howard Khan has shown how that there needs to be a change of culture in many businesses in Scotland. The culture needs to change from a macho culture, epitomized by 'blame' and 'just do as you are told', because this is leading to high levels of labour turnover, stress, and poor organizational performance. But the biggest problem is getting macho managers to admit they have faults; women make better bosses than men, because they are less inclined to be confrontational (*The Scotsman*, 24 November 1997, p. 24).

Culture and gender

Despite such assertions, organizations differ according to their gender regimes. They are both constrained by, and constitute, the practices that occur within them. Despite claims of gender neutrality, organizations are structured according to the symbolism of gender—that is, their culture is gendered (Gherardi, 1995). Organizational cultures express values and mark out places that belong to only one gender (Gherardi, 1994). People weave together the symbolic order of gender in an organizational culture as they construct their understanding of a shared world or of difference.

All cultures possess systems with which to signify sexual difference. Culture refers to the symbols, beliefs, and patterns of behaviour that are learned, produced, and created by people in an organization. This can include something as banal as appearance and the symbolic message that it transmits. Gherardi (1995: 13) asks: 'Have you ever met a woman manager with long hair worn loose to the waist?' She argues that a woman manager having loose long hair would be inappropriate—that is, she would be seen as having a 'sexiness' that clashes with the role of woman manager and the authority that this confers; it would be 'out of tune'.

Gherardi (1996) looked at women who are the first to enter a male culture—that is, at women pioneers in male occupations. She looked at the stories that these women told and realized that most of them shared the same plot: the outsider who enters an alien culture. These were women travellers in a male world. An organization's culture positions the male and female in reciprocal relation; the positioning acquired different meaning depending on whether the host culture was hostile or friendly. The female may, for example, find herself in a friendly culture in a position of the guest, while the men play host, extending a friendly and solicitous welcome, but maintaining a structure of their superior rights. An alternative might be a hostile culture, in which the female is in a position of marginality. Gherardi identifies six different types of organizational culture.

Using company materials to examine corporate culture, Mills (1995) looked at the images projected by *British Airways* in its newsletters over time. He was struck by the centrality of men and masculinities in the images. The company first consciously constructed an image of the 'heroic pilot'. Around 1919–29, air travel was associated with danger and adventure. To counter that perception and to win new passengers, the airlines used the image of the heroic First World War pilot. With changing times and the 'normalization' of flying, the emphasis shifted from safety to service, provided by the male pilot and steward (and, eventually, the stewardess). The male (and white) association of the pilot's image did not change over time; this reflected recruitment practices, and served to exclude and discourage female commercial pilots. *British Airways* did not recruit female flying crews until 1987—well after legislation against sex discrimination had been introduced. Images of women did, however, change over time. The first images—from around 1945—were of the hard-working wife and mother who stepped into the breach to do her part for the war effort. Later, a new image of the hard-working, 'girl next door' appeared as female flight attendants were employed. Throughout the decade ending in the mid-1950s, there was an increasing focus on female bodily attractiveness and an eroticized female form.

Mills is able to show, through his research, that corporate images can sanction and encourage certain types of male/female behaviour and implicitly prohibit others. Corporate images can encourage the exclusion of women from positions of power, authority, and prestige. But from where does this come? Occupational segregation is a manifestation of the symbolic order of gender that opposes the male to the female (Gherardi, 1994). Occupational segregation expresses a coherence: women do women's tasks (for example, caring and cleaning); they occupy female jobs (for example, nursing, cleaning, and secretarial); they perpetuate the symbolic system of subordination and subservience. Occupational segregation protects women from male competition and men from competition from women. Recently, research has found that, in the British army, many of 'our boys' would like to keep the girls out (Utley, 2003). Women are stereotyped as being gutsy types who would never be good enough to be 'real' soldiers. They are characterized as sexy, tomboyish, and a disruptive influence—attitudes that are to be found in policies and promotional literature. Women are seen as so different that they are incompatible with military life.

Boys, at a young age, feel that they have to identify with men, and so tend to reject any semblance of femininity and adhere instead to a rigid notion of masculinity. Because men's achievements and activities are more valued in our society, the rules of membership in the masculine 'club', and even people's notions of maleness, are more stereotypically framed and enforced than those relating to femaleness (Hort et al., 1990). Even schools help to form gendered identities, marking out 'correct' or 'appropriate' behaviour for males and females; they act as 'masculinity-making devices'. Teacher behaviour reinforces masculinity (Haywood, 1993). Having power and authority as a teacher means being a 'proper man', and keeping a class quiet usually involved discipline and force, including cuffing, shaking, and pushing; incompetence was seen as weakness—as 'womanly'.

But masculinity is not one-dimensional; rather, it has to be seen in the context of class, and sexual and ethnic relations—so, for example, there are white, working-class gays and Asian, middle-class heterosexuals. While the attributes of femininity are ingrained in the subordination relationship: 'caring'; 'compassionate'; 'willing to please others'; 'generous'; and 'sensitive', these are attributes that other marginalized or dependent groups of people also possess. Masculinity is negotiated, rejected, and accepted. The different masculinities will have differential access to power, practices of power, and differential effects (Haywood and Mac an Ghaill, 1996). Particular styles of masculinity will become dominant in certain situations; those in power will be able to define what is 'normal' or 'ordinary' male behaviour. For example, Willis (1977) found that the working-class 'lads' that he studied thought that doing mental work or having girls as friends was effeminate; manual work was the province of masculinity. Haywood (1993) studied a group of academic achievers who were labelled as having an underdeveloped masculinity and referred to as 'wankers'. The academic achievers, in turn, used terms such 'cripple', 'cabbage', and 'spanner' to describe the inadequacy of other male pupils. Yet subversion at school and 'having a laff' was seen as preparation for a shop-floor job; activities seen conventionally as 'underachieving' or 'dropping out' are, in fact, a preparation for a life at work with few intrinsic satisfactions.

How jobs are sex-typed (see Chapter 5) is one feature of organizational culture. Research by Prokos and Padavic (2002) has looked at how masculinity is created and maintained in the US police force. Male police officers equate women with feminine moral virtue, the domestic realm, social service, formal rules, administration, cleanliness, and emotions; men are equated with guns, crime fighting, a combative personality, fights, weapons, and a desire to work in high-crime areas. Many male police officers strongly believe that women are incapable of being good police officers. Male police officers cling to the image of police officers as crime fighters and downplay the femininely labelled aspects of the job, such as paperwork. Prokos and Padavic found that women in police training were treated as outsiders by means, for example, of eliminating them from classroom examples. Gendered language was pervasive, so the male pronoun, and words such as 'gentlemen' and 'guys', were used to refer to students or police officers. Women police officers were not shown how to search men, although men were shown how to search men and women. In this culture, men learned to disparage women by verbally denigrating and objectifying them, as typified by the comment: 'There oughtta be a law against bitches.'

Sharpe (1998) described similarly masculine culture in the UK police force very vividly (see also Fielding, 1994; Brown, 1998). Sharpe found that the 'cop culture' covered a multitude of sins. She could classify much of the behaviour within specific locations, as follows.

- 'Van culture' consisted largely of lavatorial humour, and farting and belching competitions.
- 'Patrol culture' included making critical and judgemental assessments of individuals—invariably ordinary members of the public going about their daily business—coloured by racist and sexist remarks.
- In the 'office culture', male and female officers would be picked out for their appearance and their sexual appetite.
- 'Custody room culture' was mostly officer-dependent.
- 'Pub culture' was a combination of van, patrol, and office culture, but heavily dominated by talk of the latest sexual conquests, sporting triumphs, and personal alcoholic consumption levels. As a researcher, Sharpe (1998) reports that she was obliged to visit licensed premises with the vice squad and drink copious amounts of alcohol; failure to keep up with them was viewed with disdain and deep suspicion.

The topics of interest to the male officers were rugby, cricket, golf, horse racing, beer, cars, and women (in that order). Women were categorized and judged by their sexual habits and activity. Sharpe (1998: 15) says: 'To a policeman, sex was rather like a crime return— the more they could claim for, the better it looked to friends and colleagues.' The easiest target for gossip was the woman police officer. Official complaints about the behaviour of male officers were not common; sexism was seen simply as part of the culture. Policewomen had to 'tough it out' or go under. In a similar way, in order to be assimilated into the dominant (male) group, certain groups of women in the professions and in politics have adopted strategies that include using deeper voices, swearing and using taboo language, adopting a more assertive style in groups, and addressing themselves in public to traditionally male topics—that is business, politics, and economics (see Coates, 1993).

But sometimes, the 'rules' change: there was, for example, a time when there were no full-time postwomen. They were not recruited in urban areas, because they were thought not to be able physically to carry the normal load; in rural areas, they were employed when no man could be obtained to perform the work (Grint, 1995: 198).

EXAMPLE **What jobs do women do: Gravedigging and terrorism?**

Gravedigging is normally a job that men do. A woman won the job of gravedigger at a cemetery in Italy after all ten male candidates failed the practical test—that is, exhuming a body— by fainting (*The Guardian*, 30 August 1997, p. 5).

Until recently, women in the UK were not allowed to work on the front line in the army. Yet research from the USA has shown that women can make better fighters than men and that women are twice as likely as their male colleagues to fire at the enemy.

Female terrorists have been said to be far more dangerous and deadly, because they are more likely to kill bystanders. Some of the Chechen terrorists who took hostages in the Moscow theatre in October 2002 were female (Myers, 2002). Released hostages claimed that the female terrorists were the cruellest (*Scotland on Sunday*, 27 October 2002). In 2002, seven women were selected for assassination by other women in a Mafia shooting incident (*The Guardian*, 28 May 2002).

Culture, gender, and hierarchy

In order to gain insight into the working of an organization, it is necessary to look at where the power and reputation in an organization or industry are held; frequently, men will be found in those areas and there will be few, if any, women. Despite the fact that nearly half of all undergraduates are women, for example, their representation at the senior levels of academia remains low (Ward, 2001). Latest figures reveal only small increases in the numbers of women working as professors, senior lecturers, and researchers: women make up, for example, only 16.5 per cent of professorial staff in higher education (HESA, 2007).

An interesting example of how culture operates in subtle ways is to be found in the unwritten rule that males dominate conversation in organizations. Men command a dominating role within conversation and gain for themselves a disproportionate amount of floor space or speaking time. Zimmerman and West (1975) found—in a study of thirty-one two-party conversations between a man and a woman—that virtually all of the interruptions and overlaps in speaking were made by the male speakers. This, they say, leads to disproportionate female silence within male–female interaction that does not occur in same-sex conversation, so men deny equal status to women as conversational partners.

Some have tried to suggest (for example, O'Barr and Atkins, 1980) that this is because males, on average, hold higher-status positions than women do. Woods (1993) put this idea to the test by examining gender and occupational status, and their relative influence on patterns of speaking time in a work setting. She found that gender tended to exert the greater influence on speaking time: while speakers in high occupational positions spent more time holding the floor than their subordinates, nevertheless, even when women held high-status occupational positions, male subordinates still dominated by, for example, interrupting more and giving less assent to women.

233

Culture, gender, and computing

The culture of computing is seen by many as a male domain: while there is no inherent gender bias in the computer itself, the computer culture is not equally neutral (Turkle, 1988). Early studies of the computing culture suggested that males heavily dominate the adult world of computing; it is transmitted to children by males (Kiesler et al., 1985). The culture values technical, rather than interpersonal, skills, hardware over software, and engineering over business backgrounds (Turkle, 1984; 1988). In addition, there is a legacy in the computer culture of images of competition, sport, and violence—and some computer operating systems still use terms such as 'killing' and 'aborting' programs. Women are said to look at computers and see more than machines; they see the culture that has grown up around computing. They see, for example, a culture associated with dedicated and expert hackers, the heroes of the larger culture who take pride in being 'nerds' (their term), who have no social rules other than the mutual tolerance and respect for radical individualism, manipulation, and mastery of the computer. Women then ask whether they belong to this culture.

Some, including Turkle (1988), argue that women are expressing a computer reticence—that is, a desire to stay away from computing, because it is a personal and cultural symbol of what a woman is not. But both men and women hold stereotypes about computer professionals. Computing is seen as a 'man's job' both in computer classes, in popular computer magazines, and by students. It is perceived as a job for the antisocial—that is, those low in social ease and frequency of social interaction (Wilson, 1997; 2003). Computer work is seen by women as a field for men and antisocial people (Newton, 1991; Shade, 1993). It is also argued that females feel that taking too much interest in technology threatens their image of themselves as women (Lage, 1991).

Whatever the reason, females make up only about 19 per cent of students studying computer science in US universities; as a result, the number of female computer professionals is low. The new and rapidly expanding information technology occupations should be providing opportunities for women, but women are under-represented in IT jobs (Panteli et al., 1997).

Culture and race

Minority groups currently comprise 11.8 per cent of the UK population (CRE, 2007). Despite this, the culture of most organizations is not only male, but it is also white. Managers involved in the recruitment process reinforce this by having a hierarchy of criteria for acceptability (Jenkins, 1985; 1988). The primary criteria involve appearance, manner, attitude, and maturity. Secondary criteria relate to 'gut feeling', employment history, experience, the ability to fit in, age, speech style, literacy, and marital status. Tertiary criteria include references and English-language competence. Minority workers are less likely to fit the stereotypical 'married with two kids and a mortgage' pattern that recruiters seem to prefer; their accent may be regarded by white recruiters as 'inferior' and they may be seen as less likely to fit in (Grint, 1998: 251).

Racism is not difficult to demonstrate. For example, the *BBC*'s Radio Five Live sent out dummy CVs to a wide range of companies in response to recruitment advertisements. For each vacancy, six applications were sent: one male and one female for each of three groups—that is, white European, Asian Muslim, and black African. All of the fictitious applicants achieved the same standards in terms of qualifications and experience, but applications were written and presented differently to increase their authenticity to recruiters. While 23 per cent of the white candidates were invited for interview, only 13 per cent and 9 per cent, respectively, were successful from the black African and Asian Muslim candidates (BBC Press Office, 12 July 2004). A similar experiment was conducted in the USA, in which white-sounding names such as 'Greg' and 'Anne' were used to compare with black-sounding applicants, such as 'Ebony' and 'Rasheed'. It was found that 'white' applicants received one response for every ten CVs, but that 'black' applicants with equal credentials received one response per fifteen (BBC News, 15 January 2003).

> **EXAMPLE** Workplace culture and racism
>
> A report by the *Equal Opportunities* Commission (2007) shows that the main reason why Bangladeshi, Pakistani, and black Caribbean women in the UK who want to work find it so difficult to fulfil their potential is workplace culture. For example, staff from ethnic minorities are repeatedly questioned about fasting, clothing, eating habits, and religious beliefs. Uniforms of dress codes rigidly impose Western fashions or do not allow women to wear trousers. And they are obliged to participate on out-of-work activities that make them feel uncomfortable: for example, going to the pub.

Several of the UK's leading corporations are, however, beginning to recognize the need to assemble a diverse staff team and have sought to devise recruitment strategies that reach out and attract qualified ethnic minority candidates. This, they realize, will help them to establish credibility and expertise to help to access increasingly diverse consumer markets.

Other aspects of culture

There are many approaches to culture. One might be to look at the moral order—that is, the ordering of expectations and moral imperatives in a work situation. A strand of the Chicago school in sociology (see Watson, 1987) suggested that we look at how an individual copes with, or adapts to, problems faced at work in maintaining his or her identity. Students were encouraged to look at the 'dirty' or deviant jobs in order to see factors of general relevance to work experience that might not be noticed in more conventional kinds of work, in which they might be taken for granted. We saw in an earlier chapter how, for example, prostitutes stress the extent to which they control their clients in order to maintain self-respect. This may also be happening when garage mechanics insist that they tell you what is wrong with your car and resent it if you diagnose the fault when they are the 'experts'.

But the 'taken-for-granted' nature of organizational rules is often hard to uncover; it is only when the rules are broken or challenged in some way that we see what they are.

Conclusion

In the chapter, we have seen how some believe that culture can be managed or engineered—that is, that it can be manipulated to the benefit of the organization. The strength of an organization's culture has a direct relationship with, or impact on, performance and productivity. This, then, is the functionalist and unitarist approach. Critical views of management doubt the ideas that lie behind the claims and instead discuss how organizational culture can best be described, highlighting some more of the realities of organizational life. They would doubt, as does Parker (2000), that organizational culture can be managed in any planned way. Organizations are not unitary entities, but more likely made up of subcultures in which organizational identities are continually contested. Power and inequalities of, for example, gender and race clearly play their part in organizational culture.

KEY POINTS

235

- Culture is a concept used to describe a company, a rationale for people's behaviour, and many other features of organizational life.

- Culture can be witnessed or researched as observable facts, meanings, norms of behaviour, symbols, values, beliefs, structures, and underlying assumptions.

- While managers may wish to see culture as a variable, subject to their manipulation and control, and management consultants have been keen to sell the idea that culture can be made stronger and managed, critics have argued that culture cannot be managed. Others have accepted that it may be malleable—but argue that change can be unpredictable, and fraught with difficulties and ethical dilemmas.

- Hofstede has looked at relationships between national and organizational cultures. His work has been criticized mainly because of his presuppositions and methodology.

- While some management consultants may claim to be able to manage and change culture with positive outcomes, organizational researchers have focused on how best to describe culture (examining the occupational culture, the corporate image, the language, the symbolic order of gender or race, or the metaphors and myths to be found in the organization), or on the outcomes of culture or culture change.

CASE STUDY
A case of company culture

In the following description of one company's culture, Schein (1990: 112) argues that it is possible for a group to hold conflicting values that manifest themselves in inconsistent behaviour while having complete consensus on underlying assumptions.

The *Action Company* is a rapidly growing, high-technology manufacturing company. Its founder manages it: he began the company thirty years ago, and holds strong beliefs and values.

A visitor to the company would notice the open office layout, and the high degree of informality, frenetic activity, confrontation, conflict, and fighting in meetings. There is an obvious lack of status symbols, such as parking spaces for senior managers or executive dining rooms. There is a sense of high energy and emotional involvement, with people staying late in the office and expressing excitement about their work. The general view appears to be that hard work, innovation, and rapid solutions to problems are essential to this rapidly growing high-technology company. New employees are carefully screened. When an employee fails, he or she is assigned to another task, rather than fired or punished.

The company operates on several critical and coordinated assumptions, as follows.

1. Individuals are assumed to be the source of all innovation and productivity.

2. Truth can only be determined by pitting fully involved individuals against each other to debate ideas until only one idea survives. An idea will not be implemented unless everyone involved in its implementation has been convinced of the validity of the idea.

3. Every individual must think for themselves and will 'do the right thing'—even if that means disobeying the boss or violating a company policy.

4. What makes it possible for people to live in this high-conflict environment is the assumption that the company is one big family, the members of which will take care of one another and protect each other even if some make mistakes or have bad ideas.

The organization appears, then, to tolerate extremely high degrees of conflict without destroying or demotivating its employees.

(*Source:* Adapted from Schein, 1990)

236

Questions

1. Is it your experience of organizations that ideas are only implemented if everyone is convinced of the validity of the idea?

2. If not, what is more usual in your experience?

3. Is this an attractive idea? What might be its disadvantages?

FURTHER READING

Alvesson, M. (2002) *Understanding Organizational Culture*, London: Sage

Brewis, J. (2007) 'Cutlture', in D. Knights and H. Willmott (eds), *Introducing Organizational Behaviour and Management*, London: Thomson Learning, ch. 9 This chapter includes mainstream, as well as critical, perspectives on the topic of culture.

Culture and Organization A journal published by Routledge with a search facility that allows you to search for the aspect of culture that interests you.

Linstead, S. (2004) 'Managing culture', in S. Linstead, L. Fulop, and S. Lilley (eds), *Management and Organization: A Critical Text*, Houndmills: Palgrave Macmillan, ch. 3 This chapter provides a good critical view of the subject.

Parker, M. (2000) *Organizational Culture and Identity: Unity and Division at Work*, London: Sage This title offers a more in-depth look at culture.

Sinclair, A. (1998) *Doing Leadership Differently: Gender, Power and Sexuality in a Changing Business Culture*, Melbourne: University of Melbourne Press This book aims to help us to think about culture, leadership, and power.

Watson, T. (2002) *Organising and Managing Work*, Harlow: Pearson Chapter 7 of this book focuses on structure, culture, and control; Chapter 8, on choice and constraint in the shaping of structure and culture.

RESEARCH QUESTIONS

1. Goffman (1961) gives us a detailed account of life in asylums. What insight can we gain from this work to help us to understand the working and culture of organizations such as universities?

2. Hopfl (1995) draws an analogy between acting and customer service. Read her paper and critically assess the similarities.

3. What evidence is there to suggest that the culture within police forces is discriminatory? (See Brown, 1998; Fielding, 1994; Sharpe, 1998; you may also want to look at newspaper and BBC sources.)

4. There is an abundance of contradictions to be found in the culture of organizations. How does Aktouf (1996) describe the contradictions that he found and what examples have you seen in your own experience?

REFERENCES

Ackroyd, S. and Crowdy, P.A. (1990) 'Can culture be managed? Working with "raw" material: The case of english slaughtermen', *Personnel Review*, 19(5): 3–13.

Aktouf, O. (1996) 'Competence, symbolic activity and promotability', in S. Linstead, R. Grafton Small, and P. Jeffcutt (eds), *Understanding Management*, London: Sage.

Alvesson, M. (1993) 'The play of metaphors', in J. Hassard and M. Parker (eds), *Postmodernism and Organizations*, London: Sage, pp. 114–31.

_____ (1999) *Cultural Perspectives on Organizations*, Cambridge: Cambridge University Press.

_____ and Billing, Y.D. (1992) 'Gender and organization: Toward a differentiated understanding', *Organization Studies*, 13(2): 73–106.

Barley, S.R. (1991) 'Semiotics and the study of occupational and organizational culture', in P.J. Frost, L.F. Moore, M.R. Louis, C.C. Lundberg, and J. Martin (eds), *Reframing Organizational Culture*, London: Sage.

Bates, B. (1988) *Communication and the Sexes*, New York: Harper & Row.

Beynon, H. (1984) *Working for Ford*, Harmondsworth: Penguin.

Brown, J.M. (1998) 'Aspects of discriminatory treatment of women police officers serving in forces in England and Wales', *British Journal of Criminology*, 38(2): 265–81.

Burrell, G. (1992) 'The organization of pleasure', in M. Alvesson and H. Wilmott (eds), *Critical Management Studies*, London: Sage, pp. 66–89.

Coates, J. (1993) *Women, Men and Language*, 2nd edn, London: Longman.

Collins, D. (1998) *Organizational Change: Sociological Perspectives*, London: Routledge.

Collinson, D.L. (1987) 'Picking women: The recruitment of temporary workers in the mail order industry', *Work, Employment and Society*, 1(3): 371–87.

_____ (1992), *Managing the Shopfloor: Subjectivity, Masculinity and Workplace Culture*, Berlin: De Gruyter.

_____ and Collinson, M. (1997) 'Delayering managers: Time–space surveillance and its gendered effects', *Organization*, 4(3): 357–407.

Commission for Racial Equality (CRE) (2007) 'Ethnic minorities in Britain', available online at http://www.cre.gov.uk

Dale, M. (1994) 'Learning organizations', in C. Mabey and P. Iles (eds), *Managing Learning*, Milton Keynes: Open University Press, ch. 2.

Deal, T.E. and Kennedy, A.A. (1982) *Corporate Cultures: The Rites and Rituals of Corporate Life*, Reading, MA: Addison Wesley.

_____ (1984) 'Tales from the trails: A journey into the existential underbelly of American business', *Hospital Forum*, May–June: 16–26.

_____ (1999) *The New Corporate Cultures: Revitalizing the Workplace After Down-sizing, Mergers and Reengineering*, London: Orion Books.

Denison, D.R. (1990) *Corporate Culture and Organizational Effectiveness*, New York: Wiley.

Detert, J.R., Schroeder, R.G., and Mauriel, J.J. (2000) 'A framework for linking culture and improvement initiatives in organizations', *Academy of Management Review*, 25(4): 850–63.

Du Gay, P. (1996) *Consumption and Identity at Work*, London: Sage.

Equal Opportunities Commission (2007) *Moving on Up? The Way Forward*, Report of the EOC's Investigation into Bangladeshi, Pakistani and Black Caribbean Women and Work, March, Manchester: EOC.

Etzioni, A. (1961) *A Comparative Analysis of Complex Organizations*, New York: Free Press.

Eveline, J. and Booth, M. (2002) 'Gender and sexuality in discourses of managerial control: The case of women miners', *Gender, Work and Organization*, 9(5): 556–78.

Fey, C.F, Nordahl, C., and Zalterstrom, H.T. (1999) 'Organizational culture in Russia: The secret to success', *Business Horizons*, 42(6): 47–63.

Fielding, N. (1994) 'Cop canteen culture', in E. Stanko and T. Newburn (eds), *Just Boys Doing Business: Men, Masculinity and Crime*, London: Routledge.

Fineman, S. (1993) 'Organizations as emotional arenas', in S. Fineman (ed.), *Emotions in Organizations*, London: Sage. ch. 1.

Geertz, G.A. (1973) *The Interpretation of Cultures*, New York: Basic Books.

Gherardi, S. (1994) 'The gender we think, the gender we do in our everyday organizational lives', *Human Relations*, 47(6): 591–610.

_____ (1995) *Gender, Symbolism and Organizational Cultures*, London: Sage.

_____ (1996) 'Gendered organizational cultures: Narratives of women travellers in a male world', *Gender, Work and Organization*, 3(4): 187–201.

Goffman, E. (1961) *Asylums*, Garden City, NY: Anchor.

Gordon, G.G. and DiTomaso, N. (1992) 'Predicting corporate performance from organizational culture', *Journal of Management Studies*, 29(6): 783–98.

Grint, K. (1995) *Management: A Sociological Introduction*, Cambridge: Polity.

_____ (1998) *The Sociology of Work*, 2nd edn, Cambridge: Polity.

Grugulis, I., Dundon, T., and Wilkinson, A. (2000) 'Cultural control and the "culture manager": Employment practices in a consultancy', *Work, Employment and Society*, 14(1): 97–116.

The Guardian (2002) 'The rise of the godmothers', 28 May, available online at http://www.guardian.co.uk/women/story/0,3604,723327,00.html

Guardian Higher (1997) 'Women behaving badly', 14 October, p. ii.

Guest, D. (1992) 'Right enough to be dangerously wrong: An analysis of the In Search of Excellence phenomenon', in G. Salaman (ed.), *Human Resource Strategies*, London: Sage.

Harris, L.C. and Ogbonna, E. (1998) 'Employee reactions to organizational culture change efforts', *Human Resource Management Journal*, 8(2): 78–92.

_____ (2002) 'The unintended consequences of culture interventions: A study of unexpected outcomes', *British Journal of Management*, 13(1): 31–49.

Harrison, R. (1972) 'Understanding your organization's character', *Harvard Business Review*, 50(May–June): 119–28.

Hatten, W., Vinter, L., and Williams, R. (2002) *Dads on Dads: Needs and Expectations at Home and at Work*, Mori Social Research Institute Research Discussion Series, Manchester: EOC.

Hawkins, P. (1997) 'Organizational culture: Sailing between evangelism and complexity', *Human Relations*, 50(4): 417–40.

Haywood, C. (1993) 'Using sexuality: An exploration into the fixing of sexuality to make male identities in a mixed sex sixth form', Unpublished MA dissertation, University of Warwick, cited in M. Mac an Ghaill (ed.), *Understanding Masculinities*, Milton Keynes: Open University Press, ch. 3.

_____ and Mac an Ghaill, M. (1996) 'Schooling masculinities', in M. Mac an Ghaill (ed.), *Understanding Masculinities*, Milton Keynes: Open University Press.

Higher Education Statistics Agency (HESA) (2007) 'Latest HE Staff Data', Press release No. 111, available online at http://hesa.ac.uk

Hofstede, G. (1980) 'Motivation, leadership and organization: Do American theories apply abroad?', *Organizational Dynamics*, Summer: 42–63.

_____ (1991) *Cultures and Organizations: Software of the Mind*, London: McGraw Hill.

_____ (1994) *Uncommon Sense about Organizations: Cases, Studies and Field Observations*, Thousand Oaks, CA: Sage.

_____ (1998) 'Attitudes, values and organizational culture: Disentangling the concepts', *Organization Studies*, 19(3): 477–92.

_____ (2002) 'Dimensions do not exist: A reply to Brendan McSweeney', *Human Relations*, 55(1): 1355–61.

Hopfl, H. (1995) 'Performance and customer service: The cultivation of contempt', *Studies in Culture, Organizations and Society*, 1: 47–62.

Hort, B.E., Fagot, B.I., and Leinback, M.D. (1990) 'Are people's notions of maleness more stereotypically framed than their notions of femaleness?' *Sex Roles*, 23(3–4): 197–212.

Jablin, F.M., Putnam, L.L., Roberts, K.H. and Porter, L.W. (eds) (1987) *Handbook of Organizational Communication*, Newbury, CA: Sage.

Jenkins, R. (1985) 'Black workers in the labour market: The price of recession', in B. Roberts, R. Finnegan, and D. Gallie (eds) *New Approaches to Economic Life*, Manchester: Manchester University Press.

_____ (1988) 'Discrimination and equal opportunity in employment: Ethnicity and "race" in the United Kingdom', in D. Gallie (ed.), *Employment in Britain*, Oxford: Blackwell.

Johnson, P. and Gill, J. (1993) *Management Control and Organizational Behaviour*, London: Paul Chapman.

_____ _____ (1989) *When Giants Learn to Dance*, London: Simon & Schuster.

Kiesler, S., Sproull, L., and Eccles, J.S. (1985) 'Pool halls, chips and war games: Women in the culture of computing', *Psychology of Women Quarterly*, 9: 451–62.

Kunda, G. (1992) *Engineering Culture: Control and Commitment in a High-Tech Corporation*, Philadelphia, PA: Temple University Press.

Lage, E. (1991) 'Boys, girls and microcomputing', *European Journal of Psychology of Education*, 1: 29–44.

Legge, K. (1994) 'Managing culture: Fact or fiction', in K. Sisson (ed.), *Personnel Management: A Comprehensive Guide to Theory and Practice in Britain*, Oxford: Blackwell, pp. 397–433.

Leidner, R. (1993) *Fast Food, Fast Talk*, Berkeley, CA: University of California Press.

Lloyd-Jones, R., Lewis, M.J., and Eason, M. (1999) 'Culture as metaphor: Company culture and business strategy at Rayleigh Industries, c1945–60', *Business History*, 41(3): 93–7.

Lupton, T. (1963) *On the Shopfloor*, Oxford: Pergamon.

Marshall, J. (1995) *Women Managers Moving On*, London: Routledge.

McIntyre, A. (1971) 'Is a science of comparative politics possible?', in A. McIntyre (ed.), *Against the Self Images of the Age: Essays in Ideology and Philosophy*, London: Duckworth.

McKinley, R., Sanchez, C.M., and Schick, A.G. (1995) 'Organizational downsizing: Constraining, cloning and learning', *Academy of Management Executive*, 14(3): 32–44.

McSweeney, B. (2002), 'Hofstede's model of national cultural differences and their consequences: A triumph of faith—A failure of analysis', *Human Relations*, 55(1): 89–118.

Mills, A.J. (1988) 'Organization, gender and culture', *Organization Studies*, 9(3): 351–69.

239

_____ (1995) 'Managing subjectivity, silencing diversity: Organizational imagery in the airline industry— The case of British Airways', *Organization*, 2(2): 243–69.

Morgan, G. (1986) *Images of Organization*, London: Sage.

Moss Kanter, R. (1985) *Change Masters: Corporate Entrepreneurs at Work*, London: Allen & Unwin.

_____ (1989) *When Giants Learn to Dance*, New York: Simon and Schuster.

Myers, K. (2002) 'The terrible sight of a female terrorist', *Daily Telegraph*, 27 October, available online at http://www.telegraph.co.uk/comment/personal-view/3583369/The-terrible-sight-of-a-female-terrorist.html

Myers, P. (2002) 'Customers, boardrooms and gossip: theme repetition and metapatterns in the texture of organizing', *Human Relations*, 55(6): 669–90.

Newton, P. (1991) 'Computing: An ideal occupation for women?', in J. Firth-Cozens and M.A. West (eds), *Women at Work: Psychological and Organizational Perspectives*, Buckingham: Open University Press, pp. 143–53.

Newton, T. and Findlay, P. (1996) 'Playing God? The performance of appraisal', *Human Resource Management Journal*, 6(3): 42–58.

O'Barr, W. and Atkins, B. (1980) '"Women's language" or "powerless language"?', in S. McConnell-Ginet, R. Baker, and N. Furman (eds), *Women and Language in Literature and Society*, New York: Praeger.

Ogbonna, E. and Harris, L.C. (1998a) 'Managing organizational culture: Compliance or genuine change?', *British Journal of Management*, 9: 273–88.

_____ _____ (1998b) 'Organizational culture: It's not what you think...', *Journal of General Management*, 9: 273–88.

_____ and Wilkinson, B. (1990) 'Corporate strategy and corporate culture: The view from the checkout', *Personnel Review*, 19(4): 9–15.

Ouchi, W. (1981) *Theory Z*, Reading, MA: Addison-Wesley.

Panteli, A., Ramsey, H., and Beirne, M. (1997) *Engendered Systems Development: Ghettoization and Agency*, Paper published in Proceedings of the Sixth International IFIP Conference, 'Women, Work and Computerization: Spinning a Web from Past to Future', Bonn, 24–27 May.

Parker, M. (2000) *Organizational Culture and Identity*, Sage: London.

Pascale, R.T. and Athos, A.G. (1982) *The Art of Japanese Management*, Harmondsworth: Penguin.

Peters, T. and Waterman, R. (1982) *In Search of Excellence*, New York: Warner Communications.

Prokos, A. and Padavic, I. (2002) 'There oughtta be a law against bitches: Masculinity lessons in police academy training', *Gender, Work and Organization*, 9(4): 439–59.

Rafaeli, A. and Sutton, R.I. (1987) 'Expression of emotion as part of the work role', *Academy of Management Review*, 12(1): 23–37.

_____ _____ (1989) 'The expression of emotion in organizational life', *Research in Organizational Behaviour*, 11: 1–42.

Roy, D. (1960) 'Banana time: Job satisfaction and informal interaction', *Human Organization*, 18(2): 156–68.

Schein, E. (1985) *Organizational Culture and Leadership*, San Francisco, CA: Jossey Bass.

_____ (1990) 'Organizational culture', *American Psychologist*, February: 109–19.

Schneider, W.E. (1994) *The Reengineering Alternative: A Plan for Making Your Current Culture Work*, New York: Irwin.

Scotland on Sunday (2002) 'Can you hear me? We are all going to be blown up', 27 October.

Shade, L.R. (1993) *Gender Issues in Computer Networking*, Paper presented at Community Networking: The International Fee-Net Conference, Ottawa, August.

Sharpe, K. (1998) *Red Light, Blue Light: Prostitutes, Punters and the Police*, Aldershot: Ashgate Publishing.

Silvester, J., Anderson, N.R., and Patterson, F. (1999) 'Organizational culture change: An intergroup attributional analysis', *Journal of Occupational and Organizational Psychology*, 72: 1–23.

Smelser, N.J. (1992) 'Culture: Coherent or incoherent', in R. Munch and N.J. Smelser (eds), *Theory of Culture*, Berkeley, CA: University of California Press, pp. 3–28.

Smircich, L. (1983a) 'Concepts of culture and organizational analysis', *Administrative Science Quarterly*, 28: 339–58.

_____ (1983b) 'Studying organizations as cultures', in G. Morgan (ed.), *Beyond Method: Strategies for Social Research*, London: Sage.

Smith, P.B. (2002) 'Review article and response: Culture's consequences—Something old and something new', *Human Relations*, 55(1): 119–35.

Thompson, W.E. (1983) 'Hanging tongues: A sociological encounter with the assembly line', *Qualitative Sociology*, 6: 215–37.

Trice, H.M. (1993) *Occupational Subcultures in the Workplace*. Ithaca, NY: ILR Press.

Turkle, S. (1984) *The Second Self: Computers and the Human Spirit*, New York: Simon & Schuster.

_____ (1988) 'Computational reticence: Why women fear the intimate machine', in C. Kramarae (ed.), *Technology and Women's Voices: Keeping in Touch*, New York: Routledge & Kegan Paul.

Tyler, M. and Wilkinson, A. (2007) 'The tyranny of corporate slenderness: Corporate anorexia as a metaphor of our age', *Work, Employment and Society*, 21(3): 537–49.

Utley, A. (2003) 'Army struggles to integrate women', *Times Higher*, 7 February, p. 4.

Ward, M. (2001) 'Gender and promotion in the academic profession', *Scottish Journal of Political Economy*, 48(3): 283–302.

Watson, R.J. (1987) *Sociology, Work and Industry*, 2nd edn, London: RKP.

Wilkinson, M., Fogarty, M., and Melville, D. (1996) 'Organizational culture change through training and cultural transmission', *Journal of Organizational Change Management*, 9(4): 69–81.

Williamson, D. (2002) 'Forward from a critique of Hofstede's model of national culture', *Human Relations*, 55(11): 1373–95.

Willis, P. (1977) *Learning to Labour: How Working Class Kids Get Working Class Jobs*, Aldershot: Saxon House.

Wilmott, H. (1993) 'Strength is ignorance, slavery is freedom: Managing culture in modern organizations', *Journal of Management Studies*, 30(4): 515–51.

Wilmott, R. (2000) 'The place of culture in organization theory: Introducing the morphogenetic approach', *Organization*, 7(1): 95–128.

Wilson, F.M. (1992) 'Language, technology, gender and power', *Human Relations*, 45(9): 883–904.

_____ (1997) 'Computing, computer science and computer scientists: How they are perceived', in R. Lander and A. Adam (eds), *Women in Computing*, Exeter: Insight Books, ch. 13.

_____ (2003) 'Can compute, won't compute: Women's participation in the culture of computing', *New Technology, Work and Employment*, 18(2): 127–42.

Woods, N. (1993) 'Talking shop: Sex and status as determinants of floor apportionment in a work setting', in J. Coates and D. Cameron (eds), *Women in their Speech Communities*, 4th edn, Harlow: Longman.

Zimmerman, D. and West, C. (1975) 'Sex roles, interruptions and silences in conversation', in B. Thorne and N. Henley (eds), *Language and Sex: Difference and Dominance*, Newbury, MA: Rowley House.

241

12 Teams and Teamworking

Introduction

We have seen how managers may attempt to manage through improving organizational culture; teams and teambuilding are other ways in which managers may manage. Teamwork has emerged in recent years as one of the most important ways in which work is being reorganized (Delarue et al., 2008). Teams may offer empowerment, job enrichment, and a vehicle for delivering better results. There are those who suggest links between teamworking and organizational performance (Womack et al., 1990; Hammer and Champy, 1993; Katzenbach and Smith, 1993).

In this chapter, we will look at what teams and teamworking potentially offer, but we will also think about why the potential benefits may not always be realized, providing a critique of prescriptive unitarist views of the topic.

This chapter covers:

- teamwork and teamworking;
- popular views of teamworking;
- a historical view of teamworking;
- making claims about teamworking;
- teamworking and gender.

Teamwork and teamworking

There is no generally accepted definition of 'teamwork' (Delarue et al., 2008). Teamworking can offer a benign alternative to repetitive Tayloristic or Fordist work routines through the process of job enrichment and self-management (Buchanan, 1993; Carr, 1994). Workers in teams might be multi-skilled, and might routinely rotate tasks, organize and allocate their own work, prioritize tasks, select team members, and assume responsibility for product or service output and quality. Teamworking can represent an extension to employee involvement by offering a degree of influence and control over day-to-day working. Teamworking can replace inflexible, dehumanizing work methods with more humanistic, involving ones. Teamwork has been advocated by socio-technical systems ideas, by the quality of working life movement during the 1960s and 1970s, and by advocates of total quality management (TQM) in the 1980s, business process re-engineering (BPR), and popular management thinkers such as Drucker (1988) and Peters (1989). The performance of teams within organizations is important to managers when considering the performance of the organization as a whole and there is evidence to support the proposition that teamwork improves organizational performance (Delarue et al., 2008). Teamworking is found in cellular manufacturing, and in high involvement or high-performance work systems (Lawler, 1992), as well as in human resource management rhetoric (Beer et al., 1984).

Teamworking has been advocated with almost religious zeal by management consultants and academics (Proctor and Mueller, 2000): Katzenbach and Smith (1993)—then partners in the New York office of *McKinsey and Company*—talk of the wisdom of teams and see them as a means to deliver results well beyond those that individuals acting alone in a non-teamworking environment could achieve.

Popular views of teamworking

Katzenbach and Smith, and the wisdom of teams

Katzenbach and Smith (1993) claim to have talked with hundreds of people in more than fifty teams in thirty companies and beyond to discover what differentiates various levels of team performance, where and how teams work best, and what management can do to enhance their effectiveness. Organizations included *Motorola*, *Hewlett-Packard*, and the *Girl Scouts*. They point out that a team is not simply any group working together; rather, to understand how teams deliver extra performance, it is necessary to distinguish between teams and other forms of working group.

A group's performance is a function of what its members do as individuals. A team's performance includes both individual results and 'collective work products' (ibid.: 112): 'A team is a small number of people with complementary skills who are committed to a common purpose, set of performance goals, and approach for which they hold themselves mutually accountable' (ibid.: 113). The essence of the team is common commitment. Teams develop direction, commitment, and momentum by working to shape a meaningful purpose. Most successful teams do this in response to a demand from higher management. Management is responsible for clarifying the charter, rationale, and performance challenge for the team, but management must leave enough flexibility for the team to develop its own specific goals, timing, and approach. The best teams invest effort in exploring, shaping, and agreeing a purpose that belongs to them both collectively and individually. They encourage open-ended discussion and active problem-solving meetings, and there is mutual accountability. The best teams also translate their common purpose into specific performance goals, such as reducing poor quality work or responding to customer demand within a shorter time period. Performance goals are symbols of accomplishment that motivate and energize. They challenge the people on the team to commit; drama, urgency, and a healthy fear of failure combine to drive them to an attainable, but challenging, goal.

Size matters: effective teams can encompass between two and twenty-five people. Small size—that is, fewer than ten members—is an indicator of success: large numbers have trouble interacting effectively, and face problems including finding enough space and time in which to meet. Teams must also develop the right mix of skills—that is, technical or functional expertise, problem solving, decision-making skills, and interpersonal skills.

Katzenbach and Smith believe that teams will become the primary unit of performance in high-performance organizations, enhancing existing structures without replacing them. But they acknowledge that, with teams, comes organizational and personal risk: for example, there may be personal career risks. Management has to share control and accept a measure of unaccustomed trust—and for cultures with an inherent orientation toward individualism, the team approach may require a leap of faith.

A critique of Katzenbach and Smith

Katzenbach and Smith do not claim to have researched team performance. Like other consultants—for example, Tom Peters—they are talking from their experience and their personal point of view. They say that they used interviews for gathering data, but beyond this admission, little is known of the interview process or how the interview data was analysed. They adopt a utilitarian or 'hard' human resource management (HRM) approach (Storey, 1995). They present a unitarist view of management in which workers and managers are in pursuit of a common aim—that is, higher productivity. While team-based

243

approaches are being criticized, downsized, and abandoned, these authors appear undaunted by the growing evidence that results of team efforts often fall short. They are also inclined to ignore public-sector, or third-sector, examples.

Katzenbach and Smith play down the intrinsic qualities and dimensions of teamworking, such as job motivation and job satisfaction, or the social benefits. Little attention is paid to team member's feelings and personal reflections (Metcalf and Linstead, 2003). Metcalf and Linstead (2003) argue that this approach to teams is 'masculinist'—that is, that it favours and privileges masculinist conceptions of teamwork behaviours and actions. It adopts a masculinist discourse that emphasizes managing control and performance, with the 'soft' components of teams—that is, the sensitivities and intimacies of team members (traditionally linked to feminine qualities)—being marginalized and subordinated.

Belbin and team roles

Because a great deal of work in organizations is now carried out in teams, it might be important to consider whether the members of the team work well together so that it is effective. One way in which effective team performance has been promoted is through looking at team roles and the work of Meredith Belbin, an early proponent of team roles. 'Team roles' are described as 'a pattern of behaviour that characterizes one person's behaviour in relationship to another in facilitating the progress of the team' (Belbin, 2000: xv), a number of which can be identified. These team roles are distinguished from functional roles. 'Functional roles' are those that relate to a person's job role and function in the organization: for example, marketing manager. They are the roles of the employees in terms of the job's technical demands, and the experience and knowledge that it requires. Most people know the functional demands of a job and often people are chosen to be members of teams on the basis of their functional roles—but a team made up of functional roles might not be effective and may benefit from learning about the importance of team roles. Team roles focus on the interface of technical or professional jobs with other people; they enable people to adjust their jobs and each other. For a team to be high performing, it needs a balance, or spread, of naturally occurring functional and team roles; the ideal blend depends on the goals and tasks that the team faces. The focus is therefore on the process through which a team of people makes decisions and implements them.

Others have also identified team roles in their research. The most team roles were identified by Davis et al. (1992), who found fifteen, while Parker (1990) found only four—the fewest. There is some overlap between different sets of roles that all of these authors describe, but some roles seem to be unique to each.

For Belbin, the development of the team role concept arose from observing, over a period of nine years, teams of managers on training courses playing management games in which team performance was measured in terms of 'winning' or 'losing'. Belbin originally described, from his research, eight team roles (Belbin, 1981), but later increased that number to nine (Belbin, 1993). He believes that there are only a limited number of ways in which people can usefully contribute in teamwork. The essential contributions are: coordinating the team's efforts; imparting drive; creating ideas; exploring resources; evaluating options; organizing the work; following up on detail; supporting others; and providing expertise. These contributions are translated into roles. Individuals outstanding in one role are often weak in another—hence the allowable weaknesses.

To identify each person's natural team roles, Belbin created the 'self-perception inventory' (SPI). Colleagues who know a team member well may also use observer checklists. Table 12.1 presents Belbin's team roles in more detail.

A team member may contribute more than one role to a team; each team member can be described in terms of his or her team role contribution pattern. The most competent managers seem to be able to function well in both a primary and a secondary team role (Belbin, 1981). Individuals vary greatly in their patterns of team role. Some combinations are unlikely to be found in the same person: for example, a shaper and teamworker are an unlikely combination (Belbin, 1981). Who combines with whom to make

TABLE 12.1 Belbin's team roles

Team role	Description	Allowable weaknesses
Plant	Creative, imaginative, serious-minded, knowledgeable, solves difficult problems, unorthodox	Inclined to ignore practical details, too preoccupied to communicate effectively
Resource investigator	Extrovert, enthusiastic, curious, explores possibilities, develops contacts, responds to challenge	Over-optimistic, loses interest once initial enthusiasm has passed
Coordinator	Mature, confident, good chair, calm, controlled, clarifies goals, promotes decision making, delegates	Can be seen as manipulative, no more than ordinary in terms of intellect or creative ability
Shaper	Challenging, thrives on pressure, has the drive to overcome obstacles, outgoing, dynamic	Prone to provocation, can be highly strung; offends people
Monitor evaluator	Strategic and discerning, sober, prudent, sees all options and judges accurately	Lacks drive and ability to inspire or motivate others
Teamworker	Cooperative, mild, perceptive, diplomatic, listens, builds, sensitive	Indecisive in difficult situations
Implementer	Disciplined, reliable, hard-working, conservative, efficient	Can be inflexible and slow to respond to new possibilities
Completer/finisher	Painstaking, conscientious, searches out errors and omissions, follows through, delivers on time	Inclined to worry unduly, reluctant to delegate
Specialist	Single-minded, dedicated, can provide rare and specialized skills	Contributes in narrow way, dwells on technicalities

an effective team is, then, of central importance. Complementary combinations of people prove to be far more effective in their work performance than people with similar profiles competing with each other.

Belbin has claimed to be able to predict the performance of teams through knowledge of each team member's team role. Given team role profiles for each team member in which all team roles were strongly represented across the profiles—that is, a 'balanced' team—the team would be predicted to be high performing; where certain team roles were absent, the team would have lower success.

A critique of Belbin

One of the criticisms of Belbin's work is that what constitutes success or high performance in real teams in real organizations, rather than in artificially constituted management games, may be more complex (Senior, 1997). Winning or losing can rarely be measured in real organizational settings; what usually counts are data such as customer complaints. There are also more concepts associated with high-performing teams than only team roles: at least thirty-five concepts have been associated with high-performing teams (ibid.). There is, in fact, little evidence to support Belbin's original premise; there is a paucity of research that attempts, in a systematic way, to test team role theories in real teams in real organizations. What evidence there is tends to concentrate on the psychometric properties of different ways of measuring individual's team roles (Furnham et al., 1993), and the relationship between self-perception measures and those used by observers who know the participants (Parkinson, 1995). There is also a lack of published research on the psychometric properties of the current nine-role version of the self-perception inventory.

Fisher and Hunter (1998) have found that the team roles might be seen to fall into only two general categories—that is, 'task' and 'relationship' roles. Relationship roles include chairman, teamworker, and resource investigator, all of whom are good communicators: the chairman knows how to use the team's combined human resources; the teamworker has a strong interest in people; and the resource investigator develops wide networks of external contacts. The company worker works for the company rather than in pursuit of self-interest; he or she will work well with a broad cross-section of people. The task roles include plant, monitor evaluator, completer finisher, and shaper. For example, the clever individualistic and solitary plant produces ideas and suggestions that fill a role that allows the team's work to proceed. The disinterested monitor evaluation, who specializes in evaluating alternate courses of action, is especially useful when the team is facing crucial decisions. And the completer finisher attends to details, while the shaper galvanizes the team into goal-directed activity.

A historical view of teamworking

It is important, then, to have an appreciation of what those who promote teams have to gain; it is also important to look at the critique of popularist views of teamworking to gain a balanced view. But where has this interest in teams come from?

Team-based work, as an approach to organizing work, has a long pedigree (Benders and Van Hootegem, 1999; Buchanan, 2000). Teams, we might argue, were used to build pyramids and to row galleys across oceans. In the management literature, the benefits of teamworking—that is, a reduction of boredom and an increase in output—were recognized in the 1920s by researchers looking at industrial fatigue. Group work was seen as affecting morale and productivity in the Hawthorne studies. Consequently—particularly in at least the last two decades—teamwork has become increasingly popular in organizations. By 1990, almost half of the largest US companies said that they were using self-managed work teams for at least some employees (Cohen et al., 1996). In the UK, team-based working was found to be used for most of their employees in 65 per cent of workplaces (Cully et al., 1998). This current wave of interest in teamworking draws on two main traditions: socio-technical theory and Japanese industry (Proctor and Mueller, 2000).

Teamworking in socio-technical theory

Socio-technical theory evolved from the work of the London-based *Tavistock Institute* in the 1950s. Trist and Bamforth (1951) studied coal-mining methods, showing how automation displaced the autonomous multi-skilled groups that had operated under the old 'hand-got' method. Trist and Bamforth reintroduced multi-skilled, self-selecting group working. They recognized, documented, and publicized the approach—but did not, as Buchanan (2000) notes, invent it: workers seem to have created autonomous group work in response to adverse working conditions. These ideas about autonomous groups were particularly picked up in Scandinavia (Benders and Van Hootegem, 1999). The most well-known and controversial example of this autonomous group working is found at *Volvo* plants at Kalmar and Uddevalla (Berggren, 1992; Sandberg, 1995), where team-based manufacturing was introduced to alleviate recruitment and retention difficulties (Buchanan, 2000). Unfortunately, in the midst of economic crisis in Sweden in November 1992, *Volvo* announced that it would close the Uddevalla plant in 1993 and Kalmar in 1994. All of *Volvo*'s Swedish assembly was concentrated in the main traditional line plant in Gothenburg.

EXAMPLE Teamworking at *Volvo*

In *Volvo*'s small car plant at Uddevalla, Sweden, in a typical example, a group of nine workers assembled a car from beginning to end. They conferred with each other while working, resulting in the completion of the entire car before the morning coffee break. The team, like all others in the plant, had no supervisor (Sandberg, 1995). The remarkable successes of the two plants at Kalmar and Uddevalla are documented by Berggren (1992). For example, during the three years for which *Volvo* Uddevalla was in operation, productivity (that is, assembly hours per car) improved by more than 50 per cent.

The *Volvo* experiment was not without its critics. For example, Womack et al. (1990: 101) disparaged both Kalmar and Uddevalla as 'neo-craft nostalgia', arguing that the Uddevalla plant's productivity was uncompetitive. Berggren (1992) and Sandberg (1995) argue the opposite.

Teamwork has been seen to 'empower' workers by providing them with the opportunity for increased control over their work (Sewell, 1998; Harley, 1999). Empowered employees are more positively disposed to workplace management, more committed to their organizations, and able to make better use of their skills and problem-solving capabilities—all of which contributes to superior organizational performance (Dunphy and Bryant, 1996; Harley, 2001). Drawing on the logic of socio-technical systems theory, as teams involve self-regulation or self-control, team members can utilize their knowledge skills and judgement to solve production problems as they arise and to devise more effective work processes, enhancing productivity and efficiency (Cohen et al., 1996). Teams enhance employee discretion, which, in turn, feeds into motivation, satisfaction, and commitment. Similar arguments are to be found in relation to empowerment and high-performance work systems (Ramsey et al., 2000).

But how much autonomy do teams have in practice? In assessing this, we must assess the extent of management trust in the team. There should be no input from management in any decision making; teams that are truly autonomous are accepted by management as full and equal partners (Murakami, 1997). The following nine task areas of teamworking are one way in which we might judge how autonomous a team is (Gulowsen, 1979; Murakami, 1997).

STOP AND THINK **How autonomous is the team?**

To establish how autonomous a team is, we might consider the following questions.

1. Who selects the team leader?
2. Who decides on new members of the team?
3. Who decides on the distribution of work within the team?
4. How flexibly can the team's time be used?
5. Who accepts additional work for the team to complete?
6. How is the team represented in the wider organization?
7. Who decides on methods of production?
8. Who decides and sets production goals in terms of output?
9. Who decides and sets production goals in terms of quality?

Murakami (1997) used similar questions to look at levels of team autonomy in 'lean' production systems in fourteen car plants across the world. He found that full autonomy was not found in any of the teams studied, but that teams can influence management's decisions to some degree. Teams are given considerable autonomy about production (that is, work distribution and quality) and in self-organization (that is, team leader selection and representation outside the team). Management's power in prime task areas of production within the car industry, however, remains unchallenged by the introduction of teamwork.

Rosabeth Moss Kanter (1994) also discusses these kinds of issues when she discusses the dilemmas of teamwork. There are four kinds of inequalities that can drive a wedge between individuals and the team. Teams can be comprised of people who have different statuses: each member will be aware that he or she will be returning to his or her original role at some stage, so may slip into deference patterns that give those with higher status more airtime, give their opinions more weight, and generally provide a privileged position in the group. The seductiveness of the hierarchy has emotional roots; the emotions that make it easy to reproduce hierarchy are principally fear and comfort. Crossing a powerful figure in a group can make individuals afraid of later retribution. The comfort factor, meanwhile, dictates that it is easy to maintain familiar patterns of relationships and interaction. Knowledge and information make some members of the team more powerful and effective in the team. Unequal distributions of skill and personal resources, such as verbal skill, access to information-bearing networks, or levels of interest, divide people. Further, outsiders or newcomers may feel more uncomfortable about participating and speaking up in teams. Declaring people a 'team', then, does not automatically make them one—just as seeking decisions in which many people have a voice does not ensure that democratic procedures prevail.

Teamwork is often seen as a way of achieving desired work attitudes. Managers in the UK and USA, in companies such as *Disney* and *IBM*, were keen to adopt this feature, which they perceived to be inherent to the way in which successful Japanese companies were working. In fact, the word 'team' was not used in Japan itself until teams became fashionable in Western countries (Benders and Van Hootegem, 2000).

Teams in Japanese industry

Teamworking in the Japanese context in 'Western' countries appears to take three forms (Benders and Van Houtegem, 2000). Firstly, it is the idea that the company or organization is the team; each individual has a responsibility for this. It refers to a collective spirit, and conveys the necessity of desired cooperative spirit when establishing Japanese companies in the West. The term 'Team *Toyota*' was used to describe the various methods used to socialize employees into the Japanese organizational culture of 'community of fate' that *Toyota* wished to create in Kentucky (Besser, 1996).

The second form is 'offline' teams: for example, quality control circles. These would usually be small regular meeting groups of volunteers who discussed, proposed, and helped to implement improvements to the production or service process. Quality circles became very popular in the USA and some European countries in the 1980s, because they were believed to be the key to Japan's economic success.

The third type embodies the principle of waste elimination in labour time, which is important for 'lean production'. Here, the basic work group is the team. Proponents of Japanese working practices would argue that the removal of 'slack'—that is, all human and material 'waste'—from the manufacturing operation is enabled by the dynamic work team (Kenney and Florida, 1993). The dynamic work team is at the heart of the lean factory (Womack et al., 1990). Team members need to acquire additional skills, such as simple machine repair, quality checking, housekeeping, and materials ordering. They need to think actively to contribute to superior performance. It must be noted, however, that the term 'team'—particularly in the *Toyota* context—should not be equated with autonomy; neither does the team have the right to determine membership.

Japanese teamworking is based on the *Toyota* model, which is little different from classic scientific management. Here, there is minimum staffing, multitasking, multi-machine operation, repetitive short-cycle work, powerful first-line supervision, and a conventional hierarchy (Buchanan, 1994: 219). British workers at the *Toyota* assembly line in Derby, for example, perform narrowly specified, individual tasks, designed in the best scientific management tradition, and supported by shelves of thick instruction manuals, continually improved and updated by the workers themselves (Buchanan, 2000).

A critique of the socio-technical and Japanese models

Group and individual autonomy is one of the key characteristics of socio-technical thinking. Japanese and socio-technical traditions differ in terms of autonomy and hierarchy (Benders and Van Hootegem, 1999). Not all teamworking will empower workers: there will be real variations in the distribution of power, resulting from how work is structured and the context in which teamworking takes place. It is possible that teamworking can lead to disempowerment and deskilling in lean production settings, characterized by direct management control, repetitive task routines, and heightened labour discipline (Danford, 1998). Others have warned about the coercive and potentially totalitarian features of 'devotional' team culture and ideology (for example, Barley and Kunda, 1992). There appears to be a small, but growing number of critical in-depth studies of teamworking (see, for example, McKinlay and Taylor, 1996; Pollert, 1996; Knights and McCabe, 2000; Procter and Mueller, 2000).

Teamworking is not, however, simply a new and more sophisticated form of managerial oppression of labour. There are likely to be positive and negative effects for employees. Employees can derive substantial benefits, as well as suffer the work intensification pressures of teamworking (Berggren, 1993). While Batt et al. (2002) report that self-directed teams and employee participation in offline problem-solving groups is linked to low quit rates from the telecommunications industry, there are occasions on which teamworking and an individual's authority over that team may clash.

EXAMPLE **When 'sorry' is the hardest word**

Manchester United manager Sir Alex Ferguson refused to apologize publicly to David Beckham for gashing his eyebrow with a football boot that he had kicked in a fit of temper. The wound was bad enough that it was reported as still bleeding two hours later. It is thought that Sir Alex believed apologizing would undermine his authority over the team. Do you agree?

(*Source: Daily Telegraph*, 29 February 2003)

Making claims about teamworking

So should we be wary of the positive claims being made about teamwork? Many researchers are sceptical about the claims for a number of reasons. Teams have been implemented overwhelmingly by management explicitly as a means to enhance performance (Proctor and Mueller, 2000). Teamwork can be fundamental to competitive advantage—particularly in relation to quality of product and of customer service, front-line problem solving, and time to market for product and service innovations (Buchanan, 2000). The managerial agenda is that satisfied and committed employees will contribute to organizational success (Applebaum et al., 2000); teamwork is not a manifestation of concern with employees' quality of working life (Proctor and Mueller, 2000). Further, not all members of a team experience enhanced job enrichment, or job motivation (Buchanan, 2000). Employees may see enhanced discretion negatively: the autonomy offered by teamworking is very much on management's terms. Employees may have little discretion over the way in which work is organized (Mulholland, 2002).

Looking at teamwork from the point of view of employees, Barker (1999) investigated how teams work to exert control over their members' behaviour. Workers are pressed to give more of their time and energy, to identify with the goals of the organization, and to collaborate effectively with their co-workers. This impacts on their individual autonomy and personal lives. Mulholland (2002) found resistance among workers to management's attempts in teamworking to disguise control—which shatters any illusion of unity that management or consultants may retain. While teamworking may be promoted for the greater unity that it may bring, there can be contradictory consequences.

STOP AND THINK **A case of contradiction in teams**

Professional football players perform their work in teams. Even though they work together in matches, they are rivals in the internal competition for limited places in the team of eleven players that a manager selects from a squad comprising sometimes more than thirty professionals. One player sums up the ruthlessness of rivalries in the following way: 'At the end of the day, you know, everyone is in it for themselves. And quite often players would shit on each other if it came to it' (Roderick, 2006: 251).

Critical accounts of teamwork discuss both positive and negative effects, arguing that while teamwork might empower employees, it also generates new forms of control that assist management in extracting labour from employees through work intensification (Marchington, 2000). If work is intensified, then we might expect to find heightened stress levels (Findlay et al., 2000a; 2000b). A combination of high demands and high production responsibility can have negative effects on employees' well-being—but teams that monitor their own, and others', behaviour do so more effectively than traditional or managerial control may. Sewell (1998) says, however, that this is done through vertical and horizontal surveillance: any employee discretion associated with teamwork is illusory and may well mask increased managerial control of production, even if that control comes from the team (Harley, 2001). For example, first, a team may decide to negotiate a consensus on how to shape its own behaviour to achieve organizational goals; this consensus will be translated into rules and procedures by, and for, the team. Rules such as 'We all need to be at work at the same time' go on to add 'And if you are more than five minutes late, you will be docked a day's pay' (Sewell, 1998: 410).

We need to be alert, then, to the petty tyranny that can arise in teams—that is, tyranny in the name of self-exploitation. Coercion and conflict can be camouflaged with the appearance of consultation and cohesion (Sinclair, 1992); managerial prerogative is likely to remain intact (Thompson and McHugh, 2002).

> **EXAMPLE** **How teamworking can create burnout contagion**
>
> Job-induced strain and burnout—that is, exhaustion, cynicism, and reduced professional efficacy—may transfer from one employee to another. This may particularly be the case in teams. Burnout develops in a social context: co-workers play an important part in the development of burnout and burnout symptoms expressed by colleagues may transfer to individual employees when they socialize with one another on the job or in informal meetings. This was found to be the case among eighty-five teams of *Royal Dutch Constabulary* officers (Bakker et al., 2006).

Ezzamel and Wilmott (1998) have looked at the introduction of teamworking to a company that they call StitchCo. Not all employees shared the same reaction to teamworking: the young, inexperienced, and least skilled, who had no family responsibilities and therefore less pressure to make up their wages through bonuses, were seen to reap the advantages of a team bonus level while working at below a minimum level of efficiency. This 'free-riding' created resentment among those who were working harder. Further, while teamwork appeared to deliver universal benefits, such as cost effectiveness and enhanced profitability for the company, it also concealed a variety of unsavoury features of work reorganization, including coercion masquerading as empowerment, and the camouflaging of managerial expediency in the rhetoric of 'clannism' and humanization (Knights and Willmott, 1987).

Knights and McCabe (2000) looked at the results of teamworking in an automobile manufacturing company. Supporting Ezzamel and Wilmott (1998), they found that there is no single experience of teamworking. They build on these findings to identify three reactions of employees to teamworking: 'bewitched'; 'bothered'; or 'bewildered'. Some are 'bewitched' by the discourse of teamworking, and internalize its norms and values. Some are 'bothered' and disturbed by its incessant intrusion into their lives, and by the reactions of colleagues, who seem enthralled by the team discourse. They are particularly bothered by the psychological warfare waged by management through an ideology of teamworking. There was distrust in management and cynicism towards teamworking; it was generally felt that management was trying to change their way of thinking in order to secure more output from employees for less return. Finally, there are those who are 'bewildered' due to teamworking's attack on established ways of doing things—that is, on working practices and trade demarcations that reflect and reinforce the employees' own sense of themselves.

Ezzamel et al. (2001) found a case in which the workforce actively resisted the introduction of teamworking. The workforce were 'unreasonably reasonable' (ibid.: 1067), arguing that teamworking was unworkable for many employees due to age and personality-related problems. The stamina of younger workers would put undue stress on older workers in the team, which was unfair. 'Lazy bastards' would be 'carried' by other team members; this would be unfair, because it would impede team performance and diminish rewards. Further, due to 'management's inability to manage 'properly', hard-working team members would be labeled 'lazy'. Some workers declared themselves 'loners'; others simply questioned the need for change. These workers revelled in the fact feeling that they knew better than management what teamwork really involved; they sought to expose an inadequate management that they supposed to be in control.

To test whether or not teamwork produced more positive or negative results, Harley (2001) analysed the British Workplace Industrial Survey. He found that while teamwork did not herald a transformation of work in which employees regained the discretion denied to them by Taylorist work organization, neither did it appear to involve reductions in discretion, increased work intensification, or stress. Put bluntly, team membership did not seem to matter much. Anderson-Connolly et al. (2002) found, however, that teamwork reduced satisfaction and contributed to worsening health among non-managers. But if we accept that teamwork is introduced to enhance performance and not to improve quality of working life for employees, it seems fanciful to expect to find major gains for employees. Further, teamwork is unlikely to present any challenge to existing hierarchical structures in which power and influence are exercised by virtue of position. Unless teams bring about a fundamental change in dominant patterns of work organization, they are unlikely to make a difference to employee discretion or orientations to work—and one person can still have a negative effect on a team.

EXAMPLE The bad apple

It is all too easy for a single negative team member to have a disproportionately bad effect on the whole group, research has found. Will Felps and his team found that there are three ways in which the team member can exert a negative influence:

- by withholding effort, which will provoke feelings of inequality;
- by having negative mood and morale, which will spread throughout the group;
- by violating personal norms—for example, making inappropriate religious or ethnic remarks—which may undermine trust.

The research concludes that organizations should take the 'bad apple' problem seriously, paying more attention to the negative dynamics produced by these people. The team should react to bad apples by attempting to motivate them or by rejecting them from the group.

(*Source: The Psychologist*, 2007)

So what does teamworking cost an organization? While organizations are eager to reap the benefits of teamworking, they may be less eager to count the cost (Dunphy and Bryant, 1996). There is a tendency to underestimate the implications that teamwork has for training—in particular, the short-term negative impact on performance that may be necessary for the benefits of teamworking to be fully exploited.

The issue of the management of teams is an interesting one. The team is supposed to be self-managing, so why would it need external management? The role of the 'team leader' has emerged as one of the most important issues for organizations introducing teamworking (Proctor and Mueller, 2000), but there are difficulties involved in recruiting team leaders. One of these is the fact that the obvious candidate is a previous supervisor—but he or she may not have the appropriate behaviour for managing a team. What leadership behaviour should he or she adopt? The encouragement of self-evaluation may be appropriate leadership behaviour in a team environment, but this will not always come easily to a former supervisor. Of course, if a team leader is brought in from the outside, this can lead to its own problems—in the form of resentment among the team.

Management, more generally, is affected by teamworking, which seems to demand a move away from command-and-control management towards a more participative style (Industrial Society, 1995). This does not, however, seem to happen in practice. For example, Proctor et al. (1995) found that the introduction of team-based cellular working brought with it a closed and uncommunicative style of management. Batt (2003) found that supervisors and middle managers opposed the use of self-managed teams. We need, then, to consider the politics of teamworking and whose interests are being served or threatened.

Teamworking and gender

While many think that teamwork offers opportunities for a high quality of working life to a broader range of employees, both men and women, compared to the hierarchical (Tayloristic) type of organization, this has been found not to be the case for all (Benschop and Doorewaard, 1998). Gender inequality is reproduced in both Tayloristic and team-based work organizations. For Taylor (1911), high pay and high output were associated with men, while women were expected to work less hard, spending as much time doing nothing or talking idly among themselves. Women were portrayed as less obedient, so their obedience needed to be encouraged through stricter control of their work by their male supervisors.

While this distinction was made at the beginning of the last century, the stereotype of the chattering female workers to whom social contacts are an important reason to engage in paid work, in addition to the pay cheque, is still well known. In contrast, one might expect the ideal worker in team-based work to be gender neutral—but a closer look suggests that there are 'common-sense' notions of masculinity attached to this type of worker, in terms of the willingness to invest in one's own talent in order to go to the top and through the characteristic of entrepreneurialism, in which the independence, responsibility, and the initiative ideally expected from group work members seem often to be linked to men and the masculinity of entrepreneurialism, rather than to women. Further, women's motivation and commitment to teamwork are seen as lessened by their care responsibilities in the home.

Conclusion

Despite sustained criticism of teamworking, the concept appears to have survived. Buchanan (2000) argues that there are a number of reasons why. Firstly, the concept of teamwork in Western societies has connotations of collaboration, mutual support, and commitment: who wants to be accused of 'not being a team player'? It has an irresistible appeal to our social and individual imperatives that are difficult to challenge or deny. Secondly, teamworking has connotations of shared skill, solving problems, and making decisions together. It provides opportunities to use and share our creativity, initiative, skill, and knowledge with others. Organizations rely on employees to provide quality of service to customers. Thirdly, the team concept is very flexible: it might involve three, or more than thirty-three, people. For example, the Italian car company, *Fiat*, created an international team of 300 to design a new vehicle for the Brazilian market. The creation of 'virtual teams' linked together through computer-supported cooperation remains to be researched.

It should be clear that the word 'team' can be used in many different ways; it assumes different meanings even within the context of Japanese-style management. The meaning of the word varies over time and between settings. We need to continue to ask how teams are used in particular situations, and to examine the politics and whose interests they serve. We also need to pay attention to both the positive and negative effects that teams can bring.

KEY POINTS

- Managing by improving or introducing teams and teamworking has been seen as a way of delivering better organizational performance and countering some of the negative effects of the routinization of work, such as boredom.

- Popularist views of teamworking include those from consultants such as Katzenbach and Smith, and Belbin. It is important to look at both the prescription and the critique of these views.

- Socio-technical theory advocated autonomous work groups or teams. This idea was applied at *Volvo* to alleviate difficulties with recruitment and retention.

- In contrast, Japanese teamworking appears to take different forms in Western countries. Japanese team-working based on *Toyota* as a model is little different from scientific management.

- There can be both positive and negative outcomes of teamworking. Not all teamworking will empower: gender inequality can be reproduced, autonomy can be very much on management's terms, and problems such as petty tyranny can arise. Politics play a part.

253

CASE STUDY

The case of S*titchco*

The following case study highlights some of the problems that may arise when implementing teamworking.

StitchCo was a family-owned, single-brand company manufacturing garments for retail stores. Under a traditional Tayloristic management system, there was a clear division between the conception and execution of work: management planned the work while labour did it. Employees were paid under a piecework payment system (that is, each was paid according to the number of 'pieces' of work that he or she made), which identified each person as the producer of the product. Each individual was responsible for maximizing his or her output and was rewarded accordingly.

A financial crisis in the company led to half of the company's manufacturing facilities being closed. *StitchCo* management thought that teamwork could provide a cost-effective, continuously improving way of enhancing profitability of the company, helping it to respond more rapidly to shifting market demands, competitive pressure, and opportunities. Management saw teamwork as a way of improving flexibility and speeds in response to fluctuating demand. It was planned to replace line work with teamwork. The change was announced without prior warning and teamwork was introduced into parts of the manufacturing operations immediately, before being gradually phased into other sites over a few years. It led to a 30 per cent increase in productivity.

The new teamwork method put machinists into self-managing teams. Teams typically comprised six machinists with mixed skill levels. With the introduction of teamwork, the division of conception from execution became blurred, because employees were expected to assume a degree of self-managed responsibility for organizing the work process collaboratively. They were rewarded for modifying work practices in ways that improved profitability. The first targets that they were now expected to meet were delivery, performance, and quality; the fourth was output.

There were a number of elements inherent in the new working practices. Workers were paid a flat-rate payment, supplemented by a team-based bonus system. The flat rate depended on an individual's skill band. He or she would be labelled high, medium, or low skilled; the higher the skills, the higher the pay. Any machinist who attained a minimum of 80 per cent efficiency in time and motion calculation tests based on the minutes required to perform a particular task was allocated to one of three bands—but skill bands could be lowered, as well as increased. The team-based bonus was designed to establish a clear link between performance and rewards. Teams were rewarded on the basis of quality and delivery, then on output and the cost/profit implications of their activities. The quality of teamwork was measured each week. The efficiency of teams was posted half-daily to motivate teams to outperform others.

The machinists in the high skill band had misgivings about the change, because they felt that they might lose by being in a team with less skilled machinists. A style change—that is, a change in the garment being produced by a team—meant lower levels of efficiency and reduction in pay. Such changes happened every three or four weeks. Management thought that it was in the interests of the higher-skilled workers to help the lower-skilled to improve their performance. Many machinists, however, were reluctant to manage themselves in the ways intended by management. Team members were not necessarily committed to improving or maximizing output, especially if that meant having to compensate for the poor performance of other team members. Machinists accused supervisors and managers of looking to the harder-working and more productive machinists to set the pace—but they were unrecognized and unpaid for this. Harder-working and more highly skilled machinists felt under pressure to get the team, as a whole, to earn an acceptable bonus.

For some, earning the bonus was comparatively unimportant. The flat-rate payment for 'just turning up' had been intended to signal a new ethos of trust, but allowed those who were least concerned about reaping the bonus to reap the benefit of others' efforts. Those who did want to maximize bonus were not willing to accept the responsibility of resolving any tensions and conflicts within teams.

(*Source:* Adapted from Ezzamel and Wilmott, 1998)

Questions

1. Why was there resistance to teamworking at *StitchCo*? (See Ezzamel and Wilmott, 1998.)

2. Ezzamel and Wilmott argue that teamworking can have the unintended effect of fermenting hostility towards management. How?

3. What could management have done differently?

FURTHER READING

Anderson-Connolly, R., Grunberg, L., Greenberg, E.S., and Moore, S. (2002) 'Is lean mean? Workplace transformation and employee well-being', *Work, Employment and Society*, 16(3): 389–413 This research provides some interesting findings on the effects of teamwork on non-managers and managers.

Barker, J.R. (2005) 'Tightening the iron cage: Concertive control in self-managing teams', in C. Grey and H. Willmott (eds), *Critical Management Studies: A Reader*, Oxford: Oxford University Press, ch. 10 This chapter tells the story of the implementation of self-managing teams in one organization. Instead of freeing the workers from Weber's iron cage of rational control, the iron cage appeared to draw tighter and constrain the organization's members more powerfully.

Belbin, R.M. (2000) *Beyond the Team*, Oxford: Butterworth Heinemann It is useful to know more about the prescriptive view of teams. Davies et al. (1992) is a book in a similar vein. A critique of Belbin can also be found in Manning et al. (2006).

Jones, O. (1997) 'Changing the balance? Taylorism, TQM and the work organization', *New Technology, Work and Employment*, 12(1): 13–23 This article presents the argument that Japanese-style teamworking is more than a passing fad.

Proctor, S. and Mueller, F. (eds) (2000) *Teamworking*, London: Macmillan This book features a selection of excellent and varied readings about teamworking, giving in-depth coverage of the subject.

Proctor, S., Fulop, L., Linstead, S., Mueller, F., and Sewell, G. (2004) 'Managing teams' in S. Linstead, L. Fulop, and S. Lilley (eds), *Management and Organization: A Critical Text*, Houndmills: Palgrave Macmillan, ch. 11 This chapter is particularly useful for making links between Taylorism and teamworking.

LINKS TO FILMS AND NOVELS

The Italian Job (1969) dir. P. Collinson This film shows a team, led by a character called Charlie Croker (played by Michael Caine), planning to rob a $4m shipment of gold from China that is being delivered to banks in Turin. Charlie assembles a team, plans the heist, and trains the team for the job.

RESEARCH QUESTIONS

1. Katzenbach and Smith (1993) talk about the wisdom of teams. How wise are they? What needs and whose needs do they serve?

2. 'Teamworking helps to obscure domination' (Sennett, 1998). Discuss.

3. Why would there be resistance to the introduction of teamworking? Whose interests does teamworking serve?

4. Wheelan (1999) describes the stages that teams go through in development. She says that you know when you are in the final stage of development when being on the team makes you feel better than Prozac. How much research evidence is there to support this very positive view? Should we be wary of the 'tyranny' of teams (Sinclair, 1992; Barker, 1993)? How much support is there for this rather negative view?

REFERENCES

Anderson-Connolly, R., Grunberg, L., Greenberg, E.S., and Moore, S. (2002) 'Is lean mean? Workplace transformation and employee well-being', *Work, Employment and Society*, 16(3): 389–413.

Applebaum, E., Bailey, T., Berg, P., and Kalleberg, A. (2000) *Manufacturing Advantage: Why High-Performance Work Systems Pay Off*, Ithaca, NY: Cornell University Press.

Bakker, A.B., Emmerik, H., and Euwema, M.C. (2006) 'Crossover of burnout and engagement in work teams', *Work and Occupations*, 33(4): 464–89.

Barker, J. (1993) 'Tightening the iron cage: Concertive control in self-managing teams', *Administrative Science Quarterly*, 38: 408–37.

_____ (1999) *The Discipline of Teamwork: Participation and Control*, Thousand Oaks, CA: Sage.

Barley, S. and Kunda, G. (1992) 'Design and devotion: Surges of rational and normative ideologies of control in managerial discourse', *Administrative Science Quarterly*, 37: 363–99.

Batt, R. (2003) 'Who benefits from teams? Comparing workers, supervisors and managers', *Industrial Relations*, 43(1): 183–212.

_____, Covin, A.J., and Keefe, J. (2002) 'Employee voice, human resource practices, and quit rates: Evidence from the telecommunications industry', *Industrial and Labor Relations Review*, 55(4): 573–94.

Beer, M., Spector, B., Lawrence, P., Quinn Mills, P., and Walton, R. (1984) *Managing Human Assets*, New York: Free Press.

Belbin, R.M. (1981) *Management Teams: Why They Succeed or Fail*, London: Butterworth-Heinemann.

_____ (1993) *Team Roles at Work*, Oxford: Butterworth-Heinemann.

_____ (2000) *Beyond the Team*, Oxford: Butterworth-Heinemann.

Benders, J. and Van Hootegem, G. (1999) 'Teams and the context: Moving the team discussion beyond existing dichotomies', *Journal of Management Studies*, 36(5): 609–28.

_____ _____ (2000) 'How the Japanese got teams', in S. Proctor and F. Mueller (eds), *Teamworking*, London: Macmillan, ch. 3.

Benschop, Y. and Doorewaard, H. (1998) 'Six of one and half a dozen of the other: The gender subtext of Taylorism and team-based work', *Gender, Work and Organization*, 5(1): 5–18.

Berggren, C. (1992) *The Volvo Experience: Alternatives to Lean Production in the Swedish Auto Industry*, Basingstoke: Macmillan.

_____ (1993) 'Lean production: The end of history', *Work, Employment and Society*, 7(2): 163–88.

Besser, T.L. (1996) *Team Toyota: Transplanting the Toyota Culture to the Camry Plant in Kentucky*, Albany: University of New York Press.

Buchanan, D. (1993) 'Principles and practice in work design', in K. Sisson (ed.), *Personnel Management in Britain*, Oxford: Blackwell, ch. 3.

_____ (1994) 'Cellular manufacture and the role of teams', in J. Storey (ed.), *New Wave Manufacturing Strategies*, Liverpool: Paul Chapman.

_____ (2000) 'An eager and enduring embrace: The ongoing rediscovery of teamworking as a management idea', in S. Proctor and F. Mueller (eds), *Teamworking*, London: Macmillan, ch. 2.

Carr, F. (1994) 'Introducing teamworking: A motor industry case study', *Industrial Relations Journal*, 25(3): 199–209.

Cohen, S., Ledford, G., and Spreitzer, G. (1996) 'A predictive model of self-managing work team effectiveness', *Human Relations*, 49(5): 643–76.

Cully, M., Woodland, S., O'Reilly, A., Dix, G., Millward, N., Bryson, A., and Forth, J. (1998) *The 1998 Workplace Employee Relations Survey: First Findings*, London: DTI.

Danford, A. (1998) 'Teamworking and labour relations in the autocomponents industry', *Work, Employment and Society*, 12(3): 409–31.

Davies, J., Millburn, P., Murphy, T., and Woodhouse, M. (1992) *Successful Team Building: How to Create Teams That Really Work*, London: Kogan Page.

Delarue, A., Van Hootegem, G.V., Proctor, S., and Burridge, M. (2008) 'Teamworking and organizational performance: A review of survey-based research', *International Journal of Management Reviews*, 10(2): 127–48.

Drucker, P. (1988) 'The coming of the new organization', *Harvard Business Review*, January–February: 45–53.

Dunphy, D. and Bryant, B. (1996) 'Teams: Panaceas or prescriptions for improved performance?', *Human Relations*, 49(5): 677–99.

Ezzamel, M. and Wilmott, H. (1998) 'Accounting for teamwork: A critical study of group-based systems of organizational control', *Administrative Science Quarterly*, 43: 358–96.

_____, _____, and Worthington, F. (2001) 'Power, control and resistance in "the factory that time forgot"', *Journal of Management Studies*, 38(8): 1053–79.

Findlay, P., McKinlay, A., Marks, A., and Thompson, P. (2000a) 'Flexible when it suits them: The use and abuse of teamwork skills' in S. Proctor and F. Mueller (eds), *Teamworking*, London: Macmillan, ch. 12.

_____ _____ _____ _____ (2000b) 'In search of perfect people: Teamwork and team players in the Scottish spirits industry', *Human Relations*, 53(12): 1549–74.

Fisher, S.G. and Hunter, T.A. (1998) 'The structure of Belbin's team roles', *Journal of Occupational and Organizational Psychology*, 71(3): 283–8.

Furnham, S., Steele, H., and Pendleton, D. (1993) 'A psychometric assessment of the Belbin team-role self-perception inventory', *Journal of Occupational and Organizational Psychology*, 66: 245–57.

Gulowsen, J. (1979) 'A measure of work-group autonomy', in L.E. Davis and J.C. Taylor (eds), *Design of Jobs*, 2nd edn, Santa Monica, CA: Goodyear, pp. 206–18.

Hammer, M. and Champy, J. (1993) *Reengineering the Corporation: A Manifesto for Business Revolution*, New York: Harper Collins.

Harley, B. (1999) 'The myth of empowerment: Work organization, hierarchy and employee autonomy in contemporary Australian workplaces', *Work, Employment and Society*, 13(1): 41–66.

_____ (2001) 'Team membership and the experience of work in Britain: An analysis of the WERS98 data', *Work, Employment and Society*, 15(4): 721–42.

Industrial Society (1995) *Self-Managed Teams*, London: Industrial Society.

Katzenbach, J.R. and Douglas, K. (1993) 'The discipline of teams', *Harvard Business Review*, 71(2): 111–25.

_____ and Smith, D.K. (1993) *The Wisdom of Teams: Creating the High Performance Organization*, Boston, MA: Harvard Business School Press.

Kenney, M. and Florida, R. (1993) *Beyond Mass Production: The Japanese System and its Transfer to the US*, Oxford: Oxford University Press.

Knights, D. and McCabe, D. (2000) 'Bewitched, bothered and bewildered: The meaning and experience of teamworking for employees in an automobile company', *Human Relations*, 53(11): 1481–517.

_____ and Willmott, H. (1987) 'Organizational culture as corporate strategy', *International Studies of Management and Organization*, 17(3): 40–63.

Lawler, E. (1992) *The Ultimate Advantage: Creating the High Involvement Organization*, San Francisco, CA: Jossey-Bass.

Manning, T., Parker, R., and Pogson, G. (2006) 'A revised model of team roles and some research findings', *Industrial and Commercial Training*, 38(6): 287–96.

Marchington, M. (2000) 'Teamworking and employee involvement: Terminology, evaluation and context', in S. Procter and F. Mueller (eds), *Teamworking*, London: Macmillan, ch. 4.

McKinlay, A. and Taylor, P. (1996) 'Power, surveillance and resistance', in P. Ackers, C. Smith, and P. Smith (eds), *The New Workplace and Trade Unionism*, London: Routledge, pp. 279–300.

Metcalf, B. and Linstead, A. (2003) 'Gendering teamwork: Rewriting the feminine', *Gender, Work and Employment*, 10(1): 94–119.

Moss Kanter, R. (1994) 'Dilemmas of teamwork', in C. Mabey and P. Iles (eds), *Managing Learning*, Milton Keynes: Open University Press, ch. 16.

Mulholland, K. (2002) 'Gender, emotional labour and teamworking in a call centre', *Personnel Review*, 31(3): 283–303.

Murakami, T. (1997) 'The autonomy of teams in the car industry: A cross-national comparison', *Work, Employment and Society*, 11(4): 749–57.

Parker, G.M. (1990) *Team Players and Teamwork: The New Competitive Business Strategy*, Oxford: Jossey Bass.

Parkinson, R. (1995) 'A silk purse out of a sow's ear', *Organizations and People*, 2: 25–31.

Peters, T. (1989) *Thriving on Chaos: Handbook for a Management Revolution*, New York: Harper & Row.

Pollert, A. (1996) '"Teamwork" on the assembly line', in P. Ackers, C. Smith, and P. Smith (eds), *The New Workplace and Trade Unionism*, London: Routledge, pp. 178–209.

Proctor, S. and Mueller, F. (2000) 'Teamworking: Strategy, structure, systems and culture', in S. Proctor and F. Mueller (eds), *Teamworking*, London: Macmillan, ch. 1.

_____ Hassard, J., and Rowlinson, M. (1995) 'Introducing cellular manufacturing operations, human resources and high-trust dynamics,' *Human Resource Management Journal*, 5(2): 46–64.

The Psychologist (2007) 'Bad apples at work', 20(4): 200.

257

Ramsey, H., Scholarios, D., and Harley, B. (2000) 'Employees and high performance work systems: Testing inside the black box', *British Journal of Industrial Relations*, 38(4): 501–33.

Roderick, M. (2006) 'A very precarious profession: Uncertainty in the working loves of professional footballers', *Work, Employment and Society*, 20: 245–65.

Sandberg, A. (ed.) (1995) *Enriching Production: Perspectives on Volvo's Uddevalla Plant as an Alternative to Lean Production*, Aldershot: Avebury.

Senior, B. (1997) 'Team roles and team performance: Is there really a link?', *Journal of Occupational and Organizational Psychology*, 70: 241–58.

Sennet, R. (1998) *The Corrosion of Character: The Personal Consequences of Work in the New Capitalism*, New York: Norton.

Sewell, G. (1998) 'The discipline of teams: The control of team-based industrial work through electronic and peer surveillance', *Administrative Science Quarterly*, 43: 397–428.

Sinclair, A. (1992) 'The tyranny of a team ideology', *Organization Studies*, 13(4): 611–26.

Storey, J. (ed.) (1995) *Human Resource Management: A Critical Text*, London: Routledge.

Taylor, F.W. (1911) *Scientific Management*, London: Harper Row.

Thompson, P. and McHugh, D. (2002) *Work Organization: A Critical Introduction*, 3rd edn, Houndmills: Palgrave.

_____ and Wallace, T. (1995) *Teamworking: Lean Machine or Dream Machine?*, Paper presented at the 13th International Labour Process Conference, University of Central Lancashire, Blackpool, April.

_____ _____ (1996) 'Redesigning Production through Teamworking: Case Studies from the Volvo Truck Corporation,' *International Journal of Operations and Production Management*, 16(2): 103–18.

Trist, E. and Bamforth, K. (1951) 'Some social and psychological consequences of the longwall method of coal getting', *Human Relations*, 4(1): 3–38.

Wheelan, S.A. (1999) *Creating Effective Teams: A Guide for Members and Leaders*, Thousand Oaks, Ca: Sage.

Womack, J.P., Jones, D.T., and Roos, D. (1990) *The Machine that Changed the World: The Story Of Lean Production—How Japan's Secret Weapon in the Global Auto Wars Will Revolutionize Western Industry*, New York: Rawson Associates.

Structure

13

Introduction

We looked at the logic and rationale of Taylorism, human relations, and job design in Chapter 4—that is, the rationale of making work more efficient and making jobs better for people: for example, applying the principles of scientific management to make the job simpler and cheaper, or redesigning jobs to make them more challenging and interesting.

In this chapter, we will be looking at bureaucracy, which represents a continuous drive towards rationalization and efficiency in organizations. Bureaucracy is designed to install rationality and eliminate emotionality. It can be viewed as 'organizational structure'—that is, a rational design for efficiency. From this point of view, creating an efficient organizational structure involves dealing with task and job division, performance, and control. This approach does not consider discussions about the allocation of people to those tasks and jobs; instead, the discussions about structure are abstract and depersonalized, rather than human-focused, which creates an image of objectivity and neutrality towards people fulfilling performance and control activities. Here, we are not thinking about job design, but about organizational design—that is, about how bureaucracy might structure an organization to make it more rational and efficient.

When discussing bureaucracy, it is usual to start with the work of Max Weber, a rational systems theorist who believed that modernity meant rationality and the spread of a scientific approach to living, of which principles bureaucracy was the embodiment. The chapter will then go on to look at rationality in the service sector—specifically, at *McDonald's* and the process of 'McDonaldization', because these represent good examples of the increasing rationalization process found in modern organizations. We also look at other forms of structure—for example, more organic structures—and how they have been researched.

By the end of the chapter, you will be able to identify the key strengths and weaknesses of the process of rationalization, of bureaucracy, and of other organizational forms. You will understand the links between bureaucracy and rationality, and structure in organizations.

This chapter covers:

- Weber on bureaucracy;
- the advantages of bureaucracy;
- the unintended consequences and dysfunctions of bureaucracy;
- bureaucracy, emotion, and gender;
- rationality and the service sector;
- the case of *McDonald's*;
- McDonaldization;
- organizational variation in structure.

Weber on bureaucracy

While Taylor had been a theorist-practitioner, Max Weber (1864–1920) was a writer on sociology and politics. Weber wrote on many topics, including the history of the piano and Freudianism (see Runciman, 1978), but is probably best known in management for his work on bureaucracy.

Weber described the process of rationalization underlying Western history—that is, a trend in which the traditional or 'magical' criteria of action were replaced by technical, calculative, or scientific criteria. Weber's (1930) study of the rise of capitalism argued that the 'spirit of capitalism' owed a lot to the practices and thoughts of the Calvinist Church, which, in turn, was enmeshed in logical, calculative thought—rationality that had spread from science, through politics, and into the new Protestant Church. Rationalization is a process whereby the means chosen to pursue ends can be determined by logical and rational calculation. The continuous drive towards greater rationalization and efficiency, according to Weber, is clear in every sphere of social, economic, and political life. With this process, relations between people increasingly come to take the form of calculations about the exchange and use of capabilities and resources. One key place in which this happens is in bureaucracies. Weber' study of bureaucracy focused on historical surveys of administrative systems, relying largely on documentary sources.

All organizations make provision for their continuance to ensure that they meet given aims; bureaucracy helps them do this. Bureaucracies are enterprises, or political parties, or other organizations (such as the Church), in which people discharge functions specified in advance, according to rules. Authority is wielded as tasks are allocated, coordinated, and supervised. Tasks are regulated through the organization's structure. The bureaucratic structure has become dominant in modern society, in both the public and private sectors. Bureaucracy is at work, for example, in the processes that try to ensure that fairness in student admission processes, in *National Health Service* waiting and treatment times, and many other everyday work processes.

EXAMPLE **Bureaucracy in further education**

Subject: Call Closed Report, Call Reference F0032397

Dear Sir

Your outstanding problem logged with the Facilities Helpdesk, call reference number F0032397, has now been closed. This is a status report with information on the last action taken by our support analyst, who has closed the call. The last action on this call took 0:05 and the call was closed at 15:45:12 on the 15/01/2008.

The solution to the call follows:

Light tube replaced above desk in J313 - DT 15.1.08

When reports of this type are prepared over something as simple as changing a light, is it any wonder that bureaucracy has become synonymous with 'red tape'?

Weber's starting point is authority. Authority gives those who have the right or legitimacy to give orders. The claims to legitimacy of authority come from three different sources, as follows.

1. *Legal authority* is based on rational grounds—that is, a belief in the rules and rights of those in authority to issue commands.

2. *Traditional authority* is based on traditional grounds—that is, the sanctity or sacredness of tradition and legitimacy of status.

3. *Charismatic authority* is based on charismatic grounds—that is, a devotion to the sanctity, heroism, or character of an individual.

In legal authority, obedience is owed to the office, whoever the incumbent may be; he or she has a right to issue commands. Legal authority is found in bureaucracy. In contrast, a monarch or a feudal lord would have traditional authority, and dynamic, influential characters would have charismatic authority. Legal authority and bureaucracy involve a levelling of status.

So in Weber's view, what are the characteristics of bureaucracy? According to Weber, modern officialdom functions in the following manner (adapted from Gerth and Wright Mills, 1948).

1. The principle of fixed and official areas of administration usually involves an order established by rules or regulations. Activities are distributed as official duties. The authority to give commands about these duties is distributed in a stable way and strictly delimited by rules concerning the coercive means that officials have. Subordinates know then whose orders they must obey and that they can be sanctioned if they fail to do so. Only suitably qualified individuals are employed.

2. Modern officialdom involves hierarchy, which means that there is a firmly ordered system in which those in lower office are under the command of those in higher office.

3. The management of the office is based upon written documents, which are preserved in their original form. The officials, the office materials, and the files make up the bureau or office.

4. Specialized office management presupposes thorough and expert training.

5. When the office is fully developed, official activity demands the full working capacity of the official.

6. The management of the office follows general rules that can be learned.

The official is in a vocation that requires work over a long period and for which the official needs to be qualified. Holding office is not to be exploited for, for example, rents or the exchange of services, as has been the case in the past. The official manages faithfully in return for security of employment. The job—at least in public authorities when Weber wrote—was held for life. Loyalty should be impersonal and functional, not personal, like that of the vassal, slave, or disciple; the official is not the personal servant of a ruler. The official enjoys social esteem. A superior authority appoints him or her, and the official receives a fixed salary for the job and is set on a career within the hierarchical order.

STOP AND THINK Weber: A world of men?

When you were reading about the 'slave', the 'vassal', and the 'official', what gender did you envisage them being? Bologh (1990: xiv) argues that Weber is describing a world of men who struggle for power—that is, men who strive to dominate their world and give meaning to, and find meaning in, that world. Would you agree?

The advantages of bureaucracy

Weber was keen to stress the technical advantages of bureaucratic organization. The decisive reason for the advance of bureaucratic organization has been its purely technical superiority over every other form of organization. There is precision, speed, lack of ambiguity, knowledge of the files, continuity, discretion, unity and uniformity, strict subordination, reduction of friction, and reduction of material and personal costs. All of these are raised to the optimum in a strictly bureaucratic organization. There are calculable rules, so there is a 'calculability' of consequences. Scientific management has a role to play in this process, because it provides the ideal vehicle for the imposition of military discipline in the factory.

Techniques such as Taylor's 'shop cards', which specify the daily routines of employees, are ideal for this process of bureaucratization.

Further, business is discharged 'without regard for persons' (Weber, 1978: 226); the division of labour in administration is put into practice according to purely objective criteria. All love, hatred, and purely personal, irrational, and emotional sentiments are excluded. In contrast, the 'lord' of older societies was capable of being moved by personal sympathy, kindness, favour, or gratitude. With rationalization comes the use of calculative devices and techniques—that is, formally rational means, including the division of labour, sets of rules, accounting methods, money, technology, and other means for increasing that rationality.

EXAMPLE Bureaucracy in pregnancy

Both women and the medical profession organize and manage productive lives, seeking to control, routinize, and make predictable the process of pregnancy and birth (Brewis and Warren, 2001). The need for this is clear in light of the fact that there were 708,708 births in England and Wales in 2008 alone (see http://www.statistics.gov.uk). An example of this organizing and planning is the 'birth plan' that Western women are usually encouraged to prepare for their labour; another example is the screening that is done to prevent genetic 'disorders'.

What other elements of bureaucracy are likely to be witnessed during pregnancy and birth?

The unintended consequences and dysfunctions of bureaucracy

There will always be unintended consequences of bureaucracy; bureaucracy can also manifest features that are 'materially irrational'. For example, bureaucracy can threaten individual freedom. Weber (1930: 181) recognized that bureaucracy might become an 'iron cage', meaning that our bureaucratic rules might ultimately confine us as solidly as if we were in a cage bound by iron bars. He speculated that the domination of the official in modern society could become more powerful than the slave owner of eras past.

Since Weber wrote about the ideal bureaucracy (an 'ideal type' being the purest, most fully developed version or benchmark), a good deal of work has focused on the dysfunctions of the bureaucratic form, or 'the menace' of bureaucracy: for example, by Merton (1936), Selznick (1949), and Gouldner (1954). As well as questioning the perfection of the 'ideal type', these writers discussed whether the opposition between organizational efficiency and the freedom of the individual was possible.

EXAMPLE Gouldner's case history of the bureaucratization of a gypsum factory

Gypsum rock is mined by blasting, like coal; the rock is pulverized and dried, and then used to make wall boards, which are used in the construction industry. In this gypsum factory, there were two production units, each with different patterns of social organization. The first—subsurface—mining operation was characterized by comparatively informal social relations and traditional work practices. In the second—that is, the surface—factory unit, there was more formal organization; practices were 'rationally' administered. In the mine, there were problems of absenteeism. Supervisors in the mine tried to enforce a 'no absenteeism' rule—only to realize that doing so in the mine was impossible: bureaucratic efforts to suppress absenteeism were not viewed as legitimate. There were, then, clear limits to the rational bureaucratic processes that could be introduced and enforced.

(*Source:* Gouldner, 1954)

Bureaucracy and the Holocaust

As we have seen, the 'ideal type' of bureaucracy is governed by a formal set of rules and procedures that ensures that operations and activities are carried out in a predictable, uniform, and impersonal manner. Personal relationships are excluded from organizational life.

Zygmunt Bauman (1989) showed the importance of bureaucratic organization to the death camps in Nazi Germany. According to Bauman, the genocide was an extreme application of bureaucratic logic, with a system of rules, uniformity, impersonality, and technical efficiency. Bauman argues that the Holocaust, rather than being a specifically German problem, was the result of modernity and bureaucracy. Modernity and bureaucracy created unintended conditions that led to the demise of moral responsibility.

Yet moral responsibility and perception played their part in the Holocaust: while killing involved technical efficiency, uniformity, and impersonality, the methods of killing were reconsidered when it was found that shooting was perceptually stressful for those who had to carry out the killings. The Nazis therefore deemed shooting to be insufficiently 'productive', not only because of the increasingly large numbers of people to be killed, but also because it resulted in unavoidable levels of perceptual stimulation for those carrying out the killing. The Nazi regime therefore found its solution in the form of permanent concrete gas chambers, in which the perpetrators need not see, hear, or feel the human consequences of their actions (Russell and Gregory, 2005).

Bureaucracy, emotion, and gender

Can bureaucracy be devoid of emotion? We think of bureaucracy, organizational order, and efficiency as matters of rational, non-emotional activity; we envisage cool, clear strategic thinking that should not be sullied by messy feelings. Good organizations are places in which feelings are managed, designed out, or tamed. We have known for four decades, since C. Wright Mills (1951) wrote about white-collar workers, of the need for workers to control their feelings and that facial expressions (for example, a smile) can become a matter of professionalism. As Wright Mills (1963: 272) wrote: 'She [sic] must smile when it is time to smile.' It is often thought that emotions interfere with rationality (Fineman, 1996)—that is, that rationality and effective leadership would be damaged by, for example, a sign that the leader cannot cope (Sachs and Blackmore, 1998). But it is only the expression of some emotions that are frowned upon: anger and competitiveness are generally condoned in bureaucratic organizations, while other emotions, such as sadness, fear, and some forms of sexual attraction and vulnerability, are taboo (Martin et al., 1998: 434). Emotion management operates through the exclusion of negative emotions—that is, emotions that are neither easy to encounter nor contribute to productivity.

STOP AND THINK

Can organizations—and, in particular, bureaucracy—be free of all unwanted emotion? Can you, for example, imagine a political party free of all public embarrassment?

Writers (for example, Acker, 1990; Martin, 1990; Brewis and Grey, 1994; Witz et al., 1996) have suggested that while the rational-legal model presents itself as gender neutral, it actually constitutes a new kind of patriarchal structure. Ferguson (1984) also argues that bureaucracy is an organization of oppressive male power. Bureaucracy is both mystified and constructed through an abstract discourse of rationality, rules, and procedures. 'Discourse', as defined in the work of Foucault, refers to what is regarded as acceptable—in terms of what is permitted to be said and thought, who can and cannot speak, and with what authority, and who is regarded as 'normal' or 'abnormal'. The reality of organizational life is constituted through discourses that have a 'normalizing' effect on individuals, defining what and who is 'normal', 'standard', and 'acceptable' (Thomas, 1996). According to this view, bureaucracy is a construction of male domination. In response, bureaucrats, workers, and clients are 'feminized' as they develop ways of managing their powerlessness that, at the same time, perpetuate their dependence.

Pringle (1989), using the case of secretaries, shows how the relationship between the boss and the secretary is the most visible aspect of a pattern of domination to be found in modern bureaucratic structures—one that, according to Pringle, is based on desire and sexuality. Secretaries seem to contradict the criteria of the ideal bureaucracy. For example, they are far from being specialized, because they can be called upon to do almost anything. Further, there may be considerable overlap between their work and that of their boss. Finally, in bringing to bear the emotional, personal, and sexual, they represent the opposite of rationality, as discursively constituted. Pringle argues that the concept of rationality itself excludes the personal, the sexual, and the feminine. According to Pringle, the personal, sexual, and the feminine are perceived as associated with chaos and disorder, and therefore in opposition to rationality; the concept of rationality can thus be seen to have a masculine base.

Pringle and others (for example, Burrell 1984; 1987; Hacker and Hacker, 1987) have questioned whether bureaucratic forms have banished sexuality from organizational life. While the complete eradication of sexuality from bureaucratic structures has been a goal that many top decision makers have pursued, many managements content themselves with the incorporation and close containment of sexual relations in the non-work field. Human features, such as love, comfort, and sexuality, have been gradually expelled from bureaucratic structures and relocated in the family. Faced with this curtailment, significant numbers of men and women have resisted, so acts of intimacy have taken place in the past and will continue to take place in the future. This view stresses how male sexuality is routinely privileged within organizational practices, because sexuality and power are intertwined in everyday social interactions.

Men, then, are more likely to meet the requirements of bureaucratic organizations than are women. It is the male body—that is, its sexuality, minimal responsibility in procreation, and, conventionally, its control of emotions—that pervades work and work organizations (Acker, 1990). Bureaucrats need to be highly controlled and regimented, and lacking in desire: this is the 'male' body being privileged (Witz et al., 1996).

STOP AND THINK

Do you agree with the view that men better meet the requirements of the bureaucratic organization? How might you argue against this view?

Rationality and the service sector

More recently, jobs in the service sector have expanded, challenging employers to rationalize workers' self-presentation and feelings, as well as their behaviour (see Chapter 11). Employers may try to specify how workers should look, how their hair should be styled, and, in the case of women, how their make-up should look. Employers may try to specify what employees say, their demeanour, their gestures, and even their thoughts. To do this, they create scripts, uniforms, dress codes, rules, guidelines for dealing with customers and co-workers, and instructions about how best to think about their work and their customers.

This 'routinization' of human interaction is disconcerting, but explicit rules have become a significant feature of employment contracts in many mass service industries. For example, the personal appearance guidelines issued to *Walt Disney World* employees include 'Fingernails should not extend more than one-fourth of an inch beyond the fingertips' (Leidner, 1993: 9). These very explicit rules also include 'feeling' rules (Fineman, 1995): 'First, we practice a friendly smile at all times with our guests and among ourselves. Second, we use friendly courteous phrases ... "May I help you" ... "Thank you" ... "Have a nice day" ... "Enjoy the rest of your stay", and many others are all part of our working vocabulary' (Walt Disney Productions, 1982: 6). The *Walt Disney World* 'Magic Kingdom'—also known as 'the smile factory'—expects each member of staff (who are referred to as 'the cast') to show a constant smile even to those who are difficult, offensive, or threatening. A system of staff surveillance attempts to ensure that the guidelines are met. But the cast seeks out blind spots (for example, behind a large rock or a concrete pillar) in which to have a rest, chat, or smoke. The staff, then, resist these 'feeling rules' by taking illegitimate breaks (Van Maanen, 1991). As research has shown, they have also been known to slap misbehaving visitors hard across their chests with the seatbelts of ride vehicles.

Values and attitudes can be constructed and influenced through training programmes and corporate culture. We discussed Hochschild's research on emotional labour in Chapter 5. Hochschild (1983) shows how recurrent training for flight attendants is aimed at reinforcing the 'inside-out' smile. She documents how flight attendants were trained to repeat 'I know just how you feel', in order to calm passengers furious over a missed connection or other failures of service. Hochschild called this 'emotion work'—that is, the work of creating a particular emotional state in others, often by manipulating your own feelings. She showed that the result of regulating 'emotion work' was that the attendants became alienated from their feelings, their faces, and their moods. Some showed signs of resistance: for example, by spilling a Bloody Mary over an offensive passenger's lap. The following is another story from Hochschild's research:

A young businessman said to a flight attendant, 'Why aren't you smiling?' She put her tray back on the food cart and said, 'I'll tell you what. You smile first, then I'll smile'. The businessman smiled at her. 'Good,' she replied. 'Now freeze and hold that for fifteen hours.'
(Hochschild, 1983: 127)

EXAMPLE **The rules: An employer in a tie is best?**

Two men working in job centres questioned the issue of men's dress code in the office. The first, working in a job centre in Stockport, objected to the dress code for men, which included wearing a collar and tie; he had been disciplined for not wearing them. He argued at a tribunal that it was unfair that men had to wear a collar and tie, when women could turn up to work wearing what they liked, including T-shirts and football shirts. This, he said, amounted to unlawful sex discrimination: males were being treated less favourably than their female colleagues. The tribunal agreed with him (Bradley, 2003; Manners and McMyn, 2003).

A second male job centre employee, in Birmingham, was banned from wearing jeans to work. In response, he turned up to work in a kilt, lumberjack shirt, and loud multicoloured tie. He argued that his employers 'seemed happy for me to go to work like this, even though I looked like a pillock' (Manners and McMyn, 2003).

Increasing rationalization does not always bring about the intended outcomes. Smiling is not always interpreted as intended by 'rational' organizations and the 'smile' is not always 'read' correctly by customers: one customer attacked a checkout operator for 'flirting' with her husband. Also, call centres are not set up to bear the brunt of obscene phone calls, yet there have been numerous examples of obscene phone calls to operators (Keenoy, 1990, reported in Burrell, 1992).

The effect of increased rationalization on the workforce is, however, not always negative. Some will accept the tight scripting, because it saves them having to make the effort of thinking of appropriate words to say or ways in which to act. The standards of good work have been clarified for them, and the routines can act as shields against the insults and indignities that the worker might have to accept from the public (Leidner, 1993: 5). Further, it is possible to resist: some will refuse to smile (Hochschild, 1983), or will insist on their right to their own style (Benson, 1986).

Finally, it is interesting to note that most of us, as customers, know how to behave with service workers in order to fit the organizational routines. We have been 'fitted into' the routine of 'involuntary unpaid labor' (Glazer, 1984): for example, when we serve ourselves petrol at the petrol station, check ourselves in at the airport, gather up, bring, and unload groceries from our baskets in the supermarket, and clear away our rubbish in fast-food restaurants. We know not to order items in fast-food restaurants that are not on the menu and we know to line up for service. The garish colours and plastic seats are designed to make sure that we do not linger too long; our behaviour as customers is then influenced by the organization to 'fit' with its intentions—in this case, to have a fast turnover of customers.

The case of *McDonald's*

McDonald's and Taylorism

The routinization to be found at *McDonald's* shows a close link with the logic of Taylorism—that is, maximizing managerial control of work and breaking work down into its constituent tasks, which can be preplanned. The key to the success of *McDonald's* is its uniformity and predictability: customers know exactly what to expect. *McDonald's* promises that every meal will be served quickly, courteously, and with a smile. It promises fast service, hot food, and clean restaurants. To do this, it needs to use the principles of scientific management, coupled with centralized planning, centrally designed training programmes, approved and supervised suppliers, automated machinery, meticulous specifications, and systematic inspections. As a result, 'a quarter-pounder is cooked in exactly 107 seconds' and 'Our fries are never more than 7 minutes old when served'. Each restaurant aims to serve any order within 60 seconds (Beynon, 1992: 180). In order to ensure that this happens, customers are channelled through the restaurant by its layout and design, by the service routines, and by the relatively restricted menu on offer.

About three-quarters of the outlets are owned by franchisees rather than the corporation—owners of the franchises are able to retain control over pay scales, for example—but *McDonald's* requires that every outlet's production methods and products meet its precise specifications. This centrally managed regimen covers food preparation, book-keeping, purchasing, dealing with workers and customers, and virtually every aspect of the business. The food production is the most visible aspect of the regimentation—that is, for the customer. For the employee, a 'bible'—that is, the operations and training manual—demonstrates the proper placement and amount of ketchup, mustard, and pickle slices on each type of hamburger available. Lights and buzzers tell the crew when to take French fries out of the fat, while the French fry scoops specify the size of portion, and allow the worker to fill a bag and set it down in one continuous motion; specially designed ketchup dispensers squirt the correct portion of ketchup. Crew are also told in what sequence the components of a customer's order are to be gathered, what arm motion is to be used in salting the batch of fries, and to double-fold each bag before presenting it to the customer. Only minor variations in the execution of its routines are allowed. Customers are referred to as 'guests', so that all customers are potentially treated with respect and courtesy. Routinization and Taylorism are clearly in evidence, then, at *McDonald's*.

STOP AND THINK Cooking a hamburger

The following is an example of the original *McDonald's* procedure for cooking hamburgers.

Those grilling the burgers were instructed to put hamburgers down on the grill moving from left to right, creating six rows of six burgers. Because the first two rows are furthest away from the heating element, they were instructed to flip the third row first, then the fourth, fifth, and sixth, before flipping the first two (Love, 1986: 141–2).

How would you feel if instructions as detailed as this were to be found in recipe books? Would you follow the instructions (a) in your own home and (b) for an employer?

While the routinization and extreme standardization is clear, *McDonald's* does allow some experimentation. When an employee produces a new idea, it can be adopted (the Egg McMuffin and the Big Mac are examples of employee ideas), but the corporation will experiment, test, and refine the idea before it is implemented in a uniform way. Some products will also be found to differ depending on national or local context, despite the uniformity of approach. For example, in Norway, *McDonald's* sells grilled salmon sandwiches with dill sauce on a wholegrain bread (Ritzer, 1998: 85).

McDonald's also issues strict rules about safety, hygiene, and uniform. All workers have to wear a clean uniform, complete with hat and nametag. Brightly coloured nail polish, wearing more than two rings, and dangling jewellery are forbidden. Leidner (1993) shows how extensively these dress code rules stretched: one window worker always wore a piece of adhesive tape on his ear to hide a gold earring; while the tape was probably more offensive to the customer than the earring would be, management considered otherwise.

Performance is rated and each worker is awarded stars (worn on a badge), which are linked to pay and promotion prospects. The performance rating is made on the basis of an assessment, which lists criteria that must be met, such as: 'Greeting the customer: 1. There is a smile 2. Greeting is pleasant, audible, sincere 3. Looks customer in the eyes.' (from *McDonald's* 'Counter Observation Checklist', quoted in Fineman, 1995). Again, training programmes are designed to ensure that employee performance matches the specified guidelines. The *McDonald's* training centre near Chicago is called 'Hamburger University': the 'university' is on a 'campus'; the director is called 'the dean'; and the trainers are 'professors'. The trainers work from scripts prepared for them. Fineman (1995) wrote that they try to produce managers 'with ketchup in their veins'. Crew, managers, and franchisees learn that there is a '*McDonald's* way' of doing business and that any diversion from this would be wrong. The full training programme requires between 600 and 1,000 hours of work, and is required of all those who wish to own a *McDonald's* outlet. This, then, is the bureaucracy—that is, the set of rules, routinization, and standardization—that helps to constitute this organization, its structure, and its everyday functioning.

267

Working in a fast-food restaurant

Gabriel (1988) documented the experience of working in a fast-food restaurant in his book on working lives in catering (see Chapter 2). He interviewed in three London outlets of one fast-food company. Virtually all of the staff were in their teens or early twenties, and management was only slightly older. About one third of the workers worked part-time and several were students; most lived with their parents and, for many, it was their first job. Few expected to stay for more than a year.

Gabriel's research found that the jobs offered little intrinsic satisfaction and very few people found their jobs enjoyable. Most respondents spent most of their time doing only one job, such as cleaning, sweeping, serving at the counter, or in the kitchen. To get through the day, they had to fantasize: nineteen of the twenty-six workers said that they kept their minds on other things while they worked; only working on the till required concentration. Many had developed a contempt for the work that they did, describing them as 'crap jobs'. Some played games: for example, catching a girl's eye as she entered the restaurant and seeing if she joined their queue (if they were heterosexual males); some added personal touches to the burgers that they put together and wrapped, or bent the rules about how many burgers to make in any one batch, to see if they could get away with it. Breaking the rules, adding personal touches, and playing games broke the drudgery of work. As Burawoy (1981; 1985) notes, these games give some degree of control to workers and are tolerated by management because, in the end, they enhance the efficiency of work.

STOP AND THINK **Does routinization really lead to efficiency?**
The research findings that show how workers behave in these routinized jobs leaves us with a question: does increasing routinization really lead to greater efficiency, or are workers undermining the rules so much that at least some of the greater efficiency is potentially lost?

McDonaldization

There is a downside to the fast-food industry, concludes George Ritzer (1998; 2000). For example, the fast-food restaurant can be a dehumanizing setting in which to eat as well as to work. It can feel like dining—as well as working—on an assembly line. It minimizes contact among human beings, and it serves food that is high in calories, fat, sugar, and salt content. It has run afoul of environmentalists as well as nutritionists. And it contributes to a homogenization around the world: diversity of food choice is being reduced or eliminated.

STOP AND THINK How much choice do fast-food restaurants offer?

Burger King has had a slogan, 'Have it your own way', that implies that the customer's wish is its command. But what do you think would happen if you were to ask for your burger to be medium rare?

George Ritzer argues that fast-food restaurants such as *McDonald's* are the new model of rationalization, which built on many ideas found in bureaucratization; *McDonald's* is an extreme version of the rationalization process. He talks of 'McDonaldization', defining it as a process by which the principles of the fast-food restaurant are coming to dominate more and more sectors of US society, as well as that of the rest of the world. Ritzer notes that *McDonald's* did not develop in a historical vacuum; there were important precursors that provided the principles of the assembly line, scientific management, and bureaucracy. But although the fast-food restaurant adopts elements of these precursors, it takes a quantum leap in the process of rationalization. He believes that 'McDonaldization' has influenced education, work, travel, the family, and every other sector of society. The *McDonald's* model has proved to be irresistible.

According to Ritzer, four basic dimensions lie at the heart of the success of *McDonald's*, as follows.

1. *McDonald's* offers efficiency—that is, the optimum method of getting from a state of being hungry to a state of being full.

2. It offers food and service that can be easily quantified and calculated. We feel that we are getting a lot of food for a modest amount of money. People roughly quantify and calculate how long it will take to get fast food; they think that it will take less time to go to *McDonald's*, eat the food, and return home than it will to prepare the food at home.

3. It offers predictability: we know that the burger that we eat in one town will be the same as that which we eat in another and that the one that we order next week will be identical to that which we eat today.

4. Control is exerted over human beings, especially through the substitution of non-human technology for human. The humans do a limited number of tasks precisely as they are told to do them. Limited menus, few options, and uncomfortable seats lead diners to do what management wants them to do—that is, eat quickly and leave. Technology replaces human labour: for example, the soft drink dispenser shuts off when the carton is full, and the programmed cash register eliminates the need for cashiers to calculate prices.

The basic dimensions of McDonaldization—that is, efficiency, calculability, predictability, and increased control through technology—are manifest not only in fast-food restaurants, but also in a wide and increasing array of social settings throughout the world, including shopping malls, home shopping, and pre-prepared meals. These dimensions are also evident in factory farming. Burrell (1997: 138) takes this point one stage further when he says that *McDonald's* is an organization that is, in fact, *dependent* on the profitable death of cattle and chickens in profusion. Without efficient and cost-effective automated death, the cost of the Big Mac would be higher—an 'irrational' outcome for an organization that aims to achieve high levels of efficiency and productivity. The Nazi concentration camps, Burrell also notes, relied upon the relative automation of death too (see also Bauman, 1989).

Ritzer (1998) has gone on to document the continuation, if not acceleration, of the rationalization process in a book called *The McDonaldization Thesis,* and in another about credit cards (Ritzer, 1995). He argues that a 'new means of consumption' (Ritzer, 1998: 1) is evident in fast-food restaurants, credit cards, tourism, shopping malls, superstores, home shopping television networks, and other examples. Ritzer believes that 'McDonaldized' systems—through their rules, regulations, scripts, and so on—encroach upon, and ultimately threaten, the ability of the people working with these systems to think intelligently. Central planning and the considerable control that is exerted over franchisees, employees, and customers bring us back to a Weberian image of an 'iron cage of rationalization'. Ritzer says that this 'iron cage' is currently being constructed, piece by piece, by the various organizations and institutions that follow the *McDonald's* model—and it may be more escape-proof than Weber ever imagined.

Credit cards and fast-food restaurants share some interesting similarities: both represent radical change in society, yet neither is highly innovative; both rely heavily on advertising; both have been forced to engage in price competition; and both have tried to target teenage populations. While *McDonald's* rationalized the delivery of prepared food, credit card companies have rationalized the consumer loans business. Prior to credit cards, the process of obtaining a loan was slow, cumbersome, and non-rationalized; it now requires little more than the filling out of a short questionnaire. Credit bureaus and computerization mean that credit records can be checked and applications approved or rejected rapidly. The unpredictability of whether a loan will be approved has been greatly reduced. Credit card loans, like fast-food hamburgers, are being served up in a highly rationalized assembly line.

There are also degrees of McDonaldization to be found in surprising areas of life. Academia might be one domain that would be thought to be immune to this process—yet Ritzer believes that *McDonald's* has influenced even academia, medicine, and law. For example, parents and students increasingly approach universities as consumers, in the same way that they approach other consumption items. In so doing, they are looking for low price, convenience, efficiency, and absence of hassle. One way in which universities have responded to this is by opening satellite campuses in suburban areas or smaller towns that have not been well served by a central university, providing plenty of parking space and advanced technology. Further, universities increasingly offer distance learning, within which courses are transmitted by television, video, or video conferencing. We confront a future of accelerating McDonaldization in which *McDonald's* will remain powerful until the nature of society changes so dramatically that it is no longer able to adapt. Like scientific management, the assembly line, and bureaucracy, it leads to an ever more rational world.

STOP AND THINK **Are graduation days as an example of McDonaldization?**

Graduation day can resemble an experience similar to that of a drive-through *McDonald's* : the individual has only a moment of personal attention at the ceremony, and finds that he or she is only one in a long list of 'customers' for graduation that day.

What other features of graduation day make it similar to the experience of *McDonald's*?

Ritzer is, of course, not without his critics. He is accused of offering an analysis that is too simple, and also of being insensitive to the variety and diversity of consumer practices and local variations. It is argued—for example, by Parker (1998; 2002)—that Ritzer is making the judgement that food and service in fast-food restaurants are not as good as they used to be in traditional restaurants; he is condemning contemporary practices and is nostalgic for an older, quieter, slower world. He is also accused of neglecting gender analysis and the meanings that *McDonald's* has for women, or for people of different classes, races and regions. He is also accused of being too pessimistic (Alfino et al., 1998).

Organizational variation in structure

So far in this chapter, we have looked at bureaucracy and its features. We have also looked at how *McDonald's* presents an extreme version of the rationalization process that bureaucracy offers. We will now look at variation in structure.

Weber provided a single model of efficient organizations—that is, the 'bureaucratic ideal' type. But when social scientists came to study the structure of organizations in the late 1950s, they found a variety of organizational types, not one single unified type. Tom Burns and G.M. Stalker (1961) studied British firms in the textiles, heavy industry, and electronics industries, and found that firm structure varied depending on whether the firm was operating in a stable or fast-changing environment. Firms in industries such as textiles produced a familiar product, using well-established technology; product characteristics and consumer demand were relatively stable. These organizations conformed to a traditional bureaucratic model that Burns and Stalker defined as 'mechanistic'. In this relatively predictable environment, centralized decision making, specialization, sharply defined duties, formal rules, and hierarchical control were efficient ways in which to organize activity.

In contrast, in the electronics industry—a highly dynamic and innovative industry—consumer tastes were changeable. In response to this, the structures of firms in the industry were looser. Job definitions and boundaries between functions were more flexible, rules were less formalized, employees exercised more discretion, and hierarchy was less pronounced. Communication moved in a lateral, rather than a vertical, direction and contained a greater proportion of consultation, as opposed to directives and decisions. Individuals worked more collaboratively and seniority was based on expertise, rather than hierarchy. Burns and Stalker called these 'organic systems'. They concluded that when novelty and unfamiliarity—in both market situations and regarding technical information—become the norm for an organization, a fundamentally different kind of management system becomes appropriate from that which is appropriate in a relatively stable commercial and technical environment. Both mechanistic and organic management systems are 'rational' in that they may both be explicitly and deliberately created and maintained in order to exploit the human resource in the most efficient manner possible, in the given circumstances.

Paul Lawrence and Jay Lorsch (1967) pursued this theme of the 'appropriate' structure for organizations. They studied firms in the plastics, container, and packaged foods industries, looking specifically at the degree to which the stability and predictability of markets and technology varied between these firms. They asked, for example: 'What types of organizations are most effective under different environmental conditions?' They inferred that firms achieve higher levels of performance when managers align 'organizational properties' with 'environmental properties'. Their results were broadly consistent with those of Burns and Stalker, but they extended the principle to departments within organizations that faced differing levels of change and uncertainty. Lawrence and Lorsch coined the term 'contingency theory' to describe the idea that the structure of successful firms is contingent on the kind of environmental or other conditions in which they function. But Starbuck and Mezias (1996) note that Lawrence and Lorsch obtained no 'objective' measures of either organizational or environmental properties; rather, all of their data were based on managers' perceptions. It is likely, however, that managers would have varied in their perceptions of the environmental properties.

Joan Woodward (1965) chose to assess the effect of technology—specifically, of production technology—on organization. Technology was not the only variable, but it was the one most easily isolated for study. She studied a hundred firms and grouped production systems into eleven categories, but found that some—such as *Remploy*, which was set up to employ disabled people—did not fit into any of the eleven categories. She classified technologies on the basis of their complexity and level of sophistication: unit and small batch production; large batch and mass production; and continuous process production. Unit and small batch production is characteristic of craft production, and is found in the tailoring industry and in the manufacture of airplanes. Large batch and mass production are found, for example, in the car industry. Continuous process production is the most highly automated, in which materials flow continuously between operations with minimum human intervention, and is found, for example, in the chemical, oil refining, or bottling industries. Woodward found that organizations using mass production technology were more bureaucratized than those using small batch technology, and their productions jobs were more Taylorized and less skilled. Organizations using continuous process technology tended to have a more organic structure, and their production jobs carried more responsibility and skill. Woodward, like Burns and Stalker, believed that historical trends favoured a less rigid and alienating form of organization than mechanized bureaucracy offers.

Derek Pugh (1973) and others from the *Aston Group* (based in Birmingham) developed the idea that context determines the form of organization, and examined the variables or dimensions on which organizations differ. Six dimensions were selected:

- *specialization*—that is, the degree to which an organization's activities are divided into specialized roles;

- *standardization*—that is, the degree to which an organization lays down standard rules and procedures;

- *standardization of employment practices*—that is, the degree to which an organization has standardized employment practices;

- *formalization*—that is, the degree to which instructions and procedures are written down;

- *centralization*—that is, the degree to which authority to make certain decisions is located at the top of the management hierarchy;

- *configuration*—that is, the shape of the organization's role structure (for example, whether the chain of management command is long or short, and the breadth of span of control for managers).

The research found that, when the dimensions were measured and applied to different organizations, no two profiles were alike. There were, however, *similarities* in the profiles of a number of the organizations studied. The researchers then went on to analyse organizational context and its relationship with size, technology, and location of the organization. This showed that context is a determining factor—perhaps *the* determining factor overall—that shapes and modifies the structure of any organization.

It now appears to be agreed that a universally applicable bureaucratic model of organization does not exist and that the appropriate structure for a particular organization (if there is one) may be at least partly contingent on variables such as environmental uncertainty, and complexity, technology, and size. But contingency theory does not escape its critics: the assumption that inappropriate structure leads to lower performance has, for example, been questioned; Child (1997) argued that management has a wide discretion in choosing the organizational form that suits its preferences and philosophy. Contingency theory has also been criticized for neglecting the role of power, choice, historical accident, fashion, ideology, norms, and values in influencing structure. And some of the dimensions proved difficult to measure—in particular, environmental uncertainty (Blau and Meyer, 1987).

The steepest hierarchies are found in traditional bureaucracies, in contrast with idealized, flat organizations with team structures in which most, or at least some, of the responsibility and decision making is distributed. Some influential theorists have argued that decentralized, participative, and more democratic systems of control offer the most viable alternatives to the confines of bureaucracy and tight authoritarian control (for example, Follett, 1941; Lewin, 1948). Contemporary writers have consequently unleashed a flood of literature announcing the 'coming demise of bureaucracy and hierarchy' (Kanter, 1989: 351)—an issue at which we will look in more depth in the next chapter.

Conclusion

In this chapter, we have looked at how bureaucracy has been described and discussed, and at its advantages and disadvantages. We have looked at its features and manifestations in different sectors, and shown how it is alive and well.

STOP AND THINK

It might be argued that this chapter and Chapter 4 are misleading. Currently, the book leads you to understand that there has been a linear development of management thinking from early theorists, such as Taylor and Babbage, to the present day; Tsoukas and Cummings (1997) present an alternative view. They argue that we should abandon the idea that there has been a development of thinking about organization and management that has been underpinned by progression—that we should abandon the idea that we are part of a continuous progress. Rather than seeing the history of management as a 'stairway to heaven' going upwards and onwards, it should be viewed as a 'kaleidoscope', containing a number of discrete fragments that reveal a pattern, as noted by Foucault (1966). The sequence of patterns from the kaleidoscope obeys no inner logic and conforms to no universal norm of reason; fragments from the past will reappear now and again.

What support do you find for this image of history as a kaleidoscope? Would you agree with Tsoukas and Cummings? What would be the rationale for presenting a non-linear view of management thinking?

272

KEY POINTS

- Bureaucracy may be seen as a rational design for efficiency.

- Weber was keen to stress the technical advantages of bureaucracy—but there are also unintended consequences.

- *McDonald's* and other fast-food restaurants have been portrayed by Ritzer as the new model of rationalization, which has built on many ideas found in bureaucracy.

- Researchers have found that context can help to determine the form of organizational structure.

CASE STUDY

Cases of organizational structure: Two churches

Churches, like other organizations, make choices about how they organize and structure themselves. The Church of Scotland has a relatively flat organizational structure and no hierarchy. It is one of the largest organizations in Scotland, with around 600,000 members and 1,200 ministers, supported by more than 2,000 professional and administrative support staff. The support staff deliver the services at national and international level for the Church—that is, the day-to-day policymaking and practical decision making; they are organized into six main councils (for example, the Social Care Council offers services and specialist resources to people in need), a number of associated committees (for example, the Legal Questions Committee advises on questions of Church and constitutional law), and departments (for example, the human resources department).

The governing system is Presbyterian, which means that authority is shared and no single person or group has more influence or say than any other. The Church does not have one person who acts as head of the faith; rather, it is governed at three levels:

- at local parish level by a kirk session (elders presided over by a minister);
- at district level by a presbytery (all of the ministers in the district, an equal number of elders, and other ordained members, including those working in industry or prisons);
- at a national level by the General Assembly, which consists of around 400 ministers, 400 elders, and other ordained members.

The General Assembly is the supreme court of the Church of Scotland, and has the authority to make laws determining how the Church of Scotland operates and to establish the priorities for the coming year. The General Assembly meets once a year and is chaired by the Moderator, whose role is honorary and held for twelve months. The Moderator is not the head or leader of the Church, nor its spokesperson; if asked for an opinion on an important issue, the Moderator is expected to have in mind the views of the General Assembly or relevant Church board or committee. A Committee of the Assembly nominates the Moderator.

Unlike the Church of England, the Church of Scotland does not need to take orders from Parliament; the Church was given freedom from interference in spiritual matters. The Church of Scotland does keep in close touch with parliamentarians and contributes to the discussion on the issues of the day. The reigning monarch is not seen as the head, although she is given a special place in that she attends, or is represented, in each General Assembly. She is not, however, able to influence debates.

In contrast, the Church of England has at its head the Archbishop of Canterbury as its most senior cleric, while the British monarch is the Supreme Governor of the Church of England. There is a direct link between Church and State. There is also a hierarchy of archbishops, bishops, and dioceses. The Church is divided into two provinces, each headed by archbishops, who are the most senior clergy in the Church. The Archbishop of Canterbury is head in the south of England and is the 'first among equals' of the bishops—that is, he is the spiritual leader. The Archbishop of York is head of the north of England, with pastoral oversight of the bishops in that province and responsibility for clergy discipline. Each of the two provinces contain a number of dioceses—that is, defined administrative areas presided over by a bishop, who has exclusive jurisdiction within it. The forty-three dioceses in England are further divided into arch-deaconries run by archdeacons, deaneries, and parishes. An archdeaconry, headed by an archdeacon appointed by the bishop, may include the whole of a diocese, but is usually smaller. A deanery, presided over by a dean, is a collection of parishes within an archdeaconry. The smallest administrative unit is the parish. A parish priest, usually called a 'vicar' or 'rector', oversees each parish; a parochial church council will collaborate with the priest in the everyday running of the parish church. The majority of the Church's 13,920 clergy are involved in parish ministry. The two archbishops and twenty-four bishops sit in the House of Lords. The Church of England is described as being 'episcopally' led by the 108 bishops and the General Synod decides its practices.

The General Synod is the central governing and legislative body that meets as a national assembly of the Church of England. It can, for example, legislate to pass measures that, if approved by resolution of each House of Parliament and granted royal assent, become part of the law of England. The General Synod has three houses: one for the diocesan bishops; one for the elected representatives of the clergy; and the other for the laity of the Church.

A system of discipline is necessary for any organization. In the last decade, the Church of England has acknowledged the need to review its governmental and disciplinary procedures (General Synod, 1996; 1997).

(*Sources:* http://www.churchofscotland.org.uk; http://www.cofe.anglican.org; http://www.bbc.co.uk/religion)

Questions

1. What are the advantages and disadvantages of the different organizational structures for:

    A the laity?

    B the management?

2. Which structure do you prefer and why?

FURTHER READING

Chandler, J. (2000) 'Organizational behaviour and the individual: A critique of a consensus' in J. Barry, J. Chandler, H. Clark, J. Johnston, and D. Needle (eds), *Organization and Management: A Critical Text*, London: Business Press, ch. 1 This chapter discusses emotion and bureaucracy as well as morality.

Handel, M (2003) *The Sociology of Organizations: Classic, Contemporary and Critical Readings*, London: Sage Chapter 1A looks at Max Weber, bureaucracy, and legitimate authority, and includes a critique.

Noon, M. and Blyton, P. (2007) *The Realities of Work*, 3rd edn, Basingstoke: Palgrave Macmillan The chapter on emotional work defines emotional labour and demonstrates why it is important. It also looks at employees' reactions to emotional labour.

Parker, M. (2002) *Against Management: Organizations in the Age of Managerialism*, Oxford: Blackwell Chapter 2 is entitled 'McBureaucracy'.

Schlosser, E. (2001) *Fast Food Nation: What the All-American Meal is Doing to the World*, London: Penguin Schlosser is a journalist who offers all sorts of interesting facts about fast food, such as that Americans now spend more money on fast food than on higher education, personal computers, or new cars. On any given day, about a quarter of the adult population in the USA visits a fast-food restaurant.

Watson, T. (2002) *Organizing and Managing Work*, Harlow: Pearson Chapter 7 on the structure, culture, and the struggle of management control contains a good section on the ubiquity and inevitability of bureaucracy, as well as its failings and contradictions.

LINKS TO FILMS AND NOVELS

Brazil (1985) dir. T. Gilliam This film incorporates drama, comedy, and fantasy to illustrate what can go wrong in bureaucracy. In an Orwellian vision of the future (see below), the people are completely controlled by the state, but technology remains almost as it was in the 1970s. Sam Lowry is a civil servant who spots a mistake in one of the pieces of paperwork passing through his office. The mistake leads to the arrest of an innocent man and, although Lowry attempts to correct the error, the situation goes from bad to worse.

Heller, J. (1961) *Catch-22* Among other things, this book is a general critique of bureaucratic operation and reasoning. It sets out the absurdity of living by the rules of others—whether friends, family, governments, systems, religions, or philosophies. Heller suggests that rules left unchecked will take on a life of their own, forming a bureaucracy in which important matters such as those affecting life and death are trivialized, and trivial matters such as clerical errors assume enormous importance. He concludes that the only way to survive such an insane system is to be insane oneself.

Huxley, A. (1931) *Brave New World* This is a science fiction novel about a utopian world state in which family, culture, art, literature, science, and religion have been eliminated. The world state is built around the principles of Henry Ford, who is worshipped by society. Humans are genetically bred and pharmaceutically anaesthetized to serve the ruling order passively. The novel warns us of the lengths to which organization and bureaucracy might potentially go to gain compliance.

Orwell, G. (1949) *Nineteen Eighty-Four* The novel depicts a fictional future—the 1984of its title—in which the hero, Winston Smith, lives in a totalitarian state within which 'Big Brother is watching you'. Pervasive surveillance is used to watch the citizens and the Thought Police have two-way telescreens in the living quarters of Party members and in public areas. Winston Smith is a bureaucrat in the Records Department of the Ministry of Truth. In this story, then, the efficiency of bureaucracy plays a big part.

Pilkington Garimara, D. (1996) *Follow the Rabbit Proof Fence* Bureaucracy can affect some lives very dramatically. This story shows the impact of government policy and bureaucracy on the lives of three Aborigine girls taken away from their family in 1931. Official government policy decreed that all 'half-caste' children (that is, those born to an Aboriginal mother and 'white' father) be taken away from kin and land in order to be 'made white'. The architect of the removal policy was the Chief Protector of Aborigines, a man driven by the vision of a society cleansed of 'half-castes'.

RESEARCH QUESTIONS

1. Why should management, thinking about rationalization, be seen as a kaleidoscope and not in a linear fashion?

2. George Ritzer argues that McDonaldization constrains or eliminates people's creativity. Discuss.

3. Filby (1992) described the everyday life in a betting shop. The management tried, and partly succeeded, in using women's bodies and personalities to promote the product—but the female employees 'turned the tables' (Thompson and McHugh, 2002: 144). How did they do this?

REFERENCES

Acker, J. (1990) 'Hierarchies, jobs, bodies: A theory of gendered organizations', *Gender and Society*, 4(2): 139–58.

Alfino, M., Caputo, J.S., and Wynyard, R. (eds) (1998) *McDonaldization Revisited: Critical Essays on Consumer Culture*, London: Praeger.

Bauman, Z. (1989) *Modernity and the Holocaust*, Cambridge: Polity.

Benson, S.P. (1986), *Counter Culture: Saleswomen, Manager and Customers in American Department Stores 1890–1940*, Urbana, IL: University of Illinois Press.

Beynon, H. (1992) 'The end of the industrial worker?', in N. Abercrombie and A. Warde (eds), *Social Change in Contemporary Britain*, Cambridge: Polity.

Blau, P.M. and Meyer, M.W. (1987) *Bureaucracy in Modern Society*, 3rd edn, New York: Random House.

Bologh, R.W. (1990) *Love or Greatness: Max Weber and Masculine Thinking—A Feminist Inquiry*, London: Unwin Hyman.

Bradley, R. (2003) 'Employers get a dressing down', *The Scotsman*, 28 March, p. 6.

Brewis, J. and Grey, C. (1994) 'Re-eroticizing the organization: An exegesis and critique', *Gender, Work and Organization*, 1(2): 67–82.

_____ and Warren, S. (2001) 'Pregnancy as project: Organizing reproduction', *Administrative Theory and Praxis*, 23(3): 383–406.

Burawoy, M. (1981) 'Terrains of contest: Factory and state under capitalism and socialism', *Socialist Review*, 11(4): 58, 83–124.

_____ (1985) *The Politics of Production*, London: Verso.

Burns, T. and Stalker, G.M. (1961) *The Management of Innovation*, Oxford: Oxford University Press.

Burrell, G. (1984) 'Sex and organizational analysis', *Organization Studies*, 5(2): 97–110.

_____ (1987) 'No accounting for sexuality', *Accounting, Organization and Society*, 12: 89–101.

_____ (1992) 'The organization of pleasure', in M. Alvesson and H. Wilmott (eds), *Critical Management Studies*, London: Sage, ch. 4.

_____ (1997) *Pandemonium: Towards a Retro-Organizational Theory*, London: Sage.

Child, J. (1997) 'Strategic choice in the analysis of action, structure, organizations and environment: Retrospect and prospect', *Organization Studies*, 18: 43-76.

Ferguson, K.E. (1984) *The Feminist Case against Bureaucracy*, Philadelphia, PA: Temple University Press.

Filby, M. (1992) 'The figures, the personality and the bums: Service work and sexuality', *Work, Employment and Society*, 6(1): 23–42.

Fineman, S. (1995) 'Stress, emotion and intervention', in T. Newton, J. Handy, and S. Fineman (eds), *Managing Stress: Emotions and Power at Work*, London: Sage, ch. 6.

_____ (1996) 'Emotion and organizing', in S.R. Clegg, C. Hardy, and W.R. Nord (eds), *Handbook of Organization Studies*, London: Sage, ch. 3.3.

Follett, M.P. (1941) *Dynamic Administration: The Collected Papers of Mary Parker Follett*, eds H.C. Metcalf and L. Urwick, London: Pitman.

Foucault, M. (1966) *The Order of Things: An Archaeology of the Humanities*, London: Tavistock & Routledge.

Gabriel, Y. (1988) *Working Lives in Catering*, London: Routledge & Kegan Paul.

General Synod (1996) *Under Authority: Report on Clergy Discipline—The Report of the General Synod Working Party Reviewing Clergy Discipline and the Working of the Ecclesiastical Courts*, London: Church House Publishing.

_____ (1997) *Synodial Government in the Church of England: A Review—Report of the Review Group Appointed by the Standing Committee of the General Synod*, London: Church House Publishing.

Gerth, H.H. and Wright Mills, C. (1948) *From Max Weber: Essays in Sociology,* trans. H.H. Gerth and C. Wright Mills, London: Routledge & Kegan Paul.

Glazer, N.Y. (1984) 'Servants to capital: Unpaid domestic labor and paid work', *Radical Political Economics*, 16: 61–87.

Gouldner, A. (1954) *Patterns of Industrial Bureaucracy*, Glencoe, IL: The Free Press.

Hacker, B.C. and Hacker, S. (1987) 'Military institutions and the labor process: Non-economic sources of technological change, women's subordination and the organization of work', *Technology and Culture*, 28: 743–75.

Hochschild, A.R. (1983) *The Managed Heart: Commercialization of Human Feeling,* Berkeley, CA: University of California Press.

Kanter, R.M. (1989) *When Giants Learn to Dance*, New York: Simon and Schuster.

Keenoy, T. (1990) Personal communication reporting research at Cardiff Business School, reported in Burrell (1992).

Lawrence, P. and Lorsch, J. (1967) *Organization and Environment: Managing Differentiation and Integration*, Boston, MA: Harvard University Graduate School of Business Administration.

Leidner, R. (1993) *Fast Food, Fast Talk: Service Work and the Routinization of Everyday Life*, Berkeley, CA: University of California Press.

Lewin, K. (1948) *Resolving Social Conflicts: Selected Papers on Group Dynamics*, New York: Harper and Row.

Love, J. (1986) *McDonald's: Behind the Arches*, Toronto: Bantam.

Manners, W. and McMyn, J. (2003) 'Tie case throws dress codes into confusion', *The Times,* Law, p. 3.

Martin, J. (1990) *Re-Reading Weber: Searching for Feminist Alternatives to Bureaucracy*, Paper presented to the Academy of Management in San Francisco.

_____, Knopoff, K., and Beckman, C. (1998) 'An alternative to bureaucratic impersonality and emotional labor: Bounded emotionality at The Body Shop', *Administrative Science Quarterly*, 43: 429–69.

Merton, R.K. (1936) 'The unanticipated consequences of purposive social action', *American Sociological Review*, 1: 894–904.

Parker, M. (1998) 'Nostalgia and mass culture: McDonaldization and cultural elitism', in M. Alfino, J.S. Caputo, and R. Wynyard (eds), *McDonaldization Revisited: Critical Essays on Consumer Culture*, London: Praeger, ch. 1.

_____ (2002) *Against Management*, Cambridge: Polity Press.

Pringle, R. (1989) 'Bureaucracy, rationality and sexuality: The case of secretaries', in J. Hearn, D.L. Sheppard, P. Tancred-Sheriff, and G. Burrell (eds), *The Sexuality of Organizations*, London: Sage, ch. 10.

Pugh, D. (1973) 'The measurement of organization structures: Does context determine form?', *Organizational Dynamics*, Spring: 19–34.

Ritzer, G. (1995) *Expressing America: A Critique of the Global Credit Card Society*, Thousand Oaks, CA: Pine Forge Press.

_____ (1998) *The McDonaldization Thesis: Explorations and Extensions*, London: Sage.

_____ (2000) *The McDonaldization of Society*, New century edn, Newbury Park, CA: Sage.

Runciman, W.G. (1978) *Max Weber: Selections in Translation*, Cambridge: Cambridge University Press.

Russell, N. and Gregory, R. (2006) 'Making the undoable doable: Milgram, the Holocaust and modern government', *The American Review of Public Administration*, 35: 327–49.

Sachs, J. and Blackmore, J. (1998) 'You never show you can't cope: Women in school leadership roles managing their emotions', *Gender and Education*, 10(3): 265–79.

Schlosser, E. (2001) *Fast Food Nation: What the All-American Meal is Doing to the World*, London: Penguin.

Selznick, P. (1949) *TVA and the Grass Roots*, Berkeley, CA: University of California Press.

Starbuck, W.H. and Menzias, J.M. (1996) 'Opening Pandora's box: Studying the accuracy of manager's perceptions', *Journal of Organizational Behavior*, 17: 99–117.

Thomas, R. (1996) 'Gendered cultures and performance appraisal: The experience of women academics', *Gender, Work and Organization*, 3(3): 143–55.

Thompson, P. and McHugh, D. (2002) *Work Organizations*, 3rd edn, Houndmills: Palgrave.

Tsoukas, H. and Cummings, S. (1997) 'Marginalization and recovery: The emergence of Aristotelian themes in organization studies', *Organization Studies*, 18(4): 655–83.

Van Maanan, J. (1991) 'The smile factory', in P. Frost, L.F. Moore, M.R. Louis, C.C. Lundberg, and J. Martin (eds), *Reframing Organizational Culture*, Newbury Park, CA: Sage.

Walt Disney Productions (1982) *Your Role in the Walt Disney World Show*, Orlando, FL: Walt Disney Productions.

Weber, M. (1930) *The Protestant Ethic and the Spirit of Capitalism*, London: Allen & Unwin.

_____ (1978) *Economy and Society: An Outline of Interpretative Sociology*, ed. G. Roth and C. Wittich, Berkeley, CA: University of California Press.

Witz, A., Halford, S., and Savage, M. (1996) 'Organized bodies: Gender, sexuality and embodiment in contemporary organizations', in L. Adkins and V. Merchant (eds), *Sexualising the Social*, London: Macmillan, ch. 8.

Woodward, J. (1965) *Industrial Organization: Theory and Practice*, Oxford: Oxford University Press.

Wright Mills, C. (1951) *White Collars: The American Middle Class*, Oxford: Oxford University Press.

_____ (1963) *Power, Politics and People: The Collected Essays of C. Wright Mills*, Oxford: Oxford University Press.

277

14

All Change?

Introduction

The media and textbooks on management often leave the impression that organizations have undergone fundamental transformation, and that new forms of work organization mean that our organizations are leaner, flatter, and more fitted to cope with change.

This chapter begins by looking at whether or not it can be claimed that new forms of work organization have emerged in recent decades. It looks at different forms of working, managing change, and technology; it also looks at the Japanese model of management, perceived in the 1970s and early 1980s as new way of improving productivity and competitiveness, how real that was, and how well it translated into Western organizations. But how much change has really happened, and is it change or only continuity? This chapter is designed to document some of the key changes that are widely celebrated and discussed in the management literature.

By the end of the chapter, you will be able to discuss these key changes and their claims. You will also be able to critique just how much change has actually happened in terms of work organization in the last two or three decades.

This chapter covers:

- new forms of organization;
- change in organizations;
- technology and change;
- the knowledge economy and knowledge workers;
- new organizations?
- the Japanese model;
- change—or continuity?

New forms of organization

Bureaucracy was a theme that dominated organization studies throughout the 1950s and represented the most common form of organizational design. As we saw in the last chapter, bureaucracy has been seen as the most technically efficient and rational form of organization. Bureaucracy is as relevant today, but some would say that new forms of organization have emerged. Now, there is also talk of 'clusters', 'networks', and 'strategic alliances' among organizations. Within organizations, some claim that the 'new work structures' (Geary, 1995) are flatter, more flexible, places in which employees can feel 'empowered', as opposed to the hierarchical bureaucratic structures that have been emphasized previously. Many writers in management talk of radical change. They speak of a 'revolution' (Kanter, 1989; Peters, 1989) and a 'transformation of industrial relations (Kochan et al., 1986), of 'new industrial relations' (Kelly and Kelly, 1991), and of the 'new workplace' (Ackers et al., 1996).

A radical change has been occurring in the way in which work is organized and experienced. For some writers (for example, Clegg, 1990), the new organizational forms are sufficiently different from bureaucracy that it is suggested that they are called 'postmodern' or 'post-bureaucratic' (Hecksher and Donnellon, 1994). Their structure has changed to become less specialist and more team-based. Throughout the 1990s, a stream of textbooks incorporated the 'Japanese model' of employment relations in order to offer an alternative to Weberian bureaucracy; the Japanese model included the active encouragement of employees in decision making and job security. And positive accounts persisted in textbooks, with some writers confirming the model's continuing vitality (Inagami and Whittaker, 2005; Vogel, 2006) even in the face of media accounts of 'the death of the Japanese model' (for example, Giddens, 2001; Macionis, 2002).

Hales (2002) noted that organizational restructuring often entails changes within the basic bureaucratic model, rather than major shifts to radically new organizational forms. But before looking at this counter-argument, we will consider how the new structures and arrangements are described—that is, as new organizational forms, to be found in both the external and internal environments.

Change in the external environment

There are a number of different types of structure emerging in the external environment, as follows.

- 'Clusters' refer to groups of usually small and medium-sized enterprises (SMEs) cooperating at a local level; each will have its own specialism in a part of a production cycle. For example, in the knitwear industry, one company may specialize in dyeing, another in sewing, and so on. Some clusters have developed as a result of state interventions: for example, in Northern Italy (Weiss, 1988) and in Germany (Herrigel, 1993).

- 'Technology parks' are also an example of a cluster, in which university research laboratories and new enterprises are grouped together in the hope of creating a synergy and new collaborations. Networks can function to exchange information, share risk, or avoid duplication of effort.

- 'Strategic alliances', meanwhile, are mechanisms that help firms to enter new markets by, for example, sharing the costs of development of new technology.

In order to meet the needs of these new external relations, internal arrangements within organizations may also have to change.

Change in the internal environment

Postmodern organizations are said to be 'decentralized' and 'networked' where there is a collaboration between people who have complementary skills, so that, together, they can achieve more. The internal network organization is conceived of as a loose federation of informally constituted, self-managing, often temporary work units of teams within which there is a fluid division of labour. Leadership has to be team-based, which means that team-building, conflict-resolution, and problem-solving skills are needed. Such a 'post-bureaucratic' internal network organization is different from bureaucracy in its absence of a rigid division of labour, hierarchy, and rules; instead, openness, trust, empowerment, and commitment characterize these organizations (Clegg and Hardy, 1996). Once in motion, 'virtuous circles' mean collaborative, open decision making, which eliminates traditional hierarchical styles of secrecy, sycophancy, and sabotage. Decisions are sought from those with the expertise and accepted.

Clegg and Hardy's view of organizations operating in this way is a very positive one. Examples of six organizations that have introduced network technology—that is, computer networks—to link different organizational units, such as branches or subsidiaries, are found in Boddy and Gunson (1996). They give a vivid account of the practical difficulties, failures, and successes of the process of implementation—and it is clear that the process of change is not necessarily easy.

Change in organizations

Organizational change is a very popular topic in management literature. Change is both influenced by, and influences, behaviour in organizations. It is a highly complex business, difficult to understand, and almost impossible to deal with systematically (Bate, 1995).

One of the perennial problems faced by management in organizations is how to bring about change. Changes may be needed as products change; with this often comes a change in working methods in jobs. But workers may resist change in a number of ways, through grievances about new piece rates that go with new methods, high labour turnover, low efficiency, restriction of output, or marked aggression against management (Coch and French, 1948; 1959). If workers respond in this way, managers will wish to know why people are resisting change so strongly and what can be done to overcome this resistance. Mainstream approaches to managing change are dominated by concerns for prescription, linearity, and the maintenance of order (Jeffcutt, 1996). The literature on managing change tends to be very functionalist and prescriptive. It tends to focus on cases of success and not on cases of failure. Some writers estimate that, in fact, up to 70 per cent of large-scale changes fail and that a 'conspiracy of silence' accompanies these failures (Scott-Morgan, 1994: 59). Kotter (1996: 4) argues that many changes result in 'carnage ... with wasted resources and burned-out, scared or frustrated employees'. These unsuccessful cases tend not to receive attention in the mainstream literature.

Research on implementing change, as a process, has its roots in the early work of Kurt Lewin (1947). Lewin is probably best known for his 'force field analysis'—that is, a method for analysing the dynamics in change processes by identifying the drivers for, and resistances to, change. He proposed that change progresses through successive phases of 'unfreezing', 'moving', and 'freezing'. Lewin worked in the 1930s with White and Lippitt on the experiments in leadership style that we saw in Chapter 7. He also worked with Coch and French on overcoming resistance to change.

Resistance to change

While managers may look to implement change, this change can often be met by resistance. It is important, then, to understand why people might want to resist change. Is it due to people simply being difficult and irrational, or are there rational reasons for this resistance? Coch and French (1948; 1959) looked at overcoming resistance to change in the Harwood Manufacturing Company in Virginia, USA. Both Coch and French had been employed at the company: John French had been director of research and labour relations, while Lester Coch had been director of personnel (Coch and French, 1948). The main plant at which the research was undertaken produced pyjamas and employed mostly women. The workers were recruited from rural mountainous areas surrounding the town and usually did not have previous industrial experience. The company appeared to care about workers' views and held plant-wide votes where possible to resolve problems affecting the whole working population.

The employees worked on an individual incentive system, on piece rates set by time study. One 'unit' was equal to one minute of standard work and 60 units was the standard efficiency rating. If a particular operation was rated at one dozen pieces equal to ten units, the operator would have to produce six dozen pieces per hour to achieve the standard rating of 60 units per hour. The skill required was quite high: in some jobs, the average trainee could take thirty-four weeks to reach the skill level necessary to perform at 60 units per hour. The amount of pay was directly proportional to the weekly average efficiency rating achieved. If an employee worked at an average efficiency rating of 75 units per hour (25 per cent higher than the standard), then he or she would receive 25 per cent more than the base pay. There was also a minimum wage. The operators saw their daily record of production each day when the supervisor spoke to them. When an operator changed from one type of work, a transfer bonus was given to that operator, who relearned at an average rate, so that he or she suffered no loss in earnings.

Despite this allowance, the general attitude toward job changes was negative. Many operators refused to change, choosing instead to leave the plant. Analysis showed that 38 per cent of operators who did transfer jobs managed to recover to the standard efficiency rating, but that the other 62 per cent either became chronically substandard operators or quit during the relearning period.

Coch and French interpreted the slow relearning that occurred after job transfer as a kind of resistance to change—that is, as primarily a motivational problem. Interviews with operators who had recently transferred revealed a common pattern of feelings and attitudes: resentment against the management for having transferred them; feelings of frustration; loss of hope of ever regaining the former level of production and status in the factors; and a low level of aspiration. The frustration led to high turnover and absenteeism. Operators with more difficult jobs quit more frequently than those on easy jobs. It was also found that employees aspired to the standard production level of 60 units per hour; those who fell below it lost status in the eyes of their fellow employees. Relatively few operators set a goal appreciably above 60 units. One reason for this was group pressure. For example, the production record of a presser (one of the jobs) was recorded over forty days. For the first twenty days, she was working in a group that was producing at about 50 units per hour. When she exceeded the production level of the other workers, she became a scapegoat for the group. Her production level then decreased toward the level of the group. After twenty days, the group was broken up: members were transferred, leaving only the scapegoat operator. Her productivity shot up to 96 units per hour in a period of four days. It is possible to conclude from this that the motivational forces of the group are more powerful than those of management.

Overcoming resistance to change

Resistance to change (where change has been due to the management's wishes, not those of the workers) is due, then, to individual reaction to frustration and strong group pressure. Coch and French (1948) suggest that a way of overcoming such resistance to change might be through group methods. They designed an experiment to employ three degrees of participation in handling groups to be transferred. In the first group, the employees did not participate in planning the changes, but the proposed changes were explained to them. The change involved stacking finished shirts in boxes, rather than on sheets of cardboard, as had happened previously. The employees were told that the change was necessary because of competitive conditions.

The second group involved participation through representation of the workers in designing the changes to be made in the jobs. They were shown two identical garments: one produced the year earlier and selling for 100 per cent more than its twin, produced one year later. The group was asked to identify the cheaper one and could not do it. This demonstration effectively shared the problem with the group and demonstrated the necessity of cost reduction. A general agreement was reached that savings could be effected by removing the 'frills' of the work from the garment without affecting the opportunity to achieve a high efficiency rating. Management then used Taylorist principles to set a plan for the new job: checking study of the job as it was being done; eliminating the unnecessary work; training operatives in the correct methods; setting piece rates on these specially trained operators; and explaining and training all operators in the new method, so that they could reach a high rate of production within a short time. The group approved this plan and operators were chosen to be specially trained. According to Coch and French (1959: 240): 'They displayed a co-operative and interested attitude and immediately presented many good suggestions.' The 'special' operators referred to the new job and piece rates as 'our job' and 'our rate'; these special operators trained the other operators in the new job.

The third group involved total participation by all of the employees. The groups were smaller and all operators were chosen as 'special' operators, because this would allow them all to participate directly in the designing of new jobs and all studied by time study. In these meetings, it is reported that suggestions were made in such quantity that there was difficulty in recording them all. The group approved the plans.

The first, 'no participation', group improved little beyond its early efficiency ratings. Resistance developed almost immediately after the change. Marked expressions of aggression against management included conflict with the methods engineer, expressions of hostility with the supervisors, 'deliberate restriction of production' (ibid.: 240), and lack of cooperation with the supervisor. Seventeen people left within the first forty days. Grievances were filed about the piece rate, but checking found it to be a little 'loose'.

The second group—that with some representation—showed an unusually good relearning curve. At the end of fourteen days, it averaged 61 units per hour. The attitude was 'cooperative and permissive'. The group worked well with supervisors and others, and there were no quits within the first forty days.

The third, 'total participation', group recovered faster than the other groups. After a slight drop on the first day of change, the efficiency ratings returned to a pre-change level and showed sustained progress to a level of about 14 per cent higher. The group worked well with supervisors and there were no quits during those initial forty days.

While Coch and French (1959) do not discuss the weakness of their research design, it is assumed that they realized that it lay in the fact that the three different groups had different jobs and were therefore not really comparable. They subsequently designed a second experiment, which used the total participation technique, again with some members of the earlier 'no participation' group, who were again transferred to a new job. This group's levels of productivity also recovered rapidly from previous efficiency ratings and continued to a new, high level of production. The researchers reported that there was no aggression or turnover for nineteen days. (We are left to question why not forty days, as in the first experiment.) Coch and French were thus able to conclude that the rate of recovery in levels of productivity is directly proportional to the level of employee participation, and that the rates of turnover and aggression are inversely proportional to the level of employee participation. The second experiment showed that the results depended on how people were treated in the experiment, rather than on personality factors, such as skill or aggression. In conclusion, total participation produces a stronger influence on productivity and lack of resistance than participation through representation. It is therefore possible for management largely to modify or remove group resistance to changes through its choice of methods of work and piece rates. This can be achieved through group meetings in which management communicates the need for change and stimulates group participation in planning the changes; participation will result in higher production, higher morale, and better labour—management relations.

STOP AND THINK Emotion and change

The following are some quotes that indicate the emotions associated with change process at a company called *ICL* (Clarke, 1994).

'I don't think the company realizes how frightened people are.'

'We feel very battered.'

'In the past, we worked hard and played hard, and people laughed. They don't anymore.'

What emotions do you think might be associated with a change process? How significant do you think are people's emotions in the process of change? How should management respond to such emotions?

Models of change

The challenge for managers is how to implement change effectively without causing resistance. The literature and research on managing change tends to be very prescriptive and make claims about how successful change can be achieved. In a very functionalist, 'how to do it' management style and building on Lewin's early work, Kotter (1995) draws lessons from watching more than a hundred companies that have tried to make fundamental changes in how business is conducted, in order to help them to cope with a new, more challenging market environment. From this analysis, Kotter is able to note that while a few efforts at change have been very successful, others have been utter failures. Most companies' success rates tend to fall in between, with a distinct tilt towards the lower end of the scale.

The general lesson to be learned from the more successful cases is that the change process goes through a series of phases over a considerable length of time. Kotter says that there are some common mistakes that companies make: for example, companies tend not to establish a great enough sense of urgency about the need for change. Successful change requires there to be a frank discussion with employees about the unpleasant facts and employees have to be motivated to act to improve the situation. According to Kotter, about 75 per cent of management have to be convinced that business as usual is no longer acceptable in order for change to take place successfully. There needs to be a powerful guiding coalition that develops a picture of the future that is relatively easy to communicate; that vision needs to be successfully communicated and obstacles to achieving it need to be removed. For example, narrow job categories, as opposed to more flexible ones, can seriously undermine efforts to increase productivity. Further, there need to be short-term improvements to keep the level of urgency up and forced detailed analysis to clarify or revise visions. Changes need to be anchored into the company structure.

There are many models of change for the practitioner to follow, but similarities can be drawn between them. As Armenakis and Bedein (1999) note, basic lessons underscore implementation models of change. The change process is, in general, seen to occur in multiple steps that take a considerable amount of time to unfold. Efforts to bypass steps seldom yield a satisfactory result and mistakes made in any step can slow implementation, as well as negate hard-won progress. Managing change is not, then, an easy process.

It is interesting to note, as does Cooke (1999), that Lewin demonstrated a belief in egalitarianism, democracy, and an opposition to hierarchy. Coch and French were working colleagues of Lewin, and were heavily influenced by him. But Lewin and the managing change literature seem to have been located in a sociology of regulation, rather than radical change. Models of change are used to change the behaviour of the workforce for managerial ends. It has been argued by Cooke (1999), for example, that there is a willingness within the change management literature to adopt a position in which the social, political, and ideological circumstances under which the change is made are assumed to be uncontested and as objectively given. It is possible to go one stage further and argue that it is only the interests of management that seem to be represented in much of the change management litera-ture. In Lewin's work and that of his followers, there appears to be no acknowledgement of how change represents the interests of the workforce.

Technology and change

Similarly, the implementation of new technology within organizations is typically described in prescriptive literature as if it is a rational and linear process, without paying attention to the social and political circumstances within which such change takes place. This has been the subject of criticism for some decades (McLoughlin, 1999). The political process is often downplayed or ignored (Dawson and Buchanan, 2005); in contrast, more critical approaches draw attention to political processes in management, organization, and in the social shaping of technology (Knights and Murray, 1994). Often, there are contrasting accounts of events of the implementation of new technology from within the same organization (Dawson, 2000). As Buchanan (2003: 16) argues: 'The notion of one unitary, accurate, authentic account of the change process and its outcomes is a delusion.'

Some believe that changes in technology and organization are causing a radical transformation of society as a whole, not only within organizations. With the widespread use of information and communication technology (ICT) comes a convergence of ways of life, as we, for example, 'log on' to exchange goods, communicate with others, and find information. In what is termed the 'information society', or the 'knowledge economy', the dominant form of work becomes information and knowledge-based (Wajcman, 2002). In the networked society, the compression of space and time—made possible by new communication technology—alters the scope and speed of decisions. For example, communication technology allows organizations to decentralize and disperse; high-level decision making can remain in world cities, with lower-level operations linking to the centre through communication networks from virtually anywhere (Castells, 1996). It can be easy to form the impression that ICT is the most important cause of social change—but as Wajcman (2002) notes, this stance verges on 'technological determinism', within which technology is seen as the driver. This argument is too simplistic, because technological change is shaped by the social circumstances in which it takes place: technology is not simply the product of rational, technical imperatives; a particular technology will not triumph simply because it is the best.

We need to look at the social decisions behind technological development: for example, why was a particular technological change seen to be compelling? When might the decision making have been challenged? And what criteria are used to define something as 'superior'? A number of options are available. Technology is a socio-technical product: a technological system is never merely technical; rather, it includes organizational, economic, and political elements. For example, history tells us that, once, there was a choice between an electric and a gas refrigerator, both of which were equally effective. The electric model took off only because *General Electric* had the financial resources to develop it, while the manufacturers of gas refrigerators lacked the resources to develop and market their machine (Cowen, 1983). History also tells us that, in the development of automatically controlled machine tools, two options existed: the record playback, in which the machine replicated the manual operations of a skilled machinist, or numerical control, in which tool movements were controlled by a mathematical program produced by a technician. The machine tool suppliers, technologists, and managers in aerospace companies deliberately suppressed record playback in favour of numerical control, in order to reduce their reliance on the unionized craft workers. Nonetheless, management found that it needed to retain skilled machinists to operate new machines effectively, so the shift of power from the shop floor was not realized (Noble, 1984). We can conclude, then, that while management makes choices about technology and skills, and may seek to reduce skill levels to reduce reliance on non-skilled craft workers, as well as to make labour cheaper, it has not always succeeded.

How technology is used is crucial to our understanding of consequences. When thinking about information technology, it is interesting to note that it appears to have two faces. On the one, for example, the Internet is seen as an environment of individual freedom, consumer convenience, shared knowledge, virtual community, and free markets; on the other, it can represent Orwellian control, computer-enabled surveillance, and a world inhabited by pornographers, hackers, unscrupulous fraudsters, and paedophiles.

STOP AND THINK

Can technology present two faces at the same time? Can you see how this might be the case?

The knowledge economy and knowledge workers

With a change away from manufacturing industries, there has been a growth in service employment and knowledge-based industries or sectors, such as those found in professional services (for example, consulting companies, legal firms, banking and finance companies, tourism, and advertising agencies) in information technology software and bioscience. We talk now of 'knowledge management'—that is, the management of knowledge to meet existing and future needs—and the 'knowledge economy'—that is, an economy characterized by knowledge-intensive firms, such as those above, as opposed to an economy based on manufacturing products.

Managing knowledge and knowledge workers is, it might be argued, the single most important challenge presently being faced by many kinds of organization (Newell et al., 2002). Knowledge management has been heralded in the last decade as an important and new approach to the problems of competitiveness and innovation confronting information-based organizations in the 'knowledge era'.

Taylorism and Fordism were both examples of ways in which knowledge was, or is, managed. In Taylorism, the responsibility for the planning and organization of work is taken away from the workers—that is, away from the head and the hands of the workers. Engineer managers can effectively extract and capture that knowledge required to standardize work and make it more efficient; they were thus managing the knowledge of the work process. More recently, there has been a resurgence of this idea of managing knowledge. The 'learning organization', at which we looked at in Chapter 10, is one recent example. The main change is that knowledge work is perhaps more apparent now in professional and service organizations (Frenkel et al., 1995).

The knowledge economy is one in which economic value is found in intangibles such as innovations, software, new services, or new information technologies. Knowledge management practices tend to be focused on improving the ways in which organizations facing highly turbulent or competitive environments can better use or mobilize their knowledge base, in order to ensure continuous innovation. Knowledge management should identify, extract, and capture the 'knowledge assets' of an organization, so that they can be fully exploited and protected as a source of competitive advantage. One place in which this is happening is in universities, which commercialize research through, for example, spin-out companies, and by selling innovative licences and technologies. Another new development is e-business.

E-business

One aspect of the knowledge economy is e-business, on which there is also a large literature (Wareham et al., 2005).

E-business—that is, electronic business—is a combination of technologies, applications, processes, business strategies, and practices that are necessary to do business electronically (Taylor and Berg, 1995). There are currently some well-known e-businesses operating, such as Amazon, eBay, and Yahoo, each of which first opened its website for business over ten years ago. E-business technologies, such as the Internet, have had a significant effect on business-to-consumer trading, but there appears to be an even bigger potential for business-to-business transactions (McCalman and Anderson, 2002).

Some have expressed the view that it may be only a 'management fad' (McCalman and Anderson, 2002)—but whether it is a fad or not, e-business has placed significant attention on the concept of the non-physical workplace. Organizational behaviour and human resource management specialists have therefore pointed out that e-business still needs some kind of organizational form, and that this needs to be carefully considered. Key organizational behaviours come to the fore in a teleworking environment: for example, issues such as work–life balance (Sparrow, 2000). Design issues include how to manage knowledge and labour, and the interaction between people in numerous workplaces. It is expected that e-business will enhance the concept of teamworking, because the technology demands multi-skilled teamworking. So new forms of working are required—forms that are more flexible in both work methods and structure.

New organizations?

There have been other management critics who have cast doubt on the extent and true character of postmodern or network organizations (Ezzamel et al., 1994; Alvesson, 1995; Thompson and O'Connell Davidson, 1995; Warhurst and Thompson, 1998; Whittington and Mayer, 2000). It is argued that there are few examples of different organizational forms to be found, and that there are only a few recurring and celebrated cases. Indeed, it is said, managers are guilty of using misleading rhetoric in their claims about the adoption of new organizational forms: many forms of organizational change have entailed only an extension or intensification of, rather than a departure from, bureaucratic control.

Hales (2002) is one researcher who has suggested that organizational change may be far less radical than is claimed and that it may occur within bureaucratic forms. His research focused on organizations that have claimed to have moved away from bureaucracy, towards decentralized or empowered organizations in which hierarchy and rules are banished, and proved that such claims were illusory: neither the forms of organization, nor the work that managers did, were all that 'new'. Hales found that the organizational units remained firmly located within a system of hierarchical control. Responsibility for unit performance continued to be vested in individual managers, who were accountable to more senior managers, and were judged on the basis of conformance with centrally imposed rules about appropriate levels of performance. Only one or two layers of management had been reduced in the cases on which Hales focused; as a result, the organizations were a little more bureaucracy-'lite', but just as—if not more—consistent with the ethos of bureaucratic control. In addition, senior managers were very reluctant to relinquish control. Other researchers have noted that public-sector organizations have actually become *more* bureaucratic as control by professionals has given way to tighter managerial control (Warhurst and Thompson, 1998). This has often arisen in response to external audit (Power, 1997).

> **EXAMPLE** *Sony* **and speed**
>
> *Sony* has been under great pressure to improve its ability to respond flexibly and speedily to market demand. The product has to be adjusted to market demand and the time taken to get the product to the consumer needs to be reduced. A step towards this goal for *Sony* was the introduction of cell-based manufacturing in the production of camcorders: lots of small groups, or cells, were introduced. Mass-production factory lines are difficult to stop once started, but cell-based manufacturing makes it possible to shift quickly for making one model of camcorder (from among 200–300 models) to another that is selling better.
>
> (*Source:* Nakamoto, 2003)

But what about the fundamental shifts in organization and management of manufacturing operations that have been witnessed, such as autonomous group working, 'flexible' and 'lean' production (Piore and Sabel, 1984; Womack et al., 1990), just-in-time (JIT), quality circles, total quality management (TQM), and the Japanese model of manufacturing management?

Autonomous work groups

In autonomous work groups, a team of workers organizes its own labour and how it is deployed; the team enjoys discretion over work methods and time (Buchanan, 1994: 204). In the Swedish model of autonomous group working, employees have enjoyed sufficient freedom to influence such matters as goal formation, performance monitoring, production methods, labour allocation, and choice of group leaders (Ramsay, 1992). This system has allowed group control over work pace through the presence of buffers and the absence of supervision (Berggren, 1993; Thompson and Sederblad, 1994).

Quality circles

'Quality circles', or problem-solving groups, normally consist of small groups of employees from the same work area who meet together regularly and voluntarily. Their chair may be a supervisor, a 'facilitator', or another employee; he or she may have received training in statistical analysis and group dynamics to help him or her to facilitate group work. As well as quality issues, groups can deal with work flow, productivity, safety, and other problems. The concept was originally developed in the USA, but quality circles were first widely adopted in Japan (Cole, 1989). Quality circles remain more common in Japan than the USA and more common in the USA than the UK (Heller et al., 1998).

Quality circles can formalize the process of workplace innovation. Employees can frequently think of ways of making their job more efficient and problem-solving teams can encourage them to reveal their innovations. Most employees can see good reasons to want to improve the quality of work from a company. In some circumstances, however, quality circle meetings may be little more than managerial pep talks, with little opportunity for employee input; alternatively, employees can find that their ideas are ignored (Wilson, 1989). They may also feel that they deserve some reward for their participation.

Sometimes, however, quality circles evolve into work teams or total quality management.

Total quality management

Total quality management (TQM) goes beyond quality circles in that it is usually an organization-wide effort involving teams of employees and managers building in quality control at every stage of production; quality circles are meetings of groups of workers usually at only one point of production. TQM focuses on satisfying the needs of 'customers', who are both internal and external to the company. It focuses on questions such as how the organization can deliver new products and services in innovative ways, and what it can do to improve its organizational processes and capabilities continually. TQM teams typically follow a procedure that starts with tracking the number and timing of problems, then analyses the source of the error, and generates alternative solutions; the team then evaluates one solution, implements it, and checks it. Thus it can contribute to organizational learning and increase participation. On the other hand, in practice, TQM often permits little real participation (Tuckerman, 1994). Recently, its popularity appears to have waned, but its core principles may be alive and well in contemporary business practice (Chiles and Choi, 2000).

The Japanese model

Japanese management practices have evoked a good deal of interest—particularly in the 1970s and 1980s. During the 1960s and 1970s, there was a dramatic increase in Japanese manufacturing exports and people around the world marvelled at the economic 'miracle' of Japanese organizations (McCormick, 2007). In 1980, *Ford Europe* began an 'After Japan' programme, following a fact-finding visit to Japan, to tighten labour discipline, increase output, and enhance worker flexibility at *Ford* plants. In the 1980s, attention shifted to the role of Japanese firms in Europe and North America, as auto, auto components, and electrical manufacturing plants were set up.

It was argued that innovative and competitive Japanese car manufacturers had developed a distinctive form of production organization, or 'lean production' (Womack et al., 1990). This was characterized by the minimization of stocks and work-in-progress through the use of 'just-in-time' (JIT) production—that is, producing and delivering finished goods 'just in time' to be sold, sub-assemblies 'just in time' to be assembled, and so on—and by an emphasis on the continuous improvement of production procedures. This was the dominant form of production used by vehicle producers in Japan (particularly *Toyota*) and the methods were apparently transferable to locations outside Japan.

Writers such as Schonberger (1982; 1986) popularized the approach to the management of stocks and material flow. The fundamental doctrine of the *Toyota* production system was the elimination of waste (Ohno, 1988). Under the JIT system, production is driven by market requirements, as information regarding demand pulls production through the processes. In contrast, the traditional mass production model pushes production scheduling as output plans are developed on the basis of historic information; production is decoupled from demand. The intention with JIT was to reduce costs through reducing stock, labour, and time. This, in turn, reduces the amount of 'buffering' between processes. Total quality management (see above) focuses on quality design and conformance to specification, using statistical process control to monitor quality and control standards; it can also involve employees with customer responsiveness and service. Kenney and Florida (1993), too, identified the leading Japanese firms as the innovators of a new model of organization of work and production that they called 'innovation-mediated production'—that is, a symbiosis between research and development, and continuous improvement in the production process, aided by the knowledge and intelligence of all employees.

Few people have not heard of the four 'sacred treasures' of Japanese management, which involve:

- *lifetime employment*—that is, employees being hired fresh out of education on a lifetime basis;
- *seniority-based wage systems and promotions*—that is, remuneration and promotion provided according to seniority as the employee accumulates skills and experience with the company;
- *consensus decision making*;
- *enterprise unions*—that is, structures within which all of the clerks, engineers, and labourers of a company join together, facilitating labour–management compromises.

It has been argued, for example, that offering lifetime employment secured a loyal and secure workforce in Japan. The organization was viewed as a collectivity to which employees belonged; there is considerable emphasis on interdependence, shared concerns, and mutual help. Once employees had joined an organization, they were guaranteed continuing employment; in return, the employees would make a lifelong commitment to the organization that they would start to see as an extension of their family.

How real was this Japanese dream? How easy would it be to transfer Japanese management practices into UK organizations? These were the questions that researchers raised in the late 1980s. Ackroyd et al. (1988) believed that there were major constraints on the implementation of Japanese forms of work organization and employment relations in UK-based organizations, because the UK and Japan had different economic and social structures with contrasting employment systems, labour markets, different organization of finance, and investment policies. Oliver and Wilkinson (1992) also emphasized how the new production methods required very specific social conditions—of the sort provided by Japanese social structures—in order for them to work. They found that the success of major Japanese corporations could not be readily assigned to a specific set of practices, such as manufacturing methods or personnel policies. What appeared to be crucial was the 'fit' between a set of business strategies and a set of wider supporting conditions. They studied UK companies that tried to emulate Japanese practices, concluding that the companies faced substantial obstacles related to the heightened dependencies of companies on their employees, suppliers, markets, and key political and economic agencies.

In the case of suppliers, they must be trusted to deliver goods of the right quality, in the right quantity, and 'just in time'; buyers have to nurture long-term relations with their suppliers and exert influence over their operations. The supplier should find the buyers constantly 'on the doorstep', should be dependent on the customer financially, and should be under intense pressure to deliver the goods. In terms of employees, many Japanese-style manufacturing practices require willing cooperation—not merely compliance—on the part of a workforce. For example, they require a willingness to perform a range of tasks, a commitment to engage in activities of continuous improvement, and a preparedness to do what is required to satisfy both internal and external customers. For the workforce, this means, on the one hand, that work is likely to be more varied and higher in involvement and 'ownership'; on the other hand, accountability and responsibility are increased, performance is more closely monitored, and the visibility of failings (and successes) is heightened. Some Japanese companies reinforce this visibility through public displays of group or individual output and quality levels. No wonder, then, that there are mixed opinions on these methods: advocates claim that the Japanese style of work organization is humanistic, while the critics see it as being manipulative and coercive.

EXAMPLE A clash of cultures

In Chapter 2, we mentioned the Funcini and Fucini (1990) study of the *Mazda* car plant in Michigan. In that plant, a dispute arose over the wearing of baseball caps. *Mazda* issued its US employees company baseball caps, with the understanding that the caps were a voluntary accessory to the mandatory blue pants and khaki shirt *Mazda* uniform. Taking the term 'voluntary' to mean that they had a choice whether or not to wear the caps, many Americans elected to come to work bareheaded. This upset the Japanese, who regarded not wearing the caps as a sign of disrespect towards the company.

There were some other interesting 'realities' that emerged about Japanese human resource strategies. The practice of lifelong employment was only applicable to an elite, favoured group of employees. It applied almost exclusively to regular, male employees and is not as widespread as was once believed. It has been estimated that no more than 30 per cent of the Japanese labour force worked for the same company throughout their career (Smith and Misumi, 1994) and that rather more Americans than Japanese continue to work for their first employer. One reason why there was so little lifetime employment was that there was widespread subcontracting (for example, 70 per cent of a *Nissan* car was produced by subcontractors) and subcontracting workers do not enjoy job security in time of cutbacks. 'Rings of defence' were built around the core workers and their activities. Employees who find themselves in the outer rings—that is, peripheral workers employed on temporary contract or employees of firms subcontracted to the main subcontractors—are likely to have a rather different experience of work (Oliver and Wilkinson, 1992). Close attention is given to hiring new permanent employees who fit into the company culture: careful screening ensures that candidates likely to endorse the company's values and philosophy are selected—and private investigators are routinely used to check a candidate's background, families, neighbours, and friends (ibid.; see also McCormick, 2007). Finally, in around 1990, the Japanese economy entered a downturn that is only now showing signs of ending. As a result of this downturn, most Japanese companies no longer offer workers jobs for life (Macionis, 2005).

The role of culture in the Japanese model

The adult Japanese male identifies with the immediate work group of peers and his superior; this identification is very intense (Dore, 1973). Comparative studies reveal that Japanese employees see work as more central to their lives than do employees in ten other countries (Meaning of Working, 1987); they also spend substantial time eating and drinking with their workmates after work. Employees are more likely to participate in company-organized sports, holidays, and outings, and companies in Japan spend twice as much on social and recreational facilities for their employees than do US companies (Smith and Misumi, 1994). The Japanese employee is obliged to develop and maintain harmonious relations with his or her work colleagues. National service through industry, fairness, harmony and

289

cooperation, a struggle for betterment, courtesy and humility, adjustment and assimilation, and gratitude are the values that employees should adopt. New recruits share overall responsibility for their team's work; commitment to the company is fostered through extensive training programmes for new recruits.

The society is not only collective, but also has a hierarchical status system based on education, age, gender, and the firm from which the individual works. Authority relations are often paternalistic, and are highly traditional and deferential. Prospects for promotion are strongly dependent upon a senior mentor within the company. Whitehill (1991) supplies a very detailed study of Japanese management practices.

As Morgan (1986: 116) has noted, some of the more distasteful aspects of work experience have been ignored in many accounts of Japanese organization. The emphasis has been on how Japanese workers arrive at work early or stay late to find ways of improving efficiency through working in quality circles, or how the dedicated *Honda* workman straightens the windshield wiper blade on all *Honda* cars that he passes on his way home in the evening. Less attention is given to the disgruntled workers, such as Satoshi Kamata (1982), who describes how he lived in a camp that was rigidly policed by company guards. There were constant pressures to achieve demanding work targets, and to fulfil the requirements of company values and norms. Day-to-day life was gruelling. According to Turnbull (1988: 44), 'Faced with the choice of going on the dole or working like the Japanese, the men so far would prefer the dole. It's as simple as that'.

Williams et al. (1994) describe the more-than-intense nature of work in a car plant press shop in Japan. The shift runs for nine hours, including one hour of unpaid meal breaks. After nine hours on shift, the workers are required to work overtime as necessary; the overtime requirement is only put up on a board halfway through the shift. Two hours of overtime are routinely required, so an eleven-hour day is the expected norm. The scheduled meal breaks are often taken up with company business, such as quality circle meetings. Workers have been obliged to work six days a week. Even their one day off may not be completely free, because loyal workers are expected to join in company sports and social events. At one point, managers decided that the plant should work over weekends, because the local electricity board charged a lower tariff at that time; the result was that workers were unable to take their day off over the weekend.

STOP AND THINK

How would you feel about working for a Japanese company?

The apparent harmony in Japanese society may therefore be overstated (Wagatsuma, 1982). There is clear evidence of conflict within and between organizations. The harmony of the work group may be sustained by a sense of obligation; this obligation may be relaxed when employees are having a few drinks together. There is also evidence to suggest that Japanese workers are less satisfied than Western workers. Many Japanese workers work extremely long hours for what they regard as inadequate pay (Smith and Misumi, 1994). When viewed in the Western cultural and socio-political contexts, many aspects of Japanese business and management systems are socially and politically unacceptable—even illegal (Sethi et al., 1984; Jones, 1991). Research demonstrates that we should question many of the beliefs about Japanese companies—especially those fuelled by articles in the popular press.

Disciplined selves

Research has consequently gone on to address the realities of working in a factory in Japan. Kondo (1990), for example, gives a vivid account of everyday life on the shop floor of a small, family-owned sweet factory in Tokyo, at which she worked for a year. At one stage in her story, she is sent to an 'ethics school' with two other employees. At this school, they are organized in groups, or 'squads'. Each squad slept in the same room, ate at the same table, exercised together, and sat together in class. The position of squad leader changed daily, giving each the opportunity to be leader and share responsibility.

EXAMPLE **Working in a Japanese company**

The following outlines the activities in which Kondo (1990) was expected to participate before breakfast each day during her time at the ethics school.

The day started at 5 a.m. with a call to rise. Waking up late was regarded as unnatural, indulgent, selfish, and slovenly. Cleaning came next and was a standard ingredient of spiritual education. Each cleaning task was to be performed with a glad heart. The counsellors would lead the group in chants of 'Fight!' as they hosed down the toilets, emptied the tins of sanitary napkins, and scrubbed the floors. After cleaning, the group would jog to the statue of the founder and, after a rousing shout of 'Good morning!', would be briefly lectured on an inspirational theme. A tape recorder played the national anthem as the flags were raised. They then had shouting practice, at which they were required to scream greetings at the tops of their voices, or shout 'I am the sun of X company! I will make X company number one in Japan!' Every word was rewarded by shouts of encouragement from the others and applause. The idea was to inculcate receptiveness, and a willingness to greet and appreciate others, and eliminate resistance towards responding positively towards authority.

The group ran for at least 2.5 kilometres as a rehearsal for the 7.5 kilometre run scheduled for the end of the programme. Shouting and chanting was required during running. Speed was not the issue; it was important to finish and not give up. Neglect of the body was seen as lack of appreciation of the gift of life. Ritual ablution ceremonies with cold water, in order to give thanks to water, followed. The morning classes were for reciting in unison phrases such as 'Hardship is the gateway to happiness' and 'Other people are our mirrors'. Students would be given instructions on how to bow at the proper angle, have a pleasant facial expression, and use the appropriate language level.

How successful do you think the ethics centre was in crafting disciplined selves?

Compliance with a particular type of behaviour is demanded, then, in Japanese culture. This theme emerges again in research by Graham (1994), who was a participant observer for six months in a Japanese car plant in the USA. She documents both the compliance and resistance to management's technical and social control strategies. Managers had attempted to gain compliance through lengthy pre-employment and selection procedures, careful handling of training of new recruits, the team concept of working, the philosophy of continuous improvement, the shaping of shop-floor culture, and technical pacing and discipline of computerized assembly lines, coupled with JIT. They used techniques such as the company song, celebrations, and team meetings. But there was worker resistance, which emerged as sabotage when the workers surreptitiously stopped the assembly line. They protested and refused to participate in company rituals, and confronted management in team and departmental meetings. Workers were seldom allowed to make even inconsequential decisions. The company was therefore far from totally successful in instituting a spirit of cooperation and a culture of egalitarianism.

Would the experience be similar in other Japanese-owned and European-owned plants? Delbridge (1998) reports his findings from two periods of study as a participant observer working on the shop-floor in a European-owned automotive components supplier and a Japanese-owned consumer electronics plant. The European company was seeking to introduce cellular manufacturing, TQM, JIT inventory control, and teamworking during the time of his study, while the Japanese company had many characteristics of lean production and had been cited as an exemplar of 'world-class manufacturing'. Delbridge found that management at the Japanese-owned company had successfully marginalized the effects of uncertainty, and that shop-floor relations were clearly and explicitly founded upon a 'negotiated order' between management and labour. Workers faced very strict coercive controls and felt that they had to comply. There was, however, no heightened sense of commitment from the workforce; rather, they remained opposed to many of management's goals, and mistrustful of the rhetoric of teamworking and mutuality. At the European-owned plant, in contrast, the managers relied on informally negotiated solutions to problems, due to the uncertainty inherent at the plant. Workers here were also sceptical of management intentions, however, and clearly favoured an oppositional stance, so needed the protection of trade unions (see also Wilkinson et al., 1997; 1998; Knights and McCabe, 1998).

Another example of a company that has imitated the Japanese model is the car company *Fiat* in Italy. The production system was reorganized and initiatives launched aimed at enhancing the involvement of the workforce (Bonazzi, 1998). Traditional bureaucratic management, with its rigid division of responsibility and unwieldy linkages between various bodies, was abandoned. The new system encouraged supervisors to assume managerial responsibilities in order to ensure maximum reactivity as and when process and product anomalies arose. In this way, *Fiat* appears to have taken some elements of the Japanese methods and used them for its own benefit.

There are, then, some clear lessons to be drawn from the research on Japanese manufacturing methods. The main conclusion is that we need to be sceptical about claims of the unitarist management writers who present workers and managers simply as working happily together to fulfil mutual goals, and who present Japanese management practices only in a positive light. There need to be serious questions asked about the ease with which Japanese management practices can be appropriated and used in both Japanese and other organizations.

Change—or continuity?

Do the types of change discussed in this chapter actually represent change or continuity? There are some writers who would say that researchers and theorists have paid more attention to change than to continuity. Roy Jacques (1996), for example, notes that many of the characteristics of 'post-industrial management' proposed for the 1990s were actually observed and reported sixty or more years ago. According to Jacques (1996: 18–19): 'It appears to be a condition of modernity for every generation to believe it is in the midst of revolutionary change'.

In a different vein, Blyton and Turnbull (1994: 298), in discussing employee relations, say that 'Nothing changes yet everything is different: as we twist around the spiral of capitalist economic development we experience progression and return, never a return to exactly the same point but always to a point that is familiar'. We should consider both continuity and change, thinking of time as moving along a 'spiral' (Burrell, 1992). Similarly, Legge (1995) would argue that all periods are characterized by both change and continuity: today's organizational forms are no less exploitative or necessarily less alienating than those that existed before (Sewell, 1998). Forms of organization may always appear to be developing and changing—but the key question is: how much of how we organize has actually changed?

Conclusion

New forms of organization have been seen to emerge in the last few decades—but the extent of change raises a number of questions: for example, how extensive or radical that change is, how radical the new structures are, or how beneficial change has been. You may want to look in more depth at the claims of those who presented Japanese management practices in such a positive light and the success of implementing these ideas in the UK. You may also want to look at the cases of change and ask, for example, whether change benefits anyone other than managers. You might ask, if you do think that it benefits workers, how that is evidenced.

While change is a popular topic in the management literature and it may be something that is desired to bring about greater efficiency, it can be difficult to achieve. Worker participation may help the process of change—but the politics of change can present some interesting challenges for managers.

KEY POINTS

- While bureaucracy has been seen as the most rational form of organization, other forms of organization and structure have been said to have emerged. These new forms have been thought by some to be less specialist and more team-based, while others have argued that organizational restructuring often entails changes within the basic bureaucratic model rather than radical shifts.

- One of the perennial problems that managers face is how to bring about change. Change can be resisted. One way in which this resistance may be reduced is allowing employee participation in the planned change.

- The literature on the topic of change appears very prescriptive and rarely acknowledges the politics of change or questions relating, for example, to whose interests are best served by the proposed change.

- Research on Japanese management practices has demonstrated the need for scepticism about some of the claims made about these practices.

CASE STUDY

Jack Welch and his change conversations with shareholders

In the chapters on leadership and personality, we encountered Jack Welch, chief executive officer of *General Electric*. The following describes how he brought about change.

General Electric's transformational change has been described as 'one of the most far-reaching programs of innovation in business history' (Tichy, 1993). It included internationalizing the operations of the company, 'delayering' (that is, taking layers out of the hierarchy), reducing bureaucracy and hierarchy, and encouraging cross-functional teamwork. Changes such as these may introduce great uncertainty in the minds of shareholders about the impact of the change on the performance of the company, but *General Electric* was apparently successful in both retaining shareholder support and growing it.

Palmer et al. (2004) looked in detail at how Jack Welch communicated with the shareholders of *General Electric*, in his letters to them, taken from annual reports during these times of transformational change (spanning twenty years). They identified five core 'change conversations' that sought to reassure shareholders and reduce uncertainty around outcomes of the organization's transformational changes.

1. He used warnings: for example, mentioning the problems and threats that the organization faced.
2. He discussed actions that the company had taken to address these problems and challenges.
3. He used explanations to provide the rationale behind these actions.
4. He described what had been achieved.
5. He predicted what was going to happen next.

This is interesting research, because it shows how one leader tried to bring about a process of change, but raises a series of questions.

(Sources in text)

Questions

1. If these are the core conversations that are found in an organization in which transformational change was considered successful, would different conversations be found in one that was unsuccessful?
2. What would happen if one, two, or more of these kinds of conversations had not taken place?
3. How do we know that the change conversations had an effect on shareholder support? Might there be other factors at play: for example, media reports?
4. Was the transformational change successfully brought about by Jack Welch or his staff?
5. What questions does this research on organizational transformation raise for you?

293

FURTHER READING

Burnes, B. (2004) *Managing Change*, 4th edn, Hemel Hempstead: Prentice Hall This is a standard textbook on change and includes case studies.

Carnell, C.A. (2007) *Managing Change in Organizations*, Harlow: Pearson This is a standard text in the literature on managing change.

Clegg, S., Kornberger, M., and Pitsis, T. (2008) *Managing and Organizations*, London: Sage Chapter 9 on 'Managing innovation and change' will be particularly useful to anyone interested in how innovation is managed.

Dawson, P. (2002) *Understanding Organizational Change: The Contemporary Experience of People at Work*, London: Sage This is a book on change management that offers an overview with case studies to help the reader to understand the process.

Knights, D. and Willmott, H. (2007) *Introducing Organizational Behaviour and Management*, London: Thomson Chapter 10 focuses on innovation and change, and includes a critical section.

McCormick, K. (2007) 'Sociologists and "the Japanese model": A passing enthusiasm?', *Work, Employment and Society*, 21(4): 751–71 This article thoroughly discusses the research evidence that supports or refutes the realities of 'the Japanese model' of organizing.

RESEARCH QUESTIONS

1. 'Japanese managers transfer as little or as much as they wish of their management practices to the new environment' (Dedoussis and Littler, 1994). How much evidence is there to suggest that this is the case? (See Delbridge, 1998: ch. 10, for sources.)

2. To its advocates, total quality management is unequivocally good; to some management researchers, it produces some bad outcomes. What are the realities? (See Wilkinson et al., 1997; 1998; Knights and McCabe, 1998; and related sources.)

3. What methods have you witnessed for trying to bring about change in an organization or group in which you have been involved? Was group participation used? If not, why not?

REFERENCES

Ackers, P., Smith, C., and Smith, P. (eds) (1996) *The New Workplace and Trade Unionism*, London: Routledge.

Ackroyd, S., Burrell, G., Hughes, M., and Whitacker, A. (1988) 'The Japanization of British industry?', *Industrial Relations Journal*, 19(1): 11–23.

Alvesson, M. (1995) 'The meaning and meaningless of postmodernism: Some ironic remarks', *Organizational Studies*, 16(6): 1047–75.

Armenakis, A.A. and Bedeian, A.G. (1999) 'Organizational change: A review of theory and research in the 1990s', *Journal of Management*, 25(3): 293–315.

Bate, P. (1995) *Strategies for Cultural Change*, Oxford: Butterworth Heinemann.

Berggren, C. (1993) *The Volvo Experience: Alternatives to Lean Production in the Swedish Auto Industry*, London: Macmillan.

Blyton, P. and Turnbull, P. (1994) *The Dynamics of Employee Relations*, London: Macmillan.

Boddy, D. and Gunson, N. (1996) *Organizations in the Network Age*, London: Routledge.

Bonazzi, G. (1998) 'Between shock absorption and continuous improvement: Supervisors and technicians in a fiat "integrated factory"', *Work, Employment and Society*, 12(2): 219–43.

Buchanan, D. (1994) 'Cellular manufacture and the role of teams', in J. Storey (ed.), *New Wave Manufacturing Strategies*, Liverpool: Paul Chapman.

_____ (2003) 'Getting the story straight: Illusions and delusion in the organizational change process', *Tamara: The Journal Of Critical Postmodern Organization Science*, 2: 7–21.

Burrell, G. (1992) 'Back to the future: Time and organization', in M. Reed and M. Hughes (eds), *Rethinking Organization*, London: Sage, pp. 165–83.

Castells, M. (1996) *The Rise of the Network Society*, Oxford: Blackwell.

Chiles, T.H. and Choi, T.Y. (2000) 'Theorizing TQM: An Austrian and evolutionary economics interpretation', *Journal of Management Studies*, 37(2): 185–212.

Clarke, L. (1994) *The Essence of Change*, Hemel Hempstead: Prentice Hall.

Clegg, S.R. (1990) *Modern Organizations: Organizational Studies in the Post-modern World*, London: Sage.

_____ and Hardy, C. (1996) 'Organizations, organization and organizing', in S.R. Clegg, C. Hardy, and W.R. Nord (eds), *Handbook of Organization Studies*, London: Sage, Introduction.

Coch, L. and French, J.R. (1948) 'Overcoming resistance to change', *Human Relations*, 1(4): 512–32.

_____ _____ (1959) 'Overcoming resistance to change', in E. Maccoby, T.M. Newcomb, and E.L. Hartley (eds), *Readings in Social Psychology*, 3rd edn, London: Methuen, pp. 233–50.

Cole, R. (1989) *Strategies for Learning: Small Group Activities—America, Japan and Sweden*, Berkeley, CA: University of California Press.

Cooke, B. (1999) 'Writing the left out of management theory: The historiography of the management of change', *Organization*, 6(1): 81–105.

Cowen, R.S. (1983) *More Work for Mother: The Ironies of Household Technology From the Open Hearth to the Microwave*, New York: Basic Books.

Dawson, P. (2000) 'Technology, work restructuring and the orchestration of a rational narrative in the pursuit of "management objectives": The political process of plant-level change', *Technology Analysis & Strategic Management*, 12(1): 39–58.

_____ and Buchanan, D. (2005) 'The way it really happened: Competing narratives in the political process of technological change', *Human Relations*, 58: 845–64.

Dedoussis, V. and Littler, C. (1994) 'Understanding the transfer of Japanese management practices: The Australian case', in T. Elger and C. Smith (eds), *Global Japanization? The Transnational Transformation of the Labour Process*, London: Routledge, pp. 175–95.

Delbridge, R. (1998) Life on the Line in Contemporary Manufacturing: *The Workplace Experience of Lean Production and the 'Japanese' Model*, Oxford: Oxford University Press.

Dore, R.P. (1973) British Factory, *Japanese Factory*, London: Allen & Unwin.

Ezzamel, M., Lilley, S., and Willmott, H. (1994) 'The "new organization" and the "new managerial work"', *European Management Journal*, 12(4): 454–61.

Frenkel, S., Korczynski, M., Donoghue, L., and Shire, K. (1995) 'Re-constituting work: Trends towards knowledge work and info-normative control', *Work, Employment and Society*, 9(4): 773–96.

Fucini, J.J. and Fucini, S. (1990) *Inside Mazda's American Auto Plant*, New York: Free Press.

Geary, J. (1995) 'Work practices: The structure of work', in P. Edwards (ed.), *Industrial Relations: Theory and Practice in Britain*, Oxford: Blackwell, pp. 368–96.

Giddens, A. (2001) *Sociology*, Cambridge: Polity Press.

Graham, L. (1994) 'How does the Japanese model transfer to the United States: A view from the line', in T. Elger and C. Smith (eds), *Global Japanization? The Transnational Transformation of the Labour Process*, London: Routledge, ch. 4.

Hales, C. (2002) 'Bureaucracy-lite and continuities in managerial work', *British Journal of Management*, 13: 51–66.

Hecksher, C. and Donnellon, A. (1994) *The Post Bureaucratic Organization: New Perspectives on Organizational Change*, Thousand Oaks, CA: Sage.

Heller, F., Pusic, E., Strauss, G., and Wilpert, B. (1998) *Organizational Participation: Myth and Reality*, Oxford: Oxford University Press.

Herrigel, G.B. (1993) 'Power and the redefinition of industrial districts: The case of Baden-Wurttemberg', in G. Graber (ed.), *The Embedded Firm: On the Socioeconomics of Industrial Networks*, London: Routledge, pp. 227–51.

Human Relations (1948) Biographical notes on Coch and French, 1(4): 512–32.

Inagami, T. and Whittaker, D.H. (2005) *The New Community Firm: Employment, Governance and Management Reform in Japan*, Cambridge: Cambridge University Press.

Jacques, R. (1996) *Manufacturing the Employee: Management Knowledge from the Nineteenth to Twenty-First Centuries*, London: Sage.

Jeffcutt, P. (1996) 'Between managers and the managed: The process of organizational transition', in S. Linstead, R. Grafton Small, and P. Jeffcutt (eds), *Understanding Management*, London: Sage, ch. 11.

Jones, S. (1991) *Working for the Japanese: Myths and Realities, British Perceptions*, Basingstoke: Macmillan.

Kamata, S. (1982) *Japan in the Passing Lane*, New York: Pantheon.

Kanter, R. (1989) 'The new managerial work', *Harvard Business Review*, 67(6): 85–92.

Kenney, M. and Florida, R. (1993) *Beyond Mass Production: The Japanese System and its Transfer to the US*, Oxford: Oxford University Press.

Kelly, J. and Kelly, C. (1991) '"Them and us": Social psychology and "the new industrial relations"', *British Journal of Industrial Relations*, 29(1): 25–48.

Knights, D. and McCabe, D. (1998) 'Dreams and designs on strategy: A critical analysis of TQM and management control', *Work, Employment and Society*, 12(3): 433–56.

_____ and Murray, F. (1994) *Managers Divided: Organization Politics and Information Technology Management*, Chichester: Wiley.

Kochan, T., Katz, H., and McKersie, R. (1986) *The Transformation of American Industrial Relations*, New York: Basic Books.

Kondo, D.K. (1990) *Crafting Selves: Power, Gender and Discourses of Identity in a Japanese Workplace*, Chicago, IL: University of Chicago Press.

Kotter, J.P. (1995) 'Leading change: Why transformation efforts fail', *Harvard Business Review*, March–April: 59–67.

_____ (1996) *Leading Change*, Boston MA: Harvard Business School Press.

Legge, K. (1995) *Human Resource Management: Rhetorics and Realities*, London: Macmillan.

Lewin, K. (1947) 'Frontiers in group dynamics', *Human Relations*, 1: 5–41.

Macionis, J. (2002; 2005) *Sociology*, New Jersey: Prentice Hall.

McCalman, J. and Anderson, C. (2002) 'Designing oases for corporate nomads: The impact of facilities management on work design and the flexible workforce', in P. Jackson and R. Suomi (eds), *eBusiness and Workplace Redesign*, London: Routledge, ch. 2.

McCormick, K. (2007) 'Sociologists and "the Japanese model": A passing enthusiasm?', *Work, Employment and Society*, 21(4): 751–71.

McLoughlin, I. (1999) *Creative Technological Change*, London: Routledge.

Meaning of Working, International Research Team (1987) *The Meaning of Working*, London: Academic Press.

Morgan, G. (1986) *Images of Organization*, London: Sage.

Nakamoto, M. (2003) 'A speedier route from order to camcorder', *Financial Times*, 12 February, p. 11.

Newell, S., Robertson, M., Scarborough, H., and Swan, J. (2002) *Managing Knowledge Work*, Houndmills: Palgrave.

Noble, D.F. (1984) *Forces of Production: A Social History of Industrial Automation*, New York: Knopf.

Ohno, T. (1988) *Just-In-Time: For Today and Tomorrow*, Cambridge, MA: Productivity Press.

Oliver, N. and Wilkinson, B. (1988; 1992) *The Japanization of British Industry*, Oxford: Basil Blackwell.

Palmer, I., King, A.W., and Kelleher, D. (2004) 'Listening to Jack: GE's change conversations with shareholders', *Journal of Organizational Change Management*, 17(6): 593–614.

Peters, T. (1989) *Thriving on Chaos: Handbook for a Management Revolution*, New York: Harper & Row.

Piore, M. and Sabel, C. (1984) *The Second Industrial Divide*, New York: Basic Books.

Power, M. (1997) *The Audit Society: Rituals of Verification*, Oxford: Oxford University Press.

Ramsay, H. (1992) 'Swedish and Japanese work methods: Comparisons and contrasts', *European Participation Monitor*, 3: 37–40.

Schonberger, R. (1982) *Japanese Manufacturing Techniques: Nine Hidden Lessons in Simplicity*, New York: Free Press.

_____ (1986) *World Class Manufacturing: The Lesson of Simplicity Applied*, New York: Free Press.

Scott-Morgan, P. (1994) 'Ringing the changes', *International Management*, September, p. 59.

Sethi, S.P., Namiki, N., and Swanson, C.L. (1984) *The False Promise of the Japanese Miracle: Illusions and Realities of the Japanese Management System*, London: Pitman.

Sewell, G. (1998) 'The discipline of teams: The control of team based industrial work through electronic and peer surveillance', *Administrative Science Quarterly*, 43(3): 397–428.

Smith, P.B. and Misumi, J. (1994) 'Japanese management: A sun rising in the west?', in C.L. Cooper and I.T. Robertson (eds), *Key Reviews in Managerial Psychology, Concepts and Research for Practice*, Chichester: John Wiley, ch. 4.

Sparrow, P.R. (2000) 'New employee behaviours, work design and forms of work organization: What is in store for the future of work?', *Journal of Managerial Psychology*, 15: 3.

Taylor, D. and Berg, T. (1995) *The Business Value of Electronic Commerce: Strategic Analysis Report*, Stanford, CT: Gartner Group.

Thompson, P. and O'Connell Davidson, J. (1995) 'The continuity of discontinuity: Managerial rhetoric in turbulent times', *Personnel Review*, 24(4): 17–33.

_____ and Sederblad, P. (1994) 'The Swedish model of work organization in transition', in T. Elger and C. Smith (eds), *Global Japanization? The Transformation of the Labor Process*, London: Routledge.

Tichy, N.M. (1993) 'Revolutionize your company', *Fortune*, 13 December, pp.114–18.

Tuckerman, A. (1994) 'The Yellow Brick Road: TQM and the restructuring of organizational culture', *Organization Studies*, 15: 727–51.

Turnbull, P. (1988) 'The limits to Japanization: Just-in-time, labour relations and the UK automotive industry', *New Technology, Work and Employment*, 3(1): 7–20.

Vogel, S. (2006) *Japan Remodeled: How Government and Industry are Reforming Japanese Capitalism*, Ithaca, NY/London: Cornell University Press.

Wagatsuma, H. (1982) 'Internationalization of the Japanese: Group model reconsidered', in H. Mannari and H. Befu (eds), *The Challenge of Japan's Internationalization: Organizations and Culture*, Tokyo: Kodansha, pp. 298–308.

Wajcman, J. (2002) 'Addressing technological change: The challenge to social theory', *Current Sociology*, 50(3): 347–63.

Wareham, J., Zheng, J.G., and Straub, D. (2005) 'Critical themes in electronic commerce research: A meta-analysis', *Journal of Information Technology*, 20: 1–19.

Warhurst, C. and Thompson, P. (1998) 'Hands, hearts and minds: Changing work and workers at the end of the century', in P. Thompson and C. Warhurst (eds), *Workplaces of the Future*, Basingstoke: Macmillan, pp. 1–24.

Weiss, L. (1988) *Creating Capitalism: The State and Small Business since 1945*, Oxford: Blackwell.

Whitehill, A.M. (1991) *Japanese Management: Tradition and Transition*, London: Routledge.

297

Whittington, R. and Mayer, M. (2000) *The European Corporation: Strategy, Structure and Social Science*, Oxford: Oxford University Press.

Wilkinson, A., Godfrey, G., and Marchington, M. (1997) 'Bouquets, brickbats and blinkers: Total quality management and employee involvement in practice', *Organization Studies*, 18(5): 799–819.

_____, Redman, T., Snape, E., and Marchington, M. (1998) *Managing with Total Quality Management: Theory and Practice*, London: Macmillan Business.

Williams, K., Mitsui, I., and Haslam, C. (1994) 'How far from Japan? A case study of Japanese press shop practice and management calculation', in T. Elger and C. Smith (eds), *Global Japanization? The Transnational Transformation of the Labour Process*, London: Routledge, ch. 2.

Wilson, F.M. (1989) 'Productive efficiency and the employment relationship', *Employee Relations*, 11(1): 27–32.

Womack, J., Jones, D., and Roos, D. (1990) *The Machine that Changed the World*, New York: Rawson Associates.

The Core of Critical Approaches

Managerial Power and Control

15

Introduction

We have looked at how managers have tried to motivate and control production through job design, and how managerial work is described; this chapter turns to look at the issue of how much power and control managers actually have, and to what extent employees resist managerial power and control. This is, again, something that the mainstream texts on management tend not to discuss; the assumption in many mainstream texts is that that if people do not do as they are asked, they are acting illegitimately. A central tension in organizations exists between obedience and resistance.

The chapter begins by looking at how power is defined and from where power comes. It looks at the limits of managerial power, and the issues of sharing power and of individual empowerment. It tackles the thorny issues of control, technology,

and surveillance; managers can gain greater control through the use of technology and surveillance, but excessive use may invite resistance. As we saw in Chapter 13, Weber discussed bureaucracy as the dominant form of modern control; here, we look briefly at other forms of control.

This chapter covers:

- the sources and definition of 'power';
- managerial prerogative;
- workers' power;
- managing to empower;
- control and surveillance;
- technology;
- technology and surveillance;
- business process engineering.

The sources and definition of 'power'

Under the medieval guild structure, masters held the power over those who were employed. Power clearly derived from ownership and control of the means of production—that is, the resources by which goods and services are created—and it was supported by surveillance. Power was also derived from knowledge, from the 'mastery' of the skills required to complete the work to the required standard. The organization's 'status hierarchy' and 'knowledge hierarchy' therefore coincided (Offe, 1976). Increasing the size and complexity of organizations—a process that was brought about by the concentration of capital into larger units and the bringing together of different production processes—meant that the unity of status and knowledge hierarchies was disrupted. Hardy and Clegg (1996) believe that modern organizations passed by the guild structures and that, as organizations grew larger, skills became increasingly fragmented and specialized, and positions became more functionally differentiated. It was unlikely that any one person would have sufficient knowledge of all of the processes to be able to control them in an adequate manner. The effect of this was that power became centralized. Modern organizations were designed to function as if they were a unitary organism, as if employers and employees together were working towards a common aim, within which a coherent integration is maintained. But power is structured into the organization design in such a way that some will have more power than others. Obedience to those with power is central and crucial to the functioning of the organization. So how is 'power' defined and understood?

'Power' has been defined by Weber (1978) as the ability to get others to do what you want them to do, even if this is against their will, or to get them to do something that they otherwise would not do (Dahl, 1957). Weber, like Marx (1976), argued that power was derived from owning and controlling the means of production, but went on to say that it was also derived from the knowledge of operations, as much as from ownership. Employees will use creativity, discretion, and agency (that is, their ability to cause effect) as power; some will do so more than others. From the employer's perspective, the employee represents the capacity to labour, which must be realized as efficiently as possible. But standing in the way of this realization is the power of employees who may vary in their willingness to work under managerial discretion and control. In response, managerial control can be increased or tightened through the hierarchy and discipline of the manager, and through rules and bureaucracy.

One of the simplest views on power can be found in French and Raven (1959), which Raven revised in 1965. This view, or framework, of power may be described as 'managerialist' in that it serves the objectives of managers by supporting the idea that organizations should be integrated with shared values, and a single source of authority and legitimacy. It offers an analysis of individual power that proposes six 'bases' of power, or six resources, that a person can use to change beliefs, attitudes, or behaviours of a 'target': reward; coercion; legitimacy; expertise; reference; and information. Power in the form of coercion and rewards can be seen in terms of tangible rewards and real threats: for example, the threat of being fired, the promise of monetary rewards, or the offer of bonuses or promotion. In addition, personal approval from someone whom we like can also constitute quite powerful reward power; a threat of rejection or disapproval from someone whom we value highly can serve as a source for powerful coercive power. 'Legitimate power' is based on a structural relationship between the influencing agent and the target. Implicitly or explicitly, the agent says: 'I have a right to ask you to do this and you have an obligation to comply.'

Legitimate power is most obvious when it is based on some formal structure, for example, in a supervisor–subordinate relationship. Legitimate power may also exist in situations involving the expectation of reciprocity—that is, 'I did that for you, so you should feel obliged to do this for me' (Gouldner, 1960)—or equity—that is, 'I have worked hard and suffered, so it is only fair that you should do something which I ask of you'—or in situations of responsibility or dependence—that is, 'I really depend on you to do this for me'. Sometimes, a third party can be invoked: for example, a supervisor might ask for the assistance of a co-worker to persuade a recalcitrant worker. Each manager may have a number of power bases from which to choose and to combine. This view of power may also, then, be described as functionalist in that it sees the employee—particularly the manager—as a functionary who can be trained and developed to use his or her bases of power to meet organizational efficiency and objectives better.

But managers are unlikely to have total power. Looking at relationship between those at the top of the organization and managerial or leadership power, it has been found that power is shared. No manager can deal with all of the dilemmas that he or she faces. Power sharing has been found to be frequent in mature businesses, but not common; research has found that, in start-ups, it is fairly common, and that in family business, it is very common (Alvarez and Svejenova, 2005).

Despite the fact that managers and other elites are unlikely to have total power, they do bring about political quiescence (that is, silence) and perpetuate the status quo—but how do they do so? According to Bachrach and Baratz (1963), managers are in a position to use their power in order to prevent decisions being taken over issues in relation to which there would be a conflict of interests; they do so by, for example, limiting decision making to 'safe' issues. Power is also being exercised when managers devote their energies to creating or reinforcing social and political values, and institutional practices that limit the issues considered by, for example, agenda setting—that is, they get to set the agenda and exclude items that they do not regard as safe.

Lukes (1974) considers that Bachrach and Baratz do not go far enough, and so provides us with a radical view of power. Lukes asks us to look at latent, unobservable conflict and at the role of ideology in shaping perceptions and preferences that are contrary to the real interests of those who hold them. Lukes' radical concept is that 'A exercises power over B when A affects B in a manner contrary to B's interests' (ibid.: 34). According to this view, power can be used to shape people's perceptions and preferences so that they accept their role in the existing order of things, thus preventing conflict. Power can help to sustain the dominance of elite groups and reduce the ability of subordinate interests to dissent.

More recently, theorists have looked at disciplinary practices and at the micro-techniques of power used in organizations, following in the steps of Foucault (1977). These are ways in which both individuals and groups become socialized and 'normalized' (that is, begin to view specific behaviours as normal or acceptable) through the routine aspects of organizations. To study managerial power, it is therefore important to consider the 'rules of the game', which both constrain and enable action (Clegg, 1975), and of how the 'disciplinary gaze' is put into action in organizations. An example of the disciplinary gaze might be an employee appraisal system—that is, a process in which current performance in a job is observed and discussed in order to improve that performance.

STOP AND THINK **Is this an example of the disciplinary gaze?**

At one university at which the author was previously employed, staff were requested, if they were making private calls, to prefix the number that they dialled with '77'. They were subsequently issued with an itemized personal bill that they were required to pay. The bill listed the numbers dialled and the names of the people or organizations called, and the cost of the call.

If this is how private calls were logged, could this be the same for all other calls that university staff make? For what other purposes could telephone number information also be used? How would you feel knowing that this information is being gathered?

The rule systems that made up Weber's bureaucracy become disciplinary practices. Power is embedded in everyday life. Central to disciplinary practices is surveillance—personal, technical, bureaucratic, legal—seeking increasingly to control the behaviour and dispositions of the employee. Discipline is both a system of correction and a system of knowledge. Power, then, is much more than the negation and repression of the actions of others. As Issac (1987: 49) wrote: 'Rather than A getting B to do something B would not otherwise do, social relations of power typically involve both A and B doing what they ordinarily do.' From a manager's point of view, this means that managers have a right to manage; managers have the prerogative and have been given the authority to control.

Managerial prerogative

Managers are seen to have a right to manage—that is, they have the managerial prerogative (Storey, 1983). The boundaries of managerial prerogatives, or rights, give management its distinctiveness and are hotly defended. Justification for the managerial prerogative comes from the fact that it is owners or managers that have the control over capital assets, and they are supported by law; it therefore follows that managers should be left to manage as they see fit. By securing legitimization of their control, managers promote willing compliance for their rules, policies, and decisions. Golding (1980) believes that the maintenance of managerial prerogative depends on it not being overtly recognized or challenged; the belief in the rule of the manager's right to control is 'blissful clarity' (ibid.: 772). It seems to go unchallenged because of employee socialization and because of the tendency to accept most aspects of the status quo. But managerial control may be impossible without a prerogative that, in some way, legitimates the right to control (Johnson and Gill, 1993).

Workers' power

Research reveals how workers resist managerial power and control. One of the early studies on this was by Crozier (1964), who looked at bureaucracy and power relations in a French, state-owned tobacco company. The focus of the research became the relationship between the male maintenance workers and the female production workers. The male maintenance workers' job was to fix machine breakdowns reported by the mainly female production workers. The production workers were paid on a piece-rate system and had been effectively deskilled by the ways in which the jobs were designed: their jobs and the workflow were tightly planned and controlled by the management.

The main cause of uncertainty during the working day of the production workers was the potential for machine stoppages. Machine stoppages were usually caused by the difficulties in conditioning the raw material and stoppages led to a decrease in the bonus that the production workers could earn. It was therefore important to the production workers for the machines to function. When the machines did not function, their earnings became dependent on the efficient working of the maintenance workers. The maintenance workers thus had a high degree of power over the production workers, because they controlled the source of uncertainty. Comparable problems seemed to be handled better in other factories; the maintenance workers in this factory kept the maintenance and repair problems a secret, and kept their skill as a 'rule of thumb' skill, completely disregarding all blueprints and maintenance directions that they were able to make 'disappear from the plants' (ibid.: 153). The maintenance workers were able, then, to maintain relative autonomy, privilege, and power through their skills and knowledge.

The rationale of bureaucracy is the elimination of power relationships and personal dependencies—but, as can be seen from this case, unintended results are often yielded: power relationships and personal dependencies *do* exist in the workplace. In Crozier's study, uncertainty, control, and power were linked as concepts; these concepts were later linked into theory.

One such theory, which arose from the work of Hickson et al. (1971), was the theory of 'strategic contingency'. Central to this theory were four sub-units connected by the major task element of the organization—that is, coping with uncertainty. The balance of power between the sub-units was dependent on how they coped with uncertainty. The most powerful were those that were least dependent on the other sub-units and which coped with the greatest systematic uncertainty. Clegg and Hardy (1996) offered a critique of this theory: it is a view that assumes a unitary, cohesive organization, whereas the units are likely to be hierarchical, with problems of consent and dissent. In this type of structure, it is difficult—if not impossible—for managers to have total control.

EXAMPLE **Dissent and sabotage**

Thompson (1983) looked at dissent and sabotage among slaughterhouse workers. He describes how there were norms of acceptable behaviour, and unacceptable behaviour that was prohibited by the management, in the slaughterhouse. While foremen, supervisors, and federal inspectors attempted to ensure that the formal norms associated with handling beef plant products were followed, the workers did not necessarily follow them.

For example, regulations required that any meat that touched the floor had to be put in tubs marked 'inedible'. While the workers realized that the product would be consumed by people (which may include their family, friends, and relatives) and rarely did anything to contaminate the product deliberately, they would pick up meat that had dropped on the floor and put it back onto the assembly line, even though this was against the rules.

It was also a fairly common occurrence for workers, covered in beef blood, to go to the tub full of swirling water that was designed to clean the tongues, and wash their hands, arms, and knives. This procedure was strictly forbidden in the rules. If witnessed by a foreman or inspector, the tub would have to be emptied, cleaned, and refilled, and all of the tongues in the tub at the time would have to be put in the 'inedible' tub—a time-consuming and costly procedure. Despite this, the workers continued to break the rule—and even seemed to delight in successfully pulling off the act.

Engaging in 'artful sabotage' was, then, challenging and fun, and served as a symbolic way in which workers could express a sense of individuality and self-worth.

Theorists within occupational or industrial psychology have also discussed the limits of managerial control. Taking a more functionalist and prescriptive view of management activity, occupational and industrial psychologists have looked at management sanctions and at their effectiveness in controlling absence from work. Absences are usually regarded as a 'management problem'. Researchers in organizational and occupational psychology have argued against punitive sanctions in absence control. Buzzard and Liddell (1963) found, when monitoring coalminers' attendance, that after receiving disciplinary interviews for poor attendance, the men subsequently tended to take fewer, but longer, absences. Nicholson (1976), looking at a management clampdown on absence in a food processing factory, also found that while spells of very short-term absences became fewer, there was an increase in the incidence of longer absences, coupled with a dramatic fall in the frequency of uncertified absence and an increase in the frequency of certified absence. Reliance on the 'stick' of punitive sanctions (as opposed to the 'carrot' of rewards for achievement) to encourage high attendance can, then, have quite the opposite effect from that intended; instead, employees appear to resist managerial attempts to control their absences from work.

Workers' resistance

Typically, workplace resistance has been thought of as reactive opposition to oppressive forces (Anderson and Englehardt, 2001). Usually, it is associated with subordinates and, historically, it has been framed largely in class terms, with the emphasis on white male workers (Jermeir et al., 1994). More recently, research has focused on resistance among women and people of colour, with a focus on the lower levels of hierarchies (for example, Fleming and Spicer, 2002). This research has indicated that the view of the subordinated appears as distinct from the view of those who have more power.

Women are often portrayed as a compliant workforce, but this is not necessarily the case. A study of work in a nursing home for older people (Lee-Treweek, 1997) shows how female nursing auxiliary workers use resistance to get through each working day. The work is physically heavy, dirty (involving tasks such as washing soiled bodies), and poorly paid (wages at the time were sometimes as low as £1 per hour). It is often assumed that this is women's work—that is, that it is easy and natural for women, who are equipped to deal with bodily substances, who are sympathetic, and who might enjoy this type of work as 'caring people'. But the main motivation for work was, in fact, 'instrumental'—that is, it was undertaken because of the need to earn a wage; their care work had little to do with caring. Conveying this view to those outside the job was problematic for the auxiliaries, because this is not a message that those outside might find palatable.

The home's brochure advertised that patients would receive 'family-type care', but in reality, there was a strong pressure to create clean and orderly patients. The main work for the nursing auxiliary was to create a sanitized 'lounge standard' patient. It could be seen, then, that the 'product' of their work was a clean, orderly, quiet patient; the work was therefore about process and order, much the same as factory work, rather than about caring. Knowing the people was not about knowing patients as individuals, but about knowing the type of work and knowing how to handle the patients. This knowledge was a source of pride, but also of resistance to the sheer drudgery and lack of control over the nature of the work. The nurses' knowledge and role was seen by the auxiliaries as inferior: in contrast to their own, it was clean work, which was neither real nor necessary. The needs of the patient were often not met: 'needy' or 'sick' patients were 'reconstructed', turned into attention-seeking, pretending, or wilfully childish individuals; they were ignored even when they were talked about in their own presence. Incidents such as being hit by a patient were referred to as 'fun', so that personal toughness was elevated to a position of importance. This, then, is what research tells us about the power of the nurses and how they may resist giving the kind of care that patients might reasonably expect.

Similarly disturbing descriptions of the realities of life for psychiatric nurses can be found (see Handy, 1990). The issue of control over patients seems to be central in studies of nursing and care, as is the idea of being tough, of 'not being a bleeding, whining Minnie' (Bates, 1990). Again, we see how nurses have power and control. Bates (1993) also shows how 16–18-year-old care assistants cope with violence, incontinence, and death in their daily work. To cope, they 'switched off' and kept 'busy'. The girls regarded a significant proportion of the work as 'shit shovelling' (ibid.: 17). The social taboo of talking about incontinence was dealt with, in part, through a humorous language strategy: for example, reversing the word 'shit' to produce the word 'tish'. The trainee care assistants rejected and scorned the college tutor's stress of the need for sensitivity and genuine caring in their work. What they contested specifically was the quality of care that they were expected to offer.

EXAMPLE Resistance in a call centre

Mulholland (2004) describes workplace conflict in an Irish call centre. In call centres, managers are dependent on workers' selling strategies—that is, on the social skills, technical competencies, and willingness to perform in the interests of the business during each transaction. The targeted productivity requires each worker to make a call every 3–4 minutes, anticipating that 80 per cent of calls are realized into sales. But workers reported that they faked sales by talking to answering machines and putting that through as a sale. Absenteeism, sickness, and leaving work without permission before the shift ends are all ways in which the workers avoided work. Smoking provided extra break time, regardless of whether people smoked or not. Leaving the job is another sign of resistance: labour turnover is persistently high in the industry, with 60 out of a total of 756 employees resigning each month.

We have discussed some of the research into managerial control by industrial and occupational psychologists. The discipline of industrial sociology has also had much to say about the limits of managerial control. One example of industrial sociology's contribution comes from Gouldner (1954). Gouldner's research was set in a remote gypsum mine, where the work was hard, dirty, and dangerous. In Gouldner's research and analysis, the sub-surface miners were indulged in their informal work cultures by management; rules and regulations were being ignored by both managers and workers. Absenteeism, lateness, pilfering, time banditry, and verbal intransigence were tolerated by managers, and it was found that the miners exercised a large degree of collective control over the management. Gouldner's explanation for this was that management's 'indulgence' was the result of an understanding of how dangerous the work was: the foremen themselves—that is, the front line of management control—worked in similarly dirty and dangerous conditions, and so identified with the workers rather than with the more senior management.

But Thiel (2007) criticizes Gouldner for neglecting to note that managerial control was also restricted by the physical space of the mines and the contingent nature of mining work knowledge. As Thiel points out, the miners had a space in which they could assert their informal collective power over managers and bosses. Similarly, the builders in Thiel's study and those in Clegg's (1987) study of the building site (see Chapter 2) might be seen to assert their power informally over management. Building work has been affected relatively little by industrial technology or scientific management techniques. Builders retain a large degree of workplace power and autonomy (Theil, 2007). On building sites, although management orchestrates the work, builders are trusted to carry out their work autonomously. If they fail to do so, of course, management holds the ultimate sanction: the ability to dismiss them.

Managing to empower

Given that managers have the ultimate power and prerogative, are they prepared to share their power and control? Do they have an interest in empowering workers?

'Employee empowerment' has become something of a managerial buzzword (Beirne 1999; 2006) and usually means 'the giving of power'. When it is defined in this way, it concerns an individual's power and control relative to those of others, as well as the sharing of power and control, and the transmitting of power from one individual to another with less power. Terms such as 'employee involvement' and 'participation' have overlapping meanings. Kanter (1977; 1979; 1984) suggests that empowerment depends on developing the conditions in an organization for the circulation of power. Participative management, with access to resources, information, and support, can benefit the whole organization. The term 'empowerment' can also have a motivational meaning when it concerns people's feeling of behavioural and psychological investment in work (Koberg et al., 1999).

Empowerment has been shown to affect managerial and organizational effectiveness (Spreitzer, 1995). The word conjures up images of positive commitment and meaningful participation of workers in everyday management. Potentially, empowerment can mean that workers take more control over their jobs and working environment. They should be able to enhance the contributions that they make as individuals and members of a team, and also seize opportunities for personal growth and fulfilment. For Bowen and Lawler (1992), 'high involvement' occurs when organizations give the lowest level employees a sense of involvement in the total organization's performance—that is, information on performance is shared, and people have the skills and power to act beyond their traditional roles, and they are rewarded for doing so. Examples of companies with high sustained involvement are hard to find, but include *W.L. Gore* (producer of Gore-Tex® fabrics and other products) and the *Body Shop* (Boddy, 2002).

EXAMPLE **Empowerment in the hospitality industry**

Marriott Hotels has a 'Whatever it takes' programme to encourage service quality improvement. The following is an extract from an advertisement for *Marriott Hotels* that neatly exemplifies what the programme means. Here, the night porter's personal feelings of commitment to customer satisfaction match the organization's commitment to its clients:

'It was more than *considerate* of the Marriot night porter to trace my lost wallet– it meant he had to retrace my entire journey through Vienna. All I could remember was that I'd been travelling on a Southern District streetcar. Miraculously, from this tiny piece of information, the night porter from the Marriott hotel managed to trace the route I'd travelled, the particular streetcar I was on, and my wallet. I was astounded that he went out of his way so much to help me. But as I now know, everyone at Marriott works this way. Personally assuming responsibility for the needs of every guest. It's called empowerment. And thankfully, they never seem to find anything too much trouble.'

(*Source:* Lashley, 1995)

In order to empower their employees, managers are asked to create an atmosphere that supports and fosters mutual trust, to give people a sense of belonging and freedom to develop their interests in work, and to reorient the organizational culture to integrate empowerment. These are all vague, woolly prescriptions for managers to follow—but Bowen and Lawler (1992) list some of the benefits of empowerment: quicker online responses to customer needs; quicker responses to dissatisfied customers; employees feel better about their jobs and themselves; and empowered employees can be a great source of service ideas.

> ### ⭐ STOP AND THINK Empowerment at *Flightpath**
>
> Good quality customer service was thought by managers at *Flightpath* to be produced by 'empowered' and 'autonomous' workers, rather than through managerial prescription (Taylor and Tyler, 2000). Empowered telephone sales agents would deliver quality customer service 'spontaneously' and 'naturally'. Yet the work of telephone sales agents was supervised and measured thoroughly. They were given individual monthly sales targets, which they were expected to surpass. There were revenue targets relating to the value of airline services sold to customers. The number of calls per agent answered was measured, as was the amount of time spent in conversation with passengers per week, and the amount of time spent between the termination of one call and the opening of a new one. Each individual had a target. Agents were further assessed on teamwork, commitment, and job skills. Appraisal of performance happened each week and performance-related pay was awarded.
>
> Does this sound like Taylorism or empowerment to you? Would you feel empowered in this situation?
>
> * *Flightpath* is a pseudonym for a major airline.

Despite the positive connotations of the term 'empowerment', research on employee empowerment offers cautionary tales (Wilkinson, 1998; Hales, 2000). For example, it tells us that managers do not always want to empower and do not always see the benefits of empowerment. There can be a gap between the employee experience of empowerment and management rhetoric (Greasley et al., 2005). One of the most commonly cited barriers to the success of employee involvement is resistance from middle managers (Fenton-O'Creevy and Nicholson, 1994). For example, Ezzamel et al. (1994) showed that middle managers were reluctant to give power to those below them, because they wanted to retain control over the responsibilities and roles of others. Senior managers, too, may hold negative attitudes to empowerment (Fenton-O'Creevy, 2001). For example, while managers might go through the motions of offering empowerment, they may, in reality, defend their own space and interests (Anthony, 1990). According to some, then, instances of greater worker 'voice' are exceptional rather than the rule (Peiperl, 1996).

Further research has shown that empowerment can mean effectively loading non-managerial jobs with managerial responsibilities, without the commensurate means to discharge them (Geary, 1994; Wilkinson, 1998). Research also tells us that the selection and development costs of empowered employees can be high: service can be slower or inconsistent; fair play can be violated; and there are dangers if empowered employees make the wrong decisions (for example, a desk clerk in a hotel going off to look for a wallet rather than staying on the desk to serve other customers—Bowen and Lawler, 1992). Guidelines on introducing empowerment into the workplace are typically vague and overgeneralized. Also, some employees might find that they become empowered due to management's decisions on other matters (for example, in the *National Health Service*—see Beirne, 1999). Sometimes, the primary aim of a company has been to cut costs by removing a layer of decision making from the organizational structure and the unintended consequence of this has been an increase in duties for those below, leading to a greater sense of empowerment. Research confirms that the impetus towards empowerment frequently comes from technical and operational priorities, often with little sensitivity being shown to the ethical and political issues: for example, if managerial prerogative is threatened by empowered workers. Further, employees can be ambivalent about taking power if they are going to be held personally accountable (Argyris, 1998). Senior managers may believe that organizational change due to the introduction of worker empowerment has led to the hierarchy being made flatter, with more trust between the management and the 'managed', and better cooperation—but, according to research, middle managers are more likely to believe that empowerment is a fiction (Doyle et al., 2000). Further, those at the bottom of the hierarchy are less likely to feel the positive effects of empowerment. In contrast, the better educated and those with higher rank are more likely to experience feelings of empowerment (Koberg et al., 1999).

As we saw in Chapter 12, while teamwork may be about empowering workers, devolving responsibility, and reversing repressive workplace control structures, it can also lead to the intensification of attention on the worker from other team members. Instead of individuals exercising a degree of influence over their own work, they can now influence the work of others in their team through suggestion, demonstration, and exhortation. Life in teams can be stressful, because individuals are subject to intense peer pressure in order to conform to group norms (see Barker, 1993, for an example). Those who stand out as either 'good' or 'bad' workers will receive the scrutiny of their peers and will then be subjected to sanction or reward, or other forces determined by the team. But teamwork does not necessarily descend into tyranny, as McKinlay and Taylor's (1996) discussion of *Pyramid* shows. Here, empowered teams were expected to use peer review to classify, rank, and divide workers so that bonuses could be allocated, but the employees subverted the idea. (See Knights and Willmott, 2007: 152, for more details.)

EXAMPLE *Kay Electronics*: **Management surveillance and control**

At *Kay Electronics* (see Sewell and Wilkinson, 1992), teams comprised between twelve and forty members who were assembling printed circuit boards (PCBs). As the PCBs progressed, they were subjected to electronic tests and the test results were relayed to a central inventory control database. At the start of each day, the team members had yesterday's quality performance information displayed above their workstations in the form of 'traffic lights'. A red card signified that a team member had exceeded acceptable quality limits. A green card signified that he or she had made no quality errors at all and an amber card signified that the operator had made some errors, but that they remained in an acceptable range.

This display of management information unambiguously identified for all those team members who are above average, or 'good' workers, as well as those who are below average. As a result, teams were likely to normalize their productive effort at the level of better performers. Persistent poor workers, identified by regular red cards, would be removed by management from the line, counselled, and retrained; repeated unsatisfactory performance would lead to dismissal. A persistent green card, on the other hand, could mean that an individual was worthy of closer attention, because he or she may have made some kind of innovation in the work process.

While this may be a high-tech company, the 'traffic light' system copies ideas generated by Robert Owen at textile mills in New Lanark, Scotland, in the early 1800s (Randell, 1994: 223). Letting employees know what was thought of their performance through the use of these 'silent monitors' was thought to encourage the 'good' to improve.

Control and surveillance

Power and prerogative give managers rights to control. Control is probably the key issue that shapes and permeates organizational life (Barker, 2005). Wherever there is a need for efficiency, effectiveness, and coordination, structures of control will be found. It is necessary for all individuals to subordinate, to some extent, their own desires to the collective will of the organization (Barnard, 1968).

Control is always problematic for an organization: hierarchical control is often seen as tainted (Jermier, 1998). And as with power, we are uncomfortable discussing struggles for control. But processes of control are integral to the way in which organizations operate. We have been made aware of the excesses of control in the writings of novelists such as George Orwell, who wrote *Nineteen Eighty-Four*, and Aldous Huxley, who wrote *Brave New World*. Their writings were designed to horrify, shock, and provoke thought and discussion.

EXAMPLE **The limits of managerial power and control in the prison and police services**

The number of prison absconders gives an impression of the limits of managerial power and control in the *Prison Service* despite high levels of control and surveillance. Recently, there has been news of a number of prison escapes; some absconders have gone on to murder and rape. Seventy-five prisoners absconded from prison in Scotland in 2006–07 alone (BBC News, 24 January 2008). More than 660 inmates have walked out of Sudbury prison in England in the last ten years (BBC News, 18 December 2007).

The limits of police power are illustrated in rising robbery statistics: for example, robbery rates increased by 3 per cent in 2006–07 in comparison with 2005 figures (available online at http://www.homeoffice.gov.uk/crime-victims/reducing-crime/robbery).

Edwards (1981) identified three broad strategies of control.

1. *Simple control* refers to the direct, authoritarian, and personal control of work and workers by the company's owner or hired bosses—best exemplified today in small, family-owned companies.

2. *Technological control* emerges for the physical technology, such as the assembly line.

3. *Bureaucratic control* is the most familiar strategy, in which control derives from the organizational hierarchy and the organization's rules, which reward compliance and punish non-compliance.

Although all organizations use a mix of strategies of control, some scholars have argued that specific strategies have become popular in specific historical periods. For example, Edwards (1979) argued that managerial practices moved away from widespread use of the simple coercive control in the late nineteenth century towards technological control (using, for example, the assembly line), and then on to bureaucratic control in the mid-twentieth century. Each shift was precipitated by changes in the nature of work and the climate of labour relations. More recently, it has been argued (Wilkinson and Wilmott, 1995) that we make more use of 'post-bureaucratic' control, which involves advanced technology and the instilling of emotions, values, and world views that are congruent with the interests of more powerful parties into the company structure and culture.

Surveillance is one way in which this can be done. New information technologies increase the scope and reach of workplace surveillance; never before have employees been subjected to such intense scrutiny and monitoring as they are now (Sewell, 1998). For example, new technology has allowed for the close monitoring of the activities of supermarket checkout operators, telesales staff, and bus, taxi, and long-distance truck drivers. Zuboff (1988) has talked about the 'information panopticon'—based on an eighteenth-century model of prison design in which inmates were kept in single cells constructed in a ring surrounding a central watchtower from which they were constantly visible. Elite groups are able to exercise control using computer-based production and information technology; armed with the new technology, they consolidate better quality information (Robey, 1981). The electronic monitoring of behaviour can be used to reduce employee theft, to increase control over work behaviour, and to increase productivity.

Researchers have asked for three decades whether or not organizations should be monitoring the activities of their employees electronically. Proponents (for example, Grant and Higgins, 1991) argue, as one might expect, that it ensures accuracy and removes bias when assessing employee performance; detractors argue that it compromises basic rights in areas such as privacy and dignity (Ambrose et al., 1998). In fact, monitoring may not cause workers to raise productivity and may lead to decreased work quality (Griffith, 1993). Those against the idea of electronic monitoring of behaviour (for example,

Davidson and Henderson, 2000) also point to the negative consequences to the worker, such as increased stress and lower quality performance. Consultation can, however, help to overcome potential negative consequences.

EXAMPLE Monitoring

Research has demonstrated that if employees are given the opportunity to have a say in the implementation of a monitoring system, this will enhance the perception of fairness (Hovorka-Mead et al., 2002): if we are unaware of when we are being monitored, we view surveillance as tantamount to spying. Research now recommends that employees have the opportunity to voice their opinions on the monitoring system and that employees should be given the right to appeal decisions made on the basis of monitoring. It is important to let employees know when they will be monitored and they should be offered the opportunity to consent to monitoring before it takes place. Monitoring practice should be formalized and communicated to employees (Zweig and Scott, 2007). It has also been found that, if monitoring that has been designed to reduce theft is not implemented in a fair manner, then it may *increase* both labour turnover and theft (Thoms et al., 2001).

EXAMPLE Monitoring: An example from practice

Holiday company *Freedom Direct* operates under the trading name *Holidaysyoulike.com* and uses an inbound call-handling system to incorporate homeworkers into its call centre team. Homeworkers make up one third of the sales team. When a customer phones *Freedom Direct*, he or she has no idea whether the person answering the call is on the company's premises or in his or her own home. The management can, however, check which homeworkers are logged on or off, how many calls they have taken, how long the calls last, and how many have been converted to sales; they can also monitor the calls for quality.

(*Source:* Twentyman, 2007)

311

Technology

So technology can assist in surveillance—but what place does technology have in other forms of power and control? How has it been considered, researched, and discussed?

Technology is not only about machines—that is, computers, washing machines, telephones, and so on—but also about social relations. These technologies encourage particular forms of interaction. There is little point in defining 'technology' merely as 'devices' and 'machines': as Kramarae (1988) noted, to do so would be like describing housework in terms of dusters and cleaning fluids, without reference to the social systems that determine *who* dusts and cleans. Technology can be described as 'the application of scientific and other knowledge to practical tasks by ordered systems that involve people and organizations, living things and machines' (Pacey, 1983), or it can be described as the transformation of science into a means of capital accumulation (Noble, 1977; 1984). Technology is, then, a human, political, and social activity. When looking at technical change, the key questions include who benefits, how they benefit, and whose interests the technological change best serves.

One of the earliest studies of the impact of technological change and its impact on social activity concerned the impact of innovation in the coal industry (Trist and Bamforth, 1951). We saw in Chapter 12 how teamworking was disturbed by the technological innovation in the coal industry. In pre-mechanized mining, coal was extracted using the 'hand-got' method under which small, self-selected groups—usually made up of a hewer and his mate, assisted by a boy 'trammer'—would be responsible for the whole process of coal extraction (cutting the coal from the face, loading it onto tubs, and taking it out the mine), using a number of skills. These small teams worked on short faces autonomously; leadership and supervision were internal to the group, and the group set its own targets for production. The small groups tended to become isolated from each other—the isolation being intensified by the darkness, under which conditions continuous supervision was impossible. Stable relationships tended to result, which frequently endured over many years. In circumstances under which a man was injured or killed, it was not uncommon for his mate to care for his family. There also were rivalries and conflicts, however. A common form of 'misbehaviour' was to bribe the deputy managers in order to secure a good length, or 'bank', of coal with a 'rack roof' under which the coal was soft and easy to work. Because supplies of tubs were often in short supply, the trammer would go early to work and turn two or three tubs on their sides in his 'gate', maintaining that he had only taken one. It was a common saying that it was he who could lie, cheat, or bully the most who made the best trammer. All of this was accepted as part of the system.

With the advent of mechanization and mass production engineering came the 'longwall method' for extracting the coal. Coal cutters and mechanical conveyors were introduced. The introduction of mechanization made it possible to work on a single long face in place of the series of short faces. With the longwall method, a direct advance was made on the coal on a continuous front. A medium-sized pit might have between twelve and fifteen longwall faces in operation simultaneously. Men were organized into groups of between forty and fifty men, their shot-firer and shift deputies working in cycles or shifts. There were four groups of task: to prepare the face for shot firing; to shift the conveyor; to build up the roof and gates; and to fire the shots and move the shot coal onto the conveyor, and prop up the roof.

This new, differentiated structure disturbed the previous simple balance of working. Now, the men were trained in only one of the seven required roles. They worked on one of three shifts and the shifts never met. Mistakes and difficulties made or encountered at one stage would be carried forward, producing yet further difficulties in the next. Tension and anxiety were consequently created, and a group culture of angry and suspicious bargaining over which both management and men were in collusion arose. A norm of low productivity was the outcome. The men clearly did not see the benefit of the new system over the old: the introduction of the technology disrupted the old system and while the new work arrangements might have given greater managerial control, they had also produced problems.

Technology is usually thought of as providing greater managerial control; it is also usually thought of as a masculine invention and activity (see Chapter 14). It is often assumed that women have not been very involved in the invention of technology. There were, for example, no women among the qualified engineering professionals responsible for the food processor or the washing machine (Cockburn and Furst-Dilic, 1994). But many technologies have been invented by women (see Trescott, 1979; Warner, 1979). Household technologies, such as refrigerators and washing machines, were originally designed and manufactured for commercial laundries, hotels, and hospitals, but have been scaled down for family use. These technologies—sold as 'labour-saving' devices—have not made the household easier to run or freed women for other activities (Cowan, 1983): as the equipment has been introduced into the homes of families who could afford it, cleaning standards have been raised and it is still women who are doing the repetitive tasks.

We also tend to think of technology as novelty and innovation as if it travels only in one way on a progressive timeline, but is this always the case? The old is always with us—and sometimes, we return to it: for example, cable television was a declining industry in the 1950s and 1960s, but re-emerged in the 1990s. Ships are the most important agent of globalization, but we think of them as old-fashioned technology. And the condom decreased in use in the 1960s with the arrival of the contraceptive pill, but came back into use on a massive scale globally in the 1980s (Edgerton, 2007).

Turning now to factory technology, technology and power have been drawn together in research initiated by Braverman (1974) on the 'labour process'. Braverman combined the concepts of power and technology through the intermediary concept of control. Power was originally seen as exercised in a 'zero-sum' power game in which one party profits at the expense of another. The classical cases were documented by Gorz (1972) and Marglin (1974). Marglin cites the case of cotton and wool merchants, who constructed a role for themselves using technology to control the activities of their workers rather than only to enhance productivity. A very different technology would be developed if maximum control were not the main aim (Gorz, 1972). Technology can have a major impact on work tasks, using judgement, discretion, and decision making, and so reduce or eliminate the individual's opportunities for resistance (Beynon, 1974; Nichols and Beynon, 1977). Other authors examining the introduction of technology into white-collar work include Watanabe (1990), who describes how labour was deskilled and degraded in the banking sector (and whose work was described in an earlier chapter), and Knights and Sturdy (1987), who argued that there had been a massive increase in routine work in the insurance industry and a polarization of skills, due to technology and the way in which jobs were designed around it.

But it would be wrong to believe that technology always deskills jobs. Zeitlin (1983) shows how the introduction of new technology in the UK engineering industry during the period 1890–1920 increased the margin of workers' control. Employers remained heavily dependent on skilled labour and vulnerable to craft militancy during boom periods, but the marginal gains by skilled employees were always short-lived. Managerial intentions towards deskilling have been limited, as Buchanan (1986), Wilson (1987), and others have shown. When computer numerically controlled (CNC) machines are introduced, new demands are made on the workforce: programs need to be debugged and the production process monitored; workers' knowledge and skills prove to be essential. How long management is dependent on skills following the introduction of new technology is probably related to products, processes, and the configuration of power (Clegg and Wilson, 1991). The locus of control cannot always be moved from workers to managers during technical change, nor from managers to workers. Control does, therefore, ultimately lie with management—although workers may resist it.

313

Technology and surveillance

Employers have always monitored the performance of their employees, but in the last twenty years, surveillance at work has increased with the introduction of information technology as managers have attempted to increase their control. Surveillance is to be found particularly in high-volume service operations, such as call centres, including those used in direct banking and insurance sales, where it is used to ensure work is being done. It has been described as 'the technological whip of the electronic age' (Fodness and Kinsella, 1990). Calls are listened to by those who are monitoring levels of service quality and data are collected on performance levels, including number of calls received or made. Those who are being monitored know that their work is being seen, but often do not know what information is being generated about them and their performance.

Kirsty Ball and David Wilson (1997; 2000) describe two case studies of the technology of surveillance: one in a debt collection department in a building society, and the other in the credit card division of a bank. In the debt collection department, work varied according to the complexity of the accounts in question and the length of time for which they had been in arrears. In the case of the credit card division, the main activity was the inputting of credit card sales vouchers onto the computer system to charge the correct amounts to the customer. In both cases, managers and supervisors could see what each operator and team had produced in a day. The performance statistics were a great source of stress to the operators, because their calculation was secret. Operators would be given feedback on their performance and, in one company, if they were persistently to fall short of their targets, they would be sacked. This was the direct result, then, of increased management control.

Given the potential negative outcomes of greater managerial control, we should therefore not be surprised if greater surveillance is met with some suspicion from employees.

EXAMPLE The 'SPY' in the sky

'Spy' devices—that is, satellite navigation technology—have been installed in dustcarts to tell the drivers which routes to take, to ensure that drivers take the shortest routes, and to give base control information on where they are, how long they have been stopped, the size of the bins being emptied, and the speed limit of the roads on which they are travelling. Management argues that the technology delivers the most efficient and effective system, and that cost savings are passed on to the taxpayer; the refuse collectors are not so sure of the motive.

(*Source: Daily Mail,* 6 November 2002)

Business process engineering

Business process engineering (BPR) represents the latest in a series of managerial 'recipes' that advocate the use of technical and organizational changes to achieve higher efficiency and performance, thereby giving managers greater control. BPR has been described as 'the fundamental rethinking and radical design of business processes to achieve dramatic improvements in critical, contemporary measures of performance, such as cost, quality, service, and speed' and as 'a manifesto for revolution' (Hammer and Champy, 1993: 32). It is the most recent in a long line of management innovations adopted by a wide spectrum of industry and commerce in the UK and the USA, and is a successor of total quality management (see Chapter 14).

The distinctiveness of BPR, for Knights and McCabe (1998), is that it focuses upon radical change and is a process-based approach to the organization of work; it is based on the analysis and redesign of how activities are organized. The process is facilitated by the increased use of information technology. The implementation of new information technology is usually the main push for transforming the organization and is closely associated with BPR. BPR can include teamworking, empowerment, flatter hierarchies, and a customer orientation; the novelty rests in packaging these together to 'transform' organizations (Grint et al., 1996).

While BPR is widely discussed among management practitioners and proponents, they have widely different perceptions as to what it means. For some practitioners within the UK financial service industry, for example, it means short-term cost savings; for others, it promises a radical future of change (McCabe et al., 1994). But examples of effective implementation are rare (Willcocks and Grint, 1997), and academics, such as Grey and Mitev (1995), are challenging the claims and promises of BPR. While practitioners may think that BPR presents the radically new, discontinuous future and recommend 'don't automate, obliterate', calling for organizational politics to be cast aside, Willcocks and Grint (1997) argue that BPR is an inherently risky and political process that does not always lead to positive outcomes.

EXAMPLE Where BPR led to loss of knowledge

Business process engineering is seen as responsible for the loss of some knowledge and expertise when whole layers of middle management are stripped out; one reason why knowledge management initiatives became so popular in the late 1990s was because they were seen as an antidote to the knowledge loss that firms had experienced, following the successful implementation of BPR programmes a few years previously (Newell et al., 2002). Newell and his colleagues give the example of a shipbuilding company in the north of England, which found, when it came to launch a new ship, that it had lost that knowledge and expertise held by middle managers when it 'downsized' the company to make it more 'efficient'.

Conclusion

Power is fundamental to organizational design. Behaviour in organizations is political. Understanding organizations as political systems is a productive image that helps us to understand more of the nature and functioning of organizations. Seeing organizations as political systems draws attention to the ways in which they can serve as sites within which different values, forms of knowledge, and interests are articulated and embodied in decisions, structures, and practices. As political systems, organizations use power and control; in so doing, they provide meaning and personal identity, as well as goods, services, and income. The issue of control is central to this book and was picked up in Chapter 11. We have seen, here, that despite managerial power and prerogative, surveillance, and managers' ability to use technology and to silence dissent, managers will never have total control; workers will resist. Managers, as functionary agents, are limited in what they can achieve.

This chapter gives you good reason to be suspicious of the claims that may be made by those advocating greater efficiency and productivity by using increasingly rational means (such as the introduction of new technologies, systems, or surveillance), because employees may find good reason to resist—particularly if they are not involved in the decision making relating to the change. We will look at this resistance—and at other misbehaviour—in the next chapter.

KEY POINTS

- Various descriptions, views, and analyses of power and how it operates in organizations exist within the management literature.

- Managers do not have total power, but they have been given the authority and prerogative to manage and control.

- Research illustrates how workers also can exert control: for example, they may not follow the rules, instructions, or expectations of management. There are many examples in the management literature of how different occupational groups exert control over their work.

- Empowerment is about managers sharing power with workers—but managers do not always want, or see the need, to empower.

- Increasing surveillance can increase management control. Technologies may assist in this process.

CASE STUDY

Resistance at Disneyland

We touched on the limits to the absorption of organizational culture in Chapter 11, but much more might be said.

Van Maanen (1991) shows the limits to which overt company propaganda in the *Disney* organization can be effective. Satirical banter, mischievous winking, and playful exaggeration are to be found in the classroom with the new recruits. As one notes: 'It is difficult to take seriously an organization that provides its retirees with "Golden Ears" instead of gold watches after 20 or more years of service' (Van Maanen, 1991: 67). All of the newcomers are aware that the label 'Disneyland' has both an unserious and artificial connotation. A full embrace of the Disneyland role would be as deviant as its full rejection.

Sometimes, customers will overstep their role, insult an operator, challenge their authority, or disrupt the routines of the job. If a customer slights a ride operator, routine practices have been developed by the operators to deal with this. Common remedies include the following.

- During the 'seatbelt squeeze', the deviant customer's seatbelt is adjusted to the extent that he or she is doubled over at the point of departure and left gasping.

- The 'brake toss' involves an operator jumping on the outside of a norm violator's car, unhitching the safety belt, then slamming on the brakes, bringing the car to an almost instant stop while the driver flies over the bonnet.

- In the 'seatbelt snap', an offending customer receives a sharp quick snap of the hard plastic belt across the face or other part of the body while entering or exiting a seatbelted ride.

- The 'break up the party' gambit is a queuing device put into officious use to separate troublesome pairs into different units, thus forcing on them the pain of strange companions for the duration of a ride.

- Offensive guests can be drenched with water as part of the submarine ride.

All of these procedures, and more, are learned on the job and enliven conversation time at breaks or after work. Naturally, though, operators are aware of the limits and, if caught, they know that restoration of corporate pride will be swift.

(*Source:* Van Maanen, 1991)

Questions

1. Is this behaviour a sign of resistance to managerial control, demonstrating how ride operators are in control of their job and how it is managed?

2. Should it be regarded as misbehaviour?

3. Does it represent ways in which the operator copes with the difficult demands of the job—especially difficult customers?

FURTHER READING

Collinson, D. (2000) 'Strategies of resistance: Power, knowledge and subjectivity in the workplace', in K. Grint (ed.), *Work and Society: A Reader*, Cambridge: Polity Press, ch. 8 This chapter discusses the options, knowledge, and agencies through which opposition to managerial power is initiated.

Gabriel, Y., Fineman, S., and Sims, D. (2000) *Organizing and Organizations*, London: Sage Chapter 3, 'Rules are rules', discusses the rationality and rules in organizations. You will see some links to the chapter about bureaucracy and rationality.

Hales, C. (2000) 'Management and empowerment programmes', *Work, Employment and Society*, 14(3): 501–19 This article compares and contrasts the rhetoric with the limited reality of empowerment. It takes evidence from a number of companies and settings to show how senior managers enthusiastically promote, while junior managers reluctantly accept, empowerment programmes.

Noon, M. and Blyton, P. (2002; 2007) *The Realities of Work*, Houndmills: Palgrave One chapter of this title discusses knowledge, work, and power.

Thompson, P. and McHugh, D. (2002) *Work Organizations*, 3rd edn, Houndmills: Palgrave Chapter 9 of this book discusses issues of power, conflict, and resistance.

Watson, T. (2002) *Organising and Managing Work*, Harlow: Pearson Chapter 10 discusses power and politics in organizations.

LINKS TO FILMS AND NOVELS

The Great Escape (1963) dir. J. Sturges Based on a true story from the Second World War, this film depicts a group of allied prisoners of war held in an 'escape-proof' camp. The group leader makes plans to lead several hundred prisoners of war in an escape. The story illustrates the limits of the Germans' managerial control. Surveillance and teamwork are also themes that arise in this film.

RESEARCH QUESTIONS

1. Sewell (1998) says that discipline can be maintained through teamwork and peer group scrutiny. Surveillance and teamwork are an unexpected combination. How are surveillance and teamwork combined?

2. What research might help you to argue that the panopticon is as diverse in its use as the contexts in which it occurs? (See Ball and Wilson, 1997.)

3. 'Many concepts used in organizational analysis, such as power, domination, control, and authority can be used as euphemisms for violence, most obviously in the police, military, and prisons' (Hearn, 1994). Discuss.

REFERENCES

Alvarez, J.L. and Svejenova, S (2005) *Sharing Executive Power: Roles and Relationships at the Top*, Cambridge: Cambridge University Press.

Ambrose, M.L., Alder, G.S., and Noel, T.W. (1998) 'Electronic performance monitoring: A consideration of rights', in M. Schminke (ed.) *Managerial Ethics: Moral Management of People and Processes*, Mahwah, NJ: Erlbaum, pp. 61–80.

Anderson, J. and Englehardt, E.E. (2001) *The Organizational Self and Ethical Conduct: Sunlit Virtue and Shadowed Resistance*, Fort Worth, TX: Harcourt College Publishers.

Anthony, P. (1990) 'The paradox of the management of culture or "he who leads is lost"', *Personnel Review*, 19: 3–8.

Argyris, C. (1998) 'Empowerment: The Emperor's new clothes', *Harvard Business Review*, 76: 98–105.

Bachrach, P. and Baratz, M.S. (1963) 'Decisions and nondecisions', *American Political Science Review*, 57: 641–51.

Ball, K. and Wilson, D. (1997) *Computer-Based Monitoring and the Electronic Panopticon: A Review of the Debate and Some New Evidence from the UK*, Working paper, Birmingham: Aston Business School.

_____ (2000) 'Power, control and computer-based performance monitoring: Repertoires, resistance and subjectivities', *Organization Studies*, 21(3): 539–65.

Barker, J.R. (1993) 'Tightening the iron cage: Coercive control in self managing teams', *Administrative Science Quarterly*, 38: 408–37.

_____ (2005) 'Tightening the iron cage: Concertive control in self managing teams', in C. Grey and H. Willmott (eds), *Critical Management Studies: A Reader*, Oxford: Oxford University Press, ch. 10.

Barnard, C. (1938; 1968) *The Function of the Executive*, Cambridge, MA: Harvard University Press.

Bates, I. (1990) 'No bleeding, whining minnies: The role of YTS in class and gender reproduction', *British Journal of Education and Work*, 3: 91–110.

_____ (1993) 'A job which is "right for me"? Social class, gender and individualization', in I. Bates and G. Riseborough (eds), *Youth and Inequality*, Buckingham: Open University Press, ch. 1.

Beirne, M. (1999) 'Managing to empower? A healthy review of resources and constraints', *European Management Journal*, 17(2): 218–25.

_____ (2006) *Empowerment and Innovation: Managers, Principles and Reflective Practice*, Cheltenham: Edward Elgar.

Beynon, H. (1974) *Working for Ford*, Harmondsworth: Penguin.

Boddy, D. (2002) *Management: An Introduction*, 2nd edn, Harlow: Pearson.

Bowen, D.E. and Lawler, E.E. (1992) 'The empowerment of service workers: What, why, how and when', *Sloan Management Review*, Spring: 31–9.

Braverman, H. (1974) *Labor and Monopoly Capital: The Degradation of Work in the Twentieth Century*, New York: Monthly Review Press.

Buchanan, D.A. (1986) *Canned Cycles and Dancing Tools: Who's Really in Control of Computer Aided Machining?*, Working Paper Series No. 1, March, Glasgow: University of Glasgow Department of Management Studies.

Buzzard, R.B. and Liddell, F.D. (1963) *Coalminers' Attendance at Work*, National Coal Board Medical Research Memorandum 3, London: National Coal Board.

Clegg, S.R. (1975) *Power, Rule and Domination*, London: Routledge.

_____ (1987) 'The language of power and the power of language', *Organization Studies*, 8(1): 61–70.

_____ and Hardy, C. (1996) 'Organizations, organization and organizing', in S.R. Clegg, C. Hardy, and W.R. Nord (eds), *Handbook of Organization Studies*, London: Sage, Introduction.

_____ and Wilson, F. (1991) 'Power, technology and flexibility in organizations', in J. Law (ed.), *A Sociology of Monsters: Essays on Power, Technology and Domination*, London: Routledge, pp. 223–73.

Cockburn, C. and Furst-Dilic, R.F. (eds) (1994) *Bringing Technology Home: Gender and Technology in a Changing Europe*, Buckingham: Open University Press.

Cowan, R.S. (1983) *More Work for Mother: The Ironies of Household Technology from the Open Hearth to the Microwave*, New York: Basic Books.

Crozier, M. (1964) *The Bureaucratic Phenomenon*, Chicago, IL: University of Chicago Press.

Dahl, R. (1957) 'The concept of power', *Behavioral Science*, 20: 201–15.

Davidson, R. and Henderson, R. (2000) 'Electronic performance monitoring: A laboratory investigation of the influence of monitoring and difficulty in task performance, mood state and self-reported stress levels', *Journal of Applied Psychology*, 30(5): 906–20.

Doyle, M., Claydon, T., and Buchanan, D. (2000) 'Mixed results, lousy process: The management experience of organizational change', *British Journal of Management*, 11(Special issue): S59–S80.

Edgerton, D. (2007) *The Shock of the Old: Technology in Global History Since 1900*, London: Profile Books.

Edwards, R.C. (1979) *Contested Terrain: The Transformation of the Workplace in the Twentieth Century*, New York: Basic Books.

_____ (1981) 'The social relations of production at the point of production', in M. Zey-Ferrell and M. Aiken (eds), *Complex Organizations: Critical Perspectives*, Glenview, IL: Scott Foresman.

Ezzamel, M., Lilley, S., and Wilmott, H. (1994) 'The "new organization" and the "new managerial work"', *European Management Journal*, 12(4): 454–61.

Fenton-O'Creevy, M. (2001) 'Employee Involvement and the middle manager: Saboteur or scapegoat?', *Human Resource Management Journal*, 11(1): 24–40.

_____ and Nicholson, N. (1994) *Middle Managers: Their Contribution to Employee Involvement*, Employment Department Research Series No. 28, London: HMSO.

Fleming, P. and Spicer, A. (2002) 'Workers' playtime? Unraveling the paradox of covert resistance in organizations', in S.R. Clegg (ed.), *Management and Organization Paradoxes*, Philadelphia, PA: John Benjamins, pp. 65–85.

Fodness, K. and Kinsella, S. (1990) *Stories of Mistrust and Manipulation: The Electronic Monitoring of the American Workforce*, Cleveland, OH: National Association of Working Women.

Foucault, M. (1977) *Discipline and Punish: The Birth of the Prison*, Harmondsworth: Penguin.

French, J.R. and Raven, B.H. (1959) 'The bases of social power', in D. Cartwright (ed.), *Studies in Social Power*, Ann Arbor, MI: Institute for Social Research, pp. 150–67.

Geary, J. (1994) 'Task participation: Employees' participation, enabled or constrained', in K. Sisson (ed.), *Personnel Management*, 2nd edn, Oxford: Blackwell, ch. 19.

Golding, D. (1980) 'Establishing blissful clarity in organizational life: Managers', *Sociological Review*, 28(4): 763–83.

Gorz, A. (1972) 'Technical intelligence and the capitalist division of labour', *Telos*, 12: 27–41.

Gouldner, A. (1954) *Patterns of Industrial Bureaucracy*, Glencoe, IL: The Free Press.

_____ (1960) 'The norm of reciprocity: A preliminary statement', *American Journal of Sociology*, 81: 82–108.

Grant, R.A. and Higgins, C.A. (1991) 'The impact of computerized performance monitoring on service work: Testing a causal model', *Information Systems Research*, 2: 116–42.

Greasley, K., Bryman, A., Dainty, A., Price, A., Soetanto, R., and King, N. (2005) 'Employee perceptions of empowerment', *Employee Relations*, 27(4): 354–68.

Grey, C. and Mitev, N. (1995) 'Reengineering organizations: A critical appraisal', *Personnel Review*, 24(1): 6–18.

Griffith, T.L. (1993) 'Monitoring performance: A comparison of computer and supervisor monitoring', *Journal of Applied Social Psychology*, 24: 873–96.

Grint, K., Case, P., and Willcocks, L. (1996) 'BPR reappraised: The politics and technology of forgetting', in W.J. Orlihowski, G.I. Walsham, M.R. Jones, and J.I. Degross (eds), *Information Technology and Changes in Organizational Work*, London: Chapman & Hull.

Hales, C. (2000) 'Management and empowerment programmes', *Work, Employment and Society*, 14(3): 501–19.

Hammer, M. and Champy, J. (1993) *Reengineering the Corporation: A Manifesto for Business Revolution*, London: Nicholas Brealy.

Handy, J. (1990) *Occupational Stress in a Caring Profession*, Aldershot: Avebury.

Hardy, C. and Clegg, S.R. (1996) 'Some dare call it power', in S.R. Clegg, C. Hardy, and W.R. Nord (eds), *Handbook of Organization Studies*, London: Sage, ch. 3.7.

Hearn, J. (1994) 'The organization(s) of violence: Men, gender relations, organizations and violences', *Human Relations*, 47(6): 731–54.

Hickson, D.J., Hinings, C.A., Lee, C.A., Schneck, R.E., and Pennings, J.M. (1971) 'A strategic contingencies theory of intraorganizational power', *Administrative Science Quarterly*, 16(2): 216–29.

Hovorka-Mead, A.D., Ross, W.H., Whipple, T., and Renchin, M.B. (2002) 'Watching the detectives: Seasonal student employee reactions to electronic monitoring with and without advance notice', *Personnel Psychology*, 55: 329–62.

Isaac, J.C. (1987) *Power and Marxist Theory: A Realist View*, Ithaca, NY: Cornell University Press.

Jermier, J.M. (1998) 'Introduction: Critical perspectives on organizational control', *Administrative Science Quarterly*, 43: 235–56.

_____, Knights, D., and Nord, W.R. (1994) 'Introduction', in J.M. Jermier, D. Knights and W.R. Nord (eds), *Resistance and Power in Organizations*, New York: Routledge, pp. 1–24.

Johnson, P. and Gill, J. (1993), *Management Control and Organizational Behaviour*, London: Paul Chapman.

Kanter, R.M. (1977) *Men and Women of the Corporation*, New York: Basic Books.

_____ (1979) 'Power failure in management circuits', *Harvard Business Review*, 57: 65–75.

_____ (1984) 'Innovation: The only hope for times ahead?', *Sloan Management Review*, 25: 51–5.

Knights, D. and McCabe, D. (1998) 'When "Life is but a dream": Obliterating politics through business process reengineering?' *Human Relations*, 51(6): 761–98.

_____ and Sturdy, A. (1987) 'Women's work in insurance: Information technology and the reproduction of gendered segregation', in M.J. Davidson and C.L. Cooper (eds), *Women and Information Technology*, Chichester: Wiley, pp. 151–75.

_____ and Wilmott, H. (2007) *Introducing Organizational Behaviour and Management*, London: Thomson Learning.

Koberg, C.S., Boss, R.W., Senjem, J.C., and Goodman, E.A. (1999) 'Antecedents and outcomes of empowerment', *Group and Organization Management*, 24(1): 71–91.

Kramarae, C. (1988) 'Gotta go Myrtle, technology's at the door', in C. Kramarae (ed.), *Technology and Women's Voices: Keeping in Touch*, London: Routledge & Kegan Paul.

Lashley, C. (1995) 'Towards an understanding of employee empowerment in hospitality services', *International Journal of Contemporary Hospitality Management*, 7(1): 27–32.

Lee-Treweek, G. (1997) 'Women, resistance and care: An ethnographic study of nursing auxiliary work', *Work, Employment and Society*, 11(1):47–63.

Lukes, S. (1974) *Power: A Radical View*, London: Macmillan.

Marglin, S.A. (1974) 'What do bosses do? The origins and functions of hierarchy in capitalist production', *Review of Radical Political Economics*, 6: 60–112.

Marx, K. (1976) *Capital*, Harmondsworth: Penguin.

McCabe, D., Knights, D., and Wilkinson, A. (1994) *Quality Initiatives in Financial Services*, Research report, Manchester: UMIST Manchester School of Management Financial Services Research Centre.

McKinlay, A. and Taylor, P. (1996) 'Power, surveillance and resistance', in P. Ackers, C. Smith, and P. Smith (eds), *The New Workplace and Trade Unionism*, London: Routledge, pp. 279–300.

Mulholland, K. (2004) 'Workplace resistance in an Irish call centre: Slammin', scammin', smokin' an' leavin'', *Work Employment and Society*, 18: 709–24.

Newton, L.H. (2006) *Permission to Steal: Revealing the Roots of Corporate Scandal—An Address to My Fellow Citizens*, Oxford: Blackwell Publishing.

Nichols, T. and Beynon, H. (1977) *Living with Capitalism*, London: Routledge & Kegan Paul.

Nicholson, N. (1976) 'Management sanctions and absence control', *Human Relations*, 29: 139–51.

Noble, D. (1977) *America by Design: Science, Technology and the Rise of Corporate Capitalism*, New York: Alfred A. Knopf.

_____ (1984) *Forces of Production*, New York: Alfred A. Knopf.

Offe, C. (1976) *Industry and Inequality*, London: Edward Arnold.

Pacey, A. (1983) *The Culture of Technology*, Cambridge, MA: MIT Press.

Peiperl, M. (1996) 'Does empowerment deliver the goods?', *Mastering Management*, 10: 2–4.

Randell, G. (1994) 'Employee appraisal', in K. Sisson (ed.), *Personnel Management: A Comprehensive Guide to Theory and Practice in Britain*, 2nd edn, Oxford: Blackwell, ch. 7.

Raven, B.H. (1965) 'Social influence and power', in I.D. Steiner and M. Fishbein (eds), *Current Studies in Social Psychology*, New York: Holt Rinehart & Winston, pp. 371–82.

Robey, D. (1981) 'Computer information systems and organization structure', *Communications of ACM*, 24: 679–87.

Sewell, G. (1998) 'The discipline of teams: The control of team-based industrial work through electronic and peer surveillance', *Administrative Science Quarterly*, 43: 397–428.

_____ and Wilkinson, B. (1992) 'Someone to watch over me: Surveillance, discipline and the just-in-time labour process', *Sociology*, 26: 271–89.

Spreitzer, G.M. (1995) 'Psychological empowerment in the workplace: Dimensions, measurement and validation', *Academy of Management Journal*, 38(5): 1442–65.

Storey, J. (1983) *Managerial Prerogative and the Question of Control*, London: Routledge & Kegan Paul.

Swallow, C. (2004) 'Protecting workers from travel rage', *Logistics and Transport Focus*, 6(9): 49.

Taylor, S. and Tyler, M. (2000) 'Emotional labour and sexual difference in the airline industry', *Work, Employment and Society*, 14(1): 77–95.

Thiel, D. (2007) 'Class in construction: London building workers, dirty work and physical cultures', *The British Journal of Sociology*, 58(2): 227–51.

Thompson, W.E. (1983) 'Hanging tongues: A sociological encounter with the assembly line', *Qualitative Sociology*, 6(3): 215–36.

Thoms, P., Wolper, P., Scott, K., and Jones, D. (2001) 'The relationship between immediate turnover and employee theft in the restaurant industry', *Journal of Business and Psychology*, 15(4): 561–77.

Trescott, M.M. (1979) *Dynamos and Virgins Revisited: Women and Technological Change in History*, Metuchen, NJ: Scarecrow Press.

Trist, E.L. and Bamforth, K.W. (1951) 'Some social and psychological consequences of the longwall method of coal-getting: An examination of the psychological situation and defences of a work group in relation to the social structure and technological content of the work system', *Human Relations*, 4(3): 3–38.

Twentyman, J. (2007) 'Staff monitoring: Keeping tabs on homeworkers', *Personnel Today*, 22 October, available online at http://www.personneltoday.com/articles/2007/10/22/42869/staff-monitoring-keeping-tabs-on-homeworkers.html

Van Maanen, J. (1991) 'The smile factory: Work at Disneyland', in P.J. Frost, L.F. Moore, M.R. Louis, C. C. Lundberg, and J. Martin (eds), *Reframing Organizational Culture*, London: Sage, ch. 4.

_____ (1995) 'Fear and loathing in organization studies', *Organization Science*, 6(6): 687–92.

Warner, D. (1979) 'Women inventors at the centennial', in M.M. Trescott (ed.), *Dynamos and Virgins Revisited*, Metuchen, NJ: Scarecrow Press.

Watanabe, T. (1990) 'New office technology and the labour process in contemporary Japanese banking', *New Technology, Work and Employment*, 5(1): 56–67.

Weber, M. (1978) *Economy and Society: An Outline of Interpretive Sociology*, ed. G. Roth and C. Wittich, Berkeley, CA: University of California Press.

Wilkinson, A. (1998) 'Empowerment: Theory and practice', *Personnel Review*, 27: 40–56.

_____ and Willmott, H. (eds) (1995) *Making Quality Critical: New Perspectives on Organizational Change*, London: Routledge.

Willcocks, L. and Grint, K. (1997) 'Re-inventing the organization? Towards a critique of business process re-engineering', in I. McLoughlin and M. Harris (eds), *Innovation, Organizational Change and Technology*, London: International Thomson Business Press, ch. 4.

Wilson, F.M. (1987) 'Computer numerical control and constraint', in D. Knights and H. Wilmott (eds), *New Technology and the Labour Process*, London: Macmillan.

Zeitlin, J. (1983) 'The labour strategies of British engineering employers, 1890–1922', in H. Gospel and C. Littler (eds), *Managerial Strategies and Industrial Relations*, London: Heinemann.

Zuboff, S. (1988) *In the Age of the Smart Machine*, New York: Basic Books.

Zweig, D. and Scott, K. (2007) 'When unfairness matters most: Supervisory violations of electronic monitoring practices', *Human Resource Management Journal*, 17(3): 227–47.

321

16 Organizational Misbehaviour

Introduction

In the last chapter, we looked at the limits of power and control, as well as at the issue of sharing power—that is, empowerment. In that chapter, we also looked at examples of resistance, which helped to explain why people resist greater managerial control exercised in a bid to increase productivity and efficiency.

This chapter looks at some examples of behaviour that people at work do not, in general, want to see—that is, organizational misbehaviour such as theft, virtual crime, and bullying. It includes misbehaviour that is not usually regarded as 'organizational behaviour' and which is therefore not included in the textbooks. But this is behaviour that takes place in organizations—swindling, lying, denying, and other forms of misbehaviour—and is seen among owners, managers, and workers alike. Such forms of misbehaviour among workers pose limits on managerial power and control. The statistics, research, and examples of organizational theft, for example, clearly demonstrate this. People are very adept at stealing from organizations in many ways—but mainstream management texts tend to ignore this topic.

By the end of this chapter, you will learn about the more 'seedy' side of organizational life and appreciate how 'sanitized' other accounts of organizational life are. By acknowledging all forms of behaviour in the workplace, including misbehaviour, you will have a more balanced and realistic view of what you might expect of people at work.

This chapter covers:

- resistance and organizational misbehaviour;
- cheating, fraud, and theft;
- virtual crime;
- swearing;
- swindling;
- lying;
- denial;
- bullying;
- sabotage;
- struggles relating to time;
- gossip;
- fun;
- managing organizational misbehaviour.

Resistance and organizational misbehaviour

Organizational misbehaviour, resistance, and crime have been relatively neglected topics in textbooks on management and business. They are seldom thought of as 'organizational behaviour'—yet cheating and theft have probably been going on since the very beginnings of 'organization', and worker resistance has been acknowledged since Karl Marx wrote about the many forms that it takes and its roots in revolutionary class consciousness. For Marx, however, class-conscious radical resistance was not very likely to occur within a capitalist system. According to Marx, this was because there is an illusion of freedom within the capitalist system—that is, members of society believe themselves to be free when, in fact, they are constrained by the system. This obscures the reality of alienation—that is, the disconnection of workers from their job and from others in the production process (see Chapter 2). Capitalism therefore appears normal and inevitable, like the laws of nature. 'Real resistance' was broken down (Jermier et al., 1994) and acts such as sabotage, theft, or the intentional withholding of output often explained as reactions to frustrations (Spector, 1997).

EXAMPLE **Misbehaviour in the fast-food industry**

A television investigation videotaped local restaurant workers sneezing into their hands while preparing food, licking salad dressing off their fingers, picking their noses, and flicking cigarette ash into food about to be served. In May 2000, three employees at *Burger King* were arrested for putting spit, urine, and cleaning products into the food. They had allegedly tampered with the *Burger King* food for eight months (Schlosser, 2001: 222). There are other stories that Schlosser tells about behaviour at work that might make you think twice about ever eating fast food again.

Bad behaviour in organizations does, of course, take all sorts of different forms.

EXAMPLE **More examples of bad behaviour**

A director of a charity would sleep through meetings with senior staff, but afterwards request and receive reassurance from them that his input would be helpful. Youth workers allowed the youth clubs for which they were responsible to fall into disuse, but falsified attendance figures to make it look as if they were still serving young people (Myers, 2002).

Almost 2,000 university students in the UK were reprimanded for bad behaviour, including drug abuse, drink-driving, harassment, vandalism, and plagiarism in only one year (Paton, 2007). Plagiarism has become a topical issue as plagiarism detection software is introduced to try to prevent students from taking another person's thoughts and passing them off as their own. A Glasgow academic said, in a letter to a newspaper, that when he was an external university examiner, one student's essay was spotted as a cheat because it ended with the phrase: 'For more information, click here' (Ditton, 2008).

Cheating, fraud, and theft

We all know people who thieve and cheat—and we may even do it ourselves. According to Ashworth (1999), middle managers—often long-serving members of staff—are among the chief culprits, because they have the best understanding of how to cheat their company and cover their tracks. But we all know how to cheat and thieve, even if we do not do so: in universities, plagiarism is one form of cheating that is much despised; theft is equally despised by most. Every now and again, newspapers report a story of theft that is bound to catch the eye: for example, it has recently been estimated that £1 billion is stolen from Scottish companies through fraud every year (Friedli, 2006). *Société Générale*, a bank, claims to have lost £3.7 billion ($7.1 billion) due to the fraudulent activities of one of its traders—losses four times greater than those made by the now infamous Nick Leeson, the city trader who brought down Barings Bank in 1995. Nick Leeson has been quoted as saying that rogue trading is probably a daily occurrence within the financial markets (BBC News, 24 and 25 January 2008).

Punch (1996) cites a number of cases of misbehaviour within organizations. For example, he describes the newspaper story about nuns who had fraudulently diverted money (about $5 million) from a hospital in order to build an indoor swimming pool and purchase television sets for all of the cells in their luxurious convent. He also details three highly dramatic cases of business deviance, including the case of Robert Maxwell, who built up *Pergamon Press* and a series of other companies, including the *Daily Mirror*, but was, after his death, accused of 'looting' his companies to pay massive debts (ibid.: 5–9). In one case cited by Punch, £300 million went missing from pension funds; in further cases, *BCCI*, a large financial institution, is estimated to have swindled $20 billion from depositors around the world (and to have run a 'black bank' within the bank). It was accused of systematically falsifying records and laundering the illegal income of drug sellers (ibid.: 9–15). And the *Savings and Loan* scandal involved mismanagement and fraud: funds were siphoned off for personal gain (ibid.: 15–21). These cases, Punch says, blow apart the rationale and 'respectable myth' of management: top managers do manipulate their companies, the regulators, and their environments for devious ends.

In *Permission to Steal*, Newton (2006) has also outlined some major corporate scandals and analysed their causes. Cases include *Enron*, in which, when business gambles failed, company losses were concealed. One *Enron* executive sold his shares for $350 million, when *Enron* stock was at its peak, knowing that the share prices were going to fall; he retired to Hawaii, while most *Enron* employees discovered that their comfortable retirements had evaporated. *Arthur Andersen*, *Enron*'s auditor in Houston, shredded bag after bag of *Enron* records in order to conceal the company's losses; the firm—one of the top accountancy firms worldwide—was convicted of conspiracy and went out of business. (The conviction was later reversed, but too late to save the company.) Newton consequently asks whether it is possible to trust our nation's wealthiest not to rob us.

Theft within the workplace happens at all levels. It is estimated that three-quarters of all employees steal from their employers at least once (McGurn, 1988; Ashworth, 1999) and that many of these repeat such actions on a regular basis (Delaney, 1993). Petty theft may include personal telephone calls, taking office stationery, and fiddling expenses. Employee theft has been blamed for 30–50 per cent of all business failures (Greenberg, 1997). Companies sacrifice about 1 per cent of annual sales to petty pilfering, which, for a major company, could cost as much as £70 million a year (Ashworth, 1999). And as much as 75 per cent of losses attributable to employee theft goes undetected (Winbush and Dalton, 1997): for example, in Ditton's (1977) classic study of British bakery workers, theft within one bakery was so extreme—and the practice so widely accepted—that supervisors had to plan for extra loaves to be baked each day in order to avoid running short.

Gerald Mars (1982), a social anthropologist, also looked at ways in which ordinary people cheat at work and at how they steal from their organizations, arguing that cheating is endemic and integral to the rewards of work. 'Fiddling' is woven into the fabric of people's everyday lives. He sorts the behaviour of people within organizations into four 'cultures': 'hawks'; 'donkeys'; 'wolves'; and 'vultures'. Each group has a distinct ideology, a set of attitudes, a set of rules, and a view of the world. What the groups have in common, however, is that each plans to rob, cheat, fiddle, or short change subordinates, customers, employers, or the state.

- Hawks are individualists, who bend the rules to suit themselves. They are entrepreneurs, innovative professionals (including academics and journalists), and those who run small businesses. Hawkish entrepreneurs are also to be found among waiters, fairground buskers, and owner taxi drivers. The individual's freedom to transact on his or her own terms is highly valued; his or her aim is to 'make it'. An example would be a journalist claiming good expenses for a good story or claiming first-class travel, but actually travelling second class, or a lawyer charging cheap time (by using trainee, unqualified, apprentice labour), but charging it at full professional rates.

- Donkeys are highly constrained by rules and isolated from each other. Unlike hawks, who have a reasonably full choice in how they spend their time, donkeys have no such freedom. Some transport workers are donkeys, because their jobs isolate them and they feel dominated by rules (for example, those governing safety). Supermarket cashiers and machine minders are also highly constrained and isolated. These people will respond—particularly where the constraints are strongest—by breaking or sabotaging the rules that constrain them; alternatively, they will 'fiddle'. These individuals can be either powerful or powerless, depending on their actions. If they passively accept the constraints, they are powerless; if they are disruptive and reject the rules, they can be extremely powerful. The example given by Mars is of a supermarket cashier who was able consistently to extract five times her daily wage in fiddled cash. She might do this by ringing up less than the total charge on the till and then pocketing the difference, or by allowing her friends and family to take goods through the checkout for which they had not paid. She hated being treated like a programmed robot and fiddled in order to make her job more interesting. Fiddling gave her new targets, a sense of challenge, and a sense of power, in that she was able to hurt her boss.

- Wolves work and steal in packs; they have a hierarchy, order, and internal controls that ensure that, when they steal, they do so with agreed rules and a well-defined division of labour. They have a leader and penalize their own deviants. Examples are a gang of dock workers, refuse collectors, airplane crews, or miners. Refuse collectors can break the rules, for example, by riding on the back of the cart or leaving it unattended. They may also break the 'no gratuities rule' and may sell dustbins to those who ask. They can also sell what they collect: for example, sofas, brass, and copper. If management attempts to exert its control over one deviant refuse collector, it will be seen by the group as an attack on all.

- Vultures need the support of the group if they are to fiddle, but will act on their own when 'at the feast'—that is, when committing the act of theft. They depend on support and information from colleagues, but they are also competitive and act in isolation for much of the time. Because they rely on both cooperation and competition, their groups can be unstable and turbulent. Examples from this group include travelling sales people, driver-deliverers, and waiters. For example, waiters can overcharge for drinks from the bar; photocopy sales staff can sell paper that they are supposed to give away; the delivery person can sell black economy clothing from the van. All rely on the actions of others to keep their 'scam' going; they rely on others to be behaving similarly and supporting (as opposed to reporting) their stealing behaviours.

Elsewhere, Mars (1989) describes in greater depth the pilferage that took place in a hotel in Blackpool at which he worked. Mars documented how, in this hotel, wages paid to waiting staff were comparatively low and labour turnover high. Using this as justification, the waiting staff would pilfer and indulge in 'the fiddle'. Mars talks about 'knock-off', which refers to a subtype of fiddle: the illicit acquisition of food, cutlery, and linen. According to Mars, such fiddles are regarded by the waiting staff as entitlement—that is, as part of the wages. This could be done, for example, by fiddling on tea and coffee. For example, a waiter would receive an order for two coffees. He would go into the kitchen and order one coffee on an order slip; he would obtain a standard coffeepot, milk jug, and one cup and saucer from the staff in the kitchen. But he needs an extra cup and saucer for his customers; he will have hidden this in a strategic area near the lounge. A 'bent helper' in the kitchen can make sure that there is enough coffee in the pot to serve two. The waiter charges the customer for two coffees, but only puts the price of one, with the order slip, into the till. 'Bent helpers' can be paid in beer rather than cash.

According to research by Nichols (1997), some employers in the manufacturing industry have tried to combat theft by locking their workers into factories during their shifts. As a result of this measure, there have been some tragic accidents: 146 workers died in a fire in a locked New York garment industry sweatshop in 1911; eighty-four died in a fire in a toy-producing company in China in 1993; and twenty-five died in fire at a poultry plant in North Carolina in 1991 (ibid.: 108).

Research (for example, Greenberg and Scott, 1996) does, however, suggest that many individuals steal from their companies because they believe that they are justified in doing so. They believe that the company is not providing them with a fair deal, so to even up the score, they appropriate company property—and the fact that such theft is often accompanied by a total absence of guilt supports this research.

STOP AND THINK

Do you believe that appropriating company property (for example, stealing paper) can sometimes be justified, or is it always simply theft?

Virtual crime

The Internet has opened up countless deviant and criminal opportunities (Capeller, 2001). This crime takes place on websites owned and managed by organizations. In the 1990s, cybercriminal activity became a problem, with increasing numbers of reports of online harassment, defamation, indecency, and the dissemination of obscene materials, and large-scale money laundering (Castells, 1998). Wall (2001) has classified cybercrime into four categories: trespass; obscenity/pornography; theft; and violence.

- Trespass is the invasion of private space on the Internet by a hacker. He or she might deliberately plant viruses, manipulate data such as web pages, break access codes and passwords to enter classified areas on computer networks, spy on classified knowledge, or bring servers to a standstill, thus halting business or even whole economies.

- In the case of obscenity and pornography, the online sex industry is one of the more successful e-commerce ventures.

- In the case of cyber theft, this might involve the appropriation of intellectual property—for example, music or video—which is then sold on, or the theft of virtual money or credit card numbers.

- Cyber violence is the term used to describe online activities that have the potential to harm others in textual, visual, or audio form, for example, homophobic or racist text, online stalkers, and virtual rape (MacKinnon, 1997).

In the USA, an annual survey of computer crime in 700 corporations found that 56 per cent of respondents had suffered computer security breaches in the preceding twelve months. In the UK, a survey of 200 companies indicated that 89 per cent had experienced some kind of computer-related crime, with viruses and worms affecting 83 per cent and 10 per cent reporting the theft of data (Williams, 2006).

Swearing

Theft and fiddling have an obvious negative effect on organizations; abusive behaviour and swearing can also have negative outcomes and can be detrimental to staff. For example, repeated occurrences of swearing, threats, and verbal abuse can lead to depression, stress, reduced morale, absenteeism, and other problems (Swallow, 2004; Baruch and Jenkins, 2007). Yet swearing can also be seen as a form of self-expression and group solidarity, and may also be instrumental in the *release* of stress. It should be taboo, however, where customers can overhear staff.

Montagu (2001) classifies swearing into 'social swearing' and 'annoyance swearing'.

- *Social swearing* is used conversationally and serves to signify membership of a social group or class, or to develop in-group solidarity. It may be used to ingratiate—that is, to increase a person's perceived attractiveness and to influence others (Linden and Mitchell, 1988). Within a close group, it can even be seen as a form of 'positive politeness' (Daly et al., 2004).

- *Annoyance swearing* provides a relief mechanism for the release of stress and tension, and is valued because it replaces physical aggression (Jay, 1999).

Levels of both social swearing and annoyance swearing are correlated with stress (Montagu, 2001): where there is little or no stress, social swearing can dominate; as stress levels rise, social swearing tends to decrease, while annoyance swearing increases. In high-stress situations, swearing tends to stop. Executives use swearing less frequently than employees at lower levels of the hierarchy.

Taking a managerial perspective, Baruch and Jenkins (2007) have asked how far swearing, seen as misbehaviour, should be allowed to penetrate the workplace. They conclude that managers may wish to consider being permissive about some swearing, but that they should eliminate abusive and offensive swearing.

Swindling

Swindling is another example of behaviour in organizations that is undesirable. None of us like being swindled by organizations, yet being cheated over food is a universal human experience. Food fraud has a long history: organizations, such as government, the *Food Standards Agency*, and others, try to stop us from being swindled, yet there appear to be reports of swindles on a regular basis in the news. Examples include rice being sold as Basmati rice, but actually being adulterated with non-Basmati rice, and food sold as organic or free range being bogus. In November 2006, for example, British police investigated claims that up to 30 million eggs had been illegally passed off as free range when they were not. More seriously, in April 2004, at least thirteen babies died in central China and hundreds more became dangerously ill after being fed fake formula milk (Wilson, 2008).

EXAMPLE **Drug industry swindling**

The drug industry has recently been accused of passing off research and review articles in medical journals as the work of academic scientists rather than of their own or contracted employees. This swindle involves 'ghost authorship': the drug company drafts the article, then passes it on to health communication agencies to write on contract; these agencies, in turn, recruit prestigious academic scientists for the articles and then disappear from view. The academics 'edit' the paper for a fee (usually of around £12,000) and are then given sole authorship.

Ghostwriting has been documented at rates of between 6 per cent and 15 per cent of medical journal articles. Public trust in clinical research is therefore at stake (Kamerow, 2008).

Lying

Lying is another behaviour that we find in organizations, but which has not been regarded as 'organizational behaviour' to date. As long ago as 1968, Albert Carr argued that business is a game and that, like other games, it is played by its own set of rules. In particular, he argued that bluffing (that is, lying) is a convention that the rules of business both support and encourage. Because business bluffing is conventional, it is not—and should not be—subject to norms applicable outside the business realm. Concern for morals appears, therefore, to have disappeared from view.

Deception and lies have received little attention in the management literature, yet we all know that they happen. Because workers must constantly report their behaviour or share information with others, people in the workplace have ample opportunity either to lie or to tell the truth in the course of their work. For example, truck drivers must report the number of hours that they spend on the road; nurses must chart vital signs; public accountants must audit; foresters must report tree censuses. Organizations generally rely on employee reports to be accurate and honest—but each of these individuals may have reason to lie. We lie to avoid embarrassment or conflict, to impress others, to cope with difficult situations, and to achieve personal gain. It has been estimated, for example, that between a half and a third of CVs contain lies (Edwards, 1998; Cole-Golomski, 1999; Prater and Kiser, 2002). But lying jeopardizes information quality and therefore the integrity of organizations.

EXAMPLE **Lying in the *Ministry of Defence***

One organization in which there are tight bureaucratic rules and in which we may therefore expect to see less lying is in the military. Nonetheless, cases of soldiers being lied to have come to light in recent years. Veterans at Porton Down in England were told that they were being given cold remedies, but were actually being exposed to a cloud of nerve agents, or nerve agents were applied to their arms. The men were ordered to keep quiet and not even tell their own doctors that they had taken part in the tests.

(*Source:* BBC News, 17 January 2008)

Grover (1993a) has also looked at the conditions under which employees tell lies. He found that employees will lie to protect their 'turf', or when faced with conflicting demands (role conflict). For example, the truck driver may lie about speeding, because there is a conflict between organizational policy (which says that speed limits must be followed) and external role demands (for example, he or she must pick his or her children up by 6 p.m.). Similarly, the nurse's time may conflict with time demands of the job assignment, leading the nurse to report vital signs not actually measured. People may also lie out of self-interest: for example, to get promoted, to prevent themselves from being admonished, or to make more money. Grover (1993b) also looked at the conditions under which professionals lie about their work behaviour. Again, he found that role conflict causes lying: when, for example, the physician has a professional ethic to cure patients by diagnosing and treating them as accurately as possible, but finds that the costs of the procedure are prohibitive.

STOP AND THINK **Lying in job applications**

Would you lie when applying for a job? Some people lie on their CVs: for example, claiming that they have degrees that they do not. But beware: Digging for 'digital dirt' is now becoming more common. Recruiters can gather information about job applicants that can be gleaned online from MySpace, Friends Reunited, or Google (*Business Week*, 2006; Quinn, 2007).

Despite Glover's findings, role conflict and self-interest cannot explain all lying. Some people may have pathological tendencies towards lying, or may lie when instructed to do so by a superior, or as revenge in response to anger. Managers may also employ deceptive strategies to lie to workers about the opportunities of advancement, or deceive overworked individuals about possible relief, or create fear and anxiety by selective public reprimands. According to research by Jackall (1980), managers may also display indiscriminate bursts of staged anger. Jackall also discusses how corporations lie: in the case of Thalidomide, in order to continue high sales of the drug as a non-toxic tranquilizer, the managerial response to reports of children born with deformities was to 'Lie, suppress, bribe and distort' (Insight Team, 1979).

Denial

While not avoiding outright lying, people or organizations can sometimes deny—either consciously or unconsciously—a reality that others may see, such as the fear and loathing that is being expressed or experienced in an organization. In addition, organizations can take on collective false images: for example, an elite university department may be riddled with conflict, but maintain a positive—if false—public image. Its members may admit privately to the strife, but in public, they will talk about how 'inspiring' or 'stimulating' it is to work there.

Stanley Cohen (2001) received acclaim for his study of denial—that is, how we black out, turn a blind eye, shut off, and see only what we want to see. There are many occasions on which individuals and organizations are perfectly justified in claiming that an event did not happen, or that an event did not happen as it was alleged to have happened, or that an event happened, but without their knowledge. Denials and simple statements of fact are made in good faith: evidence can be produced to counter evidence, claims can be checked, lies can be exposed, and proof can be presented. Games of truth are highly volatile.

There may, however, be a conscious attempt to deceive. Cohen notes that no cognitive psychology textbook lists terms such as 'denial' in its index, even though the perceptual processes that lead to a denial may include perception without awareness, perceptual defence, a use of selectively attending to facts, or simply an error of perceptual.

There are many examples of different kinds of organization and organizational behaviour to be found in Cohen's work, which draws even on the Holocaust and political murders. Concentration camps and prisons are organizations too; businesses are involved in their creation and maintenance. In the case of the Holocaust, the *Post Office* delivered notification of expropriation and deportation, the *Finance Ministry* confiscated wealth, and businesses fired Jewish workers; pharmaceutical companies tested drugs on concentration camp inmates. Travel agents booked one-way passages to camps: the same forms and procedures to book tourists going on holiday were used to send people to Auschwitz (Berenbaum, 1993: 115). Companies bid for the contract to supply gas ovens; others received the shaved hair from women's heads to process into felt, while others melted down gold (10–12 kg a week by 1944) from jewellery and dental fillings. Clerks meticulously recorded each transaction (Cohen, 2001). Many individuals and organizations were therefore either directly or indirectly involved in the Holocaust—but both personal and collective denials of involvement are commonplace. Denial—in the sense of shutting out others' suffering—is the normal state of affairs.

329

Bullying

Bullying is another significant workplace problem (Hodson et al., 2006). Research on bullying—sometimes referred to as 'mobbing' (particularly if it has involved singling a person out for victimization)—has been described as a 'silent epidemic' (McAvoy and Murtagh, 2003). Attention to the topic has grown substantially since the term was introduced and defined as a workplace problem in the early 1990s (Adams, 1992), and since The House of Lords passed anti-bullying legislation in the UK in 2002 (the Dignity at Work Act 2002).

There have been several high-profile nationwide surveys of bullying (for example, Hoel and Cooper, 2000; Rayner et al., 2002; Einarsen et al., 2003). Bullying can take many forms: for example, persistent insults or offensive remarks, teasing, ridicule, persistent criticism, or personal or even physical abuse. It usually involves a person with power in a hierarchy bullying a subordinate (Hoel et al., 2001). Victims of bullying can suffer from severe psychological stress symptoms such as anxiety, depression, irritability, and self-hate (Zapf et al., 1996).

If persistent bullying is defined as exposure to two acts of bullying per week for at least six months, then figures reveal that between 2.7 per cent and 8 per cent of employees are exposed to persistent bullying. If defined as at least one negative act in a week for six months, then between 8 per cent and 25 per cent of employees can be classified as victims of bullying (Mikkelson and Einarsen, 2001). A recent survey has shown that almost half of employees say that they have worked for a bully (Eversheds, 2006). Just over a quarter believed that management styles were too harsh. Another survey by the *Chartered Institute of Personnel and Development* found that one in five employees has been a victim of bullying or harassment at work in the last two years, with black, Asian, women, and disabled employees most likely to face the problem (Haurant, 2006). The *Health and Safety Executive* in the UK estimates that bullying accounts for up to 50 per cent of stress-related workplace illnesses, which means that, every year, bullying is costing UK employers 80 million lost working days (Equality Challenge Unit, 2007). A study of Finnish business school graduates showed 8.8 per cent reported exposure to bullying, at least occasionally, during the previous twelve months (Salin, 2001); a study of male workers in a Norwegian shipyard revealed the prevalence of bullying to be as high as 17 per cent (Einarsen and Skogstad, 1996). Some have shown that women are significantly over-represented among those classifying themselves as bullied (Hoel et al., 2001), but others have found approximately equal victimization rates for men and women (Leymann, 1992; Einarsen and Skogstad, 1996). Younger workers and ethnic minorities are considered to be particularly vulnerable (Westhuses, 2004).

EXAMPLE Bullying

Jeanette, a bank employee, reported that when she questioned a decision, her supervisor made it clear that she was free to leave at any time: 'However when I stated that was not my intention, he looked at me with contempt, telling me that I might come to regret that decision later' (Rayner et al., 2002: 15).

Greater pressure on managers for increased competitiveness can create an environment that is ripe for bullying (Lewis, 1999). Organizational restructuring is one time at which workplace bullying may be facilitated, because restructuring can lead to job insecurity when people worry about possible redundancies and the extra demands that it can put on remaining employees (Kearns et al., 1997). One study found that 60 per cent of managers had experienced large-scale restructuring in the previous twelve months; such processes feed perceptions of job insecurity that make employees feel vulnerable (Worral and Cooper, 1999). But poor work design, deficient leadership, a socially exposed victim, unresolved escalated conflict. (Zapf, 1999), and a low moral standard in a department (Einarsen, 1999) can also contribute to bullying

Some would argue that the very act of managing can be seen as bullying. 'Institutionalized tyranny' divests employees of their former identities and drives home the overriding importance of compliance. Some researchers (for example, Ashforth, 1994) believe that organizations simply facilitate petty tyranny, rather than actively promote it; others take a less generous view and argue that management requires the exercise of power, and that, by its very nature, it promotes tyranny of varying degrees of subtlety (Alvesson and Deetz, 1996; Mumby and Stohl, 1996).

Most research in this area has looked at the percentages of employees being bullied by using a survey—that is, the questionnaire method. Respondents are given a list of 'items', such as 'incidence of verbal abuse' or 'practical jokes', and are asked how often they have been subjected to that negative act in the last six months. The person may not, however, interpret some of these incidents as bullying: research on bullying has shown that many victims are either unaware of the fact that they are being bullied or will not admit that this is the case (Mikkelsen and Einarsen, 2001). When Finnish professionals with a university degree in business studies were provided with a definition of bullying, only 8.8 per cent of respondents (as we have seen) reported they had at least occasionally been bullied during the past twelve months. When presented with a list of thirty-two predefined negative and potentially harassing acts, however, as many as 24 per cent reported that they had been subjected to at least one of the negative acts on a weekly basis (Salin, 2001).

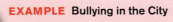

EXAMPLE Bullying in the City

While many graduates might aspire to a job in the City of London's financial sector, a 2003 survey of over 300 City workers found that one in three said that they have been subject to bullying behaviour. There have recently been some cases of bullying that have made headline news. Helen Green became the target of a 'relentless campaign of mean and spiteful behaviour from work colleagues' at *Deutsche Bank* and was awarded £800,000 in damages in respect of psychiatric injury. Steven Horkulak, another City worker, was awarded close to £1 million after he pursued his case through the courts (Cartwright and Cooper, 2007).

Sabotage

Sabotage is often a rational and calculative act: it is a deliberate action, or inaction, that is intended to damage, destroy, or disrupt some aspect of the workplace environment (that is, its property, product, process, or reputation). Although few academic studies exist on sabotage, those who have studied the topic estimate that between 75 per cent and 96 per cent of employees routinely behave in a manner that can be described as either deliberately deviant or intentionally dysfunctional (Harper, 1990; Slora, 1991; Harris and Ogbonna, 2002). Examples offered include destroying machinery or goods, work slowdowns, passing on defective work, flattening tyres, scratching cars, intentionally misplacing important paperwork, offering a chemical company's new formula to a competitor, erasing financial records, or introducing a computer virus. Taylor and Walton (1971: 219) define sabotage as 'the conscious act of mutilation or destruction', which may serve to reduce tension and frustration in the individual carrying out the sabotage. They quote the cases of a frustrated salesman in a Knightsbridge store who demobilized a machine that shuttled change around the store by ramming a cream bun down its gullet and a half-mile of Blackpool rock in a sweet-producing factory that had to be thrown away because it carried the terse words 'F*** off'. Industrial sabotage may be an attempt to reduce tension and frustration, an attempt to ease the work process (by creating a break time), a way of having fun, or an attempt to assert control. It also may be an important index of underlying industrial conflict.

Harris and Ogbonna (2006) argue that service sabotage—that is, behaviour intentionally designed to affect customer service negatively—may represent an insidious form of resistance, and even equalization, in labour management relations. While the ideology of consumption and customer sovereignty has become a central aspect of management thinking (Thompson and Ackroyd, 1995; Du Gay, 1996), the frontline employees might reconstruct this ideology to suit themselves. Not only is service sabotage a way of getting back at management's espoused levels of customer satisfaction, but it is also a way of responding to dysfunctional customers.

An early study of sabotage can be found in Dubois (1979), who argues that, while sabotage may be committed by workers, it can also be committed by management. Lockouts and strikes bring production to a halt, and can be caused by managers or workers. Non-productive time is also a form of sabotage: machines that are out of order, poor planning, a shortage of raw materials, and an inadequate consideration of the situation of machinery can all be seen as forms of management sabotage. And sabotage by management is far more serious than sabotage by workers. LaNuez and Jermier (1994) argue that sabotage is a result of low levels of control; both managers and workers can experience low levels of control due to mergers and restructuring, increased use of monitoring and other control techniques, technological changes that replace skilled labour with less skilled labour, and displacement.

Sabotage can be seen as a strategic weapon that can be used by any person to revise power imbalances, or to re-establish control of their work or workplace. Similarly, they may choose to 'whistleblow'— that is, to disclose illegal, unethical, or harmful practices in the workplace to parties who might take action (see Rothschild and Miethe, 1994; Miceli and Near, 1997).

EXAMPLE Sabotage

Recently, sabotage at *Wikipedia* has hit the headlines. It has been reported that *Ministry of Defence* employees have been responsible for more than 4,600 anonymous edits in the past four years on *Wikipedia*. For example, they are accused of editing the entry on the Faslane Peace Camp. The CIA has also been accused of editing articles relating to casualties in Iraq.

(*Source: Scotland on Sunday*, 26 August 2007, p. 3; http://www.scotlandonsunday.com)

Struggles relating to time

It is easy to see how tangible organizational resources can be sabotaged; there can also be sabotage of productive time and other struggles relating to time. The control over working time is always a source of struggle between workers and managers: throughout the nineteenth century, employers opposed the retention, in Birmingham, of 'Saint Monday' (a traditional holiday). Workplace studies have shown that time is both struggled over and negotiated. The accounts demonstrate that action relating to time might be in an effort to relieve the monotony of work, as in Roy's (1960) study of machine operators, or as a way of creating time away from work, as in Ditton's (1979) study of a factory bakery.

Heyes (1997) has shown how workers in a chemical plant created opportunities for overtime and enhanced earnings through what management termed 'illegitimate' absenteeism, and what the workers called 'knocking'. Heyes showed that knocking took two forms. In one form, a pair of workers from separate shifts would collaborate: for example, a worker might deliberately go sick for a shift while his workmate would voluntarily provide cover at an overtime premium. The following week, the roles would be reversed and the gains from knocking were thus shared. The second form was known as the '8 plus 4' system, in which a worker on an eight-hour shift would volunteer to work the extra four hours for someone who had been unable to fulfil (that is, had 'knocked off') his or her own twelve-hour shift. Again, there was an explicit, reciprocal agreement in order to enhance joint incomes. Workers also regarded occasional absences (3.5 per cent of contractual hours, on average) as a necessary means of gaining relief from the pressures of a hard, physically intensive, and dangerous job.

Gossip

Gossip can also be regarded as organizational misbehaviour if it is negative, or malicious—but it is similarly intrinsic to organizational life (Noon and Delbridge, 1993). Gossip can be defined as idle chat or conversation that can be positive or negative (Fine and Rosnow, 1978), can be malicious or harmless (Guendouzi, 1996), can praise or blame (Elias and Scotson, 1965), and can be cooperative or competitive (Guendouzi, 2001). Gossip is associated almost exclusively with women, as studies of oral culture confirm (for example, Jones, 1980), but men also participate in gossip and can be the subject of study (see Johnson, 1994).

Gossip flourishes in close-knit communities and facilitates social bonds between people (Harrington and Bielby, 1995). In organizational behaviour, gossip is informal communication of value-laden information about members of a social setting (Noon and Delbridge, 1993). It is about exchange of information between at least two people about a non-present third party (Blum-Kulka, 2000). Gossip serves many functions. In a negative sense, it can provide the gossiper with a means of indirect attack that has lower risk than a direct attack. It can also be used to impart information, to influence others, or as entertainment. It may secure personal gain or status for the gossipers, if they have information that is considered to be important, and it can be motivated by self-interest among rivals. The power dynamics of gossip tend to be a balance tilted in favour of the 'producer' of gossip rather than the 'consumer' (Harrington and Bielby, 1995).

According to Shibutani (1966), the most interesting gossip is information that deals with violations of moral codes. The more scandalous the information and the more it concerns people within the group, the more gossip-worthy the information. But this could be dangerous information to spread, so the potential gossiper has to consider who to tell and the impact that the information might have.

For women, in particular—among whom the social conventions of femininity carry with them obligations of 'behaving nicely' (Coates, 2000)—the risk for malicious gossip instigators is being labelled a 'bitch' (Guendouzi, 2001).

STOP AND THINK Deceit or impression management?

The gossip in one company was that the managing director, who was rumoured to be in personal debt, was said to 'dress down' when she met tax inspectors in an attempt to conceal her spending and engender their sympathy (Myers, 2002). Is this an example of deceit or of 'impression management'?.

Gossip and power are linked (Kurland, 2000). One effect of negative gossip is that it may enhance 'coercive power'—that is, power that achieves compliance through threat (see Chapter 15). When the gossiper relates negative news about a third party, recipients may infer that the gossiper could also spread negative information about them. Positive gossip, in contrast, is likely to affect 'reward power', because the recipient may infer that the gossiper could spread positive information about them. Gossip is likely to influence 'expert power' if it facilitates the exchange of data and helps to build a knowledge base, and it may detract from the 'referent power' of the gossiper if it is seen as a small or petty activity, but positive gossip can enhance the reputation of people.

The business literature deals with gossip as bad and something that should be eradicated by managers: employees who are gossiping are seen not to be working hard enough. But gossip plays a vital role in group formation, regulation, and perpetuation, so the removal of gossip is not possible unless there is a complete ban on all communication. Other commentators suggest that managers should accept the existence of gossip as a natural part of organizational life and attempt to manipulate it for their own benefit (Davis, 1973; Hirschhorn, 1983). Gossip can help the functioning of an organization: it can communicate rules, values, and morals. It facilitates the diffusion of organizational tradition and history, and maintains the exclusivity of the group. It may provide an explanation of matters that otherwise would not have been clear, and so can relieve feelings of insecurity and anxiety. It can smooth interpersonal and intergroup strains, and it may be a vehicle for social change (Noon and Delbridge, 1993). And gossip may also be fun.

Fun

Fun has been touched upon in other chapters—particularly where we have looked at how individuals resist organizational culture's constraints. The presence of horseplay and humour is also found in research on hospitals (Goffman, 1968), coalmines (Pitt, 1979), building sites (Riemer, 1979), civil engineering (Watts, 2007), schools (Willis, 1977), and shop floors (Roy, 1960; Burawoy, 1979; Pollert, 1981).

Humour serves many purposes. As we saw in Chapter 2, Donald Roy (1960) described how the machinists avoided 'going nuts' by teasing and using mock aggression. Racial hostility was found to be diluted by humour by Burawoy (1979). Linstead (1985) found, however, that joking was closely related to resistance and sabotage: joking helped to establish an informal world outside the constraints of management control.

Collinson (1998) also looked at the role of joking within organizations. Showing the collective elements of joking, and exploring the contradictions and divisions that characterize shop-floor relations, Collinson focuses on gender identity and working-class resistance in a lorry-producing factory. He shows that humour serves as resistance both to the tightly controlled repetitive work tasks and to the organization of production. The men wanted to make the best of the situation and enjoy the company of others.

They were concerned to show that they could laugh at themselves. The use of nicknames—such as 'Fat Rat', 'Bastard Jack', 'Big Lemon', and 'The Snake'—created a mythical and imaginary world: 'Electric Lips' was unable to keep a secret; 'Pot Harry' had broken all of the drinking pots and mugs by dropping them.

The workers also wanted to differentiate themselves from white-collar staff and managers. They did this by, for example, expressing how manual work was the very essence of masculinity. The joking culture was a symbol of freedom and autonomy. The uncompromising banter of the shop floor, permeated with swearing, ridicule, displays of sexuality, and pranks, was contrasted, exaggerated, and elevated above the middle-class politeness, cleanliness, and more restrained demeanour of office white-collar staff.

In this context, humour might also mean conformity: there were demands of group conformity—that is, specific rules that led to social survival. Individuals had to be able to take a joke and laugh at themselves, and expected others to do the same. They needed to be aggressive, critical, and disrespectful. Apprentices had to learn to accept degrading initiation ceremonies. In this way, humour also meant control: it was used as a way to pressure people to conform to routine shop-floor values and practices, mutual control, and discipline. There was, for example, a steady stream of cutting remarks to control 'deviants'—that is, lazy workers.

EXAMPLE Humour

Humour is often used to deride or deprecate a company or its staff. The first example is a joke told by Gabriel et al. (2000) and is disparaging of the board of directors: 'Our chairman meets the presidents of America and France at an international conference. The American President says: "My problem is that I have 12 security advisers. One of them is a foreign spy but I don't know which." The French President says: "Funny you should say that. I have 12 mistresses; one of them is unfaithful and I don't know which." "Your problems are nothing compared to mine," says our chairman. "I have 12 directors on the board. One of them is competent but I don't know which."

Another joke heard on BBC Radio 2 tells the following tale: 'Human resource departments sometimes use "exit" interviews or questionnaires to ask why employees leave a company. One employee was reported as saying that he was leaving the organization because he wanted to join the circus "and work with professional clowns next time".'

EXAMPLE More misbehaviour: Fear and loathing

Fear and loathing can be a feature of organizational life. It is documented in subject areas, such as organization studies (Van Maanen, 1995: 687), when controversy breaks out between academics, in an 'academic blood sport called debate'. It happens in departments—sometimes, to such an extent that a department is closed (Hayes, 1998: 24): 'Several of the key professors had come to hate each other for reasons known only to themselves and their mutual animosity grew so severe that they began putting obstacles in each other's paths and in the paths of the students of their rival professors. The bitterness became so intense that not a single student escaped having to undergo a great deal of pain and inconvenience. There were no victors, but every single person, whether student or professor, became a victim of this uncontrolled childish hatred.'

Managing organizational misbehaviour

Within the framework of functionalism, it is clear that there are choices in how managers view the issues discussed here: they may clamp down on the activities and exercise greater control, but this is likely to lead to further resistance; alternatively, they may learn to live with these realities, as authors such as Mars (1982; 1989) suggest.

In his discussion of industrial relations, Fox (1973) offers another framework that helps us to consider potential conflict. He says that there are two frames of reference: the unitarist and pluralist perspectives. If managers adopt a unitarist perspective, they believe that, within their organization, there is the potential for unity, partnership, and harmony, if it does not already exist. In this organization, there will be one source of authority and one focus of loyalty; the organization could—and perhaps does—function much like a healthy sports team. According to this view, logic, or perspective, management and workers should be striving jointly to meet company goals: individuals should accept the authority of those who manage, and managers are the best qualified to manage; managers, meanwhile, motivate and promote an *esprit de corps*—that is, mutual pride in the company. Any conflict in this environment would be either negligible, caused by poor communication, stupidity, or the work of agitators. This view, Fox would argue, denies that theft, strikes, conflict, and sabotage exist—and it is maintained only because it suits the needs of management. Denial of conflict may be one way in which managers cope with conflict; psychologists have found that denial of reality is one way in which individuals cope (Edwards, 1990).

A pluralist perspective, however, would represent a more accurate description of what really happens: it would accept the existence of several different, but related, interest groups, each with its own leaders, loyalties, and objectives. Management and workers are two different groups, who have conflicting interests. In this environment, conflict, sabotage, and so on, are seen as inevitable and natural components of work. And a certain amount of overt conflict is welcomed as a sign that aspirations are neither being drowned by hopelessness, nor suppressed by power (see Armstrong and Dawson, 1989).

Finally, a third—radical—approach to considering conflict and misbehaviour might be to argue that a pluralist ideology does not address the full extent of conflict—that is, that it does not fully appreciate the differences in power between managers and workers. This approach would focus on the power differences between various groups and would show that management's power is greater than it appears. Employees would be seen as being totally dependent on the organization, with little power or influence. Sabotage, theft, fun, and so on would simply be seen as some of the few ways in which employee undermine managerial power and control.

Conclusion

In this chapter, we have looked at different aspects and examples of resistance and misbehaviour. For example, we have looked at fraud, plagiarism, theft, swearing, swindling, lying, swearing, sabotage, and fun. Considering these behaviours as organizational behaviour gives us insight into the realities of organizational life. This chapter also potentially counteracts some of the more positive, sanitized, prescriptive, and functionalist views of management.

KEY POINTS

- Organizational behaviour is not all positive, yet the less positive behaviour has tended not to have been given much room in the textbooks.

- Bad behaviours take many and very varied forms. They can have a very negative impact on the organization and/or on individuals within it.

- Acknowledging the more 'seedy' side of organizational life may give us a more realistic perspective on the facts to be uncovered.

- Managers have choices in relation to the perspective that they wish to take on such issues and how to manage them.

CASE STUDY

The 'game of making tips' and cheating in casinos

The following is one example of how cheating occurs in one setting.

Worker solidarity in the casino industry in the USA is induced by the industry's shared tip structure in which individual dealers' tips are pooled together and split evenly among all workers (Sallaz, 2002). Tipping constitutes 75–85 per cent of a dealer's income. Because the most experienced dealer's income was dependent on the tip-making ability of the least experienced and newest of dealers, new workers were 'taken under the wings' of veteran dealers and taught the group's tip-making tactics.

The standard method of tipping is to offer a 'toke bet'. The player places a smaller side bet 'for the dealer' next to his or her own bet before the game begins. If the player wins, the dealer earns a tip, which is deposited in a 'toke box' and evenly distributed among all of the dealers at the end of the shift. The dealer is only tipped when the player wins; otherwise, both bets go to the house. The maximum tips will be made if dealing is fast. Non-tippers are treated rudely and forced off the table. Novice players (who are likely not to know about toke bets and tipping) find that attention will be drawn to the tipping structure by, for example, the dealer thanking a tipper in an exaggerated tone. Having made players aware of the toke system, dealers must make clear that tips are not gratuities or gifts, but rather a fee for service rendered. Dealers might whisper advice to a player, improving the 'service'. Veteran roulette dealers can, with varying degrees of accuracy and consistency, 'set the ball down' in particular numbers by coordinating their spinning of the ball with that of the wheel (ibid.).

Dealers have regularly cheated. They might slyly pocket money when supervisors are out of sight or use special shuffling techniques to 'set the deck' for a confederate playing at the table (Nelson, 1978). In the past, despotic control managers and owners of casinos have used severe tactics to stop cheating. Owners would walk the floor and monitor workers. If dealers were caught cheating, they were fired on the spot (Binion, 1973; Nelson, 1978). If the cheating was serious, two others would hold the dealer down; a third 'goon' would wield a baseball bat and bring it down on the dealer's hands, smashing them beyond repair. 'The dealer was then dragged through the casino, with the blood dripping from his crushed fingers' (Reid and Demaris, 1963: 52).

Actions designed to stop cheating, with less serious consequences, involved instructing workers never to display emotions while dealing. The advice was to 'dummy up and deal' (Solkey, 1980). Talking to players was seen as risky behaviour and seldom necessary. Shuffling machines and multideck shoes served to maximize the speed and security of dealing by eliminating dealer skill and discretion. Electronic surveillance technology is used to monitor workers closely: a black ceiling globe houses a video camera above each table and relays images to a central control room staffed by surveillance specialists. Even the dealers' uniforms are designed to maximize security: tight cuffs on long-sleeved shirts ensure that they do not slide chips up their sleeves; aprons prevent them from accessing their pockets while at the tables. (For more examples of surveillance in the gaming industry, see Earley, 2001; Austrin and West, 2005.)

(Sources in text)

Questions

1. What other examples have you seen of shared tipping?

2. Do individuals try to cheat the system?

3. What other examples of cheating at work have you witnessed, and how have management and workers tried to deal with it?

FURTHER READING

Ackroyd, S. and Thompson, P. (1999) *Organizational Misbehaviour*, London: Sage This book documents all kinds of misbehaviour. You will see lots of connections between this book and many of the chapters here.

Brewis, J. (2000) 'Sex, work and sex at work: Using Foucault to understand organizational relations', in J. Barry, J. Chandler, H. Clark, R. Johnston, and D. Needle (eds), *Organization and Management: A Critical Text*, London: Thompson Learning, ch. 5 You will find links here with the chapters on power and control, and rationality and bureaucracy.

Gabriel, Y., Fineman, S., and Sims, D. (2000) *Organizing and Organizations* (2nd edn.), London: Sage Chapter 13 focuses on sex in organizations.

Giacalone, R.A. and Greenberg, J. (1997) *Antisocial Behaviour in Organizations*, London: Sage.

Noon, M. and Blyton, P. (2007) *The Realities of Work*, 3rd edn, Basingstoke: Palgrave Macmillan See the chapter entitled 'Time and work' and that on survival strategies, which discuss how and why employees 'fiddle'. These chapters help challenge the view that all rule bending is problematic.

Punch, M. (1996) *Dirty Business: Exploring Corporate Misconduct—Analysis and Cases*, London: Sage.

LINKS TO FILMS AND NOVELS

Orwell, G. (1937) *The Road to Wigan Pier* In this novel, the author laments the 'filthy chemical by-product that people will pour down their throats under the name of beer' (Orwell, 1937:190).

_____ (1939) *Coming Up for Air* In this novel, the protagonist, George Bowling, is reduced to eating fake foodstuffs.

RESEARCH QUESTIONS

1. Compare and contrast two of the cases of organizational misdemeanour described by Punch (1996).

2. Even when people are trained, paid, and told to be nice, it is hard for them to do so all of the time. Why? (See, for example, Van Maanen, 1991.)

3. 'Sabotage is bound up with the private ownership of the means of production and will disappear only when that does' (Dubois, 1979: 213). Discuss.

REFERENCES

Adams, A. (1992) *Bullying at Work: How to Confront and Overcome It*, London: Virago Press.

Alfred Marks Bureau (1991) *Meeting Your Partner at Work: A Quantitative Report on the Frequency and Effects of Relationships at Work*, December, Borehamwood: Alfred Marks Bureau.

_____ (1995) *Does Cupid Work in Your Office?*, February, Borehamwood: Alfred Marks Bureau.

Alvesson, M. and Deetz, S. (1996) 'Critical theory and post modernism: Approaches to organizational studies', in S.R. Clegg and C. Hardy (eds), *Studying Organization: Theory and Method*, London: Sage.

Armstrong, P. and Dawson, C. (1989) *People in Organizations*, 4th edn, Cambridge: ELM Publications.

Ashforth, B. (1994) 'Petty tyranny in organizations', *Human Relations*, 47(7): 755–78.

Ashworth, J. (1999) 'Blowing the whistle on the office fraudsters', *The Times*, 26 January, p. 17.

Austrin, T. and West, J. (2005) 'Skills and surveillance in casino gaming: Work, consumption and regulation', *Work, Employment and Society*, 19: 305–26.

Baruch, Y. and Jenkins, S. (2007) 'Swearing at work and permissive leadership culture: When anti-social becomes social and incivility is acceptable', *Leadership and Organizational Development Journal*, 28(6): 492–507.

Berenbaum, M. (1993) *The World Must Know: The History of the Holocaust as Told in the United States Holocaust Museum*, Boston, MA: Little, Brown & Co.

Binion, L.B. (1973) *Some Recollections of a Texas and Las Vegas Gaming Operator*, Reno: University of Nevada Oral History Program, cited in Sallaz (2002).

Blum-Kulka, S. (2000) 'Gossipy events at family dinners: Negotiating sociability, presence and the moral other', in J. Coupland (ed.), *Small Talk*, Harlow: Pearson.

Brewis, J. (1998) 'What is wrong with this picture? Sex and gender relations in disclosure', in J. Hassard and R. Holliday (eds), *Organization Representation: Work and Organizations in Popular Culture*, London: Sage, ch. 4.

Burawoy, M. (1979) *Manufacturing Consent*, Chicago, IL: Chicago University Press.

Business Week (2006) 'Working Life: You are what you post—Bosses and headhunters are using Google to peer into places interviews can't take them', 27 March, p. 52.

Capeller, W. (2001) 'Not such a neat net: Some comments on virtual criminality', *Social and Legal Studies*, 10: 229–49.

Carr, A.Z. (1968) 'Is business bluffing ethical?', *Harvard Business Review*, 46(1): 143–53.

Cartwright, S. and Cooper, C.L. (2007) 'Hazards to health: The problems of workplace bullying', *The Psychologist*, 20(5): 284–7.

Castells, M. (1998) *The End of the Millennium: The Information Age: Economy, Society and Culture, Vol. II*, Oxford: Blackwell.

Coates, J. (2000) 'Small talk and subversion: The female speakers backstage', in J. Coupland (ed.), *Small Talk*, Harlow: Pearson.

Cohen, S. (2001) *States of Denial: Knowing about Atrocities and Suffering*, Cambridge: Polity Press.

Cole-Gomolski, B. (1999) 'Job applicants finding fake credentials on the web', *Computerworld*, 7 September, 32(36): 6.

Collinson, D.L. (1988) 'Engineering humour: Masculinity, joking and conflict in shop floor relations', *Organization Studies*, 9(2): 181–99.

Daly, N., Holmes, J., Newton, J., and Stubbe, M. (2004) 'Expletives as solidarity signals in FRAs on the factory floor', *Journal of Pragmatics*, 34: 1683–1710.

Davis, K. (1973) 'The care and cultivation of the corporate grapevine', *Management Review*, 62: 53–5.

Delaney, J. (1993) 'Handcuffing employee theft', *Small Business Report*, 18: 29–38.

Ditton, J. (1977) *Part-Time Crime: An Ethnography of Fiddling and Pilferage*, London: Macmillan.

_____ (1979) 'Baking time', *Sociological Review*, 27: 157–67.

_____ (2008) 'Letters', *The Guardian*, 21 January.

Dubois, P. (1979) *Sabotage in Industry*, Harmondsworth: Penguin.

Du Gay, P. (1996) *Consumption and Identity at Work*, London: Sage.

Earley. P. (2001) *Super Casino: Inside the New Las Vegas*, New York: Bantam.

Edwards, A. (1998) 'True or false?', *Business Journal: Serving Jacksonville and Northeast Florida*, 7 August, 13(443): 33.

Edwards, J.R. (1990) 'The determinants and consequences of coping with stress', in C. Cooper and R. Payne (eds), *Causes, Coping and Consequences of Stress at Work*, Chichester: John Wiley, ch. 8.

Einarsen, S. (1999) 'The nature and causes of bullying at work', *International Journal of Manpower*, 20(1–2): 16–27.

_____ and Skogstad, A. (1996) 'Bullying at work: Epidemiological findings in public and private organizations', *European Journal of Work and Organizational Psychology*, 5: 185–201.

_____, Hoel, H., Zapf, D., and Cooper, C.L. (eds) (2003) *Bullying and Emotional Abuse in the Workplace*, London: Taylor and Francis.

Elias, N. and Scotson, J.L. (1965) *The Established and the Outsiders*, London: Frank Cass.

Equality Challenge Unit (2007) *Dignity at Work: A Good Practice Guide for Higher Education Institutions on Dealing with Bullying and Harassment in the Workplace*, January, London: ECU.

Eversheds (2006) 'UK infested with bad managers', available online at http://www.management-issues.com/2006/8/24/research/uk-infested-with-bad-managers.asp

Fine, G.A. and Rosnow, R.L. (1978) 'Gossip, gossipers and gossiping', *Personality and Social Psychology Bulletin*, 4(1): 161–8.

Fox, A. (1973) 'Industrial relations: A social critique of pluralist ideology', in J. Child (ed.), *Man and Organization*, London: Allen & Unwin.

Friedli, D. (2006) 'Rich pickings for fraudsters as £1bn is stolen from Scottish Companies', *Scotland on Sunday*, 26 February.

Gabriel, Y., Fineman, S., and Sims, D. (2000) *Organizing and Organizations*, 2nd edn, London: Sage.

Giacalone, R.A. and Greenberg, J. (1997) *Antisocial Behaviour in Organizations*, London: Sage.

Goffman, E. (1968) *Asylums*, Harmondsworth: Penguin.

Greenberg, J. (1997) 'The steal motive: Managing the social determinants of employee theft', in R.A. Giacalone and J. Greenberg (eds), *Antisocial Behaviour in Organizations*, London: Sage, ch. 5.

_____ and Scott, K.S. (1996) 'Why do workers bite the hands that feed them? Employee theft as a social exchange process', in B.M. Staw and L.L. Cummings (eds), *Research in Organizational Behavior*, Greenwich, CT: JAI Press, pp. 111–56.

Grover, S.L. (1993a) 'Lying, deceit and subterfuge: A model of dishonesty in the workplace', *Organizational Science*, 4(3): 478–95.

_____ (1993b) 'Why professionals lie: The impact of professional role conflict on reporting accuracy', *Organizational Behavior and Human Decision Processes*, 55: 251–72.

_____ (1997) 'Lying in organizations: Theory, research and future directions', in R.A. Giacalone and J. Greenberg (eds), *Antisocial Behaviour in Organizations*, London: Sage, ch. 4.

Guendouzi, J. (1996) 'Gossip: Some problematics for definitions and gendered talk', in *Papers in Linguistics for the University of Manchester, Vol I*, Manchester: University of Manchester Press, pp. 61–75.

_____ (2001) 'You'll think we're always bitching: The functions of cooperativity and competition in women's gossip', *Discourse Studies*, 3(1): 29–51.

Harper, D. (1990) 'Spotlight abuse—save profits', *Industrial Distribution*, 79(10): 47–51.

Harrington, C.L. and Bielby, D.D. (1995) 'Where did you hear that? Technology and the social organization of gossip', *Sociological Quarterly*, 36(3): 607–28.

Harris, L.C. and Ogbonna, E. (2002) 'Exploring service sabotage: The antecedents, types and consequences and frontline, deviant antiservice behaviors', *Journal of Service Research*, 4(3): 163–83.

_____ _____ (2006) 'Service sabotage: A study of antecedents and consequences', *Journal of the Academy of Marketing Science*, 34: 543–58.

Haurant, S. (2006) 'Workplace bullying affects one in five', *Guardian Unlimited*, 24 October.

Hayes, R.P. (1998) *Land of No Buddha: Reflections of a Sceptical Buddhist*, Birmingham: Windhorse Publications.

Heyes, J. (1997) 'Annualized hours and the "knock": The organization of working time in a chemicals plant', *Work, Employment and Society*, 11(1): 65–81.

Hirschhorn, L. (1983) 'Managing rumors during retrenchment', *SAM Advanced Management Journal*, 48: 5–11.

Hodson, R., Roscigno, V.J., and Lopez, S.H. (2006) 'Chaos and the abuse of power: Workplace bullying in organizational and interactional context', *Work and Occupations*, 33: 382–416.

Hoel, H. and Cooper, C.L. (2000) *Destructive Conflict and Bullying at Work*, Manchester: UMIST Manchester School of Management.

_____, _____, and Faragher, B. (2001) 'The experience of bullying in Great Britain: The impact of organizational status', *European Journal of Work and Organizational Psychology*, 10(4): 443–65.

Insight Team of The Sunday Times of London (1979) *Suffer the Children: The Story of Thalidomide*, New York: Viking (esp. ch. 7).

International Labour Organization (ILO) (1999) *Safe Work: Introduction to Violence at Work*, Geneva: ILO.

Jackall, R. (1980) 'Structural invitations to deceit: Some reflections on bureaucracy and morality', *Berkshire Review*, 15: 49–61.

Jay, T. (1999) *Why We Curse: A Neuro-Psycho-Social Theory of Speech*, Philadelphia, PA: John Benjamins.

Jermier, J.M., Knights, D., and Nord, W.R. (eds) (1994) *Resistance and Power in Organizations*, London: Routledge.

Johnson, S. (1994) 'A game of two halves: On men, football and gossip', *Journal of Gender Studies*, 3(2): 145–54.

Jones, D. (1980) 'Gossip: Notes on women's oral culture', *Women's Studies International Quarterly*, 3: 193–8; reprinted in D. Cameron (ed.), *The Feminist Critique of Language: A Reader*, London: Routledge, pp. 242–50.

Kamerow, D. (2008) 'Who wrote that article?', *British Medical Journal*, 3 May, p. 989.

Kearns, D., McCarthy, P., and Sheehan, M. (1997) 'Organizational restructuring: Considerations for workplace rehabilitation', *Australian Journal of Rehabilitation Counselling*, 3(1): 21–9.

Kurland, N.B. (2000) 'Passing the word: Toward a model of gossip and power in the workplace', *Academy of Management Review*, 25(2): 428–39.

LaNuez, D. and Jermier, J.M. (1994) 'Sabotage by managers and technocrats: Neglected patterns of resistance at work', in J.M. Jermier, D. Knights, and W.R. Nord (eds), *Resistance and Power in Organizations*, London: Routledge.

Lewis, D. (1999) *UK Workplace Bullying: HRM Friend or Foe?*, Paper presented at the Ninth European Congress on Work and Organizational Psychology, Helsinki, Finland, cited in Liefooghe and Mackenzie Davey (2001).

Leymann, H. (1992) *Adult Bullying at Swedish Workplaces: A Nationwide Study Based on 2438 Interviews*, Stockholm: Swedish National Board of Occupational Safety and Health.

Liefooghe, A.P. and Mackenzie Davey, K. (2001) 'Accounts of workplace bullying: The role of organization', *European Journal of Work and Organizational Psychology*, 10(4): 375–92.

Linden, R.C. and Mitchell, T.R. (1988) 'Ingratiatory behaviors in organizational settings', *Academy of Management Review*, 13: 572–87.

Linstead, S. (1985) 'Breaking the "purity rule": Industrial sabotage and the symbolic process', *Personnel Review*, 14(3): 12–19.

MacKinnon, R.C. (1997) 'Virtual rape', *Journal of Computer-Mediated Communication*, 2: 4.

Mars, G. (1982) *Cheats at Work*, London: Allen & Unwin.

_____ (1989) 'Hotel pilferage: A case of occupational threat', in C. Littler (ed.), *The Experience of Work*, Milton Keynes: Open University Press, ch. 21.

McAvoy, B.R. and Murtagh, J. (2003) 'Workplace bullying: The silent epidemic', *British Medical Journal*, 326(7393): 776–7.

McGurn, T. (1988) 'Spotting the thieves who work among us', *Wall Street Journal*, 7 March, p. 16A.

Miceli, M.P. and Near, J.P. (1997) 'Whistle-blowing as antisocial behavior', in R.A. Giacalone and J. Greenberg (eds), *Antisocial Behaviour in Organizations*, London: Sage, ch. 7.

Mikkelsen, E.G. and Einarsen, S. (2001) 'Bullying in Danish work life', *European Journal of Work and Organizational Psychology*, 10(4): 393–413.

Montagu, A. (2001) *The Anatomy of Swearing*, Philadelphia, PA: University of Pennsylvania Press.

Mumby, D.K. and Stohl, C. (1996) 'Disciplining organizational communication studies', *Management Communication Quarterly*, 10(1): 50–72.

Myers, P. (2002) 'Customers, boardrooms and gossip: Theme repetition and metapatterns in the texture of organizing', *Human Relations*, 55(6): 669–90.

Nelson, W. (1978) *Gaming from the Old Days to Computers*, Reno, NV: University of Nevada Oral History Program.

Newell, S., Robertson, M., Scarborough, H., and Swan, J. (2002) *Managing Knowledge Work*, Houndmills: Palgrave.

Newton, L.H. (2006) *Permission to Steal: Revealing the Roots of Corporate Scandal*, Oxford: Blackwell.

Nichols, T. (1997) *The Sociology of Industrial Injury*, London: Mansell.

Noon, M. and Delbridge, R. (1993) 'News from behind my hand: Gossip in organizations', *Organization Studies*, 14(1): 23–36.

Orwell, G. (1937) *The Road to Wigan Pier*, Harmondsworth: Penguin

_____ (1939) *Coming Up for Air*, London: Secker and Warburg.

Paton, G. (2007) 'Universities reprimand 2,000 students in year hall of shame', *Daily Telegraph*, 29 December, p. 13.

Pitt, M. (1979) *The World on Our Backs*, London: Lawrence & Wishart.

Pollert, A. (1981) *Girls, Wives, Factory Lives*, London: Macmillan.

Prater, T. and Kiser, S.B. (2002) 'Lies, lies and more lies', *SAM Advanced Management Journal*, 67(2): 9–14.

Punch, M. (1996) *Dirty Business: Exploring Corporate Misconduct—Analysis and Cases*, London: Sage.

Quinn, C. (2007) 'Beware of being caught out by the net', *The Scotsman*, 27 January.

Raynor, C., Hoel, H., and Cooper, C.L. (2002) *Workplace Bullying*, London: Taylor and Francis.

Reid, E. and Demaris, O. (1963) *The Green Felt Jungle*, New York: Trident Press.

Riemer, J.W. (1979) *Hard Hats*, London: Sage.

Rothschild, J. and Miethe, T.D. (1994) 'Whistleblowing as resistance in modern work organizations', in J.M. Jermier, D. Knights, and W.R. Nord (eds), *Resistance and Power in Organizations*, London: Routledge, ch. 8.

Roy, D.F. (1960) 'Banana time: Job satisfaction and informal interaction', *Human Organization*, 18: 158–68.

Salin, D. (2001) *Bullying Among Professionals: The Role of Work Overload and Organizational Politics*, Paper presented at the Tenth European Congress on Work and Organizational Psychology, Prague, May; cited in Mikkelsen and Einarsen (2001).

Sallaz, J.J. (2002) 'The house rules: Autonomy and interests among service workers in the contemporary casino industry', *Work and Occupations*, 29(4): 394–427.

Schlosser, E. (2001) *Fast Food Nation: The Dark Side of the All-American Meal*, London: Penguin.

Shibutani, T. (1966) *Improvised News: A Sociological Study of Rumor*, Indianapolis, IN: Bobbs-Merrill.

Slora, K.B. (1991) 'An empirical approach to determining employee deviance base rates' in J. Jones (ed.), *Pre-Employment Honesty Testing: Current Research and Future Directions*, Westport, CT: Quorum Books.

Solkey, L. (1980) *Dummy Up and Deal*, Las Vegas, NV: GBC Press.

Spector, P.E. (1997) 'The role of frustration in antisocial behaviour at work', in R.A. Giacolone and J. Greenberg (eds), *Antisocial Behaviour in Organizations*, London: Sage, ch. 1.

Swallow, C. (2004) 'Protecting workers from travel rage', *Logistics and Transport Focus*, 6(9): 49.

Taylor, L. and Walton, P. (1971) 'Industrial sabotage: Motives and meanings', in S. Cohen (ed.), *Images of Deviance*, Harmondsworth: Penguin, pp. 219–45.

Thompson, P. and Ackroyd, S. (1995) 'All quiet on the workplace front? A critique of recent trends in British industrial sociology', *Sociology*, 29(4): 615–33.

Van Maanan, J. (1991) 'The Smile Factory: Work at Disneyland', in P.J. Frost, L.F. Moore, M.R. Louis, C.C. Lundberg, and J. Martin (eds), *Reframing Organizational Culture*, London: Sage, ch. 4.

_____ (1995) 'Fear and loathing in organization studies', *Organization Science*, 6(6): 687–92.

Wall, D.S. (2001) 'Maintaining order and law on the Internet', in D. Wall (ed.), *Crime and the Internet*, London: Routledge, ch. 1.

Watts, J. (2007) 'Can't take a joke: Humour as resistance, refuge and exclusion in a highly gendered workplace', *Feminism Psychology*, 17: 259–66.

Westhuses, E. (2004) *Workplace Mobbing in Academe*, Lewiston, NY: Edwin Mellen Press.

Williams, M. (2006) *Virtually Criminal: Crime, Deviance and Regulation Online*, London: Routledge.

Willis, P. (1977) *Learning to Labour*, London: Saxon House.

Wilson, B. (2008) *Swindled: From Poison Sweets to Counterfeit Coffee—The Dark History of Food Cheats*, London: John Murray.

Winbush, J.C. and Dalton, D.R. (1997) 'Base rate for employee theft: Convergence of multiple methods', *Journal of Applied Psychology*, 82: 756–63.

Worral, L. and Cooper, C.L. (1999) *Quality of Working Life 1998 Survey of Manager's Changing Experiences*, London: Institute of Management.

Zapf, D. (1999) 'Organizational, work group related and personal causes of mobbing/bullying at work', *International Journal of Manpower*, 20(1–2): 70–85.

_____, Knorz, C., and Kulla, M. (1996) 'On the relationship between mobbing factors, and job content, social work environment and health outcomes', *European Journal of Work and Organizational Psychology*, 5(2): 215–37.

Voluntary and Alternative Organizations

Introduction

This book has discussed many of the problems associated with work design and how those problems might be overcome. It has looked at alienation, lack of control, boredom, theft, sabotage, problems created by bureaucracy and hierarchy, and other organizational ills. Voluntary work, cooperatives, or other alternative organizations might help to solve a lot of these problems, because the organization can be flatter, can appear less bureaucratic, can offer equality and democracy, and can involve employees more, which may mean that the employees are less bored and have more control over their work. Alternative organizations, such as cooperatives, and workplace schemes, such as profit sharing and share ownership, can potentially reduce levels of industrial conflict and enhance productivity by aligning the interests of workers with those of the firm.

Cooperatives are jointly owned and democratically controlled by their members, and it is the members who are the beneficiaries of the activities of the business. In principle, cooperatives offer a model of a more humane and productive alternative to bureaucratic organization (Rothschild-Whitt, 1982). Some (for example, Mellor et al., 1988) may claim that, in cooperatives, the dispossessed seek to control the very existence of work itself; ultimately, cooperatives exist because of a desire to change the whole basis of control and radically shift it towards those who have so little. Similarly, the kibbutz is a collective endeavour, as was self-management.

In all of these examples of the many alternative ways in which we can currently organize ourselves (Parker et al., 2007), workers' interests are aligned with those of the organization and, potentially, they have more control over what work they do, how work is shared, and the benefits to them as individuals.

This chapter covers:

- voluntary work;
- cooperatives;
- the Israeli kibbutz;
- Yugoslav self-management;
- employee involvement—profit sharing and share ownership.

Voluntary work

Voluntary work—characterized by that absence of payment for work undertaken—has, for the most part, been ignored by research on organizational behaviour, but it is an important form of labour (Harris, 1990; MacDonald, 1997). Regular surveys by the *National Centre for Volunteering* consistently find that just under a half of all adults engage in 'informal' voluntary work (Taylor, 2004). The voluntary sector is now a major employer. In 2004, the Labour Force Survey found that 2.2 per cent of the overall workforce was employed in the voluntary sector (see http://www.ncvo-vol.org.uk). The voluntary sector is highly diverse and includes organizations, such as charities, not-for-profit and cooperative organizations, and sports clubs, all of which differ in terms of origin, structure, governance, degree of participation, and objectives.

There has been a rapid growth in the number of charities and it is estimated that half a million people are employed in the sector (Halfpenny and Reid, 2002). Levels of voluntary work have been high, and can help to give insight into the changing nature of what work and unemployment mean to people. In rural areas, participation in voluntary groups is heavily skewed towards the relatively affluent, who use them as vehicles for improving their social networks (Williams, 2002). In economically depressed areas, volunteering has been taken up increasingly by people not in employment. Middle-class people are more likely to engage in formal voluntary organizations (Egerton and Mullan, 2006).

MacDonald's (1997) research on volunteer workers gives us some useful information. It showed that volunteers are predominantly engaged in looking after the disadvantaged as carers or as fund-raisers. A minority work for only a few hours a week; most work virtually full-time. All are motivated by a moral concern for the disadvantaged in their communities. Some—particularly middle-aged and older women— use volunteering to rebuild lives left empty through redundancy or bereavement (after husbands have died, children left home, or employment ceased). Volunteering gives them the opportunity to maintain self-identity despite their socially ascribed roles as carers at home.

Voluntary work was also found by MacDonald to be a semi-permanent response to being excluded from employment—particularly for middle-aged men. They had realized that unemployment could be the norm for them: volunteering provided new opportunities and challenges, and the chance to give up images of 'worker' and 'breadwinner'. Further, the new work had the potential to broaden their work aspirations and expectations. For teenagers and young adults, meanwhile, volunteering can be a strategy for finding 'proper jobs'. They were gaining work experience, skills, contacts, and references through volunteering—although it must be noted that some suggested that the work could be physically and emotionally hard, and that they could be treated like 'skivvies'. Their treatment could consequently come close to exploitation because the work is unpaid.

EXAMPLE   How voluntary work can provide a 'space'

A different perspective on voluntary work is to be found in Gold and Fraser (2002). They describe how voluntary work can also provide a 'career space'—that is, an opportunity to balance working and non-work life. It can, then, provide an alternative career for those with employment.

What would doing voluntary work mean to you?

Cooperatives

A cooperative is a business that is wholly or substantially owned and controlled by those who work in it; it is run for their mutual benefit. Control is exercised on the basis of 'one person, one vote'; membership is open, as far as possible, to all workers.

Cooperatives are based on values of self-help, self-responsibility, democracy, equality, equity, and solidarity. The following are the 'Rochdale Principles of Cooperation', established by the Rochdale pioneers of the cooperative movement in the 1840s (see http://www.ica.coop/coop/principles.html and http://www.ica.coop/coop/principles-revisions.html)—the basic principles that we would expect to find in a cooperative.

1. *Open, voluntary membership* Membership in a cooperative should be voluntary and available without restriction or discrimination to all persons who can make use of its services, and who are willing to accept the responsibilities of membership.

2. *Democratic control* Cooperatives are democratic organizations. Their affairs should be administered by persons elected or appointed in a manner agreed to by the members and accountable to the members. Members should enjoy equal rights of voting and participation in decisions affecting the coop. No member has greater control than any other. Members must 'cooperate' to govern their business effectively.

3. *Limited return, if any, on equity capital* Share capital should receive a strictly limited rate of interest. This means that cooperatives do not seek speculative investments that care more about profits than people; investments in the cooperative are for the good of the whole.

4. *Net surplus belongs to user-owners* The net savings from the operations of a coop belong to the members of that coop and should be distributed in an equitable manner. This usually means one of three things: (a) setting aside money for the development of the coop; (b) providing a service to its members; or (c) distributing money to the members in proportion to their transactions with the coop.

5. *Education* All cooperatives should make provision for the education of their members, officers, and employees, and of the general public in the principles and techniques of cooperation, both economic and democratic. Members who understand the social vision of cooperatives—and who understand how their coop works—can, and do, play a more active role in controlling their business.

6. *Cooperation among cooperatives* All cooperative organizations, to best serve their members' interests and their communities, should actively cooperate in every practical way with other cooperatives at local, national, and international levels. In the same way as coops seek to help and protect their members through the implementation of these principles, coops can do so for each other. Through helping one another, coops can strengthen the movement and broaden the social vision.

STOP AND THINK **Do these principles of cooperation appeal to you?**

France, Spain, and Italy have seen a rise in the strength of the cooperative movement: thousands of worker cooperatives employ over 200,000 worker members. In Italy, cooperatives account for up to 30 per cent of total trade. Cooperation is also well established in France. In Spain, cooperatives lead all other enterprises in national productivity (Williams, 2007). Government legislative and financial support for cooperatives has continued in both France and Italy, in marked contrast to the experience of the UK. In western Germany, a network of business projects was initiated in the alternative sector. These businesses did not necessarily adopt formal cooperative status, but shared many of their characteristics, such as collective ownership and democratic management. They also had a strong commitment to providing a socially useful product or service, and aimed to pay an income equivalent to the general level of wages. In the USA, as in Europe, the new wave of cooperative development was associated with the alternative movement (see Ehrenreich and Edelstein, 1983; Lichtenstein, 1986).

EXAMPLE **A North American cooperative**

Ocean Spray is an agricultural cooperative owned by more than 600 cranberry and over a hundred grapefruit growers in the USA and Canada. The cooperative was formed in the 1930s and currently employs more than 2,000 people worldwide. Three cranberry growers started the cooperative in order to expand the market for cranberries and make juice drinks.

Interest in cooperatives has waxed and waned in the UK over the years. In 1945, there were just forty-four cooperatives (Mellor et al., 1988); their numbers reached a low point in the early 1970s, when there were about thirty-five registered. But an alternative movement in the 1970s brought about a number of idealistic cooperatives. With growing unemployment in the late 1970s and early 1980s, interest in cooperatives increased—and by 1985, there were over a thousand cooperatives in the UK. Local authorities and government agencies—such as the *Highlands and Islands Development Board* in Scotland—promoted cooperatives as a means of job creation. Cooperatives across the UK now collectively represent 237,000 jobs and 10.8 million members (see http://www.cooperatives-uk.coop). The average size of cooperatives in the UK is, however, not large: the mean size is about seven workers and the median only four. They are concentrated in particular sectors, such as clothing, printing, catering, wholefoods, and bookshops (Cornforth et al., 1988).

EXAMPLE **A British cooperative: *Suma***

Suma has no chief executive or managing director, but does have an elected management committee to implement decisions made at regular general meetings with the consent of cooperative members. Day-to-day work is carried out by self-managing teams. All of the employees are paid the same wage and enjoy an equal stake in the success of the business. Members are encouraged to get involved in more than one area of the business, so perform more than one role, in order to broaden skills and give insight into the workings of the cooperative. The company is the UK's largest independent wholefood wholesaler-distributor.

What, then, is the experience of cooperative working? In a study of sixteen British case studies, Cornforth et al. (1988) found that cooperative working was intense and involving—whether for better or worse. The individuals felt a heightened emotional involvement with their work. Their worries could be severe, but when cooperative working was going well, it gave rise to feelings of great excitement and satisfaction that were far more stimulating than those related to conventional employment had ever been. While instrumental benefits, such as job security, were important and a powerful spur to founding or working in a cooperative, social benefits were also an advantage. It was a welcome luxury to work with people who were congenial, both politically and personally. Working in a cooperative is a way in which self-esteem and self-identity needs can be met within a work environment. Many of the members of the cooperatives had joined because they felt attracted to the radical products or services and egalitarian working practices. Many found it difficult to think of the things that they liked least about their work, but there were costs, such as low pay (especially at the start of the cooperative) and tiredness due to long hours. Workers in cooperatives were able to secure more control over organization and management of work on the shop floor than is usually the case, although there were limits imposed by the need for efficiency, the nature of technology, the workers themselves, knowledge, and experience. The cooperatives' achievements included less supervision, more flexible working arrangements, more variety of work, lower wage differentials, and more direct control over how workers carry out their jobs. Over time, however, the increasing complexity of some businesses and pressures for continuity have led to limits being placed on job rotation, and the introduction of small differentials due to the increasing specialization. Some may argue that the principles of cooperation are eroded by these changes that may have taken place over time.

Cooperatives and the labour process

We have seen how cooperatives can give a greater sense of job ownership—but it cannot be assumed that ownership of a job bestows control over that job: the nature of the labour process in the particular industry or service will affect the control that an individual has. The labour process can be defined as 'the means by which raw materials are transformed by human labour, acting on the objects with tools and machinery: first into products for use and, under capitalism, into commodities to be exchanged on the market' (Thompson, 1983: xv). Raw materials are transformed by people and technology—and when it comes to technology in cooperatives, there is often little choice about the technology that is purchased or hired. Inappropriate or outdated equipment might even contribute to the demise of a cooperative (Wajcman, 1983). A fledgling cooperative might be tied to previous production methods and even to previous suppliers or customers; others will be constrained by the amount of money available, making it difficult to upgrade technology. Machinery itself will impose its own limits on how jobs can be designed. The workforce, will, however—within certain parameters—have some choice about specific equipment as well as over work design. They might choose less efficient machinery that is safer; they may choose to situate workers facing each other in pairs to allow them to talk; they might also allow workers discretion over unscheduled breaks or flexibility in relation to hours of work.

Because cooperatives are unlikely to find themselves in a monopoly selling position or a market leader, due to the limitations of resource, such as funding for investment, they are unlikely to be able to determine the type, quantity, or price of the product—particularly if linked to a single buyer. The speed and skill required to produce competitively conflicts with the ability of cooperatives to practise preferred forms of work organization, such as job rotation. Worker cooperatives can, then, face stark choices in often very unfavourable circumstances and poor economic climates. There are therefore both positive and more negative outcomes of the cooperative working experience.

Mondragon

In 1956, Father Jose Maria Arizmendi-Arieta inspired workers in the Basque region of Spain—where the ideas of egalitarianism and industrial democracy are intrinsic elements of Basque identity (Kasmir, 1996)—to take over a redundant factory in a town known in Spanish as 'Mondragon'. By 1982, over 18,000 people were employed by what became known as the 'Mondragon group of cooperatives', and they had created their own network of financial and welfare services; in 1986, the numbers employed were 19,500. In the 1980s, the Spanish economy was more severely affected by recession than those of other Western industrialized nations—yet the Mondragon cooperatives coped with the extreme economic adversity.

In Mondragon, there are primary cooperatives that produce a variety of manufactured products, including electrical goods, refrigerators, and machine tools. The difficulty of obtaining funding, and the need to provide social and welfare services, led to the establishment of secondary cooperatives to support the primary cooperatives, of which the most important is the *Caja Laboral Popular*, a savings bank. The *Caja* lays down a democratic governing structure and a code of practice for each cooperative (Mellor et al., 1988), and provides about 60 per cent of the funding for new cooperatives. Workers, however, must make an investment; this provides incentive to workers' commitment to the cooperative's success. All profits return to workers or to community welfare (Hacker, 1987).

Participation by workers is mediated though a committee system. Directors are elected on the basis of 'one person, one vote'; they are then accountable to a general assembly. The general assembly meets at least annually and members of the firm have an obligation to vote. The governing council is the top policymaking body and may call meetings. This governing council is elected by the members, who are all workers; non-members may attend. A works or social council effectively replicates the role of trade unions and could, for example, question abuses committed by management, and make suggestions on safety and health, social security, systems of compensation, and social work activities or projects. Many of the cooperatives employ no non-members and, under their own constitution and by-laws, no cooperative may employ more than 10 per cent non-members.

STOP AND THINK What is your opinion of Mondragon?

What are the pros and cons of an organization such as Mondragon for you? Does it have any appeal to you as an organization?

For a fuller discussion of Mondragon, see, for example, Benello (1996), or some of the web-based discussion of this cooperative endeavour.

Until the early 1970s, worker participation at Mondragon was limited to governance. In the late 1970s, this was extended to the organization and management of work. Foote Whyte and King Whyte (1988: 113–14) note that a manager, asked to look at personnel and human relations, concluded that:

- the personnel department should play a leading role in linking the economic and technological objectives of the firm with the social concerns of the members;

- the growing tensions in the workplace revealed the inherent contradiction between the democratic system of cooperative governance and the rigid authoritarian system for organizing work, according to the scientific management principles of Taylor;

- management should explore the possibility of creating new forms of work organization that would be economically efficient, yet more in harmony with the social values on which the cooperative movement was based. Personnel should work with line managers to do this.

Changes were consequently made to work organization at Mondragon: for example, an assembly line for the manufacture of thermostats was removed and substituted with work tables. Workers could now set their own work rhythm, and freely exchange information and ideas. All workers were expected to perform all of the tasks and could rotate tasks as they themselves decided. As they gained skill and confidence, they began to take over supervisory and staff functions, such as requisitioning tools and materials, and recording their output. As a result of reorganization, the workers could more readily visualize their contribution to the total product; they were better able to respond to customer needs and improve the planning process; the inventory of work in progress was reduced, and the research and development process strengthened. Both managers and workers were in favour of the new ways of working. The monotony of work was relieved. The work groups increased workers' self-esteem and made individuals feel responsible to the group for their performance. Workers welcomed the opportunity to learn new skills and improve relationships with supervisors. And improved productivity and quality reduced scrap and stock levels.

But Mondragon is not without its critics. For example, Kasmir (1996) is disappointed that the more or less democratic entrepreneurial decisions are implemented through a hierarchy of managers, experts, and skilled workers. Further, Hacker (1987) claims that empirical research on work democracy has tended to ignore issues of gender, with studies of Mondragon failing to note the situation of women or to ask questions about gender before Hacker arrived. In fact, Foot Whyte and King Whyte (1988) do look briefly at the situation of women and find that, at the outset, single women had been required to leave the firm when they married, but by the mid-1960s, this policy had been abandoned. They also note the efforts made to establish a women's cooperative within Mondragon.

Sally Hacker's (1987) study (which was aided by Clara Elcorobairutia) does suggest that women fared somewhat better in Mondragon cooperatives than in private firms in the region, in terms of employment, earnings, and job security. But the concentration of technical and scientific skill lay with the men in the cooperatives: women workers were found clustered at the bottom of the pay and occupational hierarchies.

The studies of Mondragon show, then, some very positive features—balanced against research evidence that Mondragon may not have overcome some of the inequalities found in other non-cooperative organizations.

The Israeli kibbutz

A kibbutz is a collective community, or settlement, found in Israel and is a logical extension of cooperative working. The kibbutz movement in Israel remains a viable attempt to provide an alternative to capitalism, without managerial authority, worker subordination, and worker exploitation (Warhurst, 1998). The kibbutz movement was founded at the beginning of the twentieth century and grew rapidly in the two decades after 1931. The pioneers wished to create an economy and society that was free, working, and classless. The organizational design uses socialist principles, within which the means of production are owned by the community, and all work is shared equally and rotated to give every member experience of every activity, including the most routine and demeaning work. In the kibbutz, members live and work communally. Membership is voluntary, but subject to the approval of the community. A common 'household' and treasury exist. Nobody receives payment, but all basic needs are met on an agreed basis and with equality; all members receive a small, personal, and equitable allowance, regardless of contribution. A general assembly is the source of power, to which every member has equal access. This assembly is supplemented by several committees: of work branches, of work allocation, of culture, of services, of economic planning, and others. The typical kibbutz will have as many as thirty different committees, in which between 30 and 50 per cent of members annually participate. General managers are elected and the position is open to regular rotation approximately every five to seven years. In recent years, however, the situation has become less favourable, as support for socialist solutions has dwindled (Heller et al., 1998). Today, there are 269 kibbutzim, with a total population of 123,900 members (Yad Tabenkin, 1997); the average size of a kibbutz is just fewer than 500 members.

Warhurst (1998) has produced a case study of a kibbutz through open participant observation—that is, by living and working there. In this kibbutz, he found that the role of managers was to coordinate rather than to control. There were no job descriptions, no direction, monitoring, or evaluation by managers of work or workers, and no records of individual workers or work group performance or attendance. Workers decided their own specific tasks and how to do them. It was, then, the antithesis of Taylorism. Labour discipline came about, in part, due to the commitment of individual members and their identification with the purposes of the kibbutz. There is a common framework of norms, values, and beliefs about the organization and the importance of work to which all members, as workers, consent and conform. At least one alternative form of workplace organization and control is possible then, Warhurst concludes.

Yugoslav self-management

Another alternative form of organization was the self-management system found in the former Yugoslavia until the 1990s. Until the break-up of Yugoslavia around 1992, Yugoslav workers enjoyed social ownership and worker self-management. For about three decades, social scientists studied the Yugoslav self-management system, which was based on the assumption that organizations could be run by their employees operating through elected workers' councils. Workers' councils had the right to hire and fire management, and to make major decisions. Theoretically, all decisions were made by workers; the role of management was simply one of implementing those decisions. Technically, managers were prohibited from becoming members of workers' councils, although they were allowed to attend and speak.

Research showed, however, that top management did become members of the workers' councils and, in fact, tended to dominate discussions on strategic issues; most top management proposals were accepted (Heller et al., 1998). There was, therefore, a great gap between the expectations of what self-management could achieve and what it did achieve, in reality. Much of this gap could be explained by differences in experience and knowledge of managers and workers: it may have been a mistake to expect all employees (most of whom came from peasant backgrounds) to take part in decisions on technology, marketing, and innovation, and to think that professional managers would carry out decisions without having a say. And despite the ideals of self-management, the Tayloristic scientific division of labour was widespread; democratic management was curbed. Self-management degenerated into little more than self-interest—a situation reinforced by the personal financial remuneration of workers within these enterprises (Warhurst, 1998).

There were, nonetheless, some successes. Yugoslav industries were shown to be the most participative of the industries studied in eleven countries. Self-management educated the workers, and created a feeling of collective ownership and responsibility. It did much to transform a traditional hierarchical society. Self-management also trained a generation of managers (Heller et al., 1998). Self-management, as an organizing principle within industry, disappeared when the Yugoslav state broke apart in the 1990s. But research by Pusic since self-management disappeared from Yugoslav industries (see Heller et al., 1998) shows that Croatian managers continue to feel quite positively about self-management. Further, in Slovenia, a new structure has emerged based in codetermination. So while Yugoslav workers' self-management has now largely disappeared, its experience provides some important lessons about how social ownership can be achieved and how that social ownership goes hand in hand with more participative, less hierarchical, organization.

STOP AND THINK Would self-management suit you?

Imagine, when being asked by your boss to do a particular job, being able to say: 'No, I prefer to do something else.' This is how a worker in Warhurst's (1998) case study explained his relationship with his line manager. The manager can only ask you to do something; he cannot *tell* you to do it. How would you feel about having this opportunity?

Employee involvement: Profit sharing and share ownership

Each of the examples at which we have looked so far has involved employees in decision making. Interest in employee participation in organizational decision making peaked in the 1970s, but continued interest in the subject is maintained by, for example, financial participation. One such form of financial participation is profit sharing. In profit sharing, employees are given the opportunity to take some of their income from employment in a form related to their employer's profits. Profit sharing is thought to foster greater identification among employees with their employer, and is seen as a means by which employees can bear some of the risks and rewards of the enterprise.

Profit sharing was initially introduced in the mid-nineteenth century to prevent or inhibit union activity. During this time, however, schemes would often be withdrawn when company profits declined or when the threat of union influence was raised (Baddon et al., 1989). Further surges of interest in profit sharing emerged just before the First World War, during the inter-war period, and following the Second World War. Such a fluctuating history suggests that the schemes were introduced for two main purposes: as an act of faith by employers towards their employees, or as a means of securing employee compliance (Baddon et al., 1989). Interest in profit sharing has grown again in recent years (Gomez-Mejia and Balkin, 1992; Bhargara, 1995; Morris and Pinnington, 1998): it is now estimated that 24 per cent of private-sector employees in the UK (that is, 3.7 million) currently receive profit-related pay (Robinson and Perotin, 1997).

Profit sharing can be effective in eroding the 'them and us' divide between owner and employees, and in increasing commitment to enterprise goals, and raising efficiency and profitability. There is very strong research evidence to show that profit sharing does act to increase company productivity (Robinson and Perotin, 1997). With profit sharing, there is the potential incentive effect of a payment system that links workers' productive performance with their remuneration; it can also be seen as offering an incentive to employees to increase profitability as a group. One disadvantage is that it loses the directness of the effort–pay relation, which can create 'free-rider' problems (Kim, 1998) when workers do not put in the expected effort, because they only receive a small part of the profits generated by their effort.

Another form of employee financial participation is share ownership. Share ownership means that employees are able to acquire a degree of ownership of the assets of the employer. The purpose is to allow employees to develop a sense of belonging to the company and, as with profit sharing, to break down the 'them and us' divide. In theory, employee share ownership should generate more favourable attitudes towards the company and greater organizational commitment (Kelly and Kelly, 1991). This, in turn, will lead to changes in employee behaviour, such as greater personal effort, a reduced propensity to quit, and greater scrutiny of colleagues' work behaviour (Pendleton et al., 1998). In time, these changes should be reflected in improvements in collective performance, as measured by productivity and profitability.

EXAMPLE A share ownership company

Tullis Rusell Group Ltd, a papermaking and paper coating company, became employee-owned in 1994. In this case, a pioneering capital reorganization programme transferred ownership of the company from the family who owned it to the employees, using legislation governing employee share owner-ship trusts in the UK. A 'share council' comprising thirteen employee members advises the board on the distri-bution of shares and dividend payments. The company employees nearly 800 people.

(*Sources:* http://www.tullis-russell.co.uk; http://www.employeeownership.co.uk)

Like profit sharing, employee share ownership schemes have become widespread in the UK (Millward et al., 1992), some parts of the European Union (Uvalic,1991), the USA (Blasi and Kruse, 1991), the former Eastern bloc countries (Karsai and Wright, 1994), and Japan (Jones and Kato, 1995).

EXAMPLE An organization involved in social enterprise, share ownership, and profit sharing

When *Divine Chocolate Ltd* was launched in 1997, the Kuapa Kokoo farmers in Ghana, who grow the raw ingredients, owned a third of it; the rest of the ownership was split between *Body Shop International*, *Comic Relief*, *Christian Aid*, and *Twin* (the alternative trading company behind *CafeDirect*). *Divine* pays a fair price for the farmers' cocoa (guaranteed to be more than the market price), plus a fair trade premium that helps to fund social projects such as building schools and sinking wells. A share of turnover is also given to fund aspects such as training in agricultural practices, health and hygiene, and gender equality. The farmers are also paid dividends. The farmers have created a thriving democratically run cooperative with 45,000 members. *Divine Chocolate* is now a £10 million business, employing only sixteen people in London.

(*Sources: The Observer*, special report, 21 October 2007; http://www.divinechocolate.com/default.aspx)

Robinson and Perotin (1997) argue that there is a link between profit sharing and share ownership, and productivity; others, such as Baddon et al. (1989), have concluded that the evidence on increased profitability and productivity arising from profit sharing and share ownership schemes is mixed. Although employers and employees are potential beneficiaries of financial participation, there is surprisingly little hard evidence demonstrating what the benefits are or to whom they accrue.

Baddon et al. (1989) surveyed about 400 employee share ownership and profit-sharing schemes in companies. They found that companies commonly run more than one scheme of financial participation for more than one objective. The managers themselves had only a very general sense of what they were trying to achieve through these schemes. Case studies showed that, although there was a strong sense of unitary thinking in which share ownership (and, to a lesser extent, profit sharing) was seen as reinforcing employee loyalty and commitment, there was no systematic attempt by the companies to measure the benefits of running these schemes. The conclusion is that the management objectives were not being achieved and that personal financial gain is a stronger motivating factor among employees than some of the loftier objectives. The benefits that resulted from the profit-sharing and share ownership schemes tended not to be seen by employees as an essential element of pay, and therefore did not, in themselves, generate commitment—even where profit bonus benefits were quite substantial; rather, they were seen as 'just another kind of bonus' (ibid.: 275), which fell short of moving employees to a feeling of unity of purpose. The researchers found that no specific scheme held any significant advantage over others.

Similarly, Dunn et al. (1991) and, more recently, Keef (1998) also found that employee ownership does not result in expected improvements in attitudes. They offer two reasons: firstly, that employee equity stakes are too small in relation to total equity to bring about a pronounced sense of ownership; and secondly, that few opportunities are provided for employees to translate ownership into increased control and participation in decision making (Pendleton, 1997). In other words, the benefits were merely financial; a true sense of ownership, whereby the employee could become directly involved in decision making, was not provided. It would appear, then, that a 'sense of ownership' is important in bringing about attitudinal change. Opportunities for *participation* in decision making are more important than ownership per se in generating feelings of ownership. And feelings of ownership are significantly associated with higher levels of commitment and satisfaction (Pendleton et al., 1998).

Conclusion

Alternatives to highly bureaucratic, hierarchical organizations do exist. These alternatives involve greater democracy, wider decision making, ownership, and involvement. While Frederick Taylor, Henri Fayol, and Max Weber legitimated the managerial right to manage in the USA, the UK, and other parts of Europe, as well as the managers' right to analyse the work situation scientifically and rationally, thus devising the most appropriate, efficient methods to organize, this is not the *only* way in which to organize. In Scandinavia, for example, there was a 'historic compromise' between capital and labour (Burnes, 1996), with government-backed approaches to industrial democracy and extensions of workers' rights. Rules, divisions of labour, and some bureaucracy will not be eliminated entirely, but organizations can be more democratic, less hierarchical, and more collectivist. There are the circumstances under which workplace democracy is possible (Joseph, 1989). But as Joseph notes, what is striking about the UK is the extent to which alternatives to conventional management arrangements are non-issues and rarely appear to be discussed.

Greater moves could be made towards extending and renewing existing organizational forms. There are a variety of possible organizational forms of decision making, ownership, and involvement from which to choose that might result in a minimal bureaucracy. Task sharing, egalitarian rewards, democratic controls, cooperative cultures, and participation might offer solutions to the problems created by Taylorism, bureaucracy, hierarchy, and social inequality.

KEY POINTS

- Voluntary work can provide an opportunity for individuals, motivated by a moral concern, to network. It can provide work for the unemployed, present new opportunities and challenges, and broaden expectations and aspirations. It may also be difficult and demanding.

- Voluntary work will have different meanings for different individuals depending on their personal circumstances: for example, class and whether or not they have other employment.

- A cooperative is a business that is wholly or substantially owned and controlled by those who work in it for their mutual benefit. There can be both positive and negative effects of cooperative working for the individual.

- The kibbutz represents the antithesis of Taylorism because managers do not direct, monitor or control; workers decide what tasks they do and how to do them.

- In relation to self-management, the ideals have not been realized: there has been a gap between the expectations and reality, mainly due to differences in experience and knowledge of managers and workers. The Yugoslav experiment showed, however, how self-management might be achieved.

- Profit sharing and share ownership give employees the opportunity to share in some of the profits that they have helped to generate.

CASE STUDY

Payback for companies that encourage staff to do voluntary work

Organizations can encourage staff to get involved in voluntary work. Staff who undertake voluntary work appear to be better, more rounded, and capable individuals, and so better employees. Employees also like to think that they are working for a company that cares about the local community.

The *Royal Bank of Scotland* is an example of a company that encourages this. It employs a 'head of community investment'. Staff in the bank are supported in giving to the community in a number of ways. For every pound that the employee gives to a charity though a direct payroll deduction, the bank will add two. Further, staff who give time to causes are supported by cash grants from the bank: for example if an employee chooses to run a marathon to raise funds for a charity, the bank will match what he or she raises to a maximum of £1,000. If he or she acts as a treasurer to a local charity, the employee will be supported through a grant from the bank worth £250.

Marks & Spencer has a corporate and social responsibility unit. The company places employees in secondment roles with community organizations. Secondment can encourage employees to think for themselves, to listen to and get along with a broader range of people than those whom they meet at work, and to develop a different perspective. Skills, including dealing with people and successful negotiation, may be improved.

KPMG has a corporate social responsibility group that identifies and develops partnerships with organizations that provide education, social inclusion, and conservation; they then provide staff with the appropriate training. Each employee has the opportunity to dedicate half a working day each month to a volunteer programme. He or she might help primary school children with literacy or numeracy. *PricewaterhouseCoopers*, too, is reported as working to improve work–life balance and to accommodate family life or voluntary work.

(*Source:* Craig, 2008)

Questions

1. A cynic might argue that the benefits to the companies—in terms of good publicity, and employee and public relations—are greater than the costs. Would this be fair?

2. How big are the benefits to the communities compared to the benefits that the companies reap in profits? Is that fair in your view?

3. How would you make an evaluation of costs and benefits?

FURTHER READING

Hickson, D.J. and Pugh, D. (1995) *Management Worldwide*, London: Penguin In Chapter 5, there is a description of the kibbutz both in theory and in practice.

Lammers, C.J. and Szell, G. (eds) (1989) *International Handbook of Participation in Organizations: For the Study of Organizational Democracy, Cooperation and Self Management*, Oxford: Oxford University Press This book of readings covers organizational democracy, cooperatives, employee share ownership, job involvement, job design, semi-autonomous work groups, and self-management in European, Scandinavian, and other countries.

Oakshott, R. (1990) *A Case for Workers' Cooperatives*, 2nd edn, Houndmills: Macmillan Press This book provides an account of independent worker cooperatives in the UK and around other European countries, including Mondragon in Spain.

Parker, M, Fournier, V., and Reddy, P. (2007) *The Dictionary of Alternatives: Utopianism and Organization*, London: Zed Books This book disagrees with the view that there is no real alternative to market managerialism. It demonstrates that there are many alternatives to the ways in which we currently organize ourselves.

Warhurst, C. (1999) *Between Market, State and Kibbutz: The Management and Transformation of Socialist Industry*, London: Mansell Publishing This book is a 'before' and 'now' exposition and explanation of the kibbutz in Israel.

Williams, R.C. (2007) *The Cooperative Movement: Globalization from Below*, Aldershot: Ashgate This book is one of the few new books on the topic.

RESEARCH QUESTIONS

1. The impetus and motivation for cooperatives comes from a number of different sources, according to the research. What motivation for the establishment of alternative organizations can you find in your reading?

2. There are examples from all over the world of people taking control of their own economic destiny. The Rochdale pioneers are one such example; another is the Antigonish Movement in Nova Scotia (Coady, 1967; Gherardi et al., 1989). What were the advantages for these people of being involved in owning and controlling their enterprises? What were the drawbacks?

3. Credit unions help to provide financial support to people in their local communities and are regulated by the Financial Services Authority in England and Wales. What advantages and disadvantages (apart from the obvious financial ones) do they offer to their members?

REFERENCES

Baddon, L., Hunter, L., Hyman, J., Leopold, J., and Ramsay, H. (1989) *People's Capitalism? A Critical Analysis of Profit-Sharing and Employee Share Ownership*, London: Routledge.

Benello, G. (1996) 'The challenge of Mondragon', in H. Ehrlich (ed.), *Reinventing Anarchy Again*, Edinburgh: AK Press, ch. 17.

Bhargara, S. (1995) 'Profit sharing and financial performance of companies: Evidence from UK panel data', *Economic Journal*, 104: 1044–56.

Blasi, J. and Kruse, D. (1991) *The New Owners: The Mass Emergence of Employee Ownership in Public Companies and What it Means to American Business*, New York: Harper Business.

Burnes, B. (1996) *Managing Change: A Strategic Approach to Organizational Dynamics*, 2nd edn, London: Pitman.

Coady, M.M. (1967) *Masters of Their Own Destiny: The Story of the Antigonish Movement of Adult Educaton through Economic Cooperation*, New York: Harper & Row.

Cornforth, C., Thomas, A., Lewis, J., and Spear, R. (1988) *Developing Successful Worker Cooperatives*, London: Sage.

Craig, T. (2008) 'Keep them engaged: How three employers work with Generation Y-ers', *Personnel Today*, 14 September, available online at http://www.personneltoday.com/articles/2008/09/14/47304/keep-them-engaged-how-three-employers-work-with-generation-y-ers.html

Drago, R. and Turnbull, G.K. (1996) 'On the incidence of profit sharing', *Journal of Economic Behaviour and Organization*, 31: 129–38.

Dunn, S., Richardson, R., and Dewe, P. (1991) 'The impact of employee share ownership on worker attitudes: A longitudinal case study', *Human Resource Management Journal*, 1(1): 1–17.

Earle, J. (1986) *The Italian Cooperative Movement*, London: Allen & Unwin.

Egerton, M. and Mullen, K. (2006) *An Analysis and Monetary Valuation of Formal and Informal Voluntary Work by Gender and Educational Attainment*, Institute for Social and Economic Research working paper, Colchester: University of Essex ISER.

Ehrenreich, R.C. and Edelstein, J.D. (1983) 'Consumers and organizational democracy: American new wave cooperatives', in C. Crouch and F. Heller (eds), *Organizational Democracy and Political Processes*, New York: Wiley.

Foote Whyte, W. and King Whyte, K. (1988) *Making Mondragon: The Growth and Dynamics of the Worker Cooperative Complex*, New York: ILR Press/New York State School of Industrial and Labor Relations, Cornell University.

Gherardi, S., Strati, A., and Turner, B. (1989) 'Industrial democracy and organizational symbolism', in C.J. Lammers and G. Szell (eds), *International Handbook of Participation in Organizations, Vol. I*, Oxford: Oxford University Press, ch. 13.

Gold, M. and Fraser, J. (2002) 'Managing self-management: Successful transitions to portfolio careers', *Work, Employment and Society*, 16(4): 579–97.

Gomez-Mejia, L. and Balkin, D. (1992) *Compensation, Organizational Strategy and Firm Performance*, Cincinnati, OH: South Western Publishing.

Hacker, S. (1987) 'Women workers in the Mondragon system of industrial cooperatives', *Gender and Society*, 1: 358–79.

Halfpenny, P. and Reid, M. (2002) 'Research on the voluntary sector: An overview', *Policy and Politics*, 30(4): 533–50.

Harris, M. (1990) 'Working the UK voluntary sector', *Work Employment and Society*, 4(1): 125–40.

Heller, F., Pusic, E., Strauss, G., and Wilpert, B. (1998) *Organizational Participation: Myth and Reality*, Oxford: Oxford University Press.

Jahoda, M. (1982) *Employment and Unemployment: A Social Psychological Analysis*, Cambridge: Cambridge University Press.

Jones, D. and Kato, T. (1995) 'The productivity effects of Japanese employee stock ownership plans: Evidence from Japanese panel data', *American Economic Review*, 85: 391–414.

Joseph, M. (1989) *Sociology for Business*, Cambridge: Polity in association with Basil Blackwell.

Karsai, J. and Wright, M. (1994) 'Accountability, governance and finance in Hungarian buy-outs', *Europe-Asia Studies*, 46: 997–1016.

Kasmir, S. (1996) *The Myth of Mondragon: Cooperatives, Politics and Working Class Life in a Basque Town*, Albany, NY: SUNY Press.

Keef, S.P. (1998) 'The causal association between employee share ownership and attitudes: A study based in the long framework', *British Journal of Industrial Relations*, March: 73–82.

Kelly, J. and Kelly, C. (1991) '"Them and ys": Social psychology and the new industrial relations', *British Journal of Industrial Relations*, 29: 25–48.

355

Kim, S. (1998) 'Does profit sharing increase firms' profits?', *Journal of Labor Research*, 19(2): 351–70.

Kruse, D.L. (1996) 'Why do firms adopt profit sharing and employee ownership plans?', *British Journal of Industrial Relations*, 34(4): 515–38.

Lichtenstein, P.M. (1986) 'The concept of the firm in the economic theory of alternative organizations', in S. Jansson and A.-B. Hellmark (eds), *Labour-Owned Firms and Workers' Cooperatives*, London: Gowe.

MacDonald, R. (1997) 'Informal working, survival strategies and the idea of an "underclass"', in R. Brown (ed.), *The Changing Shape of Work*, Basingstoke: Macmillan, ch. 6.

Mellor, M., Hannah, J., and Stirling, J. (1988) *Worker Cooperatives in Theory and Practice*, Milton Keynes: Open University Press.

Millward, N., Stevens, M., Smart, D., and Hawes, W. (1992) *Workplace Industrial Relations in Transition: The ED/ESRC/PSI/ACAS Surveys*, Aldershot: Dartmouth.

Morris, T. and Pinnington, A. (1998) 'Patterns of profit-sharing in professional firms', *British Journal of Management*, 9: 23–9.

Parker, M., Fournier, V., and Reedy, P. (2007) *A Dictionary of Alternatives*. London: Zed Books.

Pendleton, A. (1997), 'Shareholders as stakeholders', in A. Gamble, D. Kelly, and G. Kelly (eds), *Stakeholder Capitalism*, Basingstoke: Macmillan, ch. 15.

_____, Wilson, N., and Wright, M. (1998) 'The perception and effects of share ownership: Empirical evidence from employee buy-outs', *British Journal of Industrial Relations*, 36(1): 99–123.

Robinson, A. and Perotin, V. (1997) 'Is profit sharing the answer?', *New Economy*, 4: 112–16.

Rothschild-Whitt, J. (1982) 'The collectivist organization', in F. Lindenfeld and J. Rothschild-Whitt (eds), *Workplace Democracy and Social Change*, Boston, MA: Porter Sargent.

Russell, R. (1995) *Utopia in Zion: The Israeli Experience with Worker Cooperatives*, Albany, NY: SUNY Press.

Taylor, R.F. (2004) 'Extending conceptual boundaries: Work, voluntary work and employment', *Work, Employment and Society*, 18(1): 29–49.

Thompson, P. (1983) *The Nature of Work*, London: Macmillan.

Uvalic, M. (1991) *Social Europe: The PEPPER Report*, Brussels: European Commission.

Wajcman, J. (1983) *Women in Control*, Milton Keynes: Open University Press.

Warhurst, C. (1998) 'Recognizing the possible: The organization and control of a socialist labour process', *Administrative Science Quarterly*, 43: 470–97.

Williams, C.C. (2002) 'Harnessing voluntary work: A fourth sector approach', *Public Studies*, 23(3–4): 247–60.

Williams, R.C. (2007) *The Cooperative Movement: Globalization from Below*, Aldershot: Ashgate.

Yad Tabenkin (1997) *Kibbutz: Facts and Figures*, Efal: Yad Tabenkin.

Health, Well-being, Emotion, and Stress

Introduction

Because organizations have historically often been perceived as rational, unemotional entities, issues of health and well-being (other than stress) are not usually dealt with in most texts on organizational behaviour. Yet work-related illness incurs very large personal and organizational costs, as do violence and abuse. While we might hope that we would be able to take respect for individuals' dignity, health, and well-being at work for granted, they seem threatened in the world of employment.

The aim of this final chapter is to give a more complete view of the realities of life and work, both within and without organizations, and to uncover some of the more hidden realities.

This chapter covers:

- violence and abuse;
- stress;
- the management of emotions;
- being unemployed;
- being 'on the fiddle' or working 'on the side';
- 'non-work'.

Violence and abuse

In some organizations, violence is legitimated: for example, in the military and police, or in a martial arts organization (Hearn and Parkin, 2007). Violence may also be found in relationships between workers and managers, between organizational peers, or between clients and professionals. Violence and abuse can lead to employees taking time off work. Occasionally, we see a newspaper headline about violence at work: a flight attendant may be attacked with a broken bottle, for example, or there may be found to be a tripling of assaults on railway workers. Shop workers in the UK suffer 20,000 physical assaults a year (*Personnel Today*, 2005b), while more than two-thirds of refuse collectors have faced physical and verbal abuse, including attacks with guns, knives, and drug needles. They report being attacked with shovels and grabbed around the throat by angry members of the public and road rage motorists stuck behind refuse trucks (*Personnel Today*, 2005a). The very threat of violence or abuse—particularly if accepted as 'part of the job' and occurring on a daily basis—can increase job stress. Research by the *Nuffield Foundation* (Baty, 2003; *The Guardian*, 2003) shows that even lecturers in higher education are increasingly at risk of violent attack; employees in all sectors of education have been found to be at significantly higher risk of work-related stress, anxiety, and depression than most other occupational groups (Kinman and Jones, 2004). Those working as call handlers in call centres are also mentioned as at higher risk of mental health problems (Sprigg et al., 2003).

Stress

The chief executive of the UK's *Health and Safety Executive* believes that stress is a major problem in British workplaces, and that there is a clear link between poor work organization and subsequent ill health. The *Health and Safety Executive* says that 2.2 million people were suffering from illness that they believed was caused or made worse by their current job in 2006–07 (see http://www.hse.gov.uk). Its survey indicated that around 13 million working days were lost due to work-related stress in 2004–05 (Equality Challenge Unit, 2007). The UK economy loses £12 billion every year due to sickness absence, representing an estimated cost of around £500 per employee (Masterton, 2003). Yet because stress and other negative emotions are not seen as productive, they are rarely acknowledged to exist within organizations.

A classic study of job stress came from William Foot Whyte's (1948) research on 'weeping wait-resses' in the restaurant industry. The waitresses quite often cried because the way in which work was organized caused them stress. The customers put pressure on the waitresses to deliver their order to the table quickly, but the waitresses could not satisfy the demand until the counter hand gave them the ordered food. The counter hand did not like being told by the waitresses to speed up order delivery, so he made them wait. He then felt as though he were the boss rather than someone being bossed. The solution was that the waitresses would write out order slips, then put them on a prong. The counter hand could then decide how to fill the orders without feeling that the waitresses were ordering him what to do. Sometimes, then, managers or workers will be able to change the way in which work is done to reduce the stress.

Boring repetitive jobs can lead to mental strain. As early as 1965, Kornhauser's research with Detroit car workers was showing that the higher the occupation level, the better the mental health of the worker—that is, better jobs with greater work skill, variety, responsibility, and pay lead to better mental health. The lower the occupational level, the more likely workers are to have little support or discretion in their jobs. Recent research also shows how low job control and high demand makes for stress (Schnall and Landbergis, 1994; Bosma et al., 1997). Marmot et al. (1997), in the Whitehall studies, found that stress associated with low control in the workplace is linked to coronary heart disease. In addition to low control, Bosma et al. (1998) found that an imbalance between workers' effort and their rewards was linked to heart disease. It has also been found that the higher the status of the worker, the more likely they are to admit or believe that they have stress problems (Fletcher, 1990). This may be explained by the fact that many of those in white-collar jobs—not least in the public sector (for example, university lecturers, schoolteachers, and social workers)—have experienced a deterioration in their work conditions and that these people are more articulate than most (Nichols, 1998). For example, recently, clinical researchers were reported as experiencing stress as an outcome of extensive work pressure, a lack of control over the work situation, and unsatisfactory interpersonal relationships (Styhre et al., 2002). Perhaps this is why most courses on stress management are aimed at professional employees.

....

STOP AND THINK **Does technology cause stress?**

Do you think that technology can increase stress? A training company found that one in three people complained that technology at work contributes directly to rising stress levels. Referring to this as 'digital depression', the managing director noted how he had recently come across a person who had 19,400 emails in his inbox (Hilpern, 2003).

More recently, researchers have found that more than a third of workers say that they feel stressed out by the number of emails that they receive and the pressure to respond promptly. Some workers viewed their inbox up to forty times each hour, leaving them tired and frustrated. Only 38 per cent of workers were relaxed enough to wait a day or longer before replying to an email.

(*Source:* BBC News, 13 August 2007)

....

But employment is not the only environment in which we experience stress: stressful events include moving house, getting married, having fights and conflicts, and bereavement. When people are under high stress, they tend to fail to sleep for a full eight hours, fail to eat full meals, and tend to stay up late at night. In this way, it is clear that stressful events affect health by decreasing health-sustaining behaviours, which, in turn, plays a role in physical and psychological illnesses.

Stress has been a topic of interest to researchers since the Second World War. Newton et al. (1995) note how an interest in stress arose out of ideas within social Darwinism eugenics and a concern for maintaining a healthy race, with writers such as Walter Cannon and Graham Wallas. Cannon studied the effects of stress on animals and people, focusing on the 'fight or flight' reaction—that is, whether they choose to stay and fight or try to escape when confronting extreme danger. Post-war laboratory research later reflected military concerns, because stress was assumed to affect the performance of pilots, gunners, and others. In the 1970s, however, role stress gathered interest, with 200 articles being written on the topic between 1970 and 1983 (Jackson and Schuler, 1985).

Hans Seyle, researching in 1946, described three stages to a person's response to stress: alarm, resistance, and exhaustion (Seyle, 1976). In the first stage, the muscles tense, and the respiration, heart, and blood pressure rates increase. Next, the person experiences anxiety, anger, and fatigue, as he or she resists stress; he or she may consequently make poor decisions or experience illness at this stage. The person will not be able to sustain this resistance and, if the level of stress continues, he or she will experience exhaustion and stress-induced illness (such as headaches and ulcers). Seyle claims that all individuals go through the same pattern of response and that we can only tolerate so much stress before a serious debilitating condition is brought about. But critics of Seyle's work argue that it ignores both the psychological impact of stress upon an individual, and the individual's ability to recognize stress and act in various ways to change his or her situation (Cooper et al., 1988; Cooper and Payne, 1990). Later theories of stress have emphasized the interaction between a person and their environment; others have added to this by discussing the individual's reaction. For example, Lazarus (1976) has suggested that an individual's stress reaction depends on how the person interprets or appraises (consciously or unconsciously) the significance of a harmful, threatening or challenging event. All is dependent, then, on whether the person feels that he or she can cope with a threat.

Cooper and Cummings (see Cooper et al., 1988) believe that stress results from a misfit between individuals and their environments. This helps to explain why one person seems to flourish in a setting, while another suffers. They suggest that individuals, for the most part, try to keep their thoughts, emotions, and relationships in a 'steady state'; they have a range of stability with which they feel comfortable. When forces disrupt the emotional and physical state, the individual must act or cope to restore a feeling of comfort. If he or she fails to cope, the stress will continue. Symptoms of stress can be manifested physically in, for example, lack of appetite or craving for food, headaches, skin problems, insomnia, fainting spells, and high blood pressure. Mental symptoms may include irritability, feeling unable to cope, difficulty in concentrating, and a lack of interest in life.

So what are the causes of stress? The following are a few of the factors that have been shown to contribute towards stress and strain:

- *the physical environment*—for example, being exposed to hazardous and noxious substances, density and crowding, lack of privacy, high noise levels, high or low temperature, and poor quality lighting;

- *role conflict*—that is, when the individual is torn by conflict in job demands or doing things that he or she neither wants to do, nor believes are part of the job—or *role ambiguity*—that is, when an individual does not have a clear picture about work objectives, co-workers' expectations, or the scope and responsibilities of the job;

- *the characteristics of the job*—for example, work overload, lack of career progression, lack of autonomy, underutilization, too many meetings, shift work, or long hours;

- *relationships with others*—for example, poor relationships with supervisors, or work–family conflict.

For more factors, see Cooper et al. (1988: ch. 4), and Cartwright and Cooper (1997: ch. 1).

Shift work is a common stress factor affecting blood temperature and blood sugar levels, metabolic rate, mental efficiency, work motivation, sleep patterns, family, and social life (Arnold et al., 1995). A study of offshore oil-rig workers showed work patterns—including shift work, physical conditions, and travel—to be one of the most important sources of stress (Sutherland and Cooper, 1987). The longer the work shift (for example, twenty-eight days on, twenty-eight days off, versus fourteen days on, fourteen days off), the greater the stress. The shift patterns were a predictor of mental and physical ill health—particularly when the oil-rig workers were married and had children.

Research on the relationship between stress and balancing the needs of work and family shows that mothers who work outside the home have better mental and physical health than those who do not. But if partners contribute little to domestic tasks, they will have poorer mental health—and the vast majority of mothers had partners who contributed less than 20 per cent to the domestic tasks (Khan and Cuthbertson, 1994). The home is, therefore, a source of stress for women, as they try to balance the dual needs of work and domestic responsibilities (Wheeler and Lyon, 1992; Ginn and Sandell, 1997), but it would appear that work probably impacts on family more than family impacts on work. Interestingly, husbands' attitude towards wives working has been studied extensively, but wives' attitudes towards husbands' employment has not been so extensively researched. Also, research on the impact of children on job stress has focused more on women than on men: while mothers might experience stress due to role overload, fathers might experience some stress as they attempt to fulfil the role of good provider (Gutek et al., 1990).

STOP AND THINK **Stress and dreams**

Have you noticed that, if you are under stress, you have more vivid dreams? Work stress is thought to contribute to nightmares about killing the boss. Stress at work is contributing to a regular nightmare for one in two adults (Womack, 2003). Research in the UK found that 51 per cent of respondents suffered work-related nightmares at least once a week, with the figure rising to 61 per cent among Londoners. A row with the boss was the most common dream, followed by arriving late for a meeting. Worryingly, 7 per cent confessed to dreams in which they wanted to murder the boss.

STOP AND THINK **Stress in the City**

Nicola Horlick hit the headlines by losing a top City job. She had a very large salary, a high-pressured job, and five children, but gave up her job after being falsely accused by a colleague.

The costs of holding highly paid, but high-pressured, jobs can be high: for example, an increasing number of senior women are likely to be found in second or third marriages. Women in top jobs are more likely to suffer from stomach problems, reflecting their struggle with stress. Few women will have been mentored for top jobs. And some are beginning to wonder if they can 'have it all'—that is, a high-powered job and a family.

Do men face these issues of whether they can have both a high-powered job and a family? Is this, then, really 'equality'?

Individual differences are involved in the stress process. There may be collections of traits that protect people from stress: for example 'hardiness' (Maddi and Kobasa, 1984), positive self-image or self-esteem, flexibility. Their personality, coping strategies, personal history, and social support may similarly affect the individual's vulnerability to stress. Some jobs are more stressful than others: the uniformed professions (that is, the *Prison Service*, police force, or civil aviation) have the highest average stress ratings (Cooper et al., 1988); there is also concern about the psychological health of doctors. Rates of suicide among doctors are two or three times those among non-medical populations of comparable social class. In 1996, doctors hit headline news when the *British Medical Association* published a report showing how doctors were turning to drink and drugs to cope with increased stress. One in five doctors had thought about killing themselves (*Daily Mail*, 10 April 1996, p. 21; The Scotsman, 13 April 1996, p. 10). Substance abuse may be up to thirty times more common among doctors than the general population (King et al., 1992). There is also a relatively high suicide rate among nurses (*The Observer*, 19 March 1995, p. 1) and other health service workers (Rees, 1995).

It may be that some individuals have personalities that predispose them to the effects of stress. One such difference that has been examined is 'Type A' coronary-prone behaviour. 'Type A' behaviour is characterized by sustained drive towards poorly defined goals, a preoccupation with deadlines, competitiveness, and a desire for advancement and achievement. Mental and behavioural alertness or aggressiveness, chronic haste, and impatience are also characteristic. This type of behaviour has been shown to be an important risk factor in the development of coronary heart disease—a leading cause of death in the UK and North America. It kills more than 150,000 people a year—that is, one person every three or four minutes (Arnold et al., 1995). In contrast, 'Type B' personality types—a more relaxed type—have a low risk of coronary heart disease.

Typically, more than 50 per cent of the workforce would be classified as 'Type A'. (Completing the questionnaire in Cooper et al., 1988: 51, or Arnold et al., 1995: 376, will give you a rough idea of the degree to which you might be a 'Type A' personality.) While there are some studies that offer contradictory results in relation to the relative risks of heart disease (see Cooper et al., 1988: 48), there are other dilemmas that face those characterized as 'Type A'. 'Type A' behaviour may lead to heart disease—but it is consistently found to predict career success (Steffy et al., 1989). The individual thus faces a conflict: should he or she work hard (going beyond what is expected is a virtue), or should he or she take care not to suffer the psychological and physiological effects of overwork? It is the individual that faces the dilemma, of course, not the organization—that is, the individual has to adjust to work.

If an individual finds that he or she is suffering from stress, there are a number of ways in which he or she can cope—that is, in which he or she can 'transform maladaptive behaviour' (Cooper et al., 1988). The techniques that Cooper et al. recommend include developing assertiveness, identifying the incidents that cause distress by keeping a stress diary, and noting what action was taken and how effective it proved. The individual needs then to attempt to eliminate, or change, the problem or stressor; if the problem or stressor cannot be changed, he or she must find ways of coping with the problem, then monitor and review the outcome (Arnold et al., 1995).

We have—through the measure of 'Type A' behaviour and other measures of stress, such as the General Health Questionnaire—a view of 'normality' that is operationally defined through reference to 'abnormality' (see Newton et al., 1995: 65). There are, however, other ways of looking at stress: for example, taking a sociological approach and looking at the subjective experience of the distress of dealing with the impending closure of a factory, as did Anna Pollert (1981; see Handy, 1995). Most current models of work stress fit firmly within a functionalist paradigm, but this is not the only way in which the subject matter might have been treated.

Using highly individualized methods, some organizations have tried to answer the negative effects of stress by pre-empting it. Companies such as *Federal Express*, *Hewlett Packard*, and *Conoco* have adopted Stephen Covey's programme, 'The Seven Habits of Highly Effective People' (Vecchio, 1995). Stress can be managed in a number of different ways, including employment assistance programmes (EAPs), stress management training, and stress reduction or intervention (Murphy, 1988; Newton et al., 1995). EAPs generally refer to the provision of employee counselling for problems such as alcoholism, drug abuse, and mental health. Stress management training is designed to provide employees with improved coping skills and so includes techniques, such as meditation, biofeedback, and muscle relaxation, to help the individual. Stress reduction or intervention would usually change a job to reduce job stressors—but most workplace initiatives focus on stress management training, or counselling and health promotion, not changing jobs.

The US *Department of Health and Human Services* found that more than 60 per cent of US worksites offered some form of stress management or health promotion activity (Cooper and Cartwright, 1994): for example, the *New York Telephone Company* introduced a 'wellness' programme for cardiovascular fitness, while *PepsiCo* created a physical fitness programme. Evidence of the success of such schemes is generally confusing and imprecise—possibly reflecting the idiosyncratic nature of the form and content of courses (Arnold et al., 1995: 383). The growing evidence that individual and company performance is adversely affected by stress has, however, had little effect on companies in the UK (Wheeler and Lyon, 1992). Companies such as *Anglia Railways*, *Cummings Engineering*, and *Pfizer* are among those few in the UK that have been using techniques such as EAPs and stress management training (Industrial Society, 2001; Hilpern, 2003).

EXAMPLE **How schools have coped with stress**

A pilot project across five schools in York claims to have reduced absence rates among teachers from 10.5 days to 8.9 days a year. An assessment of mental and physical health was completed, and those with higher stress levels were given extra support, such as mentoring and counselling. The project also identified the main causes of stress and drew up a calendar of workload hotspots, so plans could be prepared to cope with peak times. The marking policy was changed to stagger that workload better and an extra teacher was employed.

(*Source:* Hilpern, 2003)

Stress and burnout—that is, exhaustion, cynicism, and reduced professional efficacy—can be treated by organizations as everyday work life problems with which the individual is expected to deal (Kunda, 1982). But Martin et al. (1998) studied the use of personal counselling as a method of reducing the negative effects of stress, concluding that, 'however helpful such a counsellor may be, the implicit message is that work stress is an abnormal response that must be controlled, with the blame for the problem and the responsibility for fixing it resting primarily with the individual experiencing the stress' (ibid.: 458). Being able to handle one's self and stressful situations is, then, seen as the mark of the professional.

EXAMPLE **Stress, overwork, and death**

Overwork can lead to death. There have been reports in the Japanese newspapers of deaths due to overwork—that is, what the Japanese call *karoshi*. If a death is judged as *karoshi*, surviving family members may receive compensation.

(*Source: The Economist*, 2007)

While programmes such as EAP may have genuine benefits for employees, they may also represent an extension of corporate control over staff, who are now expected not only to sell their skills and time, but also to ensure that their total lifestyle ensures maximum corporate gain (Handy, 1988). Newton et al. (1995) argue that stress management techniques are not impartial and are not applied by caring progressive management; in fact, they may be 'nakedly coercive'—that is, a tool of cunning management, intent upon domination and control of its workforce. Fineman (1995) offers the example of managers at a nuclear research establishment undertaking a study of employee role stress: the managers were so alarmed by the results that they immediately suppressed the findings and tried to discredit the analysis. Stress, Fineman (1995) therefore argues, has much to do with the organization and social context of the job. It is an emotional product of the social and political features of work and organizational life. The individual is actively involved in reproducing the social structures and there may be little that he or she can do to affect them—either because they are tacit, taken-for-granted features of organizational life, operating at a more or less preconscious level, or because the individual is relatively powerless to affect them.

EXAMPLE Changing attitudes towards long work hours

Jeffrey Pfeffer (2004) argues that long work hours and short holidays do not pay. Americans work more hours a year than employees in any other industrialized country and earn only twelve days of holiday a year. Yet there is a growing awareness that excessive work hours contributed to the soaring medical costs of many US companies. He argues that the European model is best: for example, *Airbus* recently surpassed its bigger US rival *Boeing* in aircraft sales. *Airbus* managers take five weeks of holiday, while their most critical knowledge workers—junior engineers—get and take as much as nine weeks per year and do not work weekends.

The management of emotions

Emotions are seen and discussed in various ways in the research literature:

- as a psychological state, such as a sense of well-being or frustration;
- as a perception of value—that is, as a response, such as gratitude or anger;
- as transformation—that is, an experience that enhances understanding and provides meaning, such as a belief, a source of energy, or a motivation.

Emotion guides the individual in appraising social situations and responding to them. They can be pleasant and exciting (positive), or unpleasant and disturbing (negative), depending on the interpretations given by individuals and tested though their relation with others. They can be learned aspects of behaviour. We have seen in earlier chapters how emotional labour is described; there is also talk in the literature of emotion labour that represents the psychological work expended in reconciling personal feelings with socially sanctioned displays of emotion (Fineman and Gabriel, 2000; Antonacopoulou and Gabriel, 2001).

We saw, in Chapter 5, how men and women are required—due to the expectations of sex-typed jobs—to manage their emotions. Because emotion management is typically performed in the presence of others, individuals who frequently interact with people at work are thought to spend a significant amount of time controlling their emotions (Sloan, 2004). We learn 'feeling rules': we have learnt how much emotion to display, how to appear, and what is appropriate demeanour for the workplace. Some of the rules will reflect our gender, age, or class; others will reflect the nature of the business in which we work—for example, the academic world (Bellas, 1999), the service sector (McCammon and Griffin, 2000), or the fast-food industry (Leidner, 1993). Our social status may affect our emotional experience and expression (Gibson and Schroeder, 2002): higher status is linked to freer expression of negative emotions, such as anger (Tiendens, 2001); individuals of lower status report more intense and longer-lasting anger than those of higher status (Stets and Tsushima, 2001).

EXAMPLE Emotion management among paralegals

Lively (2000) showed that paralegals—that is, non-lawyers practising law—of similar status turn to each other for help in performing the emotion management required in the workplace. Being unable to express anger directly to higher status lawyers or attorneys, the paralegals sought the aid of co-workers for emotional support—a process that Lively termed 'reciprocal emotion management'. This did not, however, stop the superiors venting their anger on their subordinates.

> **EXAMPLE** Emotion and football management
>
> Gilmore (2006) studied football managers and how the emotionality of the game is found in the relationships that managers have with their players. She argues that the relationship between manager and player is similar to that of 'good mother' and infant. Football managers also have to balance paradoxical activities, engaging in collaboration and competition, provoking and containing conflict, and ensuring love from, for, and between, players, to whom the manager is 'everything'.

Crucially, we all privately labour with, and work within, our feelings in order to create the socially desired emotional expression and impression. Stress feelings, such as anxiety, fear, and dread, will have to be dressed up for managers, customers, clients, and colleagues. In doing the 'face work' (Goffman, 1961)— that is, camouflaging our feelings—we create new tensions: the polite automatic smile from the waitress may be relatively stress-free, but the emotional labour cost rises when the waitress starts to hate her work and the people whom she serves. We have discussed the explicit feeling rules in Chapter 5 and when looking at Hochschild's (1983) work on emotions. There are also implicit feeling rules. These would include, for example, the rules on what should remain a private doubt and worry and what can be openly expressed. Fineman (1995) shows how social workers provide much illustration of this. The social workers did not share their concerns with their colleagues and 'played a charade' with each other's stresses; they did not admit to their own stresses and would fail to care for colleagues. Their coping mechanism took the form of absenteeism—that is, sickness or holiday leave—because this was organizationally acceptable. It is apparent, then, that these tacit assumptions and rules about emotion and stress are not going to emerge easily from the results of interviews or questionnaires; rather, they will be the unintended product of a lengthy process of establishing a relationship with individuals in a study.

> **EXAMPLE** Stress in a computer consulting firm
>
> A Seattle-based computer consulting firm lost an important client and a project worth over $100,000 when an employee, who was managing the project, had a personal crisis and disappeared for three days. The job was not completed due to the disappearance (Solomon, 1999). It is implied that the absence was caused by stress: 'He began showing signs of stress but no one really thought much about it because he was well regarded' (ibid.: 48). His sister rang the company three days later and 'explained that he had started drinking again'.
>
> Other examples of stress that Solomon mentions include throwing food in the cafeteria, finding employees standing in the rubbish bin smoking pot, and crying in the hallways.

A more positive discussion of emotion management can be found in a study of *The Body Shop* (Martin et al., 1998). Here, the constrained expression of emotions at work was encouraged because it facilitated a sense of community and personal well-being. Employees of *The Body Shop* frequently discussed intimate personal issues with co-workers; employees felt that they could 'be themselves at work' (ibid.: 460). Most employees shared a strong sense of being part of *The Body Shop* community. Anita Roddick, herself, repeatedly and persuasively articulated values such as caring, sharing, and love; these values were enacted by employees in practices such as one intimate self-disclosure encouraging another, and hugs and kisses as common ways of saying 'hello', 'thank you', and 'goodbye'.

Being unemployed

It is not only the experience of employment that can impact our well-being; the experience of being unemployed can weigh heavily. Those of us in work are in fear of becoming unemployed—and the burden of unemployment is not evenly spread throughout the social classes. While unemployment occurs largely among the semi-skilled and unskilled, it is not restricted to those at the bottom of the socio-economic hierarchy; the managerial and professional middle classes also feel anxious and insecure about their jobs (Pahl, 1996). Increases in managerial redundancy have followed in the wake of recession and fiercer competition. And because managers may believe that they are less vulnerable when it comes to redundancies, having invested a lifetime of service in return for job security (Hallier and Lyon, 1996), when job loss comes, it can consequently be a fundamental shock to their personal identity and financial security (Kozlowski et al., 1993).

Those with qualifications and job experience can, however, usually face redundancy with greater confidence than those without, because they have skills, competencies, and networks that others may lack. The highest rates of unemployment therefore tend to be among those with no qualifications, from the working class, among the chronically sick and disabled, and those from ethnic minorities. And it is those who are the most vulnerable to unemployment who are also the most likely to have fewer resources with which to protect themselves and their families from a loss of earning power.

The media are inclined to present unemployment as social disintegration occasioned by male job loss. Pit closures, for example, focused on male job loss, the loss of community pride in the wake of male redundancy, and the loss of the community's 'heart' with the closure of the colliery. Yet women in these communities suffered in parallel ways to men: what emerged from Dicks's (1996) study of pit closures in two communities was that women's ability to cope with the aftermath of pit closure was not decided so much by their spouses' employment fate as by the material, social, and emotional resources on which they could draw. Because the women remained largely responsible for household management and childcare, the tasks of budgeting and catering on a reduced income, as well as the provision of emotional support to distressed partners, fell squarely on their shoulders.

Responses to unemployment consequently vary from depression, through stoic acceptance, to celebration (Ezzy, 2001). The emphasis in the literature has, however, tended to focus on the negative effects and research since the 1930s has very clearly shown the negative effects of unemployment on well-being (Warr, 1987; Warr et al., 1988; Fryer, 1992). For most individuals, unemployment manifests itself in ill health, despair, and chronic lethargy—that is, symptoms remarkably like those to be found in bereaved individuals (Archer and Rhodes, 1987). For the majority, unemployment impairs mental health, involving increased psychological distress, and including anxiety and depression, lowered self-esteem, resigned apathy, helplessness, powerlessness, social isolation, and disintegration. These disorders have been confirmed in many countries (Fryer, 1992). The effect may not be universal, however: a small minority will show gains in mental health after job loss. These people will have been in stressful jobs or will be happy to tolerate unemployment, taking jobs as they come along; a small minority even see unemployment as a challenge and an opportunity to develop skills or interests. It will be factors such as a person's age, gender, income, social support, reason for job loss, commitment to employment, satisfaction with previous work, expectation of returning to work, and length of unemployment that will vary the experience of the unemployed (Winefield, 1995).

EXAMPLE Is work life?

John Lennon is quoted as saying 'Work is life, you know, and without it, there's nothing but fear and insecurity' (Solt and Egan, 1988: 75). Do you agree? What would be your reaction to facing unemployment?

An integral part of the experience of unemployment is the task of actively seeking paid work. Many—particularly those in employment—impose a moral imperative on the unemployed to seek work actively; otherwise, they will be labelled 'scrounger' or 'undeserving'. The logical corollary of this attitude is that the unemployed only have themselves to blame if they fail—and this is an attitude that ignores facts such as that there are far more registered unemployed than there are job vacancies.

Classic studies in the 1930s began to detail what it meant to people to be unemployed (Jahoda et al., 1933; Bakke, 1934; Eisenberg and Lazarsfeld, 1938; Komarovsky, 1940). Jahoda et al. (1933) lived, for some months, in an Austrian village that had suffered from the demise of the textile industry.

Their research reported that, although the unemployed inhabitants of the village spent more time in bed to shorten the length of the day, they were unable to account for other ways in which their days had been spent. They reported that they were slower moving about and were unpunctual for fixed arrangements, such as meals. Weekends blended into weekdays and they lost 'structured meaning'—that is, their sense of time disintegrated (Jahoda, 1982). Women's sense of time was less disrupted, because they still had a domestic routine to follow, but many wanted to return to work because they missed the social contact of the factory. Despite the economic stringencies caused by unemployment, the researchers reported that people chose to do 'irrational' acts: for example, spending money on a cream cake, or growing flowers instead of vegetables, when there was a food shortage.

Jahoda (1982; 1987) provides five categories of psychological experience that she says are not only conducive to feelings of well-being, but also vital:

- *time structure*—that is, work imposes a time structure on the waking day;
- *social contact*—that is, work compels contact and shared experiences with others outside the family;
- *collective effort or purpose*—that is, work demonstrates that there are goals and purposes that are beyond the purpose of the individual, but which require collectivity;
- *social identity or status*—that is, work imposes status or social identity through the division of labour;
- *regular activity*—that is, work enforces activity.

For a more detailed discussion of the categories, see Haworth (1997: 25).

As unemployed people are deprived of these experiences, so their well-being declines. The employed take these categories of experience for granted, but the unemployed have to search for experiences within these categories: 'What preoccupies them is not the category, but the quality of experience within it' (Jahoda, 1982: 39). She does, however, recognize that the quality of experience in some jobs can be very poor, and stresses the importance of improving and humanizing employment.

Jahoda has been criticized for missing the fact that lack of money and contending with bureaucracy are two of the features of unemployment that contribute to feelings of lack of well-being. Also, it is noted that the unemployed *can* gain access to the five categories of experience—and that those unemployed who have better access will have better well-being. Jahoda concludes, however, that the employed have better access to the categories of experience than the unemployed: unemployment destroys the very structures that the employed take for granted—that is, structures of time, routine, status, and social networks—as Bostyn and Wright (1987) also suggest. Given the excessive amount of time that the unemployed have on their hands, they ought not to be late for interviews, but they are (Miles, 1983); they ought to have more time for leisure activities, but yet retreat from such social interaction (Grint, 1998).

Warr (1987) has built on the categories of experience by proposing a model of mental health. This model incorporates the five categories of experience advocated by Jahoda and emphasizes nine principal environmental influences:

- *opportunity for control*—that is, the opportunity for a person to control activities and events;
- *environmental clarity*—that is, feedback about the consequences of actions, certainty about the future, and clarity of understanding about what is expected in the job;
- *opportunity for skill use*;
- *externally generated goals*;
- *variety*;
- *opportunity for interpersonal contact*;
- *valued social position*;
- *the availability of money*;
- *physical security*.

These nine principal environmental influences, or environmental categories of experience, are seen to be acting together in conjunction with personal factors to help or hinder psychological well-being or mental health. Warr likens these influences to vitamins: some will improve mental health up to a certain point and have no further effect; others will produce benefits up to a certain level beyond which increases would be detrimental. He argues that there can be good and bad jobs, and good and bad unemployment, depending on how much of these influences are present in the individual's experience.

The nine-factor framework tells us a good deal about what work means to people in a psychological sense. There is also a widespread view among the unemployed that they should not be seen as lazy, even if this means taking a job that pays only marginally more than unemployment benefit (Turner et al., 1985). Being a 'breadwinner' is also important to men for a sense of masculine identity (Yankelovich, 1973; McKee and Bell, 1986).

Becoming unemployed typically changes a person's life story (Ezzy, 2001). Different people tell different types of story and the type of story that someone tells about his or her experiences shapes whether he or she becomes depressed as a consequence of becoming unemployed. Ezzy argues that there are three types of job loss narrative that can be identified: romances, tragedies, and more complex stories. Fourteen of the thirty-three people whom he interviewed described their job loss as romance—that is, as a clearly positive experience. Unemployment brought both release from an oppressive job and the freedom to pursue alternative highly valued goals. Twenty-four, however, were tragic stories in which the experience of unemployment was painful and unerring. People described the trauma of losing their job; the focus of the trauma was the loss of certainty about the future that secure employment provides, and a sense of being unwanted and worthless when unable to find work led them into periods of depression and self-deprecation. For seven of the interviewees, the situation was more complex, because other events in their lives were at least as important as the consequences of their job loss: for example, two were involved in marriage separation, two had chronic illness, and one was having a 'faith crisis'. This, then, provides us with a more complex analysis of the effect of unemployment on individuals.

One of the responses to massive rises in unemployment has been the growth of agencies, schemes, and initiatives designed to spread the gospel of enterprise and to encourage new businesses (MacDonald and Coffield, 1991). The new jobs tend to be in the service sector: clothes retailers, beauticians, car valets, sandwich deliverers, sign writers, car mechanics, private detectives. Yet we do not seem to be witnessing the birth of a local enterprise culture: new small firms—even those that seem to do well initially—are unable to continue in the long term (ibid.); the smallest and youngest firms are the least likely to survive and grow (Chittenden and Caley, 1992). Instead, this can be seen as 'survival self-employment' (MacDonald, 1997), in which individuals trade with skills informally learnt and experienced from hobbies and pastimes—only to find that competition is too fierce and the marketplace is saturated with similar businesses, so that the local economy cannot support them all.

Callender (1987) argues that women's experience of job search and job acquisition can be different from that of men. The demand and supply side of men's and women's labour are not the same: her study of a group of married women who had experienced redundancy through the partial closure of a clothing factory showed that all of the redundant women wanted to work again, and were very flexible about the conditions and type of paid work that they were prepared to accept; many were even willing to take a reduction in pay. The women had an astute view of the state of the labour market, and of the way in which demand structured their choices and opportunities; they had little choice, so were prepared to accept any job. They organized and marshalled resources for coping with their paid and unpaid work, including assistance with childcare and dependent relatives, but paid work was not a moral imperative for them, unlike men. The most effective strategy for finding work was through informal social networks, such as family and friends, and by word of mouth. Those women who succeeded in finding work were highly reliant upon other people in their social network for information about jobs and recommendations. These networks were closed, restricted, and home and female-centred; this, then, determined the type of jobs that the women obtained and their opportunities. If the women got jobs, they were similar jobs to those that their female contacts had—that is, typical 'women's work'.

Those of us in work are in fear of becoming unemployed. Unemployment is not restricted to those at the bottom of the socio-economic hierarchy; the managerial and professional middle class also feel anxious and insecure about their jobs (Pahl, 1996). Increases in managerial redundancy have followed in the wake of recession and fiercer competition. Managers may believe they are less vulnerable when it comes to redundancies, having invested a lifetime of service in return for job security (Hallier and Lyon, 1996), so when job loss comes, it can be a fundamental shock to their personal identity and financial security (Kozlowski et al., 1993). Those with qualifications and job experience can, however, usually face redundancy with greater confidence than those without, as they have skills, competencies, and networks that others may lack. The highest rates of umemployment tend to be amongst those with no qualifications, from the working class, amongst the chronically sick and disabled, and from ethnic minorities.

Being 'on the fiddle' or working 'on the side'

Sometimes, those who are officially 'unemployed' will undertake work 'on the side'—that is, work that is carried out for pay by those who are also claiming social security or unemployment benefits to which they would not be wholly entitled if they were to declare this work to the benefit authorities. Some research (for example, Pahl, 1984; Bradshaw and Holmes, 1989), however, shows that the unemployed are far less likely than the employed to engage in illicit work. Jordan et al. (1992), for example, have found that around two-thirds of poor households benefit from undeclared work. Of MacDonald's (1997) sample of non-standard employed—that is, those who are self-employed in very small businesses, those in voluntary work, those 'on the fiddle', or those in community enterprise and cooperatives—one third were found to have been 'on the fiddle'. These jobs were not preferred to 'proper' jobs; rather, combining 'fiddly' work with unemployment benefits was a survival strategy initiated in the face of mass, structural unemployment and a system of benefits that failed to meet material needs. For the poor and long-term unemployed, MacDonald describes the 'fiddle' as a necessary way of maintaining individual self-respect and household income. Fiddly work is therefore better understood as representing a culture of enterprise, rather than one of dependency: those engaged in it fitted the model of 'entrepreneur', showing high degrees of personal motivation, initiative, local knowledge, and risk taking.

Fiddly jobs tended to be short-lived, irregular, infrequent, and poorly rewarded. One young woman in the sample had worked thirty hours in one week as a care assistant in a residential home on the 'fiddle'. Together with her Income Support, she had netted the grand sum of £75. Fiddly jobs were most common in subcontracted labour at steelworks, in construction, as car mechanics, and in taxi driving, cleaning, and bar work. Some contractors cut their costs and won tenders by offering low pay to people whom they knew to be in receipt of benefit and therefore able to 'afford' to work cheaply. For those involved in fiddly work, the material experience of unemployment was ameliorated. The social psychological impact of unemployment was softened and individuals were helped to reconnect with work culture. The majority of those on the fiddle were white working-class males in their twenties and thirties, in neighbourhoods of high and long-term unemployment, with tradable skills and/or a reliable record of manual work experience. The work was distributed through local, pub-centred social networks.

The picture painted by MacDonald (1997) is not one of a dangerous, parasitical underclass; rather, there was an incipient culture of survival, resilience, and getting by. Williams and Windebank (2003) critically evaluated women's paid informal work, which included cleaning, shopping, ironing, hairdressing, making and repairing clothes, and babysitting. Following 400 interviews, in low-income neighbourhoods, they concluded that the vast majority of this work is conducted for family, friends, and neighbours for motives more associated with redistribution—that is, to help people out and to cement or forge social networks—than economic gain.

Reorganization of work in the late twentieth century is forcing an increasingly large proportion of people to seek the means for their economic and social survival through various types of disorganized, insecure, risky, and casualized work. Jones' (1997) research, for example, does not support the assumption that homeless youth represent a distinct and dangerous underclass; on the contrary, this group indicates a desire to achieve conventional goals, such as a home, a family, and a job. In fact, research on homeless youth finds that the overwhelming majority would be interested in finding paid employment (Gaetz and O'Grady, 2002). The homeless do not avoid legitimate paid employment. To make ends meet, they have very varied ways of making money in the informal economy. Some are paid 'under the table' for childminding or for short-term casual jobs, but this paid employment is unlikely to be taxed or regulated. They also beg (which they regard as work activity), wash car windscreens, and are involved in the sex trade (street prostitution, escort services, exotic dancing, Internet sex, and phone sex). About 18 per cent are involved in criminal activity, such as selling drugs or stolen property. Those who are windscreen washers and beggars are the most likely to be without adequate shelter, while, ironically, those involved in crime and employment are most likely to be staying in temporary hostels and shelters.

'Non-work'

Finally, given some of the findings on the impact that work can have on health and well-being, it is unsurprising that the rejection of paid labour entirely is seen as one way in which to improve life.

Gypsies are one group that has consciously rejected waged labour. Judith Okley (1983) lived alongside a group of gypsies in a trailer caravan for about two years. She went out to work with them, calling for scrap metal, and joined a potato-picking gang. She found that the identity of gypsies served as a political weapon for non-gypsies: gypsies could be rejected as 'counterfeit' in contrast to a mythically 'real Romany'; through this discrimination, harassment, and oppression could be legitimated. They had a huge variety of occupations, but spoke of wage labour with contempt: they could not—or would not—be 'trained' for 'ordinary' employment.

Conclusion

Violence is a feature of some organizational life and work for those who are employed in, for example, the military or martial arts organizations. Employees, such as shop assistants and flight attendants, are frequently assaulted while at work—violence that is likely to have a negative impact on the individual. Even the threat of such violence can be stressful. Stress is a negative emotion, which can be caused by work or lack of work, but stress—and some other negative emotions generated by work—can remain hidden. Doing emotional labour may mean that employees do not admit to their own stresses; they may not even be conscious of their stress. This may make research on the topic particularly difficult. Just as employment can be stressful, so, too, can unemployment—and just as there can be good and bad jobs, so, too, can there be good and bad unemployment.

KEY POINTS

- Negative features of organizational life, such as violence and stress, make up part of the everyday reality of organizational life and can lead to further negative behaviours, such as absenteeism.

- Stress is a particularly difficult topic for research, because much may be unconscious or hidden as a result of the good reasons that individuals may have not to admit to their stress.

- Unemployment research shows that the experience of unemployment varies depending on age, gender, income, social class, social support, and other factors.

- Research on unemployment, non-work, and being 'on the fiddle' may give us insight into issues of employment and what work means to those who do it.

CASE STUDY

A company attempting to minimize stress

Companies have an interest in trying to reduce or minimize stress. At *What If!*, a London-based inventing consultancy, stress in the workplace is minimized by creating a fun and supportive working environment that emphasizes the idea of staff bringing their 'whole self' to work. Each employee has a mentor—usually his or her manager—with whom they can discuss work, as well as domestic, sources of stress.

Company partner Helen Clements explains: 'We encourage staff to chat about their long-term vision for their life and we offer flexible working contracts that reflect the balance that people want to make between their career and personal responsibilities.' That means that staff with children can choose to complete a nine-month contract over the year to free up enough time to cover school holidays. People who only want to work three days a week can do so too.

The company has found that stress, for many people, is generated by an outside source: money. To help staff to deal with financial problems, it has set up a loan scheme—to help people to cope with short-term difficulties such as maternity leave—and a crisis fund, which helps with emergencies and does not need to be paid back. The fund has, so far, helped one staff member to jump on a plane to see a sick relative and another to buy essential furniture after a burglary.

The company also has a regular Friday afternoon—usually four times a year—on which everyone downs tools to enjoy an alternative slice of life. Past events have included playing bingo, meditation sessions, and belly-dancing lessons. 'These sessions are about having fun and seeing something, doing something that you might otherwise not experience. They are good for morale, they enhance creativity, induce loyalty and take the pressure off for a while,' says Helen Clements.

Other stress-relieving features at the company include a quiet room in which staff can 'take five' on a futon, a massage chair in the lobby, and a 'well-being fund', which part-pays for groups of staff to undertake relaxation activities such as yoga, kung fu, and pilates.

(*Source:* Siddall, 2002)

Questions

1. Is this a company for which you would want to work?

2. Is it really attempting to reduce stress, or just get more out of its employees?

3. If an employee is stressed, does the source of the problem lie with the individual or the organization?

FURTHER READING

Bjarnason, T. and Sigurdardottir, T.J. (2003) 'Psychological distress during unemployment and beyond: Social support and material deprivation among youth in six northern European countries', *Social Science & Medicine*, 56(5): 973–85 Psychological distress is a serious problem among unemployed youth, and may lead to various social and psychological problems. This study examines patterns of distress among previously unemployed youth in Denmark, Finland, Iceland, Norway, Scotland, and Sweden.

Noon, M. and Blyton, P. (2007) *The Realities of Work*, 3rd edn, Houndmills: Palgrave This book covers hidden work and includes voluntary work.

Sayer, A. (2007) 'Dignity at work: Broadening the agenda', *Organization*, 14: 565–81 This article discusses dignity, bullying, and harassment, and their links with hierarchy and inequality.

Strandh, M. (2000) 'Different exit routes from unemployment and their impact on mental well-being: The role of the economic situation and the predictability of the life course', *Work, Employment and Society*, 14(3): 459–79 This article discusses the earlier research on unemployment and effects on mental health, but goes on to look at different outcomes of exiting unemployment for different groups. For example, it determines that exit to permanent employment is better for mental well-being than exit to temporary or self-employment.

Thompson, P. and McHugh, D. (2002) *Work Organizations*, 3rd edn, Houndmills: Palgrave Chapter 18, entitled 'Putting the pressure on: Stress, work, and emotion', makes some interesting connections.

Watson, T. (2002) *Organizing and Managing Work*, Harlow: Pearson Pages 148–54 focus on stress, and make connections between home and work.

LINKS TO FILMS AND NOVELS

The Full Monty (1997) dir. P. Cattaneo This film depicts a group of unemployed Sheffield steelworkers. There are some very moving moments in the film relating to the despair and desolation of unemployment.

Supersize Me (2004) dir. M. Spurlock This is a documentary that takes a pop at *McDonald's* and the fast-food industry, and challenges how they contribute to our health and well-being. Although living with his vegan girlfriend, the documentary maker decides to eat a *McDonald's* every meal for a month. He also reduces the amount of exercise that he takes to match that of the average American. The results on his health and well-being are telling.

RESEARCH QUESTIONS

1. According to some, women cope better with stress in demanding jobs than men. What evidence can you find to support or refute this statement?

2. 'Customer abuse is perpetuated by a range of cost-rational and profit-centred policies' (Boyd, 2002). Discuss.

3. 'Some 700,000 people phone in sick on a Monday morning. One in three are faking it' (Channel 5, 2002, *UK Undercover*, 'Throwing a sickie'). These bare facts raise more questions: for example, what kinds of people 'throw a sickie'? Is it mainly those who are in stressful, repetitive, routine work, or professional workers? Is it because they feel that they are not given enough holiday entitlement? How would you investigate the reasons behind this behaviour?

4. By looking at unemployment, we can understand more about what employment might mean to people. What can be learned about what work means by looking at research on unemployment? And what are the personal and social consequences of unemployment? Are the consequences different for different groups of individuals? If yes, how?

REFERENCES

Antonacopoulou, E.P. and Gabriel, Y. (2001) 'Emotion, learning and organizational change: Towards an integration of psychoanalytic and other perspectives', *Journal of Organizational Change Management*, 14(5): 435–51.

Archer, J. and Rhodes, V. (1987) 'Bereavement and reactions to job loss: a comparative review', *British Journal of Social Psychology*, 26(3): 211–24.

Arnold, J., Cooper, C.L., and Robertson, I.T. (1995) *Work Psychology: Understanding Human Behaviour in the Workplace*, London: Pitman Publishing, chs 17 and 18.

Bakke, E. (1934) *The Unemployed Man*, New York: E.P. Dutton & Co.

Baty, P. (2003) 'Violent students terrorise staff', *Times Higher Education Supplement*, 28 February, p. 1.

Bellas, M. (1999) 'Emotional labour in academia: The case of professors', *Annals of the American Academy of Political and Social Science*, 561: 96–110.

Bosma, H., Marmot, M.G., Hemingway, H., Nicholson, A.C., Brunner, E., and Stansfield, S.A. (1997) 'Low job control and risk of coronary heart disease in Whitehall II (prospective cohort) study', *British Medical Journal*, 22 February: 558–65.

_____, Peter, R., Siegrist, J., and Marmot, M. (1998) 'Two alternative job stress models of the risk of coronary heart disease', *American Journal of Public Health*, 88(1): 68–74.

Bostyn, A. and Wright, D. (1987) 'Inside a community: Values associated with money and time', in S. Fineman (ed.), *Unemployment: Personal and Social Consequences*, London: Tavistock.

Boyd, C. (2002) 'Customer violence and employee health and safety', *Work, Employment and Society*, 16(1): 151–69.

Bradshaw, A. and Holmes, H. (1989) *Living on the Edge*, Tyneside: Tyneside Child Poverty Action Group.

Callender, C. (1987) 'Women seeking work', in S. Fineman (ed.), *Unemployment: Personal and Social Consequences*, London: Tavistock, ch. 3.

Cartwright, S. and Cooper, C.L. (1997) *Managing Workplace Stress*, London: Sage.

Chittenden, F. and Caley, K. (1992) 'Current policy issues and recommendations', in K. Caley, E. Chell, F. Chittenden, and C. Mason (eds), *Small Enterprise Development*, London: Paul Chapman Publishing.

Cohen, S., Kessler, R.C., and Gordon, L.U. (eds) (1995) *Measuring Stress: A Guide for Health and Social Scientists*, Oxford: Oxford University Press.

Cooper, C.L. and Cartwright, S. (1994) 'Healthy mind; healthy organization: A proactive approach to occupational stress', *Human Relations*, 47(4): 455–71.

_____ and Payne, R. (1990) *Causes, Coping and Consequences of Stress at Work*, Chichester: Wiley.

_____, Cooper, R.D., and Eaker, L.H. (1988) *Living with Stress*, Harmondsworth: Penguin.

Dicks, B. (1996) 'Coping with pit closure in the 1990s: Women's perspectives', in J. Pilcher and A. Coffey (eds), *Gender and Qualitative Research*, Aldershot: Avebury, ch. 2.

The Economist (2007) 'Death by overwork in Japan: Jobs for life', 19 December, available online at http://www.economist.com/world/asia

Eisenberg, P. and Lazerfield, P.F. (1938) 'The psychological effects of unemployment', *Psychological Bulletin*, 35: 358–90.

Equality Challenge Unit (2007) *Dignity at Work: A Good Practice Guide for Higher Education Institutions on Dealing with Bullying and Harassment in the Workplace*, January, London: ECU.

Ezzy, D. (2001) *Narrating Unemployment*, Aldershot: Ashgate.

Fineman, S. (1995) 'Stress, emotion and intervention', in T. Newton (ed.), *Managing Stress: Emotion and Power at Work*, London: Sage.

_____ and Gabriel, Y. (2000) *The Study of Organizational Emotions: Psychoanalytic and Social Constructionist Perspectives*, Paper presented at the Annual Symposium of the International Society for the Psychoanalytic Study of Organizations, London.

Fletcher, B. (1990) 'The epidemiology of occupational stress', in C.L. Cooper and R. Payne (eds), *Causes, Coping and Consequences of Stress at Work*, Chichester: Wiley, ch. 1.

Fryer, D. (1992) 'Psychological or material deprivation: Why does unemployment have mental health consequences?', in E. McLaughlin (ed.), *Understanding Unemployment*, London: Routledge.

_____ and McKenna, S. (1987) 'The laying off of hands: Unemployment and the experience of time', in S. Fineman (ed.), *Unemployment: Personal and Social Consequences*, London: Tavistock, ch. 4.

Gaetz, S. and O'Grady, B. (2002) 'Making money: Exploring the economy of young homeless workers', *Work, Employment and Society*, 16(3): 433–56.

Gibson, D.E. and Schroeder, S. (2002) 'Grinning, frowning, and emotionless: Agent perceptions of power and their effect on felt and displayed emotions in influence attempts', in N.M. Ashkanasy, W.J. Zerbe, and C.E.J. Hartel (eds), *Managing Emotions in the Workplace*, Armonk, NY: M.E. Sharpe, pp. 184–211.

Gilmore, S. (2006) 'The mother's breast and football managers', in J. Brewis, S. Linstead, D. Boje, and T. O'Shea (eds), *The Passion of Organizing*, Malmö: Liber and Copenhagen Business School Press, ch. 9.

Ginn, J. and Sandell, J. (1997) 'Balancing home and employment: Stress reported by social services staff', *Work, Employment and Society*, 11(3): 413–34.

Goffman, E. (1961) *Asylums*, Harmondsworth: Penguin.

Grint, K. (1998) *The Sociology of Work: An Introduction*, 2nd edn, Cambridge: Polity.

The Guardian (2003) 'Student violence on increase', 28 February, available online at http://education.guardian.co.uk/higher/news/story/0,9830,904449,00.html

Gutek, B.A., Repetti, R.L., and Silver, D.L. (1990) 'Non-work roles and stress at work', in C.L. Cooper and R. Payne (eds), *Causes, Coping and Consequences of Stress at Work*, Chichester: Wiley, ch. 5.

Hallier, J. and Lyon, P. (1996) 'Job insecurity and employee commitment: Managers' reactions to threat and outcomes of redundancy selection', *British Journal of Management*, 7(1): 107–23.

Handy, J.A. (1988) 'Theoretical and methodological problems with occupational stress and burnout research', *Human Relations*, 41(5): 351–69.

_____ (1995) 'Rethinking stress: Seeing the collective', in T. Newton (ed.), *Managing Stress: Emotion and Power at Work*, London: Sage, ch. 4.

Haworth, J. (1997) *Work, Leisure and Well-Being*, London: Routledge.

Hearn, J. and Parkin, W. (2007) 'The emotionality of organizational violations: Gender relations in practice', in P. Lewis and R. Simpson (eds), *Gendering Emotions in Organizations*, Palgrave Macmillan, Basingstoke, ch. 9.

Hilpern, K. (2003) 'Office house: Boiling over', *The Guardian*, 17 March.

Hochschild, A.R. (1983) *The Managed Heart: Commercialization of Human Feeling*, Berkeley, CA: University of California Press.

Industrial Society (2001) *Managing Best Practice*, Occupational Stress Report No. 83, London: Industrial Society.

Jackson, S.E. and Schuler, R.S. (1985) 'A meta-analysis and conceptual critique of research on role ambiguity and role conflict in work settings', *Organizational Behaviour and Human Decision Processes*, 36: 16–78.

Jahoda, M. (1982) *Employment and Unemployment: A Social Psychological Analysis*, Cambridge: Cambridge University Press.

_____ (1987) 'Unemployed men at work', in D.M. Fryer and P. Ullah (eds), *Unemployed People: Social and Psychological Perspectives*, Milton Keynes: Open University Press.

_____, Lazarsfeld, P., and Zeisel, H. (1933; 1971) *Marienthal: The Sociography of an Unemployed Community*, London: Tavistock.

Jones, G. (1997) 'Youth homelessness and the underclass', in R. McDonald (ed.), *Youth, the Underclass and Social Exclusion*, London: Routledge, ch. 7.

Jordan, B., James, S., Kay, H., and Redley, M. (1992) *Trapped in Poverty? Labour-Market Decisions in Low-Income Households*, London: Routledge.

Khan, H. and Cuthbertson, J. (1994) *Mothers Who Work and Mothers Who 'Only' Stay at Home: Are the Stressors Different?*, Paper presented to the Annual Conference of the Scottish Branch of the British Psychological Society, Crieff Hydro, November.

373

King, M.B., Cockcroft, A., and Gooch, C. (1992) 'Emotional distress in doctors: Sources, effects and help sought', *Journal of the Royal Society of Medicine*, 85: 605–8.

Kinman, G. and Jones, F. (2004) *Working to the Limit: Stress and Work–Life Balance in Academic and Academic-Related Employees in the UK*, November, London: AUT.

Komarovsky, M. (1940) *The Unemployed Man and his Family*, New York: Dryden Press.

Kozlowski, S.W., Chao, G.T., Smith, E.M., and Dedlund, J. (1993) 'Organizational downsizing: Strategies, interventions and research implications', in C.L. Cooper and I.T. Robertson (eds), *International Review of Industrial and Organizational Psychology*, London: John Wiley, pp. 263–332.

Kunda, G. (1982) *Engineering Culture*, Philadelphia, PA: Temple University Press.

Lazarus, R.S. (1976) *Patterns of Adjustment*, New York: McGraw Hill.

Leidner, R. (1993) *Fast Food, Fast Talk: Service Work and the Routinization of Everyday Life*, Berkeley, CA: University of California.

Lively, K.J. (2000) 'Client contact and emotional labour: Upsetting the balance and evening the field', *Work and Occupations*, 29(2): 32–63.

MacDonald, R. (1997) 'Informal working, survival strategies and the idea of an "underclass"', in R. Brown (ed.), *The Changing Shape of Work*, Basingstoke: Macmillan, ch. 6.

_____ and Coffield, F. (1991) *Risky Business? Youth and the Enterprise Culture*, Basingstoke: Falmer Press.

Maddi, S.R. and Kobasa, S.C. (1984) *The Hardy Executive: Health Under Stress*, Homewood, IL: Dow Jones-Irwin.

Marmot, M.G., Bosma, H., Hemingway, H., Brunner, E., and Stansfeld, S. (1997) 'Contribution of job control and other risk factors to social variations in coronary heart disease incidence', *Lancet*, 350(9073): 235–9.

Martin, J., Knopoff, K., and Beckman, C. (1998) 'An alternative to bureaucratic impersonality and emotional labor: Bounded rationality at The Body Shop', *Administrative Science Quarterly*, 43(2): 429–69.

Masterton, V. (2003) '"Stressed" staff should face sack', *Scotland on Sunday*, 23 February, p. 6.

McCammon, H. and Griffin, L. (2000) 'Workers and their customers and clients: An introduction', *Work and Occupations*, 27: 278–93.

McKee, L. and Bell, C. (1986) 'His unemployment, her problem: The domestic and marital consequences of male unemployment', in S. Allen, A. Waton, K. Purcell, and S. Wood (eds), *The Experience of Unemployment*, Basingstoke: Macmillan.

Miles, I. (1983) *Adaptation to Unemployment?*, Occasional Paper No. 20. Brighton: Science Policy Review Unit.

Murphy, L.R. (1988) 'Workplace interventions for stress reduction and prevention', in C.L. Cooper and R. Payne (eds), *Causes and Coping and Consequences of Stress at Work*, Chichester: Wiley.

Newton, T., Handy, J., and Fineman, S. (1995) *Managing Stress: Emotions and Power at Work*, London: Sage.

Nichols, T. (1998) 'Health and safety at work', *Work, Employment and Society*, 12(2): 367–74.

Okley, J. (1983) *The Traveller-Gypsies*, Cambridge: Cambridge University Press.

Pahl, R. (1984) *Divisions of Labour*, Oxford: Blackwell.

_____ (1996) 'Reflections and perspectives', in C.H.A. Verhaar, P.M. de Klauer, M.P.M. de Goede, J.A.C. van Ophem, and A. de Vries (eds), *On Challenges of Unemployment in Regional Europe*, Aldershot: Avebury Press.

Personnel Today (2005a) '"Bin rage" leads to assaults on refuse collectors' 1 August, available online at http://www.dailymail.co.uk/news/article-469802/Bin-rage-Assaults-collectors-soar-backlash-fortnightly-calls.html

_____ (2005b) 'Employers and unions target retail rage', 13 July, available online at http://www.personneltoday.com/articles/2005/07/13/30807/employers-and-unions-target-retail-rage.html

Pfeffer, J. (2004) 'All work, no play? It doesn't pay: European companies get it, but when will their workaholic American counterparts? Longer hours don't always add up to better work', *Business 2.0 Magazine*, 1

August, available online at http://money.cnn.com/magazines/business2/business2_archive/2004/08/01/377377/index.htm

Pollert, A. (1981) *Girls, Wives, Factory Lives*, London: Macmillan.

Rees, D.W. (1995) 'Work-related stress in health service employees', *Journal of Managerial Psychology*, 10(3): 4–11.

Schnall, P.L. and Landsbergis, P.A. (1994) 'Job strain and cardiovascular disease', *Annual Review of Public Health*, 15: 381–411.

Seyle, H. (1976) *The Stress of Life*, New York: McGraw Hill.

Siddall, R. (2002) 'Managing stress at work', available online at http://www.channel4.com/health/microsites/0-9/4health/stress/saw_manage.html

Sloan, M. (2004) The effects of occupational characteristics on the experience and expression of anger in the workplace, *Work and Occupations*, 31(1): 38–72.

Solomon, C.M. (1999) 'Stressed to the limit', *Workforce*, 78(9): 48–54.

Solt, A. and Egan, S. (1988) *Imagine: John Lennon*, London: Bloomsbury.

Sprigg, C.A., Smith, P., and Jackson, P.R. (2003) *Psychosocial Risk Factors in Call Centres: An Evaluation of Work Design and Well-Being*, Health and Safety Executive Research Report No. 169, London: HSE.

Steffy, B.D., Shaw, K., and Noe, A.W. (1989) 'Antecedents and consequences of job search behaviours', *Journal of Vocational Behavior*, 3: 254–69.

Stets, J.E. and Tsushima, T.M. (2001) 'Negative emotion and coping responses within identity control theory', *Social Psychology Quarterly*, 64(3): 283–95.

Styhre, A., Ingelgard, A., Beausang, P., Castenfors, M., Mulec, K., and Roth, J. (2002) 'Emotional management and stress: Managing ambiguities', *Organization Studies*, 23(1): 83–103.

Sutherland, V. and Cooper, C.L. (1987) *Man and Accidents Offshore*, London: Lloyds.

Tiendens, L.Z. (2001) 'Anger and advancement versus sadness and subjugation: The effect of negative emotion on social status conferral', *Journal of Personality and Social Psychology*, 80(1): 86–94.

Turner, R., Bostyn, A.M., and Wight, D. (1985) 'The work ethic in a Scottish town with declining employment', in B. Roberts, R. Finnegan, and D. Gallie (eds), *New Approaches to Economic Life*, Manchester: Manchester University Press, pp. 476–89.

Vecchio, R.P. (1995) *Organizational Behaviour*, 3rd edn, London: Dryden Press.

Warr, P. (1987) *Work, Unemployment and Mental Health*, Oxford: Clarendon Press.

_____, Jackson, P., and Banks, M. (1988) 'Unemployment and mental health: Some British studies', *Journal of Social Issues*, 44: 37–68.

Wheeler, S. and Lyon, D. (1992) 'Employee benefits for the employer's benefit: How companies respond to employee stress', *Personnel Review*, 21(7): 47–63.

Whyte, W.F. (1948) *Human Relations in the Restaurant Industry*, New York: McGraw Hill.

Williams, C.C. and Windebank, J. (2003) 'Reconceptualizing women's paid informal work: Some lessons from lower-income urban neighbourhoods', *Gender, Work and Society*, 10(3): 281–300.

Winefield, A. (1995) 'Unemployment: Its psychological costs', *International Review of Industrial and Organizational Psychology*, 10: 169–212.

Womack, S. (2003) 'Worried staff find that work is a nightmare', *Daily Telegraph*, 11 February, available online at http://www.telegraph.co.uk/news/uknews/4185773/Worried-staff-find-that-work-is-a-nightmare.html

Yankelovich, D. (1973) 'The meaning of work', in R. Rosnow (ed.), *The Worker and the Job*, New York: Columbia University Press/Prentice Hall, pp. 19–47.

375

Glossary

alienation A term used by Karl Marx to describe the effects of the process of production on workers. Alienation happens in a number of different ways. Firstly, the work is external to the worker, rather than part of their nature; it does not fulfil, gives a feeling of misery, and leaves them physically exhausted and mentally debased. At work, they feel homeless. The work is not voluntary, but imposed. It is not the satisfaction of a need, but only a means for satisfying other needs. As soon as there is no physical or other compulsion to work, it is avoided. Finally, the alienated character of work for the worker appears in the fact that it is not his or her work, but work for someone else; in work, he or she does not belong to him- or herself, but to another person. For original writings and meaning, see K. Marx (1961) 'Alienated labour', in *Economic and Philosophical Manuscripts of 1844*, Moscow: Foreign Languages Publishing House, pp. 85–6.

attention The process of selecting one aspect of the sensory information that we are receiving on which to focus while disregarding the rest.

attribution theory This theory was developed in the 1950s and 60s by Fritz Heider and Harold Kelley. The theory is concerned with the ways in which individuals attribute causes to events. For example it suggests that we observe a person's behaviour and then try to establish whether internal or external forces caused it.

authoritarian Favours obedience to authority. An authoritarian leadership style would favour providing clear expectations for what needs to be done, when it should be done, and how it should be done. Authoritarian leaders would be inclined to make decisions independently with little or no input from the rest of the group.

autonomy The amount of freedom that a person has in his or her job to make judgements and decisions about how that job is done.

banana time This was one of the times or informal short breaks designated by workers in Donald Roy's study of machine operators for the consumption of food and drink. The creation of these times helped operators to alleviate the monotony and tiring nature of their jobs. Without fail, each day one operator would consume the banana brought by another operator for their lunch; just before eating it he would announce "banana time".

bourgeois Members of the middle class. The term is often used in a derogatory fashion to indicate that the speaker feels that the subject has become selfish or materialistic.

burnout contagion This happens when symptoms of strain or burnout (e.g. exhaustion, cynicism) expressed by colleagues are transferred to other employees when they socialize at work.

centralization This is found where the authority to make certain decisions is located at the top of the management hierarchy.

charities These are not for profit organizations focused on activities helping those in need.

cloning This is the process of reproducing identical individuals.

competence These are qualities such as skill, knowledge or ability.

conditioning The learning of a response. The concept is crucial in understanding behaviourism and learning. In classical (or Pavlovian) conditioning, learning depends on a stimulus being given, which results in a response. For example, a learned response to hearing a fire alarm might be to get up and leave the building. Operant (or instrumental) conditioning shapes behaviour using conditioning techniques. For example, one person can condition another to increase the number of opinions that he or she gives by reinforcing his or her statements. When the subject starts a sentence with 'I think' or 'In my opinion', the reinforcer might respond with 'I agree', or a sound that suggests agreement. Conversely, he or she might decrease the statements of opinion by disagreeing in response, or simply by being silent.

confucian dynamism A term which comes from Geert Hofstede's work on national cultures and refers to the extent to which societies adopt a short-term or long-term approach to life.

content theory This is a theory of motivation that would attempt to describe the individual's needs, drives, and goals.

coop This is short for cooperative: an organization fully owned and controlled by its members.

decentralization This is found where authority for decision making is dispersed widely throughout an organization.

deskilling Taking the skill out of work.

deviant work This is work that may be considered somehow morally dubious by the public. It is another term for "dirty work".

"dirty work" This is a term originally coined by Everett Hughes, a North American sociologist, in 1951, to describe jobs that are physically disgusting, which symbolize degradation, which wound the individual's dignity, or which 'run counter to the more heroic of our moral conceptions'.

e-business This is short for electronic business—a combination of technologies, applications, processes, business strategies, and practices that are necessary to do business electronically.

embourgeoisement Working-class people adopting middle-class lifestyles and values.

emotional intelligence (EI) This is the ability to perceive emotions, to access and generate emotions so as to assist thought, to understand emotions and emotional knowledge, and to reflectively regulate emotions so as to promote emotional and intellectual growth.

emotional labour The effort that workers must make to bring their feelings and/or visible emotional displays in line with organizational or managerial requirements.

eugenics This is the 'science' of improving stock, taking into account all influences that tend to give the preferred races, or strains of blood, a better chance of prevailing speedily

over the others than they would otherwise have had.

fordism This is the application of scientific management to jobs coupled with employment policy which creates a system of mass production.

formalization This is the degree to which formal procedures and rules are applied in an organization.

functionalism This is a model or framework that assumes that workers and managers are working together with consensus. Activities continue to exist because they perform the indispensible function of maintaining coherent integration within the organization.

Gestalt A German word meaning a form or configuration in which the sum is greater than the parts.

globalization The term 'globalization' was originally used to describe the gradual connection between different societies. It is a shorthand term to describe the global circulation of goods, services and capital, information, ideas, and people.

halo effect The 'halo effect', or 'halo error', which involves a tendency to let our assessment of an individual be influenced by only one trait or characteristic. We see a person as better than he or she really is, because we associate that person with one positive attribute.

inclemency rule This was a rule found in Stewart Clegg's work on a construction site. If the weather was inclement (poor or harsh) the employees did not have to work outside.

ingroups These are groups we tend to perceive favourably, one to which the individual feels loyalty and respect.

kibbutz A kibbutz is a collective community, or settlement, found in Israel and is a logical extension of cooperative working.

lucifer effect This concept is described by Phillip Zimbardo. The book with the same title describes the point in time when a normal person first crosses the boundary between good and evil to engage in an evil action. It represents a transformation of human character that is significant in its consequences. Such transformations are more likely to occur in novel settings where social situational forces are sufficiently powerful to overwhelm, or set aside temporally, personal attributes of morality, compassion, or sense of justice and fair play.

mcDonaldization This is a concept discussed extensively in the work of George Ritzer. He defines it as a process by which the principles of the fast-food restaurant are coming to dominate more and more sectors of US society, as well as that of the rest of the world. It is a new model of rationalization, which built on many ideas found in bureaucratization; McDonald's is an extreme version of the rationalization process.

mondragon This is a town in the Basque region of Spain where a group of cooperatives was established.

narcissism This is a personality trait encompassing grandiosity, arrogance, self-absorption, entitlement, fragile self-esteem, and hostility. Narcissists lack empathy, value competition over cooperation, and are interpersonally dismissive and abrasive.

net surplus This is the profit remaining in an organization after subtracting operating costs and other costs.

new economy A term coined in the late 1990s to describe a move in industrialized developed countries away from a manufacturing-based wealth-producing economy to a service-sector asset-based economy, more reliant on knowledge workers, in which there is global competition and better information access. For one view of the new economy, see R.B. Reich (2002) *The Future of Success: Working and Living in the New Economy*, New York: First Vintage Books.

not-for-profit organization An organization that does not distribute its surplus funds to owners or shareholders, but instead uses them to help pursue its goals. An example of this type of organization may be a charity or a trade union.

outgroups Groups to which we do not belong and which we accordingly evaluate unfavourably.

prescribed behaviour Instructions given to employees about how to behave in order to do their job.

profit sharing An incentive based compensation program to award employees a percentage of the organization's profits.

psychometric test A psychometric test is a way of assessing a person's ability or personality in a measured and structured way. It is usually a test that has been thoroughly investigated to examine its reliability (that is, to ensure that it gives similar answers on various occasions) and validity (that is, that it measures what it says it measures). There are three main types of test: ability; personality; and interest.

quality circles These are usually small regular meeting groups of volunteers who discuss, propose, and help to implement improvements to the production or service process.

rationalized A situation in which measures have been taken to increase the efficiency, or improve the effectiveness, of work practices. For example, shirt manufacture might be rationalized so that, instead of sewing different parts of the shirt, one worker will make only buttonholes.

reciprocal leadership A form of leadership discussed by Mary Parker Follett in which 'the leader guides the group and is at the same time himself guided by the group'.

sex stereotyping When the term is used alongside jobs it means that jobs become sex-typed as masculine or feminine for example a secretary's job is sex stereotyped as female.

social identity theory A theory concerned with how we categorize and understand our own identity in relation to others.

social mobility Social mobility describes the movement or opportunities for movement between different social groups, and the advantages and disadvantages that go with this for example income, security of employment, opportunities for advancement.

taylorism This means applying the principles of scientific management and Frederick Taylor.

time and motion study An analysis of the time spent in going through the different motions of a job or series of jobs. The study is designed to improve the methods of work by subdividing the different operations of

379

a job into measurable elements. They are then used as aids to standardization of work and in checking the efficiency of people and equipment.

trait theory The earliest research in leadership looking at the traits of leaders—that is, trying to identify the characteristics of effective leaders.

virtual crime Term used to describe crime that takes place on websites owned and managed by organizations.

virtuous circles These mean collaborative, open decision making, which eliminates traditional hierarchical styles of secrecy, sycophancy, and sabotage. Decisions are sought from those with the expertise and accepted.

yugoslav self-management This was based on the assumption that organizations could be run by their employees operating through elected workers' councils. Workers' councils had the right to hire and fire management, and to make major decisions.

 For further definitions of key terms and concepts, including exclusive access to definitions from OUP's *Dictionary of Business and Management*, please visit the Online Resource Centre that accompanies this book.

Index

N

O

389